lonely planet

Shanghai

"All you've got to do is decide to go
and the hardest part is over.

So go!"

TONY WHEELER, COFOUNDER – LONELY PLANET

D0034253

THIS EDITION WRITTEN AND RESEARCHED BY

Damian Harper,
Dai Min

Apr 2015

Contents

(left) **Noodles** Casual street dining in Shànghǎi

(above) **Chinese New Year** Celebrations in the Yùyuán Gardens shopping area (p80)

(right) **Traditional Chinese Door**

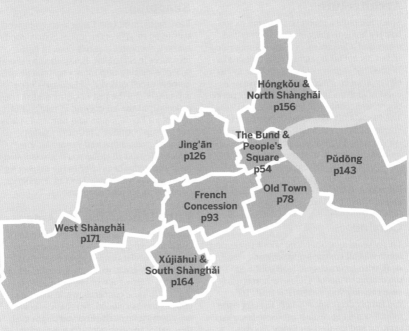

Hóngkǒu & North Shànghǎi p156

Jìng'ān p126

The Bund & People's Square p54

Pǔdōng p143

French Concession p93

Old Town p78

West Shànghǎi p171

Xújiāhuì & South Shànghǎi p164

Welcome to Shànghǎi

Shànghǎi: few world cities evoke so much history, glamour, mystique and exotic promise by name alone.

Architecture

Shànghǎi pulls a rabbit or two from its top hat. It's home to the world's second-tallest tower and a host of other neck-craning colossi, but it's not all sky-scraping razzamatazz. Beyond the crisply cool veneer of the modern city typified by Pǔdōng, there's a treasure chest of architectural styles. The city's period of greatest cosmopolitan excess – the 1920s and 1930s – left the city with pristine examples of art deco buildings, most of which survived the 20th-century vicissitudes that assailed Shànghǎi. And there's more: from Jesuit cathedrals, Jewish synagogues and Buddhist temples to home-grown *lòngtáng* laneway and *shíkùmén* housing, Shànghǎi's architectural heritage is like nowhere else.

Cuisine

Thirty years ago, Shànghǎi's dour restaurant scene was all tin trays and scowling waiting staff, with international food confined to the dining rooms of 'exclusive' hotels. Chinese cooking was pedestrian stuff. Today, you simply don't know where to start – the mouth-watering restaurant scene is varied, exciting and up-to-the-minute. Food is the hub of Chinese social life. It's over a meal that people catch up with friends, celebrate and clinch business deals, and spend hard-earned cash.

Shopping

Bearing in mind that Chinese shoppers constitute up to 47% of the global luxury-goods market, shopping is rarely done in half-measures in Shànghǎi. Retail therapy is one way of spending new money and the Shanghainese aren't called 小资 (*xiǎozī* – 'little capitalists') by the rest of China for nothing, especially at the luxury end of things. But it's not all Prada, Gucci and Burberry. There are pop-up boutiques, bustling markets, funky vintage shops and young designer outlets. Beyond clothing you're also spoiled for choice, whether you're in the market for antiques, ceramics, art, Tibetan jewellery... whatever is on your shopping list.

Entertainment & the Arts

Běijīng often hogs the limelight as China's cultural nexus, but for what is essentially a town of wheelers and dealers, Shànghǎi is surprisingly creative. Many art galleries are exciting, offering a window onto contemporary Chinese concerns, while nightlife options have exploded. Acrobatics shows are always a favourite and you might grab the chance to catch some Chinese opera. Shànghǎi's music and club scene is vibrant: from unpretentious jazz and indie venues to all-night hip-hop and electro dance parties, the city swings with the best of them.

Why I Love Shànghǎi

By Damian Harper, Author

I first visited Shànghǎi in 1993, when the Oriental Pearl TV Tower was going up, the Peace Hotel Jazz Band was already *old* and Xīntiāndì wasn't even on the back of an envelope. I sat on the Bund by the Huángpǔ River, opposite the flatland of Pǔdōng, and felt a buzz in the air: this city was going places. Why do I love Shànghǎi? It's the food, the people, the European streets and art deco buildings, the narrow alleys and the sense of purpose. And don't get me started on the language!

For more about our authors, see p320.

Top: A shop owner at Dongtai Road Antique Market (p91)

Shànghǎi's
Top 13

1

The Bund (p54)

1 The Bund is mainland China's most iconic concession-era backdrop and a source of intense local pride. Offering a gorgeous curve of larger-than-life heritage architecture, the buildings here may be dwarfed by the city's modern high-rises, but they carry in their stones an old-fashioned gravity that simply can't be matched. As a monument to the unbridled pursuit of wealth, it's no surprise that the Bund was left to languish during the communist years, but China's economic renaissance has restored its standing among the city's most stylish panoramas.

⊙ *The Bund & People's Square*

Shànghǎi Museum (p61)

2 Shànghǎi has never been a city to bother with the rear-view mirror, and this obvious disregard for tradition is what most distinguishes it from the rest of the country. The one glaring exception, however, is the outstanding Shànghǎi Museum, an inspiring tribute to the path of beauty throughout the millennia, from ancient bronzes to gorgeous ceramic masterpieces from the Qing dynasty. Come here for Chinese landscape paintings, sea-green celadon jars, Buddhist statuary and a taste of a world that has since disappeared.

BELOW: SHÀNGHǍI MUSEUM (P61), DESIGNED BY ARCHITECT XING TONGHE

⊙ *The Bund & People's Square*

PETER STUCKINGS / GETTY IMAGES ©

LONELY PLANET / GETTY IMAGES ©

French Concession Fashion (p118)

3 In the early 20th century, Shànghăi single-handedly shaped the image of the modern Chinese woman through calendar posters, which were printed in the millions and distributed throughout the rural hinterland and beyond. Ever since, it has worn the crown of China's most fashionable city, and there's no better place to get a feel for the latest trends than the French Concession. Browse boutiques for sequin-covered shoes, Tibetan-inspired jewellery, silky summer dresses and the hip new styles of a growing crop of local and international designers.

🔒*French Concession*

Hángzhōu's West Lake (p183)

4 Whizz down to Hángzhōu on the high-speed train in a shot, but whatever you do, take your time dawdling around willow-fringed West Lake, one of the nation's top sights. The most famous city lake in China, it's vast, placid and beautiful in equal measure, and best savoured in a very low gear. With its undulating range of pagoda-capped hills to the north, picturesque causeways and lakeside gardens and parks, West Lake is even more spellbinding come nightfall, when couples come out to walk languorously along its shores. Aim for sundown for spectacular photographs across the water to the setting sun.

◉*Day Trips*

Yùyuán Gardens & Bazaar (p80)

5 Yùyuán Gardens – in Shànghăi's Old Town – is one of the nation's best examples of traditional Chinese gardens. With its ponds, trees, flowers, bridges, pavilions and harmonic compositions, Yùyuán Gardens encourages contemplation and reflection – elusive moods in today's frantic Shànghăi. The gardens are popular though, so get here early in the day while it's still quiet. After exploring, join the hectic throb of shoppers in the attached bazaar, an excellent place to pick up skilfully made handicrafts and keepsakes.

◉*Old Town*

Dining in the French Concession (p101)

6 An incomparable melange of regional Chinese restaurants, stylish Shanghainese eateries, international dining and no-frills street food, the French Concession is the epicentre of the city's culinary revolution. On a single strip you might find explosively hot Sichuanese, a Hong Kong–style diner, Shanghainese seafood and MSG-free noodles – venture just a little bit further and you can travel to the end of the Middle Kingdom and back. BELOW: CAFE IN THE XÌNTIĀNDÌ AREA (P96)

✖ *French Concession*

Markets (p91)

7 Shànghǎi's air-conditioned malls can be a haven on a hot day, but if you want to see locals in their true shopping element, drop by a market. Get your haggling hat on and your elbows out, and join the push and shove – among all the jostling and banter, endless fakes and tricks of the trade, you might just find exactly what you're looking for. Don't forget: prices aren't fixed. For starters, roll up your sleeves in the Shíliùpù Fabric Market or cast a shrewd eye over the goods at the Dongtai Road Antique Market in the Old Town. TOP RIGHT: SOUVENIR SHOP IN OLD STREET (P91)

🔒 *Old Town*

7

8

Jade Buddha Temple *(p128)*

8 While Shànghăi and materialism fit together like hand and glove, the city's connection to spiritual matters can seem more tenuous, to say the least. Despite first impressions, however, the city harbours a strong affection for religious tradition, best observed in the main courtyard of this century-old Buddhist temple, which witnesses a continual stream of worshippers throughout the day. Housed on the top floor of a rear building is the temple's centrepiece and crowd-puller, a 1.9m-high statue of Sakyamuni crafted from pure Burmese jade.

⊙ *Jìng'ān*

M50 (p129)

9 Shànghǎi has traditionally eschewed the arts in favour of more commercial pursuits, but the escalating value of Chinese artwork has led to the emergence of a busy gallery scene. Located in a former cotton mill, the industrially chic M50 is the city's main creative hub and Shànghǎi's answer to the 798 Art District in Běijīng. Dozens of edgy galleries, a handful of studios and occasional events make this an absorbing place to wander. BELOW: ARTWORK BY XU ZHEN – PRODUCED BY MADELN COMPANY, COURTESY OF SHANGHART GALLERY IN M50 (P129)

👁 *Jìng'ān*

Modern Architecture (p239)

10 Through its occasionally debauched history, Shànghǎi has become synonymous with both excess and success. Today is no different. It's hard to talk about Shànghǎi without references to skyscrapers, as they have become *the* defining architectural style (even eclipsing art deco). Urban Shànghǎi's high-altitude topography is entirely constructed: walk around Lùjiāzuǐ at night and be blown away by the visuals. There's nowhere else in mainland China quite like it. TOP RIGHT: ORIENTAL PEARL TV TOWER (P147) DESIGNED BY SHANGHAI MODERN ARCHITECTURAL DESIGN COMPANY LTD

👁 *Architecture in Shànghǎi*

Nightlife (p43)

11 One-time city of sin, Shànghǎi's heady promise of lipstick-smudged martini glasses and flashing neon lights doesn't always match expectations, but there's no doubt that the place loves to party. You don't need to knock back shots of green tea and whisky or dance till dawn to have a good time. The nightlife scene continues to mature, and whatever your preference – theatre, jazz or punk rock – you can be sure that the midnight hour will always have something in store. BOTTOM RIGHT: TMSK BAR (P114) IN XĪNTIĀNDÌ

🍷 *Drinking & Nightlife*

Lĭlòng & Lòngtáng (p245)

12 When Shànghăi's superscale buildings leave you feeling totally dwarfed, get down to the city's traditional *lĭlòng* and *lòngtáng* lanes. Exploring this charming realm allows you to discover a more personable aspect to the city, so go slow. This is where you can find Shànghăi's homey and more intimate side: narrow alleys, classic three-storey buildings, a warm community spirit, history, heritage and a lethargic tempo entirely at odds with the roar of the main drag.

◉ *Architecture in Shànghăi*

Zhūjiājiăo (p194)

13 The nearest decent-sized water town to Shànghăi, Zhūjiājiăo is ideal for a day trip. Easily reached by bus, it offers quintessential traditional bridges, pinched lanes, ancient streets, hoary Qing-dynasty temples, waterside views and even some pretty fine cafes. It's fun losing your bearings, but Zhūjiājiăo is small enough to mean you never get entirely lost. If you take to the water-town culture, you can carry on from Zhūjiājiăo to other canal towns in neighbouring Jiāngsū province. ABOVE: ZHŪJIĀJIĂO'S (P194) GRAND CANAL

◉ *Day Trips from Shànghăi*

What's New

Shànghǎi Tower

Set to open in 2015, this colossal skyscraper – topping out at 632m – has further redefined the Pǔdōng skyline. Gently corkscrewing into the Shànghǎi stratus, the twisting glass-clad tower will contain a superhigh observation deck, entertainment venues, shopping outlets, offices, a luxury hotel and 'sky lobbies' bathed in natural daylight. (p146)

Bulgari Hotel

After hotel openings in London, Bali and Milan, exclusive Bulgari turned its attention to an area north of Sūzhōu Creek near the Bund for its latest address, set for a 2016 opening. The modern Foster+Partners tower will be offset by the adjacent traditional Chinese Chamber of Commerce building, housing one of the hotel's restaurants. (www.bulgarihotels.com/en-us/shanghai/)

Shànghǎi Disney Resort

Set for a 2015 unveiling, the 3.9 sq km Shànghǎi Disney Resort – China's first (Hong Kong doesn't count) – will top little emperors' wishlists for many years to come. Located in Pǔdōng, it will be served by its own metro station and will boast two themed hotels and a huge 100 acre lake. (http://en.shanghaidisneyresort.com.cn/en)

Power Station of Art

This converted power station by the Huángpǔ River has staged some intriguing and forward-thinking international contemporary art and design exhibitions. It's a magnificent addition to the artistic firmament and will be the industrial-sized venue of the Shanghai Biennale. (p151)

The Shànghǎi Metro

The Shànghǎi metro is the world's fastest-growing underground rail network, and recent developments continue to be a boon for visitors. Forthcoming extensions to lines 5, 13, 12 and 16 are under construction, with a planned line 11 link to the new Shànghǎi Disney Resort in 2015, and more than a dozen future extensions and new lines earmarked for construction in the next five years.

China Art Palace

The collection of the Shànghǎi Art Museum upped sticks and shifted to this vast new modern art space in the former World Expo site on the Pǔdōng side. Once the China Pavilion, the building is a spectacle and its international exhibitions have gained praise, although the permanent collection is less thought-provoking. (p150)

Shànghǎi Museum of Natural History

The tired old Shànghǎi Museum of Natural History moves into brand-new state-of-the-art facilities in Jìng'ān (344 Shanhaiguan Rd; 山海关路344号) at the end of 2014. It'll make a change from its old-school address on East Yan'an Rd, but we'll miss the 1970s displays and musty corridors.

For more recommendations and reviews, see **lonelyplanet. com/shanghai**

Need to Know

For more information, see Survival Guide (p251)

Currency
Rénmínbì (RMB); basic unit is the yuán (¥).

Language
Mandarin and Shanghainese

Visas
Needed for all visits to Shànghǎi except transits up to 72 hours.

Money
ATMs widely available. Credit cards less widely used; always carry cash.

Mobile Phones
Inexpensive pay-as-you-go SIM cards can be bought locally for most mobile phones. Buying a local mobile phone is also cheap. Using Skype or Viber is the cheapest way to communicate when in a wi-fi zone.

Time
China Standard Time/Běijīng Time (GMT/UTC plus eight hours).

Wi-Fi
Available in many bars, cafes, restaurants and hotels.

Daily Costs

Budget under ¥350
➡ Dorm bed: ¥50–60; double room from ¥200 (per person)

➡ Cheap hole-in-the-wall restaurants, food markets and street food: ¥50

➡ Bike hire, metro or other transport: ¥20-30

➡ Museums: some have free entry

➡ Sundries: ¥40–60

Midrange ¥350–¥1300
➡ Double room in a midrange hotel: ¥250-650 (per person)

➡ Lunch and dinner in decent local restaurants: ¥150–200

➡ Entertainment: ¥80

➡ Travelling in comfort: ¥80

Top End over ¥1300
➡ Double room in a top-end hotel: from ¥650 (per person)

➡ Lunch and dinner in excellent restaurants: from ¥300

➡ Shopping at top-end boutiques: ¥300

Advance Planning

Three months before Book a room at popular hotel accommodation.

One month before Book tables for well-known restaurants; check listings on entertainment sites such as *Time Out Shanghai* (www.timeoutshanghai.com) for art exhibitions, live music, festivals and shows, and book your tickets.

A few days before Check the weather online (www.bbc.co.uk/weather/1796236).

Useful Websites

➡ **Lonely Planet** (www.lonelyplanet.com/shanghai) Destination information, hotel bookings, traveller forum and more.

➡ **Time Out Shanghai** (www.timeoutshanghai.com) Authoritative, in-the-know entertainment listings.

➡ **City Weekend** (www.cityweekend.com.cn/shanghai) Comprehensive listings website of popular expat magazine. News stories can be weak.

➡ **Shanghaiist** (www.shanghaiist.com) Excellent source for news and reviews.

➡ **Smart Shanghai** (www.smartshanghai.com) Quality listings website with forum.

WHEN TO GO

Summer is peak season but it's hot and sticky with heavy rain; spring and late September to October are optimal. Winter is cold and clammy.

°C/°F Temp
40/104 —
30/86 —
20/68 —
10/50 —
0/32 —
-10/14 —
-20/-4 —
-30/-22 —
-40/-40 —

Rainfall inches/mm
12/300
8/200
4/100
0

J F M A M J J A S O N D

Arriving in Shànghǎi

Pǔdōng International Airport Metro into town 6am to 10pm ¥3–¥10; Maglev to Longyang Rd metro station 6.45am to 9.40pm ¥50; airport buses into town 7am to 11pm ¥16–¥30; taxi ¥160.

Hóngqiáo International Airport Metro into town 6.05am to 10.50pm ¥3–¥10; buses 6am to 11pm ¥6–¥30; taxi ¥70.

Shànghǎi Railway Station Metro into town 5.30am to 11pm ¥3–¥10; taxi ¥20–¥30.

Shànghǎi Hóngqiáo Railway Station Metro into town 5.30am to 11pm ¥3–¥10; taxi ¥70.

Shànghǎi South Railway Station Metro into town 5.30am to 11pm ¥3–¥10; taxi ¥50.

For much more on **arrival** see p252

Money-Saving Tips

Shànghǎi isn't cheap and costs can mount up. Here are some tips to help your yuán go further.

➡ **Target happy hour** Buy one and get one free, usually from 5pm to 8pm or 9pm – this can be crucial when paying ¥35-plus for a small bottle of beer.

➡ **Take the metro** It's cheap, efficient, fast and goes almost everywhere (but doesn't run late at night).

➡ **Haggle** If prices aren't displayed, haggling is often the *lingua franca,* especially in markets (but not in department stores or shops).

➡ **Stay visa-free** For stays of 72 hours and less, no need to fork out for a visa.

Sleeping

Sleeping in Shànghǎi is rarely a cheap proposition unless you snag a dorm bed or move into the suburbs. You'll need to book your room in advance to secure your top choice, and avoid the national holiday periods.

There's a great deal of choice in the main, fashionable and sight-heavy areas but some neighbourhoods, such as Pǔdōng, strictly favour the top end. Finding accommodation within reach of a metro station is rarely hard. Hotels range from budget hostels and express business hotels to heritage hotels and boutique choices, and through to five-star towers.

Useful Websites

➡ **Lonely Planet** (lonelyplanet.com/china/shanghai/hotels) Hotel bookings and forum.

➡ **CTrip** (www.english.ctrip.com) An excellent online agency, good for hotel bookings.

➡ **eLong** (www.elong.net) Hotel bookings.

For much more on **sleeping** see p199

TOURIST INFORMATION

Oddly, Shànghǎi is not well served with tourist information offices, so get chummy with your hotel concierge/reception staff for travel pointers. Pop their number into your mobile phone to communicate with taxi drivers or for any situation requiring an interpreter. Youth hostels often offer great advice and are generally well attuned to the needs of travellers. The Shànghǎi Call Centre (☎962 288) is a handy 24-hour English-language hotline.

First Time Shànghǎi

For more information, see Survival Guide (p251)

Checklist

➡ Ensure your passport is valid for at least six months past your arrival date

➡ Organise your visa

➡ Check airline baggage restrictions

➡ Check your vaccinations are up to date

➡ Get a pre-trip dental check-up

➡ Arrange for appropriate travel insurance

What to Pack

➡ Sunscreen and sunhat in summer

➡ Insect repellent to keep mosquitoes at bay

➡ Good walking shoes – Shànghǎi's concrete distances can become foot-numbing

➡ Phrasebook with Chinese characters – English is spoken fitfully

➡ An electrical adaptor

➡ Any prescribed drugs you may need

Top Tips for Your Trip

➡ Make an early start to your day – the Chinese rise early so the city's firing on all cylinders by 8am.

➡ The Shànghǎi metro will be your best friend: fast, efficient, cheap, punctual and extensive.

➡ Taxis are widespread and great value for short hops.

➡ For budget accommodation, stick to Pǔxī, not Pǔdōng.

➡ Plan your time – the metro system is excellent but criss-crossing Shànghǎi can eat into your time. Instead, choose just one or two neighbourhoods to explore in a day. For our suggested itineraries, see p22.

➡ If you've only a few days, stick to the city's core districts of the Bund, People's Sq, the French Concession and Jìng'ān, with a foray or two to Pǔdōng.

What to Wear

Shànghǎi is a fairly casual destination, so you can wear what you want most of the time, although more modest dress is required for temple and mosque visits. For fancy dinners, smart-casual should be all that's required – no restaurant will insist on jackets or ties. Winters are clammy, draining and cold, so warm clothing is crucial; summers are hot, humid and long, with epic downpours. An umbrella won't go astray in either season.

Be Forewarned

Shànghǎi is largely safe for foreign visitors, but in some cases you'll need more than mere common-sense to keep trouble at bay.

Scammers prey on foreign visitors in the Bund area, East Nanjing Rd and other tourist zones: maintain a healthy scepticism if a stranger approaches you to chat in English or asks you to photograph them. Definitely do not go to a restaurant, cafe or teahouse with them (no matter how friendly they appear to be), otherwise you will be fleeced.

Money

ATMs are widespread and generally accept Visa, MasterCard, Cirrus and Maestro cards. Most operate 24 hours. Many ATMs are linked to the main international money systems, so you should have no problem using your bank card from back home; Bank of China (中国银行; Zhōngguó Yínháng) and the Industrial & Commercial Bank of China are best bets. Credit cards are widely used in Shànghǎi hotels, restaurants and shops (but much less so in rural areas); always check beforehand and carry enough cash. Change money at hotels, large banks, some Bank of China ATMs and department stores. Travellers cheques are not widely used. **For more information, see p268.**

Bargaining

Haggling is *de rigueur* (and a common language between foreigners and Chinese vendors) in markets where goods do not have a clearly marked price, but not in department stores or high-street shops. Don't be afraid to come in really low, but remain polite.

Tipping

➡ **Restaurants** Never tip at budget eateries; some (midrange and up) restaurants will levy a service charge, so check your bill first.

➡ **Bars** No need to tip in bars or clubs.

➡ **Hotels** Porters at midrange and high-end hotels may expect around ¥5 per bag.

➡ **Taxis** No need to tip.

Taichi practitioners on the Bund (p56)

Etiquette

There are a few etiquette rules worth noting:

➡ Chinese people rarely kiss each other upon greeting, but shaking hands is fine.

➡ If visiting a local person's home, take off your shoes.

➡ Queue-barging used to be a way of life in China, but respect for getting in line is increasing, especially in Shànghǎi.

➡ Don't stick your chopsticks vertically into your bowl of rice.

➡ Avoid large, expansive physical gestures.

Tours

The following provide a good introduction to Shànghǎi:

➡ **Big Bus Tours** (p258) and **City Sightseeing Buses** (p258) Double-decker open-bus tours around town.

➡ **Insiders Experience** (p260) Fun motorbike sidecar tours.

➡ **Newman Tours** (p260) Themed guided walks around Shànghǎi.

Language

Outside hotels, English is not widely spoken, and even less so outside the city. You'll be able to get by in tourist areas, but it's useful to learn a few basic phrases. Some restaurants may not have an English menu. You'll find yourself surrounded by written Chinese wherever you travel, so a phrasebook is useful. See Language (p274) for more information.

Getting Around

For more information, see Transport (p252)

Metro

Quickest way to travel around town. The extensive system runs from 5.30am to 10.30pm or 11pm. Tickets are cheap; trains run regularly and with few delays.

Taxi

Cabs are affordable, plentiful and the way to go for short hops around town or trips late at night.

Bus

Slow-going on Shànghǎi's congested roads and difficult for non-Chinese speakers to use but useful if you get the hang of them.

Bicycle

Handy for sightseeing around smaller neighbourhoods; not so useful for large distances.

Ferry

Great for crossing the Huángpǔ River.

Walking

The central areas of town can be explored on foot; moving between neighbourhoods, Shànghǎi's sprawling expanses are hard going.

Car Hire

Because of restrictions, paperwork and an undeveloped rental network, self-drive is generally not an option, but cars with drivers can be hired.

Key Phrases

Chūzūchē (出租车) Taxi

Dìtiě (地铁) Literally the 'underground railway'; this is what the Chinese call the Shànghǎi metro. It's shorthand for *dìxià tiělù* (地下铁路; underground railway).

Dìtiězhàn (地铁站) Metro station

Dùchuán (渡船) Ferry

Gōnggòng qìchē (公共汽车) Public bus

Gōnggòng qìchēzhàn (公共汽车站) Bus stop

Jiāotōng Kǎ (交通卡) Transport Card

Piào (票) Ticket

Qǐng gěi wǒ fāpiào (请给我发票) Please give me a receipt.

Shǒubānchē/Mòbānchē (首班车／末班车) First/last train (or bus)

Zìxíngchē (自行车) Bicycle

Key Routes

Metro line 1 Links Shànghǎi Railway Station, People's Sq, South Shaanxi Rd, Changshu Rd (for French Concession West), Hengshan Rd and Xujiahui.

Metro line 2 Zooms from Pǔdōng International Airport through Century Ave, Lujiazui, East Nanjing Rd, People's Sq, West Nanjing Rd, Jing'an Temple, Hongqiao Airport Terminal 2 and Hongqiao Railway Station.

Metro line 10 Runs through East Nanjing Rd, Yuyuan Garden, Xintiandi, South Shaanxi Rd, Shànghǎi Zoo, Hongqiao International Airport and Hongqiao Railway Station.

How to Hail a Taxi

➡ Look for a taxi with an illuminated light behind the windscreen.

➡ Hail it from the street by raising your arm. The driver should pull over when they see you.

➡ You can also catch a taxi from a taxi rank.

➡ Have your destination written out in Chinese or use your mobile phone to have your hotel concierge translate for you in the event of communication problems.

TOP TIPS

➡ If you're in town for more than a week, invest in a Transport Card.

➡ Cars can still turn when the green man is lit at crossings, so stay alert.

➡ Combine taxi trips and metro journeys to get around Shànghǎi quickly.

➡ Forget about hiring a car.

➡ If taking a taxi, have your destination written down in Chinese (if you don't speak Chinese).

➡ There is no need to tip taxi drivers.

➡ Try to have some coins for the metro ticket machines, as notes sometimes don't work.

When to Travel

➡ Rush hour (gāofēng shíjiān) is roughly from 7.30am to 9.30am and 5pm to 7pm on working days, when millions of people are on the move. The metro and buses are packed out and empty taxis can be hard to find.

➡ Taxis are in short supply when one of Shànghǎi's summer downpours inundate town.

➡ The pricier taxi night-rates run from 11pm to 5am.

Travel Etiquette

➡ Passengers should stand on the right when using escalators in metro stations but this is frequently ignored; prepare for a mass of people and get your elbows out.

➡ Hand over your bag to be scanned at the security check at metro stations. A lot of locals ignore the request, but it's good form to oblige.

➡ Have your ticket or Transport Card ready when leaving the station. Locals go through the barriers without breaking pace. Transport Cards are swiped while single-fare tickets are fed into the machine, where they are retained.

➡ Wait for passengers to disembark the metro and buses before boarding at marked embarkation points.

➡ Address taxi or bus drivers as sījī (driver).

Tickets & Passes

➡ The Transport Card is a handy smartcard on which you can store credit for use on the metro, in taxis, on most buses and on some ferries. Swipe the touchpad at both ends of your metro journey, but only once for bus journeys. You won't save much money, but you will be spared queuing or hunting for change.

➡ Plastic tickets can also be used on the metro, and you can use cash on buses (drop coins into the slot on entering or pay the conductor) and in taxis. The taxi driver will ask if you want to use cash (xiànjīn) or a card (kǎ).

➡ Buy Transport Cards or top up credit at the service counter in metro stations and at numerous convenience stores and banks.

For much more on
getting around
see p20

TRAVEL AT NIGHT

The metro stops early, so you could be left high and dry from roughly 10.30pm. Buses 300 to 399 are night buses, but buses in general are not easy to use if you don't know Chinese. Taking a taxi is your best and fastest option; cabs are usually plentiful. Note that the more-expensive taxi night-rate operates between 11pm to 5pm. Shànghǎi's public transportation is generally safe at night; as anywhere though, use common sense.

Top Itineraries

Day One

The Bund & People's Square (p54)

 Follow the sweep of architectural pomp along the **Bund** and savour the art deco grandeur of the **Fairmont Peace Hotel**, before walking along the riverside promenade to view the **Pǔdōng** skyline across the river. Art lovers can swoop upon the **Rockbund Art Museum**, while architecture fans enjoy the highlights of **Yuanmingyuan Road**. Head west along East Nanjing Rd past shoppers to **People's Square**.

> **Lunch** Lost Heaven (p71): all the flavours of far-off Yúnnán province.

The Bund & People's Square (p54)

Immerse yourself in the collection of the **Shànghǎi Museum** before choosing between the **Shànghǎi Urban Planning Exhibition Hall** or discovering a pocket of greenery in People's Park. For views, shoot up in the lift to the lobby of the JW Marriott on the 38th floor of **Tomorrow Square**.

> **Dinner** Bāguó Bùyī (p153): top-notch Sìchuān classics in a smart setting.

Pǔdōng (p143)

Hop on the metro (or a sightseeing bus) from People's Sq to Lùjiāzuǐ to wander round the walkway in front of the **Oriental Pearl TV Tower**. Select between the observation towers of the **Shànghǎi Tower**, **Jinmao Tower** and the **Shànghǎi World Financial Center**, or settle for evening cocktails at **Flair**.

Day Two

French Concession (p93)

 View the architecture and boutiques of **Xīntiāndì** and explore the **Shíkùmén Open House Museum** for a lowdown on *shíkùmén* (stone-gate house) architecture before tracking down **St Nicholas Church**, the whimsical **Moller House** or taking a seat to watch locals relaxing in French-designed **Fùxīng Park**.

> **Lunch** Din Tai Fung (p105): classic, moreish Shànghǎi dumplings.

French Concession (p93)

Admire the dazzling glass creations at the **Liúli China Museum** before disappearing among **Tiánzǐfáng's** warren of lanes. Boutique window-shop around Tiánzǐfáng; take your hat off to the collection in the **Propaganda Poster Art Centre**; and hunt down contemporary art at **James Cohan**, **Art Labor** and **Space**.

> **Dinner** Jian Guo 328 (p106): Home-style Shànghǎi cooking on a fab menu.

The Bund & People's Square (p54)

Zip up the day in style by sipping cocktails and dining on the **Bund**, but most of all enjoy the mind-altering neon views. Select from a long list: the **Glamour Bar**, **New Heights**, the **Long Bar**, **Bar Rouge** or **Captain's Bar** – or don your best togs for views, booze and moves at **M1NT**. Die-hard traditionalists can lend an ear to the jazz band in the **Fairmont Peace Hotel Jazz Bar**.

Dongtai Road Antique Market (p91)

Lu Xun Park (p160)

Day Three

Old Town (p78)

 Reach the Old Town's **Yùyuán Gardens** early in the day, before the crowds arrive. Sift through the handicrafts on sale in the **Yùyuán Bazaar** before tracking down bargain collectables along **Old Street** and **Dongtai Road Antique Market**. Head east past **Dǒngjiādù Cathedral** to the **Cool Docks** for its fetching blend of *shíkùmén*, riverside warehouse architecture and views.

 **Lunch** Nánxiáng Steamed Bun Restaurant (p89): celebrated dumplings.

Jìng'ān (p126)

Weave some Buddhist mystery into your afternoon at the **Jade Buddha Temple** before sprinkling contemporary art into the mix at the fascinating galleries of **M50**. Consider a cruise along **Sūzhōu Creek** or explore the **Jìng'ān Temple** before seeking out the *lǐlòng* lanes of the **Bubbling Well Road Apartments** and shopping along West Nanjing Rd.

Dinner Fu 1088 (p138): fine Shànghǎi cuisine in dapper villa surrounds.

French Concession (p93)

Round off your day in some of Shànghǎi's best bars, all handily located in the French Concession: chill out at **Bell Bar**; seek out specialist beers at **Kaībā** or **Boxing Cat Brewery**; sink a drink in the garden of **Cotton's** or corner your perfect cocktail at **el Cóctel**.

Day Four

Xújiāhuì & South Shànghǎi (p164)

Spend the morning admiring the former Jesuit sights of Xújiāhuì, in particular the **St Ignatius Cathedral** and the **Tousewe Museum**. Pay your respects to the Buddhist **Lónghuá Temple & Pagoda**; the green-fingered can explore the foliage of the **Shànghǎi Botanical Gardens**.

 Lunch Kota's Kitchen (p169): superb Japanese dishes meets the Beatles.

Hóngkǒu & North Shànghǎi (p156)

Pay a visit to the **Ohel Moishe Synagogue** and the surrounding former Jewish neighbourhood; walk up **Duolun Road Cultural Street**; track down some of the neighbourhood's best architecture and relax in **Lu Xun Park**. In the late afternoon, head back south to the North Bund area of Hóngkǒu, near the Bund.

Dinner Guǒyúan (p161): superduper spice-infused dishes from Húnán.

Pǔdōng (p143)

Get haggling at the **AP Xīnyáng Fashion & Gifts Market** before closing time, or get a handle on local history at the **Shànghǎi History Museum**. Follow up with an evening walk along the **Riverside Promenade**, gazing over to the Bund. For fine Pǔdōng views, jump on a ferry across the river to toast the skyline from **Char Bar** in the South Bund.

If You Like...

Views

The Bund Walk the promenade for views of Pǔdōng's soaring skyline on one side and concession-era magnificence on the other. (p56)

Shànghǎi Tower The city's highest observation deck in Shànghǎi's tallest tower. (p146)

Flair An outdoor terrace gives this sky-high Pǔdōng bar the wow-factor. (p154)

New Heights This top-floor cafe-bar at Three on the Bund is a good spot to gawp at Pǔdōng. (p74)

Vue An outdoor Jacuzzi and views of both Pǔdōng and the Bund. (p162)

JW Marriott Tomorrow Square Zip to the 38th-floor lobby for stupendous vistas over People's Sq. (p205)

Cloud 9 This cool bar at the top of Jinmao Tower is a great alternative to the observation decks. (p154)

West Lake Hángzhōu's main attraction. this lake is the very definition of classical beauty in China. (p183)

Modern Architecture

Shànghǎi Tower Adding a glass twist to the Pǔdōng skyline, this 632m-high skyscraper is a breathtaking colossus. (p146)

Tomorrow Square The People's Sq supertower could easily double as the headquarters for a sci-fi corporation. (p68)

Jinmao Tower No longer the tallest, but still one of the city's most graceful buildings. (p147)

KYLIE MCLAUGHLIN / GETTY IMAGES ©

Street food vendor near Yùyuán Gardens (p80)

China Art Palace The upturned red pyramid was the symbol of the 2010 World Expo. (p150)

Oriental Art Center Way out in Pǔdōng, this classical-music venue was designed to resemble the five petals of a butterfly orchid. (p154)

Shànghǎi Grand Theatre The curving eaves of this theatre recall traditional Chinese architectural design. (p75)

Oriental Pearl TV Tower Not so subtle perhaps, but this poured-concrete tripod remains a Shànghǎi icon. (p147)

Boutique Shopping

Spin Imaginative ceramics from a new generation of designers. (p140)

NuoMi Stylish women's wear that's ecofriendly, too. (p123)

Brocade Country Jewellery, clothing and handicrafts from the Miao of Guìzhōu province. (p123)

Annabel Lee An elegant shop that specialises in embroidery and sells accessories in silk, linen and cashmere. (p76)

OOAK Concept Boutique Three small floors of inspiring jewellery and good-looking clothing designs for women. (p123)

Lolo Love Vintage For all your vintage needs. (p123)

PCS (Pop Classic Sneakers) Come here to pick up the latest canvas-shoe styles. (p121)

Heirloom An elegant range of clutches, satchels and shoulder bags. (p121)

Chouchou Chic Kids' clothes from a joint French–Chinese brand. (p119)

Urban Tribe Local fashion label inspired by the ethnic minorities of China's southwest. (p124)

Street Food

Qībǎo Poke a straw in a coconut; sample barbecued squid; or indulge in sweet dumplings: Qībǎo corners the market for delicious Shànghǎi street food. (p173)

Yunnan Road Food Street One of the best strips for unpretentious regional Chinese restaurants. (p73)

Wujiang Road Food Street The most modern snack street in the city, with Japanese and Korean options, too. (p138)

Huanghe Road Food Street Near People's Park, this strip has some big traditional restaurants, but it's most famous for its dumplings. (p73)

Yùyuán Bazaar It's crowded and overpriced, but famous spots such as Nánxiáng Steamed Bun Restaurant make it a can't-miss option. (p80)

Raffles City A good primer to mall-style food courts, with the popular Food Republic on the top floor and nonstop snacking options in the basement. (p77)

Art Deco Architecture

Fairmont Peace Hotel Built as the legendary Cathay Hotel, this is the best surviving example of art deco style in Shànghǎi. (p204)

Rockbund Art Museum Straight from the deco textbook, with some Chinese ingredients. (p65)

Park Hotel The tallest building in Shànghǎi until the 1980s and an inspiration for IM Pei. (p68)

Embankment Building An art deco landmark now housing rental holiday apartments. (p160)

For more top Shànghǎi spots, see the following:
➡ Eating (p33)
➡ Drinking & Nightlife (p43)
➡ Entertainment (p45)
➡ Shopping (p47)

PLAN YOUR TRIP IF YOU LIKE...

Art Deco Artsy boutique in the M50 complex containing a trove of period furnishings. (p141)

Cathay Theatre Catch a movie in this original 1930s French Concession theatre. (p118)

Broadway Mansions A classic 1934 apartment block north of Sūzhōu Creek that today houses a deco-style hotel. (p160)

China Baptist Publication Society Designed by Ladislaus Hudec, a Czech-Hungarian and one of Shànghǎi's most prolific architects. (p70)

Art Galleries

M50 Former manufacturing space now housing the largest collection of art galleries in the city. (p129)

Propaganda Poster Art Centre Collection of 3000 original posters from the golden age of Maoist propaganda. (p100)

Beaugeste Superb photography gallery tucked away in Tiánzǐfáng. (p98)

James Cohan Edgy New York gallery set in a French Concession art deco villa. (p101)

Art Labor Independent French Concession gallery representing Chinese and international artists. (p101)

Shanghai Gallery of Art Conceptual Chinese art on the Bund. (p65)

Leo Gallery Works by young Chinese artists. (p101)

Space Modern art gallery housed in a former Russian Orthodox church. (p100)

Temples & Churches

Jade Buddha Temple Shànghǎi's most active Buddhist temple. (p128)

Língyǐn Temple Hángzhōu's main Buddhist temple, with a remarkable series of cliff-side carvings. (p179)

Chénxiānggé Nunnery This Old Town temple shelters a gorgeous effigy of the Buddhist goddess of compassion. (p82)

Confucian Temple A tranquil spot with old trees and a Sunday book market, in an atmospheric part of the Old Town. (p83)

Jìng'ān Temple Recently rebuilt downtown Buddhist temple fashioned from Burmese teak. (p130)

Ohel Moishe Synagogue Onetime heart of Shànghǎi's Jewish ghetto, now home to the Jewish Refugees Museum. (p159)

Lónghuá Temple & Pagoda The oldest and largest monastery in the city. (p168)

Temple of the Town God Shànghǎi is one of the few cities in China whose Taoist town god weathered the vicissitudes of the 20th century. (p82)

Dǒngjiādù Cathedral Shànghǎi's oldest church, established by Spanish Jesuits in 1853. (p83)

St Ignatius Cathedral This Xújiāhuì landmark and Jesuit cathedral dates back to 1904. (p166)

Shěshān Basilica Magnificently crowning a hilltop southwest of the city. (p197)

Museums

Shànghǎi Museum Extraordinary overview of traditional Chinese art through the millennia, from ancient bronzes to Qing-dynasty ink paintings. (p61)

Sūzhōu Museum Local artefacts – jade, ceramics and carvings – housed in a gorgeous contemporary building. (p188)

Shànghǎi History Museum Fun and accessible introduction to old Shànghǎi. (p147)

Shànghǎi Urban Planning Exhibition Hall The highlight here is an incredible scale model of the megalopolis c 2020. (p68)

Rockbund Art Museum Contemporary Chinese art installations in a gorgeous 1930s building, once home to Shànghǎi's first museum. (p65)

Liúlí China Museum This unusual edifice is dedicated to the art of glass sculpture, with both ancient and contemporary pieces on display. (p98)

Post Museum Surprisingly good museum covering the history of the Chinese postal service. (p158)

Mínshēng Art Museum Excellent line-up of contemporary Chinese art exhibits. (p174)

China Art Palace Former World Expo China Pavilion reconfigured as a mammoth five-floor art museum, Pǔdōng-side. (p150)

Power Station of Art Shànghǎi's take on London's Tate Modern, with contemporary art hung within a riverside power station. (p151)

Markets

AP Xīnyáng Fashion & Gifts Market The city's largest market sells everything from tailor-made clothes to counterfeit bags. (p155)

Flower, Bird, Fish & Insect Market Pick up your city-sized pets at one of Shànghǎi's only traditional markets. (p83)

Dongtai Road Antique Market Always a fun browse through Mao memorabilia, old calendar posters and mass-produced 'antiques'. (p91)

Shíliùpù Fabric Market Have a suit, dress or blouse tailor-made for a song. (p91)

Ghost Market Climb up to the top floors of the Fúyòu Antique Market on weekends when sellers from the countryside hawk their wares. (p92)

Yùyuán Bazaar The ultimate Shànghǎi souvenir market in the Old Town: slightly tacky and extremely crowded, but always entertaining. (p80)

Qīpǔ Market Push through the crowds at this popular clothing outlet – everything must go now! (p162)

Electronics Market DVD players, speakers and various computer parts for sale. It's cheap, but you'll get no receipt. (p163)

Month by Month

January

**The Western New Year
is greeted wildly in bars
citywide.**

★ Western New Year

Lónghuá Temple (p168) has excellent New Year (元旦; Yuándàn) celebrations, with dragon and lion dances. On 1 January the abbot strikes the bell 108 times while the monks beat on gongs and offer prayers for the forthcoming year.

February

**Preparations for the
festive Chinese New Year
are under way as hundreds
of millions of people get
ready to journey home. If
you plan to travel, book
tickets well in advance.**

★ Chinese New Year

Commonly called the Spring Festival (春节; Chūn Jié), Chinese New Year is the equivalent of Christmas. Families get together to feast on dumplings, vegetate in front of the TV, hand out *hóngbāo* (red envelopes stuffed with money) and take a week-long holiday. New Year's Eve fireworks can be a chaotic but good show. The festival traditionally commences on the first day of the first moon of the traditional lunar calendar (19 February 2015, 8 February 2016, 28 January 2017), but a high-octane month-long build-up gets everyone hyped much earlier.

★ Lantern Festival

Lantern Festival (元宵节; Yuánxiāo Jié) falls on the 15th day of the first lunar month (5 March 2015, 22 February 2016, 11 February 2017). Families make *yuán xiāo* (also called *tāng yuán*; delicious dumplings of glutinous rice with a variety of sweet fillings) and sometimes hang paper lanterns. It's a colourful time to visit Yùyuán Gardens.

★ Valentine's Day

Valentine's Day (情人节; Qíngrén Jié) is taken seriously by Shànghǎi suitors as an occasion for a massive blowout: it's the chance to get their true love that Cartier wristwatch or diamond ring, or a bunch of 11 roses.

March

**March in Shànghǎi is
usually grey, cold and
clammy, though hints of
spring often appear by the
month's end.**

★ JUE Festival

Two-week arts-and-music festival (www.juefestival.com) held in both Shànghǎi and Běijīng. This is one of the best times of the year for music lovers and creative types.

★ Shanghai International Literary Festival

To counter Shànghǎi's drift towards philistinism, this highly popular festival for book lovers is staged in the Glamour Bar (p74) in March or April, with a range of famous names in attendance.

★ Birthday of Guanyin

The Buddhist goddess of mercy celebrates her

birthday (观世音生日; *Guānshìyīn Shēngrì*) on the 19th day of the second lunar month (7 April 2015, 27 March 2016, 16 March 2017).

April

Spring is springing, and transport and hotels are booked solid on Tomb Sweeping Day, now extended into a long weekend.

⚑ Tomb Sweeping Day

Qīngmíng Jié (清明节) public holiday is held every 5 April (4 April in leap years), when more than six million Shanghainese visit the graves of their dearly departed relatives.

⚑ Lónghuá Temple Fair

The two-week fair (龙华寺庙会; Lónghuá Sìmiào Huì) at Lónghuá Temple (p168) coincides with the blossoming of the local peach trees and kicks off on the third day of the third lunar month (21 April 2015, 9 April 2016, 30 March 2017).

☆ Formula One (F1)

The slick Shànghǎi International Circuit has hosted F1's Chinese Grand Prix (www.formula1.com) every year since 2004. The race usually comes to town for three days in mid-April.

May

The thermometer is starting to rocket as the month kicks off with the busy Labour Day holiday period.

⚑ Labour Day

On 1 May, the whole of China gears up for a hard-earned three-day holiday.

June

The sweltering summer heat kicks in and rainfall in Shànghǎi hits its peak.

⚑ Dragon Boat Festival

This public holiday (端午节; Duānwǔ Jié) is celebrated on the fifth day of the fifth lunar month (20 June 2015, 9 June 2016, 30 May 2017) with boat races along the Huángpǔ River, Sūzhōu Creek and Diànshān Lake.

⚑ Shanghai International Film Festival

With screenings at various cinemas around Shànghǎi, this festival (www.siff.com) brings a range of international and locally produced films to town.

July

Shànghǎi sweats it out under a summer sun and the streets are awash with school kids on holiday.

⚑ West Lake Lotuses in Bloom

Hángzhōu's lovely West Lake (p183) offers a stunning combination of long summer nights and full pink lotus blooms. The first West Lake Lotus Festival was in 2013.

September

The tail end of summer, this is one of the best times to visit as temperatures drop from August highs, although rainfall is still abundant.

⚑ Mid-Autumn Festival

The Mid-Autumn Festival (中秋节; Zhōngqiū Jié) is the time to give and receive delicious moon cakes stuffed with bean paste, egg yolk, coconut, walnuts and the like. The festival, now a one-day public holiday, takes place on the 15th day of the eighth lunar month (27 September 2015, 15 September 2016, 4 October 2017).

⚑ International Qiántáng River Tide Observing Festival

The most popular time to witness the surging river tides sweeping at up to 40km per hour along the Qiántáng River at Yánguān, outside Hángzhōu, is during the Mid-Autumn Festival, although you can catch the wall of water during the beginning and middle of every lunar month.

October

The week-long National Day holiday beginning 1 October wreaks havoc and it's best to avoid travelling. Book your hotel well in advance.

✖ Hairy Crabs

Now's the time to sample delicious *dàzháxiè* (hairy crabs) in Shànghǎi. They're at their best between October and December.

⚑ Shanghai Biennale

Held once every two years, this popular international arts festival (www.shanghai

(Top) Lantern Festival (p27) at the Yùyuán Gardens & Bazaar (p80)

(Bottom) Chinese New Year (p27) celebration at Lónghuá Temple & Pagoda (p168)

RICHARD I'ANSON / GETTY IMAGES ©

HOLGER LEUE / GETTY IMAGES ©

biennale.org) takes place on the former World Expo grounds.

November

Autumn's last gasp before winter begins.

✨ China Shanghai International Arts Festival

A month-long program (www.artsbird.com) of cultural events in October and November, which includes the Shanghai Art Fair, a varied program of international music, dance, opera and acrobatics, and exhibitions of the Shanghai Biennale.

🏃 Shanghai International Marathon

Usually held on the last Sunday of November, this annual event (www.shmarathon.com) attracts around 20,000 runners. It starts at the Bund and also includes a half-marathon.

December

Shànghǎi winters are generally unpleasant, with temperatures cold enough to cut to the bone, but rarely chilly enough for snow.

✨ Christmas

Not an official Chinese festival, Christmas (圣诞节; Shèngdàn Jié) is nevertheless a major milestone on the commercial calendar, and Shànghǎi's big shopping zones sparkle with decorations and glisten with fake snow.

With Kids

The Shànghǎi Disney Resort park in Pǔdōng, opening in late 2015, will be a must-see attraction for children visiting Shànghǎi. Until then the following sights will keep the family entertained.

Need to Know

➡ In general, 1.4m (4ft 7in) is the cut-off height for children's tickets. Children under 0.8m (2ft 7in) normally get in for free.

➡ Holidays and weekends see traffic peak, but in China 'crowded' takes on a new meaning. Try to schedule visits for weekdays if possible.

➡ For more information on events and activities, see *That's Shanghai* (http://online.thatsmags.com/city/shanghai) or *City Weekend* (www.cityweekend.com.cn/shanghai).

Acrobatics Shows

An evening with the acrobats – at Shànghǎi Circus World (p162) or the Shànghǎi Centre Theatre (p140) – will keep most kids entertained, with plate spinning, contortionism and daredevil motorcycle feats performed to *Star Wars* theme music.

Observation Decks

A bird's-eye view from a Pǔdōng skyscraper is one of Shànghǎi's top draws. Try the Shànghǎi Tower (p146), Shànghǎi World Financial Center (p145), Jinmao Tower (p147) or Oriental Pearl TV Tower (p147).

Maglev

Save this trip for your first or last day in Shànghǎi, heading from or to Pǔdōng International Airport. A trip on the hovering Maglev (p253) is thrilling (for all ages).

Museums

Shànghǎi History Museum

Waxworks and interactive exhibits make this museum (p147) fun for everyone.

Shànghǎi Science & Technology Museum

There are loads of things for kids to explore at this museum (p150), from volcano and space exhibits to sports activities and robots that can solve Rubik's cubes before your eyes. It also has IMAX and 4-D theatres.

Animal Parks

Shànghǎi Zoo

One of the best zoos in China, this one (p174) has plenty of green space to run around in and lawns to crash out on.

Shànghǎi Ocean Aquarium

One of the best in China, this acquarium (p147) is surprisingly good, with an impressive shark tunnel and intelligent exhibits. Avoid weekends if possible.

Amusement & Water Parks

Shànghǎi Disney Resort

This will be mainland China's first Disney Resort (http://en.shanghaidisneyresort.com.cn/en/). Expect epic queues.

Happy Valley

Happy Valley (p198) has scores of roller coasters, dive machines and other heart-thumping rides, with mellower attractions for younger kids plus a water park.

Dino Beach

This water park (p176) boasts Asia's largest wave pool and is a fun-filled way to beat the summer heat.

Like a Local

On the surface Shànghǎi appears more Western than anywhere else in China, bar Hong Kong. But don't be fooled by appearances – even if the Shanghainese are known for their flings with things foreign, engaging in local life quickly exposes a culture that is deeply Chinese.

Learn Chinese

True, you won't be yacking with locals in Mandarin overnight, but learning the basics – or at least trying to – will take you a long way. It's also great for your ego: you only need to master a handful of words before receiving lavish compliments about your language skills. On that note, it's good form to return the compliment when someone speaks to you in English.

If you've been hankering to learn some Shanghainese, well, we won't discourage you, but try to get Mandarin down first.

Eat Like a Local

This is actually a little trickier than it sounds. If you're wondering how you could not eat like a local, you only need to step into a Western restaurant or bar any night of the week – in Shànghǎi, temptations to stay in your comfort zone are everywhere. Eating Shanghainese-style may require an initial leap of faith (you want me to eat *what*?), but be brave and travel your taste buds: with specialities such as freshly pulled noodles, braised pork belly and quick-fried shrimp, you won't regret it.

Get on the Bus

The abundance of cheap taxis makes it all too easy to steer clear of public transport, but hopping on a bus is actually the best way to become part of the local fabric and you can see the city above ground. You will also be a rarity, as most *lǎowài* (foreigners) avoid the bus because it's challenging to use, but it's true Shànghǎi. A sense of adventure (and the name of your destination written down in Chinese) are helpful.

Practise Taichi

Head out to the nearest park in the early morning and look for a group that seems to be moving in slow motion. That's the martial art of taichi (*tàijíquán* is its full name), and if you want to try and follow along, you'll usually be welcomed. You may not learn much if you're just in town for a few days, but you can kick-start a new interest. If you're in Shànghǎi for the long haul, there are plenty of places to study. Taichi can be knackering, and some styles – such as Chen style – are seriously gruelling, even if you're 100% fit. The elderly in China are admirably active and supple.

Shop Till You Drop

The Shanghainese are Olympian shoppers. It doesn't matter whether you prefer the see-and-be-seen of megamalls or browsing in independent boutiques, creating your own individual style – no matter how crazy the look – is an essential part of Shanghainese identity. Guys, take note: many Shanghainese women expect their boyfriends to accompany them on shopping excursions and, just as importantly, to carry their purse or handbag.

For Free

Shànghǎi can dig serious holes in your wallet. And with inflation and yuán appreciation, it's only going to become a pricier destination. If you're on a budget or just want to save your cash, be sure to check out these recommendations.

Museums

Shànghǎi Museum

Shànghǎi's premier museum (p61) walks you through the pages of Chinese history via sumptuous art forms such as porcelain and landscape painting. The number of daily visitors is limited, so don't show up too late.

Power Station of Art

Inventive and thought-provoking art and design exhibitions, hosted in a vast former power station (p151) near the Huángpǔ River.

Bund History Museum

Located beneath the Monument to the People's Heroes at the north end of the Bund, this museum (p56) introduces the history of the area through a selection of old photographs and maps.

M50

M50 (p129) is the largest complex of modern-art galleries in Shànghǎi, housed in an industrial setting.

Shànghǎi Arts & Crafts Museum

OK, almost free but not quite: this gorgeous museum (p100) features live displays of traditional arts and crafts.

CY Tung Maritime Museum

Get the lowdown on the astonishing 15th-century explorer Zheng He at this museum (p167).

Communist Heritage

Make sure you have your passport with you to gain access to the Site of the 1st National Congress of the CCP (p97), Zhou Enlai's Former Residence (p98) and the Former Residence of Mao Zedong (p130).

Walks

The Bund

The Bund (p56) is the first port of call for most visitors to Shànghǎi. Thankfully, strolling the promenade and peeking inside the historic buildings here doesn't cost a cent. Restaurants and bars here are mostly upscale though.

Walking Tours

Follow one of our walking tours as they guide you around the backstreets and historic neighbourhoods of the Bund, Old Town, French Concession and Jìng'ān.

Parks

Shànghǎi parks, many of which are free, are great for people-watching. There is almost always something going on, whether it's people practising *qìgōng,* taichi, playing chess or holding impromptu music concerts.

Food preparation at street stall

Eating

Brash, stylish and forward-thinking, Shànghǎi's culinary scene typifies the city's craving for foreign trends and tastes. As much an introduction to regional Chinese cuisine as a magnet for talented chefs from around the globe, Shànghǎi has staked a formidable claim as the Middle Kingdom's trendiest dining destination.

NEED TO KNOW

Price Ranges

$ up to ¥60 per main

$$ ¥60 to ¥160 per main

$$$ over ¥160 per main

Opening Hours

In general, the Chinese eat earlier than Westerners. Restaurants serve lunch from 11am to 2pm and then often close until 5pm, when the dinner crowd start pitching up. They then carry on serving until 11pm. Smaller restaurants are more easy-going, so if you're hungry out of hours they're often happy to accommodate you, though you may be dining alone.

Ordering

Many places have English and/or picture menus, although they aren't always as comprehensive (or comprehensible) as the Chinese version. In any case, if you see a dish on someone else's table that looks delicious, just point at it when the waiter comes – no one will think you're being rude.

Tipping

Tipping is not done in the majority of restaurants. High-end international restaurants are another matter and while tipping is not obligatory, it is encouraged. Hotel restaurants automatically add a 15% service charge.

Reservations

At high-end restaurants or smaller places, it's sometimes necessary to book a week or more ahead, particularly if you want a decent table with a view. Otherwise, a couple of days in advance is fine.

Shanghainese Cuisine

Shànghǎi cuisine has been heavily influenced by the culinary styles of neighbouring provinces, and many of the techniques, ingredients and flavours originated in the much older cities of Yángzhōu, Sūzhōu and Hángzhōu. Broadly speaking, dishes tend to be sweeter and oilier than in other parts of China. Spiciness is anathema to Shànghǎi cooking.

The eastern provinces around the Yangzi River delta produce China's best soy sauces,

Dim sum

vinegars and rice wines, and the method of braising (known as 'red cooking'), using soy sauce and sugar as a base, was perfected here. As a general rule, the regional cuisine emphasises the freshness of ingredients – as with Cantonese food – using sauces and seasonings only to enhance the original flavours. Look out for the characters 本帮菜 (běnbāngcài) on restaurant shopfronts and in menus, which refers to authentic Shànghǎi homestyle cooking.

DUMPLINGS

Dumplings are the easiest way to become acquainted with Shanghainese cuisine. The city's favourite dumpling is the *xiǎolóngbāo* (小笼包; 'little steamer buns'), copied everywhere else in China but only true to form here. *Xiǎolóngbāo* are normally bought by the *lóng* (笼; steamer basket) and dipped in vinegar. They're simple, delicious, and have no annoying bones or unusual ingredients that might otherwise deter the naturally squeamish. There's an art to eating them though as they're full of a delicious but scalding gelatinous broth: the trick is to avoid both burning your tongue and staining your shirt (not easy), while road-testing your (shaky?) chopstick skills.

Tradition attributes the invention of the dumpling – filled with pork, and in more upmarket establishments with pork and crab – to Nánxiāng, a village north of Shànghǎi city.

Another Shanghainese speciality is *shēngjiān* (生煎), scallion-and-sesame-seed-coated dumplings that are fried in an enormous flat-bottomed wok, which is covered with a wooden lid. These are also

Top: Food for sale at Yùyuán Gardens & Bazaar (p80) in Old Town

Right: Diners at Nánxiáng Steamed Bun Restaurant (p89) in Old Town

pork-based; again, watch out for the palate-scorching, scalding oil, which can travel.

On the sweet side are *tāng yuán* (汤圆; also known as *yuán xiāo*), a small glutinous rice ball crammed with sweet fillings such as black-sesame paste or red-bean paste. They're traditionally eaten during the Lantern Festival and are utterly delectable. You can find them easily in Qībǎo at any time of year and are not hard to find anywhere in Shànghǎi, especially in small hole-in-the-wall eateries.

FISH & SEAFOOD

The city's position as a major port at the head of the Yangzi River delta means that you'll find plenty of fish and seafood, especially crab, river eel and shrimp. The word for fish (*yú*) is a homonym for 'plenty' or 'surplus', and fish is a mandatory dish for most banquets and celebrations. Fish commonly appearing on Shànghǎi's menus include *guìyú* (Mandarin fish), *lúyú* (Songjiang perch), *chāngyú* (pomfret) and *huángyú* (yellow croaker). Fish is usually *qīngzhēng* (steamed) but can be stir-fried, pan-fried or grilled. Squirrel-shaped Mandarin fish is one of the more famous dishes from Sūzhōu.

Dàzháxiè (hairy crabs) are a Shànghǎi speciality between October and December. They are eaten with soy, ginger and vinegar and downed with warm Shàoxīng rice wine. The crab is thought to increase the body's yin, or coldness, and so rice wine is taken lukewarm to add yang.

Sichuanese

One of China's most famous regional cuisines, Sìchuān cooking relies on six basic tastes, which can be combined together to form more than 20 distinct flavours, including 'numbing spicy', 'sour spicy', 'fish-flavour spicy' and 'chilli-oil spicy'. A key ingredient of Sichuanese cuisine is the Sìchuān peppercorn (花椒; *huājiāo*), which stimulates a characteristic tingling sensation (known as *má*) when eaten. Although spices dominate, the key to a good meal – as with all Chinese cuisines – is to balance the different flavours, so even those who don't like it hot will find something to savour.

Sichuanese cuisine uses ingredients that are inexpensive and relatively easy to find, hence a lot of restaurants across China – particularly tiny family-run places – have incorporated the standards in their menus. Look for classics such as kung pao chicken (*gōngbǎo jīdīng),* mapo tofu (*mápó dòufu*), fish-flavoured eggplant (*yúxiāng qiézi),* twice-cooked pork (*huíguōròu*) and dandan noodles *(dàndàn miàn).* In Shànghǎi, one of the most popular Sichuanese dishes is a giant bowl of tender pieces of catfish or frog suspended in hot chilli oil.

Hunanese

Known as *xiāngcài* (湘菜) in Chinese, Hunanese is another chilli-driven cooking tradition from China's wholesome heartland province of Húnán. It differs from Sichuanese cooking notably for its use of fresh chilli peppers (Sìchuān cuisine often makes use of chilli paste), which are ladled liberally onto many dishes. The heat from the peppers helps to expel moisture from the body, combatting high humidity in summer. Chicken, frog, freshwater fish and pork are key ingredients; some of the all-time classics include cumin spare ribs

---

CHEAP EATS

Shànghǎi's restaurants are in a whole other ballpark when compared to the rest of China – meal prices here exceed Běijīng, and to top it off, the portions are smaller! Thankfully, you can still eat cheaply if you know where to look. Malls are always a good place to begin; they may lack atmosphere, but you will always find food inside – check the basement or top floors. The larger malls are best as they often have decent food courts.

Street food is another sure thing, though in some neighbourhoods tiny restaurants and backstreet stalls can be hard to find. Look for corner noodle shops (面馆; *miànguǎn*) or dumpling vendors – popular stalwart chains include Yang's Fry Dumplings, Jiājiā Soup Dumplings, Wúyuè Rénjiā, Ajisen and Noodle Bull – and there are also a handful of top places to discover that are popular with Shànghǎi diners (but virtually unknown to foreign foodies without a tip-off). When in doubt, head to one of the official food streets for a good selection of restaurants that won't empty your wallet.

More and more restaurants catering to office workers offer good-value weekday lunch specials – to take advantage, ask for a *tàocān* (套餐).

TRY THIS!

Some of the most common Shanghainese dishes:

Smoked fish (熏鱼; *xūn yú*) This cold appetiser is gingery sweet and absolutely succulent when prepared correctly.

Drunken chicken (醉鸡; *zuìjī*) Another cold appetiser that consists of steamed chicken marinated overnight in Shàoxīng rice wine.

Braised pork (红烧肉; *hóngshāo ròu*) The uncontested king of Shanghainese home-cooking, this dish consists of tender, fatty pieces of pork stewed in sweet soy sauce.

Crystal shrimp (水晶虾仁; *shuǐjīng xiārén*) They may not look like much, but these quick-fried shrimp undergo an elaborate preparation that results in a unique texture that's both crispy and tender.

Lion's head meatball (狮子头; *shīzi tóu*) A large creamy meatball made of crab and minced pork, often presented as a single serving.

Crab and tofu casserole (蟹粉豆腐; *xièfěn dòufu*) Another dish that emphasises texture, this is a good way to indulge in crab without paying over-the-top prices.

(*zīrán páigǔ),* smoked-pork drypot (*gānguō tuǐròu*) and Mao Family braised pork (*máo shì hóngshāo ròu*).

Cantonese

Cantonese cuisine shares some similarities with Shànghǎi cuisine, notably light seasoning, an emphasis on natural flavours and lots of seafood (海鲜; *hǎixiān*). The Cantonese believe that good cooking does not require much flavouring, for it is the *xiān* (natural freshness) of the ingredients that mark a truly high-grade dish – hence the near obsessive attention paid to the freshness of ingredients.

Many of the smartest restaurants in Shànghǎi (often located in hotels) are Cantonese, though these cater primarily to Hong Kong tourists and businesspeople. The Cantonese restaurants that are most popular among everyday Shanghainese are entirely different; these are based on Hong Kong–style cafeterias known as 'tea restaurants' (*chá cāntīng*). Tea restaurants have a casual, downmarket atmosphere that's somewhat similar to an American diner, and feature an incredibly eclectic menu that ranges from Cantonese comfort food (beef with oyster sauce) to Italian pasta, Malaysian curries, sandwiches and an endless array of rice and noodle dishes.

The other famous tradition associated with Cantonese cuisine is, of course, dim sum (点心; *diǎnxīn*), which is served in a number of places in Shànghǎi, often incorporating local specialities (eg *xiǎolóngbāo*) in addition to Cantonese standards.

Muslim

Most of Shànghǎi's Muslim restaurants are run by Uighurs – Central Asians from Xīnjiāng, in China's far northwest. A refreshing alternative to the seafood and sweetness of Shanghainese cuisine, Xīnjiāng dishes involve lots of mutton (though chicken and fish dishes are

ANDREW ROWAT / GETTY IMAGES ©

Food stand on Sipailou Rd, Old Town (p84)

available), peppers, potatoes, cumin and delicious naan bread. Charcoal-grilled lamb kebabs are the staple here. It's not unusual for Uighur restaurants to offer evening performances of some kind (usually karaoke-style singing and dancing).

Shànghǎi's other main Muslim food vendors are tiny noodle stalls that specialise in *lāmiàn* (hand-pulled noodles), which are made fresh to order and can be served either in broth or fried.

Street Food

Shànghǎi's street food is excellent and usually quite safe to eat. It generally consists of tiny dumpling and noodle shops along with vendors selling snacks such as green onion pancakes *(cōngyóu bǐng)*, steamed buns *(bāozi)*, stinky tofu *(chòu dòufu)* and baked sweet potatoes *(dìguā)*. The city's food streets are also great places to browse for snacks. Try the following destinations:

➡ **Yunnan Rd** (p73)

➡ **Huanghe Rd** (p73)

➡ **Wujiang Rd** (p138)

➡ **Qībǎo** (p173)

➡ **North Jiangxi Rd** (p161)

Hotpot

A hugely popular winter meal is *huǒguō* (hotpot), and several chain restaurants corner the market. There are two varieties of hotpot: Sìchuān and Mongolian. A typical Sìchuān version is the circular *yuānyāng* hotpot, cleaved into hot (red) and mild (creamy coloured) sections, into which you plunge vegetables and meats. Plucking the cooked chunks from the broth, diners dip them in different sauces before consuming. It's a sweat-inducing experience that's best done with a group but can refreshingly be done solo in fast-food style hotpot restaurants. Mongolian hotpots differ in both appearance and flavour. These are typically a brass pot with a central stove and a ring-like bowl of non-spicy broth, into which are dropped thin slices of lamb and vegetables. Again, they are accompanied by sauces.

International

Shànghǎi is a destination for both global superchefs and less-established international talents trying to make a mark, so some fantastic meals can be found. Many restaurants are not averse to importing local ingredients and flavours; it's not exactly

Local farmers market

fusion cuisine, but it's not something you're likely to get back home either.

Much lower down the food chain are Shànghǎi's pubs, which are seriously happening dining destinations, for their convivial atmosphere and huge servings of comfort food. They aren't gastropubs though, so expect burgers, plates of pasta and countless sandwich variations offered by the majority of big-name drinking choices. The food is neither cheap nor particularly memorable, but venues are almost always packed. Slick, trendy cafe-restaurant chains such as Element Fresh serve an inventive and wide range of international and Asian cuisine to a largely young and dapper clientele.

Vegetarians

Chīzhāi (吃斋; vegetarianism) became something of a snobbish fad in Shànghǎi in the 1930s, when it was linked to Taoist and Buddhist groups. Growing middle-class values and attention to healthy living have encouraged a minor revival, although nothing like the zealous vegetarian and vegan populations in countries such as the UK or the USA. Beyond Buddhist dictates, very few Chinese give up meat for ethical reasons. But there is a growing band of vegetarian restaurants in Shànghǎi, and monasteries all have good meat-free restaurants.

The Chinese are masters at adding variety to vegetarian cooking and, to the bemusement of Western vegetarians, like to create so-called 'mock meat' dishes. Not only is it made to taste like any meaty food you could possibly think of, it's also made to resemble it; dishes can be made to look like everything from fish to spare ribs and chicken nuggets.

Etiquette

Strict rules of etiquette don't apply to Chinese dining; table manners are relaxed and get more so as the meal unfolds and the drinks flow. Meals commence in Confucian fashion – with good intentions, harmonic arrangement of chopsticks and a clean tablecloth – before spiralling into total Taoist mayhem, fuelled by incessant toasts with *báijiǔ* (hard liquor) or beer and furious smoking all round. Large groups in particular wreak havoc wherever they dine, with vast quantities of food often strewn across and under the table at the end of a meal.

A typical dining scenario sees a group of people seated at a round table, often with one person ordering on everyone's behalf.

Top: Traditional Chinese snacks
Middle: Chinese hotpot meal
Bottom: Chinese hairy crabs

ANDY QIANG / GETTY IMAGES ©

Roasted quail

full glasses of beer and causing consternation. Rice normally comes at the end of the meal. If you want it before, just ask.

The mainland Chinese dig their chopsticks into communal dishes, although some dishes are ladled out with spoons. Don't worry too much about your chopstick technique, especially when chasing slippery button mushroom around your plate; many Chinese are equally fazed by knives and forks.

Service

If there's one thing that drives foreigners in Shànghǎi crazy, it's the service. To be fair, some waiters really are completely disorganised and indifferent, but the underlying problem here is twofold: first, Chinese and Westerners have completely different expectations when it comes to what constitutes good service; second, overcoming the language barrier is no trifling matter. Remember that many waitstaff will only have a minimal command of English (if they speak it at all), and unless you are able to hold your own in Mandarin, there will inevitably be a few mix-ups and scowling faces somewhere along the way. Occasionally a waiter will be so intimidated by a non-Chinese-speaking customer that they will, unfortunately, completely ignore you, especially if it's a busy night. If you're having trouble, shout out *Fúwùyuán!* (Waiter!) loudly – don't be shy – and someone will usually appear.

If you're eating at a smaller place without a menu, be sure to clarify the total price *before* you finalise your order. If you don't use the wrapped serviette that is often dropped on your table and you are charged for it, ask for it to be deducted from the bill.

At Chinese restaurants, group diners never order their own dishes, but instead a selection of dishes embracing both *ròu* (meat) and *cài* (vegetables) are chosen for everyone to share. At large tables, dishes are placed on a lazy Susan, so the food revolves to each diner, occasionally knocking over

Eating by Neighbourhood

➡ **The Bund & People's Square** (p54) You'll find everything here from superchefs to food streets.

➡ **Old Town** (p78) The place to try Shànghǎi's famous dumplings.

➡ **French Concession** (p93) The epicentre of Shànghǎi dining.

➡ **Jìng'ān** (p126) Popular vegetarian restaurants and sumptuous Chinese.

➡ **Pǔdōng** (p143) Where to come for dinner with a view.

COOKING SCHOOLS

Learn how to make your own *xiǎolóngbāo* (小笼包; 'little steamer buns') dumplings at the following Shànghǎi institutions.

The Kitchen at... (☑6433 2700; www. thekitchenat.com; Ⓜ Changshu Rd) Great culinary school offering courses in regional Chinese and Western cuisines; good for both long-term residents and short-term visitors.

Chinese Cooking Workshop (Map p310; ☑5404 3181; www.chinesecooking-workshop.com) Learn different Chinese cooking styles from dim sum to Sichuanese. It also offers market tours and courses for kids.

PLAN YOUR TRIP EATING

Lonely Planet's Top Choices

Yang's Fry Dumplings (p73) Simple, greasy and oh-so-good.

Dī Shuǐ Dòng (p110) Country cookin' and Húnán chilli peppers.

Spicy Joint (p73) Blistering hot Sìchuān classics.

Din Tai Fung (p168) Glorified street food from the renegade province.

Lost Heaven (p108) A taste of paradise, from Yúnnán with love.

Fu 1039 (p111) Old-fashioned charm, succulent Shanghainese.

Best Budget Restaurants

Yang's Fry Dumplings (p73) The fried dumpling king, with branches scattered around town.

Jian Guo 328 (p106) Shanghainese homestyle, crammed with flavour, rammed with diners.

Wagas (p134) All across Shànghǎi; the town's coolest cafe chain.

Guǒyuán (p161) For the full spectrum of fiery Húnán flavours.

Best Shanghainese

Jesse (p108) (Xīnjíshì) Stand-out Shànghǎi home-cooking and a class act.

1221 (p175) Modern, smart, long-standing and unfailingly good.

Fu 1039 (p111) For a period villa atmosphere and lashings of sophistication.

Bǎoluó Jiǔlóu (p108) Ever-popular and expanded to accommodate a deluge of diners.

Best Hole-in-the-Wall Shanghainese

Lánxīn Cāntīng (p102) On-the-money family-run Shanghainese on Jinxian Rd.

Ā Dà Cóngyóubǐng (p102) The very definition of hole-in-the-wall, with long queues.

Best Gastronomic

Mr & Mrs Bund (p72) With bundles of personality and an appealing casual vibe.

T8 (p106) Elegant and stylish Xīntiāndì heavyweight in the gastronomic league.

M on the Bund (p72) Still winning plaudits for its faultless Bund-side menu and lavish views.

Ultraviolet (p72) Two-to-three month waiting list. Say no more.

Best International

Commune Social (p136) Shànghǎi's tapas-lovers are buzzing big time so join the queue.

ElEfante (p108) Romantic and alluring dining environment meets superb Mediterranean food.

Fortune Cookie (p106) Tofu chop suey and all your favourite (and hard-to-find) Chinatown specials.

Tock's (p71) Melt-in-the-mouth Montreal smoked beef.

Madison (p108) French Concession good-looker sporting a quality American menu.

Mercato (p71) For all your fine-dining Italian needs, Bund-side.

Best Dumplings

Yang's Fry Dumplings (p73) Simply scrumptious.

Din Tai Fung (p105) Pricier than the street equivalent, but outstanding xiǎolóngbāo.

Nánxiáng Steamed Bun Restaurant (p89) Shànghǎi's most famous with round-the-block lines.

Best Noodles

Noodle Bull (p161) Super-neat, super-sharp, super-tasty.

Ajisen (p71) A dab hand at swiftly served-up, full-flavoured Japanese-style noodles.

Wèixiāng Zhāi (p102) Wall-to-wall with noodle fans.

Best Vegetarian

Vegetarian Lifestyle (p136) Consistently tasty, wholesome, organic and MSG-free flavours.

Gōngdélín (p131) Buddhist ethos and flesh-free meat-look-alike dishes is its scrummy stock-in-trade.

Jen Dow Vegetarian Restaurant (p131) Three floors of goodness, slung out behind the Jìng'ān Temple.

Best Cafes

Wagas (p71) Natty, neat and snappy, with brisk staff and tempting offers.

Sumerian (p131) Small cafe, ample selection of brews plus bites.

Element Fresh (p169) Trendily cornering the smoothie, crisp salad and homemade hummus market.

Baker & Spice (p134) For all things sticky, sweet, wholesome and appetising. And ace coffee.

Fried dumplings

Best by Cuisine

Sichuanese

Yúxìn Chuāncài (p69) Past masters in the spicy-yet-numbing Sìchuān culinary arts.

Bāguó Bùyī (p153) You could eat here twice a day and still want more (not brekkie, perhaps).

South Beauty (p151) Magnificent, rich and flavoursome, with tip-top views to boot.

Cantonese

Cha's (p102) Perennially popular Canto fixture off Huaihai Rd.

Charme (p71) Full-on eclectic menu for eclectic palates.

Xian Yue Hien (p109) Delicious, dainty dim sum, in an exquisite setting.

Southeast Asian & South Asian

Pho Real (p109) *Pho* the real thing and a neat ambience, this is your place.

Vedas (p109) Sublime and aromatic Indian cuisine.

Coconut Paradise (p110) Sugar, spice and all things nice at this Thai joint.

Food Fusion (p104) Fantastic and affordable Malaysian cuisine.

Uighur

Xīnjiāng Fēngwèi Restaurant (p169) Go the whole-hog with an entire lamb roast.

Yàkēxī (p134) Spangly Jìng'ān Xīnjiāng fixture good for skewers, noodles and all things mutton.

Xībó (p109) The upscale Xīnjiāng choice, with a French Concession address.

Drinking & Nightlife

Shànghǎi adores its lychee martinis and cappuccinos to go, and with dazzling salaries and soaring property prices leaving the streets sloshing with cash, there are more than enough bars and cafes to wet the lips of the thirsty white-collar set. But don't be intimidated by the glitzy exterior: underneath is a happening nightlife scene that keeps everyone – VIP or not – entertained.

Bars

While bars today are predominantly frequented by expats and internationally minded locals, the race is on to capture the domestic market. In Běijīng a more populist approach rules, but Shànghǎi has stayed true to its roots: it's all about looking flash, sipping craft cocktails or imported wine, and tapping into the appetite for new trends. As might be expected, new bars pop up and disappear as fast as the money vanishes from your wallet, but the upside to the intense competition is weekly specials and happy hours (generally from 5pm to 8pm) that manage to keep things affordable.

Cafes

Cafe culture has long steeped Shànghǎi in caffeine and roasted coffee beans. Though decent teahouses can be as rare hen's teeth in trendy areas, lattes and sandwiches served at hip wi-fi hang-outs – some familiar names, some not – are all over the place. Also look out for street stalls selling bubble tea *(zhēnzhū nǎichá)*, a fabulously addictive Taiwanese milk tea with tapioca balls, and all sorts of related spin-offs, such as hot ginger drinks or freshly puréed papaya smoothies.

Clubbing

Shànghǎi's clubs are mostly big, glossy places devoted to playing mainstream house, techno and hip-hop. The offerings are getting better, and each year sees at least one new opening that strives to go beyond mainstream expectations. Loads of big-name DJs are flying in, which has helped boost interest among the locals, although the crowds are still predominantly made up of Westerners, Hong Kong and Taiwanese expats, and young, rich Shanghainese. Unsurprisingly, high turnover is the name of the game; check the local listings for the latest up-to-date hot spots.

Drinking & Nightlife by Neighbourhood

➡ **The Bund & People's Square** (p74) The Bund serves up glamour and gorgeous views in equal measure.

➡ **French Concession East** (p114) Fine crop of cafes and bohemian boltholes.

➡ **French Concession West** (p115) The most alcohol-saturated stretch of the city, jostling with clubs, pubs and microbreweries.

➡ **Jìng'ān** (p139) Sports bars and a few divey faves.

➡ **Pǔdōng** (p154) It's all about the views in Pǔdōng.

PUB CRAWL SHÀNGHǍI

Every Thursday, Friday and Saturday at 9.30pm, this organised **pub crawl** (http://pubcrawlshanghai.com) starts with an hour-long open bar (with free snacks), followed by a series of bars around town, with free shots and cut-price booze to follow. It's a great way to size up the Shànghǎi bar scene and make new friends. Sign up online; cost ¥150.

NEED TO KNOW

Opening Hours

➜ Many bars offer a full dining menu and open for lunch at 11am, and even earlier for weekend brunch. Bars that only serve drinks are more erratic; they might open anywhere between 4.30pm and 8pm.

➜ For the most part, last call at bars is 2am, but there's a handful of places that serve punters till 4am or 5am.

➜ Clubs generally don't get going until 10pm at the earliest and stay open until 2am on weekdays and 5am on weekends. Most close Sundays and Mondays.

➜ Sports bars will sometimes open around the clock, depending on what time the big game is on. You can even get a pancake breakfast at some places.

Prices

➜ On average, expect to spend roughly ¥35 to ¥45 for bottled beer, ¥70 for cocktails, ¥25 for coffee and ¥15 for tea and juice.

Event Listings

➜ Smart Shanghai (www.smartshanghai.com)
➜ Time Out (www.timeoutshanghai.com)
➜ City Weekend (www.cityweekend.com.cn/shanghai)

Lonely Planet's Top Choices

Glamour Bar (p74) Iconic views, great drinks and a first-rate events line-up.

Bell Bar (p114) The place to kick back in Tiánzǐfáng.

Apartment (p115) Loft-style bar with drinks, dining and dancing.

Shelter (p115) Cold War relic turned underground dance floor.

Cotton's (p115) The French Concession villa that everyone wants to call home.

Best Views

Flair (p154) Awesome nighttime panoramas from the alfresco terrace.

Vue (p162) Hop into the alfresco Jacuzzi, but don't forget your swimsuit.

Sir Elly's Terrace (p74) Find 270-degrees-worth of the best views in town.

Best Brews

Boxing Cat Brewery (p116) Much-applauded, three-floor microbrewery.

Kāibā (p139) For more draught craft beers and brews than you can shake a stick at.

Brew (p154) Putting Pǔdōng on the Shànghǎi ale map.

Dean's Bottle Shop (p114) Supercheap imported beers and a cracking range.

Best Design

Long Bar (p74) The Waldorf Astoria's re-creation of the legendary 34m-long Shànghǎi Club bar.

Bar Rouge (p74) Hip, supercrisp and stylish, with awesome views on tap.

Flair (p154) Japan's Super Potato–designed interior, almost as lovely as the view.

Best Cocktails

el Cóctel (p115) Mixology central.

Constellation (p116) A galaxy of gorgeous cocktails from the hands of master mixers.

Fennel Lounge (p139) Awesome drinks and a classy ambience.

Best Clubs

M1nt (p74) Shànghǎi all the way, with breathtaking views and sharks (the finned variety).

Geisha (p114) Japanese-inflected party spot with sake lounge, restaurant and club.

Dada (p116) When the grungy, indie-dive mood hits.

Best Wine

Burdigala 2 (p115) Top spot for Shànghǎi wine lovers.

Dr Wine (p116) Just what the doctor ordered.

Café des Stagiaires (p114) Fine wine is one of this bar's fortes.

Best Dives

Time Passage (p117) Rock-steady, unpretentious and a cut above the rest.

C's (p175) Graffiti-infested underground warren of cheap booze.

B&C (p139) Hugs from the owners and unlikely to break the bank.

Helen's (p140) Student-set fave in Jìng'ān.

⭐ Entertainment

Shànghǎi is no longer the decadent city that slipped on its dancing shoes as the revolution shot its way into town, but entertainment options have blossomed again over the past decade. Plug into the local cultural scene for a stimulating shot of gallery openings, music concerts and laid-back movie nights at the local bar.

Acrobatics

Shànghǎi troupes are among the best in the world. Spending a night watching them spinning plates on poles and tying themselves in knots never fails to entertain. *Era: Intersection of Time* is a hugely enjoyable and popular acrobatics, music, circus and dance 'multimedia and theatrical spectacular' held nightly from 7.30pm to 9pm in the Shànghǎi Circus World (p162). Feats conclude with eight motorcyclists zipping around within a globe – it's a massive hit with kids. See www.shanghaiacrobaticshow.com for an overview of other performances around town.

Music

Back in the 1920s and '30s, Shànghǎi enjoyed a brief heyday in the jazz spotlight, when big-band swing was the entertainment of choice. It remains a popular genre, and even if you won't catch many household names, there are some surprisingly good musicians here and some excellent clubs.

Classical music is also big, with both local and international orchestras performing regularly. For traditional Chinese music, check out the programs at the Oriental Art Center (p154) or Shànghǎi Grand Theatre (p75).

Shànghǎi's rock scene continues to evolve, though it is somewhat hamstrung by a lack of good venues. Nevertheless, a dedicated local following means that shows are often packed.

Chinese Opera

The shrill falsetto, crashing cymbals, expressive masks and painted faces of Běijīng opera are what most people have in mind when they think of Chinese opera, though the art form actually has a number of different styles. A local predecessor to Běijīng opera is the melodic Kūnjù or Kūnqǔ (Kun opera, from nearby Kūnshān), one of the oldest existing forms of Chinese opera, and best known for its 19-hour-long adaptation of the 16th-century erotic-love ghost story *The Peony Pavilion*. One of the only Kun opera troupes in the country is based in Shànghǎi.

The main problem with seeing a traditional opera in Shànghǎi is that there are no English surtitles and performances can be, well, quite lengthy. But the plotlines are relatively simple, which makes following the action not impossible. Nonetheless, before snatching up tickets for *A Dream of Red Mansions* at the Shànghǎi Grand Theatre, try the Běijīng opera highlights show in the Yìfū Theatre (p75) first.

Entertainment by Neighbourhood

➡ **The Bund & People's Square** (p75) Accessible entertainment: jazz, blues, classical music, ballet, soloists and Chinese opera.

➡ **French Concession** (p118) Stylish choice for live rock, theatre, jazz, and classical music.

➡ **Jìng'ān** (p140) For acrobatics and ballroom dancing.

➡ **Pǔdōng** (p154) Classical music, jazz, dance, opera and theatre, in a contemporary setting.

NEED TO KNOW

Tickets

➡ Tickets for all of Shànghǎi's performing-arts events can be purchased at the venues where the performances take place.

➡ Tickets are also available from Smart Ticket (www.smartshanghai.com/smartticket).

➡ The **Shanghai Cultural Information & Booking Centre** (☑6217 2426; www.culture.sh.cn; 272 Fengxian Rd, 奉贤路272号; ⊘9am-7pm), which is directly behind the Westgate Mall on West Nanjing Rd, often has tickets available when other places have sold out.

What's On

➡ The Shanghai Cultural Information & Booking Centre office carries a handy monthly bilingual *Calendar of Performances in Shanghai,* and you can find the same information in the expat magazine listings such as *Time Out* (www.timeoutshanghai.com) and *City Weekend* (www.cityweekend.com.cn/shanghai).

Lonely Planet's Top Choices

Shànghǎi Centre Theatre (p140) Spend an evening with the acrobats.

Shànghǎi Circus World (p162) Venue of the amazing acrobatics event *Era: Intersection of Time.*

Fairmont Peace Hotel Jazz Bar (p75) Swing with Shànghǎi's most famous – and oldest – jazz band.

Shànghǎi Grand Theatre (p75) Ballet, opera and classical music on the biggest stage in town.

Best Jazz & Rock Venues

JZ Club (p118) Backed up by a classy outfit in Hángzhōu, JZ is the jazz specialist's choice.

Cotton Club (p118) Long-established mainstay of the Shànghǎi blues and jazz scene.

Yùyīntáng (p176) Shànghǎi's premier indie venue, where the amps get cranked up to 11.

House of Blues & Jazz (p76) For all your Bund-side blues and jazz needs.

Mao Livehouse (p118) At the heart of Shànghǎi's international and local live-music circuit.

Best Classical Venues

Yìfū Theatre (p75) Shànghǎi's leading venue for traditional Chinese opera.

Shànghǎi Grand Theatre (p75) The top venue in Shànghǎi, in the heart of town.

Oriental Art Center (p154) The modern Pǔdōng choice for classical, jazz, dance, Chinese and Western opera.

Shànghǎi Concert Hall (p76) Classical concerts and international and national soloists.

Shanghai Culture Square (p118) State-of-the-art facility for musicals, drama, ballet and classical music.

Best Chinese Opera & Theatre

Yìfū Theatre (p75) Sit along with local opera-goers and enjoy the classics.

Pearl Theatre (p162) For drama, cabaret and more in a fantastic old theatre building.

Dàguān Theater (p155) Spiffing new Pǔdōng theater with cutting-edge equipment.

Píngtán Museum (p191) Live performances of Sūzhōu's musical storytelling.

Best Cinemas

Cathay Theatre (p118) Classic art deco picture-house decorating the corner of Middle Huaihai Rd and South Maoming Rd.

UME International Cineplex (p118) Right at the heart of the action in Xīntiāndì.

Shànghǎi Film Art Centre (p176) The principle venue for the Shanghai International Film Festival.

Shoe fashions on Taikang Rd, French Concession (p118)

Shopping

Shànghǎi's runaway property market and thrusting economy have filled pockets citywide: Shànghǎi shoppers buy-up big-time. While locals have a bee in their bonnet about luxury goods and designer labels, it's not all Gucci, Prada and Louis Vuitton. Whether it's boutique togs, a set of snappy heels, Chinese antiques, funky ceramics or a period poster from the Mao era, Shànghǎi is an A–Z of shopping.

Boutiques

The French Concession's bijou boutiques are where the most interesting finds are hidden, though given the sheer number of tiny shops, it can be hard to separate the wheat from the chaff. Start with recommended shopping strips to get a feel for local fashion before crossing town for a specific store. Keep in mind that unless you are petite, finding the right size can be difficult.

Tailor-Made Clothes

For perfect-fit clothing, the Old Town fabric markets may be the answer. There's all types of textiles, from synthetic to silk and cashmere. Compare fabric and prices at different stands to ensure no one is ripping you off. Suits, trousers, shirts, dresses and scarves can be made in as little as 24 hours (expect to pay extra), though a one-week turnaround is more realistic. For traditional Chinese *qípáo* (cheongsam) and jackets, head to South Maoming Rd or Tiánzǐfáng in the French Concession.

NEED TO KNOW

Opening Hours

Most shops open from 10am to 10pm daily, though government-run stores often close at 6pm while smaller boutiques may not open until noon. Yùyuán Bazaar and Dongtai Road Antique Market are best visited early in the day.

Chinese Numbers

If negotiating in pidgin Chinese, be very careful of similar-sounding numbers: 14 (十四; shísì) and 40 (四十; sìshí); and 108 (一百零八; yībǎilíngbā) and 180 (一百八; yībǎibā). These offer great potential for misunderstanding, deliberate or otherwise.

Customs

Technically, nothing older than 200 years can be taken out of China, but you'd be lucky to corner any genuine antiques that old in Shànghǎi. If buying a reproduction, make sure the dealer provides paperwork declaring it is not an antique. Dealers should also provide the proper receipts and paperwork for any antique items. Keep the receipts along with the business card of the dealer, just in case.

Phrases to Know

➡ Duōshao qián? (多少钱) – How much?

➡ Tài guì le! (太贵了) – Too expensive!

➡ Tài xiǎo (太小) – Too small.

➡ Tài dà (太大) – Too big.

➡ Bù yào (不要) – I don't want it.

Counterfeits

'In Shànghǎi, everything can be faked except for your mother', or so the saying goes. Counterfeit goods are ubiquitous; even if you've set out to buy a genuine item, there's no guarantee that's what you're going to get. Antiques in particular are almost always reproductions: the best advice is to buy something because you like it, not because you think it has historic value.

DVD stores and fake markets are drawcards for visitors and can make for a fun browse, but remember that although your purchases might not cost much (provided you're a decent bargainer), they most likely break international copyright law, and they may soon fall apart.

Haggling

In Shànghǎi markets, haggling over prices is standard practice. Most common is for the vendor to punch a price into a calculator and hand it hopefully to you for inspection. You then laugh theatrically and tap in 10% to 25% of their price, before looking the vendor in the eye. The seller shakes their head, emits a dismissive cry, adjusts the price a bit and hands the calculator back to you. This goes on until the price drops by at least 50%. At some touristy places, like Yùyuán Bazaar, vendors will go as low as 25% of the original price. But at stores where a discount is not normally offered, you may only get 10% or 20% off.

It often pays to smile, shrug and walk away to a nearby stall selling exactly the same thing. Most times the vendor will chase you down and get you to agree to a deal. Bear in mind, though, that the point is to achieve a mutually acceptable price and not to screw the vendor into the ground. It's always best to smile, which will help keep negotiations light even if you don't ultimately agree on a sale.

Shipping

Most reputable shops will take care of insurance, customs and shipping for larger items, though find out first exactly what the dealer covers. Separate charges may materialise for handling, packaging, customs duty and quarantine, driving the shipping charges above the price of the item. Also consider how much it will cost to get the goods from the shipping port to your home.

Shipping clothing, curios and household items on your own is generally not a problem. China Post (中国邮政; Zhōngguó Yóuzhèng) has an excellent packing system for airmailing light items.

Shopping by Neighbourhood

➡ **The Bund & People's Square** (p76) Luxury togs, gifts, accessories and East Nanjing Rd.

➡ **Old Town** (p91) Fabric and antique markets plus an abundance of souvenirs.

➡ **French Concession** (p118) Hip boutiques, shoe shops, vintage, jewellery, ceramics, malls and shíkùmén alleyway shopping.

➡ **Jìng'ān** (p140) Upmarket malls, designer shopping, funky ceramics and knock-offs.

➡ **Pǔdōng** (p155) Big name malls and fakes.

Lonely Planet's Top Choices

Tiánzǐfáng (p119) Great collection of shops in an artsy enclave.

Old Street (p91) All your souvenir needs, from calendar posters to Mao-era kitsch.

Spin (p140) The coolest china in China.

AP Xīnyáng Fashion & Gifts Market (p155) The mother of all fake markets.

Amy Lin's Pearls (p141) Fresh- and saltwater pearls at unbeatable prices.

Best Boutiques

NuoMi (p123) Figure-conscious clothing that's stylish and feminine, with organic fabrics and a sustainable ethos.

Heirloom (p121) Classy and eye-catching handbags and clutches.

Lolo Love Vintage (p123) Fine choice of vintage threads.

OOAK Concept Boutique (p123) Slim, trendy and full of bright and interesting jewellery and fashion ideas.

Best Souvenirs & Antiques

Dongtai Road Antique Market (p91) Delve into this sprawling market for a diamond or two from the rough.

Art Deco (p141) Choice selection of furniture from Swinging Shànghǎi's deco age.

Yùyuán Bazaar (p80) A compendium of Middle Kingdom knick-knacks, souvenirs and gifts.

Best Art

Shànghǎi Museum Art Store (p76) A cut above the rest, with quality porcelain and some great books.

Link Shanghai (p119) Individual, creative, artsy and at the heart of Tiánzǐfáng.

Propaganda Poster Art Centre (p124) The cream of Mao-era agitprop, before it became kitsch.

Best Ceramics

Spin (p140) Zestful, inspiring, beautifully crafted and affordable pieces.

Pilingpalang (p119) Bursting with colour and eye-catching deco lines.

Pottery Workshop (p120) Selling pieces from the workshop's resident potters.

Happy Clay (p125) Light-hearted and whimsical handmade pieces.

Best Local Fashion

Annabel Lee (p76) Elegant array of silk, linen and cashmere accessories, just off the Bund.

Xīntiāndì Style (p119) Host of stylish boutiques, all under one roof.

Madame Mao's Dowry (p124) Highly browsable collection of clothing, jewellery, postcards and Maoist ephemera.

Urban Tribe (p124) Ethnic-inspired natural fabric clothing and excellent handmade jewellery.

Best Markets

Shíliùpù Fabric Market (p91) Bundles of affordable silks and all manner of fabrics.

South Bund Fabric Market (p91) Stuffed with fabric stalls.

AP Xīnyáng Fashion & Gifts Market (p155) Shànghǎi's premier bonanza for knock-offs; a sprawling mass of bargains.

Explore Shànghǎi

SHÀNGHǍI'S
TOP SIGHTS

Neighbourhoods at a Glance

❶ The Bund & People's Square p54

Shànghǎi's standout landmark is the Bund, a grandiose curve of colonial-era buildings lining the western bank of the Huángpǔ River. It's the first stop for visitors, and the historic architecture houses a profusion of exclusive restaurants, bars, shops and hotels.

Running perpendicular from the waterfront is East Nanjing Rd – a maelstrom of shoppers, department stores and neon lights – which eventually runs into the city's heart, People's Sq. The de facto centre of town, this large open space is studded with museums and fenced in by skyscrapers.

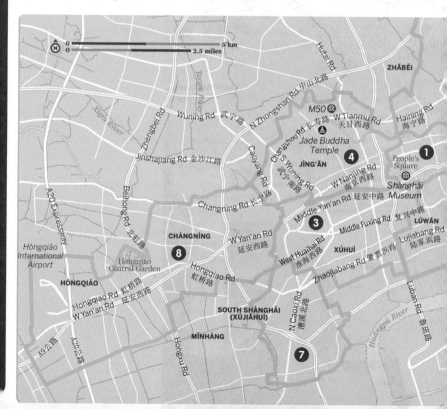

❷ Old Town p78

The original city core and the sole part of Shànghǎi to predate the 1850s, the Old Town is a favourite with visitors hoping to glimpse 'traditional' China. Many of the older buildings have been replaced with modern apartment blocks, but there are still more temples here than in the rest of the city combined, and pockets are impregnated with atmosphere and shabby charm.

❸ French Concession p93

The city's most stylish side, the former French Concession is where the bulk of Shànghǎi's disposable cash is splashed. The low-rise, villa-lined, leafy backstreets are perfectly geared to shopping, dining and entertainment, but a brood of museums makes the former concession – now a handsome melange of several distinct neighbourhoods – a cultural experience as well.

❹ Jìng'ān p126

North of the French Concession ranges the vibrant commercial district of Jìng'ān, an expat-friendly domain anchored around bustling West Nanjing Rd, and defined by its abundance of period architecture, malls, top-end hotels and enticing *lòngtáng* (laneway) architecture. Further away you run slap-bang into the grittier railway station area, not far from the city's most famous Buddhist temple and happening art enclave.

❺ Pǔdōng p143

Pǔdōng is brand-spanking-new Shànghǎi, sprawling east with seemingly infinite high-rises and skyscrapers from the Huángpǔ River's far bank. A dazzling cosmos of high-altitude five-star hotels, banks, Maglev trains, giant TV screens and faceless residential towers, it's all set to a backdrop of roaring traffic and construction work.

❻ Hóngkǒu & North Shànghǎi p156

Hóngkǒu envelops north Shànghǎi from Sūzhōu Creek and the Bund. It's a less-polished domain of old lanes, tatty working-class textures and heritage architecture. A former American (and later Japanese) controlled concession, Hóngkǒu is undergoing gradual (sometimes lavish) redevelopment, especially close to Sūzhōu Creek.

❼ Xújiāhuì & South Shànghǎi p164

An extension of the French Concession, Xújiāhuì's tantalising Jesuit heritage and the prestigious Jiāotōng University contrast spectacularly with the outsized shopping centres dominating its main intersection.

❽ West Shànghǎi p171

You don't get a sense for just how vast the city is until you start to head west, where the residential and office towers, conference centres and busy highways of Shànghǎi's suburban districts stretch into the horizon. The focal point here is Hóngqiáo's airport and railway station, but the old canal town of Qībǎo is well worth a visit.

The Bund & People's Square

THE BUND | PEOPLE'S SQUARE

Neighbourhood Top Five

1 Stroll along the **Bund** promenade (p56), and capture Pǔdōng lighting up through a martini glass.

2 Load up on Chinese culture's greatest hits at the **Shànghǎi Museum** (p61).

3 Catch up with the latest trends in contemporary Chinese art at the **Rockbund Art Museum** (p65).

4 Dine at some of Shànghǎi's signature Bund **restaurants** (p69), all with showstopping views.

5 Plunge into the neon-lit swell of **East Nanjing Road** (p65).

For more detail of this area see Map p296

Explore: The Bund & People's Square

Shànghǎi's definitive spectacle, the grand sweep of the riverside Bund (外滩; Wàitān) is a designer retail and dining strip; it's *the* address in town for the city's most exclusive boutiques, restaurants and hotels. The best strategy is just to stroll, weighing up the bombastic neoclassical contours with the pristine geometry of Pǔdōng over the water.

The streets west from the waterfront morph instantly into a less salubrious commercial district housed in the uncleaned shells of concession-era buildings, mixed with newer skyscrapers and office towers. Yet even the most casual of wanders yields sudden architectural gems.

Continuing west is People's Sq (人民广场), a swathe of open space boxed in by towers. The de facto city centre, it's the address of a host of museums, entertainment venues, malls, a park and the city hall. People's Sq is free of the rigid geometry and supervision of Běijīng's Tiān'ānmén Sq, with musicians serenading pockets of crowds.

Linking the Bund with People's Sq is East Nanjing Rd, once China's most famous shopping street. Mostly pedestrian, it's a bonanza of department stores, neon signs, determined English-speaking girls latching onto foreign men (getting kick-backs from cafes they drag their victims to), incessant offers of 'massagee', and hawkers flogging copy watches and gimmicky toys.

Local Life

➡ **Dumplings** Sample *shēngjiān* at Yang's Fry Dumplings (p73) or *xiǎolóngbāo* at Jiājiā Soup Dumplings (p73) or Nánxiáng Steamed Bun Restaurant (p73).

➡ **Museum-hopping** Spend a rainy day checking out the museums at People's Sq (p68).

➡ **Shopping** Join the throngs clogging up East Nanjing Rd, crowding into malls such as Raffles City or angling for discounts in the subterranean stalls around the People's Sq metro station (p76).

Getting There & Away

➡ **Metro** The Bund is a 10-minute walk east from the East Nanjing Rd stop (lines 2 and 10). People's Sq, one of the city's busiest stations, is served by lines 1, 2 and 8.

➡ **Pedicab** Drivers hang out in side streets along the Bund and charge ¥10 (total) to Yùyuán Gardens.

➡ **Bund Sightseeing Tunnel** Runs from the Bund to Pǔdōng under the Huángpǔ River.

➡ **Tourist train** Runs the length of East Nanjing Rd's pedestrianised section (tickets ¥5) from Middle Henan Rd to the Shànghǎi No 1 Department Store.

Lonely Planet's Top Tip

Avoid young people posing as out-of-town students who ply the main tourist drags (East Nanjing Rd, the Bund), engaging visitors in conversation. They seem friendly enough. You help them take a picture, chat about China and then they invite you to a traditional tea ceremony. It sounds welcoming, but **don't** do it. You'll get the tea all right, but you'll also get a bill for US$100 or more.

✕ Best Places to Eat

➡ Lost Heaven (p71)
➡ Yang's Fry Dumplings (p73)
➡ Mr & Mrs Bund (p72)
➡ Yúxìn Chuāncài (p69)
➡ M on the Bund (p72)

For reviews, see p69. ➡

🍷 Best Places to Drink

➡ Glamour Bar (p74)
➡ New Heights (p74)
➡ Long Bar (p74)
➡ Bar Rouge (p74)
➡ Barbarossa (p75)

For reviews, see p74. ➡

🔒 Best Shopping

➡ Annabel Lee (p76)
➡ Sūzhōu Cobblers (p76)
➡ Shànghǎi Museum Art Store (p76)
➡ Shànghǎi No 1 Food Store (p76)
➡ Blue Shànghǎi White (p76)

For reviews, see p76. ➡

FEARGUS COONEY / GETTY IMAGES ©

 TOP SIGHT
THE BUND

Symbolic of colonial Shànghǎi, the Bund was the city's Wall St, a place of feverish trading and fortunes made and lost. Originally a towpath for dragging barges of rice, it's remained the first port of call for visitors since passengers began disembarking here over a century ago. Today, however, it's the extravagant bars and restaurants and the hypnotising views of Pǔdōng that pull crowds.

Promenade

The Bund offers a host of things to do, but most visitors head straight for the riverside promenade to pose for photos in front of Pǔdōng's ever-changing skyline. The area is essentially open around the clock, but it's at its best in the early morning, when locals are out practising taichi, or in the early evening, when both sides of the river are lit up and the romance of the waterfront reaches a crescendo. The promenade begins at Huángpǔ Park; you can follow it 1km to the Bund's south end at the Meteorological Signal Tower.

Huángpǔ Park

China's first public **park** (黄浦公园; Huángpǔ Gōngyuán; Map p296; Ⓜ East Nanjing Rd) was laid out in 1886 by a Scottish gardener shipped out to Shànghǎi especially for that purpose. The park achieved lasting notoriety for its apocryphal 'No Dogs or Chinese allowed' sign (p69). Located at the northern end of the Bund, the park's anachronistic **Monument to the People's Heroes** (Map p296) hides the entrance to the **Bund History Museum** (外滩历史纪念馆; Wàitān Lìshǐ Jìniànguǎn; Map p296; ⏰ 9am-4.30pm Mon-Fri) **FREE**, which contains a collection of old maps and photographs.

DON'T MISS...

➡ The Promenade
➡ Fairmont Peace Hotel
➡ HSBC Bank Building
➡ Dining or drinks with a view

PRACTICALITIES

➡ 外滩; Wàitān
➡ Map p296
➡ East Zhongshan No 1 Rd; 中山东一路
➡ Ⓜ East Nanjing Rd

Jardine Matheson

Standing at No 27 on the Bund is the former headquarters of early opium traders **Jardine Matheson** (Map p296), which went on to become one of the most powerful trading houses in Hong Kong and Shànghǎi. Also known as EWO, it was the first foreign company to erect a building on the Bund – in 1851. It later invested in China's earliest railways and cotton mills, and even operated a popular brewery. The current building replaced the original and was completed in 1922. In 1941 the British Embassy occupied the top floor, facing the German Embassy across the road in the Glen Line Building, at No 28. Jardine Matheson now holds the House of Roosevelt, which is quite possibly China's largest wine cellar and bar.

Bank of China

Originally established in 1897, the Bank of China (中国银行; Zhōngguó Yínháng), at No 23, relocated its headquarters from Běijīng to Shànghǎi in the 1920s, undergoing a major transformation from state bureaucracy to a market-driven business. Although the bank has occupied this address since 1923, the present building was only begun in 1935 and was originally designed to be the tallest building in the city at 33 storeys high. The Sino-Japanese War interrupted construction and it finally opened in 1942, its front door guarded by a magnificent pair of art deco lions.

Fairmont Peace Hotel

Lording it over the corner of East Nanjing Rd and East Zhongshan Rd is the most famous building on the Bund, the landmark Fairmont Peace Hotel, constructed between 1926 and 1929. It was originally built as Sassoon House, with Victor Sassoon's famous Cathay Hotel on the 4th to 7th floors. It wasn't for the hoi polloi, with a guest list running to Charlie Chaplin, George Bernard Shaw and Noel Coward, who penned *Private Lives* here in four days in 1930 when he had the flu. Sassoon himself spent weekdays in his personal suite on the top floor, just beneath the green pyramid. The building was renamed the Peace Hotel in 1956.

Even if you aren't a guest, pop in to savour the wonderful art deco lobby and magnificent rotunda, or lend an ear to the old jazz band in the evening. It's also possible to arrange an hour-long tour (¥100) of the premises through the Peace Gallery (p65) a small, museum-like space displaying intriguing hotel memorabilia, hidden up a flight of stairs near the main entrance. It's recommended you book a half-day in advance.

WHAT'S IN A NAME?

The Bund gets its Anglo-Indian name from the embankments built up to discourage flooding (a *band* is an embankment in Hindi). There's some debate over how to say the word, though given its origins, it's likely the correct pronunciation is 'bunned', not 'booned'.

SHÀNGHǍI CLUB

The Shànghǎi Club, at No 2 on the Bund, originally had 20 rooms for residents, but its most famous accoutrement was its bar – at 34m said to be the longest in Asia. Once one of the most exclusive spots in the city, the building lost considerable face in the 1990s when a KFC set up inside in the foyer, but it found redemption with the opening of the Waldorf Astoria.

RIVER CRUISE

The Bund's monumental facades presented an imposing – if strikingly un-Chinese – view for those arriving in the busy port. For a glimpse of how it might have looked, take a river cruise departing from the docks in either Pǔxī or Pǔdōng.

The Bund

The best way to get acquainted with Shànghǎi is to take a stroll along the Bund. The waterfront was the seat of colonial power from the mid-19th century onward, and the city's landmark hotels, banks and trading houses all established themselves here, gradually replacing their original buildings with even grander constructions as the decades passed.

The Bund had its golden age in the 1920s and '30s before the turmoil of war and occupation brought an end to the high life enjoyed

by Shànghǎi's foreign residents. Mothballed during the communist era, it's only in the past 15 years that the strip has sought to rekindle its past glory, restoring one heritage building after another. Today, it has become China's showcase lifestyle destination, and many of the landmarks here house designer restaurants, swish cocktail bars and the flagship stores of some of the world's most exclusive brands.

Once you've wandered the promenade and ogled at the Pǔdōng skyline opposite, return

North China Daily News Building (1924)

Known as the 'Old Lady of the Bund', the *News* ran from 1864 to 1951 as the main English-language newspaper in China. Look for the paper's motto above the central windows.

Hongkong & Shanghai Bank Building (1923)

Head into this massive bank (🕘9am-4.30pm Mon-Fri) to marvel at the beautiful mosaic ceiling, featuring the 12 zodiac signs and the world's (former) eight centres of finance.

Russo-Chinese Bank Building (1902)

Custom House (1927)

Still a customs house today, the building is decorated with some delightful octagonal lobby ceiling mosaics portraying sailing junks, just within the entrance. Sadly, photography is not allowed.

Former Bank of Communications (1947)

Bund Public Service Centre (2010)

TOP TIP

The promenade is open around the clock, but it's at its best in the early morning, when locals are out practising taichi, or in the early evening, when both sides of the river are lit up and the majesty of the waterfront is at its grandest.

to examine the Bund's magnificent facades in more detail and visit the interiors of those buildings open to the public.

This illustration shows the main sights along the Bund's central stretch, beginning near the intersection with East Nanjing Road. The Bund is 1km long and walking it should take around an hour. Head to the area south of the Hongkong & Shanghai Bank Building to find the biggest selection of prominent drinking and dining destinations.

Former Palace Hotel (1909)

Now known as the Swatch Art Peace Hotel (an artists' residence and gallery, with a top-floor restaurant and bar), this building hosted Sun Yatsen's 1911 victory celebration following his election as the first president of the Republic of China.

CHRISTOPHER PITTS

Bank of China (1942)

This unusual building was originally commissioned to be the tallest building in Shànghǎi, but, probably because of Victor Sassoon's influence, wound up being one metre shorter than its neighbour.

Former Bank of Taiwan (1927)

Former Chartered Bank Building (1923)

Reopened in 2004 as the upscale entertainment complex Bund 18, the building's top-floor Bar Rouge is one of the Bund's premier late-night destinations.

CHRISTOPHER PITTS

GREG ELMS/GETTY©

Fairmont Peace Hotel (1929)

Originally built as the Cathay Hotel, this art deco masterpiece was *the* place to stay in Shànghǎi and the crown jewel in Sassoon's real estate empire.

Former Palace Hotel

The Palace Hotel was China's largest hotel and the tallest building on Nanjing Rd when completed (1909). Ravaged by fires in its early years, it was then strafed by stray Chinese bombs in 1937 (one of the Bund's most tragic moments; 720 passers-by were killed). Former guests include Sun Zhongshan, who lent his name to the road along the Bund. Today it's the Swatch Art Peace Hotel.

Custom House

The **Custom House** (Map p296; 13 E Zhongshan No 1 Rd; Ⓜ East Nanjing Rd), established at this site in 1857 and rebuilt in 1927, is one of the most important buildings on the Bund. Capping it is Big Ching, a bell modelled on London's Big Ben. Clocks were by no means new to China, but Shànghǎi was the first city in which they gained widespread acceptance and the lives of many became dictated by a standardised, common schedule. During the Cultural Revolution, Big Ching was replaced with loudspeakers that blasted out revolutionary songs ('The East is Red') and slogans.

HSBC Building

Adjacent to the Custom House, the **Hongkong & Shanghai Bank building** (HSBC Building; Map p296000) was constructed in 1923. The bank was first established in Hong Kong in 1864 and in Shànghǎi in 1865 to finance trade, and soon became one of the richest in Shànghǎi, arranging the indemnity paid after the Boxer Rebellion. The magnificent mosaic ceiling inside the entrance was plastered over until its restoration in 1997 and is therefore well preserved. Photography is not allowed inside.

Three on the Bund

With its opening 10 years ago, **Three on the Bund** (Map p296) became the strip's first lifestyle destination and the model that many other Bund edifices followed. Upscale restaurants and bars occupy the upper three floors, while the lower levels are anchored by Armani, the Evian Spa and the conceptually minded Shanghai Gallery of Art (p65).

Meteorological Signal Tower

This **signal tower** (外滩信号台; Wàitān Xìnhào Tái; Map p296; 1 East Zhongshan No 2 Rd; 中山东二路1号; ⊙10am-5pm; Ⓜ East Nanjing Rd) FREE was built in 1907 to replace the wooden original as well as to serve as a meteorological relay station for the tireless Shànghǎi Jesuits. In the early 1950s it was commandeered as a river-boat police station, and in 1995 the entire edifice was shunted 22.4m to its present location.

WINING & DINING ON THE BUND

The Bund overflows with restaurants and bars that specialise in fabulous views and period charm. Top choices:

➡ **Fairmont Peace Hotel** Tap your foot and raise a glass in its old-fashioned Jazz Bar (p75).

➡ **Swatch Art Peace Hotel** Part of Shook! (p72).

➡ **Bund 18** Features Bar Rouge (p74) and Mr & Mrs Bund (p72).

➡ **Five on the Bund** Home to M on the Bund (p72) and the Glamour Bar (p74).

➡ **Three on the Bund** With Jean Georges (p72), Mercato (p71) and New Heights (p74).

➡ **Waldorf Astoria** At No 2, with its immense and prestigious Long Bar (p74).

ALAN COPSON / GETTY IMAGES ©

TOP SIGHT
SHÀNGHǍI MUSEUM

One of the world's premier repositories of Chinese art, the Shànghǎi Museum celebrates one masterpiece after another while guiding visitors through the pages of Chinese history. Whether you prefer the meditative beauty of a landscape painting or the crafted perfection of a Song dynasty bowl, the luxurious curves of a Ming chair or the expressive face of a Nuo mask, this is the one museum in Shànghǎi you must not miss.

Although you could easily spend an entire day here, many people only come with a half-day to spare. Thus, in order to get the most out of your visit, make sure to identify your interests ahead of time. It's best to arrive in the morning, as only 8000 people are allowed in daily and lines can get long once the tour groups descend.

Ancient Chinese Bronzes Gallery

On the ground floor is the museum's star attraction, a collection of ancient bronzes. Some date back to the 21st century BC. Many visitors are unfamiliar with this early aspect of Chinese art and for this reason the exhibit may seem less appealing than others, but Asian art enthusiasts should make a point of stopping by this unrivalled collection.

These bronzes were created during a long shamanistic period that saw the development of ancestor worship and ritual – two facets of life that would go on to dominate Confucianism.

Their diversity of shapes and versatility are striking, revealing the significance of bronze in important rituals and, later, everyday life. Objects range from wine bottles, jars and goblets to weapons and even two-toned bells, once China's chief musical instrument. The most important ritual bronzes were *dǐng* (three- or four-legged food vessels

DON'T MISS...

➡ Ancient Chinese Bronzes Gallery
➡ Ancient Chinese Ceramics Gallery
➡ Chinese Painting Gallery
➡ Minority Nationalities Art Gallery

PRACTICALITIES

➡ 上海博物馆; Shànghǎi Bówùguǎn
➡ Map p296
➡ www.shanghai museum.net
➡ 201 Renmin Ave; 人民大道201号
➡ admission free
➡ ⏰9am-5pm
➡ Ⓜ People's Sq

ARCHITECTURAL INSPIRATION

Before you enter the museum, admire the exterior of the building. Designed by architect Xing Tonghe to recall an ancient bronze *dǐng* (a three-legged cooking vessel), the building also echoes the shape of a famous bronze mirror from the Han dynasty, exhibited within the museum.

The audio guide is well worth the ¥40 (¥400 deposit, or your passport). It highlights particularly interesting items as well as offering good gallery overviews and general background information.

SEAL GALLERY

Although obscure, this gallery on the 3rd floor provides a fascinating glimpse into the niche art form of miniature carving. Seals (chops) are notable both for the intricacy of their design and the special script used on the underside, which is known to only a handful of artisans and calligraphers. Look for the two orange soapstone seals that feature incredibly detailed landscapes in miniature.

used for cooking and serving) – one highlight in the collection is an enormous 10th-century *dǐng* weighing 200kg. Look for inscriptions on the vessels and you'll be able to witness the early evolution of Chinese writing.

Decoration is an intrinsic element of the beauty of ancient bronzes. The most common design is the stylised animal motif, depicting dragons, lions and the phoenix. This was replaced in the 10th century BC by zigzags (representing thunder) and cloud designs, and later by geometric shapes. As bronzes lost their ritual significance, decorative scenes from daily life made an appearance. Later still, stamped moulds, lost wax techniques and piece moulds enabled designs to become ever more complex.

When appreciating the bronzes, remember that they would have originally been a dazzling golden colour. Oxidisation has given them their characteristic dull green patina.

Ancient Chinese Sculpture Gallery

Also on the ground floor, exhibits in this gallery range from the funeral sculptures of the Qin and Han dynasties to the predominantly Buddhist sculptures of the following centuries, which were heavily influenced by the Indian and Central Asian styles that came to China via the Silk Road. If you're interested in Buddhism and the various representations of bodhisattvas, disciples and fierce-looking *lokapalas* (Buddhist protectors), it's certainly worth a visit. Note that the sculptures displayed were almost all painted, but only scraps of pigment survive.

Ancient Chinese Ceramics Gallery

On the 2nd floor, this is one of the largest and most fascinating galleries in the museum. The exhibits include so much more than the stereotypical blue-and-white porcelain that many think of when they hear the word 'china'. Even if you don't consider yourself a fan, this is one gallery that everyone should at least take a look at.

It begins with 6000-year-old pottery excavated from just outside Shànghǎi before leap-frogging ahead to the figurines of Han times; the *sāncǎi* (polychrome) pottery of the Tang; the marvellously diverse and elegant tableware of the Song; and the sea-green celadon jars, Yíxīng teapots and vast collection of porcelain produced under the Ming and Qing.

Don't worry if you don't know your 'ewer with overhead handles in *dòucǎi*' from your 'brushholder with *fěncǎi* design', it's all part of a luxurious learning curve. Look out for the 'celadon vase with ancient bronze design' and the delightful

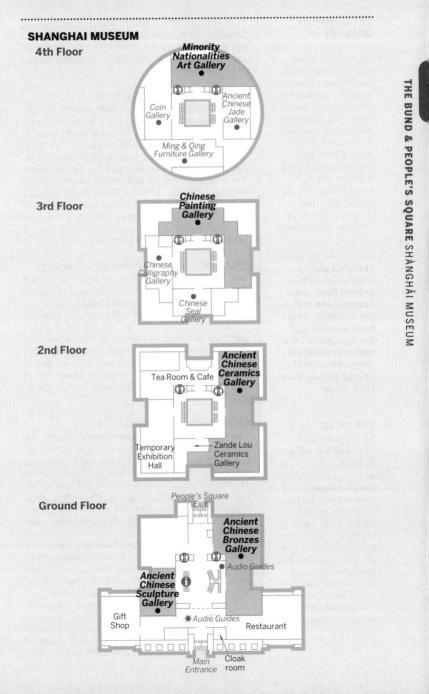

SHANGHAI MUSEUM

4th Floor

Minority Nationalities Art Gallery

Coin Gallery

Ancient Chinese Jade Gallery

Ming & Qing Furniture Gallery

3rd Floor

Chinese Painting Gallery

Chinese Calligraphy Gallery

Chinese Seal Gallery

2nd Floor

Ancient Chinese Ceramics Gallery

Tea Room & Cafe

Temporary Exhibition Hall

Zande Lou Ceramics Gallery

Ground Floor

People's Square

Exit

Ancient Chinese Bronzes Gallery

Audio Guides

Ancient Chinese Sculpture Gallery

Gift Shop

Audio Guides

Restaurant

Main Entrance

Cloak room

CALLIGRAPHY GALLERY

Chinese characters, which express both meaning as a word and visual beauty as an image, are one of the most fascinating aspects of the Chinese language. While the full scope of this 3rd-floor gallery may be unfathomable for those who don't read Chinese, anyone can enjoy the purely aesthetic balance of Chinese brush artistry.

There's a simple restaurant on the ground floor and a tearoom and cafe on the 2nd floor if you need a break, but the best place for a real meal is outside the museum at the nearby Yunnan Road Food Street.

THE FOUR TREASURES OF THE SCHOLAR'S STUDY

The basic tools of Chinese painting are the brush, ink, ink-stone (on which the ink is mixed) and paper. The brush, which is not only used for visual arts but also for writing, was instrumental in influencing the closely intertwined development of painting, poetry and calligraphy.

Ming-dynasty white-glazed porcelain statues of Guanyin, the goddess of mercy. Angled mirrors beneath each piece reveal the mark on the foot. A reproduction kiln and workshop is located at the end of the gallery.

Chinese Painting Gallery

On the 3rd floor, this gallery leads visitors through various styles of traditional Chinese painting, with many works dwelling on idealised landscapes. At first glance many appear to be similar, but upon closer inspection you'll realise that there is a vast array of techniques used to depict the natural world. There are some true masterpieces here, from painters such as Ni Zan (1301–74), Wang Meng (1308–85) and Wu Wei (1459–1508). Although works are rotated regularly, the Ming collection is generally regarded as containing the best selection of paintings. Scroll paintings are 'read' from right to left.

Minority Nationalities Art Gallery

Save something for the Minority Nationalities Art Gallery on the 4th floor, which introduces visitors to the diversity of China's non-Han ethnic groups, totalling (officially) some 40 million people. Displays focus mainly on dress: from the salmon fish-skin suit from Hēilóngjiāng and the furs of the Siberian Oroqen, to the embroidery and batik of Guìzhōu's Miao and Dong, the Middle Eastern satin robes of the Uighurs and the wild hairstyles of the former slave-owning Yi. Handicrafts include Miao silverware and Yi lacquer work.

Other 4th-Floor Galleries

The **Ancient Chinese Jade Gallery** reveals the transformation of jade use from early mystical symbols (such as the *bì*, or 'jade discs', used to worship heaven) to ritual weapons and jewellery. Exhibit 414 is a remarkable totem, with an engraved phoenix carrying a human head. Bamboo drills, abrasive sand and garnets crushed in water were used to shape some of the pieces, which date back more than 5000 years.

When it comes to the **Coin Gallery**, it's tempting to keep moving. But do look for the *bànliáng* coins, standardised during the Qin dynasty, which are pierced with a hole so they could be carried by string. Some older coins are shaped like keys or knives.

The **Ming & Qing Furniture Gallery** features rose and sandalwood furniture of the elegant Ming dynasty and heavier, more baroque examples from the Qing dynasty. Several mock offices and reception rooms offer a glimpse of wealthy Chinese home life.

👁 SIGHTS

👁 The Bund

THE BUND
ARCHITECTURE

See p56.

EAST NANJING ROAD
ARCHITECTURE

Map p296 (南京东路; Nánjīng Dōnglù; Ⓜ East Nanjing Rd) Linking the Bund with People's Sq is East Nanjing Rd, once known as Nanking Rd. The first department stores in China opened here in the 1920s, when the modern machine-age – with its new products, automobiles, art deco styling and newfangled ideas – was ushered in. A glowing forest of neon at night, it's no longer the cream of Shànghǎi shopping, but its pedestrian strip remains one of the most famous and crowded streets in China.

Shànghǎi's reputation as the country's most fashionable city was forged in part here, through the new styles and trends introduced in department stores such as the Sun Sun (1926), today the Shànghǎi No 1 Food Store (p76), and the Sun Company (1936), now the Shànghǎi No 1 Department Store (p77). Today it's shops such as the vast **Apple Store** (Map p296; www.apple.com/cn; 300 East Nanjing Rd; 南京东路300号; ◷10am-10pm; Ⓜ East Nanjing Rd) that dominate the shopping landscape. The pedestrianised section of the road is an assault course of fake-watch sellers, clinging purveyors of 'massagee' and English-speaking girls who encourage you to spend a king's ransom on cups of tea. Small 'train' tourist buses roll from one pedestrianised end to the other (¥5).

ROCKBUND ART MUSEUM
MUSEUM

Map p296 (上海外滩美术馆; Shànghǎi Wàitān Měishùguǎn; www.rockbundartmuseum.org; 20 Huqiu Rd; 虎丘路20号; adult ¥15; ◷10am-6pm Tue-Sun; Ⓜ East Nanjing Rd) Housed in the former Royal Asiatic Society building (1933) – once Shànghǎi's first museum – this private space behind the Bund focuses on contemporary Chinese art, with rotating exhibits year-round and no permanent collection. One of the city's top modern-art venues, the building's interior and exterior are both sublime. Check out the unique art deco eight-sided *bāguà* (trigram) windows at the front, a fetching synthesis of Western modernist styling and traditional Chinese design.

The interior is all textbook deco lines and curves, including the fine staircase. Head to the rooftop terrace for excellent views, despite the hulking form of the Peninsula hotel blocking out much of Lùjiāzuǐ. A cafe on the top floor dispenses free cups of tea.

BUND SIGHTSEEING TUNNEL
TUNNEL

Map p296 (外滩观光隧道; Wàitān Guānguāng Suìdào; 300 East Zhongshan No 1 Rd; 中山东一路300号; one way/return ¥50/60; ◷8am-10pm; Ⓜ East Nanjing Rd) A 647m voyage with entertainment from budget effects, garish lighting and dreadful props, the Bund Sightseeing Tunnel is a transport mode that guarantees to get you to Pǔdōng in an altered state. Stepping from the trains at the terminus, visitors are visibly nonplussed, their disbelief surpassed only by those with return tickets.

SHANGHAI GALLERY OF ART
GALLERY

Map p296 (外滩三号沪申画廊; www.shanghaigalleryofart.com; 3rd fl, 3 on the Bund, 3 East Zhongshan No1 Rd; 中山东一路三号三楼; ◷11am-7pm; Ⓜ East Nanjing Rd) FREE Take the lift up to the 3rd floor of 3 on the Bund to this neat and minimalist art gallery for glimpses of current directions in highbrow and conceptual Chinese art. It's all bare concrete pillars, ventilation ducts and acres of wall space; there are a couple of divans where you can sit to admire the works on view.

ISLAND6
GALLERY

Map p296 (六岛; Liùdǎo; www.island6.org; 17 Fuzhou Rd; 福州路17号; ◷11am-7pm; Ⓜ East Nanjing Rd) FREE This new Bund art gallery opened its doors in 2014 is part of the inspirational island6 art collective.

PEACE GALLERY
MUSEUM

Map p296 (和平收藏馆; Hépíng Shōucángguǎn; Fairmont Peace Hotel, 20 East Nanjing Rd; 南京东路20号费尔蒙和平饭店; ◷10.30am-7pm; Ⓜ East Nanjing Rd) FREE This intriguing little museum, in essence a long room stuffed with period objects and photos relating to the colourful history of the Peace Hotel, is an absorbing and atmospheric diversion. Head through the first entrance to the Peace Hotel off East Nanjing Rd (walking west from the Bund) and it's upstairs on the right.

Hour-long tours (¥100) of the Fairmont Peace Hotel are run through here.

PETER STUCKINGS / GETTY IMAGES ©

1. East Nanjing Road (p65)

Linking the Bund with People's Sq, East Nanjing Road remains one of the most famous and crowded streets in China.

2. The Bund (p56)

Extravagant bars and restaurants, and hypnotising views of Pŭdōng attract visitors to the Bund.

3. Shànghǎi Urban Planning Exhibition Hall (p68)

View exhibits such as a miniature scale model of future Tokyo (pictured) as well as photos and maps of historic Shànghǎi.

4. Glamour Bar (p74)

Iconic views, great drinks and a first-rate events line-up draw crowds to Glamour Bar.

⊙ People's Square

SHÀNGHǍI MUSEUM   ART MUSEUM
See p61.

SHÀNGHǍI URBAN PLANNING
EXHIBITION HALL   MUSEUM
Map p296 (上海城市规划展示馆; Shànghǎi Chéngshì Guīhuà Zhǎnshìguǎn; 100 Renmin Ave, entrance on Middle Xizang Rd; 人民大道100号; adult ¥30; ☺9am-5pm Tue-Sun, last entry 4pm; Ⓜ People's Sq) Some cities romanticise their past; others promise good times in the present. Only in China are you expected to visit places that haven't even been built yet. The highlight here is the 3rd floor, where you'll find an incredible model layout of the megalopolis-to-be, plus a dizzying Virtual World 3D wraparound tour. Balancing out the forward-looking exhibits are photos and maps of historic Shànghǎi.

SHÀNGHǍI MUSEUM OF
CONTEMPORARY ART (MOCA
SHÀNGHǍI)   MUSEUM
Map p296 (上海当代艺术馆; Shànghǎi Dāngdài Yìshùguǎn; www.mocashanghai.org; People's Park; 人民公园; adult/student ¥50/25; ☺10am-6pm Mon-Thu, 9am-7pm Fri-Sun; Ⓜ People's Sq) This nonprofit museum collection has an all-glass home to maximise natural sunlight when it cuts through the clouds, a tip-top location in People's Park and a fresh, invigorating approach to exhibiting contemporary artwork. Exhibits are temporary only; check the website to see what's on. On the top floor there's a funky restaurant and bar with a terrace.

PEOPLE'S PARK   PARK
Map p296 (人民公园; Rénmín Gōngyuán; ☺6am-6pm, till 7pm Jul-Sep; Ⓜ People's Sq) Oc-cupying the site of the colonial racetrack (which became a holding camp during WWII), People's Park is a green refuge from Shànghǎi's fume-ridden roads. It's home to the Shànghǎi Museum of Contemporary Art, pond-side bar Barbarossa, and a small childrens' fairground, and is overlooked by the towering form of Tomorrow Square, the old British racecourse club building and the art deco classic Park Hotel.

If you're in Shànghǎi in June, join the photographers ringing the gorgeous pink lotuses that flower in the pond.

TOMORROW SQUARE   BUILDING
Map p296 (明天广场; Míngtiān Guǎngchǎng; 399 West Nanjing Rd; 南京西路399号; Ⓜ People's Sq) This stupendous tower seizes the Shànghǎi zeitgeist with dramatic aplomb. Resembling a sci-fi corporation headquarters, the strato-spheric building is given further lift by the stylistic awkwardness of nearby rivals. The foyer of the JW Marriott Tomorrow Square hotel debuts on the 38th floor – pop up to put People's Square in the proper perspective.

PARK HOTEL   HISTORIC BUILDING
Map p296 (国际饭店; Guójì Fàndiàn; 170 West Nanjing Rd; 南京西路170号; Ⓜ People's Sq) De-signed by Hungarian architect Ladislaus Hudec and erected as a bank in 1934, the Park Hotel was Shànghǎi's tallest building until the 1980s, when shoulder-padded ar-chitects first started squinting hopefully in the direction of Pǔdōng. Back in the days when building height had a different mean-ing, it was said your hat would fall off if you looked at the roof.

Peruse the foyer for its art deco overture.

A short walk east along Nanjing Rd is the Pacific Hotel, formerly the China United Apartment Building, also equipped with some lovely lobby details.

IDENTITY & THE SHÀNGHǍI DIALECT

Older Shanghainese are highly conscious of the disappearance of the Shànghǎi dialect (Shànghǎihuà), under assault from the increased promotion of the Mandarin (Pǔtōnghuà) dialect and the flood of immigrant tongues. As a deeply tribal element of Shànghǎi culture and heritage, the vanishing of the dialect equals a loss of iden-tity. Fewer and fewer young Shanghainese and children are now able to speak the pure form of the dialect; or can understand it only and prefer to speak Mandarin. Youngsters might not care, but older Shanghainese agonise over the tongue's slow extinction. The most perfectly preserved forms of Shànghǎihuà survive in rural areas around Shànghǎi, where Mandarin has less of a toehold. The Shanghainese may re-mind themselves of the Chinese idiom – jiùde bù qù, xīnde bù lái (旧的不去新的不来; 'If the old doesn't go, the new doesn't arrive') – but it may offer scant consolation.

NO DOGS OR CHINESE

A notorious sign at Huángpǔ Park (黄浦公园; Huángpǔ Gōngyuán), then called the Public Gardens, apocryphally declared 'No dogs or Chinese allowed'. Although this widely promoted notice never actually existed, the general gist of the wording hits the mark. A series of regulations was indeed posted outside the gardens listing 10 rules governing use of the park.

The first regulation noted that 'The gardens are for the use of the foreign community,' while the fourth ruled that 'Dogs and bicycles are not admitted.' Chinese were barred from the park (as expressed in the first regulation), an injustice that gave rise to the canard.

The bluntly worded sign has, however, become firmly embedded in the Chinese consciousness. Bruce Lee destroys a Shànghǎi park sign declaring 'No dogs and Chinese allowed' with a flying kick in *Fist of Fury* and Chinese history books cite the insult as further evidence of Chinese humiliation at the hands of foreigners. For a thorough academic examination of the subject, hunt down *Shanghai's 'Dogs and Chinese not Admitted' Sign: Legend, History and Contemporary Symbol* by Robert A Bickers and Jeffrey N Wasserstrom, published in the *China Quarterly,* No 142 (June 1995).

MADAME TUSSAUDS MUSEUM
Map p296 (上海杜莎夫人蜡像馆; Shànghǎi Dùshā Fūrén Làxiàngguǎn; www.madametussauds.com; West Nanjing Rd; 南京西路; adult/student/child ¥150/110/90; ⊙10am-9pm; MPeople's Sq) The waxworks at Madame Tussauds are largely aimed at locals and cost a lot, but may make do for entertainment during one of Shànghǎi's notorious summer downpours. Irritatingly, online discounts of ¥30 on adult tickets are available on the Chinese page of the website, but not on the English page.

EATING

A Bund address is the crown jewels in Shànghǎi, luring international superchefs and hotel restaurants vying for China's first Michelin star. While the settings are often spectacular and the views are knockout, there's less diversity and charm than in the French Concession. Many local eateries are in malls or designated food streets; try Huanghe Rd or Yunnan Rd for an old-school Shànghǎi atmosphere.

The Bund

SHÀNGHǍI GRANDMOTHER CHINESE $
Map p296 (上海姥姥; Shànghǎi Lǎolao; ☎6321 6613; 70 Fuzhou Rd; 福州路70号; dishes ¥25-55; ⊙10.30am-9.30pm; MEast Nanjing Rd) This packed eatery is within easy striking distance of the Bund and cooks up all manner of home-style dishes. You can't go wrong with the classics here: braised eggplant in soy sauce, Grandmother's braised pork, crispy duck, three-cup chicken and *mápó dòufu* (tofu and pork crumbs in a spicy sauce) rarely disappoint.

NÁNXIÁNG STEAMED BUN RESTAURANT DUMPLINGS $
Map p296 (南翔馒头店; Nánxiáng Mántou Diàn; 3rd fl, Shànghǎi No 1 Food Store, 720 East Nanjing Rd; 南京东路720号上海市第一食品商店3楼; 8 dumplings from ¥16; ⊙9.30am-9pm; MEast Nanjing Rd) The purveyors of some of Shànghǎi's best-loved dumplings have several branches around town, and this is one of the less crowded.

SOUTH MEMORY HUNANESE $
Map p296 (望湘园; Wàng Xiāng Yuán; ☎6360 2797; 6th fl, Hóngyī Plaza, 299 East Nanjing Rd; 南京东路299号宏伊国际广场6楼; dishes ¥29-88; MEast Nanjing Rd) This popular Húnán place is a chopstick's throw from the waterfront with a range of spicy drypots (served in a personal mini wok), including favourites such as bamboo shoots and smoked pork, and chicken and chestnuts. Also on the menu are other *xiāngcài* (Hunanese) classics (such as steamed pork served in a bamboo tube); it's absolutely jammed at lunchtime and only early birds get window seats.

★YÚXÌN CHUĀNCÀI SICHUANESE $
Map p296 (渝信川菜; ☎6361 1777; 5th fl, Huasheng Tower, 399 Jiujiang Rd; 九江路399号华盛大厦5楼; dishes ¥20-98; ⊙11am-2.30pm & 5-9.30pm; ☎; MEast Nanjing Rd) In the top

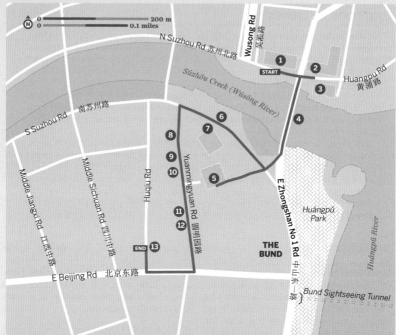

Neighbourhood Walk
The North Bund

START BROADWAY MANSIONS
END ROCKBUND ART MUSEUM
LENGTH 800M; 45 MINUTES

Begin in Hóngkǒu, where the American Settlement was established in 1848. First stop, the Orwellian brick pile ❶ **Broadway Mansions** (p160; 1934), originally an apartment block that later became a favourite with military officers and journalists for its commanding views over the harbour. The Japanese occupied the building from 1937 until the end of WWII. Not far away is the ❷ **Astor House Hotel** (p212), which first opened in 1846 as the Richards Hotel. It was Shànghǎi's most prestigious hotel until the completion of the Cathay Hotel in 1929, and from 1990 to 1998 its Peacock Ballroom found new employment as the Shànghǎi Stock Exchange. Across the street is the original ❸ **Russian Consulate** (p264), still in use today. Head south over ❹ **Wàibáidù Bridge** (Garden Bridge; 1906), the first steel bridge in China, over which trams used to glide.

Cross the street to the grounds of the ❺ **former British Consulate** (1873), one of the first foreign buildings in Shànghǎi in 1852, which went up in an 1870 fire. Continue west past the ❻ **former Shànghǎi Rowing Club** (1905) and ❼ **former Union Church** (1886) to reach lavishly restored Yuanmingyuan Rd. This street was once home to several go-downs – buildings that served as warehouses and office space – shared by traders and missionaries, such as the ❽ **China Baptist Publication Society**, whose Gothamesque offices at No 187 (1932) were designed by Ladislaus Hudec.

Further along is the Italian Renaissance ❾ **Lyceum Building** (1927), now housing a cafe-bar; the multidenominational ❿ **Associate Mission Building** (1924; No 169); the ornate deco brick and stone ⓫ **YWCA Building** (1932; No 133) and the red-brick ⓬ **Yuanmingyuan Apartments** (No 115). Turn onto Huqiu Rd to end the tour at the Royal Asiatic Society Building (1933). Once Shànghǎi's first museum, it houses the ⓭ **Rockbund Art Museum** (p65).

league of Shànghǎi's best Sìchuān restaurants, Yúxìn is a dab hand in the arts of blistering chillies and numbing peppercorns. All-stars include the 'mouthwatering chicken' starter (口水鸡; *kǒushuǐ jī*), or opt for the simply smoking spicy chicken (辣子鸡; *làzǐ jī*), the crispy camphor tea duck (half/whole ¥38/68) or catfish in chilli oil.

There's an occasionally misfiring English menu ('Impregnable Sibao' anyone?). Take the lift.

CHARME
CANTONESE $

Map p296 (港丽餐厅; Gǎnglì Cāntīng; ☑6360 7577; 4th fl, Hóngyī Plaza, 299 East Nanjing Rd; 南京东路299号宏伊国际广场4楼; dishes ¥33-168; ☉11am-10pm; MEast Nanjing Rd) This rip-roarin' Canto-style cafe unashamedly darts all over the culinary map from fiery Sichuanese and Hong Kong curries to Cantonese seafood, Italian pasta and, of course, milk tea. Reserve or come prepared to wait; service can be spotty. It's one of several choices located in the Hóngyī Plaza mall, above the East Nanjing Rd metro station.

TOCK'S
CANADIAN $

Map p296 (221 Middle Henan Rd; 河南中路221号; mains from ¥45; ☉11am-10.30pm; MEast Nanjing Rd) Unsurprisingly, this is the sole place in town serving Montreal-style smoked meat, but Shànghǎi could sorely do with more of the same. The meat – spiced and cured Australian beef, slow-smoked locally – is gorgeously tender and each sandwich comes with homemade fries, coleslaw and pickle. Canadian Moosehead lager and organic coffee is at hand for lubrication.

AJISEN
NOODLES $

Map p296 (味千拉面; Wèiqiān Lāmiàn; Basement, Hóngyī Plaza, 299 East Nanjing Rd; 南京东路299号宏伊国际广场地下一层; noodles ¥25-40; ☉11am-10pm; MEast Nanjing Rd) If it ain't broke, don't fix it. Japanese-style noodle king Ajisen still works wonders and also rules the world of glossy photo menus. Snappy, clean and done by the numbers; there's something endlessly gratifying about Ajisen's formula of black-clad, bandana and jeans-wearing staff, and the (rich, spicy) food is perennially on the money.

Ajisen is possibly the most popular chain in Shànghǎi, with more than 100 locations around town. Large cups of *dàmàichá* tea are served free; pay up front.

SHĚNJIĀMÉN LÁNSǍO HǍIXIĀN MIÀNGUǍN
NOODLES $

Map p296 (沈家门兰嫂海鲜面馆; 120 Middle Fujian Rd; 福建中路120号; mains ¥15; ☉7am-10.30pm; MEast Nanjing Road) This spot may fumble with English and décor, but it cooks up some standout seafood noodles. Noodles with yellow croaker (黄鱼面; *huángyú miàn*) and seafood noodles (海鲜面; *hǎixiān miàn*) are popular dishes, but there's also delicious *shēngjiān* (生煎; fried dumplings) and crispy *cōngyóubǐng* (fried scallion pancakes). No English menu, but a photomenu clings to the wall. Look for the blue sign.

WAGAS
CAFE $

Map p296 (沃歌斯; Wògēsī; 1st fl, Hóngyī Plaza, 288 Jiujiang Rd; 九江路288号宏伊国际广场1楼; mains ¥48-58; ☉6.30am-10pm Mon-Fri, 8.30am-10pm Sat & Sun; ☏; MEast Nanjing Rd) Just south off East Nanjing Rd, this branch of the city's favourite cafe is perfect for on-the-spot caffeination, sandwiches, wraps, pasta and Asian sets.

CAFE AT 1
CAFE $

Map p296 (45 Huqiu Rd; 虎丘路45号; mains from ¥30; ☉10am-10pm; ☏; MEast Nanjing Rd) There aren't many decent cafes within ambling distance of the Bund that are not part of a hotel, but this spot is a quiet and relaxing choice, with huge cups of coffee and colourful cushions (though losing the deer head poking from the wall is a plan). Ample bites fill the menu, from Russian soup through to sandwiches, chips and cheesecake.

★LOST HEAVEN
YUNNAN $$

Map p296 (花马天堂; Huāmǎ Tiāntáng; ☑6330 0967; www.lostheaven.com.cn; 17 East Yan'an Rd; 延安东路17号; dishes ¥50-210; ☉noon-2pm & 5.30-10.30pm; MEast Nanjing Rd) Lost Heaven might not have the views that keep its rivals in business, but why go to the same old Western restaurants when you can get sophisticated Bai, Dai and Miao folk cuisine from China's mighty southwest? Specialities are flowers (banana and pomegranate), wild mushrooms, chillies, Burmese curries, Bai chicken and superb *pǔ'ěr* (pu-erh) teas, all served up in gorgeous Yúnnán-meets-Shànghǎi surrounds.

MERCATO
ITALIAN $$

Map p296 (☑6321 9922; 6th fl, 3 on the Bund, 3 East Zhongshan No 1 Rd; 中山东一路3号6楼; mains ¥68-228; ☉5.30-11pm Sun-Wed,

THE BUND & PEOPLE'S SQUARE EATING

to 1am Thu-Sat; ☎; Ⓜ East Nanjing Rd) Chef Jean-Georges Vongerichten's celebrated Bund-side restaurant combines first-rate (and affordable) Italian cuisine with a stylishly relaxed Neri & Hu-designed setting of modern rusticity. Add an exacting level of service for an experience to savour. The rigatoni and meatballs is a faultless pleasure while the pizzas (starting at ¥68) provide a masterclass in taste and texture. Reserve, especially for a window table.

★ ULTRAVIOLET   GASTRONOMIC $$$

(www.uvbypp.cc; dinner from ¥3000; ☺ dinner Tue-Sat; Ⓜ East Nanjing Rd) You've probably paired food and wine before, but what about coupling an illuminated apple-wasabi communion wafer with purple candles, *Hell's Bells* on the stereo and a specially designed cathedral scent? Welcome to China's most conceptual dining experience. The evening's diners gather first at Mr & Mrs Bund (p72) for an apéritif before they're whisked away to a secret location.

The meal consists of 22 courses – each accompanied by a different sensory mood (sounds, scents and images). This is Paul Pairet's masterpiece, years in the making. Revolving around his signature mischievous creations, a dinner here is bound to be unlike anything you've ever experienced before.

Reservations must be made online for the one table with 10 seats, so book months in advance.

★ LOBBY, PENINSULA   BRITISH $$$

Map p296 (上海半岛酒店; http://shanghai. peninsula.com; 32 E Zhongshan No 1 Rd; 中山东一路32号; 1/2 persons ¥290/540; ☺ 2-6pm; ☎; Ⓜ E Nanjing Rd) Afternoon heritage tea for smart/casually attired visitors in the sumptuous Peninsula lobby is a decadent delight, with gorgeously presented scones, macaroons, clotted cream, jam, cookies, tea, of course, and live piano tinklings. For ¥440, a glass of champers is thrown in.

In the evenings, a live jazz band takes over. You can dine here all day à la carte from 6am to midnight.

★ M ON THE BUND   EUROPEAN $$$

Map p296 (米氏西餐厅; Mǐshì Xīcāntīng; ☎ 6350 9988; www.m-restaurantgroup.com/mbund/ home.html; 7th fl, 20 Guangdong Rd; 广东路20号7楼; mains ¥128-288, 2-course set lunch ¥188, light lunch menu ¥118; Ⓜ East Nanjing Rd) M exudes a timelessness and level of sophistication that eclipses the razzle dazzle of many other upscale Shànghǎi restaurants. The menu ain't radical, but that's the question it seems to ask you – is breaking new culinary ground really so crucial? Crispy suckling pig and a chicken tajine with saffron are, after all, simply delicious just the way they are.

The art deco dining room and 7th-floor terrace are equally gorgeous. Finish off with drinks in the Glamour Bar downstairs and reserve well in advance. It's also heavenly for a spot of afternoon tea (from ¥88 to ¥138).

★ MR & MRS BUND   FRENCH $$$

Map p296 (☎ 6323 9898; www.mmbund.com; 6th fl, Bund 18, 18 East Zhongshan No 1 Rd; 中山东一路18号6楼; mains ¥150-800, 2-/3-course set lunch ¥200/250; ☺ lunch 11.30am-2pm Mon-Fri, dinner 6-11pm Fri & Sat, 6-10.30pm Sun-Thu, night 10.30pm-2am Tue-Thu, 11pm-2am Fri & Sat; Ⓜ East Nanjing Rd) French chef Paul Pairet's casual eatery aims for a space that's considerably more playful than your average fine-dining Bund restaurant. The mix-and-match menu has a heavy French bistro slant, but reimagined and served up with Pairet's ingenious presentation. But it's not just the food you're here for: it's the post-midnight meals (discounted), the Bingo nights and the wonderfully wonky atmosphere. Reserve.

JEAN GEORGES   FUSION $$$

Map p296 (法国餐厅; Fǎguó Cāntīng; ☎ 6321 7733; 4th fl, Three on the Bund, 3 East Zhongshan No 1 Rd; 中山东一路3号4楼; mains ¥248-318, 3-course lunch/dinner ¥238/638; ☎; Ⓜ East Nanjing Rd) Pitched somewhere between Gotham City and new Shànghǎi is Jean-Georges Vongerichten's dimly lit, copper-appliquéd temple to gastronomy. Head chef Lam Ming Kin has some divine palate-pleasers on the menu, such as foie gras brûlée with sour cherries and candied pistachios, black cod with sesame and citrus confit, and seared lamb with cardamom crumbs.

It's divided into the Nougatine Bar, which has an early-bird special from 6pm to 7pm, and the formal dining room (set menu only) at night. At lunch you can get a window table with relatively little hassle. Reserve.

SHOOK!   SOUTHEAST ASIAN $$$

Map p296 (☎ 2329 8522; www.shookshanghai restaurant.com; 5th fl, Bund 18, 23 East Zhongshan No 1 Rd; 中山东一路23号5楼; 2-course weekday set lunch ¥98, mains from ¥188; ◷11.30am-2.30pm & 6-10.30pm; Ⓜ East Nanjing Rd) Like most of its Bund-side brethren, Malaysian Shook! sports trendy design and fabulous views, particularly from its rooftop terrace. There are some good ideas on the menu, which stretches from Southeast Asian classics to Japanese and Western, but the lack of a culinary focal point is telling – the kitchen's execution can be inconsistent.

✕ People's Square

★ YANG'S FRY DUMPLINGS   DUMPLINGS $
Map p296 (小杨生煎馆; Xiǎoyáng Shēngjiān Guǎn; 97 Huanghe Rd; 黄河路97号; 4 dumplings ¥6; ◷6.30am-8.30pm; Ⓜ People's Sq) The city's most famous place for sesame-seed-and-scallion-coated shēngjiān (生煎; fried dumplings) gets nil points for decor or service, but that's hardly the point. Queues can stretch to the horizon as eager diners wait for scalding shēngjiān to be dished into mustard-coloured bowls. Watch out for boiling meat juices that unexpectedly jet down your shirt (and your neighbour's). Per liǎng (两; 4 dumplings) ¥6.

Zero in on the bright-pink frontage to order at the left counter – eight dumplings and a soup (汤; tāng) should be sufficient – then join the queue on the right to pick up your order.

NÁNXIÁNG STEAMED BUN RESTAURANT   DUMPLINGS $
Map p296 (南翔馒头店; Nánxiáng Mántou Diàn; 2nd fl, 666 Fuzhou Rd; 福州路666号2楼; steamer 8 dumplings ¥25-50; Ⓜ People's Sq) This pleasant branch of Shànghǎi's most famous dumpling restaurant overlooks Fuzhou Rd and can be slightly less crowded than other branches.

SPICY JOINT   SICHUANESE $
Map p296 (辛香汇; Xīnxiānghuì; ☎400 100 1717; 4th fl, Yalong International Plaza, 500 East Jinling Rd; 金陵东路500号亚龙国际广场4楼; dishes ¥12-78; ◷11am-10pm; 📱; Ⓜ Dashijie) This branch of one of Shànghǎi's best Sichuanese joints can see excruciatingly long waits at peak times and you'll need a mobile number to secure a place in the queue. But it's worth it for some mouthwatering Sìchuān classics.

FOOD REPUBLIC   FOOD COURT $
Map p296 (大食代; Dàshídài; 268 Middle Xizang Rd; 西藏中路268号; dishes from ¥20; ◷10am-10pm; Ⓜ People's Sq) Bustling Food Republic has several locations around town – this one, on the 6th floor of the Raffles City mall, is kind of cool. Choices range from teppanyaki and curry to hotpot and noodles. Pay up-front at the entrance (¥50 or ¥100; ¥10 deposit; refunds granted) and hand over your card to the vendor of your choice. For quick snacks, desserts and juices, head to the equally bustling mall basement.

PEOPLE'S SQUARE FOOD STREETS
These streets are lined with an amazing variety of Chinese restaurants, each with its own speciality.

➡ **Huanghe Road Food Street** (黄河路美食街; Huánghé Lù Měishí Jiē; Map p296; Ⓜ People's Square) With a prime central location near People's Park, Huanghe Rd covers all the bases from cheap lunches to late-night post-theatre snacks. You'll find large restaurants such as the always popular **Táishèngyuán Restaurant** (莕圣园中华料理; Táishèngyuán Zhōnghuá Liàolǐ; Map p296; 50 Huanghe Rd; 黄河路50号), but Huanghe Rd is best for dumplings – get 'em fried at Yang's (No 97) or served up in bamboo steamers across the road at **Jiājiā Soup Dumplings** (佳家汤包; Jiājiā Tāngbāo; Map p296; 90 Huanghe Rd; 黄河路90号; ◷7am-10pm).

➡ **Yunnan Road Food Street** (云南路美食街; Yúnnán Lù Měishí Jiē; Map p296; Ⓜ Dashijie) Yunnan Rd has some great speciality restaurants and is just the spot for an authentic meal after museum-hopping at People's Sq. Look out for Shaanxi dumplings and noodles at No 15 and five-fragrance dim sum at **Wǔ Fāng Zhāi** (五芳斋; Map p296; 28 Yunnan Rd; 云南路28号; ◷7am-10pm). You can also get salted duck (盐水鸭; yán shuǐ yā) and steamed dumplings at **Xiǎo Jīn Líng** (小金陵; Map p296; 55 Yunnan Rd; 云南路55号; dumplings from ¥7; ◷8am-9pm), Mongolian hotpot and Yunnanese here.

KEBABS ON THE GRILLE INDIAN $$

Map p296 (☑3315 0132; 227 North Huangpi Rd, inside Central Plaza; 黄陂北路227号; dishes ¥60-90, set lunch ¥48-58; Ⓜ People's Sq) This handy branch of the excellent north Indian restaurant offers fantastic-value set lunches and a diverse menu of authentic Indian dishes.

WÁNG BǍOHÉ JIǓJIĀ SHANGHAINESE $$$

Map p296 (王宝和酒家; ☑6322 3673; 603 Fuzhou Rd; 福州路603号; dishes ¥19-208, set menu ¥450-800; ⊙11am-1pm & 5-9pm; Ⓜ People's Sq) More than 250 years old, this restaurant claims a fame that rests on its extravagant selection of crab dishes; its popularity reaches an apex during hairy-crab season (October to December). Most diners opt for one of the all-crabs-must-die banquets, but if you're new to hairy crab, you might want to give it a try elsewhere before 'shelling out' for an eight-course meal. Reserve.

🍷 DRINKING & NIGHTLIFE

The Bund is home to some of Shànghǎi's premier drinking spots. It's hopping come weekends so get into your glad rags. Drinks don't come cheap but a trip to at least one bar in the area is obligatory, if only for the stunning nighttime view of the Huángpǔ River and the glittering lights of Pǔdōng.

🍷 The Bund

★GLAMOUR BAR BAR

Map p296 (魅力酒吧; Mèilì Jiǔbā; www.m-glamour .com; 6th fl, 20 Guangdong Rd; 广东路20号6楼; ⊙5pm-2am; Ⓜ East Nanjing Rd) The Glamour Bar is more than just one of Shànghǎi's most popular watering holes, it's a cultural institution. It hosts the annual literary festival, chamber-music performances and China-related book launches and talks. Of course, none of that would hold up if the martinis weren't so good. Get here before midnight on weekends or be prepared to queue.

★NEW HEIGHTS BAR

Map p296 (新视角; Xīn Shìjiǎo; ☑6321 0909; 7th fl, Three on the Bund, 3 East Zhongshan No 1 Rd; 中山东一路3号7楼; ⊙11.30am-1.30am; Ⓜ East Nanjing Rd) The most amenable of the big Bund bars, this splendid roof terrace has the choicest angle on Pǔdōng's hypnotising neon performance. There's always a crowd, whether for coffee, cocktails or meals (set meals from ¥188).

★LONG BAR BAR

Map p296 (廊吧; Láng Bā; ☑6322 9988; 2 East Zhongshan No 1 Rd; 中山东一路2号; ⊙4pm-1am Mon-Sat, 2pm-1am Sun; 🛜; Ⓜ East Nanjing Rd) For a taste of colonial-era Shànghǎi's elitist trappings, you'll do no better than the Long Bar. This was once the members-only Shànghǎi Club, whose most spectacular accoutrement was a 34m-long wooden bar. Foreign businessmen would sit here according to rank, comparing fortunes, with the taipans (foreign heads of business) closest to the view of the Bund.

Now part of the Waldorf Astoria, the bar's original wood-panelled decor has been painstakingly re-created from old photographs. There's a good selection of old-fashioned cocktails as well as an oyster bar (and jazz, naturally).

★BAR ROUGE BAR

Map p296 (☑021 6339 1199; 7th fl, Bund 18, 18 East Zhongshan No 1 Rd; 中山东一路18号7楼; cover charge after 10pm Fri & Sat ¥100; ⊙6pm-late; Ⓜ East Nanjing Rd) Bar Rouge attracts a cashed-up party crowd who come for the fantastic views from the terrace and the all-night DJ parties. The lipstick-red decor is slick and the crowd is slicker, so ordinary mortals can sometimes struggle to get served on busy nights.

SIR ELLY'S TERRACE BAR

Map p296 (艾利爵士露台; 14th fl, The Peninsula Shanghai, 32 East No 1 Zhongshan Rd; 中山东一路 32号外滩32号半岛酒店14楼; ⊙5pm-midnight Sun-Thu, to 1am Fri & Sat; 🛜; Ⓜ East Nanjing Rd) Offering some of Shànghǎi's best cocktails, shaken up with that winning ingredient: 270-degree views to Pǔdōng, over Suzhou Creek and down the Bund. Of course it's not cheap, but the views are priceless.

M1NT CLUB

Map p296 (☑6391 2811; 24th fl, 318 Fuzhou Rd; 福州路318号24楼; ⊙lounge 6pm-late daily, club 9pm-late Wed-Sat; Ⓜ East Nanjing Rd) Exclusive penthouse-style club with knockout views, snazzy fusion food but not a lot of dance space. Dress to impress or you'll get thrown into the shark tank.

MUSE
CLUB

Map p296 (☑021 5213 5228; 5th fl, Yi Feng Gal-leria, 99 East Beijing Rd; 北京东路99号5楼; ⓜEast Nanjing Rd) One of the hottest clubs in the city for more than six years now – and that's no small feat – Muse has moved downtown to this swanky Bund-side location. Don't go looking for a lot of dance space; just squeeze into the crowd or jump up on a private table (minimum ¥4000 per night).

CAPTAIN'S BAR
BAR

Map p296 (船长青年酒吧; Chuánzhǎng Qīngnián Jiǔbā; 6th fl, 37 Fuzhou Rd; 福州路37号6楼; ◷11am-2am; ☏; ⓜEast Nanjing Rd) This used to be an affordable bar with decent, if slightly restricted, views of Pǔdōng's lights from its outside terrace, but it's now almost as expensive as the glitzier competition and the lift is as crummy as ever.

🍷 People's Square

★BARBAROSSA
BAR

Map p296 (芭芭露莎会所; Bābālùshā Huìsuǒ; www.barbarossa.com.cn; People's Park, 231 West Nanjing Rd; 南京西路231号人民公园内; ◷11am-2am; ☏; ⓜPeople's Sq) Set back in People's Park alongside a pond, Barbarossa is all about escapism. Forget Shànghǎi, this is Morocco channelled by Hollywood set designers. The action gets steadily more intense as you ascend to the roof terrace, via the cushion-strewn 2nd floor, where the hordes puff on fruit-flavoured hookahs. At night, use the park entrance just east of the former Shànghǎi Raceclub building (上海跑马总会; Shànghǎi Pǎomǎ Zǒnghuì).

⭐ ENTERTAINMENT

FAIRMONT PEACE HOTEL JAZZ BAR
JAZZ

Map p296 (爵士吧; Juéshì Bā; ☑6138 6883; 20 East Nanjing Rd; 南京东路20号费尔蒙和平饭店; ◷5.30pm-2am, live music from 7pm; ⓜEast Nanjing Rd) Shànghǎi's most famous hotel features Shànghǎi's most famous jazz band, a septuagenarian sextet that's been churning out nostalgic covers such as 'Moon River' and 'Summertime' since the dawn of time. There's no admission fee, but you'll need to sink a drink from the bar (draught beer starts at ¥70, a White Lady is ¥Y98).

The original band takes the stage from 7pm to 9.45pm; to get the pulse moving, a 'sultry female vocalist' does her bit from 9.45pm.

YÌFÚ THEATRE
CHINESE OPERA

Map p296 (逸夫舞台; Yìfū Wǔtái; ☑6322 5294; www.tianchan.com; 701 Fuzhou Rd; 人民广场福州路701号; tickets ¥30-280; ⓜPeople's Sq) One block east of People's Sq, this is the main opera theatre in town and recognisable by the huge opera mask above the entrance. The theatre presents a popular program of Běijīng, Kun and Yue (Shaoxing) opera. A Běijīng opera highlights show is performed several times a week at 1.30pm and 7.15pm; pick up a brochure at the ticket office.

★SHÀNGHǍI GRAND THEATRE
CLASSICAL MUSIC

Map p296 (上海大剧院; Shànghǎi Dàjùyuàn; ☑6386 8686; www.shgtheatre.com; 300 Renmin Ave; 人民广场人民大道300号; ⓜPeople's Sq) Shànghǎi's state-of-the-art concert venue hosts everything from Broadway musicals to symphonies, ballets, operas and performances by internationally acclaimed

GREAT WORLD

If you were passing through Shànghǎi in the 1920s or '30s, chances were you'd wind up at **Great World** (大世界; Dà Shìjiè; Map p296; cnr East Yan'an & Middle Xizang Rds; ⓜPeople's Sq) sooner rather than later. No place better epitomised the city's reputation as a den of escapism and vice, and at its peak it allegedly saw some 20,000 visitors daily. The six-storey building initially opened in 1917 as a place for acrobats and nightclub stars, rivalling the existing New World on Nanjing Rd. For the first decade or so it was relatively tame, gradually incorporating a movie theatre, fortune tellers and Chinese opera shows. By the time Pockmarked Huang got hold of it in 1931, however, it had become a centre for the bizarre and burlesque, its floors a farrago of singsong girls, gambling, opium and prostitution.

It's been in a state of perpetual renovation for more than a decade, and while rumours swirl around its resurrection as an entertainment venue, nothing has yet materialised.

classical soloists. There are also traditional Chinese music performances here. Pick up a schedule at the ticket office.

SHÀNGHĂI CONCERT HALL   CLASSICAL MUSIC

Map p296 (上海音乐厅; Shànghǎi Yīnyuè Tīng; ☑6386 2836; www.shanghaiconcerthall.org; 523 East Yan'an Rd; 人民广场延安东路523号; tickets ¥80-480; Ⓜ People's Sq, Dashijie) A decade or so ago, the government shunted all 5650 tonnes of this classic 1930s building 66m away from East Yan'an Rd to a quieter park-side setting, a relocation that cost more than building a new concert hall. It features smaller-scale concerts plus local and international soloists.

HOUSE OF BLUES & JAZZ   LIVE MUSIC

Map p296 (布鲁斯乐爵士之屋; Bùlǔsī Yuè Juéshì Zhīwū; ☑6323 2779; 60 Fuzhou Rd; 福州路60号; ☺4.30am-2am Tue-Sun; Ⓜ East Nanjing Rd) A classy restaurant and bar for music lovers with walls plastered in old photos of jazz legends. An in-house band (which changes regularly) delivers live music from 9.30pm (10pm on Friday and Saturday) to 1am. Sunday night is a free-for-all jam.

Jazz purists can check out the 'Highlights of the Jazz Story in the USA' poster in the foyer for the swing, bebop, cool, mainstream and fusion family-tree lowdown.

PEACE CINEMA   CINEMA

Map p296 (和平影都; Hépíng Yĭngdū; 290 Middle Xizang Rd; 西藏中路290号; Ⓜ People's Sq) People's Sq cinema with an attached IMAX theatre (巨幕影院; Jùmùyĭngyuàn).

🛍 SHOPPING

The Bund is all about luxury shopping, while beneath People's Sq, a maze of former bomb shelters has been transformed into a downmarket shopping centre known as D-Mall. Linking the two is East Nanjing Rd, which reached its peak as the most famous shopping strip in East Asia in the 1920s.

★ANNABEL LEE   ACCESSORIES

Map p296 (安梨家居; Ānlí Jiājū; No 1, Lane 8, East Zhongshan No 1 Rd; 中山东一路8弄1号; ☺10am-10pm; Ⓜ East Nanjing Rd) This elegant shop sells a range of soft-coloured accessories in silk, linen and cashmere, many of which feature delicate and stylish embroidery. Peruse the collection of shawls, scarves, table runners and purses, evening bags and nighties.

★SUZHŌU COBBLERS   ACCESSORIES

Map p296 (上海起想艺术品; Shànghǎi Qǐxiǎng Yìshùpǐn; unit 101, 17 Fuzhou Rd; 福州路17号101室; ☺10am-6.30pm; Ⓜ East Nanjing Rd) Right off the Bund, this cute boutique sells exquisite hand-embroidered silk slippers, bags, hats and clothing. Patterns and colours are based on the fashions of the 1930s, and as far as the owner, Huang Mengqi, is concerned, the products are one of a kind. Slippers start at ¥480 and the shop can make to order.

★BLUE SHÀNGHĂI WHITE   CERAMICS

Map p296 (海晨; Hǎi Chén; ☑6352 2222; unit 103, 17 Fuzhou Rd; 福州路17号103室; ☺10.30am-6.30pm; Ⓜ East Nanjing Rd) Just off the Bund, this little boutique is a great place to browse for a contemporary take on a traditional art form. It sells a tasteful selection of hand-painted porcelain teacups (from ¥150), teapots and vases, displayed together with the store's ingeniously designed wooden furniture.

★SHÀNGHĂI MUSEUM ART STORE   GIFTS

Map p296 (上海博物馆艺术品商店; Shànghǎi Bówùguǎn Yìshùpǐn Shāngdiàn; 201 Renmin Ave; 人民大道201号; ☺9.30am-5pm; Ⓜ People's Sq) Attached to the Shànghǎi Museum and entered from East Yan'an Rd, this store offers refreshing variety from the usual tourist tat. Apart from the excellent range of books on Chinese art and architecture, there's a good selection of quality cards, prints and slides. The annexe shop sells fine imitations of some of the museum's ceramic pieces, as well as scarves and bags. There's another branch near Xīntiāndì (p120).

★SHÀNGHĂI NO 1 FOOD STORE   FOOD

Map p296 (上海市第一食品商店; Shànghǎi Shì Dìyī Shípǐn Shāngdiàn; 720 East Nanjing Rd; 南京东路720号; Ⓜ People's Sq) Brave the crowds to check out the amazing variety of dried mushrooms, ginseng and sea cucumber, as well as more tempting snacks including sunflower seeds, nuts, dried fruit, moon cakes and tea, all up on the 2nd floor. Built in 1926 and redone in 2012, this used to be Sun Sun, one of Shànghǎi's big department stores.

SHIATZY CHEN   CLOTHING

Map p296 (夏姿; Xià Zī; ☑6321 9155; 9 East Zhongshan No 1 Rd; 中山东一路9号; ☺10am-10pm; Ⓜ East Nanjing Rd) One of the top names in Asian haute couture, Taiwanese designer Shiatzy Chen finds her inspiration in traditional Chinese aesthetics. The exclusive collections (women's and men's apparel) at her Bund 9 flagship store display a painstaking attention to detail, gracefully crossing cultural boundaries.

SILK KING
FABRIC

Map p296 (真丝大王; Zhēnsī Dàwáng; ☏6321 1869; 136 East Nanjing Rd; 南京东路136号; Ⓜ East Nanjing Rd) The city's largest fabric chain is good for a quick browse to see a typical selection of Chinese prints and fabric designs. In-store tailors can make you a custom-fit *qípáo* (cheongsam), shirt or jacket in three to 10 days for around ¥1800 to ¥2000. Twenty-four-hour rush jobs are also possible.

DUŌYÚNXUĀN ART SHOP
ARTS & CRAFTS

Map p296 (朵云轩; Duǒyún Xuān; ☏6360 6475; 422 East Nanjing Rd; 南京东路422号; ◷9.30am-9.30pm; Ⓜ East Nanjing Rd) A multistorey, traditional-looking building (look for the two enormous calligraphy brushes outside) with an excellent selection of art and calligraphy supplies. The 2nd floor is one of the best places for heavy art books, both international and Chinese, and the 3rd floor houses antiques and some excellent calligraphy and brush-painting galleries. You can get your own chop (seal) made here.

FOREIGN LANGUAGES BOOKSTORE
BOOKS

Map p296 (外文书店; Wàiwén Shūdiàn; 390 Fuzhou Rd; 福州路390号; ◷9.30am-6pm; Ⓜ East Nanjing Rd) There's a strong showing of English-language fiction, nonfiction and travel guides on the ground floor, with kid's literature consigned to the 4th floor.

SHÀNGHǍI BOOK TRADERS USED BOOKS
BOOKS

Map p296 (上海外文图书公司; Shànghǎi Wàiwén Túshū Gōngsi; 36 Shanxi Rd; 山西路36号; ◷9am-5.30pm; Ⓜ East Nanjing Rd) This tiny used bookstore stocks back issues of *Time, Elle* and *Vogue,* along with three walls of well-priced used English-language books, from Balzac to Dan Brown and beyond.

SHÀNGHǍI NO 1 DEPARTMENT STORE
CLOTHING

Map p296 (上海市第一百货商店; Shànghǎi Shì Dìyī Bǎihuò Shāngdiàn; 800 East Nanjing Rd; 南京东路800号; ◷9.30am-10pm; Ⓜ People's Sq) Opened in 1936, the Shànghǎi No 1 Department Store was formerly known as the Sun Company and was one of East Nanjing Rd's big department stores (with Wing On, Sun Sun and Sincere) and the first equipped with an escalator. Today it averages 150,000 shoppers a day over 11 levels of merchandise.

RAFFLES CITY
MALL

Map p296 (来福士广场; Láifúshì Guǎngchǎng; ☏6340 3600; 268 Middle Xizang Rd; 西藏中路268号; ◷10am-10pm; Ⓜ People's Sq) This seven-floor Singapore-owned mall is the most popular shopping destination by People's Sq, with everything from clothes to electronics and toys. Like most Shànghǎi malls, it's also a big-time dining destination: food courts, restaurants and juice bars occupy the basement and upper levels.

SPORTS & ACTIVITIES

HUÁNGPǓ RIVER CRUISE
CRUISE

Map p296 (黄浦江游览; Huángpǔ Jiāng Yóulǎn; 219-239 East Zhongshan No 2 Rd; 中山东二路219-239号; tickets ¥128; Ⓜ East Nanjing Rd) The Huángpǔ River offers intriguing views of the Bund, Pǔdōng and riverfront activity. The night cruises are arguably more scenic, though boat traffic during the day is more interesting – depending on when you go, you'll pass an enormous variety of craft, from freighters, bulk carriers and roll-on roll-off ships to sculling sampans and massive floating TV advertisements.

Most cruises last 90 minutes and include not one, but two trips up to the International Cruise Terminal and back.

The whole experience is a bit long, and if you can find one of the rarer 40- or 60-minute cruises (¥100), book that instead.

Departures are from the docks on the south end of the Bund (near East Jinling Rd), or, less conveniently, from the Shíliùpù Docks (十六铺; Shíliùpù), a 20-minute walk south of the Bund. Buy tickets at the departure points or from the Bund **tourist information and service centre** (Map p296), beneath the Bund Promenade, opposite the intersection with East Nanjing Rd. Departure times vary, but cruises usually run from 11am to 8.30pm.

Six 40-minute cruises also depart from the Pearl Dock (p147) in Lùjiāzuǐ between 10am and 1.30pm.

Old Town

Neighbourhood Top Five

1 Zone out from Shànghǎi's concrete-and-glass jungle in the labyrinthine **Yùyuán Gardens & Bazaar** (p80), but avoid the weekend surge.

2 Sift through the clutter for gems at **Dongtai Road Antique Market** (p91).

3 Delve into traditional Old Town **backstreets** on a walking tour (p88).

4 Quaff a cup of Chinese tea in **Old Shanghai Teahouse** (p90).

5 Pay your respects to the diverse pantheon of divinities in the **Temple of the Town God** (p82).

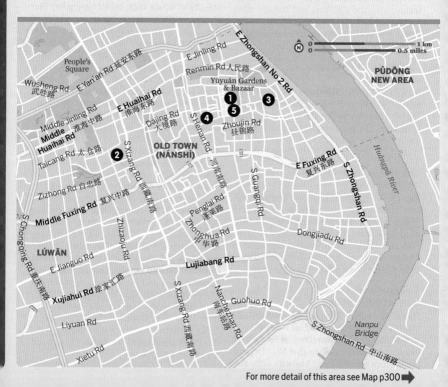

For more detail of this area see Map p300 ➡

Explore: Old Town

Known to locals as Nánshì (南市; literally 'Southern City'), the Old Town is the most traditionally Chinese area of Shànghǎi, along with Qībǎo. For long a concoction of old-fashioned textures, tatty charm and musty temples, the neighbourhood's central positioning and lucrative real estate potential have been mined by developers, squeezing out the old for the new. For glimpses of old Shànghǎi (that of the Chinese, not the foreigners), however, explore the surviving Old Town backstreets with their narrow and crowded lanes, dark alleyways and overhanging laundry.

The oval layout of the Old Town follows the footprint of its old 5km-long city walls, flung up to defend against marauding Japanese pirates. The 16th-century city wall was eventually torn down in 1912, but its outline remains along Renmin and Zhonghua Rds.

Temple buffs will adore the area's modest Confucian, Taoist, Buddhist, Christian and Muslim shrines, but most visitors are here to capture the traditional Chinese charms of the Yùyuán Gardens. You can also down pots of Chinese tea, haggle at the attached bazaar and sift through knick-knacks on Old St and Dongtai Road Antique Market.

East of the Old Town, the riverside Cool Docks and South Bund 22 have brought some pizzazz to formerly run-down areas, attracting a steady stream of diners and drinkers to their Westerner-oriented bars and restaurants.

Local Life

➡ **Lanes** Jostle with Shànghǎi locals wandering along the pinched Old Town back lanes.

➡ **Chinese medicine** Forage for the best panaceas at the Tóng Hán Chūn Traditional Medicine Store (p92).

➡ **Religious devotion** Fathom the profound Buddhist mysteries of the Chénxiānggé Nunnery (p82).

➡ **Markets** Join the critter-loving Shanghainese browsing the Flower, Bird, Fish & Insect Market (p83).

Getting There & Away

➡ **Metro** Line 10 runs from East Nanjing Rd to the French Concession, passing under the Old Town. The Yuyuan Garden station is close to most sights. Line 8, which runs south from People's Sq to the China Art Museum, intersects with line 10 at Laoximen (near the Confucian Temple), line 9 at Lujiabang Rd and line 4 at South Xizang Rd. Line 9 runs along the Old Town's southern edge and into Pǔdōng with a station at Xiaonanmen.

➡ **Bus** Route 11 circles the Old Town, following Renmin and Zhonghua Rds; bus 66 travels along Henan Rd, connecting the Old Town with East Nanjing Rd.

Lonely Planet's Top Tip

Development has called in last orders for much of Shànghǎi's Old Town. The most intriguing areas to wander are well off the main drag: the alleys north of the Confucian Temple (old roads such as Zhuangjia St) retain their old flavour, as do some of the alleys off Dajing Rd (such as Changsheng St) and the western stretch of Dongjiadu Rd.

Best Places to Eat

➡ Kebabs on the Grille (p89)
➡ Nánxiáng Steamed Bun Restaurant (p89)
➡ Wúyuè Rénjiā (p85)
➡ el Willy (p89)
➡ Table No 1 by Jason Atherton (p89)

For reviews, see p84.➡

Best Places to Shop

➡ Shíliùpù Fabric Market (p91)
➡ South Bund Fabric Market (p91)
➡ Dongtai Road Antique Market (p91)
➡ Tóng Hán Chūn Traditional Medicine Store (p92)

For reviews, see p91.➡

OLD TOWN

◉ TOP SIGHT
YÙYUÁN GARDENS & BAZAAR

With its shaded corridors, glittering pools churning with carp, pavilions, pines sprouting wistfully from rockeries, whispering bamboo, jasmine clumps, potted flowering plants and stony recesses, the labyrinthine Yùyuán Gardens (豫园; Yùyuán) are a delightful escape from Shànghǎi's hard-edged, glass-and-steel modernity. The attached bazaar (豫园商城; Yùyuán Shāngchéng) is a treasure trove of handicrafts, souvenirs and snacking opportunities, but brace for a powerful onslaught of visitors and the hard sell.

The Yùyuán Gardens

The Yùyuán Gardens were founded by the Pan family, who were rich Ming-dynasty officials. The gardens took 18 years (from 1559 to 1577) to be nurtured into existence, only to be ransacked during the Opium War in 1842, when British officers were barracked here, and again during the Taiping Rebellion, this time by the French in reprisal for attacks on their nearby concession.

Today the restored gardens are a fine example of Ming garden design. The gardens are small, but seem much bigger thanks to an ingenious use of rocks and alcoves. Nonetheless, they were simply never designed to accommodate the number of visitors that descend daily, so prepare for considerable disruption to the harmonious feng shui.

A handy map depicting the layout of the gardens can be found just inside the entrance. As you enter, **Three Ears of Corn Hall** (三穗堂; Sānsuìtáng) is the largest of the halls in the gardens. Its wood doors and beams are carved with images of corn, rice, millet and fruit, all symbolising a bountiful harvest. The **rockeries** (假山; jiǎshān) attempt to re-create a mountain setting within the flatland of the garden, so when combined with

DON'T MISS...

➡ Hall of Heralding Spring
➡ Exquisite Jade Rock
➡ Shopping and snacking in the bazaar area

PRACTICALITIES

➡ 豫园、豫园商城; Yùyuán & Yùyuán Shāngchéng
➡ Map p300
➡ Anren Jie; 安仁街
➡ admission low/high season ¥30/40
➡ ⏱8.30am-5.30pm, last entry at 5pm
➡ Ⓜ Yuyuan Garden

ponds (池塘; *chítáng*) they suggest the 'hills and rivers' (*shānshuǐ*) of China's landscapes. The largest rockery in the gardens is the **Great Rockery** (大假山; Dàjiǎshān), with its huge arranged stones, ranging west of the **Chamber of Ten Thousand Flowers** (万花楼; Wànhuālóu).

In the east of the gardens, keep an eye out for the **Hall of Heralding Spring** (点春堂; Diǎnchūn Táng), which in 1853 was the headquarters of the Small Swords Society, a rebel group affiliated to the Taiping rebels. To the south, the **Exquisite Jade Rock** (玉玲珑; Yù Línglóng) was destined for the imperial court in Běijīng until the boat carrying it sank outside Shànghǎi.

South of the Exquisite Jade Rock is the **inner garden** (内园; *nèiyuán*), where you can also find the beautiful **stage** (古戏台; *gǔxìtái*) dating from 1888, with a gilded, carved ceiling and fine acoustics, as well as the charming **Hall for Watching Waves** (观涛楼; Guāntāo Lóu).

Spring and summer blossoms bring a fragrant and floral aspect to the gardens, especially in the luxurious petals of its *Magnolia grandiflora,* Shànghǎi's flower. Other trees include the luohan pine, bristling with thick needles, and willows, towering ginkgos, cherry trees and beautiful dawn redwoods.

The Bazaar

Next to the Yùyuán Gardens entrance rises the **Mid-Lake Pavilion Teahouse** (湖心亭; Húxīntíng; Map p300; tea downstairs/upstairs ¥35/50; ⓧ8.30am-9.30pm), once part of the gardens and now one of the most famous teahouses in China. The zigzag causeway is designed to thwart spirits, who can only journey in straight lines.

Surrounding all this is the restored bazaar area, where scores of speciality shops and restaurants – including the Nánxiáng Steamed Bun Restaurant (p89) – jostle over narrow laneways and small squares in a mock 'ye olde Cathay' setting. There are some choice gift-giving ideas in the souvenir shops, from painted snuff bottles to silhouette cuttings from paper and leather, delightful Chinese kites, embroidered paintings and clever palm-and-finger paintings. Despite the skill on display, the hard sell is off-putting.

At the heart of the melee is the venerable **Temple of the Town God** (p82), dedicated to the protector of the city of Shànghǎi. Any city in China with any sense of history should have a temple to their town god, and it is always located within the old quarter.

DAWN REDWOOD

Among the trees and foliage at the Yùyuán Gardens are dawn redwood (Metasequoia), a towering (up to 200ft) and elegant fine-needled deciduous tree dating to the Jurassic period. Once considered long extinct, a single example was discovered in 1941 in Sìchuān province. Three years later, a small stand of the trees was located, from which the tree was disseminated (around China and the globe).

BEST TIME TO VISIT

More than a thousand visitors stream into the gardens daily, so arrive at midday and you'll be wedged in the entrance with camera-toting tour groups. Weekends are also overpowering so make it a weekday morning. Aim to give yourself at least an hour or two to explore the garden.

WIND & WATER

The Yùyuán Gardens are devised with the central precept of feng shui (literally 'wind water') in mind. The main gate is south-facing to maximise the *yángqì* (male, positive energy); all rockeries and ponds are arranged to maximise positive '*qi*'; and the undulating 'dragon walls' in the gardens bring good fortune.

◉ SIGHTS

YÙYUÁN GARDENS & BAZAAR GARDENS, BAZAAR

See p80.

CHÉNXIĀNGGÉ NUNNERY BUDDHIST TEMPLE

Map p300 (沉香阁; Chénxiāng Gé; 29 Chenxiangge Rd; 沉香阁路29号; admission ¥10; ⊘7am-5pm; MYuyuan Garden) Sheltering a community of dark-brown-clothed nuns from the Chénhǎi (Sea of Dust) – what Buddhists call the mortal world, but which could equally refer to Shànghǎi's murky atmosphere – this lovely yellow-walled temple is a tranquil refuge. At the temple rear, the **Guanyin Tower** guides you upstairs to a glittering effigy of the male-looking goddess within a resplendent gilded cabinet.

Carved from *chénxiāng* wood (Chinese eaglewood) and seated in *lalitasana* posture, head tilted and with one arm resting on her leg, this version is a modern copy – the original disappeared during the Cultural Revolution.

At the front, the **Hall of Heavenly Kings** (天王殿; Tiānwáng Diàn) envelops four gilded Heavenly Kings (each belonging to a different compass point) and a slightly androgynous form of Maitreya. Muttered prayers and chanted hymns fill the **Great Treasure Hall** (大雄宝殿; Dàxióng Bǎodiàn), where a statue of Sakyamuni (Buddha) is flanked by two rows of nine *luóhàn* (arhat).

TEMPLE OF THE TOWN GOD TAOIST TEMPLE

Map p300 (城隍庙; Chénghuáng Miào; Yùyuán Bazaar, off Middle Fangbang Rd; admission ¥10; ⊘8.30am-4.30pm; MYuyuan Garden) Chinese towns traditionally had a Taoist temple of the town god, but many fell victim to periodic upheaval. Originally dating to the early 15th century, this particular temple was badly damaged during the Cultural Revolution and later restored. Note the fine carvings on the roof as you enter the main hall, which is dedicated to Huo Guang, a Han-dynasty general, flanked by rows of effigies representing both martial and civil virtues.

Exit the hall north and peek into the multifaith hall on your right, which is dedicated to three female deities: Guanyin (Buddhist), Tianhou and Yanmu Niangni-

---

MOUNTAIN-WATER GARDENS

Classical Chinese gardens can be an acquired taste: there are no lawns, few flowering plants, and there are huge misshapen rocks strewn about. Yet a stroll in the Yùyuán Gardens (and the gardens of Sūzhōu) is a walk through many different facets of Chinese civilisation, and this is what makes them so unique. Architecture, philosophy, art and literature all converge, and a background in some basics of Chinese culture helps to fully appreciate the garden design.

The Chinese for 'landscape' is *shānshuǐ* (山水), literally 'mountain-water'. Mountains and rivers constitute a large part of China's geography, and are fundamental to Chinese life, philosophy, religion and art. So the central part of any garden landscape is a pond surrounded by rock formations.

This also reflects the influence of Taoist thought. Contrary to geometrically designed formal European gardens, where humans saw themselves as masters, Chinese gardens seek to create a microcosm of the natural world through an asymmetrical layout of streams, hills, plants and pavilions (they symbolise humanity's place in the universe – never in the centre, just a part of the whole).

Symbolism works on every level. Plants are chosen as much for their symbolic meaning as their beauty (the pine for longevity, the peony for nobility); the billowy rocks call to mind not only mountains but also the changing, indefinable nature of the Tao (the underlying principle of the universe in Taoist thought); and the names of gardens and halls are often literary allusions to ideals expressed in classical poetry. Painting, too, goes hand in hand with gardening, its aesthetics reproduced in gardens through the use of carefully placed windows and doors that frame a particular view.

Finally, it's worth remembering that gardens in China have always been lived in. Generally part of a residence, they weren't so much contemplative (as in Japan) as they were a backdrop for everyday life: family gatherings, late-night drinking parties, discussions of philosophy, art and politics – it's the people who spent their leisure hours there that ultimately gave the gardens their unique spirit.

ang (Taoist). Gazing fiercely over offerings of fruit from the rear Chengghuang Hall is the red-faced and bearded town god himself. Also note the Tàisuì Hall where worshippers pay respects to divine figures representing each year of the Chinese zodiac. Within the temple grounds is a small restaurant that serves vegetarian noodles (素面; sùmiàn) for ¥8.

CONFUCIAN TEMPLE   CONFUCIAN TEMPLE

Map p300 (文庙; Wén Miào; 215 Wenmiao Rd; 文庙路215号; adult/student ¥10/5; ⊙9am-5pm, last entry 4.30pm; MLaoximen) A modest and charming retreat, this well-tended temple to Confucius is cultivated with maples, pines, magnolias and birdsong. The layout is typically Confucian, its few worshippers complemented by ancient and venerable trees, including a 300-year-old elm. The main hall for worshipping Confucius is **Dàchéng Hall** (Dàchéng Diàn), complete with twin eaves and a statue of the sage outside.

The towering **Kuíxīng Pavilion** (Kuíxīng Gé) in the west is named after the god of the literati. Originally dating to 1294, when the Mongols held sway through China, the temple moved to its current site in 1855, at a time when Christian Taiping rebels were sending much of China skywards in sheets of flame. In line with Confucian championing of learning, a busy secondhand market of (largely Chinese-language) books is held in the temple every Sunday morning (admission ¥1; open from 7.30am to 4pm). There are some genuine finds, if you can read Chinese.

FLOWER, BIRD, FISH & INSECT MARKET   MARKET

Map p300 (万商花鸟鱼虫市场; Wànshāng Huā Niǎo Yú Chóng Shìchǎng; South Xizang Rd; 西藏南路; MLaoximen) One of few remaining traditional markets in town, this spot is a fascinating experience. Wander among the racket of crickets, interlaced with snatches of birdsong, to a backdrop of multicoloured fish flitting about. Crickets come in a variety of sizes and are sold in woven bamboo cages for under ¥30.

DǑNGJIĀDÙ CATHEDRAL   CHURCH

Map p300 (董家渡教堂; Dǒngjiādù Jiàotáng; 185 Dongjiadu Rd; 董家渡路185号; MNanpu Bridge) Just outside the Old Town and once known as St Francis Xavier Church, this magnificent whitewashed cathedral is Shànghǎi's oldest church, built by Spanish Jesuits in 1853. A splendid sight, the church was located within a famously Catholic area of Shànghǎi and is generally open if you want to view the well-kept interior (ring the bell at the side door).

COOL DOCKS   ARCHITECTURE

Map p300 (老码头; Lǎomǎtou; www.thecool docks.com; 479 South Zhongshan Rd; 中山南路479号; MXiaonanmen) The riverside Cool Docks consist of several shíkùmén (stonegate houses) surrounded by red-brick warehouses, near (but not quite on) the waterfront. Now full of restaurants and bars and all lit up at night, the Cool Docks' isolated positioning (it lacks the central location and transport connections of Xīntiāndì in the French Concession) has hobbled ambitions. Although high-profile and trendy restaurant, bar and hotel openings have helped give it a much-needed lift, it remains an entertainment backwater.

SUNNY BEACH   BEACH

Map p300 (老码头阳光沙滩; Lǎomǎtou Yángguāng Shātān; ☏133 1167 3735; South Zhongshan Rd; admission incl 1 soft drink ¥50; ⊙10am-10pm; MXiaonanmen) Life's a beach, even in the middle of Shànghǎi. If the sun comes out, pop down to this amusing artificial strip of sand right by the river and north of the Cool Docks. There you'll find a backdrop of Lùjiāzuǐ, a bar, deckchairs, beach volleyball, Frisbee, tents and other fun beach activities (and no jellyfish).

DÀJÌNG PAVILION   HISTORIC SITE

Map p300 (大境阁; Dàjìng Gé; 259 Dajing Rd; 大境路; admission ¥5; ⊙9am-4pm; MDashijie) Dating from 1815, this pavilion contains the only preserved section of the 5km-long city walls. Also within the pavilion is a small Guandi temple, which found a new calling as a factory during the Cultural Revolution. In the middle sits the fiery-faced Guandi, with an equally fierce God of Wealth to his left and Yuexia Laoren (月下老人) to his right. You can climb up to the restored battlements.

FǍZÀNGJIǍNG TEMPLE   BUDDHIST TEMPLE

Map p300 (法藏讲寺; Fǎzàngjiǎng Sì; 271 Ji'an Rd; 吉安路271号; admission ¥5; ⊙7.30am-4pm; MLaoximen) This simple but very active temple is curiously accessed from the west, rather than the south where the entrance to Buddhist temples usually lies. The restored main hall encloses a large modern statue

OLD SHÀNGHǍI STREET NAMES

The naming of streets in Shànghǎi once depended on which concession they belonged to, French or English, except for the central area of the city where the streets were given the names of Chinese cities and provinces. While the foreign names have disappeared, streets named after Chinese places have been retained: those named after other Chinese cities are oriented east–west and those named after provinces north–south. Below are some of Shànghǎi's former street names:

NOW	THEN
East Yan'an Rd	Edward VII Ave
Fanyu Rd	Columbia Rd
Fenyang Rd	Rue Pichon
Gaolan Rd	Rue Corneille
Guangdong Rd	Canton Rd
Huaihai Rd	Ave Joffre
Jiangsu Rd	Edinburgh Rd
Jinling Rd	Ave Foch
Jinshan Rd	Astor Rd
Tongren Rd	Hardoon Rd
West Nanjing Rd	Bubbling Well Rd
Xiangshan Rd	Rue Molière
Xinhua Rd	Amherst Rd

of Sakyamuni, seated lily-top between two walls glinting with gilded *luóhàn*.

Other lesser halls shelter a trinity of golden Buddhist effigies and there's a small shrine to the Buddhist god of the underworld, Dizang Wang. A handy vegetarian restaurant (open from 9am to 9pm) is right next door for karmic sustenance.

PEACH GARDEN MOSQUE   MOSQUE
Map p300 (小桃园清真寺; Xiǎotáoyuán Qīngzhēnsì; 52 Xiaotaoyuan Rd; 小桃园路52号; ⊙8am-7pm; MLaoximen, Yuyuan Garden) Originally dating to 1917, this famous mosque is the main place of worship for Shànghǎi's Muslims. Fridays are the best time to visit, when the faithful stream in to pray at lunch and a large market is held outside the entrance. Women can visit but cannot access the Main Prayer Hall; there is a separate smaller prayer hall for women.

BÁIYÚN TEMPLE   TAOIST TEMPLE
Map p300 (白云观; Báiyún Guàn; 239 Dajing Rd; 大境路239号; admission ¥5; ⊙8am-4.30pm; MDashijie) The recently built Taoist Báiyún (White Cloud) Temple is fronted by an entrance with twin eaves and separated from Dàjìng Pavilion, a preserved section of the city walls, by Dajing Lane. As it's not a historical temple, it has little heritage value.

LÚPǓ BRIDGE   BRIDGE
(卢浦大桥; Lúpǔ Dàqiáo; 909 Luban Rd; 鲁班路909号; adult/student ¥80/40; ⊙8.30am-5pm; 🚌17, MLuban Rd, then 🚌17) For aerial views of the World Expo grounds or for those seeking to measure the extent of Shànghǎi's urban sprawl, climb up to a viewing platform at the apex of the city's longest suspension bridge. The entrance is located at the end of Luban Rd (under the bridge). It's one elevator ride and an additional 367 wind-blown steps to the top. From metro Luban St take bus 17 for one stop to get here. If you take a taxi, insist on the address; the bridge is 4km long and the driver will probably have no idea what you are looking for.

🍴 EATING

The Yùyuán Gardens area is hardly a dining destination in itself, but if you're visiting the Old Town you needn't go hungry. There's snack food aplenty and several famous old restaurants, while a collection of zestful and stylish choices in South Bund 22 and the Cool Docks makes it easy to tie in the area's sights with dinner and drinks by the river. For all manner of Chinese snacks, try the stalls in the Yùyuán Bazaar. The Old Town also bursts with food streets, such as Shouning Rd and Sipailou Rd, the latter a heaving food market, where grilled squid, Shāndōng dumplings, stinky *dòufu* (tofu), flat breads and roast duck converge in a formidable aroma.

★ **WÚYUÈ RÉNJIĀ** NOODLES **$**

Map p300 (吴越人家; 234 Fuyou Rd; 福佑路234号; ⊙8am-9.30pm; Ⓜ Yuyuan Garden) Right next to KFC north of the Yùyuán Gardens, this upstairs place doesn't look particularly appealing but it serves typical Old Town fare and it's a well-known family name in Shànghǎi. They serve up excellent and filling bowls of Sūzhōu noodles. Choose between *tāng* (soupy) and *gān* (dry) noodles; in either case, the flavouring comes on a side plate.

Try the noodles with meat and pickled vegetables (榨菜肉丝面; *zhàcài ròusī miàn*; ¥10) or the spicy meat noodles in red oil (红油腊肉面; *hóngyóu làròu miàn*; ¥13).

DRAGON GATE MALL CHINESE **$**

Map p300 (豫龙坊; Yùlóngfáng; Middle Fangbang Rd; 方浜中路; dishes from ¥10; ⊙9am-11pm; Ⓜ Yuyuan Garden) True, eating in a mall isn't *quite* the same as wandering amid the chaos of the Yùyuán Bazaar, but if you've had enough of the push and pull of the crowds, this spot is a lifesaver. Noodle restaurants, a food court and juice bar are on the basement level while a branch of Din Tai Fung is on the 2nd floor.

The enormous dragon-arch fountain marks the entrance.

SŌNGYUÈLÓU CHINESE **$**

Map p300 (松月楼; ☏6355 3630; 23 Bailing Rd; 百灵路23号; dishes from ¥10; ⊙7am-7.30pm; 🖉; Ⓜ Yuyuan Garden) Dating to 1910, this place has decent-value vegie cheap-eats such as wonton (*tānghúndùn*; ¥10), and tofu masquerading as meat such as black-pepper beef noodle soup (¥35). Upstairs has an English menu, spotless tablecloths and a price hike. Downstairs is a Mandarin-only busy canteen-style affair where you order first, get a receipt and share tables.

OLD TOWN EATING

GUANYIN

Encountered in Buddhist temples across Shànghǎi and China, the bodhisattva Guanyin is the Buddhist Goddess of Mercy. Her full name is Guanshiyin (观世音; literally 'Observing the Cries of the World'), but she is also called Guanzizai, Guanyin Dashi and Guanyin Pusa, or, in Sanskrit, Avalokiteshvara. Known as Kannon in Japanese, Guanyam in Cantonese and Quan Am in Vietnamese, she is one of the most recognisable figures in Buddhism. Her mission is to offer sympathy to the world, from a wellspring of infinite compassion and she is most revered by female worshippers.

Guanyin can often be found at the very rear of the main hall, facing north (most of the other divinities, apart from Weituo, face south). She typically has her own little shrine and stands on the head of a big fish, holding a lotus in her hand, with attendant *luóhàn* (arhats) and children on a montage behind her. On other occasions, she has her own hall, often towards the rear of the temple (as in Shànghǎi's Chénxiānggé Nunnery (p82) in the Old Town) and sometimes she is worshipped within her very own temple. The goddess is also the presiding divinity on the island of Pǔtuóshān off the coast of Zhèjiāng, a site of great veneration for Buddhists and one of China's four sacred Buddhist mountains.

In ancient Chinese effigies, the goddess was male rather than female and can sometimes be found seated *lalitasana*, a lithe and relaxed regal posture where one of Guanyin's feet typically rests on, or near, the thigh of the other leg.

Guanyin can appear in many forms, often with just two arms, but sometimes in a multiarmed form or with a fan of arms behind her in the famous 1000-hand form (Qiānshǒu Guanyin). The 11-faced Guanyin, the fierce horse-head Guanyin, the Songzi Guanyin (literally 'Offering Son Guanyin') and the Dripping Water Guanyin are just some of her myriad manifestations. She was also a favourite subject for *déhuà* glazed porcelain figures, which are very elegant and either snow-white or creamy. Examples exist in the Shànghǎi Museum.

KARL JOHAENTGES / GETTY IMAGES ©

1. Confucian Temple (p83)
Wén Miào, a well-tended temple to Confucius, has beribboned trees, magnolias and birdsong.

2. Yùyuán Bazaar (p80)
Colourful dolls are just one of the many souvenirs for sale at this famous bazaar.

3. Courtyard
The traditional ways of life continue in the communal houses of Old Town.

4. Temple of the Town God (p82)
Dedicated to the protector of Shànghǎi, this temple was damaged during the Cultural Revolution and later restored.

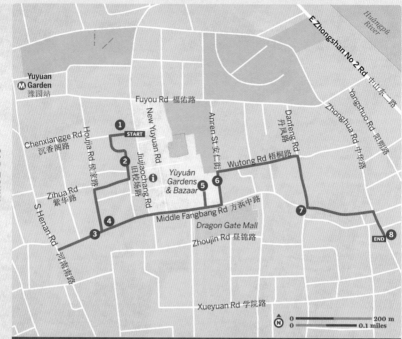

Neighbourhood Walk
Old Town

START CHÉNXIĀNGGÉ NUNNERY
FINISH SHÍLIÙPÙ FABRIC MARKET
LENGTH 1KM; TWO HOURS

Begin by visiting the charming **❶ Chén-xiānggé Nunnery** (p82) on Chenxiangge Rd, a Buddhist retreat from the surrounding clamour.

Clarity attained, exit the temple and weave south down **❷ Wangyima Alley** (王医马弄), a small and typical Old Town alley immediately facing you. Follow the alley, then turn west along Zhongwangyima Alley (中王医马弄) before turning south onto Houjia Rd.

Wander along Middle Fangbang Rd – once a canal and also known as **❸ Old Street** (p91) – and browse for Tibetan jewellery, teapots and prints of 1930s poster advertisements. Alternatively, break for a pot of refreshing oolong tea at the **❹ Old Shanghai Teahouse** (p90).

Head east down Old Street, passing the Yùyuán Bazaar, to pay your respects to the red-faced town protector at the **❺ Temple of the Town God** (p82).

Upon exiting, continue east down Middle Fangbang Rd and then turn north at the KFC onto **❻ Anren Street**. Wend your way past the outdoor mah-jong and Chinese chess matches, then turn east onto Wutong Rd and then south on Danfeng Rd, a pinched lane frequently dressed with hanging washing. Note the lovely old doorways on Danfeng Rd, such as the carved red-brick gateway at No 193.

Exit Danfeng Rd, turning east onto Middle Fangbang Rd at the old **❼ stone archway** (四牌楼; *sì páilou*). Stroll down the boisterous shopping street, which is filled with snack stands, clothing shops and booming stereo systems. As long as the eastern part of town remains standing over the next few years, there are plenty of little alleyways to explore here, particularly off to the south. When you reach the end of Middle Fangbang Rd, cross Zhonghua Rd (which marks the eastern boundary of the old city wall) to the **❽ Shíliùpù Fabric Market** (p91) for a tailor-made shirt, dress or jacket.

ELEMENT FRESH
SANDWICHES $

Map p300 (新元素; Xīnyuánsù; www.element fresh.com; 6th fl, Fraser Residence, 228 South Xizang Rd; 西藏南路228号6楼; breakfast from ¥38, meals ¥60-100; ☎; ⓜDashijie) Handy Old Town outpost of the health-conscious chain dedicated to pick-me-up breakfasts, crisp salads, sandwiches, and feel-good juices and smoothies.

QUÁNMIÀNSHÈNG GÀINIÀN MIÀNGUǍN
NOODLES $

Map p300 (全面盛概念面馆; 991 South Xizang Rd; 西藏南路991号; dishes from ¥15; ⓜLujiabang Rd) This small noodle restaurant just a short walk north of Lujiabang Rd metro station is simple and unfussy, decked out with faded photos of the owner's travel adventures. It's very popular with Shànghǎi diners for its tasty bowls of fish and meat noodles.

★EL WILLY
SPANISH $$

Map p300 (☎5404 5757; www.el-willy.com; 5th fl, South Bund 22, 22 East Zhongshan No 2 Rd; 中山东二路22号5楼; mains from ¥65, 3-course set menu ¥168; ⊙11.30am-2.30pm & 6-10.30pm Mon-Sat; ⓜYuyuan Garden) Ensconced in the stunningly converted South Bund 22, bright, vivacious, bubbly and relocated from the French Concession, Willy Trullas Moreno's fetching and fun restaurant is a more relaxed counterpoint to many other overdressed Bund operations. Seasonally adjusted scrumptious tapas and paellas are Willy's forte, paired with some serene Bund views beyond the windows. Chopsticks encourage the communal Chinese dining approach.

★KEBABS ON THE GRILLE
INDIAN $$

Map p300 (☎6152 6567; No 8, Cool Docks, 505 South Zhongshan Rd; 中山南路505号老码头8号; mains ¥45-125, set lunch Mon-Fri ¥58; ⊙11am-10.30pm; ⓜXiaonanmen) This immensely popular and busy Cool Docks restaurant is a genuine crowd-pleaser, and has alfresco seating by the pond outside. The Boti mutton (barbecued lamb pieces) is adorable. There's a delicious range of tandoori dishes, live table-top grills, vegetarian choices, smooth and spicy daal options, plus an all-you-can-eat Sunday brunch (¥150). Another central branch can be found west of People's Sq (p74).

NÁNXIÁNG STEAMED BUN RESTAURANT
DUMPLINGS $$

Map p300 (南翔馒头店; Nánxiáng Mántou Diàn; 85 Yuyuan Rd, Yùyuán Bazaar; 豫园商城豫园路85号; 1st fl per 16 dumplings ¥20; ⊙1st fl 10am-9pm, 2nd fl 7am-8pm, 3rd fl 9.30am-7pm; ⓜYuyuan Garden) Shànghǎi's most famous dumpling restaurant divides the purists, who love the place, from the younger crowd, who see an overrated tourist trap. Decide for yourself how the *xiǎolóngbāo* rate, but lines are long and you won't even get near it on weekends. There are three dining halls upstairs, with the prices escalating (and crowds diminishing) in each room.

The takeaway deal (including crab meat) is comparable to what you pay elsewhere for *xiǎolóngbāo*, but the queue snakes halfway around the Yùyuán Bazaar.

★TABLE NO 1 BY JASON ATHERTON
EUROPEAN $$$

Map p300 (☎6080 2918; www.tableno-1.com; The Waterhouse at South Bund, 1-3 Maojiayuan Rd; 毛家园路1-3号; mains ¥148-268, 3-course lunch/dinner ¥188/200; ⊙lunch & dinner; ☎; ⓜXiaonanmen) On the ground floor of the Waterhouse by the Cool Docks, English chef Jason Atherton's Table No 1 commences with a distressed industrial-chic lobby perked up with eclectic furniture. This gives way to a casual and smooth interior of candlelit wooden tables arranged in communal dining fashion with a courtyard beyond.

The excellent menu (seared sea bass with broccolini and Spanish rice or roasted lamb with smoked eggplant and tomato) is backed up by an impressive wine list.

CHAR
STEAK $$$

Map p300 (恰餐厅; Qià Cāntīng; ☎3302 9995; www.char-thebund.com; 29th-31st fl, Hotel Indigo, 585 East Zhongshan No 2 Rd; 中山东二路585号29-31楼; steaks from ¥438, burgers ¥298, mains from ¥188; ⊙6-10pm; ☎; ⓜXiaonanmen) Char has become a Shànghǎi steakhouse sensation. Park yourself on a sofa against the window or in a comfy chair facing Lùjiāzuǐ for optimum views. Or keep one eye on the open kitchen to see how your Tajima Wagyu rib-eye steak, grilled black cod or seafood tower is coming along. There's a choice of six different steak knives. Book ahead.

The views continue in spectacular fashion from the terrace of the supremely chilled-out upstairs bar (p90).

OLD TOWN EATING

SEEING SHÀNGHǍI FROM A SIDECAR

Founder of Shanghai Insiders (www.shanghaiinsiders.com; formerly Shanghai Side-ways), Thomas Chabrieres was born in France, educated in England and settled in China more than a decade ago. He speeds visitors on tours around Shànghǎi in the sidecar of his motorbike.

What is it about Shànghǎi that fires you up?

Shànghǎi is a city that one has to earn. It's not an open book and it takes a lot of getting lost to get familiar with it! After all these years, I still discover new places, even in my own neighbourhood.

What's your favourite off-beat destination in town?

The **Old Town** and **Hóngkǒu** back alleys are lovely, but the lanes of the **French Concession** are splendid too. The long lane leaving from Middle Huaihai Rd (at No 1857) immediately west of Song Qingling's former residence (p100) heads deep into the French Concession. It's like time has stopped still. It's also too narrow for cars to go through so it's as quiet as Shànghǎi ever gets.

And for a drink at the end of the day?

Burdigala 2 (p115). Red wine all the way! Yongkang Rd (p117) is also a very lively and upcoming bar street – get there early as the fun ends at 10pm.

For a romantic dinner – your top spot?

ElElefante (p108). This restaurant on Donghu Rd is my kind of place. Or a picnic with champagne on the rooftop of a residential building along Sūzhōu River.

What's your favourite building, and why?

1933 (p158). Shànghǎi's former slaughterhouse is like nothing else. With some of the craziness of Escher and Gaudi, it's simply amazing to the eye. Don't forget your camera.

And which street in Shànghǎi grabs you most, and why?

Middle Fangbang Rd. This is Shànghǎi as it disappears. Go there for the next two years, at least, to witness entire blocks being destroyed to make way for big towers – quite a visual shock.

🍷 DRINKING & NIGHTLIFE

CHAR BAR   BAR

Map p300 (恰酒吧; Qià Jiǔbā; www.char-thebund. com; 30th fl, Hotel Indigo, 585 East Zhongshan No 2 Rd; 中山东二路585号30楼; ⊙5pm-1.30am Mon-Thu, to 2.30am Fri & Sat, 2pm-1am Sun; MXiaonan-men) One of Shànghǎi's supreme alfresco bar experiences, Char Bar is a top spot for a cocktail and some neon-gazing. The terrace packs some of the finest views over the Bund, the Huángpǔ River and Pǔdōng, while inside it's chilled out and hip. From 8.30pm Thursdays to Saturdays, there's a ¥100 cover charge (including one drink). Drinks cost ¥50 between 5pm and 8.30pm from Monday to Thursday.

YAWARAGI   BAR

Map p300 (3rd fl, South Bund 22, 22 East Zhong-shan No 2 Rd; 中山东二路22号3楼; cocktails ¥80; ⊙11am-2am; 🛱; MYuyuan Garden) Lur-ing patrons with its exquisite Japanese chocolate cakes and a delectable Japanese menu, stylish Yawaragi sees the sophisti-cated cocktail crowd arriving in the even-ing to cherry-pick from its generous list of Bund-priced alcoholic infusions and fruity cocktails.

OLD SHANGHAI TEAHOUSE   TEAHOUSE

Map p300 (老上海茶馆; Lǎo Shànghǎi Cháguǎn; ☑5382 1202; 385 Middle Fangbang Rd; 方浜中路385号; tea from ¥45; ⊙9am-9pm; MYuyuan Garden) A bit like the attic of an eccentric aunt, this wonderfully decrepit 2nd-floor teahouse, overlooking the throng of Old Street, is a temple to the 1930s, with mu-sic on scratched records, period typewrit-ers, aged photos, an old fireplace, sewing machines, electric fans, an ancient fridge, oodles of charm and tea, of course.

🛍 SHOPPING

Although not originally set up as a shopping district, Yùyuán Bazaar has become exactly that. All souvenirs can be found here or on the bordering Old Street (Middle Fangbang Rd), which itself is stuffed with tourist paraphernalia and kitsch, and blasted with shrill techno spliced with Chinese opera, children's ditties and random music. You can find anything from Chinese kites to walking sticks, fans and 3D dazzle pictures of fluffy kittens. The Shílìùpù Fabric Market and the South Bund Fabric Market are both fine places to go in search of inexpensive fabric or to have a dress or shirt tailor-made.

★OLD STREET   SOUVENIRS

Map p300 (老街; Lǎo Jiē; Middle Fangbang Rd; 方浜中路; ⓂYuyuan Garden) This renovated Qing-dynasty stretch of Middle Fangbang Rd is lined with specialist tourist shops, spilling forth with shadow puppets, jade jewellery, embroidered fabrics, kites, horn combs, chopsticks, zǐshā teapots, old poster advertisements, bank notes, Tibetan jewellery, the usual knock-off Mao trash, repro 1930s posters, old illustrated books and calligraphy manuals, and surreal 3D dazzle photos of kittens.

★SHÍLÌÙPÙ FABRIC MARKET   FABRIC

Map p300 (十六铺面料城; Shílìùpù Miànliào Chéng; ☑6330 1043; 2 Zhonghua Rd; 中华路2号; ⊘8.30am-6.30pm; ⓂXiaonanmen) Having silk shirts, dresses and cashmere coats tailor-made for a song is one of Shànghǎi's great indulgences. This three-storey building, one of several fabric markets in the city, is conveniently located near the Yùyuán Bazaar. It's a far cheaper source of silk than many shops, with prices no higher than ¥200 per metre.

There are many types of fabric here in addition to silk, from wool and velvet to synthetic, but the quality of the material varies, so shop around. Most places can fill an order in 24 hours if needed, but it's best to count on at least three days.

★SOUTH BUND FABRIC MARKET   FABRIC

Map p300 (南外滩轻纺面料市场; Nán Wàitān Qīngfǎng Miànliào Shìchǎng; 399 Lujiabang Rd; 陆家浜路399号; ⊘8.30am-6pm; ⓂNanpu Bridge) This old building with more than 100 stalls has an atmospheric location not far from the markets and tailoring shops along Dongjiadu Rd. It's a bit out of the way, but popular with expats.

★DONGTAI ROAD ANTIQUE MARKET   SOUVENIRS

Map p300 (东台路古玩市场; Dōngtái Lù Gǔwán Shìchǎng; ☑5582 5254; Dongtai Rd; 东台路;

OLD TOWN SHOPPING

NAVIGATING SHÀNGHǍI ON FOOT

Unlike in other Chinese cities where street signs are in Chinese (sometimes accompanied by Pinyin), all street signs in Shànghǎi display the name of the road in Chinese script and its English translation. We use road names as they appear on street signs, to aid navigation on foot. But we also list road names in Chinese to assist you in your journey around town.

By far the majority of roads in Shànghǎi are affixed with the word lù (路), which means 'road', as in Huashan Lu (Huashan Rd). Occasionally the word jiē (街) is used, which means 'street', as in Menghua Jie (Menghua St). The other convention you may see is dàdào (大道), which means 'avenue' or 'boulevard', as in Renmin Dadao (Renmin Ave). Alleys are called lòng (弄) or lǐ (里).

Many road names are also compound words that place the road in context with others in the city, by using the points of the compass. These include:

běi – 北 (north)
nán – 南 (south)
dōng – 东 (east)
xī – 西 (west)
zhōng – 中 (middle)

So, Nanjing Donglu (南京东路) literally means East Nanjing Rd, while Huaihai Zhonglu (淮海中路) means Middle Huaihai Rd. Other words you may see are huán (环; ring, as in ring road) and numbers, such as Ruijin Erlu (瑞金二路), or Ruijin No 2 Rd.

SEDUCTION & THE CITY

Shànghǎi owes its reputation as the most fashionable city in China to calendar posters, whose print runs once numbered in the tens of millions. Distribution of these – given out as bonus gifts, a practice that began at the Shànghǎi racecourse in the late 1890s – reached from China's interior to Southeast Asia.

The basic idea behind the posters – associating a product with an attractive woman to encourage subconscious desire and consumption – today sounds like Marketing 101, but in the early 20th century it was revolutionary. Calendar posters not only introduced new products to Chinese everywhere, their portrayal of Shànghǎi women – wearing makeup and stylish clothing, smoking cigarettes and surrounded by foreign goods – set the standard for modern fashion that many Chinese women (trapped in rural lives with little freedom and certainly no nearby department stores) would dream of for decades.

Today, reproduction posters are sold throughout the Old Town for as little as ¥10, though finding a bona fide original is quite a challenge. For an in-depth look at calendar posters and Shànghǎi's role in modern China, see Wen-Hsin Yeh's *Shanghai Splendor*.

⊙9am-6pm; Ⓜ Laoximen) A block west of South Xizang Rd, this market street has more than 100 stalls strewn along both Dongtai Rd and Liuhekou Rd. It's a long sprawl of miniature terracotta warriors, Guanyin figures, imperial robes, walnut-faced *luóhàn* statues, twee lotus shoes, helicopter pilot helmets and Mao-era knick-knacks, but generally only recent stuff such as art deco (and later) ornaments are genuine.

Get haggling: a good rule of thumb is if you like the look of something and can get a fair price for it, buy it for what it is and not as an antique.

★ **TÓNG HÁN CHŪN TRADITIONAL MEDICINE STORE**   CHINESE MEDICINE
Map p300 (童涵春堂; Tóng Hán Chūn Táng; ☑6355 0308; 20 New Yuyuan Rd; 豫园新路20号; ⊙8am-9pm; Ⓜ Yuyuan Garden) An intriguing emporium of elixirs, infusions and rem-edies, this place has been selling Chinese medicinal cures since 1783. There's a vast range here, including modern medications, but it's all labelled in Chinese and little English is spoken, so take along a translator. On the 3rd floor, traditional Chinese medicine (TCM) doctors offer consultations (you'll need an appointment).

FÚYÒU ANTIQUE MARKET   ANTIQUES, SOUVENIRS
Map p300 (福佑工艺品市场; Fúyòu Gōngyìpǐn Shìchǎng; 459 Middle Fangbang Rd; 方浜中路459号; Ⓜ Yuyuan Garden) There's a permanent antique market here on the 1st and 2nd floors, but the place really gets humming for the **Ghost Market** on Sunday at dawn, when sellers from the countryside fill up all four floors and then some. The range is good, but there's a lot of junk, so you need a shrewd eye if you don't want to pay too much over the odds.

French Concession

FRENCH CONCESSION EAST | FRENCH CONCESSION WEST

Neighbourhood Top Five

1 Weave through a forest of shoppers' elbows in the charming *shíkùmén* warren of **Tiánzǐfáng** (p95).

2 Shop your socks off in the boutiques of **Nanchang** or **Xinle Roads** (p122).

3 Savour home-style Shanghainese cuisine at **Jian Guo 328** (p106).

4 Mosey around the interior of a *shíkùmén* stone-gate house at **Xīntiāndì** (p96).

5 Ease into the French Concession cocktail hour at **el Cóctel** (p115).

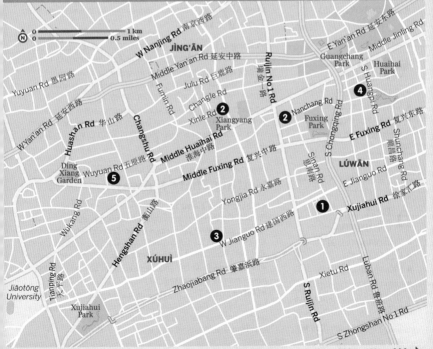

For more detail of this area see Map p302 and Map p306 ➤

Lonely Planet's Top Tip

Although most expats use the colonial-era term 'French Concession', the name means little to most Shanghainese. Locals call much of the eastern area Lúwān (卢湾) or Huángpǔ (黄浦), while the area west of South Shaanxi Rd is known as Xúhuì (徐汇), a district that extends southwest into Xújiāhuì. It's worth familiarising yourself with these official district names. The literal Chinese for the historic French Concession is Fǎzūjiè (法租界).

✕ Best Places to Eat

➡ Spicy Joint (p106)

➡ Jian Guo 328 (p106)

➡ Madison (p108)

➡ Dī Shuǐ Dòng (p104)

➡ Noodle Bull (p106)

For reviews, see p101. ➡

🍷 Best Places to Drink

➡ el Cóctel (p115)

➡ Cotton's (p115)

➡ Abbey Road (p116)

➡ Boxing Cat Brewery (p116)

➡ Dr Wine (p116)

For reviews, see p111. ➡

🛍 Best Shopping

➡ Tiánzǐfáng (p119)

➡ NuoMi (p123)

➡ Pilingpalang (p123)

➡ Lolo Love Vintage (p123)

➡ OOAK Concept Boutique (p123)

For reviews, see p118. ➡

Explore: French Concession

The French Concession is Shànghǎi sunny side up; it's the city at its coolest, hippest and most elegant. Once home to the bulk of Shànghǎi's adventurers, revolutionaries, gangsters, prostitutes and writers – ironically many of them weren't French – the former concession (also called Frenchtown) is the most graceful part of Pǔxī. Shànghǎi's erstwhile reputation as the 'Paris of the East' owes a big debt to this neighbourhood's tree-lined avenues, 1920s mansions and French-influenced architecture.

Must-see sights are thin on the ground, but the concession's leafy backstreets and European disposition make exploration a delight. Most first-time visitors start off in Xīntiāndì, which offers an all-in-one introduction to the local *shíkùmén* (stone-gate house) architecture alongside alluring dining and shopping options. South from here is the former concession's other big draw: Tiánzǐfáng, a less-polished warren of lanes and artsy boutiques that can keep you wandering (often lost) indefinitely.

The French Concession's real attraction is not sightseeing. Like Shànghǎi itself, the area thrives on its endless quest for sophistication, and its tirelessly inventive restaurant and bar scene, coupled with pop-up boutiques and diverse entertainment options, means that you should come prepared to expand your tastes – just make sure you have cash to spend.

Local Life

➡**Lǐlòng & Lòngtáng** Slip down Shànghǎi's charming alleyways for the homely rhythms of community life.

➡**Foot massages** Sink into an armchair (and maybe catch some Hong Kong action on the tube) while a masseuse kneads your tension away.

➡**Snacks** Dumplings, noodles, haute cuisine, Sichuanese, Hunanese, stinky tofu and lychee ice cream – no matter when or where, you'll find something to eat (and a local at your elbow).

Getting There & Away

➡**Metro lines 1 and 10** These two main lines serve the French Concession area, both running east–west past Xīntiāndì. Line 1 continues on to People's Sq, while line 10 serves the Old Town and East Nanjing Rd (the Bund). The two lines meet at the South Shaanxi Rd metro stop.

➡**Metro line 9** At the southern edge of the concession, line 9 serves Tiánzǐfáng.

➡**Metro line 7** This north–south line provides a handy link between the French Concession and the Jìng'ān neighbourhood; it connects with line 1 at Changshu Rd and line 9 at Zhaojiabang Rd.

TOP SIGHT
TIÁNZĬFÁNG

A shopping complex housed within a grid of traditional *lòngtáng* alleyways, Tiánzĭfáng (田子坊) is probably the most accessible, authentic, charming and vibrant example of Shànghǎi's trademark back-lane architecture. A community of design studios, local families, wi-fi cafes and start-up boutiques, it's a choice counterpoint to Shànghǎi's mega-malls and dwarfing skyscrapers (but it can get crowded).

DON'T MISS

➡ Boutique browsing
➡ Liúli China Museum
➡ Drinks or a meal at an alleyway cafe

PRACTICALITIES

➡ 田子坊
➡ Map p302
➡ www.tianzifang.cn
➡ Taikang Rd; 泰康路
➡ Ⓜ Dapuqiao

Galleries

There are three main north–south lanes (Nos 210, 248 and 274) crisscrossed by irregular east–west alleyways, which makes exploration disorienting and fun. Most shops and boutiques are slim and bijou. On the main lane is the **Deke Erh Art Centre** (Map p302; No 2, Lane 210, Taikang Rd; 泰康路 210弄2号; ⊘9am-10pm), owned by local photographer Deke Erh, where an absorbing range of books on Shànghǎi is on display. Another gallery to seek out is Beaugeste (p98), which has thought-provoking contemporary photography exhibits. It's open by appointment only on weekdays.

Just outside the complex on Taikang Rd, an enormous peony bloom covers the exterior of the Liúli China Museum (p98), dedicated to the art of glass sculpture.

Shopping & Drinking

Shopping is the main driver in Tiánzĭfáng (p119). The recent explosion of creative start-ups makes for some satisfying finds, from local fashion brands to Běijīng-style messenger bags, vintage glasses and experimental perfumes. Stalls flogging mass-produced souvenir dross have inevitably pitched up, so you'll need to hunt for the genuine boutiques; but rest assured, they're still here.

Elsewhere, a cool band of bars and cafes – such as Kommune (p105), Bell Bar (p114), Kāibā (p114) and Origin (p105) – can get you sorted for lunch, drinks and wi-fi.

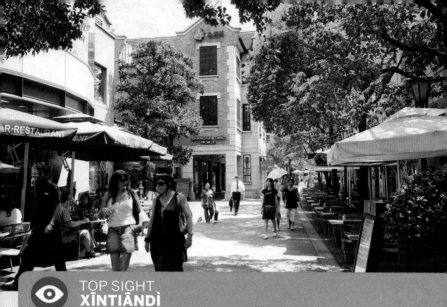

TOP SIGHT
XĪNTIĀNDÌ

With its own namesake metro station, Xīntiāndì (新天地) has been a Shànghǎi icon for a decade or more. An upscale entertainment and shopping complex modelled on traditional _lòngtáng_ (alleyway) homes, this was the first development in the city to prove that historic architecture makes big commercial sense. Elsewhere that might sound like a no-brainer, but in 21st-century China, where bulldozers were always on standby, it came as quite a revelation.

Well-heeled shoppers and alfresco diners keep things lively until late. If you're looking for a memorable meal, a drink in a dapper bar or a browse through some of Shànghǎi's more fashionable boutiques, you're in the right spot.

Museums, Restaurants & Shops

The heart of the complex, cleaved into a pedestrianised north and south block, consists of largely rebuilt traditional _shíkùmén_ (stone-gate houses), brought up-to-date with a stylish modern spin. But while the layout suggests a flavour of yesteryear, don't expect too much historic magic or cultural allure. Xīntiāndì doesn't nurture the creaking, rickety simplicity of Shànghǎi's Old Town. Beyond the two sights located in the north block – the eye-opening Shíkùmén Open House Museum (p97), which reveals the interior of a well-to-do _shíkùmén_ household, and the Site of the 1st National Congress of the CCP (p97) – it's best for strolling the pretty alleyways and enjoying a summer evening over drinks or a meal.

Serious shoppers – and diners – will eventually gravitate towards the malls at the southern tip of the south block. Beyond the first mall, which holds three top-notch restaurants on the 2nd floor (Din Tai Fung (p105); Crystal Jade (p105); and Shànghǎi Min (p105), is the Xīntiāndì Style (p119) mall, showcasing local brands and chic clobber at the vanguard of Shanghainese fashion.

DON'T MISS

➜ Shíkùmén Open House Museum

➜ Alfresco dining

➜ Window-shopping

PRACTICALITIES

➜ 新天地

➜ Map p302

➜ www.xintiandi.com

➜ 2 blocks btwn Taicang, Zizhong, Madang & South Huangpi Rds; 太仓路与马当路路口

➜ Ⓜ South Huangpi Rd, Xintiandi

SIGHTS

⊙ French Concession East

XĪNTIĀNDÌ
AREA

See p96.

SHÍKÙMÉN OPEN HOUSE MUSEUM
MUSEUM

Map p302 (石库门屋里厢; Shíkùmén Wūlǐxiāng; Xīntiāndì North Block, Bldg 25; 太仓路181弄新天地北里25号楼; adult/child ¥20/10; ⊙10.30am-10.30pm; MSouth Huangpi Rd, Xintiandi) This two-floor exhibition invites you into a typical *shíkùmén* (stone-gate house) household, decked out with period furniture. The ground-floor arrangement contains a courtyard, entrance hall, bedroom, study and lounge. There's a small kitchen to the rear and natural illumination spills down from *tiānjǐng* (light wells) above. The small, north-facing wedge-shaped *tíngzijiān* room on the landing, almost at the top of the stairs between the 1st and 2nd floors, was a common feature of *shíkùmén*, and was often rented out. The main bedrooms are all on the 2nd floor, linked together by doors.

SITE OF THE 1ST NATIONAL CONGRESS OF THE CCP
HISTORIC BUILDING

Map p302 (中共一大会址纪念馆; Zhōnggòng Yīdàhuìzhǐ Jìniànguǎn; Xīntiāndì North Block, 76 Xingye Rd; 兴业路76号; ⊙9am-5pm; MSouth Huangpi Rd, Xintiandi) FREE On 23 July 1921 the Chinese Communist Party (CCP) was founded in this French Concession building (then 106 rue Wantz). In one fell swoop this fact transformed an unassuming *shíkùmén* block into one of Chinese communism's holiest shrines. Beyond the communist narcissism, there's little to see, although historians will enjoy ruminating on the site's historic momentousness.

On the ground floor you can be present in the room where the whole party began, in what was once the house of the delegate Li Hanjun. Up the marble stairs in the 'Exhibition of Historical Relics Showing the Founding of the Communist Party of China' is a highly patriotic hymn to early Chinese communist history with exhibits such as the Chinese translation of Mary E Marcy's *The ABC of Das Kapital by Marx*.

The dizzying Marxist spin of the museum commentary is a salutary reminder that Shànghǎi remains part of the world's largest communist state. The certainties of that era – whether you sympathise with Mǎlièzhǔyì (Marxist-Leninism) or not – exude a nostalgic appeal in today's Shànghǎi, where ideology of any shade is met with a raised eyebrow. A passport is required for entry; last admission is at 4pm.

SUN YATSEN'S FORMER RESIDENCE
HISTORIC BUILDING

Map p302 (孙中山故居; Sūn Zhōngshān Gùjū; 7 Xiangshan Rd; 香山路7号; admission ¥20; audio guide ¥30; ⊙9am-4pm; MSouth Shaanxi Rd, Xintiandi) Sun Zhongshan predictably receives the complete hagiographic treatment at this shrine to China's *guófù* (father of the nation). A capacious exhibition hall next door further pampers his memory and serves as a full-on prelude to his pebble-dash 'Spanish-style' home. Once you get to his house proper – where he lived on what was rue Moliere, from 1918 to 1924 – you need to pop transparent shower caps over your shoes to protect the threadbare carpets. Don't forget to catch the lovely garden, where a *Magnolia grandiflora* deliciously flowers in summer.

FÙXĪNG PARK
PARK

Map p302 (复兴公园; Fùxīng Gōngyuán; ⊙5am-6pm; MSouth Shaanxi Rd, Xintiandi) This leafy spot with a large lawn, laid out by the French in 1909 and used by the Japanese as a parade ground in the late 1930s, remains one of the city's more enticing parks. There is always plenty to see here: the park is a refuge for the elderly and a practising field for itinerant musicians, chess players, people walking backwards and slow-moving taichi types.

Heavily shaded by big-leafed *wutong* trees, it's a choice place to take a seat and escape the summer sun, and there's even a popular kiddies' playground. Wreathed in the laughter of children, the huge stony-faced busts of Karl Marx and Friedrich Engels gaze out from a seemingly redundant epoch, and nobody seems to notice.

ST NICHOLAS CHURCH
CHURCH

Map p302 (圣尼古拉斯教堂; Shèngnígǔlāsī Jiàotáng; 16 Gaolan Rd; 皋兰路16号; MSouth Shaanxi Rd) A short walk west along Gaolan Rd from Fùxīng Park is rewarded by the distinctive shape of the vacant, and now derelict, St Nicholas Church, one of Shànghǎi's small band of Russian Orthodox houses of worship, built to service the huge influx of Russians who arrived in Shànghǎi in the 1930s.

Dating from 1934, the church has a typically varied CV, ranging from shrine to washing-machine factory to French restaurant. It was spared desecration during the Cultural Revolution by a portrait of Mao Zedong, hung strategically from the dome. The building was not open to the public at the time of writing and the space in front of the church was occupied by the terrace of Kinlock Coffee cafe next door.

ZHOU ENLAI'S
FORMER RESIDENCE   HISTORIC BUILDING

Map p302 (周恩来故居; Zhōu Ēnlái Gùjū; ☑6473 0420; 73 Sinan Rd; 思南路73号; ⊙9am-4pm; MSouth Shaanxi Rd, Xintiandi) FREE In 1946 Zhou Enlai, the much-loved (though some swear he was more sly than Mao) first premier of the People's Republic of China, lived briefly in this former French Concession Spanish villa. Zhou was then head of the Communist Party's Shànghǎi office, giving press conferences and dodging Kuomintang agents spying on him from across the road.

Zhou's age-old battered suitcase sits by his bed in the interior of this simple home, while a dormitory for his comrades and fellow communists can be found at the very top. Carry on into the charming garden and discover Zhou's Buick (actually an imitation) in his garage. For everyone but hard-boiled enthusiasts, the additional 'Exhibition of the Shanghai Office of the Communist Party' is worth skipping.

TIÁNZǏFÁNG   AREA
See p95.

LIÚLI CHINA MUSEUM   MUSEUM

Map p302 (琉璃艺术博物馆; Liúli Yìshù Bówùguǎn; www.liulichinamuseum.com; 25 Taikang Rd; 泰康路25号; admission ¥20; ⊙10am-5pm; MDapuqiao) Founded by Taiwanese artists Loretta Yang and Chang Yi, the Liúli China Museum is dedicated to the art of glass sculpture (*pâte de verre* or lost-wax casting). Peruse the collection of ancient artefacts – some of which date back more than 2000 years – to admire the early craftsmanship of pieces such as earrings, belt buckles and even a Tang-dynasty crystal *wéiqí* (go) set.

The collection transitions fluidly to more contemporary creations from around the world, before moving on to Yang's serene Buddhist-inspired creations, including a sublime 1.6m-high, 1000-armed Guanyin, which was modelled on a Yuan-dynasty mural in the Mògāo Caves near Dūnhuáng.

The museum is free for children under 18 and seniors over 65. On the 1st floor is a vegan-friendly cafe and a shop selling *liúli* crystal, where you can snag an attractive glass bracelet for ¥1000.

BEAUGESTE   GALLERY

Map p302 (比极影像; Bǐjí Yǐngxiàng; ☑6466 9012; www.beaugeste-gallery.com; 5th fl, No 5, Lane 210, Taikang Rd; 泰康路210弄5号520室田子坊; ⊙10am-6pm Sat & Sun, by appointment Mon-Fri; MDapuqiao) FREE One of Shànghǎi's top galleries, this small space is concealed high above the street-level crowds. Curator Jean Loh captures humanistic themes in contemporary Chinese photography, and his wide range of contacts and excellent eye ensure exhibits that are always moving and thought-provoking. You can also pick up previous exhibition catalogues here.

Note that the gallery is open by appointment only during the week.

SHÀNGHǍI MUSEUM OF
PUBLIC SECURITY   MUSEUM

(上海公安博物馆; Shànghǎi Gōng'ān Bówùguǎn; ☑6472 0256; 518 South Ruijin Rd; 瑞金南路518号; ⊙9am-4pm Mon-Sat; MDapuqiao) FREE It may sound turgid and dull, but this museum deals out an ace or two from an otherwise humdrum hand of traffic control and post-Liberation security milestones. The gold pistols of Sun Yatsen and 1930s gangster Huang Jinrong are worth hunting down amid the fine collection of Al Capone–style machine guns and pen-guns. Look out for the collection of hand-painted business cards once dispensed by the city's top *jìnǚ* (prostitutes).

MOLLER HOUSE   HISTORIC BUILDING

Map p302 (马勒别墅; Mǎlè Biéshù; 30 South Shaanxi Rd; 陕西南路30号; MSouth Shaanxi Rd) One of Shànghǎi's most whimsical buildings, the Scandinavian-influenced gothic peaks of the Moller House could double as the Munsters' holiday home. Swedish owner and horse-racing fan Eric Moller owned the Moller Shipping Line. Previously home to the Communist Youth League, the building now houses a hotel, the Héngshān Moller Villa. Building No 2 is a recent extension, copied in similar style. Fancifully perhaps, legend attests that a fortune teller warned Moller that tragedy would befall him on the house's completion, so the tycoon dragged out its construction (until 1949). Moller clung on for a few more years before dying in a plane crash in 1954.

SUE ANNE TAY: SHÀNGHǍI'S SHÍKÙMÉN STORIES

For almost five years, Sue Anne Tay has been photographing and penning the quotidian yet fascinating details of Shànghǎi's *shíkùmén lǐlòng* community. She reveals the underlying currents in Shànghǎi's socioeconomic fabric, including the loss of heritage architecture and the erosion of traditional community living – see www.shanghai streetstories.com.

What really grabs you about *shíkùmén* and *lǐlòng*?

The beauty and significance of *shíkùmén* (stone-gate house) and *lǐlòng* (alleyway) architecture are often overlooked by visitors. *Lǐlòng* housing is where you can still observe the native community lifestyle in the public–private space of the alley lanes. *Lǐlòng* housing (or alleyway housing) combines Western architecture – the motifs and layout of English terrace housing – with Chinese feng shui sensibilities. They are always south-facing, family-style courtyards. One could call them Shànghǎi's vernacular housing for much of the first half of the 20th century. By the end of the 1940s, more than 72% of Shànghǎi's residential space was *lǐlòng* and around three quarters was *shíkùmén* architecture. The majority of older generation Shanghainese probably lived in such housing at some point in their lives. This tightly intertwined community lifestyle has faded in Shànghǎi as such dwellings have been demolished.

Can you recommend a couple of *lǐlòng* and *shíkùmén* areas for exploration?

It's hard to not be impressed by the beautiful *shíkùmén* architecture of **Zhāng Garden** (张园; Zhāng Yuán; Map p310; Taixing Rd) located south down Taixing Rd, off West Nanjing Rd and west of Shimen No 1 Rd. Formerly known as Arcadia Hall, the site was first built in 1878 by a European merchant as a fairground for foreigners. It was then acquired in 1882 by Zhang Shuhe, a wealthy Wuxi businessman, who later opened it to the public. There was a huge garden, a dance hall, meeting rooms, a theatre for Chinese opera, a photography studio, a teahouse and restaurants. It later served as a location for political meetings and rallies against the Qing government. What you see in Zhang Garden today – mainly *shíkùmén* housing, a mix of two- and three-bay villas with tall entrance-ways, handsome windows and hanging balcony pavilions – is merely a small portion of its former site. What survives is a sign of the wealth of its former pre-1949 occupants. Today, a single *shíkùmén* villa can house 20 to even 40 families, a mix of Shanghainese residents and migrant families from neighbouring provinces. It's easy to get lost in the alleys but no worries, you'll find your way back to the main boulevard eventually.

Built in 1930, the **Cité Bourgogne** (步高里; Bùgāo Lǐ; Map p302) is a perfect example of a *shíkùmén lǐlòng* neighbourhood. As it was one of the first *lǐlòng* to be listed as an example of outstanding historic architecture in Shànghǎi, it has been relatively well preserved. There are five main entrances but only two access the compound, each with a large traditional Chinese pagoda facade (unusual for *lǐlòng* neighbourhoods). You can wander through the lane, though be respectful of residents' privacy, even if their doorways are open. There are four lanes running east to west and one central lane running north to south. Note the brick arches leading into the smaller lanes and the simplified vaulted pediments or '*shíkùmén* headers' as I like to call them. Residents will be drying laundry, playing cards or chatting in the main alleys. A friendly smile and nod will ensure a smooth passage through the lanes. Cité Bourgogne is only a few blocks away from Tiánzǐfáng, at the northeast corner of West Jianguo Rd and South Shaanxi Rd.

How does your work impact on *lǐlòng* and *shíkùmén* heritage?

A great deal has been written in Chinese, but not so much in English. Hence, by documenting them visually and sharing with a global audience the history and contemporary details of individual *lǐlòng* neighbourhoods, I can help preserve their memory when they are eventually demolished.

⊙ French Concession West

PROPAGANDA POSTER
ART CENTRE   GALLERY
Map p306 (宣传画年画艺术中心; Shànghǎi Xuānchuánhuà Yìshù Zhōngxīn; ☎6211 1845; Room B-OC, President Mansion, 868 Huashan Rd; 华山路868号B-0C室; admission ¥20; ☉10am-5pm; ⓜShanghai Library) If phalanxes of red tractors, bumper harvests, muscled peasants and lantern-jawed proletariats fire you up, this small gallery in the bowels of a residential block should intoxicate. The collection of 3000 original posters from the 1950s, '60s and '70s – the golden age of Maoist poster production – will have you weak-kneed at the cartoon world of anti-US defiance.

The centre divides into a showroom and a shop selling posters and postcards. Once you find the main entrance, a guard will pop a small business card with a map on it into your hands and point you the way. Head around the back of the apartment blocks to Building B and take the lift to the basement. It's a good idea to phone ahead (they speak some English) before heading out here to make sure it's open. The exhibition rounds off with a collection of cigarette posters from the 1920s.

SHÀNGHǍI ARTS & CRAFTS
MUSEUM   MUSEUM
Map p306 (上海工艺美术博物馆; Shànghǎi Gōngyì Měishù Bówùguǎn; 79 Fenyang Rd; 汾阳路79号; admission ¥8; ☉9am-4pm; ⓜChangshu Rd) Repositioned as a museum, this arts and crafts institute displays traditional crafts such as embroidery, paper cutting, lacquer work, jade cutting and lantern making. Watch traditional crafts being performed live by craftspeople and admire the wonderfully wrought exhibits, from jade, to ivory, to ink stones and beyond. The 1905 building itself is a highlight, once serving as the residence for Chen Yi, Shànghǎi's first mayor after the founding of the Chinese Communist Party (CCP).

After admiring the lovely garden, head up the steps to a host of splendid ivory and boxwood carvings on the first floor, where an array of divine (Guanyin) and semi-divine (Mao Zedong) beings are displayed; also look out for the exquisite ivory spider hanging from its web. Further displays include opera costumes and Shànghǎi dough modelling, while among the goods for sale, you can grab goldfish lanterns (¥30) or some intricate paper cuts (剪纸; *jiǎnzhǐ*). A framed paper cut of the Great Wall will cost you ¥450.

RUSSIAN ORTHODOX
MISSION CHURCH   CHURCH
Map p306 (东正教圣母大堂; Dōngzhèngjiào Shèngmǔ Dàtáng; 55 Xinle Rd; 新乐路55号; ☉10.30am-6pm Tue-Sun; ⓜSouth Shaanxi Rd) Built in 1934, this lovely blue-domed church was designed for the huge influx of Russian worshippers to Shànghǎi in the 1930s. Faded murals grace the cupola, but the real reason to visit today is for a meander through the contemporary art gallery **Space** (www.espace-sh.com), which shows four to five exhibits in the church's interior each year.

SONG QINGLING'S
FORMER RESIDENCE   HISTORIC BUILDING
Map p306 (宋庆龄故居; Sōng Qìnglíng Gùjū; 1843 Middle Huaihai Rd; 淮海中路1843号; admission ¥20; ☉9am-4.30pm; ⓜJiaotong University) Built in the 1920s by a Greek shipping magnate, this quiet building became home to Song Qingling, wife of Dr Sun Yatsen, from 1948 to 1963. Size up two of her black limousines

---

SHÀNGHǍI SLOGANS

Unlike Běijīng and other towns and villages across China, Shànghǎi has largely scrubbed away its slogans (政治口号; *zhèngzhì kǒuhào*) from the Cultural Revolution, despite the city's once heady revolutionary zeal. One vivid red slogan can be seen above the entrance, facing the garden, of the fabulous art deco building housing the James Cohan (p101) art gallery in the French Concession. Also in the French Concession, two almost vanished slogans decorate either side of the door to the minimalist Xīntiāndì saloon Dr Bar (p115). An imposing and well-preserved scarlet slogan survives high up on the north wall of the Huángpǔ Hotel (黄浦饭店; Huángpǔ Fàndiàn) at 106 Huangpu Rd (黄浦路), not far from the Hyatt on the Bund in Hóngkǒu. The Maoist era slogan is visible through the gate, but note that the hotel is for Chinese military and naval guests (foreigners not accepted), so be discreet if looking for it.

(one a gift from Stalin) in the garage and pad about the house, conjuring up sensations of yesteryear from its period furnishings. The highlight is the gorgeous garden, with tall magnolias and camphor trees towering over a delightful lawn, where Song entertained guests with conversation and tea.

A few personal belongings are also on display in the house, including autographed books from American journalists Edgar Snow and Agnes Smedley, and a collection of old photographs depicting the Soong sisters (p104) and various heads of state.

WUKANG ROAD TOURIST INFORMATION CENTRE ARCHITECTURE

Map p306 (武康路旅游咨询中心; Wǔkāng Lù Lǚyóu Zīxún Zhōngxīn; 393 Wukang Rd; 武康路393号; ◎9am-5pm; MShanghai Library) On one of the area's best-preserved streets, this centre displays scale-model concession buildings, photos of historic Shànghǎi architecture and maps for self-guided walking tours of Wukang Rd. It's in the former residence of Huang Xing (1874–1916), a revolutionary who co-founded the Republic of China together with Sun Yatsen. Note the fantastic art deco extension to the south along Wukang Rd.

CHINESE PRINTED BLUE NANKEEN EXHIBITION HALL MUSEUM

Map p306 (中国蓝印花布馆; Zhōngguó Lán Yìnhuābù Guǎn; ☑5403 7947; No 24, Lane 637, Changle Rd; 长乐路637弄24号; ◎9am-5pm; MChangshu Rd) Follow the blue signs through a maze of courtyards until you see bolts of blue cloth drying in the yard. Originally produced in Jiāngsū, Zhèjiāng and Guìzhōu provinces, this blue-and-white cotton fabric (sometimes called blue calico) is similar to batik, and is coloured using a starch-resist method and indigo dye bath.

This museum and shop, started by Japanese artist Kubo Mase, displays and sells items made by hand, from the cloth right down to the buttons. In business for more than 20 years, it takes pride in quality and does not give discounts.

LEO GALLERY GALLERY

Map p306 (狮语画廊; Shīyǔ Huàláng; www.leogallery.com.cn; 376 Wukang Rd; 武康路376号; ◎11am-7pm Tue-Sun; MShanghai Library, Jiaotong University) FREE Spread across two buildings in the charming Ferguson Lane complex, the Leo Gallery focuses on works by young Chinese artists.

ART LABOR GALLERY

Map p306 (www.artlaborgallery.com; Bldg 4, Surpass Court, No 570 Yongjia Rd; 永嘉路570号4号楼; ◎11am-7pm Tue-Sat, noon-6pm Sun; MHengshan Rd) FREE An independent gallery representing a balance of Chinese and international artists. Exhibits often focus on the question of identity in contemporary Shànghǎi.

JAMES COHAN GALLERY

Map p306 (www.jamescohan.com; Bldg 1, Lane 170, Yueyang Rd; 岳阳路170弄1号楼; ◎10am-6pm Tue-Sat, noon-6pm Sun; MHengshan Rd) FREE Excellent New York gallery representing international artists; this provocative Shànghǎi branch is set in a lovely art deco villa wth a gorgeously shaded garden and an original slogan from the Mao era above the door (a rarity in Shànghǎi).

BA JIN'S FORMER RESIDENCE HISTORIC BUILDING

Map p306 (巴金故居; Bājīn Gùjū; 113 Wukang Rd; 武康路113号; ◎10am-4pm Tue-Sat; MShanghai Library) FREE This charming little pebble-dash residence with a delightful garden wouldn't look out of place in a leafy London suburb. It's where the acclaimed author Ba Jin (1904–2005) lived from 1955 to the mid-1990s. Ba was the author of dozens of novels and short stories (the most famous is *Family*), many of which were published during the peak of his career in the 1930s. His house today contains a collection of old photos, books and manuscripts.

Like many intellectuals, he was persecuted mercilessly during the Cultural Revolution, during which time his wife died after being denied medical treatment. Passport may be needed for entry.

✗ EATING

The French Concession is where it's at when it comes to dining: whatever you crave, you'll probably find it here. Fancy fusion food? Check. Wild Yunnanese mushrooms? Check. Wacky *maki* rolls? Check. Tongue-tingling Sichuanese? Double check. Taojiang Rd, Dongping Rd, Fumin Rd and Xīntiāndì are the main culinary hot spots in town, and with dozens of choices between them, you'd have to eat out every night for a year to try them all. Well, what are you waiting for?

✕ French Concession East

CHA'S
CANTONESE $

Map p302 (查餐厅; Chá Cāntīng; 30 Sinan Rd; 思南路30号; dishes ¥20-55; ⏰11am-1.30am; Ⓜ South Shaanxi Rd) This crammed Cantonese diner does its best to teleport you to 1950s Hong Kong, with old-style tiled floors, whirring ceiling fans and even an antique Coca-Cola ice box to set the scene. You'll need to wait to get a table, so use the time wisely and peruse the menu of classic comfort food (curries, sweet-and-sour pork) in advance.

LÁNXĪN CĀNTĪNG
SHANGHAINESE $

Map p302 (兰心餐厅; 130 Jinxian Rd; 进贤路 130号; dishes ¥12-65; ⏰11am-2pm & 5-9pm; Ⓜ South Shaanxi Rd) Some of the best Shanghainese kitchens are hole-in-the-walls along Jinxian Rd. These aren't the domain of international superchefs and the Gucci two-shoed; they're unpretentious and family run – the last of a dying breed. Winning dishes include the classic *hóngshāo ròu* (红烧肉; braised pork), the delectable *gānshāo chāngyú* (干烧鲳鱼) quick-fried pomfret fish) and the *xiǎopái luóbo tāng* (小排萝卜汤; spare-rib-and-radish soup).

For total immersion, order up a bottle of warm *huáng jiǔ* (黄酒; traditional Chinese wine). If the wait is too long, **Hǎijīnzī** (海金滋; Map p302; 240 Jinxian Rd) at the western end of the street is a comparable experience. No reservations, no English and cash only.

WÈIXIĀNG ZHĀI
NOODLES $

Map p302 (味香斋; 14 Yandang Rd; 雁荡路14号; noodles ¥9; ⏰6.15am-9pm; Ⓜ South Huangpi Rd, Xintiandi) There aren't that many places left in Shànghǎi where you can scoop up a bowl of *májiàng miàn* (麻酱面; savoury sesame noodles) for just ¥9. For this reason Wèixiāng Zhāi is consistently packed, even at four in the afternoon. Beef noodles cost ¥18.

DIǍN SHÍ ZHĀI XIǍO YÀN
SHANGHAINESE $

Map p302 (点石斋小宴; ☎5465 0270; 320 Yongjia Rd; 永嘉路320号; dishes from ¥32; ⏰11am-2pm & 5.30-9.30pm; Ⓜ South Shaanxi Rd, Jiashan Rd) Shànghǎi cuisine can be cloyingly sweet when improperly prepared, but this elegant restaurant hits the mark with its delicate flavours. It has a wonderful range of cold appetisers and seafood dishes. Be sure to look out for the excellent Zhèjiāng dishes, including Shàoxīng drunken chicken and individual portions of tender *dōngpō ròu* (stewed pork fat).

BANKURA
JAPANESE $

Map p302 (万藏; Wànzàng; ☎6215 0373; 344 Changle Rd; 长乐路344号; noodles 30-55, lunch sets ¥39; ⏰11.30am-2pm & 5.30pm-late; Ⓜ South Shaanxi Rd) Pull up a seat at this underground Japanese noodle bar, where the focus is on soba (thin buckwheat noodles, often served cold) and udon (thick wheat noodles, often served in broth) choices, as well as delectable extras such as grilled shiitake mushrooms, curried shrimp and fried-eel rice bowls.

In the evening, the drinks menu – *shōchū* cocktails and plum wine – provides further incentive to drop by.

Ā DÀ CÓNGYÓUBǏNG
SHANGHAINESE $

Map p302 (阿大葱油饼; 2, Lane 159, South Maoming Rd; 茂名南路159弄2号; cóngyóubǐng ¥4; ⏰5am-2pm Thu-Tue; Ⓜ South Shaanxi Rd) *The* definition of a hole-in-the-wall, Ā Dà Cóngyóubǐng is a mere portal with no seats but a long queue of local diners, serving the scrummiest of that crispy Shànghǎi snacking stalwart: *cóngyóubǐng* (spring-onion pancake). You can get them all over town, but this simple place frequently edges into Top 10 lists (as voted by local diners).

Follow the aroma down the small alley off South Maoming Rd, at the intersection with Nanchang Rd.

DÀ MÁO CÓNGYÓUBǏNG
SHANGHAINESE $

Map p302 (大毛葱油饼; 213 Hefei Rd; 合肥路 213号; cóngyóubǐng from ¥2.50; ⏰6am-6pm; Ⓜ Xintiandi) Delightfully scrummy, crisp and flavoursome spring-onion pancakes (葱油饼; *cóngyóubǐng*) are the speciality at this ramshackle hole-in-the-wall snack point that sees regular lines of customers. It's *dìdào* (authentic), old school and on the money. Takeaway only.

FĒNGYÙ SHĒNGJIĀN
DUMPLINGS $

Map p302 (丰裕生煎; 41 Ruijin No 2 Rd, cnr Nanchang Rd; 瑞金二路41号; mains from ¥5; ⏰6am-10pm; Ⓜ South Shaanxi Rd) If you thought Shànghǎi dining was all white linen tablecloths, steaming hand towels and perfectly formed waitresses in cheongsam clutching gold-embossed menus, think again. Chow down on fine *xiǎolóngbāo* (dumplings; ¥6), *shēngjiān* (生煎; fried dumplings; ¥5) and *miàntiáo* (noodles; ¥8) with the hard-working

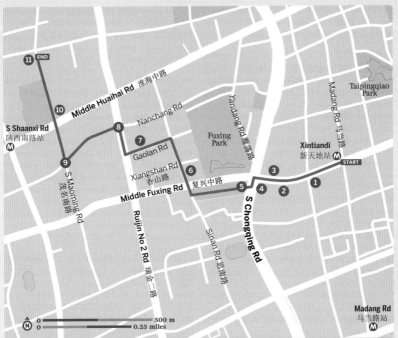

Neighbourhood Walk
French Concession Stroll

START XINTIANDI METRO STATION
END CATHAY THEATRE
LENGTH 2.5KM; 75 MINUTES

Begin walking west on Middle Fuxing Rd (formerly rue Lafayette), first passing the red-brick Italianate ❶ **All Saint's Church** (1925) and then the ❷ **Park Apartments** (1926) and smaller private villas fronted by palm trees, which date to the same era. On the northern side of Middle Fuxing Rd at No 512 is the ❸ **Former Residence of Liu Haisu** (1896–1994), a 20th-century artist who revolutionised traditional Chinese art by introducing Western painting styles. Opposite, at the corner with South Chongqing Rd, is the ❹ **Dubail Apartment Building** (1931), the one-time home of US journalist and communist sympathiser Agnes Smedley (1892–1950).

Turn into ❺ **Sinan Mansions**, a complex of luxurious 1920s private villas built south of French Park (now Fùxīng Park) and renovated as an upscale lifestyle destination; today it

houses numerous cafes and restaurants (and ultraexclusive short-term residences to the south). Exit on Sinan Rd (route Massenet) and walk north to ❻ **Sun Yatsen's Former Residence** (p97), where the father of modern China lived from 1918 to 1924. On Gaolan Rd (route Cohen) is the Russian Orthodox ❼ **St Nicholas Church** (p97), built in 1934 in dedication to the murdered tsar of Russia.

Continue on to ❽ **Nanchang Road** (rue Vallon), a shopping strip with boutiques selling jewellery, shoes, antiques and clothing. Turn onto ❾ **South Maoming Road** (route Cardinal Mercier), another shopping hot spot that specialises in *qípáo* (figure-hugging Chinese dresses) and other Chinese-style clothes. Across Huaihai Rd stands the landmark art deco ❿ **Cathay Theatre** (1932; p118) beyond which, along South Maoming Rd, is the ⓫ **Okura Garden Hotel Shanghai**, originally constructed as the French Club (Cercle Sportif Français) in 1926. Take the eastern entrance and the stairs to columns capped with stunning deco nude reliefs, concealed during the Cultural Revolution.

proletariat at Fēngyù, where plastic trays, fixed furniture and zero English rule. Pay at the entrance and join the queue.

FUNK A DELI
CAFE $

Map p302 (46 Yongkang Rd; 永康路46号; mains from ¥25; ⊙11am-late; M South Shaanxi Rd) This handy shoebox-sized bolt-hole exploits a small market crevice in bar-stuffed Yongkang Rd, dispensing coffees, wraps (nutella and banana), panini sandwiches, wine by the glass, imported beers and smiling service. Like everywhere else here, punters need to clear the streets by 10pm.

★ DĪ SHUǏ DÒNG
HUNANESE $$

Map p302 (滴水洞; ☎6253 2689; 2nd fl, 56 South Maoming Rd; 茂名南路56号2层; dishes ¥28-128; ⊙11am-12.30am; M South Shaanxi Rd) Until the chilled lagers arrive, the faint breeze from the spreading of the blue-and-white tablecloth by your waiter may be the last cooling sensation at Dī Shuǐ Dòng, a rustic upstairs shrine to the volcanic cuisine of Húnán. Loved by Shanghainese and expats in equal measure, dishes are ferried in by sprightly peasant-attired staff to tables stuffed with enthusiastic, red-faced diners.

Business is never slack, so prepare to get in line. The claim to fame is the Húnán-style cumin-crusted ribs, but there's no excuse not to sample the *làzi jīdīng* (fried chicken with chillies), one of the excellent claypot dishes or even the classic boiled frog. Cool down with plenty of beers and crowd-pleasing caramelised bananas for dessert.

FOOD FUSION
MALAYSIAN $$

Map p302 (融合; Rónghé; 8th fl, Parkson Plaza, 918 Middle Huaihai Rd; 淮海中路918号百盛8楼; dishes ¥30-168, lunch sets from ¥38; ⊙10am-11pm; M South Shaanxi Rd) Up on the 8th floor of one of Huaihai Rd's numerous shopping malls you'll find this hopping Malaysian option. Join the thronging office workers filling the lift and ascend to aromas of coriander, star anise, nutmeg, cinnamon and ginger. Crowd-pleasing classics include *rendang* beef, chilli-flecked *laksa* (coconut curry noodle soup), chicken satay, fish curry, *roti canai* and Nyonya desserts.

SOUTHERN BARBARIAN
YUNNAN $$

Map p302 (南蛮子; Nánmánzi; ☎5157 5510; http://southernbarbarian.com; 2nd fl, Gourmet Zone, 56 South Maoming Rd; 茂名南路56号生活艺术空间2楼; dishes ¥28-108; ⊙10am-10pm Mon-Fri, to midnight Sat & Sun; M South Shaanxi Rd) Despite the alarming name, there's nothing remotely barbaric about the food here. Instead, you get fine MSG-free Yúnnán cuisine served by friendly staff in a laid-back

---

THE SOONG FAMILY

The Soongs probably wielded more influence and power over modern China than any other family. The father of the family, Charlie Soong, grew up in Hǎinán and, after an American evangelical education, finally settled in Shànghǎi. He began to print bibles and money, becoming a wealthy businessman and developing ties with secret societies, during which time he became good friends with Sun Yatsen (Sun Zhongshan). Charlie had three daughters and a son.

Charlie's daughter Soong Ailing – said to be the first Chinese girl in Shànghǎi to own a bicycle – married HH Kung, the wealthy descendent of Confucius, Bank of China head and later finance minister of the Republic of China. Soong Meiling (May-ling) became the third wife of Chiang Kaishek (Kuomintang leader and future president of the Republic of China) in 1928. She went to the USA during the Japanese occupation of China and fled to Taiwan with Chiang after the communist victory. Much to the disapproval of her father, Soong Qingling (more commonly known as Song Qingling) married Sun Yatsen, 30 years her elder, studied in Moscow and was the only member of the family to live in China after 1949, until her death in 1981. TV Soong, Charlie's only son, served as the Republic of China's finance minister and premier, becoming the richest man of his generation.

Mainland Chinese say that of the three daughters, one loved money (Ailing), one loved power (Meiling) but only one loved China (Qingling). Among them, the siblings stewed up a heady brew of fascism and communism.

Song Qingling died in Běijīng and is buried at the Song Qingling Mausoleum in Shànghǎi. Her sister Meiling declined the invitation to return to China to attend the funeral; she died in the USA in October 2003, aged 105.

(though somewhat noisy) atmosphere. It's hard to fault any of the dishes, but the barbecued freshwater snapper with a cumin-and-peppercorn glaze is a sublime explosion of flavour while the goat's cheese is unmissable.

The stewed-beef-and-mint casserole is almost as good, as is the incomparable 'grandmother's mashed potatoes'. It's essential to make room for the chicken wings too, which come covered in a seriously addictive secret sauce. To top it off, there's an impressively long imported beer list. You can also enter at 169 Jinxian Rd.

CRYSTAL JADE   DIM SUM $$
Map p302 (翡翠酒家; Fěicuì Jiǔjiā; ☑6385 8752; Xīntiāndì South Block, 2nd fl, Bldg 6; 兴业路123弄新天地南里6号2楼; dim sum ¥20-42; ⏰11am-10.20pm; ⓂSouth Huangpi Rd, Xintiandi) One of Xīntiāndì's long-standing success stories, Crystal Jade still draws lines out the door. What separates it from other dim-sum restaurants is the dough: dumpling skins are perfectly tender; steamed buns come out light and airy; and the freshly pulled noodles are just plain delicious. Go for lunch, when both Cantonese and Shanghainese dim sum are served. It's in the mall; reserve ahead.

ORIGIN   CAFE $$
Map p302 (源于自然; Yuányú Zìrán; ☑159 2183 2324; Tiánzǐfáng, No 39, Lane 155, Middle Jianguo Rd; 建国中路155弄39号田子坊; mains ¥48-98; ⏰10.30am-11pm; 🌐🍴; ⓂDapuqiao Rd) With a wood finish, a feel-good vibe and funktastic music backdrop, Origin is a cool two-storey space devoted to healthy and sustainably sourced food, with a strong line-up of vegetarian choices. The menu bursts with welcome suggestions: from panzanella salad (Italian bread and tomato salad; ¥48) to seared Norwegian ahi tuna (¥98), sandwiches crammed with goodness and, of course, pasta and homemade gelato.

Arrive early for seats on the upstairs terrace in sunny weather. Stop by on Mondays to buy a vegie main and get one for free.

DIN TAI FUNG   DUMPLINGS $$
Map p302 (鼎泰丰; Dǐng Tài Fēng; ☑6385 8378; Xīntiāndì South Block, 2nd fl, Bldg 6; 兴业路123弄新天地南里6号楼2楼; 10 dumplings ¥60-96; ⏰10am-midnight; ⓂSouth Huangpi Rd, Xintiandi) Scrummy dumplings – with a price tag – and classy service from Taiwan's most famous chain. It's on the 2nd floor, inside the Xīntiāndì mall. Reserve ahead.

YÈ SHÀNGHǍI   SHANGHAINESE $$
Map p302 (☑6311 2323; Xīntiāndì North Block, 338 South Huangpi Rd; 黄陂南路338号新天地北里; dishes ¥40-88, set lunch menu ¥68-88; ⏰11.30am-2.30pm & 5.30-10.30pm; ⓂSouth Huangpi Rd, Xintiandi) Yè offers sophisticated, unchallenging Shanghainese cuisine in classy Xīntiāndì surroundings. The drunken chicken and smoked fish starters are an excellent intro to local flavours; the crispy duck comes with thick pancakes and the sautéed string beans and bamboo shoots dish doesn't disappoint either. An affordable wine list gives it another tick.

KABB   AMERICAN $$
Map p302 (凯博西餐厅; Kǎibó Xīcāntīng; ☑3307 0798; Xīntiāndì North Block, Bldg 5; 太仓路181弄新天地北里5号楼; mains ¥65-125; ⏰7am-midnight; 🌐; ⓂSouth Huangpi Rd, Xintiandi) When the hunger blues strike, this smart Xīntiāndì grill has all the answers, serving up authentic American-portioned comfort food (main-course sandwiches, burgers and quesadillas) at midrange prices. The outdoor cafe-style seating is particularly popular for a slower-paced weekend brunch, when the menu stretches to French toast with bananas and eggs Benedict.

VEGETARIAN
LIFESTYLE   CHINESE, VEGETARIAN $$
Map p302 (枣子树; Zǎozishù; ☑6384 8000; www.jujubetree.com; 77 Songshan Rd; 嵩山路77号; dishes ¥25-70; 🍴; ⓂSouth Huangpi Rd) Head into a courtyard off Songshan Rd to find a branch of this popular vegetarian restaurant, where organic, MSG-free and oil-light dishes are the order of the day.

KOMMUNE   CAFE $$
Map p302 (公社; Gōngshè; Tiánzǐfáng, The Yard, No 7, Lane 210, Taikang Rd; 泰康路210弄7号田子坊; meals from ¥68; ⏰7am-1am; 🌐; ⓂDapuqiao Rd) The original Tiánzǐfáng cafe, Kommune is a consistently bustling hang-out with outdoor seating, all-day big breakfasts (¥88), sandwiches and barbecue on the menu.

SHÀNGHǍI MIN   SHANGHAINESE $$
Map p302 (小南国; Xiǎo Nán Guó; ☑400 820 9777; Xīntiāndì South Block, 2nd fl, Bldg 6; 兴业路123弄新天地南里6号楼2楼; dishes ¥38-158; ⓂSouth Huangpi Rd, Xintiandi) Even with the smart banquet halls and classy presentation, this is still one of Shànghǎi's more affordable (and delicious) chains. First-rate dishes include tofu-and-crab casserole,

lion's head meatballs, pork trotters braised for six hours and the usual run of Shanghainese dumplings and noodles. Finish off with sweet rice dumplings in osmanthus juice. Located in the Xīntiāndì mall.

★**T8** FUSION $$$
Map p302 (☎6355 8999; http://t8shanghai.com; Xīntiāndì North Block, Bldg 8; 太仓路181弄新天地北里8号楼; set lunch weekdays ¥168, 2-/3-course lunch weekends ¥258/328; ☻11.30am-2pm & 6.30-11.30pm; MSouth Huangpi Rd, Xintiandi) T8 aims to seduce, which it does exceptionally well. Catalan chef Jordi Servalls Bonilla is at the helm, bringing a preference for molecular cuisine with dishes such as watermelon salad 2.0, *tataki* of sesame-crusted tuna and Sìchuān high pie. The renovated grey-brick *shíkùmén* (stonegate house) with its striking feng shui–driven entrance is the perfect setting.

The dark, warm interior is decorated with antique Chinese cabinets and a carved wooden screen. Reserve ahead.

✖ French Concession West

★**JIAN GUO 328** SHANGHAINESE $
Map p302 (328 West Jianguo Rd; 建国西路328号; mains from ¥12; ☻11am-9.30pm; MJiashan Rd) Frequently crammed, this boisterous two-floor MSG-free spot tucked away on Jianguo Rd does a roaring trade on the back of fine Shànghǎi cuisine. You can't go wrong with the menu, but for pointers the deep-fried spare ribs feature succulent pork in a crispy coating, while the eggplant in casserole is a rich, thick and thumb-raising choice, high on flavour. Each table comes primed with a bottle of Shànghǎi Worcestershire sauce, for further splashes of seasoning.

★**NOODLE BULL** NOODLES $
Map p306 (狠牛面; Hěnniú Miàn; ☎6170 1299; unit 3b, 291 Fumin Rd; 富民路291号3b室; noodles ¥28-35; ☻11am-midnight; ☏☏; MChangshu Rd, South Shaanxi Rd) Noodle Bull is the bees-knees: far cooler than your average street-corner noodle stand (minimalist concrete chic and funky bowls), inexpensive, and boy is that broth slurpable! It doesn't matter whether you go vegetarian or for the roasted beef noodles (¥38), it's a winner both ways. Vegetarians can zero in on the carrot-and-cucumber-sprinkled sesame-paste noodles (¥32), which are divine. The cherry on the cake? No MSG. Enter on Changle Rd.

★**SPICY JOINT** SICHUANESE $
Map p302 (辛香汇; Xīnxiānghuì; ☎6470 2777; 3rd fl, K Wah Center, 1028 Middle Huaihai Rd; 淮海中路1028号嘉华中心3楼; dishes ¥12-60; ☻11am-10pm; ☏; MSouth Shaanxi Rd) If you only go to one Sìchuān joint in town, make it this one, where the blistering heat is matched only by its scorching popularity. Dishes are inexpensive by the city's standards; favourites include massive bowls of spicy catfish in hot chilli oil, an addictive garlic-cucumber salad, smoked-tea duck and chilli-coated lamb chops.

Be forewarned that the wait can be excruciatingly long at peak times; you'll need a mobile number to secure a place in the queue.

SOUTH BEAUTY SICHUANESE, CANTONESE $
Map p306 (俏江南; Qiào Jiāngnán; ☎6445 2581; 28 Taojiang Rd; 桃江路28号; dishes from ¥18; MChangshu Rd) This popular branch of the stylish and upmarket Sichuanese chain serves outstanding food, including the fiery *mápō dòufu* (tofu with pork crumbs in a spicy sauce; ¥38) and other classics.

MIA'S YÚNNÁN KITCHEN YUNNAN $
Map p306 (香所云南菜; Xiāngsuǒ Yúnnán Cài; 45-47 Anfu Rd; 安福路45-47号; mains from ¥20; ☻11am-10pm; MChangshu Rd) In the balance, Shànghǎi has more popular Yúnnán restaurants, but titchy Mia's offers a more homely and rustic French Concession ambience, with lashings of wild vegetables. The fried goat's-milk cheese is spot on.

FARINE BAKERY $
Map p306 (http://farine-bakery.com; Ferguson Lane, 378 Wukang Rd; 武康路378号1楼; ☻7am-8pm; MShanghai Library, Jiaotong University) It can be hard to find a seat on the outdoor terrace facing Wukang Rd at this boulangerie during the weekend crush hour. Choose a quieter off-peak moment to sink some well-executed pastries, sandwiches, fantastic breads (baked with imported stone-ground flour) and coffee at this eye-catching Ferguson Lane spot.

FORTUNE COOKIE AMERICAN CHINESE $
Map p306 (簽語餅; Qiānyǔ Bǐng; ☎6093 3623; www.fortunecookieshanghai.com; 4th fl, 83

Changshu Rd; 常熟路83号4楼; mains from ¥36; ⏱11.30am-10pm Sun-Thu, to 11pm Fri & Sat; Ⓜ Changshu Rd) Selling coals to Newcastle and fridges to Eskimos was always high-risk, but Fortune Cookie's owners have cashed in on the nostalgic expat demand for Chinatown staples and the curiosity of Shànghǎi diners. Now you don't have to fly to the US to find Brooklyn *kung po* chicken, tofu chop suey, *moo shu* pork, orange chicken or sweet-and-sour pork.

Chase it all down with some fried ice cream (¥65). For purists the 4th-floor setting is distinctly un-Chinatown.

WHISK CAFE
ITALIAN $

Map p306 (1250 Middle Huaihai Rd; 淮海中路1250号; brownies ¥50; ⏱10.30am-11.30pm Tue-Sun; ☎; Ⓜ Changshu Rd) Luring a trendy crowd and tucked away down a recess off Middle Huaihai Rd, Whisk dishes up an addictive line of luxurious desserts (chocolate tarts and brownies), as the delectable icing on the cake of a popular Italian menu. When lights dim in the evening, it's a romantic spot to boot, with ambient sounds. It's a crucial stop for chocaholics. Cash only.

LA CRÊPERIE
FRENCH $

Map p306 (☎5465 9055; www.lacreperie.com.cn; 1 Taojiang Rd; 桃江路1号; mains from ¥38, set lunch ¥79-98; ⏱11am-11pm; Ⓜ Changshu Rd) This appetising slice of Brittany in Shànghǎi is a great stop-off for expertly made, delicious savoury or sweet crêpes (from ¥38) and galettes (from ¥55), with matching lighthouse salt and pepper shakers, lovely cider and home-style service.

GRAPE RESTAURANT
SHANGHAINESE $

Map p306 (葡萄园酒家; Pútáoyuán Jiǔjiā; ☎5404 0486; 55 Xinle Rd; 新乐路55号; dishes ¥18-68; ⏱11am-midnight; Ⓜ South Shaanxi Rd) This longstanding fave from the 1980s still serves up reliable and inexpensive Shanghainese in its bright premises beside the old Russian Orthodox church. Try the crab dishes – you won't find them cheaper elsewhere.

COFFEE TREE
CAFE $

Map p306 (Ferguson Lane, 376 Wukang Rd; 武康路376号; mains from ¥50; ⏱9am-10pm; ☎; Ⓜ Shanghai Library) Full of well-heeled diners come weekend brunch-time, this cafe in Ferguson Lane is a pleasant spot for a coffee. Sit on the patio in the sun-filled courtyard out front, ringed by well-composed brickwork and verdant foliage. The brunches are

deservedly popular; you can fill yourself up with two courses and a bottomless coffee for ¥138.

GREEN & SAFE
ORGANIC $

Map p306 (6 Dongping Rd; 东平路6号; mains from ¥25; ⏱8am-10pm; Ⓜ Changshu Rd) Overflowing with organic vegetables, fruits, free-range meat, wine and more, this healthy and roomy two-floor Dongping Rd hits the healthy sweet spot. It divides into a huge downstairs market and cafe for all your organic needs, with a popular upstairs (MSG-free) restaurant.

WAGAS
CAFE $

Map p306 (沃歌斯; Wògēsī; 7 Donghu Rd; 东湖路7号; mains ¥48-58; ⏱7am-10pm; ☎; Ⓜ South Shaanxi Rd) Conveniently located branch of the city's favourite cafe. Come for vanilla iced coffees and 50% off breakfast sandwiches before 10am (Monday to Friday).

BAKER & SPICE
CAFE $

Map p306 (195 Anfu Rd; 安福路195号; mains from ¥40; ⏱6am-10.30pm; ☎; Ⓜ Changshu Rd) Its wooden table a solitary slab of rustic wholesomeness, this bakery-cafe serves stuff the doctor did and didn't order, all lovingly presented: sandwiches on dense, fibre-rich bread; cellophane-packed nuts; yoghurt cups; muffins; *pains au chocolate*; tarts; cakes; and sizeable vanilla custard Berliners. A couple of box tables are flung outside for sun-catching.

ZEN LIFESTORE & CAFE
CAFE $

Map p306 (钲艺廊; 7 Dongping Rd; 东平路7号; ⏱2pm to 10.30pm; Ⓜ Changshu Rd) Tucked away upstairs in the rafters of a shop selling Oriental bits-and-bobs, trendy decorative gifts, ceramics and home furnishings, this lovely little cafe is well away from the Shànghǎi hurly-burly (although it can still fill up).

SÌCHUĀN CITIZEN
SICHUANESE $

Map p306 (龙门阵茶屋; Lóngménzhèn Cháwū; ☎5404 1235; 30 Donghu Rd; 东湖路30号; dishes ¥28-98, set lunch ¥38-58; ⏱11am-10.30pm; ☎; Ⓜ South Shaanxi Rd) The subdued evening lighting and welcoming service creates a warm and homely atmosphere at this popular outpost of Sìchuān cuisine in Shànghǎi. With a full photo menu, it's foreigner friendly, easy to use and sees a regular stream of diners. The spicy *dan dan* noodles are textbook spicy while the pork wontons in hot oil (¥10) are spot on.

Not all dishes hit the *chuāncài* (川菜; Sìchuān food) nail on the head, though, and the *mápó dòufu* (tofu and pork crumbs in a spicy sauce; ¥26) is sadly wide of the mark. Quench it all with a large bottle of Budweiser for ¥30.

★ELEFANTE   MEDITERRANEAN $$

Map p302 (☏5404 8085; www.el-efante.com; 20 Donghu Rd; 东湖路20号; ☉11am-3pm & 6-10.30pm Tue-Sun; Ⓜ South Shaanxi Rd) Willy Trullas Moreno's latest Shànghǎi creation sits squarely at the heart of the French Concession – in the same spot as his first venture – with a choice patio and romantic 1920s villa setting. It's tantalising Mediterranean menu with tapas-style dishes has pronounced Spanish and Italian inflections, and has local gastronomes buzzing.

★JESSE   SHANGHAINESE $$

Map p306 (吉士酒楼; Jíshì Jiǔlóu; ☏6282 9260; 41 Tianping Rd; 天平路41号; dishes ¥38-98; ☉11am-4pm & 5.30pm-midnight; Ⓜ Jiaotong University) Jesse specialises in packing lots of people into tight spaces, so if you tend to gesture wildly when you talk, watch out with those chopsticks. This is Shanghainese home-cooking at its best: crab dumplings, Grandma's braised pork and plenty of fish, drunken shrimp and eel.

There are several branches around town, including one at **28 Taojiang Road** (新吉士; Xīnjíshì; Map p306; ☏6445 0068; 28 Taojiang Rd; Ⓜ Changshu Rd) but serious foodies should make the effort to trek out to the original.

★MADISON   AMERICAN $$

Map p302 (☏6437 0136; www.madisonshanghai.com; Bldg 2, 3 Fenyang Rd; 汾阳路3号2号楼; mains from ¥60; ☉11.30am-11.30pm Tue-Fri, 11am-10.30pm Sat & Sun) Madison's Saturday and Sunday brunch is where it's at, but any day is a delight. Austin Hu's latest restaurant maintains a skilled focus on quality ingredients sourced from across China, and a deft and accomplished demonstration of classic new American cuisine.

Formerly up the street on Donghu Rd, the design is modish, white, bright and wood-floored but casual enough to welcome a relaxed crowd. The bar – Madi – is a good spot for a premeal cocktail (or sandwiches and small plates).

GARLIC   TURKISH $$

Map p306 (www.garlicshanghai.com; 698 Yongjia Rd; 永嘉路698号; mains from ¥78; ☉noon-11pm; ♿; Ⓜ Hengshan Rd) The ancestral homeland of much of China's northwestern Uighur cuisine, Turkish food gets a swish French Concession revamp at smart Garlic, where the *hunkar begendi* ('Sultan's Favorite' lamb in tandoori with charcoal-grilled aubergine; ¥160) is delightful and typical of the rich flavours coursing through an ample menu.

There's a strong showing of Turkish wines plus, for feasting families, a downstairs kids' zone with Playstation.

BǍOLUÓ JIǓLÓU   SHANGHAINESE $$

Map p306 (保罗酒楼; ☏6279 2827; 271 Fumin Rd; 富民路271号; dishes ¥58; ☉11am-3am; Ⓜ Changshu Rd, Jing'an Temple) Gather up some friends to join the Shanghainese at this expanded, highly popular Fumin Rd venue. It's a great place to get a feel for Shànghǎi's famous buzz. Try the excellent baked eel (保罗烤鳗; *bǎoluó kǎomán*) or pot-stewed crab and pork.

HAIKU   JAPANESE $$

Map p306 (隐泉之语; Yǐnquán Zhī Yǔ; ☏6445 0021; www.haikushanghai.com; 28b Taojiang Rd; 桃江路28号乙; maki rolls ¥62-128; Ⓜ Changshu Rd) The name suggests the minimalist beauty of a butterfly perched upon a temple bell, but the name of the game at Haiku is 'let's see how many different things we can fit into a maki roll'. The Dynamite roll wraps up raw tuna with a killer spicy sauce, while the Moto-roll-ah is a deep-fried spicy tuna, snow crab and avocado combo.

Can't make up your mind? Pimp My Roll may be the one for you – it's loaded with everything. Reserve ahead.

LOST HEAVEN   YUNNAN $$

Map p306 (花马天堂; Huāmǎ Tiāntáng; ☏6433 5126; 38 Gaoyou Rd; 高邮路38号; dishes from ¥48-88; ☉11.30am-1.30pm & 5.30-10.30pm; Ⓜ Shanghai Library) Located on a quiet street in Shànghǎi's most desirable neighbourhood, Lost Heaven is stylish and atmospheric with subdued red lighting and a giant Buddha dominating the main dining area. The Yunnanese food is delicately flavoured and nicely presented, although purists may bemoan the way some dishes, such as the Dali chicken, aren't as spicy as they should be.

The Yúnnán vegetable cakes come with a salsa-like garnish and make a fantastic starter. There's another branch on the Bund. Book ahead.

GŬYÌ HÚNÁN RESTAURANT   HUNANESE $$

Map p306 (古意湘味浓; Gǔyì Xiāngwèinóng; ☑6249 5628; 87 Fumin Rd; 富民路87号; dishes ¥28-100; ☺11am-2pm & 5.30-10.30pm; ☎; ⓂJing'an Temple, Changshu Rd) Gǔyì is a fine Húnán choice for a romantic dinner. It has a classy atmosphere equalled by a comprehensive menu, which includes great *huǒguō* (hotpot) featuring beef, chicken, crab or frog and delectable cumin ribs. Reserve.

VEDAS   INDIAN $$

Map p306 (www.vedascuisine.com; 3rd fl, 83 Changshu Rd; 常熟路83号3楼; mains from ¥68; ☺11.30am-2pm & 6-10.30pm; ▣🖉; ⓂChangshu Rd) Vedas hides the sterility of its modern tower-block setting with good-looking woodwork, warm service and a generous menu of full-flavoured Indian dishes. The delightful Bombay prawn curry (¥88) is piquant and creamy in equal measure, while the basmati rice is cooked to perfection and arrives in steaming abundance.

At the tongue-blistering end of the spectrum are chicken Chettinad (¥68) and lamb vindaloo (¥78) and vegetarians will find much to coo about. Set meals are good value and the naan is tip-top.

XĪBÓ   CENTRAL ASIAN $$

Map p306 (锡伯新疆餐厅; Xībó Xīnjiāng Cāntīng; ☑5403 8330; www.xiboxinjiang.com; 3rd fl, 83 Changshu Rd; 常熟路83号3楼; mains ¥35-92; ☺noon-2.30pm & 6pm-midnight; ⓂChangshu Rd) Trust Shànghǎi to serve up a stylish Xīnjiāng joint, because this isn't the type of place you're likely to find out in China's wild northwest. But who's complaining? When you need a mutton fix, beef skewers or some spicy 'big plate chicken', Xībó will do you right (and the restaurant donates healthily to charities in West China).

PHO REAL   VIETNAMESE $$

Map p306 (166 Fumin Rd; 富民路166号; noodles from ¥52, set lunch ¥60-70; ☺11am-2pm & 6-10pm; ⓂChangshu Rd, Jing'an Temple) This pint-sized eatery, overhung with woven fishing traps suspended from the ceiling, does a brisk trade in *pho* (beef noodle soup flavoured with mint, star anise and cilantro), spring rolls and good-value set lunches. Round it all out with a chilled Saigon lager (¥40). It only seats about 20, with no reservations, so pitch up early and prepare to wait.

There's another branch at **1465 Fuxing Rd** (Map p306; ☑6437 2222; 复兴中路1465号; ☺11am-2pm & 6-10pm Mon-Fri, 11am-3.30pm & 6-10pm Sat-Sun; ⓂChangshu Rd), which does take reservations.

GLO LONDON   BRITISH $$

Map p306 (☑6466 6565; www.glolondon.com; 1 South Wulumuqi Rd; 乌鲁木齐南路1号; mains from ¥98, 2-/3-course set lunch ¥83/110; ☺7am-midnight; ⓂChangshu Rd, Hengshan Rd) This four-storey affair wants to be everything to everyone, and, amazingly enough, it seems to be working. The 1st floor is a casual bakery and cafe (sandwiches, pastries, smoothies, UK corner-shop sweets and pork scratchings), while the slick 2nd floor (the Gastro Grill) serves the greatest hits of British cuisine: from tandoori lamb chops to beer-battered cod (and chips).

The 3rd floor is the swish Glo Lounge (p117), while the top-floor terrace is set to become the hickory-smoked BBQ ribs hangout in warmer weather.

XIAN YUE HIEN   DIM SUM $$

Map p306 (申粤轩酒楼; Shēnyuèxuān Jiǔlóu; ☑6251 1166; 849 Huashan Rd; 华山路849号; dim sum ¥17-25; ☺11am-2.30pm & 5.30-11pm Mon-Fri, from 9am Sat & Sun) The Dǐng Xiāng Garden, originally built for the concubine of a Qing-dynasty mandarin, is reserved for retired Communist Party cadres, so to peek behind the undulating dragon wall, you need to dine here. At the pointy end, seafood dishes can get very expensive, but the real draw is the dim sum, served overlooking the lawn on mornings and afternoons.

Stroll past the octogenarian officials in wheelchairs reminiscing about the good old days. Take a taxi here and reserve ahead.

FERGUSON LANE   ITALIAN, FRENCH $$

Map p306 (武康庭; Wǔkāng Tíng; www.fergusonlane.com.cn; 378 Wukang Rd; 武康路378号; mains ¥48-130; ⓂShanghai Library, Jiaotong University) On those rare days when Shànghǎi's skies are cloud-free, the secluded Ferguson Lane courtyard fills up in the blink of an eye with sun-starved diners. There are several tempting options here, including the Coffee Tree (p107), which features panini, pasta, salads and organic coffee, and Farine (p106), for breads and pastries.

NEPALI KITCHEN   NEPALESE $$

Map p306 (尼泊尔餐厅; Níbó'ěr Cāntīng; ☑5404 6281; No 4, Lane 819, Julu Rd; 巨鹿路819弄4号; mains ¥45-85; ☺11am-2pm & 6-11pm; ⓂJing'an Temple, Changshu Rd) Reminisce about that Himalayan trek over a plate of Tibetan

EATING ORGANIC

The organic movement in China has only recently sprouted, but it has quickly spread in Shànghǎi. With the quality of produce and manufactured products in China becoming increasingly dubious, there's been enough negative publicity (including the discovery of bean sprouts being soaked in a banned chemical solution at local markets, glass noodle samples that contained aluminium, and mutated eggs that bounced 'like ping-pong balls') that Shanghainese are starting to get interested. Organic farms in the area have gone from five to 30 in just three years. Upscale restaurants (including Jean Georges (p72)) usually use at least some organic produce, while the following restaurants specialise in local organic ingredients:

➡ Organic Kitchen (p110)
➡ Green & Safe (p107)
➡ Origin (p105)
➡ Vegetarian Lifestyle (p105)

momos (dumplings) or a *choila* (spicy chicken) amid prayer flags in this homey, lodge-like place. For a more laid-back meal, take your shoes off and recline on traditional cushions, surrounded by colourful *thangkas* and paper lamps. Both the set lunch and dinner are a good bet.

PĪNCHUĀN
SICHUANESE $$

Map p306 (品川; ✆400 820 7706; 47 Taojiang Rd; 桃江路47号; dishes ¥39-89; ⊗11am-2pm & 5-11pm; Ⓜ Changshu Rd) Fire fiends love Sìchuān cooking, where the sophistication goes far beyond merely smothering everything with hot peppers. The telltale blend of chillies and peppercorns is best summed up in two words: *là* (spicy) and *má* (numbing). Even though Pǐnchuān has hit the upscale button repeatedly in the past few years, it's still a fine place to experience the tongue tingling. Try the sliced beef in spicy sauce, baked spare ribs with peanuts or *làzi jī* (spicy chicken). The duck with sticky rice will help mitigate the damage to your tastebuds. Reserve ahead.

SIMPLY THAI
THAI $$

Map p306 (天泰餐厅; Tiāntài Cāntīng; ✆6445 9551; 5c Dongping Rd; 东平路5号C座; dishes ¥48-68; ⊗11am-10.30pm; Ⓜ Changshu Rd) This popular branch of Shànghǎi's favourite Thai has a tree-shaded patio, perfect for alfresco dining. Expect reasonably priced classics such as green and red curries, tom yum soup and fiery green papaya salad.

★ DĪ SHUǏ DÒNG
HUNANESE $$

Map p306 (滴水洞; ✆6415 9448; 5 Dongping Rd; 东平路5号; dishes ¥25-128; ⊗10am-12.30am; Ⓜ Changshu Rd) This branch of the spicy

Húnán favourite isn't the most popular but it's less crowded than others and the menu's equally good.

ORGANIC KITCHEN
CAFE $$

Map p306 (www.organickitchenshanghai.com; 57 West Fuxing Rd; 复兴西路57号; mains from ¥46, breakfast sets ¥78-88; ⊗8am-10pm; 🖥📶; Ⓜ Shanghai Library, Changshu Rd) 🍃 A cosy brick-walled cafe, the Organic Kitchen is a welcome change from the usual coffee chains that dominate the Shànghǎi landscape. The focus is on health-conscious comfort food, and the menu stretches from all-day breakfast sets and salads to falafel wraps, Indian curries and banana muffins.

DA MARCO
ITALIAN $$

Map p306 (大马可餐厅; Dàmǎkě Cāntīng; ✆6210 4495; 103 Dong Zhu'anbang Rd, inside Metro Park Apts; 东诸安浜路103号; pasta & pizza ¥68-88, mains ¥108-168; ⊗noon-11pm; Ⓜ Jiangsu Rd) This homey spot is one of the most popular Italian restaurants in town and remains a steal after fifteen years in business (an eternity in Shànghǎi). Daily specials such as pear-and-gorgonzola pizza and fettuccine porcini are chalked up on the blackboard. Reserve.

COCONUT PARADISE
THAI $$

Map p306 (椰香天堂; Yēxiāng Tiāntáng; ✆6248 1998; 38 Fumin Rd; 富民路38号; dishes ¥68-138; ⊗11.30am-3.30pm & 5pm-late; Ⓜ Jing'an Temple) Coconut Paradise is a tropical delight, its lush garden seating and dimly lit interior making for a decidedly romantic venue. Curries, fish salads and Chiang Mai soup will bring back memories of days spent lazing around in northern Thailand, and by the end of the meal, you might even forget you're in Shànghǎi. No MSG. Reserve two days ahead.

ELEMENT FRESH
CAFE $$

Map p306 (新元素; Xīnyuánsù; ☑6279 8682; 4th fl, K Wah Centre, 1028 Middle Huaihai Rd; 淮海中路1028号嘉华中心4楼; sandwiches & salads ¥45-98, dinner from ¥128; ⊙7am-11pm; 🔊⚟; Ⓜ South Shaanxi Rd) This sleek and good-looking branch of the health-conscious eatery is a cool choice, with an inviting bar area and a largely faultless menu.

SHÀNGHǍI MIN
SHANGHAINESE $$

Map p306 (小南国; Xiǎo Nán Guó; ☑400 820 9777; 4th fl, Dichan Bldg, 9 Donghu Rd; 东湖路9号地产大厦4楼; dishes ¥38-158; ⊙11am-2pm & 5-10pm; Ⓜ South Shaanxi Rd) This branch of the popular Shanghainese restaurant that dots town is superbly placed for French Concession diners.

★ FU 1039
SHANGHAINESE $$$

Map p306 (福一零三九; Fú Yāo Líng Sān Jiǔ; ☑5237 1878; 1039 Yuyuan Rd; 愚园路1039号; dishes ¥60-108; Ⓜ Jiangsu Rd) Set in a three-storey 1913 villa, Fu attains an old-fashioned charm. Foodies who appreciate sophisticated surroundings and Shanghainese food on par with the decor, take note – Fu is a must. The succulent standards won't disappoint: the smoked fish starter and stewed pork in soy sauce are recommended, with the sautéed chicken and mango and the sweet-and-sour Mandarin fish a close second.

The entrance, down an alley and on the left, is unmarked and staff speak little English. There's a minimum charge of ¥200 per head here.

SHINTORI NULL II
FUSION $$$

Map p306 (新都里无二店; Xīndūlǐ Wú'èr Diàn; ☑5404 5252; 803 Julu Rd; 巨鹿路803号; dishes ¥80-160, tasting menu ¥380; ⊙6-10.30pm; Ⓜ Jing'an Temple) The industrial-chic interior here resembles a set from a Peter Greenaway film, from the eye-catching open kitchen, to the sleek staff running around like an army of ninjas. The dishes (Běijīng duck rolls, cold noodles served in an ice bowl, beef steak on *pu-erh* leaves) are excellent, but they maintain the minimalist theme, so make sure to order enough. Finish with black-sesame-seed ice cream. Reserve.

KAGEN
TEPPANYAKI $$$

Map p306 (隐泉源铁板烧; Yǐnquán Yuán Tiěbǎnshāo; ☑6433 3232; 28d Taojiang Rd; 桃江路28号丁; all-you-can-eat teppanyaki ¥288; ⊙5.30-11pm Mon-Fri, 11.30am-2pm Sat & Sun; Ⓜ Changshu Rd) Opened by the folks at Haiku next door, supersleek Kagen takes Shànghǎi's all-you-can-eat-and-drink teppanyaki craze into the upper echelon. Wagyu beef, tiger prawns and foie gras are some of the finer ingredients on the menu, and quality sushi, sashimi, sake and wine are all part of the buffet deal. Reserve.

AZUL
TAPAS $$$

Map p306 (☑5405 2252; www.azultapaslounge.cn; 8th fl, 378 Wukang Rd; 武康路378号8楼; tapas ¥45-90, weekend brunch ¥138-148; ⊙11am-midnight; 🔊; Ⓜ Shanghai Library, Jiaotong University) Peruvian restaurateur Eduardo Vargas specialises in hip fusion food slanted towards South American flavours. With a new location on the top floor of Ferguson Lane's extension – terrace included – Azul keeps the tapas tradition going strong with temptations that run from prawn *ceviche* (marinated raw prawns) to reinvented standards such as *patatas bravas*.

The weekend brunch, pisco sours and Margaritas remain as popular as ever.

LÈ SHĒNG
SHANGHAINESE $$$

Map p306 (乐生; ☑5406 6011; leshengsh.com; 308 Anfu Rd; 安福路308号; dishes ¥38-138; ⊙11.30am-11pm; Ⓜ Changshu Rd) For those looking for a high-end introduction to Shanghainese cuisine, Lè Shēng will certainly fit the bill. Intimate enough to be romantic and with haute cuisine presentation, it caters well to couples and provides a refreshing change from Shànghǎi's larger banquet halls. No surprise, perhaps, that it was opened by an Australian (David Laris), but don't translate this to mean inauthentic – the food is on par with expectations.

🍷 DRINKING & NIGHTLIFE

Home to the largest concentration of bars and cafes in the whole of Shànghǎi, the French Concession offers drinkers a choice between elegant bars housed in colonial-era villas, foreign pubs around the north end of Hengshan Rd, as well as a brand-new crop of places springing up along the alcohol-sodden Yongkang Rd.

1. Tiánzǐfáng (p95)

Burrow into the alleyways for a rewarding haul of creative boutiques, selling everything from hip jewellery and yak-wool scarves to funky footware.

2. Glass artwork

One of many fascinating exhibits at a museum in the complex Xīntiāndì (p96).

3. Xīntiāndì (p96)

This upscale area has many former *shíkùmén* (stone-gate houses) that have been converted into restaurants.

🍴 French Concession East

⭐**CAFÉ DES STAGIAIRES**　　　BAR

Map p302 (www.cafestagiaires.com; 54-56 Yongkang Rd; 永康路54-56号; mains from ¥40; ⏰10am-midnight; 🕿; Ⓜ️South Shaanxi Rd) The best bar by far on buzzing Yongkang Rd, this hip oasis of Francophilia spills over with slightly zany Gallic charm. There's a coke bottle chandelier and a (French) geography lesson via the wine list: Languedoc, Provence, Côte du Rhône, Loire, Alsace, Bourgogne, Bordeaux and, *bien sûr*, Rest of the World. Each table is regularly stocked with addictive chilli peanuts. If that's insufficient, sample the quality charcuterie, cheese and pizzas.

⭐**BELL BAR**　　　BAR

Map p302 (bellbar.cn; Tiánzǐfáng, back door No 11, Lane 248, Taikang Rd; 泰康路248弄11号后门田子坊; ⏰11am-2am; 🕿; Ⓜ️Dapuqiao) This eccentric, unconventional boho haven is a delightful Tiánzǐfáng hideaway, with creaking, narrow wooden stairs leading to a higgledy-piggledy array of rooms to the tucked-away attic slung out above. Expect hookah pipes, mismatched furniture, warped secondhand paperbacks and a small, secluded mezzanine for stowaways from the bedlam outside. It's in the second alley (Lane 248) on the right.

Watch the narrow steps on the way down, if you've had a few.

⭐**DEAN'S BOTTLE SHOP**　　　BAR

Map p302 (40 Yongkang Rd; 永康路40号; beers from ¥15; ⏰noon-10pm; Ⓜ️South Shaanxi Rd) This well-priced nirvana for lovers of the grain (and, to a lesser extent, grape) has row upon row of imported bottled bliss – Moosehead lager, Old Rasputin, Young's double chocolate, Bombadier ale, pear cider – all at bargain prices. With more than enough labels to test even the most well-travelled palates, it's more shop than bar, but you can sit down.

It's a great start or concluding point to a trawl along the bars of Yongkang Rd. There's another shop on nearby **Shaoxing Rd** (Map p302; 37 Shaoxing Rd; 绍兴路37号; Ⓜ️Dapuqiao).

CITIZEN CAFÉ　　　CAFE

Map p302 (天台餐厅; Tiāntái Cāntīng; 222 Jinxian Rd; 进贤路222号; ⏰11am-12.30am; 🕿; Ⓜ️South Shaanxi Rd) Decked out with small lamp-shades and panelled walls like a private living room, this is a romantic and quiet spot, and candlelit come sundown as smooth ambient sounds manage a relaxed tempo. Recharge with a club sandwich or sit back with one of the much-loved ginger cocktails while watching street scenes unfold from the 2nd-floor terrace. Smokers get to sit by the door.

VIENNA CAFÉ　　　CAFE

Map p302 (维也纳咖啡馆; Wéiyěnà Kāfēiguǎn; 📞6445 2131; 25 Shaoxing Rd; 绍兴路25号; ⏰8am-8pm; 🕿; Ⓜ️Jiashan Rd) With a small sun-flecked conservatory at the rear, this European-style cafe does striped-wallpaper and round marble-top tables; it's ideal for unwinding with a Kafka and a coffee. Sign up for one of the breakfasts for endless caffeine on tap and nod off to the soft jazz accompaniment. Movie nights are held every Thursday at 7.30pm; call to reserve a spot. No wi-fi connection on weekends.

KĀIBĀ　　　BAR

Map p302 (开巴; www.kaiba-beerbar.com; Tiánzǐfáng, 2nd fl, 169 Middle Jianguo Rd; 建国中路169号2楼田子坊; ⏰11am-2am; 🕿; Ⓜ️Dapuqiao) This branch of the Kāibā beer specialists is a popular Tiánzǐfáng choice in the add-on Taikang Terrace development.

BOXING CAT BREWERY　　　BREWERY

Map p302 (拳击猫啤酒屋; Quánjīmāo Píjiǔwū; unit 26a, Sinan Mansions, 519 Middle Fuxing Rd; 复兴中路519号思南公馆26a; ⏰11am-2am; Ⓜ️Xintiandi) This branch of Boxing Cat Brewery in the Sinan Mansions complex isn't as popular as its West Fuxing Rd outfit (p116), but is a staple among Shànghǎi's beer-o-philes, with a strong showing of craft brews.

GEISHA　　　BAR, CLUB

Map p302 (www.thegeisha-shanghai.com; 390 South Shaanxi Rd; 陕西南路390号; ⏰5pm-2am; 🕿; Ⓜ️South Shaanxi Rd) Although the Geisha unfortunately falls well short of its claim to provide a 'surreal high-class brothel atmosphere' (sorry guys), it's definitely on the radar for a fun evening out, with a dance club on the 2nd floor, sake lounge on the 3rd floor and an equally popular California-style Japanese restaurant on the 1st.

TMSK　　　BAR

Map p302 (透明思考; Tòumíng Sīkǎo; 📞021 6326 2227; Xīntiāndì North Block, Bldg 11; 太仓路181弄新天地北里11号楼; ⏰11.30am-1am; 🕿;

South Huangpi Rd, Xintiandi) A place to visit as much for the decor as for the drinks, TMSK is designed within an inch of its life. The whole place is full of swirled pastel-coloured glass (*liúli*), but the interior design pales into insignificance once the house band gets going with its unholy fusion of techno and traditional Chinese music (Fridays and Saturdays at 8.30pm).

BURDIGALA 2 — WINE BAR
Map p302 (www.theburdigala.com; 2nd fl, 301 Jiashan Rd; 嘉善路301号2楼; ◎11.30am-late; ☎; Ⓜ Jiashan Rd) For Bordeaux wine enthusiasts, welcoming Burdigala 2 is an affordable choice in a city increasingly dotted with wine bars. Knowledgeable staff are at hand for pointers, while a decent French bistro menu takes care of evening dining and weekend brunches.

YY'S — BAR
Map p302 (轮回酒吧; Lúnhuí Jiǔbā; ☎6466 4098; basement, 125 Nanchang Rd; 南昌路125号; ◎6pm-4am; ☎; Ⓜ South Shaanxi Rd) Once home to the Shànghǎi underground scene (way back in the 1990s), YY's has successfully remained on the fringes of the city's consciousness without ever becoming too hip. Now relegated to the basement, it continues to attract an alternative crowd and has its own rough-edged appeal, which increases as night blurs into dawn.

DR BAR — BAR
Map p302 (Xintiandi North Block, Bldg 15, Lane 181, Taicang Rd; 新天地北里太仓路181弄15号楼; ◎4pm-1am; Ⓜ South Huangpi Rd, Xintiandi) This neat bar is just what the doctor ordered: all in black and chrome; pupil-dilating minimalist cool. Note the almost obliterated Maoist slogans outside, on either side of the *shíkùmén* (stone-gate) door.

LÒUSHÌ — CAFE
Map p302 (陋室; www.loushispace.com; 145 Nanchang Rd; 南昌路145号; ◎10am-11pm; ☎; Ⓜ South Shaanxi Rd) An antique-store-cum-cafe, this homey space is cluttered with Shànghǎi antiques and collectibles, from the chairs you sit in to the stone bodhisattvas, and to the art deco light fixtures and attractive furniture fashioned from recyled wood. Regardless of whether or not you're in the market for home furnishings, it's a great place to get off your feet for a spell.

🍷 French Concession West

★COTTON'S — BAR
Map p306 (棉花酒吧; Miánhuā Jiǔbā; ☎6433 7995; www.cottons-shanghai.com; 132 Anting Rd; 安亭路132号; ◎11am-2am Sun-Thu, to 4am Fri & Sat; Ⓜ Hengshan Rd, Zhaojiabang Rd) This excellent bar is perhaps the most pleasant spot in the Concession to raise a glass. Ensconced in a converted 1930s villa, the bar's interior has cosy sofas and fireplaces to snuggle around in the winter and a tiny outdoor terrace on the 2nd floor. The real draw, though, is the garden, which is intimate yet still big enough not to feel cramped.

The drinks and bar snacks, pizzas, burgers, salads and sandwiches are reasonably priced and the crowd is a good mix of locals and expats. You'll have to get here early on weekends to grab a table outside, or book ahead.

★EL CÓCTEL — BAR
Map p306 (☎6433 6511; 2nd fl, 47 Yongfu Rd; 永福路47号; ◎5pm-3am; Ⓜ Shanghai Library) What do you get when you cross an ever-inventive Spanish chef with a perfectionist bartender from Japan? El Cóctel, of course – an artsy, retro cocktail lounge that mixes up some damn fine drinks. The mixology list goes beyond the usual suspects: sample old-school temptations such as the black Manhattan or the Bermuda mule, but come with cash to spare.

If you don't reserve you might find it hard to get in, but don't worry, as there's a line of bars downstairs, including a surprisingly popular French pirate rum bar (Bounty Rhumerie).

★SHELTER — CLUB
Map p306 (5 Yongfu Rd; 永福路5号; ◎9pm-4am Wed-Sat; Ⓜ Shanghai Library) The darling of the underground crowd, Shelter is a reconverted bomb shelter where you can count on great music, cheap drinks and a nonexistent dress code. They bring in a fantastic line-up of international DJs and hip-hop artists; the large barely lit dance area is the place to be. Cover for big shows is usually around ¥30.

★APARTMENT — BAR
Map p306 (☎6437 9478; www.theapartment-shanghai.com; 3rd fl, 47 Yongfu Rd; 永福路47号; ◎5pm-late; ☎; Ⓜ Shanghai Library) This trendy loft-style bar is designed to pull in

the full spectrum of 30-something professionals, with a comfort-food menu; a dance space and lounge zone; a retro bar room; and topping it all a terrace for views and the summer BBQ action.

★ BOXING CAT BREWERY — BREWERY

Map p306 (拳击猫啤酒屋; Quánjīmāo Píjiǔwū; www.boxingcatbrewery.com; 82 West Fuxing Rd; 复兴西路82号; ⊙5pm-2am Mon-Thu, 3pm-2am Fri, 10am-2am Sat & Sun; 🛜; MShanghai Library, Changshu Rd) A deservedly popular three-floor microbrewery, with a rotating line-up of fresh beers that range from the Standing 8 Pilsner to the Right Hook Helles. But that's not all – the omnipresent restaurateur Kelley Lee has paired Southern classics (gumbo) and sandwiches (Cali-Cajun chicken club) to go with the drinks. Come for a pint; stay for dinner.

★ ABBEY ROAD — BAR

Map p306 (艾比之路; Aìbǐ Zhī Lù; www.abbey-road-shanghai.com; 45 Yueyang Rd; 岳阳路45号; ⊙4pm-2am Mon-Fri, 10am-2am Sat & Sun; 🛜; MChangshu Rd) The cheap beer with classic rock combination works its stuff again, attracting plenty of regulars to this pub. Once the weather becomes nice, the tree-shaded outdoor patio adds the final ingredient to make this an irresistible favourite. There are gigantic portions of Swiss pub food too, and live moptop sounds from the Shanghai Beatles (and other bands).

DADA — CLUB

Map p306 (115 Xingfu Rd; 幸福路115号; ⊙8pm-late; MJiaotong University) This friendly no-frills place stuffed away down an alley near Jiāotōng University is one of Shànghǎi's most popular dives, specialising in cheap drinks, Tuesday-night slasher flicks (free popcorn) and popular weekend dance parties.

★ DR WINE — WINE BAR

Map p306 (177 Fumin Rd; 富民路177号; ⊙11am-2am; 🛜; MJing'an Temple) Black-leather armchairs, salvaged *shíkùmén* brick walls and worn-in tables set the mood at this casual, two-storey wine bar on Fumin Rd. Wines are sold by both the glass and bottle, and the prices are reasonably affordable. The usual French accompaniments – cheese and charcuterie (saucisson, pâté etc) – are on the menu, as well as weekday set-lunch deals.

CONSTELLATION — BAR

Map p306 (酒池星座; Jiǔchí Xīngzuò; ☑5404 0970; 86 Xinle Rd; 新乐路86号; ⊙7pm-2am; MSouth Shaanxi Rd) The bow-tied staff at the Japanese-run Constellation take their drinks seriously – you're not going to get any watered-down cocktails here. A choice selection of whiskies (including a samurai-helmeted Nikka), Van Gogh prints on the walls and overhead black lights make this a classy yet appealingly eccentric place.

CAMEL — SPORTS BAR

Map p306 (www.camelsportsbar.com; 1 Yueyang Rd; 岳阳路1号; ⊙11am-2am Mon-Fri, 10am-2am Sat & Sun; MChangshu Rd) The French Concession's go-to sports bar, Camel has pool tables, dartboards, foosball, big screens at all angles and nightly meal and drink offers, plus a big Tuesday quiz night. Pints are sensibly priced and the bar often stays open until odd hours so that fans can catch that crucial 4am game.

EDDY'S BAR — GAY BAR

Map p306 (嘉浓休; Jiānóng Xiūxián; 1877 Middle Huaihai Rd; 淮海中路1877号, 近天平路; ⊙8pm-2am; MJiaotong University) Shànghǎi's longest-running gay bar is a friendly place with a flash, square bar to sit around, as well as a few corners to hide away in. It attracts both locals and expats, but it's mostly for the boys rather than the girls. The entrance is on Tianping Rd.

LOLA — CLUB

Map p306 (www.lolaclubshanghai.com; Bldg 4, Surpass Court, 570 Yongjia Rd; 永嘉路570号4号楼; ⊙6pm-late; MHengshan Rd) A superior sound system and wall-to-ceiling video projections that sync with the beat pull in the crowds at this first-rate club, opened by a trio of Catalan DJs. Plus, it serves tapas.

SHÀNGHǍI BREWERY — BREWERY

Map p306 (www.shanghaibrewery.com; 15 Dongping Rd; 东平路15号; ⊙10am-2am Sun-Thu, to 3am Fri & Sat; 🛜; MChangshu Rd, Hengshan Rd) Hand-crafted microbrews, a big range of comfort food, pool tables and sports on TV... this massive two-storey hang-out might have it all. Well, it certainly has enough to stand out on a strip already bursting with established names. Try the Czech-style People's Pilsner or the Hong Mei Amber Hefeweizen, which start at a mere ¥20 during happy hour (from 2pm to 8pm).

GLO LOUNGE
BAR

Map p306 (www.glolondon.com; 1 South Wulumuqi Rd; 乌鲁木齐南路1号; ⏰5pm-2am Mon-Fri, 11am-2am Sat & Sun; Ⓜ Changshu Rd, Hengshan Rd) Glo London's lounge bar is angling to become the neighbourhood's sophisticated option – no rowdy guys cheering on their favourite teams here. Instead you get an extensive mojito list, proper dry martinis, candlelit tables and all the requisite pretty young things.

PEOPLE 7
BAR

Map p306 (人间荧七; Rénjiān Yíngqī; ☎5404 0707; 803 Julu Rd; 巨鹿路803号; ⏰11.30am-2pm & 6pm-midnight; Ⓜ Jing'an Temple, Changshu Rd) Getting into this superstylish bar is an achievement in itself. That's not because there's a door policy, but because the shiny steel doors only open if you insert your hand into one of the nine holes set into the wall. Once inside, there's a long steel bar on which to rest the oddly shaped glass your cocktail arrives in.

With white armchairs scattered throughout the dimly lit interior and bathrooms that are even harder to work out than the front door, this place could be oppressively trendy. But it isn't. They do affordable Chinese food, too.

ENOTERRA
WINE BAR

Map p306 (53-57 Anfu Rd; 安福路53-57号; ⏰10am-2am; ☎; Ⓜ Changshu Rd) Wine bars have hit Shànghǎi big time. With its convivial atmosphere and affordable wines by the glass and bottle, Enoterra was the first to provide a winning formula. There's a definite focus on French wines – from sunny Corbières to powerful Vacqueyras – but there's a good selection of New World wines as well. Meals are also served.

SHÀNGHǍI STUDIO
GAY BAR

Map p306 (嘉浓休闲; Jiānóng Xiūxián; www.shanghai-studio.com; No 4, Lane 1950, Middle Huaihai Rd; 淮海中路1950弄4号; ⏰9pm-2am;

Ⓜ Jiaotong University) This hip addition to the Shànghǎi gay scene has transformed the cool depths of a former bomb shelter into a laid-back bar, an art gallery, and a men's underwear shop – MANifesto (open from 2pm to 2am). There's a ¥100 open bar on Thursday and wine at ¥99 a bottle on Wednesdays.

TIME PASSAGE
BAR

Map p306 (昨天今天明天; Zuótiān Jīntiān Míngtiān; No 183, Lane 1038, Caojiayan Rd; 曹家堰路1038弄183号; ⏰4.30pm-2am; ☎; Ⓜ Jiangsu Rd) Smacked by backhand volleys and aces from the adjacent tennis courts, Time Passage has real staying power, clocking up almost 20 years in the business of cheap beer and good music. Beyond its no-nonsense Gucci-free vibe – not a suit in sight – it's a relaxing, down-to-earth spot for an evening beer or a daytime coffee.

There's live music on Friday and Saturday nights, and a daily happy hour from 5.30pm to 7.30pm.

SASHA'S
BAR

Map p306 (萨沙; Sàshā; ☎6474 6628; 11 Dongping Rd, cnr Hengshan Rd; 东平路11号, 近衡山路; ⏰11am-2am; ☎; Ⓜ Changshu Rd, Hengshan Rd) Housed in a fine old mansion that once belonged to the Soong family, Sasha's large garden is one of Shànghǎi's most splendid summer spots. There's a pricey expat restaurant on the premises, but this place is renowned not so much for blow-out dinners as it is for the weekend brunches and outdoor lounging in warmer weather.

390 BAR
GAY CLUB

Map p306 (www.390shanghai.com; 390 Panyu Rd; 番禺路390号; ⏰6pm-late; ☎; Ⓜ Jiaotong University) One of the only LGBT clubs in Shànghǎi, the 390 Bar was opened up by the owner of Shànghǎi Studio and his partner, who runs local vinyl store Uptown Records. The club is divided into several sections, with live music, a dance floor and two bars.

YONGKANG ROAD BAR STREET

A new bar street suddenly formed – largely overnight – during 2013 in the French Concession, kicked off by the peerless Café des Stagiaires (p114), which still leads the way. The small strip of Yongkang Rd between South Xiangyang Rd and Jiashan Rd was suddenly crammed with bars, making it a convenient catch-all similar to Hong Kong's Lan Kwai Fong entertainment area (albeit much smaller and quieter) for a night on the Shànghǎi tiles. A pavement curfew at 10pm reigns, however, to appease locals living on the road, who were up in arms over the sudden, noisy transformation of their neighbourhood.

BEAVER   BAR

Map p306 (28 Yueyang Rd; 岳阳路28号; ⏲5.30pm-late; Ⓜ Chengshan Rd, Hengshan Rd) For a grungy ambience, this chipped and bruised bar gets straight to the point, hoovering up no-nonsense beer hounds with affordable booze, an undemanding music menu tilted towards US rock, and table football. A bottle of Xīnjiāng black beer will set you back ¥25 (less during happy hour).

 ENTERTAINMENT

MAO LIVEHOUSE   LIVE MUSIC

Map p302 (www.mao-music.com; 3rd fl, 308 South Chongqing Rd; 重庆南路308号3楼; Ⓜ Dapuqiao) One of the city's best and largest music venues, MAO is a stalwart of the Shànghǎi music scene, with acts ranging from rock to pop to electronica. Check the website for schedules and ticket prices.

JZ CLUB   LIVE MUSIC

Map p306 (☎6385 0269; www.jzclub.cn; 46 West Fuxing Rd; 复兴西路46号; ⏲9pm-2am; Ⓜ Changshu Rd) JZ is one of the best places in town for serious music lovers. The schedule rotates local and international groups, with sounds ranging from fusion, Latin and R&B to Chinese folk-jazz; music generally gets going around 9pm. There's a ¥50 cover on Monday, Friday and Saturday nights. It also organises the annual JZ Shànghǎi Jazz Festival.

COTTON CLUB   LIVE MUSIC

Map p306 (棉花俱乐部; Miánhuā Jùlèbù; ☎021 6437 7110; www.thecottonclub.cn; 8 West Fuxing Rd; 复兴西路8号; ⏲7.30pm-2am Tue-Sun; Ⓜ Changshu Rd) Harlem it ain't, but this is still the best and longest-running bar for live jazz in Shànghǎi. It features blues and jazz groups throughout the week. Wynton Marsalis once stepped in to jam, forever sealing the Cotton Club's reputation as the top live-music haunt in town. The music gets going around 9pm.

CATHAY THEATRE   CINEMA

Map p302 (国泰电影院; Guótài Diànyǐngyuàn; 870 Middle Huaihai Rd; 淮海中路870号; tickets from ¥40; Ⓜ South Shaanxi Rd) This 1932 art deco theatre is one of the cheaper and more centrally located French Concession cinemas. If you want to know if the film is in the original, ask if it's the *yuánbǎn* (原版) version.

SHÀNGHǍI CONSERVATORY
OF MUSIC   CLASSICAL MUSIC

Map p306 (上海音乐学院; Shànghǎi Yīnyuè Xuéyuàn; ☎64311792; 20 Fenyang Rd; 汾阳路20号; ⏲ticket office 9am-5pm; Ⓜ South Shaanxi Rd) The auditorium here holds classical-music performances (Chinese and Western) daily at 7.15pm, and the musicians are often the stars of the future. The ticket office (售票处; *shòupiàochù*) is in the southern part of the campus. Ask for directions once you're at the school.

SHANGHAI CULTURE SQUARE   THEATRE

Map p302 (上海文化广场; Shànghǎi Wénhuà Guǎngchǎng; 597 Middle Fuxing Rd; 复兴中路597号; Ⓜ South Shaanxi Rd) State-of-the-art theatrical facility with a focus on musicals, drama, ballet and classic traditional Chinese and international productions.

UME INTERNATIONAL CINEPLEX   CINEMA

Map p302 (国际影城; Guójì Yǐngchéng; www.ume.com.cn; Xīntiāndì South Block, 5th fl, Bldg 6; 新天地南里6号楼5楼; Ⓜ South Huangpi Rd) This thoroughly modern cinema complex at Xīntiāndì screens Hollywood and Chinese films, with half-price tickets during the day on Tuesdays.

SHÀNGHǍI GǓQÍN
CULTURAL FOUNDATION   CULTURAL CENTRE

Map p306 (上海古琴文化会; Shànghǎi Gǔqín Wénhuà Huì; ☎6437 4111; www.yhgy-guqin.com; 1801 Middle Huaihai Rd; 淮海中路1801号; ⏲9am-5pm; Ⓜ Shanghai Library) This cultural centre offers classes in a handful of traditional arts: Chinese ink painting, *wéiqí* (go) and the *gǔqín* (seven-string zither). It's possible to drop by just to visit the old 1930s villa, and on Friday nights there are sometimes free music performances at 7pm (call first).

🛍 SHOPPING

Huaihai Rd in the French Concession area is *the* modern shopping street in Shànghǎi. The avenue's packed with towering department stores and global chains. To seek out local boutiques and trendy shoe shops, however, head along leafy backstreets such as Nanchang or Xinle Rds. Xīntiāndì has plenty of high-end brands, but for sheer diversity, nothing beats Tiánzǐfáng, one of the best shopping destinations in the city.

French Concession East

★TIÁNZǏFÁNG CLOTHING, SOUVENIRS

Map p302 (田子坊; Lane 210, Taikang Rd; 泰康路210弄; MDapuqiao) Burrow into the *lǐlòng* (alleys) here for a rewarding haul of creative boutiques, selling everything from hip jewellery and yak-wool scarves to retro communist dinnerware. **Shànghǎi 1936** (Map p302; Unit 110, No 3, Lane 210; ⌚10am-8pm; MDapuqiao) is the place to pick up a tailored *wàitào* (Chinese jacket) or *qípáo* (figure-hugging Chinese dress); it also has a nearby **men's store** (Map p302; Unit 910, No 9, Lane 210; ⌚10am-8pm; MDapuqiao).

Further along is **Harvest** (Map p302; Rm 18, Bldg 3, Lane 210, Taikang Rd; 泰康路210弄3号楼118室田子坊; ⌚9.30am-8pm; MDapuqiao), which sells Miao embroidery from southwest China, and the courtyard at No 7, Lane 210 (aka the Yard): look for Himalayan jewellery and tapestries at **Joma** (Map p302; Unit 6, No 7, Lane 210, Taikang Rd; 泰康路210弄7号-6田子坊; MDapuqiao) and local fashion designers at La Vie (p120). For funky ceramics, cloisonné and lacquer, stop by excellent **Pilingpalang** (噼呤啪啷; Map p302; http://pilingpalang.com; No 220, Lane 210, Taikang Rd; 泰康路210弄22号田子坊; ⌚10am-9pm; MDapuqiao). Pop into colourful Link Shanghai (p119) for imaginative art work and books and Shanghai Code (p119) for vintage spectacle frames.

You'll find 1960s propaganda prints and old calendar posters at **Unique Hill Gallery** (Map p302; www.uniquehillgallery.com; No 10, Lane 210, Taikang Rd; 泰康路210弄10号田子坊; ⌚9am-10pm; MDapuqiao). The vibrant and colourful selection of crafts at **Esydragon** (Map p302; ☎021 6467 4818; No 51, Lane 210, Taikang Rd; 泰康路210弄51号田子坊; MDapuqiao) makes for excellent gifts; Zhēnchálín Tea (p119) has Chinese herbal teas in nifty packaging. Other stand-out stores are **Chouchou Chic** (Map p302; No 5, Lane 248, Taikang Rd; 泰康路248弄5号 ; MDapuqiao) and **Urban Tribe** (Map p302; No 14, Lane 248, Taikang Rd; 泰康路248弄14号; MDapuqiao).

★XĪNTIĀNDÌ CLOTHING, ACCESSORIES

Map p302 (新天地; www.xintiandi.com; 2 blocks btwn Taicang, Zizhong, Madang & South Huangpi Rds; 太仓路与马当路路口; MSouth Huangpi Rd, Xintiandi) There are few bargains to be had at Xīntiāndì, but even window-shoppers can make a fun afternoon of it here. The North Block features embroidered accessories at Annabel Lee (p120), high-end fashion from Shanghai Tang (p120) and home furnishings at Simply Life (p120) and a few scattered souvenir shops. The South Block has not one, but two malls, including **Xīntiāndì Style** (新天地时尚; Xīntiāndì Shíshàng; Map p302; 245 Madang Rd; 马当路245号).

Serious shoppers should make for Xīntiāndì Style, which features a handful of local designers including La Vie, Heirloom, the Thing, Shànghǎi Trio, Even Penniless and Xi Su.

LIÚLI CHINA MUSEUM SHOP ARTS & CRAFTS

Map p302 (琉璃艺术博物馆商店; Liúli Yìshù Bówùguǎn Shāngdiàn; 25 Taikang Rd; 泰康路25号; ⌚10am-10pm Tue-Sun; MDapuqiao) At this crystal art shop you can marvel at iridescent cast-glass creations such as contemplative monks, majestic dragons or exquisite earrings and pendants, or browse through the quality collection of English-language books and other knick-knacks.

LINK SHANGHAI ARTS & CRAFTS

Map p302 (搭界; Dājiè; www.olinksh.com; No 5, Lane 248, Taikang Rd, Tiánzǐfáng; 泰康路248弄5号田子坊; ⌚10.30am-9pm; MDapuqiao) This tiny and colourful shop for local designers and artists always has something fascinating going on, from the rivetingly good surreal paintings of Shan Jiang to eye-catching books, notepads, posters and the fun 'letter girl' T-shirts.

ZHĒNCHÁLÍN TEA TEA

Map p302 (臻茶林; Zhēnchálín; No 13, Lane 210, Taikang Rd, Tiánzǐfáng; 泰康路210弄13号田子坊; ⌚10am-8.30pm; MDapuqiao) From the entrance this looks like just another tea shop, but poke around inside and you'll find specially blended herbal teas from Ayako, a traditional Chinese medicine–certified nutritionist. Peruse the hand-wrapped *puerh* teas, ceramic and crystal teaware and water-colour postcards of Shànghǎi while staff ply you with tiny cups of ginseng oolong to keep you lingering.

SHANGHAI CODE VINTAGE

Map p302 (上海密码; Shànghǎi Mìmǎ; No 9, Lane 274, Taikang Rd, Tiánzǐfáng; 泰康路274弄9号田子坊; ⌚2.30-9.30pm; MDapuqiao) This kooky Tiánzǐfáng shop sells rows of vintage-style glasses frames, old alarm clocks and duffed-up old spectacles cases. Frames kick off from around ¥300.

LA VIE
CLOTHING

Map p302 (生; Shēng; ☑6445 3585; Tiánzǐfáng, The Yard, No 7, Lane 210, Taikang Rd; 泰康路210弄7号13室; ◎10.30am-8.30pm; Ⓜ Dapuqiao) Local designer Jenny Ji has made a name for herself with her stylish take on street fashion, including patterned jeans and nicely cut shirts, and clothing blending art deco glamour with traditional Chinese charms. None of it comes cheap, though: even the T-shirts go for a couple thousand *yuán* (¥). There are further shops at **306 Changle Road** (Map p302; 306 Changle Road; 长乐路306号; ◎1-10pm; Ⓜ South Shaanxi Rd) and in **Xīntiāndì Style** (Map p302; L 227, Xintiandi Style, 245 Madang Rd; 马当路245号新天地时尚; ◎10am-10pm).

AVOCADO LADY
FOOD & DRINK

Map p306 (红峰副食品商店; Hóngfēngfù Shípǐn Shāngdiàn; 274 South Wulumuqi Rd; 乌鲁木齐南路274号; ◎5.30am-9.30pm; Ⓜ Changshu Rd) If the eye-watering prices levied by some Shànghǎi importers of foreign foods and fruits drives you round the bend, join the scrum (literally) of expats at this small vegetable shop on South Wulumuqi Rd. There's fantastically priced bottles of wine piled up on the floor, avocados, mangoes, refrigerated imported cheeses, coffees, cereals and much more; it's crammed to the rafters with goods (and shoppers).

Colloquially, Shànghǎi shoppers call the owner the Avocado Lady, but her shop's Chinese name is Hóngfēngfù Shípǐn Shāngdiàn.

POTTERY WORKSHOP
CERAMICS

Map p302 (乐天陶社; Lètiān Táoshè; www.potteryworkshop.com.cn; Tiánzǐfáng, 220 Taikang Rd; 泰康路220号田子坊; ◎10am-8pm; Ⓜ Dapuqiao) Originally founded in Hong Kong, the Pottery Workshop is a community arts centre offering classes in ceramic design. The diverse creations of the workshop's resident artists – including those in China's ceramics capital Jǐngdézhèn – are on display in this shop at the entrance to Tiánzǐfáng.

ANNABEL LEE
ACCESSORIES

Map p302 (安梨家居; Ānlí Jiājū; Xīntiāndì North Block, Bldg 3; 太仓路181弄新天地里3号楼; ◎10.30am-10.30pm; Ⓜ South Huangpi Rd, Xintiandi) Xīntiāndì branch of this local designer where you'll find an emphasis on cashmere and silk, and a fine collection of scarves, shawls and purses.

SHANGHAI TANG
CLOTHING

Map p302 (上海滩; Shànghǎi Tān; Xīntiāndì North Block, Bldg 15; 太仓路181弄新天地北里15号楼; Ⓜ South Huangpi Rd) Hong Kong-based Shanghai Tang flies the flag for the Middle Kingdom in the world of high-end fashion. The designs are classic Chinese with a twist, incorporating fluorescent colours, traditional motifs and luxury fabrics such as silk and cashmere into the clothes and accessories. More affordable items include slinky tops and scarves, but if you have to ask the price of an item here, you probably can't afford it.

GIFT ZEN
GIFTS

Map p302 (钲艺廊; www.zenlifestore.com; L130, Xīntiāndì Style, 245 Madang Rd; 马当路245号新天地时尚L130; ◎10am-10pm; Ⓜ Xintiandi) Small but serene shop with a highly browse-worthy collection of design-led gift ideas with a modernist slant, including Frank Lloyd-Wright style bookmarks, pieces from the V&A and Tate Modern in London, MoMA in New York as well as some fabulous and eye-catching ceramics and cloisonné.

SHÀNGHǍI TRIO
ACCESSORIES, CLOTHING

Map p302 (上海组合; Shànghǎi Zǔhé; Store 129, Xīntiāndì Style, 245 Madang Rd; 马当路245号新天地时尚129屋; ◎10am-10pm; Ⓜ Xintiandi) *Ravissant! C'est tout moi!* French women go crazy for the chic ecofriendly fabrics here, which incorporate traditional Chinese motifs into much of the collection. Among the finds: cute children's clothes, purses, scarves and quilt (duvet) covers. It's located in the Xīntiāndì Style mall.

SHÀNGHǍI MUSEUM SHOP
GIFTS

Map p302 (上海博物馆商店; 123 Taicang Rd; 太仓路123号; ◎11am-7pm; Ⓜ South Huangpi Rd) A two-floor outpost of the excellent Shànghǎi Museum Art Store, with a choice selection of ceramics, calligraphy brushes, jade and other collectibles.

SIMPLY LIFE
HOMEWARES

Map p302 (逸居生活; Yìjū Shēnghuó; ☑6387 5100; Xīntiāndì North Block, Unit 101, 159 Madang Rd; 马当路159号新天地北里101单元; ◎10.30am-10pm; Ⓜ South Huangpi Rd, Xintiandi) Upmarket household knick-knacks, including hand-painted teasets, crockery and pottery, all locally made.

HEIRLOOM ACCESSORIES

Map p302 (78 Xinle Rd; 新乐路78号; ⊙10.30am-10pm; Ⓜ South Shaanxi Rd) Heirloom's staple is a range of eye-catching, vibrant and stylish clutches, satchels and handbags, as well as smaller accessories such as leather wallets and bracelets. Prices range from ¥195 for a coin purse to around ¥4000.

CHOUCHOU CHIC CLOTHING

Map p302 (喆缤豆小童生活馆; Zhébīndòu Xiǎotóng Shēnghuó Guǎn; www.chouchouchic. com; 164 South Shaanxi Rd; 陕西南路164号; Ⓜ South Shaanxi Rd) French Chinese hybrid Chouchou Chic sells kids' clothes (up to age eight) that are infinitely cuter than what you find at the souvenir stalls. Most of the clothing is Western-style, but you can find some attractive floral-patterned fabrics and Chinese-style cotton dresses as well. Prices start at ¥148; the entrance is on Changle Rd.

100 CHANGE & INSECT SHOES

Map p302 (百变虫; Bǎibiànchóng; 318 Nanchang Rd; 南昌路318号; ⊙10.30am-10.30pm; Ⓜ South Shaanxi Rd) Strange name, funky footwear – for those who want to add sparkle to their tootsies and have their heels seen in the dark. Browse Hong Kong designs blinged up with rhinestones, sequins, pink glitter, and silver and gold accents. There's another branch at **76 Xinle Rd** (百变虫; Bǎibiànchóng; Map p302; ☑021 5404 0767; 76 Xinle Road; 新乐路76号; ⊙10.30am-10pm; Ⓜ South Shaanxi Rd). No English name on the door.

YÚNWÚXĪN JEWELLERY

Map p302 (云无心; 142 Nanchang Rd; 南昌路142号; ⊙11am-9pm; Ⓜ South Shaanxi Rd) Drop by this incense-filled boutique to peruse the collection of handmade Tibetan-themed jewellery, fashioned from mother-of-pearl, red coral and turquoise.

PCS (POP CLASSIC SNEAKERS) SHOES

Map p302 (130 Nanchang Rd; 南昌路130号; ⊙1-10pm; Ⓜ South Shaanxi Rd) This tiny shoebox of a store has a fantastic collection of men's canvas sneakers, all sold at unbeatable prices. Try on a pair of original Feiyue, Warrior or spruced-up Ospop worker boots.

XI SU CLOTHING

Map p302 (熙素; http://xisushanghai.com; 425 Xīntiāndì Style, 245 Madang Rd; 马当路245号新天地时尚; ⊙10am-10pm; Ⓜ Xintiandi) Delightfully elegant, diaphanous and light women's clothing in a mix of classical Chinese and traditional lines.

HUĀYÀNG NIÁNHUÁ CLOTHING

Map p302 (花样年华; 145 South Maoming Rd; 茂名南路145号; ⊙11am-9pm; Ⓜ South Shaanxi Rd) Huāyàng Niánhuá takes its name from the Chinese title of the smouldering Wong Kar Wai movie *In the Mood for Love,* which featured Hong Kong actress Maggie Cheung in an array of stunning *qípáo* (figure-hugging Chinese dresses). Fittingly, you can get fine tailor-made *qípáo* here from ¥1200, but

FRENCH CONCESSION SHOPPING

TEA TASTING

It may be a rather clichéd choice, but there's no doubt that a Yíxīng teapot and a package of oolong tea makes for a convenient gift. But how do you go about a purchase? Two things to remember: first of all, be sure to taste (品尝; *pīncháng*) and compare several different teas – flavours vary widely, and there's no point in buying a premium grade if you don't like it. Tasting is free (免费; *miǎnfèi*) and fun, but it's good form to make some sort of purchase afterwards. Second, tea is generally priced by the *jīn* (斤; 500g), which may be more tea than you can finish in a year. Purchase several *liǎng* (两; 50g) instead – divide the list price by 10 for an idea of the final cost. Some of the different types of tea for sale include oolong (*wūlóng*), green (*lǜ*), flower (*huā*) and pu-erh (*pǔ'ěr*) – true connoisseurs have a different teapot for each type of tea.

Try the following stores:

Huìfēng Tea Shop (汇丰茶庄; Huìfēng Cházhuāng; Map p302; ☑021 6472 7196; 124 South Maoming Rd; 茂名南路124号; ⊙9am-9.30pm; Ⓜ South Shaanxi Rd)

Yányè Míngchá (严叶茗茶; Map p306; 170 Fumin Rd, 富民路170号; ⊙8am-10pm; Ⓜ Jing'an Temple)

Tiānshān Tea City (p176)

Zhēnchálín Tea (p119)

there's no guarantee you'll look like Ms Cheung once you slip one on.

GARDEN BOOKS   BOOKS
Map p302 (韬奋西文书局; Tāofèn Xīwén Shūjú; 325 Changle Rd; 长乐路325号; ◎10am-10pm; 📷; Ⓜ South Shaanxi Rd) The ice-cream parlour occupies about as much space as its well-stocked bookshelves. For all those Penguin paperback, gelato-to-go moments.

THING   CLOTHING
Map p302 (276 Changle Rd; 长乐路276号; ◎10am-9pm; Ⓜ South Shaanxi Rd) Shànghǎi urbanwear specialists: hoodies, messenger bags, shoes and Chinglish T-shirts.

APPLE STORE   ELECTRONICS
Map p302 (Hong Kong Plaza North Block, 282 Middle Huaihai Rd; 淮海中路282号香港广场北座; ◎10am-10pm; 📷; Ⓜ South Huangpi Rd) Stop by the Genius Bar for advice or troubleshooting, get online or browse the latest wonders of the tech world in this two-floor (genuine) Apple outlet.

FÓ GUĀNG   ARTS & CRAFTS
Map p302 (佛光; 594 South Shaanxi Rd; 陕西南路594号; ◎11am-8pm; Ⓜ Jiashan Rd) Permeated with the aroma of incense and sedated by Buddhist music, this tiny shop has an abundance of Tibetan Buddhist mystery: statuettes, *dorjes* (ritual objects; from ¥400), jade amulets, pendants, bracelets and other accoutrements. The name literally means 'Light of the Buddha'.

XĪNGGUĀNG PHOTOGRAPHY EQUIPMENT   PHOTOGRAPHY
(星光摄影器材城; Xīngguāng Shèyǐng Qìcái Chéng; 288 Luban Rd; 淮海中路288号; ◎7am-7pm; Ⓜ Dapuqiao, Luban Rd) There are three main floors of photography equipment here. While prices vary (you need to bargain; no guarantees) there are some good buys awaiting among the cameras, lenses, tripods and bags. A real find is Shen-Hao (申豪) on the 4th floor, which sells its hard-to-find field cameras. There's a repair shop on the 3rd floor.

YĚ HUŎ HÙWÀI YÒNGPĬN DIÀN   OUTDOOR EQUIPMENT
Map p302 (野火户外用品店; 296 Changle Rd; 长乐路296号; ◎10.30am-10pm; Ⓜ South Shaanxi Rd) A great stop for outdoor gear. Osprey packs and Vasque boots are available, in addition to quality Gore-Tex clothing, tents and sleeping bags.

LA FORMAGGERIA   FOOD
Map p302 (芙蕾玛吉亚; Fú Lái Mǎ Jí Yà; www.vivi shanghai.com/shop; 434 South Shaanxi Rd; 陕西南路434号; ◎10am-9pm; Ⓜ South Shaanxi Rd) This *piccolo* Italian cheese shop is at hand for all your crucial mozzarella, Gran Moravia, Grana Padano and mascarpone needs.

LOMOGRAPHY   PHOTOGRAPHY
Map p302 (www.lomography.com; 126 Jinxian Rd; 进贤路126号; ◎noon-9pm Sun-Thu, to 10pm Fri & Sat; Ⓜ South Shaanxi Rd) Analogue camera and film buffs will enjoy this shop ranging

---

BEST SHOPPING STRIPS

Looking for the best spots in Shanghai's French Concession to wander and window-shop? Around the South Shaanxi Rd metro station there are a few blocks that are a must for serious clothes shoppers. Afternoons and evenings are the best hours for browsing: some smaller shops don't open their doors until noon, but most stay open until 10pm.

➡ **Nanchang Road** A good street for general browsing, with shoes, antiques, and men's and women's clothing.

➡ **Changle Road** Young designers and emerging local brands have taken over a one-block stretch of Changle Rd east of Ruijin No 1 Rd. Check out La Vie (p120), Thing (p122), **Eblis Hungi** (Map p302; No 139-18, Changle Rd; ◎noon-10pm) and **Even Penniless** (Map p302; No 139, Changle Rd) to see where local fashion is headed.

➡ **Xinle Road** This two-block stretch has less-high-end fashion than Changle Rd but ultimately greater variety. Pop into Heirloom (p121), 100 Change & Insect (p121), **Source** (Map p306; No 158, Xinle Rd) and NuoMi (p123) for a taste of the 'Hai's urban style.

➡ **South Maoming Road** South of Huaihai Rd you'll find custom-tailored traditional women's clothing (such as the *qípáo*; figure-hugging Chinese dress); north of Huaihai Rd there's tailored men's suits and dress shoes.

over multiple floors with bundles of photographic accessories, a big range of film (colour, slide, black-and-white and infrared), lenses, nondigital cameras, bags, hoodies, cotton T-shirts and more.

🏠 French Concession West

⭐ NUOMI
CLOTHING

Map p306 (糯米; Nuòmǐ; www.nuomishanghai.com; 196 Xinle Rd; 新乐路196号; ⏱11am-10pm; Ⓜ Changshu Rd) This Shànghǎi-based label seems to do everything right: gorgeous dresses made from organic cotton, silk and bamboo; eye-catching jewellery fashioned from recycled materials; a sustainable business plan that gives back to the community; and even an irresistible line of kids' clothes.

⭐ PILINGPALANG
CERAMICS

Map p306 (噼吟啪啷; Pīlìngpālāng; www.pilingpalang.com; 183 Anfu Rd; 安福路183号; Ⓜ Changshu Rd) Gorgeously coloured and trendy ceramics, cloisonné and lacquer, in pieces that celebrate traditional Chinese forms while adding a funky modern and deco-inspired slant.

⭐ OOAK CONCEPT BOUTIQUE
JEWELLERY

Map p302 (OOAK设计师品牌概念店; OOAK Shèjìshī Pǐnpái Gàiniàndiàn; www.theooak.com; 124 Taiyuan Rd; 太原路124号; ⏱11am-9pm; Ⓜ Jiashan Rd, Hengshan Rd) Tall and skinny OOAK ('One of a Kind') has three floors of inspiring jewellery; catchy and attractive modern clothing for women; and bags and shoes from a host of talented big-name and aspiring independent designers from Europe and far flung parts of the globe.

⭐ LOLO LOVE VINTAGE
VINTAGE

Map p306 (2 Yongfu Rd; 永福路2号; ⏱noon-10pm; Ⓜ Shanghai Library, Changshu Rd) There's rock and roll on the stereo and a huge white rabbit, stuffed peacock and plastic cactus outside at this whacky shrine to vintage 1940s and '50s glad rags, behind the blue steel door on Yongfu Rd. It's stuffed with frocks, blouses, tops, shoes, brooches and sundry togs spilling from hangers, shelves and battered suitcases. There's a lovely garden out the front, where an old worn sofa sits.

XINLELU.COM
CLOTHING

Map p306 (www.xinlelu.com; 87 Wuyuan Rd; 五原路87号; ⏱noon-10pm Tue-Sun; Ⓜ Changshu Rd)

Local style mavens XinleLu.com have ventured out into the offline world with this original showroom, displaying the best of their hand-picked bags, shoes and dresses from local designers.

BROCADE COUNTRY
HANDICRAFTS

Map p306 (锦绣纺; Jǐnxiù Fǎng; 616 Julu Rd; 巨鹿路616号; ⏱10am-7.30pm; Ⓜ South Shaanxi Rd) Peruse an exquisite collection of minority handicrafts from China's southwest, most of which are secondhand (ie not made for the tourist trade) and personally selected by the owner Liu Xiaolan, a Guìzhōu native. Items for sale include embroidered wall hangings (some of which were originally baby carriers), sashes, shoes and hats, as well as silver jewellery. The butterfly, a homonym for 'mother' in the Miao language, is a popular motif.

BA YAN KA LA
BEAUTY

Map p306 (巴颜喀拉; Bā Yán Kā Lā; www.bayankala.com; 1221 Changle Rd; 长乐路1221号; ⏱10am-9pm; Ⓜ Changshu Rd) Taking its name from the Tibetan mountain range that separates the Yellow and Yangzi watersheds, Ba Yan Ka La offers a line of natural beauty products derived from Chinese herbs. Goji berry (skin revitalisation), lotus seed (skin nourishment) and mulberry (detoxification) are all familiar ingredients in traditional Chinese medicine, and match well with Ba Yan Ka La's natural elegance. The scented candles, shampoos, Tibetan (crystal of wisdom) bath salts and facial scrubs can also be found in several hotels around town.

PARAMITA
HANDICRAFTS

Map p306 (波罗蜜多西藏工艺品; Bōluómìduō Xīzàng Gōngyìpǐn; ☎6248 2148; 850-851 Julu Rd; 巨鹿路850-1号; Ⓜ Changshu Rd, Jing'an Temple) If you can't make it to Tibet, at least swing by Paramita for its inspiring collection of souvenirs, including yak-bone amulets, masks, jewellery, framed mandalas and other Buddhist treasures from the Himalayas. It's a nonprofit organisation, founded to help Tibetans with minimal education find employment.

IAPM MALL
MALL

Map p302 (999 Middle Huaihai Rd; 淮海中路999号; ⏱10am-11pm; Ⓜ South Shaanxi Rd) There are top names (Stella McCartney, Alexander McQueen, Prada) in this high-end mall, but it's worth a look for the spectacular and well-considered interior design alone.

MADAME MAO'S DOWRY
CLOTHING, SOUVENIRS

Map p306 (毛太设计; Máotài Shèjì; ☎5403 3551; madamemaosdowry.com; 207 Fumin Rd; 富民路 207号; ◉10am-7pm; Ⓜ Jing'an Temple) What better way to brighten up your hall than with a bust of chairman Mao? Or a poster of jubilant socialist workers? Beyond the Cultural Revolution paintings and prints, there's a collection of locally designed clothing and jewellery and some fantastic cards.

POTTERY WORKSHOP
CERAMICS

Map p306 (乐天陶社; Lètiàn Táoshè; www.potteryworkshop.com.cn; 176 Fumin Rd; 富民路176 号; ◉10am-8pm; Ⓜ Jing'an Temple) A retail shop from Shànghǎi's community ceramics centre.

URBAN TRIBE
CLOTHING

Map p306 (城市山民; Chéngshì Shānmín; 133 West Fuxing Rd; 复兴西路133号; Ⓜ Shanghai Library) Urban Tribe draws inspiration from the ethnic groups of China and Southeast Asia. The collection of loose-fitting blouses, pants and jackets are made of natural fabrics, and are a refreshing departure from the city's on-the-go attitude and usual taste for flamboyance. Don't miss the collection of silver jewellery, nor the lovely tea garden behind the store.

CULTURE MATTERS
SHOES

Map p306 (15 Dongping Rd; 东平路15号; ◉1-9pm; Ⓜ Hengshan Rd, Changshu Rd) Sneaker freaks should stop by this small Dongping Rd shop to ogle its fine selection of funky Feiyue and Warrior trainers.

MAYUMI SATO
CLOTHING

Map p306 (www.mayumisato.com; 169 Anfu Rd; 安福路169号; ◉10am-7pm; Ⓜ Changshu Rd) Japanese designer Mayumi Sato uses organic cotton, silk and wool to create a playful collection of limited-edition skirts, dresses and tops. Nothing is mass produced, and off-cuts are recycled into her line of signature accessories.

SIMPLY LIFE
HOMEWARES

Map p306 (逸居生活; Yìjū Shēnghuó; 9 Dongping Rd; 东平路9号; ◉10.30am-10.30pm; Ⓜ Changshu Rd) A branch of the local home-furnishings store, with neat and stylish household knick-knacks and ceramics.

PROPAGANDA POSTER ART CENTRE
ARTS & CRAFTS, SOUVENIRS

Map p306 (上海宣传画艺术中心; Shànghǎi Xuānchuánhuà Yìshù Zhōngxīn; ☎139 0184 1246, 6211 1845; Rm B-OC, 868 Huashan Rd; 华山路 868号B-OC房间; admission ¥20; ◉10am-5pm; Ⓜ Shanghai Library) If socialist art is your thing, check out this gallery, which houses a huge collection of propaganda posters. Increasingly prized by collectors, some posters are very rare and prices are correspondingly high.

SPOILED BRAT
JEWELLERY

Map p306 (www.spoiledbratjewelry.com; No6, Lane 123, Yanqing Rd; 延庆路123弄6号; ◉11am-8pm;

TRADITIONAL CHINESE MASSAGE

In the 17th and 18th centuries, Qing-dynasty barbers developed the current form of Chinese massage, known as tuīná (推拿; literally push-grab). In addition to cutting hair, skilled barbers learned to use acupressure points to treat different ailments and the practice, which was cheaper, less painful and safer than acupuncture, soon became quite popular – even late Qing emperors employed tuīná masseurs. In 1822, the Daoguang emperor decried acupuncture as unsafe and banned the practice, helping tuīná to secure its position as an integral part of Chinese medical treatment.

The general idea behind Chinese massage is that it stimulates your qì (vital energy that flows along different pathways or meridians, each of which is connected to a major organ) and removes energy blockages, through which you can treat specific ailments, from muscular and joint pain to the common cold.

Interestingly, the hairdresser-massage association is still quite common in China, though the roles have again changed: many businesses that advertise themselves as hairdressers are now nothing more than brothels, with rows of young girls seated beneath lurid pink lighting waiting to provide 'massage services' to their clients. This doesn't mean that tuīná has disappeared – getting a real massage has never been easier, and in Shànghǎi, they come at a fraction of the price you'd pay at home.

Ⓜ Changshu Rd) This bijou shop sells a fine selection of exquisite jewellery pieces styled with refinement and an understated, classical temperament.

KAVA KAVA   FURNITURE
Map p306 (www.kavakavahome.com; 810 Julu Rd; 巨鹿路810号; ⊙10am-6pm; Ⓜ Jing'an Temple) Seriously good-looking modern but traditionally styled lacquer cabinets, chairs, tables and cabinets.

PARSONS MUSIC   MUSIC
Map p302 (柏斯琴行; Bǎisī Qínháng; 16 Fenyang Rd; 汾阳路16号; Ⓜ Changshu Rd, South Shaanxi Rd) All your musical instrument needs are met at this professional store near the Shànghǎi Conservatory of Music. You'll find mouth organs to *pípá* (lute), *èrhú* (two-stringed fiddle), *gǔzhēng* (zither), trumpets, violins, flutes and pianos – brand new and some secondhand. This section of Fenyang Rd is stuffed with small music shops – hunt around and you can pick up fantastically cheap, quality handmade violins.

HAPPY CLAY   CERAMICS
Map p302 (Donghu Rd; 东湖路; ⊙noon-9pm Tue-Sun; Ⓜ South Shaanxi Rd) Small shop displaying fun, wonky and naively fashioned handmade ceramic pieces; it's at the end of the alley by ElEfante.

🏃 SPORTS & ACTIVITIES

★ DOUBLE RAINBOW MASSAGE HOUSE   MASSAGE
Map p302 (双彩虹保健按摩厅; Shuāng Cǎihóng Bǎojiàn Ànmó Tīng; 45 Yongjia Rd; 永嘉路45号; massage ¥68; ⊙noon-midnight; Ⓜ South Shaanxi Rd) Perhaps Shànghǎi's best neighbourhood massage parlour. The visually impaired masseuses here will have you groaning in agony in no time as they seek out those little visited pressure points. It's ¥68 for a 45-minute foot or back massage.

SUBCONSCIOUS DAY SPA   MASSAGE
Map p306 (桑格水疗会所; Sāngkē Shuǐliáo Huìsuǒ; ☑6415 0636; www.subconsciousday spa.com; 183 Fumin Rd; 富民路183号; massage per 60/90 minutes ¥150/225; ⊙10am-midnight; Ⓜ Changshu Rd, Jing'an Temple) The scent of lemongrass fills the air as you enter this serene ecofriendly spa. A veritable centre for mind-body rejuvenation, Subconscious offers an array of traditional massages, from *tuīná* (traditional) and hot-stone to Thai, as well as six-person yoga classes, nutrition counselling and beauty treatments such as manicures and waxing.

DRAGONFLY   MASSAGE
Map p306 (悠庭保健会所; Yōutíng Bǎojiàn Huìsuǒ; ☑5403 9982; www.dragonfly.net.cn; 206 Xinle Road; 新乐路206号; massage per 60 mins ¥188; ⊙10am-2am; Ⓜ South Shaanxi Rd) One of the longest-running massage services in Shànghǎi, the soothing Dragonfly offers Chinese body massages, foot massages and Japanese-style shiatsu in addition to more specialised services such as aroma oil massages and beauty treatments. Prices include a private room and a change of clothes. Book ahead.

GREEN MASSAGE   MASSAGE
Map p302 (青籁养; Qīnglài Yǎngshén; ☑5386 0222; www.greenmassage.com.cn; 58 Taicang Rd; 太仓路58号; massages & spa treatments ¥198-318; ⊙10.30am-2am; Ⓜ South Huangpi Rd) Calming fragrances envelop guests at this plush midrange spa, which offers foot, *tuīná* (traditional) and shiatsu massages. In addition to traditional practices such as cupping and moxibustion, it also provides waxing and other beauty treatments. Reserve ahead.

LÓNGWǓ KUNG FU CENTER   MARTIAL ARTS
Map p302 (龙武功夫馆; Lóngwǔ Gōngfu Guǎn; ☑6287 1528; www.longwukungfu.com; 1 South Maoming Rd; 茂名南路1号; 1-/2-/3-month lesson ¥100/450/700; Ⓜ South Shaanxi Rd) Hone your rusty Wing Chun *bong sao,* brush up on your Taekwondo *poomsae* or simply learn a few taichi moves to help slip aboard the bus at rush hour. The largest centre in the city, it also offers children's classes on weekend mornings and lessons in English.

WǓYÌ CHINESE KUNGFU CENTRE   MARTIAL ARTS
Map p302 (武懿国术馆; Wǔyì Guóshù Guǎn; ☑137 0168 5893; Room 311, 3rd fl, International Artists' Factory, No 3, Lane 210, Taikang Rd; 法租界泰康路210弄3号3楼311; Ⓜ Dapuqiao) English-language taichi classes on Thursdays and Sundays and *wǔshù* (martial arts) classes on Wednesdays and Sundays for adults and kids. Call for the latest schedules and prices.

Jìng'ān

WEST NANJING ROAD | SHÀNGHǍI RAILWAY STATION

Neighbourhood Top Five

❶ Fathom the fantastic at Shànghǎi's most sacred shrine, the **Jade Buddha Temple** (p128).

❷ Catch up with the latest trends in the Chinese art world at postindustrial **M50** (p129).

❸ Delve into the *lǐlòng* lanes of the **Bubbling Well Road Apartments** (p135) on our walking tour.

❹ Pixelate the **Jìng'ān Temple** (p130) against a skyscraper backdrop.

❺ Catch the acrobats at the **Shànghǎi Centre Theatre** (p140).

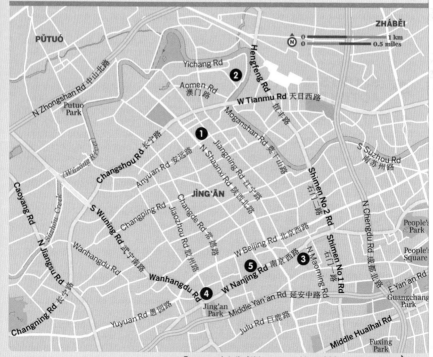

For more detail of this area see Map p309 and Map p310 ➡

Explore: Jìng'ān

In the early days of the International Settlement, West Nanjing Rd was known as Bubbling Well Rd; its far western end was where city stopped and countryside began. By the swinging 1920s, the fields were being swallowed up by the rapidly expanding city, and Bubbling Well Rd was one of Shànghǎi's busiest and most exclusive streets. Apart from its name, not much has changed since then. The main thoroughfare of today's Jìng'ān district (静安), West Nanjing Rd today is the address of some of the city's glitziest malls, high-end shops and five-star hotels.

Pǔdōng may have taller towers and the French Concession more charm, but this part of Jìng'ān is still the city's most exclusive neighbourhood. Even the skyscrapers here suggest harmony – a change from the disjointed skyline in other districts – while the traditional *lòng* (alleyways) are unexpectedly well preserved. The heart of all the consumer action is the Shànghǎi Centre, a focal point both for tourists and the many expats who work in the district.

Head north of West Nanjing Rd and you're plunged into grittier, more authentic areas. The first stop on many tours of Jìng'ān is the Jade Buddha Temple. A short hike to the north from here are the M50 art galleries along Sūzhōu Creek. Good streets to explore for a taste of an authentic working-class Shànghǎi neighbourhood include the bustling Jiangning and North Shaanxi Rds.

Local Life

→ **Temple life** Join worshippers at the Jade Buddha (p128) and Jìng'ān Temple (p130), followed by a Buddhist vegetarian meal.

→ **Art** Join the Shànghǎi Chinese looking at art in edgy M50 (p129).

→ **Snack attack** When the munchies strike, follow the crowds to Wujiang Road Food Street (p138).

Getting There & Away

→ **Metro** Line 2 runs parallel to West Nanjing Rd, stopping at People's Sq, West Nanjing Rd, Jing'an Temple and Jiangsu Rd. Line 7 runs north–south and intersects with line 2 at Jing'an Temple and line 1 at Changshu Rd in the French Concession. When completed, line 13 will link Changshou Rd in north Jìng'ān with West Nanjing Rd.

→ **Bus** Bus 19 links the North Bund area to the Jade Buddha Temple area; catch it at the intersection of Tiantong and North Sichuan Rds. Bus 112 zigzags north from the southern end of People's Sq to West Nanjing Rd, and up Jiangning Rd to the Jade Buddha Temple.

Lonely Planet's Top Tip

Jìng'ān has some remarkably well-preserved *lòng* (alleyways). The gentrified Bubbling Well Road Apartments are a great place to start exploration, and architecture buffs should also seek out the handful of lanes off Yuyuan Rd in the west of the district, particularly those at Nos 395 and 361, near the intersection with West Beijing Rd.

✖ Best Places to Eat

→ Wujiang Road Food Street (p138)
→ Commune Social (p136)
→ Jen Dow Vegetarian Restaurant (p131)
→ Sumerian (p131)
→ Fu 1088 (p138)

For reviews, see p131. ➡

🍷 Best Places to Drink

→ Fennel Lounge (p139)
→ Kāibā (p139)
→ Malone's (p139)
→ Spot (p139)
→ B&C (p139)

For reviews, see p139. ➡

🏃 Best Sports & Activities

→ Apsara Spa (p142)
→ Green Massage (p142)
→ Oz Body Fit (p142)

For reviews, see p142. ➡

JÌNG'ĀN

TOP SIGHT
JADE BUDDHA TEMPLE

One of Shànghǎi's few active Buddhist monasteries, this temple was built between 1918 and 1928. The highlight is a transcendent Buddha crafted from pure jade, one of five shipped back to China by the monk Hui Gen at the turn of the 20th century. In February, during the Lunar New Year, the temple is very busy, as some 20,000 Chinese Buddhists throng to pray for prosperity.

Entrance Courtyard
Festooned with red lanterns, the first courtyard is located between the **Hall of Heavenly Kings** and the twin-eaved **Great Treasure Hall**, where worshippers pray to the past, present and future buddhas. Also within the main hall are splendidly carved *luóhàn* (arhats), lashed to the walls with wires and a copper-coloured statue of Guanyin at the rear.

Jade Buddha Hall
Follow the right-hand corridor past the Hall of Heavenly Kings and the Guanyin Hall to arrive at the **Jade Buddha Hall** (admission ¥10). The absolute centrepiece of the temple is the 1.9m-high pale-green jade Buddha, seated upstairs. Photographs are not permitted.

Other Halls & Sights
Near the Jade Buddha Hall downstairs are the **Hall of Manjusri Bodhisattva**, to whom students pray before exams, and the **Hall of Ksitigarbha Bodhisattva**, lord of the Buddhist underworld. Both halls stand before the Ancestral Hall. At the rear of the temple is the peaceful **Jingyi Pool** (净意潭; Jìngyì Tán), which swarms with koi and multicoloured floating artificial lotus blooms, its floor glittering with coins.

DON'T MISS...

➡ Hall of Heavenly Kings
➡ Great Treasure Hall
➡ Jade Buddha Hall

PRACTICALITIES

➡ 玉佛寺; Yùfó Sì
➡ Map p309
➡ cnr Anyuan & Jiangning Rds; 安远路和江宁路街口
➡ admission high/low season ¥20/10
➡ ⏱ 8am-4.30pm
➡ 🚌 19 from Broadway Mansions along Tiantong Rd, Ⓜ Changshou Rd

HOLGER LEUE / GETTY IMAGES ©

TOP SIGHT
M50

Chinese contemporary art may not lead the international field, but it's long been boom-time in a market that came of age at the same time as China's economic drive hit the accelerator. Collectors around the globe are still paying top whack for the works of top Chinese artists. Edgier Běijīng still dominates the art scene, but swanky Shànghǎi's own gallery subculture is centred on this complex of industrial buildings down dusty and graffiti-splashed Moganshan Rd in the north of town.

Although the artists who established the M50 are long gone, it's worth taking a half-day to visit the galleries here. There are a lot of mass-produced commercial prints (especially in buildings 3 and 4), but there are also some challenging, innovative galleries if you're persistent and explorative. Most galleries are open from 10am to 6pm; some close Monday.

DON'T MISS...

→ ShanghART
→ island6
→ m97

PRACTICALITIES

→ M50 创意产业集聚区; M50 Chuàngyì Chǎnyè Jíjùqū; FREE
→ Map p309
→ 50 Moganshan Rd; 莫干山路50号
→ M Shanghai Railway Station

Galleries & Shops

The most established gallery, **ShanghART** (Xiānggénà Huàláng; Map p309; www.shanghartgallery.com; Bldg 16 & 18; M50 创意产业集聚区16和18号楼) has a big, dramatic space to show the work of some of the 40 artists it represents. The forward-thinking and provocative **island6** (Map p309; www.island6.org; 2nd fl, Bldg 6: M50 创意产业集聚区6号楼2楼) focuses on collaborative works created in a studio behind the gallery; it has a smaller gallery on the 1st floor of building 7. Other notable galleries include **Other Gallery** (Map p309; Bldg 9: M50 创意产业集聚区9号楼) and **OFoto** (Map p309; 2nd fl, Bldg 13: M50 创意产业集聚区13号楼2楼), featuring China-related photography exhibitions. Across the street is **m97** (Map p309; www.m97gallery.com; 2nd fl, 97 Moganshan Rd; 莫干山路97号2楼), another innovative photography gallery. For paint and art materials, artists can visit Espace Pébéo (p142). For photo-developing courses and prints, pop into **Dark Room** (Map p309; ☎6276 9657; Rm 107, Bldg 17, 50 Moganshan Rd; M50 创意产业集聚区 17号楼 107 室).

◉ SIGHTS

◉ West Nanjing Road

JÌNG'ĀN TEMPLE
BUDDHIST TEMPLE

Map p310 (静安寺; Jìng'ān Sì; 1686-1688 West Nanjing Rd; 南京西路1686-1688号; admission ¥50; ⏰7.30am-5pm; Ⓜ Jing'an Temple) Its roof work an incongruous, shimmering mirage amid West Nanjing Rd's soaring skyscrapers, Jing'an Temple is a much-restored sacred portal to the Buddhist world that partially, at least, underpins this metropolis of 24 million souls. There are fewer devotees than at the neighbourhood's popular Jade Buddha Temple, but over a decade's restoration has fashioned a workable temple at the very heart of Shànghǎi. Its spectacular position among the district's soaring skyscrapers makes for eye-catching photos while the temple emanates an air of reverence.

Constructed largely of Burmese teak, the temple has some impressive statues, including a massive 8.8m-high, 15-tonne silver Buddha in the main **Mahavira Hall**; a 3.86m-high white jade Sakyamuni in the side halls; and a five-tonne Guanyin statue in the **Guanyin Hall**, carved from a 1000-year old camphor tree. The temple still rattles away to the sounds of construction, while in the bunker beneath the main hall is an unfinished space, housing 18 glittering *luóhàn* (arhats), but little else. The complex has been designed to incorporate shops and restaurants around its perimeter (including a fantastic vegetarian restaurant at the rear), which goes around the block. The ¥50 admission charge is steep, however, for such a modest and thoroughly modern place of worship.

Khi Vehdu, who ran Jìng'ān Temple in the 1930s, was one of the most remarkable figures of the time. The nearly 2m-tall abbot had a large following as well as seven concubines, each of whom had a house and a car. During the Cultural Revolution the temple was shorn of its Buddhist statues and transformed into a plastics factory before burning to the ground in 1972.

Good times to visit include the Festival of Bathing Buddha on the eighth day of the fourth lunar month and at the full moon.

FORMER RESIDENCE OF MAO ZEDONG
HISTORIC BUILDING

Map p310 (毛泽东旧居; Máo Zédōng Jiùjū; No 5-9, 120 North Maoming Rd; 茂名北路120 弄 5-9号;

SHÀNGHǍI'S COMMUNIST VESTIGES

In its bid to recast itself as a modern metropolis, Shànghǎi is at odds with its more mundane communist heritage. The colourless residue of the communist period – still nominally the presiding epoch, lest we forget – still lurks among the swell and neon of town like a CD at the bottom of the pile that no one plays any more. Nonetheless, middle-aged Chinese on the 'Red Tour' (红色旅游; Hóngsè Lǚyóu) of town get nostalgic at several places of note.

China's communist bandwagon first rolled out from the Site of the 1st National Congress of the CCP (p97), one of communist China's holiest places of pilgrimage, possibly on par with Mao Zedong's birthplace at Sháoshān in Húnán province.

A palpable air of sanctity hangs over the Former Residence of Mao Zedong (p130), a pretty *shíkùmén* (stone-gate house) that includes his bedroom, study and photos of the ex-chairman doing his thing. Others on the Chairman Mao trail can check out the building at 168 Anyi Rd (安义路168号), where the Great Helmsman once stayed in 1920.

Visits to Fùxīng Park (p97) turn up anachronistic statues of Karl Marx and Friedrich Engels, godfathers to China's communist destiny. Astonishingly, the effigies were only carved in 1985, when Marxist dogma in Shànghǎi was already irreversibly pear-shaped.

The Shànghǎi Exhibition Centre (p131) is a classic example of socialist bravado, and for a lavish blast of hardcore communist spin, pop into the Propaganda Poster Art Centre (p100). Then visit another notable stop on the heritage trail (though the architecture may be concession era), Zhou Enlai's Former Residence (p98). Don't overlook hunting down some of Shànghǎi's surviving slogans (p100) from the Cultural Revolution.

⊙9-11.30am&1-4.30pm; Ⓜ Jing'an Temple) FREE
The Great Helmsman Mao Zedong lived here in the latter half of 1924 with his second wife, Yang Kaihui, and their two children at the time, Anying and Anqing.

The residence has old photos and newspaper clippings on display, but for many foreigners the real highlight is the building itself, a beautiful example of *shíkùmén* (stone-gate house) architecture. A passport or mobile telephone number is required to enter.

SHÀNGHǍI
CHILDREN'S PALACE
ARCHITECTURE

Map p310 (少年宫; Shàonián Gōng; West Nanjing Rd; 南京西路; admission weekday/weekend ¥20/50; ⊙9-11.30am & 1.30-5pm Wed-Sun; ♿ Ⓜ Jing'an Temple) A striking, white two-storey 1920s building, this was formerly Kadoorie House, named after its wealthy Jewish owner. Architecture buffs can still peek in the rooms of Elly Kadoorie's 1920s mansion, once the site of Shànghǎi's most extravagant balls. It now hosts activities for children.

SHÀNGHǍI
EXHIBITION CENTRE
ARCHITECTURE

Map p310 (上海展览中心; Shànghǎi Zhǎnlǎn Zhōngxīn; ✆6279 0279; 1000 Middle Yan'an Rd; 延安中路1000号; Ⓜ Jing'an Temple) The hulking monolith of the Shànghǎi Exhibition Centre can be seen from West Nanjing Rd. It was built as the Palace of Sino-Soviet Friendship – a friendship that soon turned sour and even led to the brink of war in the 1960s. Architecture-lovers will appreciate its monumentality and bold, unsubtle Bolshevik strokes – there was a time when Pǔdōng was set to look like this. The site of the Exhibition Centre was originally the gardens of Jewish millionaire Silas Hardoon.

⊙ Shànghǎi Railway Station

JADE BUDDHA TEMPLE
BUDDHIST TEMPLE
See p128.

M50
GALLERY
See p129.

🍴 EATING

Business lunches and after-dinner drinks are the rule in Jìng'ān. Most of the dining options here have long been first-rate, and those on a culinary tour of Shànghǎi need to pack this area into their itinerary.

🍴 West Nanjing Road

★ JEN DOW VEGETARIAN
RESTAURANT
CHINESE, VEGETARIAN $

Map p310 (人道素菜小吃; Réndào Sùcài Xiǎochī; 153 Yuyuan Rd; 愚园路153号; mains from ¥18; ⊙9am-midnight; ♿; Ⓜ Jing'an Temple) Your body is a temple, they say, so treat it with respect by dining at this fab ground-floor meat-free eatery slung out behind the Jing'an Temple. You can slurp up a vast, tasty bowl of noodles densely sprinkled with crisp and fresh mushroom, bamboo shoots, cabbage and carrots for a mere ¥18 – it's a meal in itself.

Also at hand are vegetarian hotpots and a host of other choices, plus egg tarts and other baked delicacies at the door. Order fast-food style from the counter. Upstairs, the smarter 2nd floor – with glass jars of herbs and dried grains lining the walls – is a civilised and tasty choice, and has a Chinese and Western menu. The blistering and salty *mápó dòufu* (tofu and pork crumbs in a spicy sauce) hits the Sìchuān nail squarely on the head, with mushrooms in place of meat, and the sizzling seafood bake with melted cheese is crisp and filling. Service is efficient; the only fly in the ointment is the Richard Clayderman musak.

The 3rd floor is smart self-service; 4th floor is exclusive set meals.

★ SUMERIAN
CAFE $

Map p310 (415 North Shaanxi Rd; 陕西北路415号; mains from ¥20; ⊙7.30am-7.30pm; ☎; ♿ Ⓜ West Nanjing Rd) Run by a bright and sunny Californian and a sprightly Chinese, good-looking Sumerian packs a lot into a small space, with bagels, pumpkin soup, roasted vegetable salads, wraps and standout coffees (Mexican Pluma Real Organic, Colombian Popayan decaf) on the menu.

GŌNGDÉLÍN
CHINESE, VEGETARIAN $

Map p310 (功德林; ✆6327 0218; 445 West Nanjing Rd; 南京西路445号; dishes ¥18-68;

JING'AN EATING

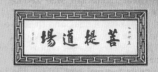

1. Shànghǎi Centre Theatre (p140)
Marvel at the feats of Shànghǎi's acrobats at the Shànghǎi Centre Theatre.

2. Jade Buddha Temple (p128)
Shànghǎi's best known shrine has striking yellow-and-red walls.

3. Jìng'ān Temple (p130)
Find peace among the district's skyscrapers at this restored Buddhist temple.

4. Plaza 66 (p141)
Fake palms, a live pianist and haute couture brands are on offer in this upmarket mall.

⊘11am-3pm & 5-9pm; ✐; Ⓜ People's Sq)
Shànghǎi's second-oldest vegetarian restaurant (opened in 1922), Gōngdélín never fails to perplex Western vegetarians – almost everything on the menu is prepared to resemble meat, down to sinewy textures and bony chunks. Don't worry though, the beef with shacha sauce and the sesame chicken rolls are actually made of tofu, no matter how convincing they look.

The interior is a blend of stone and wood with Venetian blinds, honeycombed lamps and a couple of Buddhist statues thrown in for good fortune.

CYCLO
VIETNAMESE $

Map p310 (☑6135 0150; 678 North Shaanxi Rd; 陕西北路678号; mains ¥30-75; ⊘11am-2.30pm & 6.30-10.30pm Tue-Fri, 11.30am-10.30pm Sat & Sun; Ⓜ Changping Rd) Set up by a father-and-son duo, Cyclo - named after Vietnam's version of the local *sānlúnchē* that infest Ho Chi Minh City and Hanoi – is spot on. It propels all the scrumptuous flavours of China's southwesterly neighbour into Shànghǎi, with delicious spring rolls, *pho, banh mi,* Vietnamese salads and an unwavering focus on fresh ingredients.

GOLDEN POT
HOTPOT $

Map p310 (金涮盘; Jīn Shuànpán; 142 Yuyuan Rd; 愚园路142号; lunch sets/meals from ¥29/40; ⊘11am-10pm; Ⓜ Jing'an Temple) You'll be sure to receive an enthusiastic welcome at this choose-it-yourself hotpot place, which is full to bursting during the lunch rush. Pull up a stool at the central counter and select your broth, dipping sauce and whatever ingredients you're in the mood for: thinly sliced Mongolian lamb, squid, crunchy lotus roots, mushrooms, potato slices...the list goes on. Feeling thirsty? Wash it all down with a carafe of kumquat-lemon juice.

YÀKÈXĪ
XINJIANG $

Map p310 (亚克西; 379 Xikang Rd; 西康路379号; mains from ¥18; ⊘11.30am-10pm; Ⓜ Changping Rd, West Nanjing Rd) Not a single inch of wall space survives undecorated at this Xīnjiāng restaurant and although the spangled, overblown interior only vaguely channels Kasghar, the food summons up the pungent aromas of China's mighty northwest. The staples – lamb kebabs (¥6 each), *shaozi* noodles (¥Y18), naan bread (¥6) – are tasty and filling.

If you aim high on the picture menu (trotting towards smoked horse meat), the

bill can quickly mount up. Gather together enough mates and the whole lamb (¥1498) makes an entertaining feast, but you'll need to order well in advance. Uighur dancing shakes tail feathers from 7pm nightly (apart from Mondays).

BAKER & SPICE
CAFE $

Map p310 (Shànghǎi Centre, 1376 West Nanjing Rd; 南京西路1376号; dishes from ¥40; ⊘7am-10pm; 🎧✐; Ⓜ Jing'an Temple, West Nanjing Rd) This jam-packed cafe at the Shànghǎi Centre has long wooden tables and a tempting array of fresh pastries, bread, salads and sandwiches – don't miss the nutty carrot cake.

Ā BǍO
NOODLES $

Map p310 (阿宝; 4th fl, Han City Fashion & Accessories Plaza, 480 West Nanjing Rd; 南京西路480号南政大厦 B 座 4楼; mains from ¥14; ⊘10am-10pm; Ⓜ West Nanjing Rd, People's Sq) On the 4th floor of Han City Fashion & Accessories Plaza, and cooking up Shànghǎi noodles since 1981, small Ā Bǎo serves 'a bowl of noodles, each with a story'. It's a mere counter in a food court, but don't be put off: the noodles are supreme and perfect for restoring calories on a Jìng'ān shopping jaunt.

Order up steaming and ample bowls of pork-rib noodles (阿宝大排烤葱面; *Ā Bǎo dàpái kǎocōng miàn;* ¥20) or the vegie *sùjiāo miàn* (素交面; ¥16).

WAGAS
CAFE $

Map p310 (沃歌斯; Wògēsī; B11A, Citic Sq, 1168 West Nanjing Rd; 南京西路1168号中信泰富地下一层 11A 室; mains ¥48-60; ⊘7am-10pm; 🎧; Ⓜ West Nanjing Rd) Express sandwiches are half-price before 10am weekdays; there are after-6pm deals; and you can hang out here for hours with your tablet and no one will shoo you away – need we say more? Hip Wagas is the best and most dependable of the local cafes, with chilled beats, tantalising wraps, salads and sandwiches, and prices displayed on an overhead blackboard menu.

Locations abound (this one is hidden behind a McDonald's).

AWFULLY CHOCOLATE
CAFE $

Map p310 (www.awfullychocolate.com; No 120 Inpoint Plaza, 169 Wujiang Rd; 吴江路169号四季坊商场 120号; cakes from ¥27; ⊘10am-10pm; Ⓜ West Nanjing Rd) A paradise for sweet-toothed chocoholics and slaves to the cocoa bean, this cafe brings an indulgent focus to chocolate goodies, from cupcakes to

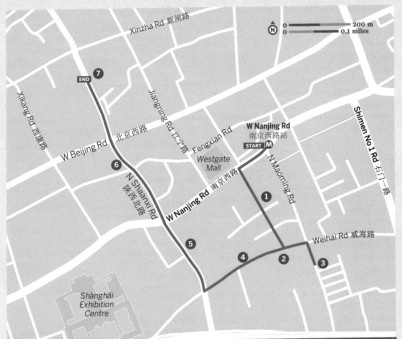

🏃 Neighbourhood Walk
Jìng'ān

START WEST NANJING RD METRO STATION
FINISH OHEL RACHEL SYNAGOGUE
LENGTH 1.7KM; 1½ HOURS

Begin by walking through the ❶ **Bubbling Well Road Apartments** (静安别墅; Jìng'ān Biéshù), which you can enter off West Nanjing Rd. One of the most delightful surviving new-style *lìlòng* housing complexes in Shànghǎi, with three-storey red-brick houses built between 1928 and 1932, it's a great spot to catch daily residential life – people walking their dogs, playing cards or hanging out laundry to dry. Note how the architecture blends Chinese motifs with European-style terraced housing. Exit at the south end of the complex, which faces ❷ **Sun Court**, a 1928 apartment block, and turn left onto Weihai Rd. Continue right onto North Maoming Rd and explore the lovingly preserved *shíkùmén* (stone-gate house) architecture of the ❸ **Former Residence of Mao Zedong** (p130), where a 30-year-old Mao once lived for several months in 1924.

Retrace your steps and return to Sun Court, continuing west down Weihai Rd and passing a ❹ **tea shop** (小叶名茶; Xiǎoyè Míngchá) at No 686, with a fabulous collection of aged *pǔ'ěr* cakes lining the walls. Turn right onto North Shaanxi Rd, where you'll eventually catch a glimpse of an enormous ❺ **garden residence** (1918) at No 186, which once belonged to Wúxī native Rong Zongjing, one of Shànghǎi's most powerful industrialists. Rong Zongjing's nephew, Rong Yiren, was one of the rare individuals with a capitalist background to succeed in communist China, becoming vice mayor of Shànghǎi in 1957 and later vice-president of the PRC from 1993 to 1998.

Follow Shaanxi Rd north, past ❻ **Grace Baptist Church** (怀恩堂; Huáiēn Táng) at No 375. Continue north till you reach the Sassoon-built ❼ **Ohel Rachel Synagogue** (1920) at No 500, the first of seven synagogues built in Shànghǎi (only two remain). It's currently closed to the public but can be visited on tours with Shanghai Jews (www.shanghai-jews.com).

tiramisu, truffles, crème brûlée, ice cream and other supremely decadent delights.

LILLIAN BAKERY
BAKERY $

Map p310 (莉莲; Lilián; 121 Wujiang Rd; 吴江路121号; pastries from ¥5; ⊙8am-10pm; MWest Nanjing Rd) A smash hit for its outstanding Macau egg tarts as well as pastries, cakes, croissants, doughnuts and all things sticky, sweet and waistline-expanding. Branches all over town.

CITY SHOP
SUPERMARKET $

Map p310 (城市超市; Chéngshì Chāoshì; ☑400 811 1797; www.cityshop.com.cn; B1, Shànghǎi Centre, 1376 West Nanjing Rd; 南京西路1376号; ⊙8am-10.30pm; MJing'an Temple) For all those imported goodies you just can't get anywhere else – at a price.

★COMMUNE SOCIAL
TAPAS $$

Map p309 (食社; Shíshè; www.communesocial.com; 511 Jiangning Rd; 江宁路511号; mains ¥58-398; ⊙noon-2.30pm & 6-10.30pm Tue-Fri, noon-3pm & 6-10.30pm Sat, till 3pm Sun; MChangping Rd) Dividing neatly into upstairs cocktail bar with terrace, downstairs open-kitchen tapas bar and dessert bar, this natty Neri & Hu–designed Jason Atherton venture blends a stylish, yet relaxed, vibe with some sensational international dishes, exquisitely presented by chef Scott Melvin. It's the talk of the town, but has a no-reservations policy, so prepare to queue.

★HǍI DǏ LĀO
HOTPOT $$

Map p310 (海底捞; ☑6258 9758; 3rd fl, 1068 West Beijing Rd; 北京西路1068号3楼; hotpot per person from ¥100-120; ⊙10.30am-late; ☎; MWest Nanjing Rd) This Sichuanese hotpot restaurant is all about service, and the assault begins the minute you walk in the door. Predining options include complimentary shoe shines, manicures and trays of fresh fruit; once you've actually sat down, the buzz of activity continues with the donning of matching red aprons and a YouTube-worthy noodle-stretching dance performance (order *lāo miàn;* 捞面).

Hǎi Dǐ Lāo sets the standard for sauce bars across the country – make sure your table has enough bowls to fully appreciate the range of flavours available. While it's great for group meals, this is definitely not a place to dine alone or to go on a date.

★DIN TAI FUNG
DUMPLINGS $$

Map p310 (鼎泰丰; Dǐng Tài Fēng; ☑6289 9182; Shànghǎi Centre, 1376 West Nanjing Rd; 南京西路1376号; 10 dumplings ¥58-88; ⊙10am-10pm; ☎; MJing'an Temple, West Nanjing Rd) To-die-for dumplings and flawless service from Taiwan's most famous dumpling chain. Reserve ahead.

LYNN
SHANGHAINESE $$

Map p310 (琳怡; Lín Yí; ☑6247 0101; 99-1 Xikang Rd; 西康路99-1号; dishes ¥50-125; ⊙11.30am-10.30pm; MWest Nanjing Rd) Lynn offers consistently good, cleverly presented dishes in plush but unfussy surroundings. The lunch dim-sum menu offers a range of delicate dumplings, while for dinner there are more traditional Shanghainese dishes, such as eggplant with minced pork in a garlic-and-chilli sauce. More adventurous stand-outs include the sautéed chicken with sesame pockets, and deep-fried spare ribs with honey and garlic.

Weekends feature all-you-can-eat dim sum for brunch. Book ahead.

VEGETARIAN
LIFESTYLE
CHINESE, VEGETARIAN $$

Map p310 (枣子树; Zǎozishù; ☑6215 7566; www.jujubetree.com; 258 Fengxian Rd; 奉贤路258号; dishes ¥25-70; ⊙11am-9.30pm; ☎; MWest Nanjing Rd) These folks are maximising meat-free goodness with organic, vegetarian fare fashioned for the masses. There are loads of clever dishes, including soup served in a pumpkin, but tops are the sweet Wúxī 'spare ribs', stuffed with lotus root of course, and claypots galore. It's MSG-free and cooks go light on the oil.

GǓYÌ HÚNÁN RESTAURANT
HUNANESE $$

Map p310 (古意湘味浓; Gǔyì Xiāngwèinóng; ☑6232 8377; 8th fl, City Plaza, 1618 West Nanjing Rd; 南京西路1618号8楼久百城市广场; dishes ¥38-98; MJing'an Temple) Classy Hunanese dining and mouth-watering cumin ribs next to Jìng'ān Temple.

PǏNCHUĀN
SICHUANESE $$

Map p310 (品川; ☑6288 8389; www.pinchuan-china.com; 5th fl, Plaza 66, 1266 West Nanjing Rd; 南京西路1266号恒隆广场5楼; dishes ¥45-89; ⊙10am-10pm; MWest Nanjing Rd) Stop by the top floor of the swish Plaza 66 shopping mall for excellent, fine-dining Sichuanese. Try the smoked duck, marinated beef or the pork spare ribs.

CRYSTAL JADE DIM SUM $$

Map p310 (翡翠酒家; Fěicuì Jiǔjiā; ☑5228 1133; 7th fl, Westgate Mall, 1038 West Nanjing Rd; 静安 南京西路1038号7楼; mains¥20-42; ⊘10.30am-11pm; Ⓜ West Nanjing Rd) This outpost of the stellar Singapore dim sum restaurant serves moreish *chā shāo, xiǎolóngbāo* (little steamer buns) and other classic dishes in a smart setting.

ELEMENT FRESH CAFE $$

Map p310 (新元素; Xīnyuánsù; ☑6279 8682; www.elementfresh.com; Shànghǎi Centre, 1376 West Nanjing Rd; 南京西路1376号; sandwiches & salads ¥45-98, dinner from ¥128; ⊘7am-11pm; ☎; Ⓜ Jing'an Temple, West Nanjing Rd) Perennially popular, Element Fresh hits the spot with its tempting selection of healthy salads, pasta dishes (Western and Asian) and hefty sandwiches. Vegetarians may well faint with excitement at the roasted eggplant on ciabatta bread or the Italian tofu sandwich smothered in pesto. Then there are the imaginative smoothies, big breakfasts, coffee and after-work cocktails.

THE GREAT JEWISH FAMILIES

The Sassoon family consisted of generations of shrewd businesspeople from Baghdad to Bombay, whose achievements brought them wealth, knighthoods and far-reaching influence. Though it was David Sassoon who initiated cotton trading out of Bombay (now Mumbai) to China, and son Elias Sassoon who had the ingenuity to buy and build his own warehouses in Shànghǎi, it was Sir Victor Sassoon (1881–1961) who finally amassed the family fortune and enjoyed his wealth during Shànghǎi's heyday. Victor concentrated his energies on buying up Shànghǎi's land and building offices, apartments and warehouses; at one time he owned an estimated 1900 buildings in Shànghǎi. Victor left the city in 1941, returning only briefly after the war to tidy up the business, and then he and his assets relocated to the Bahamas. He had plenty of romantic affairs but remained a bachelor until he finally married his American nurse when he was 70.

Today the Sassoon legacy lives on in the historic Fairmont Peace Hotel (p204) and Sassoon Mansion (known to Sassoon as 'Eve')– now the Cypress Hotel in Hóngqiáo – each the site of some infamously raucous Sassoon soirées. For one of his celebrated fancy-dress parties, he requested guests to come dressed as if shipwrecked.

The company of David Sassoon & Sons gave rise to several other notables in Shànghǎi, among them Silas Hardoon and Elly Kadoorie. Hardoon began his illustrious career as a night guard and later, in 1880, as manager of David Sassoon & Sons. Two years later he set out to do business on his own and promptly went bust. His second independent business venture in 1920 proved successful and Silas Hardoon made a name for himself in real estate. In his father's memory he built the Beth Aharon Synagogue near Sūzhōu Creek, which later served as a shelter for Polish Jews who had fled Europe. It has since been demolished. Once a well-respected member of both the French and International Councils, Hardoon's reputation turned scandalous when he took a Eurasian wife, Luo Jialing, and adopted a crowd of multicultural children. He then began to study Buddhism. His estate, including the school he had erected (now the grounds of the Shànghǎi Exhibition Centre), went up in smoke during the Sino-Japanese War. At the time of his death in 1931, he was the richest man in Shànghǎi.

Like Silas Hardoon, Elly Kadoorie began a career with David Sassoon & Sons in 1880 and he too broke away and amassed a fortune – in real estate, banking and rubber production. His famous mansion is the result of too much money left in the hands of an unreliable architect; after returning from three years in England, Kadoorie found a 19.5m-high ballroom aglow with 5.4m chandeliers and enough imported marble to warrant the name Marble Hall. Architecture detectives can still visit the staircases and peek at the ballroom of the former mansion, once the site of Shànghǎi's most extravagant balls and now home to the Children's Palace (p 131). Kadoorie died a year before the end of WWII; you can visit his mausoleum in the International Cemetery (p174).

With their immense wealth, many Jewish families were pivotal in aiding the thousands of refugees who fled to Shànghǎi, principally Jewish refugees, between 1933 and 1941. The Kadoorie family now resides in Hong Kong and is still involved in charity work.

WUJIANG ROAD FOOD STREET

The original food street (吴江路休闲街; Wújiāng Lù Xiūxián Jiē) may have been replaced by a more sanitised pedestrian area in the run-up to the World Expo, but when it comes to snack food, **Wujiang Road Food Street** (Map p310; Wujiang Rd; 吴江路; meals from ¥30; Ⓜ West Nanjing Rd) has still got the goods.

If you can beat the mealtime rush, the first spot to try is the multistorey building at No 269 (above a West Nanjing Rd metro exit). The 2nd floor here has two of the city's most famous chains: the **Nánxiáng Steamed Bun Restaurant** (南翔馒头店; Nánxiáng Mántou Diàn; Map p310; 2nd fl, 269 Wujiang Rd; 吴江路269号2楼; 4 dumplings ¥16; ☺10am-10pm; Ⓜ West Nanjing Rd) and a much-too-small outlet of **Yang's Fry Dumplings** (小杨生煎馆; Xiǎoyáng Shēngjiān Guǎn; Map p310; 2nd fl, 269 Wujiang Rd; 吴江路269号2楼; 4 fried dumplings ¥6; ☺10am-10pm; Ⓜ West Nanjing Rd).

Down at street level, you'll find plenty of cafes, ramen chains, ice-cream vendors and stalls selling more-traditional snacks such as roasted chestnuts. Also look out for the famous Japanese treat *takoyaki* (ball-shaped octopus waffles) at No 122, and Korean noodles and *bibimbap* (a rice bowl topped with seasoned vegetables and an egg) at No 200.

PIZZA EXPRESS   ITALIAN $$

Map p310 (比萨马上诺; Bǐsà Mǎshàngnuò; ☏6289 8733; Shànghǎi Centre, 1376 West Nanjing Rd; 南京西路1376号; pizza ¥80-129; ☺11am-11pm; ☎; Ⓜ Jing'an Temple, West Nanjing Rd) Part of the British Pizza Express group (founded in 1965), this restaurant serves a tempting selection of delicious thin-crust Neapolitan pizzas and even thinner-crust Roman-style pizzas that are definite contenders for the city's best. From the *quattro formaggi* and the Sicilia to the Peking duck, toppings are excellent quality and sprinkled on liberally. There's pasta and bruschetta on the menu, too.

BALI LAGUNA   INDONESIAN $$

Map p310 (巴厘岛; Bālí Dǎo; ☏6248 6970; 1649 West Nanjing Rd; 南京西路1649号; mains ¥40-188; ☺11am-2.30pm & 6-10.30pm; ☎; Ⓜ Jing'an Temple) This restaurant has a tranquil lakeside setting in Jìng'ān Park, and the open long-house interior decked out in dark wood and rattan has a genuine tropical feel. Waiters in sarongs serve up excellent dishes, such as seafood curry in a fresh pineapple, gado gado (vegetable salad with peanut sauce) and *kalio daging* (beef in coconut milk, lemongrass and curry sauce).

MÉILÓNGZHÈN JIǓJIĀ   CHINESE $$

Map p310 (梅陇镇酒家; ☏6253 5353; No 22, Lane 1081, West Nanjing Rd; 南京西路1081号22弄号; dishes ¥30-120; ☺11am-2pm & 5-9pm; Ⓜ West Nanjing Rd) This esteemed *lǎozìhào*

('old name') restaurant has been serving delighted diners since the 1930s. The menu mixes Sìchuān and Shanghainese tastes and ranges from the pricey (crab with tofu) to the more reasonable, such as the fish slices with tangerine peel.

The rooms once housed the Shanghai Communist Party headquarters, but are now bedecked in wood carvings, huge palace lamps and photos of foreign dignitaries.

★FU 1088   SHANGHAINESE $$$

Map p310 (☏5239 7878; 375 Zhenning Rd; 镇宁路375号; ☺11am-2pm & 5.30pm-midnight; Ⓜ Jiangsu Rd) Exclusive Fu 1088 has 17 rooms filled with Chinese antiques. Rooms are rented out to individual patrons, with white-gloved service and an emphasis on elegant Shanghainese fare such as shredded crab and drunken chicken. There's a minimum charge of ¥400 per person, excluding drinks. Reserve ahead.

✕ Shànghǎi Railway Station

JADE BUDDHA TEMPLE VEGETARIAN RESTAURANT   CHINESE, VEGETARIAN $

Map p309 (玉佛寺素斋; Yùfó Sì Sùzhāi; 999 Jiangning Rd; 江宁路999号; dishes ¥18-36; ☏; Ⓜ Changshou Rd) Pull up a seat alongside the monks, nuns and lay worshippers for a vegetarian feast at this two-storey Buddhist banquet hall.

DRINKING & NIGHTLIFE

Jìng'ān drinking options don't match the diversity of the area's restaurants, and cater almost exclusively to the expat and business crowd.

West Nanjing Road

★FENNEL LOUNGE
BAR

(回香; Huí Xiāng; ☎3353 1773; 217 Zhenning Rd, entrance on Dongzhu'anbang Rd; 镇宁路217号; ⊗6pm-2am; ☜; MJiangsu Rd) Fennel is a classy cocktail lounge divided into dining room, a cosy living-type room with a tiny stage, and a lounge area, featuring a sunken bar and casual seating. An impressive drinks list, skilled bar staff and an eclectic line-up of live acoustic performances (everything from jazz to traditional Chinese music) make it a favourite with hip, cashed-up 30-somethings.

★KĀIBĀ
BAR

Map p310 (开巴; www.kaiba-beerbar.com; 479 Wuding Rd; 武定路479号; ⊗4pm-2am Mon-Fri, 2pm-2am Sat & Sun; ☜; MChangping Rd) Beer-o-philes who have endured too many bottles of Shànghǎi's watery Reeb may do cartwheels at the Trappist brews, the 20 craft beers on tap and the free-flow lager brunches (Saturdays and Sundays) served up in a chilled-reclaimed concrete, wood and brick setting.

★SPOT
BAR

Map p310 (☎6247 3579; 331 Tongren Rd; 铜仁路331号; ⊗11am-late; ☜; MJing'an Temple) The district's upscale watering hole, Spot offers two sections: dining (nonsmoking) and the bar (smoking). It's much slicker than the competition, with fluorescent-coloured chairs, a tank of moon jellyfish, fancy dining options plus live music. But when push comes to shove, it's still a sports bar, best for catching football and rugby matches in the middle of the night.

Match fixtures go up on the whiteboard outside.

★MALONE'S
BAR

Map p310 (www.malones.com.cn; 255 Tongren Rd; 新闻路255号; ⊗11am-3am; MJing'an Temple) Malone's is *the* Shànghǎi old-timer (we've been visiting for nigh on 20 years), though you wouldn't guess it from the spring in its step. Filipino bands crank it up downstairs (from Monday to Saturday), while sports TV fills all corners and a big burger menu takes on all comers. Heritage comes in the form of the old Texaco gas pump by the door.

★B&C
BAR

Map p309 (685 Xikang Rd; 西康路685号; ⊗6pm-2am; MChangping Rd) You get welcoming hugs from sociable co-owner Candy at this huge old-school bar. Prices are low – in dive territory – with pool and darts for those unable to just sit and yak bar-side, while Bon Jovi and Duran Duran transport everyone back to the good-old days of big and bad hairstyles. Two other B&C bars are a five minute stumble away at different compass points: the more introverted, quiet space at 3 Changping Rd and the busier, slightly more charismatic one at 326 Xinfeng Rd.

BIG BAMBOO
BAR

Map p310 (132 Nanyang Rd; 南阳路132号; ⊗9.30am-2am; ☜; MJing'an Temple) Big Bamboo is a shamelessly out-and-out sports bar on two floors, that also serves up decent Western food to a backdrop of pool, darts and all the big games on TV.

FRESH JUICE IN A JIFFY

Fresh juice (果汁; *guǒzhī*) made on the spot sells for as little as ¥10 a cup and is vital for staying hydrated in the sweltering summer heat. Of course, you could always sink an orange juice or a mango smoothie, but why not try something a little more adventurous? Here are some of Shànghǎi's more exotic creations:

➡ Dragon fruit and pear
➡ Aloe and cucumber
➡ Bittermelon
➡ Durian and yoghurt
➡ Pineapple and cabbage

I LOVE SHÀNGHǍI
BAR

Map p310 (我爱上海; Wǒ Ài Shànghǎi; ☑5228 6899; 3rd fl, 1788 Xinzha Rd; 新闸路1788号3楼; ⊙5pm-2am; Ⓜ Jing'an Temple) Despite the name, this bar has little to do with Shànghǎi and everything to do with getting hammered and having fun along the way. Pitchers of beer, strong island ice tea and absinthe shots are all the ammo you'll need. Each night is a theme night of some sort, the climax coming with Saturday's open bar (¥100). It's above the Orchard Restaurant.

HELEN'S
BAR

Map p310 (148 North Maoming Rd; 茂名北路148号; ⊙10am-2am; Ⓜ West Nanjing Rd) Had enough of wall-to-wall suits and sky-high prices? Helen's speciality is the bargain basement, no-frills, student-set dive-end of the bar market. Enjoy.

CAFÉ 85°C
CAFE

Map p310 (85 度 C 咖啡店; Bāwǔ Dù C Kāfēidiàn; 408 North Shaanxi Rd; 陕西北路408号; ⊙24hr; Ⓜ West Nanjing Rd) This Taiwanese chain offers the cheapest caffeine fix in town.

Shànghǎi Railway Station

BANDU CABIN
CAFE

Map p309 (半度音乐; Bàndù Yīnyuè; ☑6276 8267; www.bandumusic.com; Bldg 11, 50 Moganshan Rd; 莫干山路50号11号楼; ⊙10am-6.30pm Sun-Fri, to 10pm Sat; Ⓜ Shanghai Railway Station) With charmingly eclectic and mismatched furniture, this laid-back cafe-cum-record label serves up noodles, drinks and snacks, along with traditional Chinese music concerts on Saturday at 7.30pm (¥50). Phone ahead on Friday to reserve seats. There's also a quality selection of Chinese folk-music CDs.

⭐ ENTERTAINMENT

⭐ SHÀNGHǍI CENTRE THEATRE
ACROBATICS

Map p310 (上海商城剧院; Shànghǎi Shāngchéng Jùyuàn; ☑6279 8948; Shànghǎi Centre, 1376 West Nanjing Rd; 南京西路1376号; tickets ¥180, ¥240 & ¥300; Ⓜ Jing'an Temple) The Shànghǎi Acrobatics Troupe has popular performances here most nights at 7.30pm. It's a short but fun show and is high on the to-do list of most first-time visitors. Buy tickets a couple of days in advance from the ticket office on the right-hand side at the entrance to the Shànghǎi Centre.

PARAMOUNT BALLROOM
DANCE

Map p310 (百乐门; Bǎilèmén; ☑6249 8866; 218 Yuyuan Rd; 豫园路218号; tea dances ¥80, ballroom dancing ¥100; ⊙tea dances 1-4.30pm, ballroom dancing 4.30-8pm; Ⓜ Jing'an Temple) This old art deco theatre was the biggest nightclub in the 1930s, and today has sedate tea dances in the afternoon to the sounds of old-school jazz and tango, followed by ballroom dancing. It makes for a nice nostalgia trip for those with a sense of humour. Dance partners cost ¥35 to ¥45 for 10 minutes.

STUDIO CITY
CINEMA

Map p310 (环艺电影城; Huányì Diànyǐngchéng; 10th fl, Westgate Mall, 1038 West Nanjing Rd; 静安南京西路1038号10楼; Ⓜ West Nanjing Rd) Modern cinema complex in the Westgate Mall.

🛍 SHOPPING

West Nanjing Rd is more upmarket and elitist than the eastern end. It's home to the high-end Western fashion brands and luxury items, as well as Shànghǎi's most exclusive malls, such as Plaza 66. Behind People's Sq is Dagu Rd, with a number of large DVD stores.

⭐ SPIN
CERAMICS

Map p310 (旋; Xuán; 360 Kangding Rd; 康定路360号; ⊙11am-8pm; Ⓜ Changping Rd) High on creative flair, Spin brings Chinese ceramics up to speed with its oblong teacups, twisted sake sets and all manner of cool plates, chopstick holders, and 'kung fu' and 'exploded pillar' vases. Pieces are never overbearing, but trendily lean towards the whimsical, geometric, thoughtful and elegantly fashionable.

Prices are reasonable, too – you can pick up funky (and beautiful) spiral tea cups for ¥70, which make perfect gifts. Spin ranges over three floors in a brick building on the corner of North Shaanxi Rd and Kangding Rd.

TAICHI TIPS

In his thirties, Tu Jianfeng (屠建峰) is a teacher of taichi at Pure Taichi (www.puretaichi.com) in Shànghǎi. We caught up with him to get the lowdown on 'Supreme Harmony Boxing' (Tàijíquán).

Why did you first start learning taichi?

I heard from a friend of mine who was practising taichi that it was good for the eyes, so that sparked my interest. I learn out of deep interest, as a physical discipline, for self-cultivation and peace of mind.

How did you learn taichi?

I first started learning from books, then went to study with teachers in the Taoist mountain of Wǔdāng Shān (武当山) in Central China's Húběi province and Chénjiāgōu (陈家沟), traditional home of the strenuous Chen style of taichi.

Are there any weapons in the taichi arsenal?

For sure. There's the straight taichi sword (剑; jiàn), the broadsword (刀; dāo), the spear (枪; qiāng), the pole (杆; gān; which can be 12 feet in length) and the mace (锏; jiǎn).

Have you ever seen some truly remarkable taichi skill performed?

Once a fellow student tried to punch the belly of my teacher Wang Zhanjun and was sent flying back several steps and almost damaged his wrist!

Is push hands (a two-person training routine) important?

It's very important, as it's the path from taichi forms to actual combat. You can test the results of your practice and derive a better understanding of the movements. And of course doing push hands in itself is particularly absorbing.

How long does it take to study taichi?

A lifetime!

★ **AMY LIN'S PEARLS** PEARLS

Map p310 (艾敏林氏珍珠; Àimǐn Línshì Zhēnzhū; Room 30, 3rd fl, 580 West Nanjing Rd; 南京西路580号3楼 30号; ⊙10am-8pm; Ⓜ West Nanjing Rd) This is the most reliable retailer of pearls of all colours and sizes in Shanghai. Both freshwater pearls (from ¥80), including prized black Zhèjiāng pearls (from ¥3000), and saltwater pearls (from ¥200) are available here. The staff speaks English and will string your selection for you. This place sells jade and jewellery, too.

HAN CITY FASHION & ACCESSORIES PLAZA CLOTHING

Map p310 (韩城服饰礼品广场; Hánchéng Fúshì Lǐpǐn Guǎngchǎng; 580 West Nanjing Rd; 南京西路580号; ⊙10am-10pm; Ⓜ West Nanjing Rd) This unassuming-looking building is a popular location to pick up knock-offs, with hundreds of stalls spread across four floors. You can scavenge for bags, belts, jackets, shoes, suitcases, sunglasses, ties, T-shirts and electronics. Amy Lin's Pearls is located here. Prices can be inflated, so bargain hard.

ART DECO ANTIQUES

Map p309 (凹凸家具库; Āotū Jiājù Kù; ✆6277 8927; Bldg 7, 50 Moganshan Rd; 莫干山路50号7号楼; ⊙10am-6pm Tue-Sun; Ⓜ Shanghai Railway Station) For stylish period furnishings, stop by artist Ding Yi's gallery in the M50 complex. His stand-out antique collection includes folding screens, armoires, tables and chairs, with a few vintage poster girls on the walls to help cast that 1930s spell.

JĪNGDÉZHÈN PORCELAIN ARTWARE CERAMICS

Map p310 (景德镇艺术瓷器; Jǐngdézhèn Yìshù Cíqì; ✆6253 8865; 212 North Shaanxi Rd; 陕西北路212号; ⊙10am-9pm; Ⓜ West Nanjing Rd) This is one of the best places for high-quality traditional Chinese porcelain. Blue-and-white vases, plates, teapots and cups are some of the many choices available. Credit cards are accepted, and shipping overseas can be arranged.

PLAZA 66 MALL

Map p310 (恒隆广场; Hénglóng Guǎngchǎng; ✆6279 0910; 1266 West Nanjing Rd; 南京西路1266号; Ⓜ West Nanjing Rd) Staff outnumber

MASSAGE & SPAS

In Shànghǎi, a body or foot massage will come at a fraction of the price that you'd pay at home. Options range from neighbourhood foot-massage parlours – where everyone kicks back on an armchair and watches TV – to midrange and luxury hotel spas, which offer private rooms, a change of clothes and a wonderfully soothing atmosphere. The latter two usually offer beauty treatments (waxing, manicures etc) as well. Just remember, traditional massage (*tuīná*) is not particularly gentle. As your masseuse might very well tell you: no pain, no gain. Our favourites:

➡ Double Rainbow Massage House (p125)

➡ Green Massage (p142)

➡ Dragonfly (p125)

➡ Subconscious Day Spa (p125)

➡ Apsara Spa (p142)

shoppers at this upmarket mall, featuring fake palms, a live pianist and an entire line-up of haute couture fashion brands straight from Paris' Triangle D'or. Even if you're not in the market for a little pick-me-up from Chanel or Hermès, there are some decent dining options here on the top floor.

ESPACE PÉBÉO
ART

Map p309 (http://en.pebeo.com/Pebeo; 0-101, Bldg 0, M50 Moganshan Rd; 莫干山路M50号0号楼1楼; ⊙9.30am-6pm; MShanghai Railway Station) For a quality range of oil paints and other art supplies, come to this well-stocked outlet at M50.

🏃 SPORTS & ACTIVITIES

⭐ APSARA SPA
MASSAGE

Map p310 (馨园水疗; Xīnyuán Shuǐliáo; ☑6258 5580; www.apsara.com.cn; 457 North Shaanxi Rd; 陕西北路457号; massages & spa treatments ¥160-1560; ⊙10am-10pm; MWest Nanjing Rd) Angkor-style massage therapy with treatments such as a 60-minute *qì* re-energising massage, facials (Tibetan black-mud purification), body wraps, manicures and waxing.

⭐ GREEN MASSAGE
MASSAGE

Map p310 (青籁养身; Qīnglài Yǎngshén; ☑6289 7776; www.greenmassage.com.cn; 2nd fl, Shànghǎi Centre, 1376 West Nanjing Rd; 南京西路1376号2楼; massages & spa treatments ¥198-318; ⊙10.30am-2am; MJing'an Temple, West Nanjing Rd) Soothing midrange spa, with foot, *tuīná* (traditional massage) and shiatsu massages. Book ahead.

⭐ OZ BODY FIT
MARTIAL ARTS

Map p309 (☑6288 5278; www.ozbodyfit.com; 717 Huai'an Rd; 淮安路717号; 10 classes ¥1100; MHanzhong Rd) Popular Thai kickboxing work-outs, for those who want to keep fit using martial-arts training.

ONE WELLNESS
GYM

Map p310 (咪猫健身; Mīmāo Jiànshēn; ☑6267 1550; www.onewellness.com.cn; 2nd fl, 98 Yanping Rd; 静安区延平路98号2楼; ⊙6am-11pm; MJing'an Temple) A boutique fitness club located in a renovated factory, One Wellness has a gourmet cafe on the premises and in-house massage therapy. Classes range from yoga and taichi to bodypump and aerobics, and the equipment is all state-of-the-art. It also boasts the claim of being China's first carbon-neutral gym. The day rate is ¥300; a month-long membership starts at ¥1588.

SŪZHŌU CREEK BOAT TOURS
CRUISE

Map p309 (苏州河游览船; Sūzhōu Hé Yóulǎn Chuán; ☑4008 800 862; www.sz-river.com; Changhua Rd Dock; 昌化路码头; single/return ¥80/130) Trips along Sūzhōu Creek are possible, although services dry up during the colder, greyer months and at the time of writing were only running at 1.30pm Saturdays and Sundays. Boats go from Danba Rd Dock out in Pǔtuó (West Shànghǎi) to Changhua Rd Dock (near M50), and there are plans to extend the route to Wàibáidù Bridge north of the Bund.

Check to see if the boats are still running before heading out here.

Pǔdōng

PŬDŌNG | CENTURY AVENUE AREA | WORLD EXPO SITE

Neighbourhood Top Five

1 View Shànghǎi from low-orbit altitude in the observation decks of the **Shànghǎi Tower** (p146) and adjacent **SWFC** (p145).

2 Sink an evening alfresco cocktail and bathe in Pǔdōng's neon glow at **Flair** (p154).

3 Aim your point-and-shoot westwards from the **Riverside Promenade** (p147) as the sun sets over Pǔxī.

4 Leaf through the colourful pages of history at the **Shànghǎi History Museum** (p147).

5 Take a crash course in haggling at the Science & Technology Museum metro station's **AP Xīnyáng** (p155).

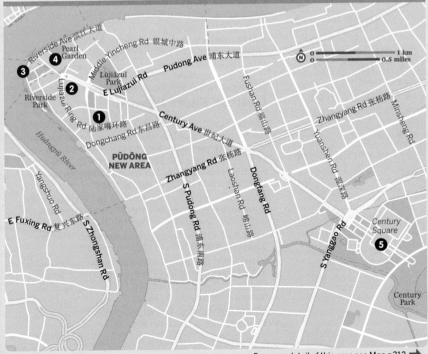

For more detail of this area see Map p312

Lonely Planet's Top Tip

The best time to see Lùjiāzuǐ's modern architecture is during late afternoon or at twilight/early evening, especially during summer (the wide Pǔdōng roads make the sun merciless). Sky-high views from observation decks, bars and restaurants allow you to contrast day, dusk and evening views. Walk around the elevated walkway by the Oriental Pearl TV Tower for show-stopping evening visuals.

Best Places to Eat

→ Hǎi Dǐ Lāo (p154)
→ South Beauty (p151)
→ Yi Cafe (p153)
→ Bāguó Bùyī (p153)
→ Sproutworks (p151)

For reviews, see p151.➡

Best Places to Drink

→ Cloud 9 (p154)
→ Flair (p154)
→ 100 Century Avenue (p154)
→ Brew (p154)

For reviews, see p154.➡

Explore: Pǔdōng

With its neck-craning tourists, scurrying suits and dazzling evening neonscapes, Pǔdōng is a place many Westerners know of before setting foot in China. More than 1.5 times bigger than urban Shànghǎi, the economic powerhouse of the Pǔdōng New Area (浦东新区; Pǔdōng Xīnqū) swallows up the eastern bank of the Huángpǔ River.

The high-rise area directly across from the Bund is the Lùjiāzuǐ Finance and Trade Zone, where China's largest stock market (the Shànghǎi Stock Exchange) makes or breaks China's nouveau riche. There's no obvious focal point where people congregate, although a swirl of sightseers rotates around the elevated walkway by the Oriental Pearl TV Tower.

For visitors, the main attractions are the high-altitude observation decks, hotels, restaurants and bars in the rocketing towers, offering ringside seats onto some of China's most mind-altering urban panoramas.

And what of the next top sight? Aiming for a 2015 launch date, the Shànghǎi Disney Resort in Pǔdōng promises to suck in legions of thrill-seeking tots and young ones.

Local Life

→**Shop** Flee the slick malls and make a beeline to the AP Xīnyáng Fashion & Gifts Market (p155) to haggle among local shoppers.

→**Take a ferry** Hop aboard the ferry across the Huángpǔ River with a scrum of Shànghǎi workers (and take your bike with you).

Getting There & Away

→**Metro** Line 2 powers through Lùjiāzuǐ, Century Ave and the Science & Technology Museum. Line 9 cuts through the southern part of the French Concession and on to Century Ave. Lines 4 and 6 also slice through Pǔdōng, all four lines converging at Century Ave. Other connections include metro lines 7, 8, 11 and the Maglev train.

→**Ferry** Run regularly between Pǔxī and Pǔdōng for the six-minute trip across the river (¥2). It's a 10-minute walk to the Jinmao Tower from the dock.

→**Bus** Both City Sightseeing Buses (p258) and Big Bus Tours (p258) have lines to Lùjiāzuǐ from Pǔxī.

→**Taxi** A taxi ride from the Bund will cost you around ¥30, as you'll have to pay the ¥15 tunnel toll heading eastwards. There is a useful taxi queue in front of the Science & Technology Museum.

→**Bund Sightseeing Tunnel** Travel underneath the Huángpǔ River in a tunnel dedicated to kitsch.

TOP SIGHT
SHÀNGHǍI WORLD FINANCIAL CENTER

Although trumped by the adjacent Shànghǎi Tower as the city's most stratospheric building, the awe-inspiring 492m-high Shànghǎi World Financial Center (SWFC; designed by Kohn Pedersen Fox Associates), is an astonishing sight. The SWFC is even more impressive come nightfall when its 'bottle opener' top dances with lights.

There are three **observation decks** – on levels 94, 97 and 100 – each with head-spinningly altitude-adjusted ticket prices and wow-factor elevators thrown in. The top two (located at the bottom and top of the trapezoid) are known as Sky Walks. It's debatable whether the top Sky Walk (474m) is the best spot for Shang-high views, though. The hexagonal space is bright and futuristic, and some of the floor is transparent glass, but the lack of a 360-degree sweep – windows only face west or east – detracts somewhat. But you get to look down on the top of the Jinmao Tower, which might be worth the ticket price alone.

A clear, smog-free day is imperative, so check the weather and pollution index up front. If you want to make a meal (or a cocktail) of it, or if lines are long, you can sashay into restaurant-bar 100 Century Avenue (p154) on the 91st floor instead. Access to the observation deck is on the west side of the building off Dongtai Rd; access to the Park Hyatt is on the south side of the building.

DON'T MISS...

➡ Observation decks
➡ 100 Century Avenue

PRACTICALITIES

➡ 上海环球金融中心; Shànghǎi Huánqiú Jīnróng Zhōngxīn
➡ Map p312
➡ ☎5878 0101
➡ http://swfc-shanghai.com
➡ 100 Century Ave; 世纪大道100号
➡ observation deck: adult 94th fl/94th, 97th & 100th fl ¥120/180, child under 140cm ¥60/90
➡ ◷8am-11pm, last entry 10pm
➡ Ⓜ Lujiazui

YONGYUAN DAI / GETTY IMAGES ©

TOP SIGHT
SHÀNGHǍI TOWER

China's tallest tower dramatically twists skywards from the firmament of Lùjiāzuǐ. The 121-storey, 632m-tall Gensler-designed Shànghǎi Tower topped out in August 2013 and is set to fully open in 2015. The spiral-shaped tower will house office space, entertainment venues, retail outlets, a conference center, a luxury hotel and 'sky lobbies'.

The gently corkscrewing form – its nine interior cylindrical units wrapped in two glass skins – is the world's second-tallest building and will remain so unless plans for the superhigh 'Sky City' in Chángshā reach fruition. The twist is introduced by the outer skin of glass that swivels though 120-degrees as it rises. Atrium 'sky gardens' in the vertical spaces sandwiched between the two layers of glass open up a large volume of the tower to public use. The tower is sustainably designed: as well as providing insulation, the huge acreage of glass will vastly reduce electrical consumption through the use of sunlight. The tower's shape furthermore reduces wind loads by 24%, which generated a saving of US$58m in construction costs. Before the tower even went up, engineers were faced with building the 61,000 cu metre concrete mat that would support its colossal mass in the boggy land of Pǔdōng.

Uppermost floors of the tower will be reserved for that obligatory Shànghǎi attraction – the world's highest skydeck above ground level – with passengers ferried skywards in the world's fastest lifts (40mph), designed by Mitsubishi, in the world's tallest single-lift elevator. Visitors will be able to gaze down on the both the Jinmao Tower and Shànghǎi World Finance Center below. A six-level luxury retail podium will fill the base of the tower.

DON'T MISS
→ Observation deck
→ Sky gardens
→ Retail podium

PRACTICALITIES
→ 上海中心大厦; Shànghǎi Zhōngxīn Dàshà
→ Map p312
→ www.shanghaitower.com.cn
→ cnr Middle Yincheng & Huayuanshiqiao Rds
→ Ⓜ Lujiazui

⊙ SIGHTS

⊙ Pǔdōng

SHÀNGHǍI TOWER
NOTABLE BUILDING

See p146.

SHÀNGHǍI WORLD FINANCIAL CENTER
NOTABLE BUILDING

See p145.

JĪNMÀO TOWER
BUILDING

Map p312 (金茂大厦; Jīnmào Dàshà; ☑5047 5101; 88 Century Ave; 世纪大道88号; adult/student/child ¥120/90/60; ⊙8.30am-9.30pm; MLujiazui) Resembling an art deco take on a pagoda, this crystalline edifice is a beauty and by far the most attractive of the Shànghǎi World Financial Center (SWFC), Shànghǎi Tower, Jīnmào Tower triumvirate. It's essentially an office block with the high-altitude Grand Hyatt (p211) renting space from the 53rd to 87th floors. You can zip up in the elevators to the 88th-floor **observation deck**, accessed from the separate podium building to the side of the main tower (aim for dusk for both day and night views).

Alternatively, sample the same view through the carbonated fizz of a gin and tonic at Cloud 9 (p154) on the 87th floor of the Grand Hyatt (accessed on the south side of the building), and photograph the hotel's astonishing barrel-vaulted atrium.

ORIENTAL PEARL TV TOWER
BUILDING

Map p312 (东方明珠广播电视塔; Dōngfāng Míngzhū Guǎngbō Diànshì Tǎ; ☑5879 1888; ⊙8am-10pm, revolving restaurant 11am-2pm & 5-9pm; MLujiazui) Love it or hate it, it's hard to be indifferent to this 468m-tall poured-concrete tripod tower, especially at night, when it dazzles. Sucking in streams of visitors, the Deng Xiaoping–era design is inadvertently retro, but socialism with Chinese characteristics was always cheesy back in the day. The highlight is the excellent Shànghǎi History Museum (p147), in the basement. You can queue up for views of Shànghǎi, but there are better views elsewhere and the long lines are matched by a tortuous ticketing system (p150).

Boat tours on the Huángpǔ River operate from the **Pearl Dock** (明珠码头; Míngzhū Mǎtou; Map p312; 1 Century Ave; tickets ¥100), next to the tower.

SHÀNGHǍI HISTORY MUSEUM
MUSEUM

Map p312 (上海城市历史发展陈列馆; Shànghǎi Chéngshì Lìshǐ Fāzhǎn Chénlièguǎn; ☑5879 8888; Oriental Pearl TV Tower basement; admission ¥35, English audio tour ¥30; ⊙8am-9.30pm; MLujiazui) The entire family will enjoy this informative museum with a fun presentation on old Shànghǎi. Learn how the city prospered on the back of the cotton trade and junk transportation, when it was known as 'Little Sūzhōu'. Life-sized models of traditional shops are staffed by realistic waxworks, amid a wealth of historical detail, including a boundary stone from the International Settlement and one of the bronze lions that originally guarded the entrance to the HSBC bank on the Bund. Some exhibits are hands-on or accompanied by creative video presentations. The city's transport history gets a look-in, where you can size up an antique bus, an old wheelbarrow taxi and an ornate sedan chair.

RIVERSIDE PROMENADE
WATERFRONT

Map p312 (滨江大道; Bīnjiāng Dàdào; ⊙6.30am-11pm; MLujiazui) Hands down the best stroll in Pǔdōng. The sections of promenade alongside Riverside Ave on the eastern bank of the Huángpǔ River offer splendid views to the Bund across the way. Choicely positioned cafes look out over the water.

SHÀNGHǍI OCEAN AQUARIUM
AQUARIUM

Map p312 (上海海洋水族馆; Shànghǎi Hǎiyáng Shuǐzúguǎn; ☑5877 9988; www.sh-aquarium.com; 1388 Lujiazui Ring Rd; 陆家嘴环路1388号; adult/child ¥160/110; ⊙9am-6pm, last tickets 5.30pm; MLujiazui) Education meets entertainment in this slick and intelligently designed aquarium that children will love. Join them on a tour through the aquatic environments from the Yangzi River to Australia, South America, the frigid ecosystems of the Antarctic and the flourishing marine life of coral reefs. The 155m-long

---

PǓDŌNG TO PǓXĪ FERRY

To get to the Cool Docks in the South Bund area from Pǔdōng, consider taking the ferry (东复线; ¥2, every 10 to 20 minutes from 5am to 11pm) from the Dongchang Rd dock to the Fuxing Rd dock. For the Old Town and the Bund, hop on the ferry (东金线; ¥2, every 15 minutes from 7am to 10pm) to the Jinling Rd dock.

LOTHAR KNOPP / GETTY IMAGES ©

TAO / ROBERT HARDING ©

1. Jīnmào Tower (p147)
Resembling an art deco take on a pagoda, Jīnmào Tower is essentially a stunning office block with an observation deck and a Grand Hyatt.

2. Shànghǎi History Museum (p147)
Visitors can get a handle on local history at this fun and accessible museum.

3. IFC Mall (p155)
This glam and glitzy mall hosts a variety of top brands and dining options.

ORIENTAL PEARL TV TOWER TICKETS

TICKET	PRICE*	INCLUDES
A	¥180	bottom and upper bauble & 'space cabin' plus Shànghǎi History Museum
B	¥150	upper & bottom bauble plus Shànghǎi History Museum
C	¥120	upper bauble plus Shànghǎi History Museum
Revolving Restaurant	lunch ¥288, dinner ¥318	ticket B plus lunch or dinner (lunch 11am to 2pm, dinner 5pm to 9pm)
Boat Tours	¥100	boat tours from the dock (10am to 8pm)
Package	¥180	top sphere, museum & cruise
Museum	¥35	Shànghǎi History Museum

*Children from 1m to 1.4m tall enter for half-price.

underwater clear viewing tunnel has gob-smacking views. Feeding times for spotted seals, penguins and sharks are between 9.45am and 11.10am, and 2.15pm and 3.40pm.

WÚ CHĀNGSHUÒ MEMORIAL HALL
HISTORIC BUILDING

Map p312 (吴昌硕纪念馆; Wú Chāngshuò Jinìànguǎn; 15 East Lujiazui Rd; 陆家嘴东路15号; admission ¥10; ☉9.30am-4pm Tue-Sun; MLujiazui) The lack of English captions badly hobbles the displays of this small museum detailing the life and work of artist, poet, calligrapher and seal carver Wu Changshuo (1844–1927). Nevertheless it's well worth exploring for the architecture of the historic building itself, once the residence of Chen Guichun, a rich merchant. Built between 1914 and 1917, there's some superb tiling on its floors, an old fireplace, lovely woodwork and carved door frames plus a gorgeous courtyard.

⊙ Century Avenue Area

SHÀNGHǍI SCIENCE & TECHNOLOGY MUSEUM
MUSEUM

Map p313 (上海科技馆; Shànghǎi Kējìguǎn; ☑6862 2000; www.sstm.org.cn; 2000 Century Ave; 世纪大道2000号; adult/student/child under 1.3m ¥60/45/free; ☉9am-5.15pm Tue-Sun, last tickets 4.30pm; MScience & Technology Museum) You need to do a huge amount of walking to get about this seriously spaced-out museum but there are some fascinating exhibits, from relentless Rubik's-cube-solving robots to mechanical archers. There's even the chance to take penalty kicks against a computerised goalkeeper. Four theatres (two IMAX, one

4-D and one outer space) show themed films throughout the day (tickets ¥20 to ¥40; 15 to 40 minutes). When you need a break, there's a good food court for lunch.

HIMALAYAS MUSEUM
MUSEUM

Map p313 (喜玛拉雅美术馆; Xǐmǎlāyǎ Měishùguǎn; www.himalayasart.cn; Himalayas Center, 1188 Fangdian Rd; 喜玛拉雅中心芳甸路1188弄1号; ☉10am-6pm Tue-Sun; MHuamu Rd) In the eye-catching Himalayas Center (attached to the Jumeirah Himalayas Hotel) and formerly the Zendai Museum of Art, this art gallery has become a fixture on the Pǔdōng art scene, with an emphasis on contemporary exhibitions in a modern art space.

CENTURY PARK
PARK

Map p313 (世纪公园; Shìjì Gōngyuán; 1001 Jinxiu Rd; 锦绣路1001号; admission ¥10; ☉7am-6pm; MCentury Park) This modern park at the eastern end of Century Ave is strong on hard edges and synthetic lines, but there's an attractive central lake (with expensive boat hire). Children will enjoy themselves, and the spacious paved area between the Science & Technology Museum and the park is great for flying kites (for sale from hawkers) and roller-blading. You can also hire tandem bikes.

⊙ World Expo Site

CHINA ART PALACE
MUSEUM

(中华艺术宫; Zhōnghuá Yìshùgōng; 205 Shangnan Rd; 上南路205号; ☉9am-5pm Tue-Sun; MChina Art Museum) FREE This 160,000 sq metre five-floor modern-art museum has invigorating international exhibitions and the inverted red pyramid building is a modern icon of Shànghǎi; however, the permanent Chinese art collection is prosaic and there's lots of propaganda. Occasional quality surfaces, such as *Virgin* (初潮的处女) by Xiang Jing, a moving, tender and comic sculptural work depicting awakening sexuality, while the Shànghǎi and Paris gallery looks absorbingly at the influence of impressionism on Shànghǎi art. Captions are clumsily translated. From the Power Station of Art, hop on bus 1213.

EATING

Most dining in Pǔdōng is about feasting on priceless views through floor-to-ceiling windows in five-star hotel restaurants. The gargantuan Superbrand Mall in Lùjiāzuǐ has restaurants spread out across 10 floors. For hole-in-the-wall dining, try roads such as the eastern end of Dongchang Rd (off South Pudong Rd), where budget *dōngběi* (northeastern) and Xīnjiāng eateries are concentrated. The spectacular new Himalayas Center complex (attached to the Jumeirah Himalayas Hotel) also boasts an impressive selection of restaurants.

✕ Pǔdōng

★ **SOUTH BEAUTY** SICHUANESE, CANTONESE **$**
Map p312 (俏江南; Qiào Jiāngnán; ☎5047 1817; 10th fl, Superbrand Mall, 168 West Lujiazui Rd; 陆家嘴西路168号正大广场10楼; dishes from ¥20; ◷11am-10pm; ⓂLujiazui) This smart restaurant with vermilion leather furniture and silky white table cloths on the 10th floor of the Superbrand Mall cooks up classic dishes from fiery Chóngqìng, Chéngdū and the south. The scorching boiled beef with hot pepper in chilli oil (¥48) opens the sweat pores, while the piquant *mápō dòufu* (tofu with pork crumbs in a spicy sauce; ¥38) arrives in a scarlet oily sauce. Divine.

Alternatively, if you don't like it hot, go for the delicious pan-fried scallion buns (¥26). Check the back pages of the menu for the cheaper dishes. You'll need to reserve for the coveted Bund-facing window seats on the terrace. Branches throughout Shànghǎi.

★ **SPROUTWORKS** HEALTH FOOD **$**
Map p312 (豆苗工坊; Dòumiáo Gōngfáng; www.sproutworks.com.cn; B2-06-07, Superbrand Mall, 168 West Lujiazui Rd; 陆家嘴西路168号正大广场B2楼; mains from ¥35, lunch sets from ¥50; ◷10am-10pm;📷;ⓂLujiazui) For a healthy recharge, Sproutworks offers a natural and earthy focus on fresh, wholesome food,

---

WORLD EXPO SITE

Most pavilions at the 2010 World Expo site (世博会区; Shìbó Huì Qū) were dismantled. However, at least five structures on the Pǔdōng side of the river remain standing and continue to host exhibits and events, including the iconic **China Pavilion** (中国国家馆; Zhōngguó Guójiā Guǎn), **Expo Center** (世博中心; Shìbó Zhōngxīn) and the galactically styled UFO **Mercedes-Benz Arena** (梅赛德斯奔驰文化中心; Méisàidésī Bēnchí Wénhuà Zhōngxīn; www.mercedes-benzarena.com).

Also Pǔdōng-side, there's the underwhelming **Moon Boat** (月亮船; Yuèliàng Chuán; Mon-Fri ¥60, Sat & Sun ¥80, holidays ¥100; ◷9am-6pm Tue-Sun) – the former Saudi Pavilion – and the **Shànghǎi Italian Centre** (上海意大利中心; Shànghǎi Yìdàlì Zhōngxīn; admission ¥60; ◷9am-5pm Tue-Sun) in the former Italian World Expo Pavilion. With 64,000 sq metres of exhibition space, the China Pavilion was relaunched as the China Art Palace (p150) and is the only thing worth visiting (though it is also missable). If you only have five days or less in Shànghǎi, don't bother.

Things are more interesting on the other side of the river. Hosting the Shànghǎi Biennale, the **Power Station of Art** (上海当代艺术博物馆; Shànghǎi Dāngdài Yìshù Bówùguǎn; Lane 20 Huayuangang Rd; ◷9am-5pm Tue-Sun; ⓂSouth Xizang Rd) **FREE** in the disused Nánshì Power Plant has seen some thought-provoking exhibitions.

Engaging highlights of the Expo are displayed in the **Expo 2010 Commemoration Exhibition** (上海世博会纪念展; Shànghǎi Shìbóhuì Jìniànzhǎn; cnr Mengzi & East Longhua Rds; admission ¥30; ◷9am-5pm Tue-Sun; ⓂLuban Rd) on the Pǔxī side, including exhibits and parts of the original pavilions. Sadly, there are no English captions.

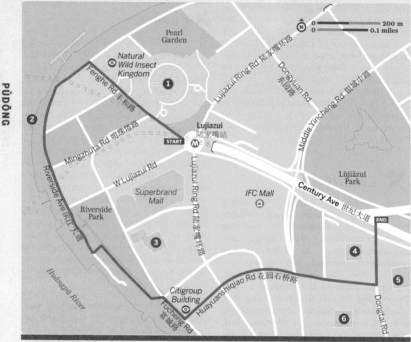

🏃 Neighbourhood Walk
Pǔdōng

START LUJIAZUI METRO STATION
FINISH SHÀNGHǍI WORLD FINANCIAL
CENTER (SWFC)
LENGTH 3.5KM; TWO HOURS

Looming above you like a sci-fi control tower a short walk from the Lujiazui metro station is the ❶ **Oriental Pearl TV Tower** (p147), one of Lùjiāzuǐ's most opinion-dividing edifices. Make sure you take a walk around the circular overhead walkway above the main intersection south of the tower, especially at night. Inside the tower, the absorbing Shànghǎi History Museum on the basement level is worth exploration.

Walk up Fenghe Rd past the Natural Wild Insect Kingdom on your right and turn left on to Riverside Park to reach a section of the ❷ **Riverside Promenade** (p147) for glorious images of the Bund across the water.

Follow a further stretch of the Riverside Promenade before cutting through River-

side Park and exiting onto Fucheng Rd by the Citigroup Building. Note the dramatic V-form of Tower Two of the ❸ **Pudong Shangri-La hotel** (p211).

Immediately after the Citigroup Building, turn onto Huayuanshiqiao Rd to walk past the twin towers of the International Financial Centre (IFC) on your left; you will see the vast Shànghǎi Tower on your right before reaching the elegant ❹ **Jinmao Tower** (p147). You're spoiled for high-altitude views all about – you can rocket to the 88th-floor observation deck of the Jinmao; cross the street to the decks in the ❺ **Shànghǎi World Financial Center** (p145), or top them all with views from the top of the awesome ❻ **Shànghǎi Tower** (p146). Alternatively, select a bar or restaurant in either tower, but have a table booked for sunset visits. To return to metro line 2, the Lujiazui metro stop is a short walk west along Century Ave.

in a clean-cut (but rather square) setting. Cleanse your insides with delicious smoothies; load up with brown rice, tasty soups and crisp, panini sandwiches; try freshly tossed salads, fresh juices, home-made desserts and lunch sets. Most dishes are pre-prepared and ready to go.

At the time of writing, a branch was about to open in Xīntiāndì.

YANG'S FRY DUMPLINGS · DUMPLINGS $

Map p312 (小杨生煎馆; Xiǎoyáng Shēngjiān Guǎn; 1406 Lujiazui Ring Rd; 陆家嘴环路1406号; 4 dumplings ¥6 ; ⊗8.30am-9pm; Ⓜ Lujiazui) A short walk from the Oriental Pearl TV Tower brings you to a string of restaurants, including the city's best sesame-seed-and-scallion-coated fried dumplings (生煎; shēngjiān), ideal for snacking on the move around Lujiazui. Per *liǎng* (两; 4 dumplings) costs ¥6.

★ BĀGUÓ BÙYĪ · SICHUANESE $

(巴国布衣; ☎3111 8055; Rm 110, 1368 Shibo Avenue; 世博大道1368号110室; mains from ¥35; Ⓜ China Art Palace) Pretty much the most authentic Sìchuān food in town is cooked up by the diligent chefs at this famous restaurant in the World Expo Site, originally founded in Chéngdū. With no concessions to the dainty Shànghǎi palate, prepare for a spicy firecracker of a meal. Make it an evening visit and catch the spectacularly lit Mercedes Benz Arena next door.

RAMEN PLAY · NOODLES $

Map p312 (拉面玩家; Lāmiàn Wánjiā; www.ramen-play.com.sg; B2, Superbrand Mall, 168 West Lujiazui Rd; 陆家嘴西路168号正大广场B2楼; mains from ¥30, sets from ¥49; ⊗10am-10pm; Ⓜ Lujiazui) Located within Food Opera in the Superbrand Mall and founded in Niigata, Japan, in 1967, this noodle spot has a simple and steady focus on tasty Japanese ramen in a utilitarian and unfussy setting. The spicy shoyu ramen (¥32) is a good place to start. There are also stone-pot rice dishes and good-value sets.

FOOD OPERA · ASIAN $

Map p312 (食代馆; Shídàiguǎn; B2, Superbrand Mall, 168 West Lujiazui Rd; 陆家嘴西路168号B2楼; dishes from ¥15; ⊗10am-10pm) Grab a card from the booth (¥10 deposit), load up with credits and then spend, spend, spend on a whole host of open kitchens in this hopping food court. There's Korean, teppanyaki, nasi padang, Hong Kong dishes, Japanese noodles, pasta and much more. Just point at what you want and hand over your card.

★ YI CAFE · CAFE $$$

Map p312 (怡咖啡; Yí Kāfēi; ☎5877 5372; 2nd fl, Pudong Shangri-La, 33 Fucheng Rd; 富城路33号2楼; meals lunch/dinner ¥298/368; ⊗breakfast, lunch & dinner; ☎; Ⓜ Lujiazui) If you're squabbling over what to eat for lunch, brunch or dinner, settle your differences at smart-casual Yi Cafe. With 10 open kitchens and a walk-through layout, it's a veritable Asian/Southeast Asian/international food fest with endless menus. Be sure to cultivate a real hunger before you stop by. The buffet breakfasts easily match Pǔdōng's sightseeing calorific demands.

ON 56 · INTERNATIONAL $$$

Map p312 (意庐; Yìlú; ☎5047 1234; 54th-56th fl, Grand Hyatt, Jinmao Tower, 88 Century Ave; 世纪大道88号君悦大酒店; meals from ¥200; ⊗11.30am-2.30pm & 5.30-10.30pm; ☎; Ⓜ Lujiazui) This swish selection of restaurants all come with breathtaking vistas into the Shànghǎi void from the Grand Hyatt. **Cucina** serves delectable Italian dishes from Campania, with breads and pizzas fresh from the oven. The line at **Grill** is fine imported meats and seafood, while **Kobachi** features excellent sushi, sashimi and yakitori. The flagship **Canton** showcases Cantonese food and afternoon dim sum.

Sit in any restaurant of your choosing and order food from another. After dinner, retire to the **Patio Lounge** (Grand Hyatt, Jinmao Tower, 88 Century Ave; 世纪大道88号君悦大酒店; afternoon tea ¥248; ⊗11.30am-11pm Sun-Thu, to midnight Fri & Sat) on the same floor for a drink with the spectacular 33-floor atrium towering above you.

On the 54th floor (the Grand Hyatt lobby), the **Grand Café** (Grand Hyatt, Jinmao Tower, 88 Century Ave; 世纪大道88号君悦大酒店; lunch/dinner from ¥248/358; ⊗24hr) offers stunning panoramas through its glass walls and a good-value lunchtime buffet during the week, which allows you to choose a main course and have it prepared fresh in the show kitchen. To reserve a table by the window, book well in advance.

KITCHEN SALVATORE CUOMO · ITALIAN $$$

Map p312 (☎5054 1265; Riverside Ave, 2967 West Lujiazui Rd, near Fenghe Rd; 陆家嘴西路2967号滨江大道近丰和路; mains lunch/dinner from ¥128/198; ⊗11.30am-2.30pm & 6-10pm; ☎; Ⓜ Lujiazui) The hefty price of the wood-fired pizzas will have your eyes as big as the margaritas at this swish riverside restaurant, and the views of fairy-light-festooned boats gliding up and down the night-time Huángpǔ River could keep them that way. The pizzas are sublime, however, and alfresco tables out front beckon for long summer evenings, with the Oriental Pearl TV Tower rocketing overhead.

✗ Century Avenue Area

★ **HĂI DĬ LĀO** HOTPOT $$
Map p313 (海底捞; ☑3871 3936; 6th fl, 588 Zhangyang Rd; 张杨路588号6楼; hotpot per person ¥100; ⏰24hr; ☎; ⓜShangcheng Rd) Faultless and resourceful service is the name of the game at this Pǔdōng outpost of the West Nanjing Rd restaurant chain, which concocts an effortlessly enjoyable Sìchuān hotpot experience. Not for solo diners or romantic soirées.

🍷 DRINKING & NIGHTLIFE

Most Pǔdōng bars are in hotels (where you occasionally have to deal with condescending staff).

★ **FLAIR** BAR
Map p312 (58th fl, Ritz-Carlton Shanghai Pudong, 8 Century Ave; 世纪大道8号58楼; cocktails ¥90; ⏰5am-2am; ☎; ⓜLujiazui) Wow your date with Shànghǎi's most intoxicating nocturnal visuals from the 58th floor of the Ritz-Carlton, where Flair nudges you that bit closer to the baubles of the Oriental Pearl TV Tower. If it's raining, you'll end up inside, but that's OK as the chilled-out interior is supercool and there's a minimum price (¥400) for sitting outside.

CLOUD 9 BAR
Map p312 (九重天酒廊; Jiǔchóngtiān Jiǔláng; ☑5049 1234; 87th fl, Jinmao Tower, 88 Century Ave; 世纪大道88号金茂大厦87楼; wine from ¥65, cocktails ¥88; ⏰5pm-1am Mon-Fri, 11am-2am Sat & Sun; ⓜLujiazui) Watch day fade to night as the neon slowly flickers on. After an espresso martini or two, you'll probably find out what it means to be *shanghaied* (in the very best sense of the word). Access to Cloud 9 is through the lobby of the Grand Hyatt.

100 CENTURY AVENUE BAR
Map p312 (世纪大道100号; Shìjì Dàdào Yìbǎi Hào; ☑3855 1428; 91st & 92nd fl, Park Hyatt,

Shànghǎi World Financial Center, 100 Century Ave; 世纪大道100号柏悦酒店91-92楼; coffee/cocktails ¥65/85, wine ¥110-180; ⏰8pm-1am Mon-Thu, to 2am Fri & Sat; ☎; ⓜLujiazui) Pǔdōng keeps its edged honed with one of the highest bars in the world at 100 Century Avenue. It's pretty impressive inside, but the restaurant on the 91st floor has better views than the bar (on the floor above), as you can get up close to the windows. The bar is closed on Sunday.

Access is through the lobby of the Park Hyatt, on the south side of the building. There are six open kitchens in the restaurant area, but there's a minimum spend per table of ¥500 on Wednesdays (ladies' night), Fridays and Saturdays.

BREW BAR
Map p313 (酿; Niàng; ☑6169 8886; Kerry Hotel, 1388 Huamu Rd; 上海浦东嘉里大酒店花木路1388号; beer half/pint ¥48/68; ⏰11am-2am; ☎; ⓜHuamu Rd) Ale connoisseurs can earmark this nifty microbrewery bar in the Kerry Hotel, where resident brew-master Leon Mickelson dispenses six on-tap handmade beers (Skinny Green, pils, White Ant, Indian pale ale, Dugite vanilla stout, Mash) and a cider (Razorback). There's a huge range of other bottled beers, and Heineken for those who prefer it.

The bar is sleek and cool without being impersonal and you can hit the terrace for alfresco park views. Prices are steep, though, so target happy hour (from 4pm to 8pm Monday to Friday).

CAMEL BAR
Map p312 (www.camelsportsbar.com; 116 West Weifang Rd; 潍坊西路116号; ⓜCentury Avenue) If the slick and serene five-star hotel bar scene leaves you cold, two-floor sports pub Camel has a huge lively branch in Pǔdōng. It covers all the sporting action, on 17 screens, backed up by a strong showing of draught beers and cider, plus pub grub.

⭐ ENTERTAINMENT

ORIENTAL ART CENTER CLASSICAL MUSIC
Map p313 (上海东方艺术中心; Shànghǎi Dōngfāng Yìshù Zhōngxīn; ☑6854 1234; www.shoac.com.cn; 425 Dingxiang Rd; 浦东丁香路425号; tickets ¥30-680; ⓜScience & Technology Museum) Home of the Shànghǎi Symphony Orchestra, the Oriental Art Center was designed to resemble five petals of a butterfly

orchid. There are three main halls that host classical, jazz, dance and Chinese and Western opera performances. Saturday brunch concerts (10am, held on the first and third Saturday of the month) cost from ¥30 to ¥80. Free tours of the centre are conducted on the first Saturday of the month (from 1.30pm to 4.30pm).

DÀGUĀN THEATER THEATRE

Map p313 (大观舞台; Dàguān Wǔtái; www.daguan theatre.cn; Himalayas Center, 1188 Fangdian Rd; 喜玛拉雅中心芳甸路1188弄1号; MHuamu Rd) This new state-of-the-art 1100-seat theatre in the impressive Himalayas Center, attached to the Jumeirah Himalayas Hotel, stages Chinese opera, other traditional performance arts and Western theatre. The theatre has retractable seating, and also hosts films from the Shanghai International Film Festival.

🛍 SHOPPING

Pǔdōng is mostly about glittering malls, exclusive hotel arcades and heart-stopping prices, but further out, all the material goods you'll ever need in one lifetime converge in the market in the Science & Technology Museum metro station.

IFC MALL MALL

Map p312 (上海IFC商场; Shànghǎi IFC Shāngchǎng; www.shanghaiifcmall.com.cn; 8 Century Ave; 世纪大道8号; ⊙10am-10pm; MLujiazui) This incredibly glam and glitzy six-storey mall beneath the Cesar Pelli–designed twin towers of the Shànghǎi International Finance Center hosts a swish coterie of top-name brands, from Armani via Prada to Vivienne Westwood, and a host of dining options. It's rather like an extended version of a customer-free five-star hotel arcade, but it's certainly awesome (and an air-conditioned oasis on a sweltering day).

SHANGHAI TANG CLOTHING

Map p312 (上海滩; Shànghǎi Tān; www.shanghai tang.com; Lobby level, Pudong Shangri-La, 33 Fucheng Rd; 富城路33号浦东香格里拉大酒店; ⊙10am-10pm; MLujiazui) Sumptuous Shanghai Tang's shops add splashes of vibrant colour to the greyest of Shànghǎi days: elegant blouses, vivacious silk dresses, gorgeous tops, eye-catching glassware, Chinese-style shirts, scarves, cardigans, handbags, clutches, neat chopsticks, napkin holders, picture frames and more. The main branch is in the French Concession.

CITY SHOP SUPERMARKET

Map p312 (城市超市; Chéngshì Chāoshì; ☏6215 0418; www.cityshop.com.cn; 1st fl, Citigroup Tower, 33 Huayuanshiqiao Rd; 花园石桥路33号花旗集团大厦1楼; ⊙8am-10pm; MLujiazui) Imported goodies from shampoo to champagne, Scrumpy Jack cider, spam, Stolichnaya, Trappist Chimay beer, cheeses, wines and other treats for homesick foreign foodies, at a price. There are seven branches in town, including the main branch in Jìng'ān. Free delivery.

SUPERBRAND MALL MALL

Map p312 (正大广场; Zhèngdà Guǎngchǎng; 168 West Lujiazui Rd; 陆家嘴西路168号; ⊙10am-10pm; MLujiazui) Always busy, this gargantuan shopping mall is also ultrahandy for its dining options, its supermarket in the basement, a kids' arcade on the 6th floor and a cinema on the 8th floor.

★AP XĪNYÁNG FASHION & GIFTS MARKET SOUVENIRS

Map p313 (亚太新阳服饰礼品市场; Yàtài Xīnyáng Fúshì Lǐpǐn Shìchǎng; ⊙10am-8pm; MScience & Technology Museum) This huge underground market by the Science & Technology Museum metro station is Shànghǎi's largest collection of shopping stalls. There's tons of merchandise and fakes, from suits to moccasins, glinting copy watches, Darth Vader toys, jackets, Lionel Messi football strips, T-shirts, Indian saris, Angry Birds bags, Great Wall snow globes: everything under the sun.

It includes a branch of the Shíliùpù Fabric Market and a separate market devoted to pearls, the Yada Pearl Market (Yàdà Zhēnzhū Shìchǎng). Shop vendors are highly persistent and almost clawing, sending out scouts to wait at the metro exit turnstiles to ensnare shoppers. Haggling is the *lingua franca* – mixed with much huffing and puffing – so start with a very low offer and take it from there.

Hóngkǒu & North Shànghǎi

Neighbourhood Top Five

❶ Get history-hunting at the **Ohel Moishe Synagogue** (p159) and delve down surrounding streets for flavours of Jewish Shànghǎi.

❷ Track down Hóngkǒu's concession-period and art deco **architecture** (p160).

❸ Get lost along the labyrinth of concrete walkways in cool **1933** (p158).

❹ Poke among the bric-a-brac of **Dàshànghǎi** (p162) and other shops along Duolun Rd.

❺ Raise a glass to the Bund and the Pǔdōng skyline from **Vue** (p162), a bar with a view.

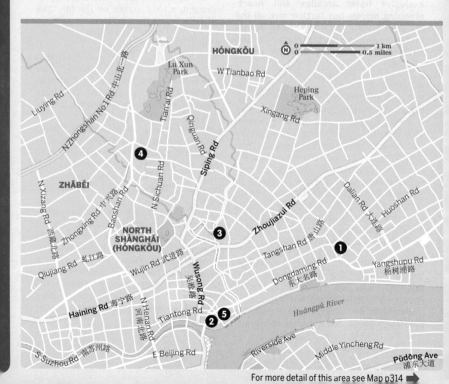

For more detail of this area see Map p314 ➡

Explore: Hóngkŏu & North Shànghăi

Hóngkŏu and North Shànghăi (虹口区·北上海) may not have the lion's share of sights in town, but prize chunks of heritage architecture rise up from the swirl of street life and an authentic grittiness survives.

The up-and-coming North Bund area beyond Sūzhōu Creek is worth exploring for its impressive buildings – including the granddaddy of heritage hotels, the Astor House Hotel – looming art deco blocks and noteworthy concession-era classics. The American Settlement was originally here, merging with the British Settlement in 1863 to form the prosperous International Settlement. To the west, Zhábĕi became infamous for its sweatshops and factories and was later flattened by the Japanese in 1932.

A rich vein of Jewish heritage survives towards Yángpŭ in the east, dating from the days when Hóngkŏu was home to thousands of Jewish refugees, mostly from Germany, who transformed 'Little Tokyo' (where 30,000 Japanese lived) into 'Little Vienna'. The Ohel Moishe Synagogue stands as a testament to this era. Wander round this neighbourhood and you'll also find examples of Shànghăi's trademark terrace-style *shíkùmén* (stone-gate house) architecture, *lòngtáng* (alleyway) houses and narrow alleyways filling in the gaps.

Close to the Bund, Hóngkŏu has some well positioned accommodation options and while notable restaurants may seem thin on the ground, work your shoe leather and you can find excellent options from across China.

Local Life

➡ **Snacking** Join locals along North Jiangxi Rd (p161) for a profusion of local titbits and hunger-busting bites.

➡ **Hóngkŏu backstreets** Wander the lanes around the Ohel Moishe Synagogue to soak up the local 'Little Vienna' flavour (p158).

➡ **Park life** Catch the locals performing taichi or honing ballroom-dancing spins in Lu Xun Park (p160).

➡ **Shopping** Sift for bargain threads with throngs of shoppers at Qīpŭ Market (p162).

Getting There & Away

➡ **Metro** Line 10 runs north from East Nanjing Rd to Fùdàn University, passing Tiantong Rd, North Sichuan Rd and Hailun Rd stations. Line 3 also runs north, offering access to Duolun Rd and Lu Xun Park. Lines 4 and 8 loop east–west. Main interchange stations are Baoshan Rd (lines 3 and 4), Hailun Rd (lines 4 and 10) and Hongkou Football Stadium (lines 3 and 8).

➡ **Bus** Nos 22, 37 and 135 run up Dongdaming Rd and back down Changyang and Dongchangzhi Rds.

Lonely Planet's Top Tip

Basing yourself in south Hóngkŏu – at the Astor House Hotel (p212), Chai Living Residences (p212) or the soon-to-open Bulgari – allows you to hang your Shànghăi fedora within easy reach of the Bund across Wàibáidù Bridge (Garden Bridge) and the nearby concession architecture of the North Bund district.

✕ Best Places to Eat

➡ Guŏyúan (p161)
➡ Noodle Bull (p161)
➡ Xīndàlù (p161)
➡ Yang's Fry Dumplings (p161)

For reviews, see p161. ➡

🔒 Best Shopping

➡ Qīpŭ Market (p162)
➡ Dàshànghăi (p162)
➡ Details Gallery (p162)
➡ Duolun Rd (p158)

For reviews, see p162. ➡

◉ SIGHTS

POST MUSEUM   MUSEUM

Map p314 (邮政博物馆; Yóuzhèng Bówùguǎn; 2nd fl, 250 North Suzhou Rd; 北苏州路250号2楼; ⊙9am-5pm Wed, Thu, Sat & Sun, last entry 4pm; M Tiantong Rd) FREE This fascinating museum in the stunning Main Post Office building explores postal history in imperial China, which dates back to the 1st millennium BC. The system used an extensive pony express to relay messages; Marco Polo estimated there were 10,000 postal stations in 13th-century China. Check out the collection of pre- and post-Liberation stamps (1888–1978) in a special climate-controlled room; the 250cc Xingyue motorbikes used by postal workers to burn up and down Shànghǎi's roads; and a mechanised mail sorter.

Downstairs, you can also inspect a historic mail-train carriage and two old post vans, one horse-drawn, plus a re-creation of a Qing-dynasty mail room. Sadly, the roof garden is closed indefinitely.

1933   HISTORIC BUILDING

Map p314 (上海1933老场坊; Shànghǎi 1933 Lǎochǎngfáng; 10 Shajing Rd; 沙泾路10号; M Hailun Rd) This vast concrete former abattoir is one of Shànghǎi's unique buildings, today converted to house boutiques, bars, shops and restaurants. An extraordinary place built around a central core, its structure is a maze of flared columns, skybridges (across which cattle would be led to slaughter), ramps, curved stairwells – and jostling photo opportunities. The shops are not of much interest, but a well-positioned branch of trendy Noodle Bull makes the most of its concrete setting.

DUOLUN ROAD CULTURAL STREET   STREET

Map p314 (多伦文化名人街; Duōlún Wénhuà Míngrén Jiē; M Dongbaoxing Rd) This pleasantly restored but sleepy street of fine old houses, just off North Sichuan Rd, was once home to several of China's most famous writers (as well as several Kuomintang generals), when the road was known as Doulean Rd. Today it is lined with art-supply stores, curio and Burmese jade shops, galleries, teahouses and cafes. The main appeal of the street is its galleries and antique shops, including **Dàshànghǎi** (p162).

The **Shànghǎi Duōlún Museum of Modern Art** (上海多伦现代美术馆; Shànghǎi Duōlún Xiàndài Měishùguǎn; Map p314; ☑6587 6902; 27 Duolun Rd; 多伦路27号; adult/student ¥10/5; ⊙10am-5pm Tue-Sun) has a focus on experimental contemporary art. Further along the street, you may find the 1928 **Hóngdé Temple** (鸿德堂; Hóngdé Táng; Map p314; ☑5696 1196; 59 Duolun Rd; 多伦路59号) open,

---

HISTORIC HÓNGKǑU

For a mini walking tour of the streets of the Jewish Quarter – aka 'Little Vienna' – surrounding the Ohel Moishe Synagogue, turn right outside the synagogue, then right again past the former Jewish tenements of Zhoushan Rd (formerly Ward Rd), once the commercial heart of the district. At Huoshan Rd (formerly Wayside Rd), head southwest past the art deco facade of the former **Broadway Theatre** (百老汇大戏院; Bǎilǎohuì Dàxìyuàn; Map p314; 57 Huoshan Rd; 霍山路57号; M Tilanqiao) to the Ocean Hotel. Turn right up Haimen Rd (Muirhead Rd), past Changyang Rd, to what was once a row of Jewish shops and a kosher delicatessen. Until just a couple of years ago, faded painted signs from the 1940s above the shops declared 'Horn's Imbiss Stube' (Horn's Snack Bar) and 'Cafe Atlantic', but the shops were recently demolished.

At the top of the road (the crossing with Kunming Rd) you'll see the largely rebuilt **Xiàhǎi Buddhist Monastery** (下海庙; Xiàhǎi Miào; Map p314; Kunming Rd; 昆明路; admission ¥5; ⊙7am-4pm). Take a right turn, then another right, down Zhoushan Rd once again to complete the circle back to the synagogue.

Zhoushan Rd is also home to the British-built **Ward Road Jail** (Map p314; Zhoushan Rd; 舟山路; M Dalian Rd), once Shànghǎi's biggest. Used by the Japanese during WWII, it's still functioning as a prison and is probably as close as you'll get, or would want to get, to a Chinese detention facility. You can catch bus 33 here from the Bund.

If you're interested in learning more about Hóngkǒu's Jewish heritage, contact Dvir Bar-Gal, an Israeli Shànghǎi resident who offers informative English and Hebrew **tours** (☑130 0214 6702; www.shanghai-jews.com; half-day tour ¥400) of the area.

TOP SIGHT
OHEL MOISHE SYNAGOGUE

The Ohel Moishe Synagogue was built by the Russian Ashkenazi Jewish community in 1927 and lies in the heart of the 1940s Jewish ghetto.

Today it houses the Shànghǎi Jewish Refugees Museum, a moving introduction to the lives of the approximately 20,000 Central European refugees who fled to Shànghǎi to escape the Nazis. Slip a pair of shower caps over your shoes to look at the synagogue itself (in the main building) and the exhibitions upstairs. The photographs and exhibits on the Holocaust are graphic, but highly educational. Considerable emphasis falls on the Soviet Red Army's liberation of death camps, but seems to skip mention of US and Allied efforts. Two other halls in the courtyard below detail the individual stories of notable Jewish refugees in Shànghǎi through their photographs and possessions.

The exhibition is rounded off with a moving quote from the writer, Nobel Laureate and Holocaust survivor Elie Wiesel: 'The past is in the present, but the future is still in our hands.' English-language **tours** (⊘9.30am-4.15pm, every 45min) are included in the admission price.

DON'T MISS...

➡ Synagogue
➡ Upstairs exhibition
➡ Courtyard exhibition halls

PRACTICALITIES

➡ 摩西会堂; Móxī Huìtáng
➡ Map p314
➡ 62 Changyang Rd; 长阳路62号
➡ admission ¥50
➡ ⊘9am-5pm, last entry 4.30pm
➡ Ⓜ Dalian Rd

HÓNGKŎU & NORTH SHÀNGHǍI SIGHTS

---

its grey-brick interior adorned with pictures of the Stations of the Cross and simple wooden pews; upstairs is a lovely hall with a wooden ceiling. The church was built in a Chinese style as the Great Virtue Church.

The League of Left-Wing Writers was established down a side alley on 2 March 1930. Today the building serves as a **political museum** (左联会址; Zuǒlián Huìzhǐ; Map p314; No 2, Lane 201, Duolun Rd; 多伦路201弄2号; adult/student ¥5/3; ⊘9am-4pm Tue-Sun), worth a look for the architecture alone.

Duolun Rd ends in another Kuomintang residence, the Moorish-looking, private **Kong Residence** (孔公馆; Kǒng Gōngguǎn; Map p314; 250 Duolun Rd; 多伦路250号), built in 1924.

If you need a break, try the Old Film Café (p162), next to the 18.2m-high **Xīshí Bell Tower** (夕拾钟搂; Xīshí Zhōnglóu; Map p314; Duolun Rd; 多伦路; Ⓜ East Baoxing Rd) at the bend in the road. There's a statue of Charlie Chaplin outside.

LU XUN MEMORIAL HALL   MUSEUM

Map p314 (鲁迅纪念馆; Lǔ Xùn Jìniànguǎn; Lu Xun Park, 2288 North Sichuan Rd; 鲁迅公园内, 四川北路2288号; ⊘9am-4pm; Ⓜ Hong-kou Football Stadium) **FREE** An excellent museum, this modern hall charts the life and creative output of author Lu Xun with photographs, first editions, videos and waxworks. Detailed English captions throughout.

LU XUN FORMER RESIDENCE   HISTORIC BUILDING

Map p314 (鲁迅故居; Lǔxùn Gùjū; ☎5666 2608; No 9, Lane 132, Shanyin Rd; 山阴路132弄9号; adult/child ¥8/4; ⊘9am-4pm; Ⓜ Dongbaoxing Rd) Lu Xun buffs will adore ferreting around this three-floor domicile on lovely Shanyin Rd, where an excellent English-speaking guide can fill you in on all the period bits and bobs, including the author's tea cosy and the clock that stopped at his time of death.

Don't overlook wandering along Shanyin Rd and peeking into its lovely alleyways and traditional *lòngtáng* houses (for example at Nos 41 to 50, Lane 180, Shanyin Rd). Around the corner at 2050 North Sichuan Rd is the site of the Uchiyama Bookstore, where Lu Xun used to stock up on literature (it's now a branch of the ICBC bank).

LOCAL KNOWLEDGE

HÓNGKŎU ARCHITECTURE

Hóngkŏu has a rich crop of architectural gems, from run-down terraced houses and dilapidated *shíkùmén* (stone-gate houses) to riverside art deco apartment blocks, noble concession-period classics, heritage hotels and converted abattoirs. At the time of writing, the lavish Foster+Partners Bulgari Hotel project was proceeding apace on North Suzhou Rd by Sūzhōu Creek, further revitalising the North Bund area.

Examples of *shíkùmén* architecture can be found if you stroll north along Zhapu Rd from Kunshan Rd and pop into the first pinched alley at No 313 (乍浦路313弄) on your left, where a line of typical *shíkùmén* awaits, decorated with distinctively carved lintels. Emerging from the alley, turn right along Baiguan Jie (百官街) for a short walk north to admire a further cluster of *shíkùmén* through the archway on your right. Other areas that are good for *shíkùmén* buildings are Zhoushan Rd, especially at its southern end. The market street of Dongyuhang Rd (东余杭路), which it crosses, also has some interesting *shíkùmén* entrances. Shanyin Rd is a pleasant tree-lined street with a number of *shíkùmén*-filled alleyways branching off it.

Notable buildings to look out for:

1933 (p158) A magnificent concrete slaughterhouse transformed into a shopping complex. The shops themselves are of less interest but the very photogenic 'air bridges' are intact.

Hongkew Methodist Church (景灵堂; Jǐnglíng Táng; Map p314; 135 Kunshan Rd; 昆山路135号) Dating from 1923, this is the church where Chiang Kaishek, leader of the Republic of China, married Soong Meiling. It's generally closed to the public, but the caretaker may let you in.

New Asia Hotel (新亚大酒店; Xīnyà Dàjiǔdiàn; Map p314; ☎info 6324 2210; fax 6356 6816; 422 Tiantong Rd; 天潼路422号) One of Shànghǎi's rich brood of art deco wonders.

Main Post Office (国际邮局; Guójì Yóujú; Map p314; 250 North Suzhou Rd; 北苏州路250号; Ⓜ Tiantong Rd) Overlooking Sūzhōu Creek, this supremely grand building dates from 1924. It is topped with a cupola and clock tower, and ornamented with bronze statues coated in a green patina. Sadly, the roof-top garden has closed 'indefinitely'.

Broadway Mansions (上海大厦; Shànghǎi Dàshà; Map p314; 20 North Suzhou Rd; 苏州北路20号) Looming over Sūzhōu Creek, this classic brick pile (resembling a Ministry of Truth) was built to great fanfare in 1934 as an apartment block and later used to house American officers after WWII. Today it's a hotel.

Astor House Hotel (p212) Bursting with history, this classic old-timer has a yarn to tell and a lot of admirers: it's an excellent place to base oneself for swift access to the Bund.

Embankment Building (河滨大厦; Hébīn Dàshà; Map p314; 400 North Suzhou Rd; 苏州北路400号) Designed by architects Palmer & Turner, dating from 1935 and home to Chai Living Residences (p212).

Russian Consulate (俄罗斯领事馆; Éluósī Lǐngshìguǎn) This grand red-roofed concession building rises up just north of Wàibáidù Bridge.

LU XUN PARK
PARK

Map p314 (鲁迅公园; Lǔ Xùn Gōngyuán; 146 East Jiangwan Rd; 江湾东路146号; ⊙6am-6pm; Ⓜ Hongkou Football Stadium) Particularly photogenic in spring and summer when the trees are in blossom, Lu Xun Park is one of the city's most pleasant green spaces. Here you'll find elderly Chinese practising taichi or ballroom dancing, and even retired opera singers testing out their pipes. It's a big shame about the fenced-in lawn, but the **Plum Garden** (admission ¥15; ⊙7.30am-6pm) is an attractive diversion.

The English Corner on Sunday mornings is one of the largest in all of Shànghǎi and it's a good place to natter to locals in English. You can take boats out onto the small lake. The park used to be called Hóngkŏu Park but was renamed because it holds Lu Xun's Tomb, moved here from the International Cemetery in 1956, on the 20th anniversary of his death.

GÒNGQĪNG FOREST PARK   PARK

(共青森林公园; Gòngqīng Sēnlín Gōngyuán; ☑6574 0586; www.shgqsl.com; 2000 Jungong Rd; 军工路2000号; adult/child ¥15/7.5; ⏱9am-6pm, last entry 4pm; ☒; ⓂNenjiang Rd, Shiguang Rd) This vast expanse of forested parkland on the western shore of the Huángpǔ River is a leafy, wooded and tranquil slice of countryside in Shànghǎi. This is about as wild as you get in Pǔxī, with acres of willows, luohan pines, magnolias, hibiscus and nary a skyscraper in sight. Aim to spend half if not a whole day picnicking and wandering around this huge area, or hop into one of the buggies (¥10) for express tours around the grounds.

For kids there's a roller coaster, rock climbing, go-carting, horse riding, paintball and other activities. Nenjiang Rd and Shiguang Lu stations near the northern terminus of metro line 8 will get you close to the western edge of the park; a taxi from the metro station will cost around ¥14. Alternatively, take line 8 to Xiangyin Rd metro station and hop aboard bus 102 from exit 2. If you want to spend the night in the park, check into the **Hongsen Forest Park Hotel** (☑6532 1296; 2300 Jungong Rd; 军工路2300号; r/cabin ¥280/580).

GALLERY MAGDA DANYSZ   GALLERY

(www.magda-gallery.com; 188 Linqing Rd; 临青路188号; ⏱11am-6pm Tue-Sun; ⓂNingguo Rd) Well worth a cultural diversion, this bold and vibrant art space for both emerging and established Chinese and international names is twinned with its Paris gallery, bringing an artistic frisson to Yángpǔ district in north Shànghǎi. Exhibitions at the Gallery Magda Danysz range through an inspiring and thoughtful spectrum of visual media – check the website for details. Take metro line 12 to Ningguo Rd and then a taxi (¥14).

✕ EATING

For local Shànghǎi snacks and eats from across China, North Jiangxi Rd (江西北路) is stuffed with chefs wilting over steamers, boisterous kebab sellers and red-cheeked *málàtàng* (麻辣烫; spicy soup with meat and vegetables) vendors. You'll also find Shāndōng *dàbǐng* (山东大饼; flatbread; ¥2) from north China and the ever-scrummy *ròujiāmó* (肉夹馍; bun stuffed with pork and peppers; ¥6). Several Buddhist vegetarian restaurants cooking up meat-free pot-stickers and other veggie dishes are flung out down Haimen Rd from the Xiàhǎi Buddhist Monastery.

★GUǑYÚAN   HUNANESE $

Map p314 (果园; 524 Dongjiangwan Rd; 东江湾路524号; mains from ¥18; ⏱11am-2pm & 5-10pm Mon-Fri, 11am-3pm & 5-10pm Sat & Sun; ⓂHongkou Football Stadium) The cool lime-green table-cloths do little to tame the tempestuous flavours of this fantastic Húnán restaurant. The *tiěbǎn dòufu* (铁板豆腐; sizzling tofu platter; ¥30) here is a magnificent dish, but its fiery flavours are almost eclipsed by the enticing *xiāngwèi qiézibāo* (湘味茄子煲; Húnán aubergine hotpot; ¥20) and the lovely *zīrán yángròu* (孜然羊肉; lamb with cumin; ¥32).

Otherwise go for the *málà dòufu* (麻辣豆腐; spicy tofu) or the cracking *tiěbǎn niúròu* (铁板牛肉; sizzling beef platter; ¥35). There's sadly no English menu; instead you get a green paper Chinese menu to tick off what you want, so use the suggestions above or point at what others are eating.

★NOODLE BULL   NOODLES $

Map p314 (狠牛; Hěn Niú; 1-234, 1933, 10 Shajing Rd; 沙泾路10号1933老场坊1-234; mains from ¥32; ⏱11am-9pm; ⓂHailun Rd) Perfectly attuned to the concrete lines and contours of the 1933 complex, this is possibly Noodle Bull's best opening. If you don't want to celebrate 1933's former employment as a slaughterhouse, the gorgeous and superhealthy sesame-paste noodles (¥32) are the way to go. There's no MSG; you'll have a choice of different thickness of hand-pulled noodles; and the ambience simply oozes with cool panache.

YANG'S FRY DUMPLINGS   DUMPLINGS $

(小杨生煎馆; Xiǎoyáng Shēngjiān Guǎn; 810 Quyang Rd; 曲阳路810号; 4 dumplings ¥6; ⏱6.30am-7.30pm; ⓂQuyang Rd) Hoover up Yang's time-honoured and much-applauded fried *shēngjiān* dumplings – you're set for brekkie, lunch or (early) dinner. Order per *liǎng* (两; 4 dumplings; ¥6)

XĪNDÀLÙ   PEKING DUCK $$

Map p314 (新大陆; ☑6393-1234, ext 6318; 1st fl, Hyatt on the Bund, 199 Huangpu Rd; 黄浦路199号外滩茂悦大酒店1楼; half/whole roast duck ¥218/298, dishes from ¥68; ⏱11.30am-2.30pm & 6-11pm; ⓂTiantong Rd) Although definitive *Běijīng kǎoyā* (Peking duck) really needs to be flamed up within quacking distance of the Forbidden City, Shànghǎi's best roast-duck experience imports all the necessary ingredients (including chefs and a special brick oven) direct from Běijīng. In addition to its sleek open kitchen, this place is unusually intimate inside.

Other first-rate dishes on offer include beggar's chicken (a Hángzhōu speciality), which needs to be ordered at least four hours in advance. Reserve.

🍷 DRINKING & NIGHTLIFE

★VUE
BAR

Map p314 (非常时髦; Fēicháng Shímáo; 32nd & 33rd fl, Hyatt on the Bund, 199 Huangpu Rd; 外滩茂悦大酒店黄浦路199号32-33楼; ⊙6pm-1am; MTiantong Rd) Located in the Hyatt on the Bund, Vue offers extrasensory nocturnal views of the Bund and Pǔdōng, with an outdoor Jacuzzi to go with your raised glasses of bubbly or Vue martinis (vodka and mango purée).

OLD FILM CAFÉ
CAFE

Map p314 (老电影咖啡馆; Lǎodiànyǐng Kāfēiguǎn; ☎5696 4763; 123 Duolun Rd; 多伦路123号; coffee/tea from ¥25/35; ⊙9.30am-midnight; MDongbaoxing Rd) Celebrating the golden age of Shànghǎi cinema, this place is also good for a coffee if you're in the Duolun Rd area. There's some fantastic woodwork, comfy armchairs plus an atmospheric loft, and photos of Chinese and Western legends of the silver screen. There are also regular screenings of classic films from the 1930s, and a wide range of teas and alcohol.

☆ ENTERTAINMENT

SHÀNGHǍI CIRCUS WORLD
ACROBATICS

(上海马戏城; Shànghǎi Mǎxìchéng; ☎6652 7501; www.era-shanghai.com/era/en/; 2266 Gonghexin Rd; 闸北区共和新路2266号; admission ¥120-600; MShanghai Circus World) Out on the far northern outskirts of town you'll find this impressive complex. The show – *Era: Intersection of Time* – combines awesome acrobatics with new-fangled multimedia elements. Shows start at 7.30pm. Tickets are available at the door, but booking ahead is advised.

PEARL THEATRE
THEATRE

Map p314 (☎137 6488 9962; www.thepearl.com.cn; 471 Zhapu Rd; 乍浦路471号; ⊙8pm-2am; MNorth Sichuan Rd) Formerly known as Chinatown, this three-floor place in an old Buddhist temple north of the Bund is set in a magnificent old theatre (with boxes!). It stages drama, cabaret and other shows.

🛍 SHOPPING

Head for the area north of Sūzhōu Creek to see where the masses shop.

QĪPǓ MARKET
CLOTHING

Map p314 (七浦服装市场; Qīpǔ Fúzhuāng Shìchǎng; 168 & 183 Qipu Rd; 七浦路168、183号; ⊙5am-5pm west side, 7am-7pm east side; MTiantong Rd) Qīpǔ Market is where ordinary Shànghǎi goes shopping for clothes. Consisting of two run-down, rabbit-warren-like department stores surrounding the North Henan Rd intersection, it's one big permanent 'everything must go now' sale. Do as locals do and push through the hordes of people trawling for T-shirts, shoes, tank tops, dresses, shorts and pretty much any item of clothing you can think of, all selling for around ¥50. Haggle hard; you should be paying at least 50% below the asking price.

DETAILS GALLERY
ANTIQUES

Map p314 (www.chailiving.com; Embankment Bldg, 370-380 North Suzhou Rd; 苏州北路370-380号; ⊙noon-8pm Tue-Fri, 11am-7pm Sat & Sun; MTiantong Rd) Located on the corner of the Embankment Building, this smart and sedate gallery from Chai Living apartments showcases good-looking antique Chinese chests, wardrobes, silks, art and other antiques.

DÀSHÀNGHǍI
ANTIQUES

Map p314 (大上海; 181 Duolun Rd; 多伦路181号; ⊙9am-5.30pm, to 6pm in summer; MDongbaoxing Rd) Explore keenly at this Duolun Rd shop, where shelves spill forth with all manner of historic collectables from pre-Liberation China: books and catalogues; 1950s maps of Běijīng and Shànghǎi; genuine posters and authentic memorabilia from the Cultural Revolution; black-and-white-photos; unopened matchboxes and cigarette packs from the 1960s; Republican-era lipsticks; toothbrushes and more.

You may not find a Shakespeare & Company first edition of *Ulysses* among all the

SHÀNGHǍI'S JEWS

Shànghǎi has two centuries of strong Jewish connections. Established Middle Eastern Sephardic Jewish families such as the Hardoons, Ezras, Kadoories and Sassoons built their fortunes in Shànghǎi, establishing at least seven synagogues and many Jewish hospitals and schools. It was Victor Sassoon who famously remarked: 'There is only one race greater than the Jews and that's the Derby.'

A second group of Jews, this time Ashkenazi, arrived via Siberia, Hǎ'ěrbīn and Tiānjīn from Russia after anti-Jewish pogroms in 1906. The biggest influx, however, came between 1933 and 1941, when 30,000 mostly Ashkenazi Jews arrived from Europe by boat from Italy or by train via Siberia. Many had been issued with visas to cross China by Ho Fengshan, Chinese consul-general in Vienna, who was recently honoured as the 'Chinese Schindler'.

Shànghǎi was one of the few safe havens for Jews fleeing the Holocaust in Europe, as it required neither a passport nor visa to stay. Gestapo agents followed the refugees and, in 1942, tried to persuade the Japanese to build death camps on Chongming Island. Instead, in 1943, the Japanese forced Jews to move into a 'Designated Area for Stateless Refugees' in Hóngkǒu.

The Jewish ghetto (stateless Russians didn't have to live here) became home to Jews from all walks of life. It grew to shelter a synagogue, schools, a local paper, hospitals and enough cafes, rooftop gardens and restaurants to gain the epithet 'Little Vienna'. Those Jews who held jobs in the French Concession had to secure passes from the Japanese, specifically the notoriously unpredictable and violent Mr Goya. Poorer refugees were forced to bunk down in cramped hostels known as *Heime*, and had to rely on the generosity of others. As the wealthy Anglophile Jewish trading families had left in 1941, the situation was tight. Still, the refugees heard of events in distant Europe and realised perhaps that they were the lucky ones.

Today there are a few remainders of Jewish life in Shànghǎi, such as the Ohel Moishe Synagogue (p159) and the former Jewish Club (1932) in the grounds of the Conservatory of Music, where concerts are still performed. The Ohel Rachel Synagogue was built by Jacob Elias Sassoon in the early 20th century. Unfortunately, it remains closed to the public. Nearby are the remains of the school founded on the grounds by Horace Kadoorie.

For information and tours of Jewish Shànghǎi, contact the **Centre of Jewish Studies Shànghǎi** (上海犹太研究中心; Shànghǎi Yóutài Yánjiū Zhōngxīn; Map p302; ☑5306 0606, ext 2476; www.cjss.org.cn; Room 476, No 7, Lane 622, Middle Huaihai Rd; 淮海中路622弄7号476屋; tours US$80; ☺9am-4pm). The centre offers one-day tours (for groups only) of Jewish Shànghǎi with English- and Hebrew-speaking guides; it also has a fine library of books and periodicals.

clutter, but it's worth a good browse. The owner seems haggling-resistant (but you can give it a shot).

ELECTRONICS MARKET   ELECTRONICS
Map p314 (电子市场; Diànzǐ Shìchǎng; Qiujiang Rd; 虬江路; ☺9.30am-5.30pm; Ⓜ Baoshan Rd) If you want to put together your own computer, replace a processor, soup-up an MP3 player or score a pair of speakers, try this market located right under the elevated train tracks that lead into Baoshan Rd metro. Prices are low and negotiable, but how long everything will last is another matter, and you may not get a receipt or a guarantee.

Xújiāhuì & South Shànghǎi

XÚJIĀHUÌ | SOUTH SHÀNGHǍI

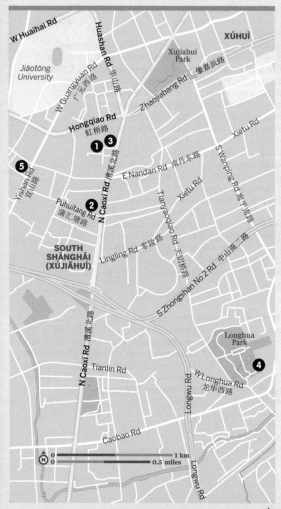

Neighbourhood Top Five

❶ Swoon over the brilliant blues and crimsons of the stained glass illuminating **St Ignatius Cathedral** (p166).

❷ Admire the elegant fusion of Chinese and Western art within the unique **Tousewe Museum** (p166).

❸ Explore the well-preserved **Jesuit heritage** of Xújiāhuì (p167).

❹ Divine the Buddhist heritage of South Shànghǎi in the **Lónghuá Temple & Pagoda** (p168).

❺ Go all out for a Uighur lamb feast at **Xīnjiāng Fēngwèi Restaurant** (p169).

For more detail of this area see Map p316 ➡

Explore: Xújiāhuì & South Shànghǎi

Bordering the southwestern end of the stylish French Concession and a zip away on the metro from People's Sq, Xújiāhuì (徐家汇) was known to 1930s expats as Zícawei or Sicawei. Most locals come here today to shop at the outsized Grand Gateway 66 mall, but Xújiāhuì was originally an attractive Jesuit settlement dating back to the 17th century. A Catholic flavour still clings to the neighbourhood, holding firm against the ever-encroaching office blocks and shopping malls. As elsewhere in Shànghǎi, you have to explore a bit to pull all the historical threads together, but if you've an eye for architectural heritage, a trip here makes for rewarding exploration.

A day's exploration of Xújiāhuì should suffice. Accessed directly on the metro at its namesake station, the area is dominated by giant shopping malls and department stores that circle a five-way intersection that's insanely busy even by Shànghǎi standards. It's one of the most popular shopping areas in the city and packed at weekends.

History, heritage architecture, green lawns and academia converge on the tranquil campus of Jiāotōng University along Huashan Rd, north of the main Jesuit sights, while a host of local dining options means you won't be caught hungry at lunch or dinner time. Of course, shopping needs are all met in Xújiāhuì's high-profile malls.

Further out from Xújiāhuì, South Shànghǎi is marked by one of the city's most famous temples, the ancient Lónghuá Temple and its pagoda, as well as an amusement park that can help occupy children rebelling against sightseeing.

Local Life

➡ **Greenery** Join the students relaxing on the lawn of Jiāotōng University (p167).

➡ **Dumplings** Find out what all the fuss is about – follow Shànghǎi's pernickety local diners to Din Tai Fung (p168).

➡ **Shopping** See how the Shanghainese spend, spend, spend at Grand Gateway 66 (p170).

Getting There & Away

➡ **Metro** Lines 1, 4, 9 and 11 run through the district. Xujiahui (lines 1, 9 and 11) and Shanghai Indoor Stadium (lines 1 and 4) are the main interchange stations. Line 1 runs through the French Concession and down to the South Shanghai Railway Station; line 9 can whisk you to Pǔdōng; line 11 stops at Jiāotōng University and heads south to Lónghuá Temple.

Lonely Planet's Top Tip

With its harried shopping hordes and hectic roads, Xújiāhuì can be breathlessly busy. Escape to some of Shànghǎi's best-tended areas of greenery: the gorgeous and inviting lawn a short walk from the main entrance of Jiāotōng University on Huashan Rd, where students lie down on the grass reading and chatting in warm weather.

⊙ Best Sights

➡ St Ignatius Cathedral (p166)

➡ Tousewe Museum (p166)

➡ Bibliotheca Zi-Ka-Wei (p166)

➡ Lónghuá Temple & Pagoda (p168)

For reviews, see p166.➡

✕ Best Places to Eat

➡ Din Tai Fung (p168)

➡ Xīnjiāng Fēngwèi Restaurant (p169)

➡ Kota's Kitchen (p169)

➡ 1001 Noodles House (p169)

For reviews, see p168.➡

XÚJIĀHUÌ & SOUTH SHÀNGHǍI

SIGHTS

⊙ Xújiāhuì

ST IGNATIUS CATHEDRAL
CHURCH

Map p316 (徐家汇天主教堂; Xújiāhuì Tiānzhǔjiàotáng; ☑6438 4632; 158 Puxi Rd; 蒲西路 158号; ◷9-11am & 1-4pm Mon-Sat, 2-4pm Sun; Ⓜ Xujiahui) The dignified twin-spired St Ignatius Cathedral (1904) is a major Xújiāhuì landmark. A long span of Gothic arches, its nave is ornamented on the outside with rows of menacing gargoyles; note how the church spires find reflection in much of the more recently built local architecture. The original stained glass was destroyed in the Cultural Revolution, but the vivid colours of the recent red, azure and purple replacements (with archaic Chinese inscriptions from the Bible) are outstanding.

Mass is held on Sundays at 7am, 8am, 10am, noon (in English) and 6pm; on weekdays at 6.15am and 7am and on Saturdays at 4.30pm and 6pm. Exit 3 from Xujiahui metro station is right by the church.

TOUSEWE MUSEUM
MUSEUM

Map p316 (土山湾博物馆; Tǔshānwān Bówùguǎn; Tǔshānwān Museum; 55-1 Puhuitang Rd; 蒲汇塘路55-1号; admission ¥10; ◷9am-4.30pm Tue-Sun; Ⓜ Shanghai Indoor Stadium, Xujiahui) Alongside a middle school along Puhuitang Rd, this fascinating museum is dedicated to the arts and crafts of the former redbrick Tousewe Orphanage, established here by the indefatigable Jesuits in 1864. The Catholics taught orphans the techniques of Western art: one of the first things you see as you enter the museum is a small, exquisite and exact copy of the former Tiānníng Pagoda in Běijīng and a magnificent wooden *páilou* (decorative arch), the Tǔshānwān Archway, carved in 1913.

There's a wealth of objects either produced or relating to the orphanage, from religious ornaments to Jesuit literature. Woodcraft was particularly productive at the orphanage, so some splendid items can be admired; look out for the expertly carved *Li Kui and his Double*, fashioned from boxwood, and the Madonna from the 1920s. Filling out the rest of the fascinating collection are paintings and stained glass. Audio tours are available.

BIBLIOTHECA ZI-KA-WEI
LIBRARY

Map p316 (徐家汇藏书楼; Xújiāhuì Cángshūlóu; ☑5425 9260; www.xjh.sh.cn/pages/cangshulou; 80 North Caoxi Rd; 漕溪北路80号; Ⓜ Xujiahui) The magnificent St Ignatius Catholic Library, the Bibliotheca Zi-Ka-Wei is one of several Jesuit monuments defining historic Xújiāhuì. Established in 1847 by the local Jesuit mission, its priceless book collection in the main library (大书房; Dà Shūfáng) can only be seen by application (☑5425 9260; limited English) as the free Saturday guided tours are no longer running. The collection of antiquarian tomes, arranged on one floor with a gallery above, is a rare and astonishing treasure.

SHÀNGHǍI'S CHRISTIANS

Christianity is the fastest-growing faith in China, and Shànghǎi alone has at least 140,000 Catholics, largely due to its history of Jesuit communities. St Ignatius Cathedral is the largest church in the city proper but Shěshān Basilica, in the suburbs, is even larger. Relations between the government and the Holy See are uneasy, as the state-run overseeing Chinese Patriotic Catholic Association does not acknowledge the authority of the Vatican and appoints its own bishops. China's one-child policy does not sit well with the Catholic stand on abortion either. For these reasons, the Vatican maintains diplomatic relations with Taiwan, much to China's consternation.

To see or take part in prayer, Catholics can visit the **Christ the King Church** (君王天主堂; Jūnwáng Tiānzhǔtáng; Map p302; cnr Julu & Maoming Rds) in the French Concession, St Ignatius Cathedral or the splendid Catholic Church (p173) in Qībǎo. Protestants can visit the lively **Community Church** (Map p306; ☑6437 6576; 53 Hengshan Rd), near South Wulumuqi Rd in the French Concession, which has a Sunday school for children and a small nursery for toddlers. There is also a growing flock of modern, newly built churches throughout Shànghǎi, including in Pǔdōng. Other historic Catholic churches can be found in Zhūjiājiǎo and Hángzhōu.

JESUIT XÚJIĀHUÌ

Beyond St Ignatius Cathedral and the Bibliotheca Zi-Ka-Wei, keep your eyes peeled to unearth a small treasure trove of historic architecture around Xújiāhuì.

A tourist information centre can be found on Puxi Rd, in between St Ignatius Cathedral and the Xújiāhuì Observatory; it has a specific focus on the neighbourhood. For more information on the area, click on www.xjh.sh.cn.

➡ **Xúhuì Public School** (徐汇中学; Xúhuì Zhōngxué; Map p316; Hongqiao Rd) This red-and-grey-brick building on the south side of Hongqiao Rd across from Grand Gateway 66 mall was established in 1850 by the Jesuit priest Claude Gotteland.

➡ **Former St Ignatius Convent** (Map p316; North Caoxi Rd) The former St Ignatius Convent, standing across North Caoxi Rd from St Ignatius Cathedral, is now a restaurant. It once belonged to the Helpers of the Holy Souls.

➡ **Xújiāhuì Observatory** (Map p316; 166 Puxi Rd; 蒲西路166号) The elegant Jesuit-built Xújiāhuì Observatory dates to 1872 and is currently part of the Shànghǎi Meteorological Bureau. Although inaccessible, it is partially visible to visitors from the gate.

➡ **Former Major Seminary** (Map p316; East Nandan Rd; 南丹东路) This Jesuit-constructed building is currently undergoing massive restoration.

Home to 560,000 volumes in Greek, Latin and other languages, the edifice consists of two buildings, with the main library itself housed in the lower, two-storey, east-facing building that partially arches over the pavement of North Caoxi Rd.

If you can gain access, wander past rare books on ecclesiastical history, Philosphica, Res Sinenses (Things Chinese) and other erudite branches of Jesuit learning. Photography is not allowed. Adjacent to the magnificent library to the south is the Priest's Residence.

Visitors can freely access the main reading room of the building, up the stairs on the 2nd floor between the hours of 9am and 4.30pm, where a video revealing the main library can be watched. There is also an art gallery, open to the public, on the ground floor.

CY TUNG MARITIME MUSEUM   MUSEUM

Map p316 (董浩云航运博物馆; Dǒng Hàoyún Hángyùn Bówùguǎn; ☑6293 3035; Jiāotōng University, 1954 Huashan Rd; 华山路1954号交通大学内; ◐1.30-5pm Tue-Sun; MJiaotong University) FREE Named after the Shànghǎi-born shipping magnate, this small but fascinating museum in Jiāotōng University explores Chinese maritime history, with model ships and early trade-route maps. A large portion of the 1st floor is devoted to Zheng He, the 15th-century admiral and explorer who was born a Hui Muslim in Yúnnán; was later captured and made a eunuch at the Ming court; and eventually went on to command

vast Chinese fleets on journeys to east Africa, India and the Persian Gulf.

JIĀOTŌNG UNIVERSITY   UNIVERSITY

Map p316 (交通大学; Jiāotōng Dàxué; http://en.sjtu.edu.cn; 1954 Huashan Rd; 华山路1954号; MXujiahui) Founded in 1896, Jiāotōng University (Transport University) has an attractive campus, especially the lawn a short walk beyond the main gate and the old library building (图书馆; túshūguǎn) opposite. Climb to the 3rd floor of the library for a small two-hall **museum** on the history of the university, complete with English captions. If the sun's out, make like a student and collapse with a book on the grass among the magnolias.

QIAN XUESEN
LIBRARY & MUSEUM   MUSEUM

Map p316 (钱学森图书馆; Qián Xuésēn Túshūguǎn; Jiāotōng University, 1800 Huashan Rd; 交通大学华山路1800号; ◐9am-4pm; MJiaotong University) FREE A former graduate of Jiāotōng University, Qian Xuesen (Hsueshen Tsien) was a pioneering aviation and rocket scientist, trumpeted as the father of China's aeronautical industry and space program. Qian receives a spotlessly patriotic appraisal by this overproduced three-floor museum in Jiāotōng University. The displays trumpet the milestones of the scientist's life, including his triumphant return to China from the US, where he began his career and endured house arrest after being labelled a communist during the McCarthy era.

GUĀNGQǏ PARK
PARK

Map p316 (光啟公园; Guāngqǐ Gōngyuán; Nandan Rd; 南丹路; MXujiahui) Dominated by an imposing white marble cross, this serene park is dedicated to 17th-century Christian scholar and scientist Xu Guangqi, whose tomb (a large mound) is also located within the grounds. Locals congregate here to practise taichi and amble about in the shade of gingko trees, magnolias, palms and bamboo. There's also a decorative archway and a small **memorial hall** (Map p316; Guangqi Park, Nandan Rd; 光启公园; ☉9am-4.30pm Wed-Sun; MXujiahui) FREE dedicated to the Shànghǎi Catholic.

◎ South Shànghǎi

LÓNGHUÁ
TEMPLE & PAGODA
BUDDHIST TEMPLE

Map p316 (龙华寺、龙华塔; Lónghuá Sì & Lónghuá Tǎ; ☑6457 6327; 2853 Longhua Rd; 龙华路2853号; admission ¥10; ☉7am-4.30pm; MLonghua) Southeast from Xújiāhuì, Shànghǎi's oldest and largest monastery is named after the pipal tree (lónghuá) under which Buddha achieved enlightenment. The much-renovated temple is said to date from the 10th century, its five main halls commencing with the **Laughing Buddha Hall**; note the four huge Heavenly Kings, each in charge of a compass point. The temple is particularly famed for its 6500kg bell, cast in 1894.

A large effigy of Sakyamuni seated on a lotus flower resides within the main hall – the **Great Treasure Hall**.

Other halls include the **Thousand Luóhàn Hall**, sheltering a huge legion of glittering arhat. Also within the temple is a vegetarian restaurant and a further imposing structure – the **Sānshèngbǎo Hall** – with a golden trinity of Buddhist statues.

Opposite the temple entrance rises the seven-storey, 44m-high **Lónghuá Pagoda**, originally built in AD 977. Sadly, visitors are not allowed to climb it.

The best time to visit is during the Lónghuá Temple Fair, in the third month of the lunar calendar (usually during April or May).

SHÀNGHĂI
BOTANICAL GARDENS
GARDENS

(上海植物园; Shànghǎi Zhíwùyuán; ☑5436 3369; 1111 Longwu Rd; 龙吴路1111号; admission ¥20; ☉7am-5pm; MShilong Rd) The location off a busy road is hardly idyllic, but the Botanical Gardens offer an escape from Shànghǎi's synthetic cityscape. The **Tropicarium** gives you the chance to get close to tropical flora, and once inside you can take the lift to the 6th floor for an impressive view of the gardens.

The northern side of the gardens has a dusty memorial temple, originally built in 1728. It's dedicated to Huang Daopo, who supposedly kick-started Shànghǎi's cotton industry by bringing the knowledge of spinning and weaving to the region from Hǎinán.

JĪNJIĀNG ACTION PARK
AMUSEMENT PARK

(锦江乐园; Jīnjiāng Lèyuán; ☑5421 6858; 201 Hongmei Rd; 虹梅路201号; 2/6 rides ¥50/80; ☉9am-10pm summer, to 5pm winter; MJinjiang Park) If the kids are in mutiny against sightseeing, the roller coasters, rides and huge Ferris wheel at this amusement park may mollify them. It's a bit out of town, but easy to get to, as it has its own metro station.

MARTYRS MEMORIAL
PARK

Map p316 (龙华烈士陵园; Lónghuá Lièshì Língyuán; Longhua Rd; 龙华路; admission ¥1, memorial hall ¥5; ☉6am-5pm, museum 9am-4pm; ☐44 from Xújiāhuì, MLongcao Rd) This park marks the site of an old Kuomintang prison, where 800 communists, intellectuals and political agitators were executed between 1928 and 1937. A modern underground tunnel leads to the original jailhouses and the small execution ground. Scattered throughout the manicured lawns are epic socialist-realist sculptures of workers and soldiers. During WWII this area was a Japanese internment camp and airfield, as depicted in the JG Ballard novel and Spielberg film *Empire of the Sun*.

✖ EATING

The 5th and 6th floors of the Grand Gateway 66 mall and food courts cater to the hardened shoppers of Xújiāhuì, but cast your net wider and discover some further flung gems.

★ DIN TAI FUNG
SHANGHAINESE $

Map p316 (鼎泰丰; Dǐng Tài Fēng; ☑3469 1383; 5th fl, Grand Gateway 66; 港汇广场5楼; mains from ¥29; ☉10.30am-9pm; MXujiahui) This brightly lit and busy Taiwan-owned restaurant chain may still be peddling its 'Top 10 restaurants of the world' mantra after a two-decades-old review in the *New York*

Times, but it still delivers some absolutely scrummy Shànghǎi *xiǎolóngbāo* dumplings. Not cheap perhaps (five for ¥29, or 10 for ¥58), but they're worth every *jiǎo.*

The mildly tangy hot-and-sour soup with pork and bean curd (¥35) is a great companion dish, or go for the lovely braised ox brisket soup with vegetables (¥50). Service is top-notch and you can watch masked chefs prepare your dumplings through sheet glass on arrival, where you can also peruse pictures of Tom Cruise giving his thumbs up. There are some good vegetable *xiǎolóngbāo* options.

★ XĪNJIĀNG FĒNGWÈI RESTAURANT
UIGHUR $

Map p316 (维吾尔餐厅; Wéiwú'ěr Cāntīng; ✆6468 9198; 280 Yishan Rd; 宜山路280号; dishes from ¥15; ⊙10am-2am; MYishan Rd, Xujiahui) Kashgar kitsch perhaps at this raucous upstairs Uighur restaurant, but you can feed an army on the whole roast lamb, or simply settle down to some tasty *dàpánjī* – a spicy stew of chicken, peppers and potatoes. There's also fresh yoghurt, *plov* (mutton pilaf), lamb kebabs, onion-laced tiger salad and *naan* (flat bread); wash it all down with some Xīnjiāng black beer. Things start hopping come evening when the music kicks in and dancers start twirling.

KOTA'S KITCHEN
JAPANESE $

Map p316 (烤串烧酒吧; Pītóushì Kǎochuànshāo Jiǔbā; ✆6481 2005; www.kotaskitchen.com; 2905 Xietu Rd; 斜土路2905号; mains from ¥35, skewers from ¥15; ⊙6pm-1am; MShanghai Stadium, Shanghai Indoor Stadium) This entertaining, funky, very welcoming and bijou Japanese yakitori restaurant-bar, with a Beatles theme, cooks up some enticing grilled meat skewers, perfectly accompanied by a heady range of homemade *shochu* spirits. The effect is an enticing blend of

1960s musical nostalgia and Japanese culinary skill: book ahead.

ELEMENT FRESH
SANDWICHES $

Map p316 (新元素; Xīnyuánsù; www.element fresh.com; Shop 163, 1st fl, Grand Gateway 66; 港汇广场1楼163室; mains from ¥45, dinner from ¥128; ⊙7am-11pm Mon-Thu, to midnight Fri & Sun; 🛜; MXujiahui) The Grand Gateway 66 branch of the health-conscious salads, sandwiches and smoothies restaurant can pep you up with a chilled gazpacho or get you firing on big breakfasts.

WAGAS
CAFE $

Map p316 (www.wagas.com.cn; Room 151, Grand Gateway 66, 1 Hongqiao Rd; 虹桥路1号港汇广场151室; mains ¥48-58; ⊙7am-10pm; 🛜; MXujiahui) The enthusiastic black-bandana-wearing staff keep things zipping along at this snappy Xújiāhuì branch of Wagas. Perfect for restorative doses of caffeine after shopping at the attached mall or seeing the local sights, with pre-10am and post-6pm deals on the menu.

1001 NOODLES HOUSE
NOODLES $

Map p316 (Unit 502, 5th fl, Grand Gateway 66, 1 Hongqiao Rd; 虹桥路1号港汇广场5楼502室; noodles from ¥22; ⊙10am-10pm; MXujiahui) The *yúxiāng* shredded-pork noodles or pork-chop noodles arrive in ample bowls at this neat noodle house in Grand Gateway 66. With soft jazzy music, snappy black-and-white decor and a long table for solo diners, it's aimed at the dapper window-shopping set and the office crowd, but prices are low. Spoon in the *làjiāo yóu* (辣椒油; chilli oil) if you like it hot and don't miss out on the scrumptious curry potato cakes.

BAKER & SPICE
CAFE $

Map p316 (www.bakerandspice.com.cn; Unit 150, Grand Gateway 66, 1 Hongqiao Rd; 虹桥路1号港汇广场150室; mains from ¥40; ⊙8am-10pm; 🛜;

XU GUANGQI

Xújiāhuì (the Xu family gathering) is named after Xu Guangqi (1562–1633), a Chinese renaissance man. Xu was an early student of astronomy, agronomy and the calendar, and he established a meteorological observatory that relayed its information to the tower on the Bund. He was then converted to Catholicism by Matteo Ricci and baptised with the name Paul. Xu became a high official in the Ming court and bequeathed land to found a Jesuit community, which eventually led to the construction of St Ignatius Cathedral. Xu's tomb and memorial hall can still be visited in nearby Guǎngqǐ Park, next to the historic Xújiāhuì Observatory, and stands as an inspirational symbol of Shànghǎi's openness to foreign ideas.

Ⓜ️Xujiahui) A handy branch of the excellent bakery-cafe, where there's 20% off bread after 7pm. A croissant and coffee is ¥28 before 10am weekdays.

⭐ ENTERTAINMENT

KŪN OPERA HOUSE   CHINESE OPERA
(上海昆剧团; Shànghǎi Kūnjù Tuán; ☎6437 7756; 295 South Zhongshan No 2 Rd, South Shànghǎi; 中山南二路295号; Ⓜ️Damuqiao Rd) Shànghǎi's Kun opera troupe has moved to a new home south of the city. There are usually monthly performances, but you'll have to call ahead for the schedule. No English.

🛍️ SHOPPING

Xújiāhuì is best known for its collection of department stores and malls that ring an insanely busy intersection. Don't try crossing the roads; use the underground metro tunnels to get to the stores.

GRAND GATEWAY 66   MALL
Map p316 (港汇恒隆广场; Gǎnghuì Hénglóng Guǎngchǎng; ☎6407 0111; 1 Hongqiao Rd; 虹桥路1号; ◎10am-10pm; Ⓜ️Xujiahui) Fed by the metro station below ground, Grand Gateway 66 is a vast, airy space and one of Shànghǎi's most popular malls. It has a decent range of Western brands such as Benetton, Diesel, DKNY, Jack Jones and Levi's, as well as a constellation of cosmetics and sports gear outlets.

The complex also has an excellent range of restaurants on the 5th and 6th floors, an outside food strip, a cinema, and seating for resting weary shopping legs.

HANYU JADEITE   JEWELLERY
Map p316 (漢玉工房; Hànyù Gōngfáng; www.hanyujadeite.com; Shop 221A, level 2, Grand Gateway 66, 1 Hongqiao Rd; 虹桥路1号港汇广场2楼221A室; ◎10am-10pm; Ⓜ️Xujiahui) If you want to guarantee quality and authenticity, this smart jade, jadeite and amber jewellery shop has pieces starting at around ¥900 for a small dragon ornament necklace. Limited English.

METRO CITY   ELECTRONICS
Map p316 (美罗城; Měiluó Chéng; ☎6426 8380; 1111 Zhaojiabang Rd; 肇嘉浜路1111号; ◎10am-10pm; Ⓜ️Xujiahui) Half of this mall is about technology, with shops selling electronics, computers and software; the other half is all about fun, with a Sega arcade, a handy branch of Food Republic on the 6th floor and, on the 5th floor, **Kodak Cinema World** (柯达电影世界; Kēdá Diànyǐng Shìjiè; Map p316; ☎6426 8181; 1111 Zhaojiabang Rd; 肇嘉浜路1111号; tickets from ¥80), which has four screens and shows some English-language films.

West Shànghǎi

CHÁNGNÍNG & GǓBĚI | HÓNGQIÁO AIRPORT AREA

Neighbourhood Top Five

1 Squeeze into the narrow alleyways of old **Qībǎo** (p173) for flavours of traditional China.

2 Take in a modern-art exhibit at the often overlooked **Mínshēng Art Museum** (p174).

3 Rock out at **Yùyīntáng** (p176), one of Shànghǎi's premier music venues.

4 Get lost in the park-like expanse of the **Shànghǎi Zoo** (p174).

5 Sample countless varieties of tea at **Tiānshān Tea City** (p176).

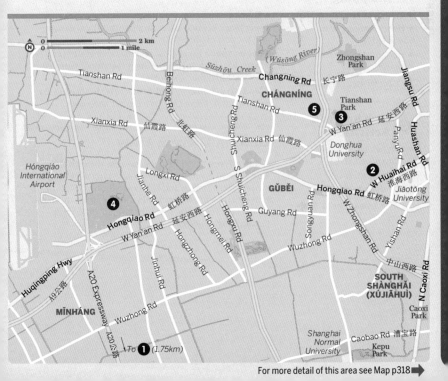

For more detail of this area see Map p318

Lonely Planet's Top Tip

Come weekends, the main sights – Qībǎo and the Shànghǎi Zoo – are absolutely teeming with people, so unless you enjoy crowds and sharp elbows, try to plan your visit for a weekday.

Best Places to Eat

➡ 1221 (p175)
➡ Băinián Lóngpáo (p175)
➡ Hongmei Road Entertainment Street (p175)
➡ Bellagio Café (p175)
➡ Carrefour (p175)

For reviews, see p175.➡

Best Shopping

➡ Tiānshān Tea City (p176)
➡ Henry Antique Warehouse (p176)
➡ Hóngqiáo International Pearl City (p176)

For reviews, see p176.➡

Best Sports & Activities

➡ Míngwǔ International Kungfu Club (p176)
➡ Dino Beach (p176)
➡ Mandarine City (p176)

For reviews, see p176.➡

Explore: West Shànghǎi

West Shànghǎi is far more a residential and business zone than a tourist drawcard, though that's not to say you should immediately scratch it from your itinerary. Enveloping a huge swathe of land, it's divided into two main districts (长宁; Chángníng and 闵行, Mǐnháng) and is the site of the Hóngqiáo airport and Hóngqiáo Railway Station (Shànghǎi's high-speed rail link), as well as the ancient waterside town of Qībǎo.

Mǐnháng runs along the southern and western borders of Chángníng district, which includes well-known neighbourhoods such as the middle-class and expat enclave of Gǔběi (古北) and Hóngqiáo (虹桥) airport. West Shànghǎi was once countryside and a playground for the rich to retreat to at weekends, and some of the city's largest parks are found here. The old Sassoon country estate is now the Cypress Hotel, while the Shànghǎi Zoo sits on what was once the British Golf Club.

Parents with kids should investigate the entertainment options here: in addition to the zoo and other pockets of green space, you'll also find an aquarium and fun-filled water park.

Local Life

➡**Snacks** From stinky tofu and squid on a stick to sweet black-sesame-paste dumplings, Qībǎo has you – and the rest of Shànghǎi – covered.

➡**Green space** Escape the relentless concrete sprawl in Zhōngshān Park (p174), the Song Qingling Mausoleum (p174) or Shànghǎi Zoo (p174).

➡**Modern art** Stop by Red Town (p174) for private art galleries and one of the city's top art museums.

Getting There & Away

➡**Metro** Lines 2 and 10 run east–west through the area (line 10 is more central), converging at Hóngqiáo airport (Terminal 2) and Hóngqiáo Railway Station. Lines 3 and 4 mirror each other, running north–south. Line 9 is to the south, passing through Qībǎo and terminating at Sōngjiāng.

◉ TOP SIGHT
QĪBǍO

When you tire of Shànghǎi's incessantly urban overture, tiny Qībǎo (七宝) is a mere hop, skip and metro ride away. An ancient settlement that prospered during the Ming and Qing dynasties, it's littered with historic traditional architecture, threaded by small, busy alleyways and cut by a picturesque canal. If you can tolerate crowds, Qībǎo brings you the flavours of old China along with doses of entertainment and snacking opportunities. Avoid weekends, when the narrow lanes are gridlocked.

Sights

Nine sights are included in the through ticket, or you can skip the ticket and pay ¥5 to ¥10 per sight instead. The best include the **Cotton Textile Mill**, **Old Trades House** (a waxworks museum) and the **Shadow Puppet Museum**, where you can catch performances from 1pm to 3pm Wednesdays and Sundays. Half-hour **boat rides** (per person ¥10) slowly ferry passengers from Number One Bridge to Dōngtángtān (东塘滩) and back, from 8.30am to 5pm. The 1866 **Catholic Church** (天主教堂; 50 Nanjie), adjacent to a convent off Qibao Nanjie, is south of the canal.

Shopping & Snacking

Wander along **Bei Dajie** north of the canal, for shops selling fans, jewellery and wooden handicrafts. Excellent crab dumplings await at Bǎinián Lóngpáo (p175) by the main bridge. South of the canal, **Nan Dajie** has every Chinese snack under the Shànghǎi sun: No 26 cooks up sweet, steaming *tāng yuán* (汤圆) dumplings, and No 9 is a traditional teahouse with Chinese **storytelling performances** (admission plus pot of tea ¥2; from 12.30pm to 2.30pm). Beggar's chicken (¥28) can be found at several spots, including No 12. Also look out for candy floss, glazed strawberries on a stick, jujubes, chestnuts, white rabbit sweets and Qībǎo spirits (0.5L should set you back ¥22).

DON'T MISS

➡ Cotton Textile Mill
➡ Bei Dajie souvenirs
➡ Nan Dajie snacks

PRACTICALITIES

➡ 七宝
➡ 2 Minzhu Rd, Mǐnháng district; 闵行区民主路2号
➡ admission high/low season ¥45/30
➡ ⊘ sights 8.30am-4.30pm
➡ Ⓜ Qibao

⊙ SIGHTS

⊙ Chángníng & Gǔběi

MÍNSHĒNG ART MUSEUM   MUSEUM
Map p318 (民生现代美术馆; Mínshēng Xiàndài Měishùguǎn; www.minshengart.com; 570 West Huaihai Rd; 淮海西路570号; admission ¥20; ⊙10am-6pm Tue-Sun; ⓂHongqiao Rd) Although sponsored mainly by the Mínshēng Bank, this edgy art space also counts the Tate, Centre Pompidou, MoMA and Guggenheim among its partners, so it should come as no surprise that the exhibits (about three per year) are generally excellent. Adding to its street cred is artistic director Zhou Tiehai, one of Shànghǎi's most well known artists.

RED TOWN   GALLERY
Map p318 (红坊; Hóng Fāng; www.redtown570. com; 570 West Huaihai Rd; 淮海西路570号; ⊙10am-5pm Tue-Sun; ⓂHongqiao Rd) FREE The No 10 Steel Factory has come to life again with an enormous display of large-scale sculpture pieces dotting the lawn, offices and studios of this creative cluster. While the majority of the premises is taken over by the so-so Shànghǎi Sculpture Space, there are a couple of other private galleries here, as well as Red Town's main highlight, the Mínshēng Art Museum.

SONG QINGLING MAUSOLEUM   MAUSOLEUM
Map p318 (宋庆龄陵园; Sòng Qìnglíng Língyuán; ☑6474 7183; 21 Songyuan Rd; 宋园路21号; adult/student ¥20/10; ⊙9am-5pm, last entry 4.30pm; ⓂSongyuan Rd) Despite the hard-edged communist layout, this green park is good for a stroll. Song Qingling, wife of Dr Sun Yatsen (co-founder of the Republic of China), is interred in a low-key tomb here. She is memorialised in the **Song Qingling Exhibition Hall** (宋庆龄陈列馆; Sòng Qìnglíng Chénlièguǎn) straight ahead from the main entrance, which resembles a Chinese imperial tomb. Among the displays of Song memorabilia (including her black *qípáo* or Chinese-style dress) is a photograph of Marxist Westerners reading from Mao's Little Red Book back in the day when it was cool.

The **international cemetery** (Map p318; cnr Hongqiao & Songyuan Rds) here also contains a host of foreign gravestones, including those of Jewish, Vietnamese and Western settlers of Shànghǎi.

ZHŌNGSHĀN PARK   PARK
(中山公园; Zhōngshān Gōngyuán; 780 Changning Rd; 长宁路780号; ⊙6am-6pm; ⓔ; ⓂZhongshan Park) Called Jessfield Park by the British and today named after 'Father of the Nation' Sun Zhongshan (Sun Yatsen), this interesting park is located in the northeast, in the former 'Badlands' area of 1930s Shànghǎi.

LIU HAISU ART GALLERY   MUSEUM
Map p318 (刘海粟美术馆; Liú Hǎisù Měishùguǎn; ☑6270 1018; 1660 Hongqiao Rd; 虹桥路1660号; ⊙9am-4pm Tue-Sun; ⓂShuicheng Rd) FREE This hulking gallery exhibits works of the eponymous painter, and also hosts visiting exhibitions.

CHÁNGFĒNG OCEAN WORLD   AQUARIUM
(长风海底世界; Chángfēng Hǎidǐ Shìjiè; ☑6233 8888; www.oceanworld.com.cn; Gate No 4, Chángfēng Park, 451 Daduhe Rd; 大渡河路451号长风公园4号门; adult/child ¥160/110; ⊙9am-5pm; ⓔ; ⓂLoushanguan Rd, then taxi) Adults may find this subterranean aquarium dank, dingy and dear, but the little people will adore the clownfish and shark tunnel. There are performances every half-hour.

⊙ Hóngqiáo Airport Area

QĪBǍO   VILLAGE
See p173.

SHÀNGHǍI ZOO   ZOO
Map p318 (上海动物园; Shànghǎi Dòngwùyuán; ☑6268 7775; www.shanghaizoo.cn; 2381 Hongqiao Rd; 虹桥路2381号; adult/child ¥40/20, tour buggy trips ¥15; ⊙6.30am-6pm Apr-Sep, to 5pm Oct-Mar; ⓔ; ⓂShanghai Zoo) On the grounds of a former golf course, this is one of China's greenest and most pleasant zoos, and makes for a great day with the kids, especially if the sun's out. There's a decent selection of animals – from woolly twin-humped Bactrian camels to spindly legged giraffes, lots of different monkeys and giant pandas – but some of their enclosures are a bit grim. Shànghǎi folk flock here for one of the city's best-tended acreages of grass.

Picnic-goers dive onto the lawns for a spot of sun, while electric tour buggies whirr along shaded paths every 10 to 15 minutes. The whole menagerie is navigable on foot with a map from the information kiosk at the entrance or by following the signs.

Not far from the zoo, in the grounds of the Cypress Hotel, is the former Sassoon Mansion, now building 1. You can take a peek at the exterior, but there's not much left to see.

EATING

Chángníng & Gǔběi

BÌ FĒNG TÁNG
DIM SUM $

Map p318 (避风塘; ☎6208 6388; 37 South Shuicheng Rd; 水城南路37号; dim sum ¥17-22; ⓂShuicheng Rd) This popular branch of the bustling chain is an excellent choice for consistently good Cantonese and dim sum dishes.

CARREFOUR
SUPERMARKET $

Map p318 (家乐福; Jiālèfú; ☎6278 1944; www.carrefour.com.cn; 268 South Shuicheng Rd; 水城路268号; Ⓣ 7.30am-10pm; ⒨Shuicheng Rd) This French supermarket chain is the epicentre of Gǔběi, and you can find everything from wine and cheese to cheap bikes and crockery. Also here is a popular food court, with a bakery and branches of Wagas and Food Republic.

★1221
SHANGHAINESE $$

Map p318 (Yī Èr Èr Yī; ☎6213 6585; 1221 West Yan'an Rd; 延安西路1221号; dishes from ¥26) No one has a bad thing to say about this dapper expat favourite, and rightly so: it has never let its standards dip over the years. Meat dishes start at ¥50 for the beef and dough strips *(yóutiáo)*, and the plentiful eel, shrimp and squid dishes cost around twice that. Other tempting fare includes the roast duck and braised pork.

Things are backed up by a four-page vegetarian menu, including the sweet-and-sour vegetarian spare ribs, which are out of this world. The pan-fried sticky rice and sweet bean paste (from the dim-sum menu) makes a grand dessert. It's also worth ordering the eight-fragrance tea just to watch it served in spectacular fashion out of 60cm-long spouts. The setting (tucked away in an alley) is white table cloths, cream walls and brown leatherette furniture. Service is fantastic. Reserve. There's no nearby public transport; take a taxi.

BELLAGIO CAFÉ
CHINESE $$

Map p318 (鹿港小镇; Lùgǎng Xiǎozhèn; ☎6270 6866; 101 South Shuicheng Rd; 水城南路101号; dishes ¥29-69; Ⓣ 11.30am-2am; ⒨Shuicheng Rd) This popular branch of the Taiwanese restaurant draws crowds of Taiwan expats for its *sānbēijī* (three-cup chicken), fried bean curd and shaved-ice desserts.

Hóngqiáo Airport Area

★BǍINIÁN LÓNGPÁO
DUMPLINGS $

(百年龙袍; 15 Bei Daijie, Qībǎo; 七宝古镇北大街15号; 8 dumplings from ¥15; Ⓣ 6.30am-8.30pm; ⒨Qibao) This tiny spot at the foot of Qībǎo's main bridge has as many dumpling makers in the kitchen as it does seats. But pay no mind to the cramped premises, as these are by far and away the best *xiǎolóngbāo* (little steamer buns) on the block. Dumpling fillings include crab, shrimp and pork. For takeaway, the slow-moving queue heads out of the door.

CITY SHOP
SUPERMARKET $

Map p318 (城市超市; Chéngshì Chāoshì; ☎400 811 1797; www.cityshop.com.cn; 3211 Hongmei Rd; 虹梅路3211号; Ⓣ 8am-10pm; ⒨Longxi Rd) For all those imported goodies you just can't get anywhere else – at a price. Goods can be delivered, too.

HONGMEI ROAD ENTERTAINMENT STREET
FOOD STREET $$

Map p318 (老外街; Lǎowài Jiē; Lane 3338, Hongmei Rd; 虹梅路3338弄虹梅休闲步行街; ⒨Longxi Rd) This popular strip has a selection of Asian and Western restaurants and bars for those who don't want to head into town. In addition to tapas, Indian and Iranian options, there are also branches of Shànghǎi Brewery, Big Bamboo and Simply Thai here.

DRINKING & NIGHTLIFE

C'S
BAR

Map p318 (685 Dingxi Rd; 定西路685号; Ⓣ 7.30pm-late; ⒨West Yan'an Rd) The king of all Shànghǎi dives, this graffiti-strewn basement warren won't impress your date, but the echoing music and rock-bottom prices guarantee devoted (student-based) droves of drinkers.

☆ ENTERTAINMENT

★ YÙYĪNTÁNG
LIVE MUSIC

Map p318 (育音堂; www.yytlive.com; 851 Kaixuan Rd; 凯旋路851号; ⏰9pm-midnight Tue-Sun; Ⓜ West Yan'an Rd) Small enough to feel intimate, but big enough for a sometimes pulsating atmosphere, Yùyīntáng has long been one of the top places in the city to see live music. Any Shànghǎi rock band worth its amps plays here, but you can also catch groups on tour from other cities in China and beyond. Rock is the staple diet, but anything goes, from hard punk to gypsy jazz.

SHÀNGHǍI FILM ART CENTRE
CINEMA

Map p318 (上海影城; Shànghǎi Yǐngchéng; ☎6280 4088; 160 Xinhua Rd; 新华路160号; Ⓜ Jiaotong University) This cinema is the main venue for the Shanghai International Film Festival. The nearest metro station is a 10-minute walk so consider a taxi.

🛍 SHOPPING

★ TIĀNSHĀN TEA CITY
TEA

Map p318 (天山茶城; Tiānshān Cháchéng; 520 West Zhongshan Rd; 中山西路520号; ⏰9am-6pm; Ⓜ Zhongshan Park, West Yan'an Rd) Running low on loose-leaf oolong and aged *pu-erh* cakes? This three-storey sprawl is hands down the largest collection of tea shops in the city. You probably won't need to leave the ground level, but you'll find a decent selection of teaware and porcelain on the 2nd floor, and teapots and jewellery on the 3rd.

HENRY ANTIQUE WAREHOUSE
ANTIQUES

Map p318 (亨利古典家具; Hēnglì Gǔdiǎn Jiājù; ☎6401 0831; www.h-antique.com; 3rd fl, Bldg 2, 361 Hongzhong Rd; 虹中路361号2号楼3层; ⏰9am-6pm) This enormous showroom, with more than 2000 high-quality antique pieces, both large and small, is a good first stop for antiques hunters. It's down a lane off Hongzhong Rd in a not-so-obvious location; take a taxi and look for the signs. The Traditional Furniture Research Department of Tongji University is based here.

HÓNGQIÁO INTERNATIONAL PEARL CITY
MARKET

Map p318 (虹桥国际珍珠城; Hóngqiáo Guójì Zhēnzhū Chéng; ☎6465 0183; 2nd fl, Hóngqiáo Craft Market, 3721 Hongmei Rd; 虹梅路3721号虹桥市场2楼; ⏰10am-9pm; Ⓜ Longxi Rd) Popular with local expats, the 2nd floor of this market has a selection of freshwater and saltwater pearls that is worth a browse. There's a relaxed atmosphere and you can bargain here. On the 1st floor there are clothes and golf gear; on the 3rd floor carpets and luggage.

FOREIGN LANGUAGES BOOKSTORE
BOOKS

Map p318 (外文书店; Wàiwén Shūdiàn; 71 South Shuicheng Rd; 水城南路71号; ⏰9.30am-9.30pm; Ⓜ Shuicheng Rd) A small branch that stocks foreign-language books and magazines.

🏃 SPORTS & ACTIVITIES

MANDARINE CITY
SWIMMING

Map p318 (明都城游泳池; Míngdūchéng Yóuyǒng Chí; ☎6405 0404; 788 Hongxu Rd, entrance cnr Guyang & Shuicheng Rds, Hóngqiáo; 虹桥虹许路788号; ⏰7.30am-9pm Jun-Oct; Ⓜ Shuicheng Rd) Popular outdoor pool.

MÍNGWǓ INTERNATIONAL KUNGFU CLUB
MARTIAL ARTS

Map p318 (明武国际功夫馆; Míngwǔ Guójì Gōngfu Guǎn; ☎6465 9806; www.mingwukungfu.com; 3rd fl, Hongchun Bldg, 3213 Hongmei Rd; 虹梅路3213号红春大厦3楼; 🔞) This versatile gym offers bilingual classes in a wide range of martial arts, from taichi and *qìgōng* to *wǔshù* and karate, for both children and adults. There's also a shop on-site, selling clothing and weapons.

DINO BEACH
SWIMMING

(热带风暴; Rèdài Fēngbào; ☎6478 3333; www.64783333.com; 78 Xinzhen Rd; 新镇路78号; admission Mon, Tue & Thu ¥100-120, Wed & Fri ¥100-150, Sat & Sun ¥150-200, child under 0.8m free; ⏰1-11pm Mon, 10am-11pm Wed & Sun, 10am-midnight Tue, Thu, Fri & Sat Jun-Sep; 🔞; Ⓜ Xinzhuang then bus 763 or 173) Way down south in Mǐnháng district, this popular summer place has a beach, a wave pool, water slides and tube hire to beat the Shànghǎi summer heat and keeps going late. But it's absolutely heaving at weekends. To get here, take metro line 1 to Xinzhuang, or catch a cab from Qībǎo.

MARTIAL ARTS

China lays claim to a huge range of martial arts styles (see p238), some of which have either fallen by the wayside or completely disappeared, perhaps due to their exclusivity. Other styles became part of the mainstream and have flourished; Wing Chun in particular has been elevated into a globally recognised art, largely due to its associations with Bruce Lee.

Unlike Korean and Japanese arts such as taekwondo or karate-do, China's individual martial arts frequently have no international regulatory body that oversees the syllabus, tournaments or grading requirements. Consequently students of China's myriad martial arts may be rather unsure of where they stand or what level they have attained. With no standard syllabus, it is often down to the individual teacher to decide what to teach students, and how quickly. It is not hard to find a teacher in Shànghǎi.

Early morning taichi (太极拳; *tàijí quán*) on the Bund is one of the classic images of Shànghǎi. If you're interested in learning either taichi or one of the harder martial arts (武术; *wǔshù*) styles, there are a number of schools around town offering a range of classes for everyone from kids to adults. There are also aikido, karate-do and taekwondo groups.

SHÀNGHǍI YÍNQĪXĪNG INDOOR SKIING SKIING
(银七星市内滑雪场; Yínqīxīng Shìnèi Huáxuěchǎng; ☑5485 3248; www.yinqixing.com; 1835 Qixing Rd, Xīnzhuāng; 莘庄七星路1835号; per hr adults/child Mon-Fri ¥98/80, Sat & Sun ¥118/100; ☺9.30am-10.30pm Mon-Thu & Sun, to midnight Fri & Sat; ☒; Ⓜ Xinzhuang) The slope is aimed at first-timers so don't expect anything overly long or steep, but children will love it. The snowboard park is more challenging. To get here take the metro to Xinzhuang (line 1) and then hop in a taxi. Shut at the time of writing, so check ahead.

Day Trips from Shànghǎi

Hángzhōu p179

Hángzhōu's gorgeous and placid West Lake sits comfortably among China's top sights.

Sūzhōu p187

China's best-known water town, Sūzhōu is a rewarding bundle of classical gardens, canals, bridges, silk, temples and fab museums.

Tónglǐ p193

One of Jiāngsū's best-looking water towns, with a racy museum dedicated to China's erotic culture.

Zhūjiājiǎo p194

Quaint canalside town within Shànghǎi municipality, dotted with temples, ancient bridges and pinched lanes.

Zhōuzhuāng p195

Lovely traditional architecture, charming back alleys and bridges make this small Jiāngsū town an eye-catching diversion.

Shěshān p197

Divine views and an imposing hilltop Catholic church, accessible on the metro from Shànghǎi city centre.

Hángzhōu

Explore

The dreamy West Lake panoramas and fabulously green and hilly environs of Hángzhōu (杭州), the former Southern Song dynasty capital, have been eulogised by poets and applauded by emperors. Religiously cleansed by armies of street sweepers and litter collectors, Hángzhōu's scenic vistas draw you into a classical Chinese vignette of willow-lined banks, ancient pagodas, mist-covered hills, wooden boats, smoky temples, flaming sunsets and shimmering evening waters.

The Best...

➡ **Sight** West Lake (p183)

➡ **Place to Eat** Green Tea Restaurant (p184)

➡ **Place to Drink** Maya Bar (p185)

Top Tip

Hop aboard Hángzhōu's excellent public bicycle-hire network to cycle around West Lake and beyond. See p184 for more info. For more info on the town, click on www.more-hangzhou.com and www.gotohz.com.

Getting There & Away

Bus Frequent buses (¥68, two hours, regularly from 6.40am to 7.20pm) run from Shànghǎi South Long-Distance Bus Station to Hángzhōu's main bus station (客运中心站; *kèyùn zhōngxīn zhàn*) at Jiǔbǎo, north bus station and south bus station. Hángzhōu's main bus station is linked to the centre of town by metro line 1 (¥5). Buses (¥68) also run to Hángzhōu from Shànghǎi Long-Distance Bus Station, north of Shànghǎi Railway Station. Hourly buses (¥85, two hours) also run to Hángzhōu from Hóngqiáo International Airport long-distance bus station and six buses daily (¥100) leave from Pǔdōng International Airport.

Train The best way to go. Very regular G-class trains (1st/2nd class ¥124/78, one hour, 6.38am to 9.31pm) to Hángzhōu depart from Shànghǎi Hóngqiáo Railway Station in Shànghǎi's west. The last G-class train back to Shànghǎi Hóngqiáo Railway Station is at 8.48pm. There are also four G-class trains (1st/2nd-class ¥148/93, 1½

hours) daily to Hángzhōu from Shànghǎi Railway Station and frequent slower trains (¥29; 2½ hours) from Shànghǎi South Railway Station to Hángzhōu.

Getting Around

Metro Hángzhōu's new metro line 1 (tickets ¥2 to ¥7; line 1 first/last train 6.06am/11.32pm) runs from the southeast of town, through the main train station, the east side of West Lake and on to the east train station, Jiǔbǎo bus station and the northeast of town.

Need to Know

➡ **Area code** ☑0571

➡ **Location** 170km from Shànghǎi

➡ **Tourist Office** (杭州旅游咨询服务中心; Hángzhōu Lǚyóu Zīxún Fúwù Zhōngxīn; ☑0571 8797 8123; Léifēng Pagoda, Nanshan Lu; ⊗8am-5pm)

⊙ SIGHTS

LÍNGYǏN TEMPLE BUDDHIST

(灵隐寺; Língyǐn Sì; Lingyin Lu; 灵隐路; grounds ¥35, grounds & temple ¥65; ⊗7am-5pm) Hángzhōu's most famous Buddhist temple, Língyǐn Temple was built in AD 326, but has been destroyed and restored no fewer than 16 times. During the Five Dynasties (AD 907–960) about 3000 monks lived here. The Hall of the Four Heavenly Kings is astonishing, with its four vast guardians and an ornate cabinet housing Milefo (the future Buddha). The **Great Hall** contains a magnificent 20m-high statue of Siddhartha Gautama (Sakyamuni), sculpted from 24 blocks of camphor wood in 1956 and based on a Tang-dynasty original.

Behind the giant statue is a startling montage of Guanyin surrounded by 150 small figures, including multiple *luóhàn* (arhat), in a variety of poses. The earlier hall collapsed in 1949, crushing the Buddhist statues within, so it was rebuilt and the statue conceived. The Hall of the Medicine Buddha is beyond.

The walk up to the temple skirts the flanks of Fēilái Peak (*Fēilái Fēng*; Peak Flying from Afar), magically transported here from India according to legend. The Buddhist carvings (all 470 of them) lining the riverbanks and hillsides and tucked away

Hángzhōu

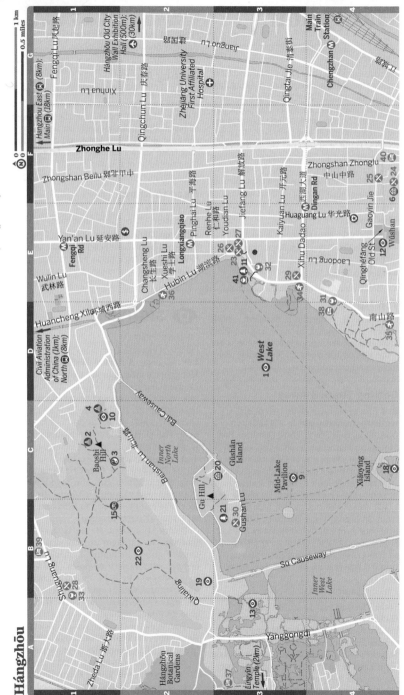

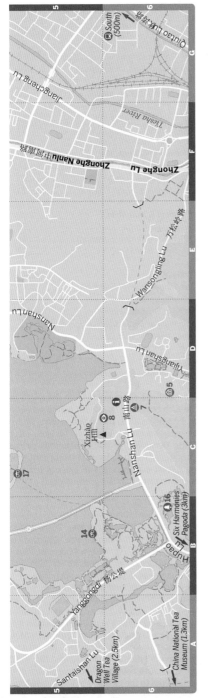

inside grottoes date from the 10th to 14th centuries. To get a close-up view of the best carvings, including the famed 'laughing' Maitreya Buddha, follow the paths along the far (east) side of the stream.

There are several other temples near Língyǐn Temple that can be explored, including Yǒngfú Temple and Tāoguāng Temple.

Behind Língyǐn Temple is the Northern Peak (*Běi Gāofēng*), which can be scaled by cable car (up/down/return ¥30/20/40). From the summit there are sweeping views across the lake and city.

Bus K7 and tourist bus Y2 (both from the train station), and tourist bus Y1 from the roads circling West Lake go to the temple.

TÀIZǏWĀN PARK PARK

(太子湾公园; Nanshan Lu; 南山路; ⊙24hr) This exquisite and serene park just south of the Sū Causeway off West Lake offers quiet walks among lush woodland, ponds, lakes, rose gardens and lawns along a wooden walkway. Just take off and explore. It's heavenly in spring, with gorgeous beds of tulips and daffodils and flowering trees.

QŪYUÀN GARDEN GARDENS

(曲院风荷; Qūyuàn Fēnghé) On the northwest shore of West Lake, this lovely collection of gardens spreads out over numerous islets and is renowned for its fragrant spring lotus blossoms.

LÉIFĒNG PAGODA PAGODA

(雷峰塔, Léifēng Tǎ; Nanshan Lu; 南山路; adult/child ¥40/20; ⊙8am-8.30pm Mar-Nov, 8am-5.30pm Dec-Feb) Topped with a golden spire, the eye-catching Léifēng Pagoda can be climbed for fine views of the lake. The original pagoda, built in AD 977, collapsed in 1924. During renovations in 2001, Buddhist scriptures written on silk were discovered in the foundations, along with other treasures.

JÌNGCÍ TEMPLE BUDDHIST TEMPLE

(净慈寺; Jìngcí Sì; Nanshan Lu; 南山路; admission ¥10; ⊙6am-5.15pm summer, 6.30am-4.45pm winter) The serene yet monastically active Chan (Zen) Jìngcí Temple was originally built in AD 954 and is now fully restored. The splendid first hall contains the massive, foreboding Heavenly Kings and an elaborate red and gold case encapsulating Milefo (the future Buddha) and Weituo (protector of the Buddhist temples and teachings). The main hall – the **Great Treasure Hall** – contains a

Hángzhōu

Top Sights (p183)
1 West Lake D3

Sights (p179)
2 Bǎochù Pagoda C1
3 Bàopǔ Taoist Temple C1
4 Big Buddha Temple C1
5 China Silk Museum D6
6 Húqìngyú Táng Chinese Medicine Museum F4
7 Jìngcí Temple C6
8 Léifēng Pagoda C6
9 Mid-Lake Pavilion C3
10 Ming-Dynasty Effigies C1
11 No 1 Park E3
12 Qīnghéfāng Old Street E4
13 Qūyuàn Garden A3
14 Red Carp Pond B5
Seal Engravers Society ..... (see 30)
15 Sunrise Terrace B1
16 Tàizǐwān Park B6
17 Three Pools Mirroring the Moon C5
18 Xiǎoyíng Island C4
19 Yuè Fēi Temple B2
20 Zhèjiāng Provincial Museum C3
21 Zhōngshān Park B3
22 Zǐyún Cave B2

Eating (p184)
23 Bì Fēng Táng E3
24 Cafe de Origin F4
25 Dōngyīshùn F4
26 Grandma's Kitchen E3
27 Green Tea Restaurant E3
28 La Pedrera B1
29 Lǎomǎjiā Miànguǎn E3
30 Lóuwàilóu B3

Drinking & Nightlife (p185)
31 Eudora Station E4
32 JZ Club E3
33 Maya Bar B1

Sports & Activities
34 Bicycle Rental E3
35 Bicycle Rental - Nanshan Lu D4
36 Small Boat Hire E2

Sleeping (p186)
37 Four Seasons Hotel Hángzhōu A3
38 Mingtown Youth Hostel D4
39 Tea Boutique Hotel B1
40 Wúshānyì International Youth Hostel F4

Transport
41 Boats to Xiǎoyíng Island E3

vast seated effigy of Sakyamuni (Buddha). Hunt down the awesome 1000-arm Guanyin (千手观音) in the Guanyin Pavilion, with her huge fan of arms. The temple's enormous bronze bell is struck 108 times for prosperity on the eve of the Lunar New Year. There's a vegetarian restaurant attached.

CHINA SILK MUSEUM MUSEUM

(中国丝绸博物馆; Zhōngguó Sīchóu Bówùguǎn; 73-1 Yuhuangshan Lu; 玉皇山路73-1号; ⌚9am-5pm Tue-Sun, noon-5pm Mon) FREE This fascinating museum has excellent displays of silk samples, silk-making techniques, a room of looms with workers, a textile conservation gallery where you can watch conservationists in action, a superb gallery devoted to silks from Dūnhuáng, silk embroideries and exhibitions on silkworm anatomy.

YUÈ FĒI TEMPLE TEMPLE

(岳庙; Yuè Miào; Beishan Lu; 北山路; admission ¥25; ⌚7.30am-5.30pm) Commander of the southern Song armies, General Yue Fei (1103–42) led a series of successful battles against Jurchen invaders from the north in the 12th century. Despite his initial successes, he was recalled to the Song court, where he was executed along with his son, after being deceived by the treacherous prime minister Qin Hui. In 1163 Song emperor Gao Zong exonerated Yue Fei and had his corpse reburied at the present site.

HÁNGZHŌU OLD CITY WALL EXHIBITION HALL MUSEUM

(杭州古城墙陈列馆; Hángzhōu Gǔchéngqiáng Chénlièguǎn; 1st fl, Qingchun Men, Qingchun Lu; 庆春路1号庆春门1楼; ⌚9am-4.30pm Wed-Mon) FREE Hángzhōu is famed for its lake, but the lake was a (glorious) appendage to a once-flourishing and magnificent city. The historic city of Hángzhōu – directly east of West Lake – has vanished, its monumental city wall long gone. This exhibition hall within the reconstructed gate of Qingchun Men celebrates the vanished bastion. For anyone keen to understand what it looked like until the early 20th century, there are photos and testaments to the old city (but no English).

The names of the city gates only survive in place names (such as Qingbo Men and Yongjin Men), but the old city of Hángzhōu (and its temples) has been buried beneath endless department stores and malls, leaving virtually nothing behind. This exhibition hall puts that tragic disappearance in its proper context.

Bus K212 from Yan'an Lu passes by.

CHINA NATIONAL TEA MUSEUM — MUSEUM

(中国茶叶博物馆; Zhōngguó Cháyè Bówùguǎn; http://english.teamuseum.cn; 88 Longjing Lu; 龙井路88号; ⊗8.30am-4.30pm Tue-Sun) FREE Not far into the hills of Hángzhōu, you'll begin to see fields of tea bushes planted in undulating rows, the setting for the China Tea Museum – 3.7 hectares of land dedicated to the art, cultivation and tasting of tea. Further up are several tea-producing villages, all of which harvest China's most famous variety of green tea, *lóngjǐng* (dragon well), named after the spring where the pattern in the water resembles a dragon.

You can enjoy one of Hángzhōu's most famous teas at the **Dragon Well Tea Village** (龙井问茶; Lóngjǐng Wènchá; ⊗8am-5.30pm), near the first pass. Tourist bus Y3 or K27 will take you to the museum and the village.

QĪNGHÉFĀNG OLD STREET — STREET

(清河坊历史文化街; Qīnghéfāng Lìshǐ Wénhuà Jiē; Hefang Jie; 河坊街) At the south end of Zhongshan Zhonglu is this touristy, crowded and bustling pedestrian street, with makeshift puppet theatres, teahouses and gift and curio stalls, selling everything from stone teapots to boxes of *lóngxūtáng* (龙须糖; dragon whiskers sweets), ginseng and silk. It's also home to several traditional medicine shops, including the **Húqìngyú Táng Chinese Medicine Museum** (中药博物馆; Zhōngyào Bówùguǎn; 95 Dajing Xiang; admission ¥10; ⊗8.30am-5pm), which is an actual dispensary and clinic.

SIX HARMONIES PAGODA — PAGODA

(六和塔; Liùhé Tǎ; 16 Zhijiang Lu; 之江路; grounds ¥20, grounds & pagoda ¥30; ⊗6am-6.30pm) Three kilometres southwest of West Lake, an enormous rail and road bridge spans the Qiántáng River. Close by rears up the 60m-high octagonal Six Harmonies Pagoda, first built in AD 960. The stout pagoda also served as a lighthouse, and was said to possess magical powers to halt the 6.5m-high tidal bore that thunders up Qiántáng River. You can climb the

TOP SIGHT
WEST LAKE

West Lake (西湖) appeared in the 8th century, when the governor of Hángzhōu had the marshy expanse dredged. As time passed, the lake's splendour was slowly cultivated.

The poet Su Dongpo had a hand in the lake's development, constructing the 3km-long **Sū Causeway** (苏堤; Sūdī) during his tenure as local governor in the 11th century, to accompany the **Bái Causeway** (白堤; Báidī). Lined by willow, plum and peach trees, today the traffic-free causeways with their half-moon bridges make for excellent outings.

Connected to West Lake's northern shores by the Bái Causeway is **Gūshān Island** (孤山; Gū Shān), the lake's largest island. It's the site of the modest Zhèjiāng Provincial Museum, Zhōngshān Park and the intriguing Seal Engravers Society.

Across from the entrance to the Sū Causeway stands Yuè Fēi Temple. At the far end of the Sū Causeway is **Red Carp Pond** (花港观鱼; Huāgǎng Guānyú), a collection of gardens on the southern shore home to a few thousand red carp. East along the shore rises splendidly eye-catching Léifēng Pagoda (p181), across the road from tranquil Jìngcí Temple (p181).

DON'T MISS...

➡ Sū and Bái Causeways
➡ Léifēng Pagoda (p181)
➡ Gūshān Island

PRACTICALITIES

➡ 西湖; Xīhú

CRUISING HÁNGZHŌU'S WEST LAKE

Cruise boats (游船; *yóuchuán*) shuttle frequently to the **Mid-Lake Pavilion** and **Xiǎoyíng Island** (小瀛洲; Xiǎoyíng Zhōu) from four points: No 1 Park (一公园; Yī Gōngyuán), Red Carp Pond, Zhōngshān Park, and the Mausoleum of General Yue Fei at Yuè Fēi Temple.

From Xiǎoyíng Island you can look over at the **Three Pools Mirroring the Moon** (三潭印月; Sāntán Yìnyuè), a string of three small towers in the water, each of which has five holes that release shafts of candlelight on the night of the Mooncake Festival in mid-autumn.

Trips take 1½ hours and depart every 20 minutes between 7am and 4.45pm. Tickets cost ¥70/35 per adult/child and include entry to the Three Pools Mirroring the Moon on Xiǎoyíng Island.

Alternatively, hire one of the six-person boats (小船; *xiǎo chuán*) that are rowed by boatmen. These cost ¥80/160 per person/boat. Look for them across from the Overseas Chinese Hotel or along the causeways. Paddle boats (¥15 per 30 minutes, ¥200 deposit) on the Bái Causeway are also available for hire.

pagoda, while behind stretches a charming walk through terraces dotted with sculptures, bells, shrines and inscriptions.

✕ EATING

The top restaurant strip in town is Gaoyin Jie (高银美食街), parallel to and immediately north of Qīnghéfáng Old St.

★ GREEN TEA RESTAURANT HÁNGZHŌU $

(绿茶; Lùchá; 250 Jiefang Lu, 解放路250号; mains from ¥20; ⊙10.30am-11pm; M Longxiangqiao) Often packed, this excellent Hángzhōu restaurant has superb food. With a barebrick finish and decorated with rattan utensils and colourful flower-patterned cushions, the dining style is casual. The long paper menu (tick what you want) runs from salty and more-ish pea soup (¥18), to gorgeous eggplant claypot (¥20), lip-smacking Dōngpō Chicken (¥48) and beyond. Seven branches in town.

★ GRANDMA'S KITCHEN HÁNGZHŌU $

(外婆家; Wàipójiā; 3 Hubin Lu; 湖滨路3号; mains ¥6-55; ⊙lunch & dinner; M Longxiangqiao) Besieged by enthusiastic diners, this restaurant cooks up classic Hángzhōu favourites; try the *hóngshāo dōngpō ròu* (红烧东坡肉; braised pork), but prepare to wait for a table. There are several other branches in town.

BÌ FĒNG TÁNG CANTONESE $

(避风塘; 256 Jiefang Lu; 解放路256号; mains from ¥15; ⊙10am-9pm Sun-Thu, 10am-10pm Fri & Sat; M Ding'an Rd or Longxiangqiao) The

charcoal and silver piping on the seats is rather garish, but the dim sum is fabulous at this restaurant right in the action by West Lake. Canto classics include: roasted duck rice (¥26), steamed barbecue pork buns (¥20), fried dumplings (¥23), vegetable and mushroom buns (¥15) and deep fried bean curd stuffed with shrimp (¥25) – all lovely.

If the waiting staff hand you a menu in Chinese, ask for the picture menu (图片菜单; *túpiàn càidān*).

CAFE DE ORIGIN CAFE $

(瑞井; Ruìjǐng; 53 Dajing Xiang; 大井巷53号; mains from ¥15; ⊙11am-10pm Mon-Fri & 10am-midnight Sat & Sun; M Dingan Rd) With a pleasant alfresco terrace upstairs and stylish downstairs cafe area, Origin is a good place to relax with a coffee, sink a beer or grab a snack (vegetarians and vegans also catered for).

DŌNGYĪSHÙN MUSLIM $

(Dōngyīshùn; 101 Gaoyin Jie; 高银街101号; mains ¥12-50; ⊙11am-9pm) Specialising in food from China's Muslim Hui minority, this busy Gaoyin Jie spot has lamb kebabs (羊肉串; *yáng ròu chuàn;* ¥10 for four), roast mutton (¥40) and roast chicken (¥48) like all the others, but you'll also find hummus, felafel, cheese omelets (¥28) and even cheese spring rolls (¥22). There's a take-out hatch for kebabs and *náng* bread. Picture menu.

LǍOMǍJIĀ MIÀNGUǍN NOODLES $

(老马家面馆; 232 Nanshan Lu; 南山路232号; mains from ¥12; ⊙7am-10pm) Simple and popular Muslim restaurant stuffed into an old *shíkùmén* (stone-gate houses) tenement building with a handful of tables and spot-on *niúròu lāmiàn* (牛肉拉面; beef noodles) and scrummy beef-filled *ròujiāmó* (肉夹馍; meat in a bun, with onion if you want). No English menu.

LÓUWÀILÓU
HÁNGZHŌU $$

(30 Gushan Lu; 孤山路30号; mains ¥20-200; ⊙10.30am-2.15pm & 4.30-8.15pm) Founded in 1838, this is Hángzhōu's most famous restaurant. The local speciality is *xīhú cùyú* (西湖醋鱼; sweet and sour carp) and *dōngpō* pork, but there's a good choice of other well-priced standard dishes.

LA PEDRERA
SPANISH, TAPAS $$$

(巴特洛西班牙餐厅; Bātèluò Xībānyá Cāntīng; ☑0571 8886 6089; 4 Baishaquan, Shuguang Lu; 曙光路白沙泉4号; tapas from ¥30, meals ¥200; ⊙11am-11pm) This fine two-floor Spanish restaurant, just off Shuguang Lu bar street, has tapas diners in a whirl, paella-aficionados applauding and Spanish-wine fans gratified. Prices may take a sizeable bite out of your wallet, but the convivial atmosphere and assured menu prove popular and enjoyable.

DRINKING & NIGHTLIFE

Shuguang Lu (曙光路), northwest of West Lake, is the main place for beers.

MAYA BAR
BAR

(玛雅酒吧; Mǎyǎ Jiǔbā; 94 Baishaquan, Shuguang Lu; 曙光路白沙泉94号; ⊙10am-2am) Jim Morrison, Kurt Cobain, Mick Jagger, Bob Dylan, the Beatles and a mural of a shaman/spirit warrior watch on approvingly from the walls of this darkly lit and rock-steady bar. Just as importantly, the drinks are seriously cheap; Tuesdays and Thursdays see Tsingtao and Tiger dropping to ¥10 a pint (¥20 at other times) and a DJ from 9.30pm.

EUDORA STATION
BAR

(亿多瑞站; Yìduōruìzhàn; 101-107 Nanshan Lu; 南山路101-107号; ⊙9am-2am) A fab location by West Lake, roof terrace aloft, outside seating, a strong menu and a sure-fire atmosphere conspire to make this welcoming watering hole a great choice. There's sports TV, live music, a ground-floor terrace, a good range of beers, and barbecues fire up on the roof terrace in the warmer months.

DAY TRIPS FROM SHÀNGHǍI HÁNGZHŌU

BĀOSHÍ SHĀN WALK

Hángzhōu's West Lake area is littered with fine walks – just follow the views. For a manageable and breezy trek into the forested hills above the lake, however, walk up a lane called Qīxiálíng, immediately west of the Yuè Fēi Temple. The road initially runs past the temple's west wall to enter the shade of towering trees, with stone steps leading you up. At **Zǐyún Cave** the hill levels out and the road forks; take the right-hand fork to head in the direction of the **Bàopǔ Taoist Temple** (抱朴道院; Bàopǔ Dàoyuàn; admission ¥5; ⊙6am-5pm), 1km further, and the **Bǎochù Pagoda** (保俶塔; Bǎochù Tǎ).

At the top of the steps, turn left and, passing the **Sunrise Terrace** (初阳台; Chūyáng Tái), again bear left. Down the steps, look out for the tiled roofs and yellow walls of the charming Bàopǔ Taoist Temple to your right; head right along a path to reach it.

Come out of the temple's back entrance and turn left towards the Bǎochù Pagoda and, after hitting a confluence of three paths, take the middle track towards and up **Toad Hill** (蛤蟆峰; Hámá Fēng), which affords supreme views over the lake, before squeezing through a gap between huge boulders to see the Bǎochù Pagoda rising ahead. Restored many times, the seven-storey grey-brick pagoda was last rebuilt in 1933, although its spire tumbled off in the 1990s.

Continue on down and pass through a **páilou** (牌楼) – or decorative arch – erected during the Republic (with some of its characters scratched off) to a series of stone-carved **Ming-dynasty effigies**, all of which were vandalised in the tumultuous 1960s, save two effigies on the right. Turn left here and walk a short distance to some steps heading downhill to your right past the remarkable weathered remains of a colossal stone **Buddha head** by the cliff-face (with square niches cut in him) – all that remains of the **Big Buddha Temple** (大佛寺; Dàfó Sì). Continue on down to Beishan Lu.

JZ CLUB
CLUB

(黄楼; Huáng Lóu; ☎0571 8702 8298; www.
jzclub.cc; 6 Liuying Lu, by 266 Nanshan Lu; 柳营
路6号; ⏱7pm-2.30am) The folk that brought
you JZ Club in Shànghǎi have the live jazz
scene sewn up in Hángzhōu with this neat
three-floor venue in a historic building near
West Lake. There are three live jazz sets
nightly, with music kicking off at 9pm (till
midnight). There's no admission charge,
but you'll need to reserve a seat on Fridays
and Saturdays. Smokers get to go upstairs.

🛏 SLEEPING

If you don't stay in a hotel within easy reach
of the lake, you'll be kicking yourself later.
Prices rise on Fridays and Saturdays, when
beds are scarce, so aim for a weekday visit.

MINGTOWN YOUTH HOSTEL
HOSTEL $

(明堂杭州国际青年旅舍; Míngtáng Hángzhōu
Guójì Qīngnián Lǚshè; ☎0571 8791 8948;
101-11 Nanshan Lu; 南山路101-11号; dm/s/d
¥65/200/295; ✳🛜) With its pleasant lakeside location, this friendly and highly popular hostel is often booked out so reserve
well ahead. It has a relaxing cafe/bar, offers ticket booking, internet access, rents
bikes and camping gear and is attractively
decked out with orchids.

WÚSHĀNYÌ INTERNATIONAL YOUTH HOSTEL
HOSTEL $

(吴山驿国际青年旅社; Wúshānyì Guójì
Qīngnián Lǚshè; ☎0571 8701 8790; 22 Zhongshan Zhonglu, 中山中路22号; dm ¥55 rm ¥158-
178 d ¥248-268 tr/q ¥298/358; ✳@🛜) With
a healthy mix of Chinese and Western
travellers, this quiet, unhurried and comfy
hostel has clean rooms and excellent, helpful staff plus a charmingly tucked-away
location off Qinghefang Jie (and not too
far from West Lake either). There are female dorms available (¥65) and cheap
attic tatami rooms. Note that prices for
non-dorm rooms go up by at least ¥30 on
Friday and Saturday.

FOUR SEASONS HOTEL HÁNGZHŌU
HOTEL $$$

(杭州西子湖四季酒店; Hángzhōu Xīzihú Sìjì
Jiǔdiàn; ☎0571 8829 8888; www.fourseasons.
com/hangzhou; 5 Lingyin Lu, 灵隐路5号; d
¥3800, ste from ¥8200; ⊖✳@🛜🛁) More of
a resort than a hotel, the fabulous 78-room,
two-swimming pool Four Seasons enjoys a
seductive position in lush grounds next to
West Lake. Low-storey buildings and villas
echo traditional China, a sensation ampli-
fied by the osmanthus trees, ornamental
shrubs, ponds and tranquillity.

HÁNGZHŌU'S GIANT WAVE

An often spectacular natural phenomenon occurs every month on Hángzhōu's
Qiántáng River, when the highest tides of the lunar cycle dispatch a wall of water –
sometimes almost 9m tall – that thunders along the narrow mouth of the river from
Hángzhōu Bay at up to 40km/h.

Occasionally sweeping astonished sightseers away and luring bands of intrepid
surfers, this awesome tidal bore (钱塘江潮; qiántáng jiāngcháo) is the world's largest.
It can be viewed from the riverbank in Hángzhōu, but one of the best places to witness
the action is on the north side of the river at **Yánguān** (盐官), a delightful ancient town
about 38km northeast of Hángzhōu.

The most popular viewing time is during the Mid-Autumn Festival, which falls in
September or October, on the 18th day of the eighth month of the lunar calendar,
when the **International Qiántáng River Tide Observing Festival** takes place. You
can, however, see it throughout the year when the highest tide occurs at the begin-
ning and middle of each lunar month; access to the park in Yánguān for viewing the
tide is ¥25. The Hángzhōu Tourist Information Centre can give you upcoming tide
times. Tie it all in with a through-ticket (¥100) on a day-trip to explore the charming
historic temples and buildings of Yánguān.

It is possible to reach Yánguān by bus K868 (90 minutes) direct from Hángzhōu
train station. Alternatively, either take the bus (¥25, one hour) from Hángzhōu's main
bus station at Jiǔbǎo to Hǎiníng (海宁) and change to bus 106 (¥8, 25 minutes) to
Yánguān; or take a bus from Hángzhōu train station (45 minutes) and change to bus
109 to Yánguān. You can also take train T109 from Hǎiníng train station to Yánguān.

HÁNGZHŌU BY BIKE

The best way to hire a bike is to use the public **bike hire scheme** (☎0571 8533 1122; www.hzzxc.com.cn; ¥200 deposit, ¥100 credit; ☺6.30am-9pm Apr-Oct, 6am-9pm Nov-Mar). Stations (2700 in total) are dotted in large numbers around the city, in the world's largest network. Apply at one of the booths at numerous bike stations near West Lake where you will need ¥300 and your passport as ID. Fill in a form, receive a swipecard, and swipe the pad at one of the docking stations till you get a steady green light. Then simply free a bike and Bob's your uncle. You can return bikes to any other station (ensure the bike is properly docked before leaving it).

The first hour on each bike is free, so if you switch bikes within the hour, the rides are free. The second hour on the same bike costs ¥1, the third ¥2 and after that it's ¥3 per hour. Your deposit and unused credit are refunded to you when you return your swipecard (check when it should be returned as this can vary).

Note: you cannot return bikes outside booth operating hours as the swipe units deactivate. If you miss opening hours you will be charged a whole night's rental.

Youth hostels also rent out bikes, but these are more expensive.

TEA BOUTIQUE HOTEL   HOTEL $$$
(杭州天伦精品酒店; Hángzhōu Tiānlún Jīngpǐn Jiǔdiàn; ☎0571 8799 9888; www.teaboutiquehotel.com; 124 Shuguang Lu, 曙光路124号; d from ¥1098, ste ¥2280; ☜✲@☎) The simply but effectively done wood-sculpted foyer area with its sinuously shaped reception is a presage to the lovely accommodation at this hotel where a Japanese-minimalist mood holds sway among celadon teacups, muted colours and – interestingly for China – a Bible in each room.

Sūzhōu

Explore

Famed for its gardens, canals and silk production, Sūzhōu (苏州) is a pleasant, though overhyped, Jiāngsū canal town. If you don't go expecting an impeccable portrait of traditional China but a melange of modern town planning embedded with picturesque chunks of history, Sūzhōu is a rewarding diversion from Shànghǎi, especially for its traditional walled gardens, excellent museums, riveting temples and charming canalside streets.

The Best...

➡ **Sight** Sūzhōu Museum (p188)
➡ **Place to Eat** Zhūhóngxìng (p192)
➡ **Place to Drink** Bookworm (p192)

Top Tip

For tips on visiting Sūzhōu, visit www.livingsu.com, www.moresuzhou.com, www.classicsuzhou.com or www.visitsz.com.

Getting There & Away

Bus Regular buses (¥28 to ¥38, 90 minutes, 6.27am to 7.30pm) to Sūzhōu's south and north long-distance bus stations run from Shànghǎi South Bus Station. Regular services also run to Sūzhōu from Shànghǎi Long-Distance Bus Station (¥30 to ¥46, 7am to 7.40pm), Shànghǎi Hóngqiáo Airport Long-Distance Bus Station (¥53, 10am to 9pm) and Pǔdōng International Airport (¥84, three hours). Buses (¥72) also travel to Sūzhōu from Hángzhōu's north bus station.

Train The best way to reach town. High-speed G-class trains (1st/2nd class ¥60/40, 30 minutes, frequent) run to Sūzhōu from Shànghǎi Railway Station. Regular high-speed D-class trains (1st/2nd class ¥31/26, 34 minutes, 6.33am to 8.09pm) run to Sūzhōu from Shànghǎi Hóngqiáo Railway Station.

Getting Around

Bicycle You can rent **bikes** (Renmin Lu; per day ¥20, deposit ¥200; ☺6.30am-7pm) at hostels or down the alley beside 2061 Renmin Lu.

Metro Line 1 of Sūzhōu's spiffing new metro (tickets ¥2 to ¥4, first/last train 6.45am/10.30pm) runs along Ganjiang Lu, connecting Mùdú in the southwest with Zhongnan Jie in the east. Line 2 runs north–south from Sūzhōu North railway station to Baodaiqiaonan in the south, via Sūzhōu Railway Station.

....

Need to Know

→ **Area Code** ☐ 0152

→ **Location** 85km from Shànghǎi

→ **Tourist Office** (苏州旅游咨询中心, Sūzhōu Lǚyóu Zīxún Zhōngxīn; ☐ 6530 5887; www.classicsuzhou.com; 101 Daichengqiao Lu; 带城桥路101号)

◎ SIGHTS

The delightful gardens *(yuánlín)* of Sūzhōu were small, private compounds attached to family residences in the Ming and Qing dynasties. They were designed to help achieve the intellectual ideal of balancing Confucian social duties (in the city) with Taoism's worldly retreat (in nature).

Gardens are generally open from 7.30am to 5.30pm during high season (March to mid-November) but close at 5pm in winter. Peak prices are from mid-April to October.

★ SŪZHŌU MUSEUM   MUSEUM

(苏州博物馆; Sūzhōu Bówùguǎn; 204 Dongbei Jie; 东北街204号; audioguide ¥30; ◎9am-5pm; ☐Y5) **FREE** An architectural triumph, this IM Pei–designed museum is a modern interpretation of a Sūzhōu garden, a confluence of water, bamboo and clinical geometry. Inside is a fascinating array of jade, ceramics, wooden carvings, textiles and other displays, all with good English captions. Look out for the boxwood statue of Avalokiteshvara (Guanyin), dating from the republican period. No flip-flops.

HUMBLE ADMINISTRATOR'S GARDEN   GARDENS

(拙政园; Zhuōzhèng Yuán; 178 Dongbei Jie; 东北街178号; high/low season ¥70/50, audioguide free; ◎7.30am-5.30pm) First built in 1509, this 5.2-hectare garden is clustered with water features, a museum, a teahouse and at least 10 pavilions such as 'the listening to the sound of rain' and 'the faraway looking' pavilions – hardly humble, we know. The largest of the gardens, it's often considered to be the most impressive. With zigzagging bridges, pavilions, bamboo groves and

fragrant lotus ponds, it should be an ideal place for a leisurely stroll, but you'll be battling crowds for right of way.

SŪZHŌU SILK MUSEUM   MUSEUM

(苏州丝绸博物馆; Sūzhōu Sīchóu Bówùguǎn; 2001 Renmin Lu; 人民路2001号; ◎9am-5pm; Ⓜ Sūzhōu Train Station) **FREE** By the 13th century Sūzhōu was the place for silk production and weaving, and the Sūzhōu Silk Museum houses fascinating exhibitions detailing the history of Sūzhōu's 4000-year-old silk industry. Exhibits include a section on silk-weaving techniques and silk fashion through the dynasties, while you can amble among mulberry shrubs outdoors. You can also see functioning looms and staff at work on, say, a large brocade.

PINGJIANG LU   STREET

(平江路; Ⓜ Lindun Lu or Xiangmen) While most of the town canals have been sealed and paved into roads, the pedestrianised Pingjiang Lu (平江路) offers clues to the Sūzhōu of yesteryear. On the eastern side of the city, this canal-side road has whitewashed local houses, many now converted to guesthouses, teahouses or trendy cafes selling overpriced beverages, sitting comfortably side-by-side. Duck down some of the side streets that jut out from the main path for a glimpse at slow-paced local life.

TWIN PAGODAS   BUDDHIST TEMPLE, PAGODA

(双塔; Shuāng Tǎ; Dinghuisi Xiang; 定慧寺巷; admission ¥8; ◎8am-4.30pm; Ⓜ Lindun Lu) Beautifully enhanced with flowering magnolias in spring, this delightful courtyard and former temple contains a pair of sublime pagodas. It's one of the more relaxing, peaceful and composed parts of town. It's also home to the small **Sūzhōu Ancient Stone Carving Art Museum**.

NORTH TEMPLE PAGODA   PAGODA

(北寺塔; Běisì Tǎ; 1918 Renmin Lu; 人民路1918号; admission ¥25; ◎7.45am-5pm) The tallest pagoda south of the Yangzi, the nine-storey North Temple Pagoda dominates the northern end of Renmin Lu. Part of Bào'ēn Temple (报恩寺; Bào'ēn Sì), you can climb the pagoda (塔; tǎ) for sweeping views of hazy modern-day Sūzhōu.

The complex goes back 1700 years and was originally a residence; the current reincarnation dates back to the 17th century. Off to one side is **Nánmù Guānyīn Hall** (楠木观音殿; Nánmù Guānyīn Diàn), which was rebuilt in the Ming dynasty with some features imported from elsewhere.

GARDEN OF THE MASTER OF THE NETS GARDENS

(网师园, Wǎngshī Yuán; high/low season ¥30/20; ☺7.30am-5pm) Off Shiquan Jie, this pocket-sized garden is considered one of Sūzhōu's best preserved. Laid out in the 12th century, it went to seed and was later restored in the 18th century as part of the home of a retired official turned fisherman (hence the name). A striking feature is the use of space: the labyrinth of courtyards, with windows framing other parts of the garden, is ingeniously designed to give the illusion of a much larger area.

★ PÁN GATE SCENIC AREA LANDMARK

(盘门; Pán Mén; 1 Dong Dajie; admission Pán Gate only/with Ruìguāng Pagoda ¥25/31; ☺7.30am-6pm; ☐Y2) This stretch of city wall, straddling the outer moat in the southwest corner of the city, has Sūzhōu's only remaining original coiled gate, Pán Gate, which dates from 1355. This overgrown, double-walled **water gate** was used for controlling waterways, with defensive positions at the top. From the gate, you can view the exquisite arched **Wúmén Bridge** (Wúmén Qiáo) to the east, the long moat and the crumbling Ruìguāng Pagoda (瑞光塔; Ruìguāng Tǎ), constructed in 1004.

The gate is also connected to 300m of the **ancient city wall**, which visitors can walk along, past old women harvesting dandelions. The gate also backs onto a delightful scenic area, dotted with old halls, bell towers, bridges, pavilions and a lake as well as the small **Wǔxiàng Temple** (Wǔxiàng Cí). It's far less crowded than Sūzhōu's gardens and, in many ways, more attractive. To get here, take tourist bus Y2 or a taxi.

TEMPLE OF MYSTERY TEMPLE

(玄妙观; Xuánmiào Guàn; Guanqian Jie; 观前街; admission ¥10; ☺7.30am-5pm; ☐Lindun Lu or Leqiao) Lashed by electronic music from the shops alongside, the Taoist Temple of Mystery stands in what was once Sūzhōu's old bazaar, a rowdy entertainment district with travelling showmen, acrobats and actors. The temple dates from 1181 and is the sole surviving example of Song architecture in Sūzhōu. The complex contains several elaborately decorated halls, including the huge **Sānqīng Diàn** (三清殿; Three Purities Hall),

which is supported by 60 pillars and capped by a double roof with upturned eaves.

The hall is home to three huge statues of **Yuqing**, **Shangqing** and **Taiqing** (the Three Purities); look out for the **one-horned ox** (独角神牛; *dújiǎo shénníu*) that conveyed Laozi on his travels; there are also shrines to Tianhou, clothed in a pink robe, and the Jade Emperor. Note the antique carved **balustrade** around the hall, which dates to the Five Dynasties period (10th century). The blank **Wordless Stele** stands just east of the hall. The first main hall of the temple now serves as a jewelry showroom.

BLUE WAVE PAVILION GARDENS

(沧浪亭; Cānglàng Tíng; Renmin Lu; 人民路; high/low season ¥20/15; ☺7.30am-5pm) Originally the home of a prince, the oldest garden in Sūzhōu was first built in the 11th century, and has been repeatedly rebuilt since. Instead of attracting hordes of tourists, the wild, overgrown garden around the Blue Wave Pavilion is one of those where the locals actually go to chill and enjoy a leisurely stroll. Lacking a northern wall, the garden creates the illusion of space by borrowing scenes from the outside.

SŪZHŌU ART MUSEUM MUSEUM

(苏州美术馆; Sūzhōu Měishùguǎn; 2075 Renmin Lu; 人民路2075号; ☺9am-5pm Tue-Sun; ☐Sūzhōu Train Station) **FREE** There's a dazzling use of daylight and design in this brand new museum, creating a seemingly infinite white space hung with contemporary landscapes, calligraphy and modern art. The interior composition includes a lovely courtyard, sprouting bamboo. It's an element of a large complex that also includes the Sūzhōu Cultural Center and a theatre.

CONFUCIAN TEMPLE CONFUCIAN TEMPLE

(文庙, Wénmiào; 613 Renmin Lu; 人民路613号; ☺6.30am-4pm) **FREE** The restored Confucian Temple is a haven and place of solitude in a busy town, with several ancient (one is 830 years old) gingkos and rows of bonsai trees, plus a statue of the temperate sage. The highlight is the fabulous stelae carved during the Southern Song dynasty (1137–1279). One features a map of old Sūzhōu, detailing the canal system (much now paved over and blocked), old roads and the city walls.

LIONS' GROVE GARDENS

(狮子林; Shīzi Lín; 23 Yuanlin Lu; 园林路23号; admission high/low season ¥30/20) The one-

Sūzhōu

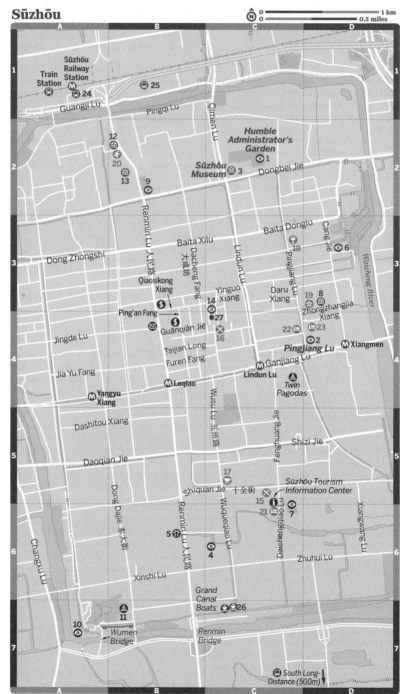

Sūzhōu

hectare **Lions' Grove** garden, constructed in 1350 by the monk Tian Ru, is famed for its strangely shaped rocks, meant to resemble lions, protectors of the Buddhist faith.

COUPLE'S GARDEN GARDENS
(耦园; Ǒu Yuán; 6 Xiaoxinqiao Xiang; 小新桥巷6号; admission high/low season ¥20/15; ⊙8am-4.30pm; Ⓜ Xiangmen) The tranquil Couple's Garden is off the main tourist route and sees fewer visitors (a relative concept in China), though the gardens, pond and courtyards are quite lovely.

KŪNQǓ OPERA MUSEUM MUSEUM
(昆曲博物馆; Kūnqǔ Bówùguǎn; 14 Zhong-zhangjia Xiang; 中张家巷14号; ⊙8.30am-4pm) FREE Down a warren of narrow lanes, the small Kūnqǔ Opera Museum is dedicated to kūnqǔ, the opera style of the region. The beautiful old theatre houses a stage, musical instruments, costumes and photos of famous performers. It also puts on regular performances of kūnqǔ.

PÍNGTÁN MUSEUM PERFORMING ARTS
(评弹博物馆; Píngtán Bówùguǎn; 3 Zhong-zhangjia Xiang; 中张家巷3号; admission ¥4, performance tickets ¥6; ⊙9.30am-noon & 3.30-5pm) Almost next to the Kūnqǔ Opera Museum is the Píngtán Museum, which puts on wonderful performances of píngtán, a singing and storytelling art form sung in the Sūzhōu dialect. Two-hour shows are at 1.30pm daily.

TIGER HILL PARK
(虎丘山; Hǔqiū Shān; ☏6723 2305; Huqiu Lu; 虎丘路; admission high/low season ¥60/40; ⊙7.30am-6pm, to 5pm winter; ⓆY1, Y2) In the far northwest of town, Tiger Hill is popular with local tourists. The beacon drawing the visitors is the leaning **Cloud Rock Pagoda** (云岩塔; Yúnyán Tǎ) atop the hill. The octagonal seven-storey pagoda was built in the 10th century entirely of brick, an innovation in Chinese architecture at the time. It began tilting over 400 years ago, and today the highest point is displaced more than 2m from its original position.

The hill itself is artificial and is the final resting place of He Lu, founding father of Sūzhōu. He Lu died in the 6th century BC and myths have coalesced around him – he is said to have been buried with a collection of 3000 swords and be guarded by a white tiger. Tourist buses Y1 and Y2 from the train station go to Tiger Hill.

WEST GARDEN TEMPLE GARDENS
(西园寺; Xīyuán Sì; Xiyuan Lu; 西园路; admission ¥25; ⊙8am-5pm; ⓆY1, Y3) This magnificent temple, with its mustard-yellow walls and gracefully curved eaves, was burnt to the ground during the Taiping Rebellion and rebuilt in the late 19th century. Greeting you as you enter the stunning **Arhat Hall** (罗汉堂; Luóhàn Táng) is an amazing four-faced and thousand-armed

statue of Guanyin. Beyond lie mesmerising and slightly unnerving rows of 500 glittering *luóhàn* (arhats – monks who have achieved enlightenment and passed to nirvana at death) statues, each unique and near life-size.

GRAND CANAL CANAL

(大运河; Dà Yùnhé) The Grand Canal passes to the west and south of Sūzhōu, within a 10km range of the town. Suburban buses 13, 14, 15 and 16 will get you there. In the northwest, bus 11 follows the canal for a fair distance, taking you on a tour of the surrounding countryside.

EATING

Sūzhōu's most-celebrated restaurants are in and around the pedestrianised shopping street of Guanqian Jie (观前街), while loads of cheap restaurants cluster at the eastern end of Shizi Jie (十梓街), immediately south of the university.

For cute cafes by the canal and traditional(ish) teahouses, take a wander along the charming cobblestone street of Pingjiang Lu.

BISTRONOMY FRENCH $$$

(☑6572 5632; 711 Shiquan Jie; 十全街711号; mains from ¥88; ⊙11.30am-2.30pm & 5.30-9.30pm Tue-Sun) With low-volume funky beats and two nifty and sleek floors, grey brick walls, drapes, spot lights and white linen tablecloths, this elegant restaurant is a choice stop on Shiquan Jie. Crowd-pullers include cheese fondue (¥118), rich and smooth onion soup (¥58) – in an over-the-top bowl – and braised rack of lamb served with gratin Dauphinois (¥148), and homemade cassoulet (¥138).

The homemade lasagne (¥88) is also excellent. You could go for the monster burger (3kg; ¥198) if you haven't eaten for a few days, or settle for pizzas (from ¥78).

ZHŪHÓNGXĪNG NOODLES $

(朱鸿兴; Taijian Long; mains from ¥15; ⊙6.45am-8.45pm; Ⓜ Lindun Lu) Popular with locals, this red-wood furniture bedecked eatery, with several branches across town, has a long history and wholesome, filling noodles – try the scrummy *xiàrén miàn* (虾仁面; noodles with baby shrimp) or the *xuěcài ròusīmiàn* (雪菜肉丝面; meat and vegetable noodles).

🍷 DRINKING & NIGHTLIFE

Largely iffy bars and sports pubs are slung out along Shiquan Jie. Pingjiang Lu is the place for serene cafe culture.

LOCKE PUB BAR

(240 Pingjiang Lu; 平江路240号; ⊙10am-midnight) Any place that plays Tom Waits is good in our book. This charming spot has ample space, comfy sofas, homemade ice cream, a whole wall of English books, hot whisky, Leffe, Corona and Guinness, all set in a traditional building along Pingjiang Lu.

BOOKWORM CAFE, BAR

(老书虫; Lǎo Shūchóng; 77 Gunxiu Fang; 滚绣坊77号; ⊙9am-1am) Běijīng's Bookworm wormed its way down to Sūzhōu, although the book selection isn't as good as Běijīng's. The food is crowd pleasing (lots of Western options) and the cold beers include Tsingtao and Erdinger. There are occasional events and books you can borrow or buy. Just off Shiquan Jie.

🏃 SPORTS & ACTIVITIES

Evening boat tours wind their way around the outer canal leaving nightly from 6pm to 8.30pm (¥120, 55 minutes, half-hourly), passing Pán Gate. Bring bug repellent as the mosquitoes are tenacious. Tickets can be bought at the **Tourist Boat Wharf** (游船码头; Yóuchuán Mǎtóu) down the alley east of Rénmín Bridge. Buses 27 or 94 run to the wharf.

Eight-person row boats (per boat ¥150) ply the canals by Pingjiang Lu where, towards the northern end of the lane, you'll find a ticket office.

🛏 SLEEPING

★**SŪZHŌU MINGTOWN YOUTH HOSTEL** HOSTEL $

(苏州明堂青年旅舍; Sūzhōu Míngtáng Qīngnián Lǚshè; ☑6581 6869; 28 Pingjiang Lu; 平江路28号; 6-bed dm ¥50, rm ¥125-185; ❈@; Ⓜ Xiangmen or Lindun Lu) This is a well-run youth hostel with a Thai sleeping Buddha at the door, a charming lobby and rooms and dorms with dark wooden 'antique' furniture. The only downside is that rooms aren't soundproof and hot water can misfire. There's free internet, free laundry, and bike rental. Rooms are around ¥20 pricier on Friday and Saturday.

★ GARDEN HOTEL   HOTEL $$$
(苏州南园宾馆; Sūzhōu Nányuán Bīnguǎn; ☑6778 6778; www.gardenhotelsuzhou.com; 99 Daichengqiao Lu; 带城桥路99号; r from ¥1558; ◉@☎) Within huge, green grounds, the very popular and recently redone five-star Garden Hotel has lovely, spacious and attractively decorated accommodation. Washed over with Chinese instrumental *pípá* music, the lobby is a picture of Sūzhōu, with a clear pond, grey bricks and white walls. Serene stuff and an oasis of calm.

PÍNGJIĀNG LODGE   BOUTIQUE HOTEL $$$
(苏州平江客栈; Sūzhōu Píngjiāng Kèzhàn; ☑6523 2888; www.pingjianglodge.com; 33 Niujia Xiang; 钮家巷33号; d¥988-1588, ste¥1888-2588; ✳@; MXiangmen or Lindun Lu) Capturing the white-washed walls and canal-side Sūzhōu aesthetic, this 17th-century, traditional courtyard building has well-kept gardens and 51 rooms bedecked in traditional furniture. Rooms at the pointy end are suites with split-level living spaces; standard rooms are bit bashed and could do with new carpets. Staff speak (faltering) English. Discounts of up to 50% are available.

Tónglǐ

Explore
With its sights neatly parcelled together in a picturesque and easily navigable setting, the charming canal town of Tónglǐ (同里) is a great day out. The ¥100 admission fee to the town includes all sights, except the Chinese Sex Culture Museum.

The Best...
➡ **Sight** Gēnglè Táng (p193)
➡ **Place to Sleep** Zhèngfú Cǎotáng (p194)

Top Tip
Tónglǐ is best reached by bus from Sūzhōu. Admission to the town gets you admission to the sights (except the Chinese Sex Culture Museum); however, there is no charge if you just want to wander the old town's streets.

Getting There & Away
Bus Day-trip buses (¥130 return including admission to town, 1¾ hours) depart daily from the Shànghǎi Sightseeing Bus Centre at 8.30am, returning from Tónglǐ at 4.30pm. You will be dropped off 2km from town at Tónglǐ Lake, from where there's a shuttle (¥4) to the gate. Half-hourly public buses (¥36, 6.25am to 3.10pm) leave Tónglǐ bus station for the Shànghǎi Long-Distance Bus Station, just north of Shànghǎi Railway Station. Regular buses (¥8, 50 minutes, every 30 minutes, from 6am to 7pm) also run to Tónglǐ bus station from Sūzhōu's north and south long-distance bus stations, from where it's a 15-minute walk to the old town. Frequent buses (¥6, 30 minutes) and local bus 263 (¥2) run between Zhōuzhuāng and Tónglǐ.

Need to Know
➡ **Area Code** ☑0152
➡ **Location** 80km from Shànghǎi

◉ SIGHTS

TÓNGLǏ OLD TOWN   VILLAGE
(老城区; Lǎochéngqū; ☑6333 1140; admission ¥100, after 5.30pm free) This lovely Old Town, only 18km southeast of Sūzhōu, boasts a rich, historical canalside atmosphere and weather-beaten charm. Many of the buildings have kept their traditional facades, with whitewashed walls, black-tiled roofs, cobblestone pathways and willow-shaded canal views adding to a picturesque allure. The town is best explored the traditional way: aimlessly meandering along the canals and alleys until you get lost. You can reach Tónglǐ from either Sūzhōu or Shànghǎi, but (due to crowds) aim for a weekday visit.

A restrained carnival atmosphere reigns here but the languorous tempo is frequently shredded by marauding tour groups that sweep in like cricket swarms, especially at weekends.

The admission fee to the town includes access to the best sights, except the Chinese Sex Culture Museum.

GĒNGLÈ TÁNG   HISTORIC BUILDING
(耕乐堂; ◷9am-5.30pm) There are three old residences in Tónglǐ that you'll pass at some

point and the most pleasant is this elegant and composed Ming-dynasty estate with 52 halls spread out over five courtyards in the west of town. The buildings have been elaborately restored and redecorated with paintings, calligraphy and antique furniture while the black-brick-faced paths, osmanthus trees and cooling corridors hung with *mǎdēng* (traditional Chinese) lanterns conjure up an alluring charm.

TUÌSĪ GARDEN
GARDENS

(退思园; Tuìsī Yuán; ☉9am-5.30pm) This beautiful 19th-century garden in the east of the Old Town delightfully translates as the 'Withdraw and Reflect Garden', so named because it was a Qing government official's retirement home. The 'Tower of Fanning Delight' served as the living quarters, while the garden itself is a meditative portrait of pond water churning with koi, rockeries and pavilions, caressed by traditional Chinese music.

CHINESE SEX CULTURE MUSEUM
MUSEUM

(中华性文化博物馆; Zhōnghuá Xìngwénhuà Bówùguǎn; admission ¥20; ☉9am-5.30pm) This private museum, located east of Tuìsī Garden, is quietly housed in a historic but disused girls' school campus and you won't miss it. Despite occasionally didactic and inaccurate pronouncements ('there were globally three abnormal sexual phenomena: prostitution, foot-binding and eunuchs'), it's fascinating, and ranges from the penal (sticks used to beat prostitutes, chastity belts) and the penile (Qing-dynasty dildos), to the innocent (small statues of the goddess of mercy) and the positively charming (porcelain figures of courting couples).

PEARL PAGODA
PAGODA

(珍珠塔; Zhēnzhū Tǎ; ☉9am-5.30pm) In the north of town, this compound dates from the Qing dynasty. Inside, you'll find a large residential complex decorated with Qing-era antiques, an ancestral hall, a garden and an opera stage. It gets its name from a tiny pagoda draped in pearls.

SPORTS & ACTIVITIES

Slow-moving six-person boats (¥90 per person, 25 minutes) ply the waters of Tónglǐ's canal system.

SLEEPING

Guesthouses (客栈; *kèzhàn*) are everywhere.

TONGLI INTERNATIONAL YOUTH HOSTEL
HOSTEL $

(同里国际青年旅舍; Tónglǐ Guójì Qīngnián Lǚshè; ☑63339311; 10 Zhuhang Jie; 竹行街10号; dm¥55, r from¥110; ❄@🛜) This youth hostel has two locations. The main one, slightly off Zhongchuan Beilu and near Zhongchuan Bridge, is 300m west of Zhèngfú Cǎotáng. With a charming wooden interior, rooms here have traditional furniture (some with four-poster beds), oozing old-China charm. The lobby area is attractive, decked out with international flags and sofas draped in throws.

ZHÈNGFÚ CǍOTÁNG
BOUTIQUE HOTEL $$

(正福草堂; ☑6333 6358; www.zfct.net; 138 Mingqing Jie, 明清街138号; s/d/ste ¥480/680/1380; ❄@🛜) *The* place to stay in town. Each one unique, the 14 deluxe rooms and suites are all aesthetically set with Qing-style furniture and antiques, with four-poster beds in some. Facilities like bathrooms and floor heating are ultramodern.

Zhūjiājiǎo

Explore

Thirty kilometres west of Shànghǎi, the pleasant canal town of Zhūjiājiǎo (朱家角) is an easy day trip from Shànghǎi. Although the settlement is far older, the town prospered during the Ming dynasty, when a commercial centre developed on its network of waterways. What survives today is a charming tableau of Ming- and Qing-dynasty alleys, bridges and old town (古镇; *gǔzhèn*) architecture.

The riverside settlement is small enough to wander completely in three hours. You'll be tripping over souvenir shops and vocal vendors, and you can buy anything from a pair of children's tiger shoes to 'antique' Chinese eyeglasses. Admission to town, including entry to four/nine of the main sights, costs ¥30/90.

The Best...

➡ **Sight** Fàngshēng Bridge

➡ **Place to Sleep** Cǎo Táng Inn

Top Tip
Visit Zhūjiājiǎo during the week; on weekends and holidays the canal town's narrow streets are packed with sightseers.

Getting There & Away
Bus The best way to reach Zhūjiājiǎo from Shànghǎi is from Pu'an Road Bus Station (普安路汽车站; Pǔ'ān Lù Qìchē Zhàn), just south of People's Square. From here Hùzhū Gāosù Kuàixiàn buses (沪朱高速快线; ¥12, one hour, every 20 minutes from 6am to 10pm, less frequently in low season) run direct to the town. Nine daily buses (¥15.50, one hour, 8.25am to 4.15pm) run between Tónglǐ bus station and Zhūjiājiǎo; they drop you on the main road, a 10-minute walk from the old town (古镇; *gǔzhèn*). Several tours head to Zhūjiājiǎo from Shànghǎi, including Insiders Experience (p260).

Need to Know
➡ **Area Code** ☑021
➡ **Location** 30km west of Shànghǎi
➡ **Tourist Office** (http://en.zhujiajiao.com; Xinfeng Lu; English guide half-/whole day ¥120/200; ☺8am-4.30pm)

◉ SIGHTS

FÁNGSHĒNG BRIDGE　　　　　BRIDGE
(放生桥; Fàngshēng Qiáo) Of Zhūjiājiǎo's quaint band of ancient bridges, the standout must be the graceful, 72m-long, five-arched Fángshēng Bridge, first built in 1571 with proceeds from a monk's 15 years of alms-gathering.

CITY GOD TEMPLE　　　TAOIST TEMPLE
(城隍庙; Chénghuáng Miào; Caohe Jie; 漕河街; admission ¥10; ☺7.30am-4pm) Moved here in 1769 from its original location in Xuějiābāng, this temple stands on the west side of the recently built City God Temple bridge.

YUÁNJĪN BUDDHIST TEMPLE　　BUDDHIST TEMPLE
(圆津禅寺; Yuánjīn Chánsì; Caohe Jie; 漕河街; admission ¥5; ☺8am-4pm) Yuanjin Buddhist Temple is near the distinctive **Tai'an Bridge** (泰安桥).

ZHŪJIĀJIĂO CATHOLIC CHURCH OF ASCENSION　　CHURCH
(朱家角耶稣升天堂; Zhūjiājiǎo Yēsū Shēngtiāntáng; 27 Caohe Jie, No 317 Alley; 漕河街27号317弄) Hunt out the peerless Zhujiajiao Catholic Church of Ascension, dating from 1863, its belfry rising in a detached tower.

 SLEEPING

CĂO TÁNG INN　　　　HOSTEL $
(草堂客栈; Cǎotáng Kèzhàn; ☑021 5978 6442; 31 Dongjing Jie; 东井街31号; dm ¥100, d ¥300-320; ✳@☎) This friendly and cozy hostel not far from Fángshēng Bridge has considerable old town charm, with clean and well-kept dorms, traditionally-dressed doubles and twins plus a lovely courtyard garden and bar.

✗ EATING & DRINKING

Food sellers line Bei Dajie, flogging everything from pigs' trotters, beggar's chicken and plump coconuts. Cafes have squeezed in along Caohe Jie, Xihu Jie and Donghu Jie, and even a creperie has set up shop near Yongquan Bridge.

✦ SPORTS & ACTIVITIES

At various points, including Fángshēng Bridge, you can hop aboard six-person row boats (per boat 15/30min ¥60/120) for waterborne tours of the town.

Zhōuzhuāng

Explore
Propelled to national fame by Chen Yifei's idyllic old paintings, Zhōuzhuāng (周庄) is Jiāngsū's best-known water town. Sixty kilometres from Shànghǎi, the picturesque canal town is regularly inundated with visitors. There's no denying the appeal of its waterside views, quaint bridges and ancient households.

If you can steal a lead on the crowds, it's possible to eke out classical red-lantern vignettes of water-town China and some enthralling courtyard architecture. Admission to Zhōuzhuāng costs ¥100, which includes 16 sights; make sure you get your photo digitally added to the ticket at purchase; this entitles you to a three-day pass. Free access after 8pm.

The Best...

→ **Sight** Shen's House
→ **Place to Drink** Zhōuzhuāng International Youth Hostel

Top Tip

It's straightforward to tie Zhūjiājiǎo, Zhōuzhuāng, Tónglǐ and Sūzhōu together by bus, without having to return to Shànghǎi.

Getting There & Away

Bus Buses (¥140 return including admission, 90 minutes, from 7am) depart for Zhōuzhuāng regularly from the Shànghǎi Sightseeing Bus Centre. From the drop-off at the bus station, turn left and walk for 15 minutes over Zhōuzhuāng Bridge (周庄大桥; Zhōuzhuāng Dàqiáo) to the old town and the ticket office by the gate. A taxi will cost around ¥10; pedicabs charge roughly the same. The last bus back to Shànghǎi is at 5pm. Buses also run from Shànghǎi long-distance bus station (¥25, six per day) and Shànghǎi south long-distance bus station (¥25, two per day). Buses (¥16, 90 minutes, 6.55am to 5.20pm) leave for Zhōuzhuāng every half-hour from the north long-distance bus station in Sūzhōu. Hourly buses (¥10, 50 minutes, 6.30am to 4.30pm) run to Zhōuzhuāng from Zhūjiājiǎo's small bus stand opposite the bus station on Xiangningbang Lu. Frequent buses (¥6, 30 minutes) and local bus 263 (¥2) shuttle between Zhōuzhuāng and Tónglǐ.

Boat Boats (one-way/return ¥180/250, 20 minutes) also run along the waterways to Tónglǐ from Zhōuzhuāng.

Need to Know

→ **Area Code** ☑ 0152
→ **Location** 60km west of Shànghǎi
→ **Tourist Office** (周庄游客中心; Zhōuzhuāng Yóukè Zhōngxīn; ☑ 5721 1655; Quanfu Lu , near memorial archway)

◉ SIGHTS

TWIN BRIDGES BRIDGE

A total of 14 bridges grace Zhōuzhuāng, but the most attractive is this pair of Ming-dynasty bridges (双桥; Shuāngqiáo) gorgeously standing at the intersection of two waterways in the heart of this canal town. **Shìdé Bridge** (世德桥; Shìdé Qiáo) is a humpbacked bridge while the connecting **Yǒngān Bridge** (永安桥; Yǒngān Qiáo) is the one with a square arch. The bridges were depicted in Chen Yifei's *Memory of Hometown*, which shot the whole town to fame from the 1980s onwards.

SHEN'S HOUSE HISTORIC BUILDING

(沈厅; Shěntīng; Nanshi Jie; 南市街; ◎8am-7pm) Near Fú'ān Bridge, this property of the Shen clan is a lavish piece of Qing-style architecture boasting three halls and over 100 rooms. The first hall is particularly interesting as it has a water gate and a wharf where the family moors their private boats. You can picture the compound entirely daubed in Maoist graffiti circa 1969 (note the crudely smashed carvings above the doors). You'll need a separate ticket (¥10) for the **Zǒumǎ Lóu** (走马楼; 8am to 4.30pm) where a further six courtyards and 45 rooms await.

ZHANG'S HOUSE HISTORIC BUILDING

(张厅; Zhāngtīng; ◎8am-7pm) To the south of the Twin Bridges, this beautiful 70-room, three-hall structure was built in the Ming era and bought by the Zhang clan in early Qing times as their residence. There's an opera stage to keep the ladies entertained (they were not supposed to leave home or seek entertainment outside). Also note the chairs in the magnificently named Hall of Jade Swallows. Unmarried women could only sit on those with a hollow seatback, symbolising that they had nobody to rely on!

Activities

One-hour and 80-minute boat trips (from ¥100 to ¥180) float along Zhōuzhuāng's waterways. Speedboats (¥80) tour South Lake from Bàoēn Bridge (报恩桥; Bàoēn Qiáo).

✖ EATING

Impregnated with the clinging smell of stinky *dòufu* (tofu), Zhōuzhuāng has no shortage of dining options. Breakfast can be difficult to source, unless you want a glistening hunk of pork; you can get a good cappuccino at the youth hostel, which also cooks up pizza, bacon sandwiches, seafood spaghetti, tuna salad and so forth.

SLEEPING

Prices peak on Fridays and Saturdays when the water town is at bursting point, so try to visit on a weekday. There are endless *kèzhàn* (客栈; guesthouses) dotted around the old town, with rooms in the ¥80 to ¥100 mark.

ZHŌUZHUĀNG INTERNATIONAL YOUTH HOSTEL HOSTEL $
(周庄国际青年旅舍; ☎5720 4566; 86 Beishi Jie; 北市街86号; dm/s/d ¥45/120/140; ❄@📶) Near an old opera stage, this efficient youth hostel occupies a converted courtyard. It has tidy rooms and a clean (but dim) dorm, and offers free laundry. The hostel owner is a barista, so enjoy a perfect brew in the ground-floor cafe. When it's slow, dorms go for ¥35; singles go for ¥100 and doubles for ¥120 on weekdays.

GŬZHÈN HOTEL GUESTHOUSE $
(古镇客房; Gŭzhèn Kèfáng; ☎135 1162 7032; 83 Beishi Jie; 北市街83号; d from ¥180) If the youth hostel is booked out, try this handy family-run place next door with clean, tile-floor rooms and one room with a four-poster and balcony.

ZHÈNGFÚ CĂOTÁNG BOUTIQUE HOTEL $$
(正福草堂; ☎5721 9333; www.zfct.net; 90 Zhongshi Jie; 中市街90号; d/ste ¥680/1080; ❄@📶) This lovingly presented five-room boutique hotel – a converted historic residence, restored to within an inch of its life – combines antique furniture with top-notch facilities, wood flooring and a lovely courtyard to fashion the best hotel in Zhōuzhuāng.

Shěshān

Explore

Easily accessed on the Shànghǎi metro, Shěshān is worth a half-day or day trip for its fantastic cathedral and the surrounding views from the hills.

Top Tip

At the foot of West Hill is one of several bike stations where you can hire green-coloured bikes (from 8am to 4.30pm) to explore the Shěshān area. You will need your passport and a deposit of ¥200; the first hour is free, thereafter ¥1 per hour.

Getting There & Away

Metro Take metro line 9 from Shànghǎi to Shěshān station and then take free bus 9 (九号线; *jiŭhào xiàn*), which runs every 20 minutes from 9am, towards Happy Valley amusement park, and drops off at West Hill; alternatively, jump on bus 92. Both depart from the bus stop outside the metro station.

Need to Know

➡ **Area Code** ☎021

➡ **Location** 35km southwest of Shànghǎi city centre

SIGHTS

Sights are contained within the Shěshān National Forest Park, divided into two areas: the West Hill area (西景区; Xījĭngqū) and the East Hill area (东景区; Dōngjĭngqū). The most famous historic attractions can be found in the West Hill area. At the time of writing, access to the West Hill was free, while admission to the East Hill (with a forest park, aviary and butterfly garden) was ¥45.

SHĚSHĀN BASILICA CHURCH
(Shěshān Shèngmŭ Dàdiàn; ⊙8am-4pm; Ⓜ Sheshan) FREE A very pleasant walk up through the trees from the road and the bus drop-off to the top of the hill, this cruciform red-brick and granite church is the highlight of the West Hill area. Glorious views range out from the hill over the suburbs of Shànghǎi. The original Holy Mother Cathedral was built here between 1863 and 1866, and the current Basilica of Notre Dame was finished in 1935. All the stained glass was destroyed during the Cultural Revolution and is being restored; the glass in the church at present is film-coated. Nonetheless, the interior is splendidly illuminated when the sun shines in. Every May sees hordes of local Catholics

making a pilgrimage to the church, climbing up the hill along the Via Dolorosa from the south gate.

SHÀNGHǍI ASTRONOMICAL MUSEUM
MUSEUM

(上海天文博物馆; Shànghǎi Tiānwén Bówùguǎn; admission ¥12; ⊙8.15am-5pm, last tickets 4.30pm; Ⓜ Sheshan) The Former Shěshān Observatory is right alongside the Shěshān Basilica on West Hill, founded by the Jesuits in 1900. The museum contains exhibitions on the history of observatories and astronomical research in China, as well as a collection of ancient telescopes.

XIÙDÀOZHĚ PAGODA
PAGODA

(秀道者塔; Xiùdàozhě Tǎ; Ⓜ Sheshan) Rising from the east flank of West Hill, this graceful 20m-high pagoda dates to the 10th century.

HAPPY VALLEY
AMUSEMENT PARK

(欢乐谷; Huānlè Gǔ; adult/child/child under 1.2m ¥200/100/free; ⊙9am-6pm; Ⓜ Sheshan or Dongjing) Happy Valley is a wildly popular national amusement park with four locations around China. This one opened in late 2009. The rides in other parks get good reviews; the Shànghǎi branch will even have a dive machine and the country's first wooden roller coaster, the Fireball. It's located in Songjiang county, in the town of Sheshan.

🛏 Sleeping

There's never been a better time to find a bed in Shànghǎi. From ultrachic, carbon-neutral boutique rooms to sumptuous five-star hotels housed in glimmering towers, grand heritage affairs and snappy, down-to-earth backpacker haunts, the range of accommodation in town is just what you would expect from a city of this stature.

Hotels

Top-end stays tend to drop into three categories: trendy boutique hotels; historic heritage hotels, where guests can wrap themselves in nostalgia; and top-of-the-range modern tower hotels, bristling with the latest amenities and sparkling with highly polished service (and often glorious views).

The midrange hotel market also offers boutique and heritage choices. The budget end has neat, comfortable but largely soulless express hotels, sometimes offering bigger rooms than hostels, but without the Western-friendly facilities or instant language skills.

Be prepared for surprisingly rudimentary English-language ability, except at the very best hotels (and youth hostels). Almost all the hotels we recommend have air-conditioning, and usually have wi-fi (sometimes at expensive daily rates or just in the lobby) or broadband.

Treat star rankings in Shànghǎi with a raised eyebrow. Some Shànghǎi hotels have secured five-star rankings, despite having no swimming pool.

Hostels

At the budget end, Shànghǎi has a good crop of youth hostels. Usually staffed by versatile English speakers, they offer well-priced dorm beds and private rooms (sometimes better than their hotel equivalent) as well as wi-fi, communal internet terminals, bike rental, kitchen and laundry rooms, and even the odd pool table, table tennis table or rooftop garden. Most have small and cheap bar-cafe-restaurant areas. Hostels also provide handy travel advice to guests and are exclusively attuned to travellers' needs.

Rates

Expect discounts of up to 50% off standard prices at most hotels, except during national holiday periods or the Formula One grand prix weekend. Rates can be bargained down at many budget and midrange hotels, but not at express hotels or hostels. All hotel rooms are subject to a 10% or 15% service charge; many cheaper hotels don't bother to charge it.

Dorm beds go for around ¥50 or ¥55, but double rooms under ¥200 can be hard to find. Expect to pay at least ¥500 for a midrange room. The fancier boutique hotels will charge more. A standard room in a top-end place will almost certainly top ¥1000, even after discount. Many of the better hotels, especially those aimed at business travellers, have cheaper weekend rates.

Longer-Term Rentals

The cheapest way to stay in Shànghǎi is to share a flat or rent local accommodation from a Chinese landlord. Classified ads in listings magazines such as *City Weekend* (www.cityweekend.com.cn/shanghai) are a good place to start. You will need to register with the local Public Security Bureau (PSB; 公安局; Gōng'ānjú) within 24 hours of moving in.

Some hostels and hotels also rent out long-let rooms. Chai Living Residences (p212) is a stylish and recommended option.

NEED TO KNOW

Price Ranges
The following represent the price per night of an en-suite double room in high season:

$	less than ¥500
$$	¥500 to ¥1300
$$$	over ¥1300

Reservations
➡ Reserve ahead, especially during high season.

➡ Online agencies **CTrip** (p271) and **eLong** (p271) are handy for reservations.

➡ **Lonely Planet** (lonelyplanet.com/shanghai/hotels) Offers bookings.

Checking In & Out
➡ You need your passport to check in. You'll fill in a registration form, or the hotel may simply scan your passport, a copy of which is sent to the local Public Security Bureau (PSB; 公安局; Gōng'ānjú) office.

➡ A deposit is required at most hotels, paid either with cash or by providing credit-card details.

➡ Check-out is usually midday.

Hotel Terms
The Chinese term for a hotel can vary. Many smaller, midrange hotels are called *bīnguǎn* (宾馆; literally 'guest house'), while larger hotels are often called *jiǔdiàn* (酒店; 'wine shop'), *dàjiǔdiàn* (大酒店; 'big wine shop') or less commonly *dàfàndiàn* (大饭店; 'big restaurant').

Lonely Planet's Top Choices

Fairmont Peace Hotel (p204) The grand dame of the Bund: restored, revitalised and renewed.

Astor House Hotel (p212) Classic old-Shànghǎi heritage and a mere foxtrot from the Bund.

Magnolia Bed & Breakfast (p206) An exquisite French Concession bijou, with only five rooms.

Waterhouse at South Bund (p209) Swish and supercool boutique style with views to match.

Best by Budget

$
Le Tour Traveler's Rest (p208) Fabulous youth hostel facilities combined with old Shànghǎi textures in a former towel factory.

Mingtown E-Tour Youth Hostel (p202) Supercentral, traditional charms and fab split-level lounge.

Mingtown Nanjing Road Youth Hostel (p202) Pretty much all your budget needs met, one step from the action.

$$
Marvel Hotel (p203) One of Shànghǎi's best midrange hotels, in a historic building and pole-position for People's Sq.

Kevin's Old House (p206) French Concession charmer, full of traditional-style elegance.

$$$
Peninsula Hotel (p204) For full-on pampering, lovely river views and exclusive surrounds.

Waldorf Astoria (p204) Home of the Long Bar, the

Waldorf is classic Shànghǎi all the way.

Mandarin Oriental Pudong (p210) For sumptuous stays and outstanding service in Pǔdōng.

Best Boutique Hotels

Le Sun Chine (p207) Fine French Concession mansion exuding yesteryear elegance.

Urbn (p208) Nifty, carbon-neutral hotel with a trendy, urban mood.

88 Xīntiāndì (p207) Stylish studios, all mod-cons, fab locale.

Best B&Bs

Quintet (p206) Another reason to bed down in the French Concession.

Kevin's Old House (p206) The three Cs: charming, comfortable, competitively priced.

Best Historic Hotels

Fairmont Peace Hotel (p204) Shànghǎi's premier art deco classic, revitalised and restored.

Waldorf Astoria (p204) Prestigious and grand, in the former Shànghǎi Club on the Bund.

Astor House Hotel (p212) Steeped in the sensations of Concession-era Shànghǎi.

Best for Views

Park Hyatt (p211) Awesome panoramas, as standard.

Ritz-Carlton Shanghai Pudong (p210) Beyond the knockout design, the views are breathtaking.

Peninsula Hotel (p204) Five-star views.

Where to Stay

Neighbourhood	For	Against
The Bund & People's Square	Luxury hotels on the Bund; close to the main sights; ubercentral with good transport links; iconic views and exclusive restaurants	Busy and expensive
Old Town	Traditional part of town; river views from stylish and happening South Bund area	Little choice; transport options limited; busy areas; ramshackle parts
French Concession	Dapper neighbourhood; vibrant, leafy and central; tip-top range of hotels; heritage architecture; standout restaurant choice; fab transport links	Few iconic views; expensive
Jìng'ān	Good transport links; fine range of accommodation choices; shopping zone; central and stylish	Sights light and spread out
Pǔdōng	Luxury, stylish and high-altitude hotels; killer views; fantastic restaurants; good transport links	Few sights, spread out; big distances; little character
Hóngkǒu & North Shànghǎi	Heritage and stylish long-stay options; good transport links; parts close to centre; off the beaten trail	Grittier and less fashionable; sprawling area with spread-out sights
West Shànghǎi	Close to Hóngqiáo International Airport; trade zone	Not much character; far from main sights; huge sprawl; not central

SLEEPING

🛏 The Bund & People's Square 外滩、人民广场

⭐MINGTOWN E-TOUR YOUTH HOSTEL
HOSTEL $

Map p296 (明堂上海青年旅舍; Míngtáng Shànghǎi Qīngnián Lǚshè; ☑6327 7766; 57 Jiangyin Rd; 江阴路57号; d ¥50, d with/without bathroom ¥260/160, tw ¥240; ✳@🛜; Ⓜ People's Sq) One of Shànghǎi's best youth hostels, E-tour has fine feng shui, a historic alleyway setting and pleasant rooms. But it's the tranquil courtyard with fish pond and the superb split-level bar-restaurant with comfy sofas that really sell it, plus there's a free pool table and plenty of outdoor seating on wooden decking.

There are both women-only and mixed dorms.

⭐MINGTOWN NANJING ROAD YOUTH HOSTEL
HOSTEL $

Map p296 (明堂上海南京路青年旅舍; Míngtáng Shànghǎi Nánjīng Lù Qīngnián Lǚshè; ☑6322 0939; 258 Tianjin Rd; 天津路258号; dm ¥50, s ¥150, d ¥200-270, tr ¥250; ✳@🛜; Ⓜ East Nanjing Rd) This sociable and friendly Mingtown hostel is located halfway between the Bund and People's Sq, a short hop from the nearest metro station. The six-bed dorms each have a private bathroom, laminated wood flooring and simple particle-board decor; perks include laundry, a kitchen, ground-floor bar-restaurant, a DVD room and a pool table.

MINGTOWN HIKER YOUTH HOSTEL
HOSTEL $

Map p296 (明堂上海旅行者青年旅馆; Míngtáng Shànghǎi Lǚxíngzhě Qīngnián Lǚguǎn; ☑6329 7889; 450 Middle Jiangxi Rd; 江西中路450号; dm with/without window ¥55/50, s/d ¥160/220; ✳@🛜; Ⓜ East Nanjing Rd) This justifiably popular hostel is just a short stroll from the famous esplanade, on the southern corner of the grand old Hengfeng Building. It offers tidy four- and six-bed dorms with pine bunk beds and clean communal shower facilities, plus decent private rooms, including cheapies with shared bathrooms.

There's a pool table, a bar-restaurant, movies, and a useful noticeboard in the lobby. Wi-fi in the lobby only.

BLUE MOUNTAIN BUND
HOSTEL $

Map p296 (蓝山国际青年旅舍; Lánshān Guójì Qīngnián Lǚshè; ☑3366 1561; www.bmhostel.com; 6th fl, 350 South Shanxi Rd; 山西路350号6楼; dm ¥55-70, d ¥160-260, tr/q ¥290/340; ✳@🛜; Ⓜ East Nanjing Rd) This hostel gets kudos for its central location – a short hop to the East Nanjing Rd metro station and not much further to the Bund or People's Sq. Eight-bed dorms are a bit small and the cheapest standard rooms have no window, but the staff is friendly and there's a decent bar and common area with a pool table, plus a colossal outside terrace.

There are also four- and six-bed dorms. Prices are slightly higher in August.

FISH INN BUND
HOTEL $

Map p296 (子鱼居; Zǐyújū; ☑3330 1399; www.fishinn.com.cn; 639 Middle Henan Rd; 河南中路639号; 🛜; Ⓜ East Nanjing Rd or Tianlong Rd) With a handy location around a 10 minute walk from the Bund and East Nanjing Rd, this friendly little place has decent rooms, although they are a bit dark. Deluxe rooms come with balcony/patio, however. The staff is eager to please and the tariff is excellent value for the hotel's positioning. Some rooms have steps up to the bed area.

There are suites for more room and comfort.

HOME INN
HOTEL $

Map p296 (如家酒店; Rújiā Jiǔdiàn; ☑6323 9966; www.homeinns.com; Lane 26, Sijing Rd; 泗泾路26弄; d ¥219-379, tr ¥399; ✳@🛜; Ⓜ East Nanjing Rd) Housed in a delightful lòngtáng (lane), overhung with laundry and accessed from Sijing Rd, this is one of the better branches of the dependable Home Inn chain. The pastel interior may not be everyone's cup of chá, but it means clean, functional rooms are nice and bright.

PHOENIX
HOSTEL $

Map p296 (老陕客栈; Lǎoshǎn Kèzhàn; ☑6328 8680; www.thephoenixshanghai.com; 15-17 South Yunnan Rd; 云南南路17号; dm ¥55, s ¥198, d ¥230-258; ✳@🛜; Ⓜ Dashijie) Although decorated with slapdash graffiti, this place has clean and bright rooms and the staff is jolly. Dorms sleep eight people; there's a rooftop bar; and the ground-floor Shaanxi dumpling restaurant adds to the appeal. Good location close to People's Sq. Bike rental costs ¥60 per day.

CAPTAIN HOSTEL
HOSTEL **$**

Map p296 (船长青年酒店; Chuánzhǎng Qīngnián Jiǔdiàn; ☑6323 5053; 37 Fuzhou Rd; 福州路37号; dm ¥75, r from ¥358; ❄@🛜; ⓂEast Nanjing Rd) Despite being hands-down the least friendly youth hostel in Shànghǎi, this naval-themed backpackers' favourite still reels in punters with its fantastic location and decent rooftop bar. There's a microwave, washing machine and lobby cafe, but all bathrooms are communal. Wi-fi is in the communal area only.

MOTEL 168
HOTEL **$**

Map p296 (莫泰连锁旅馆; Mòtài Liánsuǒ Lǚguǎn; ☑5153 3333; www.motel168.com; 531 East Jinling Rd; 金陵东路531号; r ¥309-359; ❄@; ⓂDashijie) Pricier rooms come with computer at this handy branch of Motel 168, sharing space with a branch of Home Inn. It rarely lifts itself above the functional, but this is all about location and value. English levels at reception can misfire. For discounts at any of this chain's branches, buy a ¥99 lifetime members' card (会员卡; huìyuán kǎ).

MOTEL 268
HOTEL **$**

Map p296 (莫泰连锁旅馆; Mòtài Liánsuǒ Lǚguǎn; ☑5179 3333; www.motel168.com; 50 Ningbo Rd; 宁波路50号; d/tr ¥339 /419; ❄@🛜; ⓂEast Nanjing Rd) This refurbished choice is good value. Modern doubles feature huge beds, wood-trimmed furnishings and smartly tiled chrome and glass bathrooms. But when push comes to shove, it's all about location. And for an extra ¥50 you get a room with its own PC. The only quibble: wafer-thin walls mean you need to be lucky with your neighbours.

JINJIANG INN
HOTEL **$**

Map p296 (锦江之星旅馆; Jǐnjiāng Zhīxīng Lǚguǎn; ☑6326 0505; www.jinjianginns.com; 33 South Fujian Rd; 福建南路33号; d ¥349; ❄; ⓂDashijie) This central hotel, which looks like it may have struck a deal with Ikea (think cream bedding, pine-coloured furniture and laminated wood flooring), has bright, spacious, functional twins and doubles with TVs, kettles, broadband and clean shower rooms.

JINJIANG INN
HOSTEL **$**

Map p296 (锦江之星; Jǐnjiāng Zhīxīng; www.jinjianginns.com; 680 East Nanjing Rd; 南京东路680号; d from ¥300; ❄@🛜; ⓂPeople's Sq) Located in the former Shanghai Sincere Department Store (which opened in 1917), the erstwhile East Asia Hotel has been grabbed by the folk at Jinjiang Inn and re-presented with smartish rooms with showers. It's often booked out due to its prime location.

★MARVEL HOTEL
HOTEL **$$**

Map p296 (商悦青年会大酒店; Shāngyuè Qīngniánhuì Dàjiǔdiàn; ☑3305 9999; www.marvelhotels.com.cn; 123 South Xizang Rd; 西藏南路123号; d ¥1080-1280, ste ¥1580; ❄@🛜; ⓂDashijie) Occupying the former YMCA building (1931) just south of People's Sq, the Marvel is one of the city's better midrange hotels. Beyond the chintzy corridors, the brown and cream rooms offer a reassuring degree of style. The building resembles Běijīng's Southeast Corner Watchtower (although the blurb compares it to Qiánmén), with a traditional hammerbeam ceiling.

The lobby is somnolent and dim, but the central location and modern comforts makes it one of Shànghǎi's best-value hotels. Online discounts can slash room rates in half.

SOFITEL HYLAND HOTEL
HOTEL **$$**

Map p296 (索菲特海仑宾馆; Suǒfēitè Hǎilún Bīnguǎn; ☑6351 5888; www.sofitel.com; 505 East Nanjing Rd; 南京东路505号; d ¥1150-2110; ❄🛜; ⓂEast Nanjing Rd) Rising up halfway along East Nanjing Rd, the Sofitel is a solid choice for those insisting on location without breaking the bank. The uncluttered and cool lobby area is dominated by open space and geometric lines. Standard rooms are rather dated, with a crisper and more modern finish in the executive rooms.

Facilities include a spa, two restaurants, a bar and a French bakery.

CENTRAL HOTEL SHANGHAI
HOTEL **$$**

Map p296 (王宝和大酒店; Wángbǎohé Dàjiǔdiàn; ☑0400 155-5008; www.centralhotel-shanghai.com; 555 Jiujiang Rd; 九江路555号; d from ¥850; ⓂEast Nanjing Rd) This hotel has a choice location at the heart of the action just south of East Nanjing Rd. It offers good value for travellers who don't want to go totally overboard but require comfort and convenience. Doubles are pleasant and well done, if rather unsurprising, with smallish bathrooms. Discounts add good value to the equation.

Food in the hotel's restaurants is OK (the breakfast is good), but with so many great restaurants nearby you're spoiled for choice – so eat out.

SLEEPING THE BUND & PEOPLE'S SQUARE

PARK HOTEL
HISTORIC HOTEL **$$**

Map p296 (国际饭店; Guójì Fàndiàn; ☑6327 5225; http://park.jinjianghotels.com; 170 West Nanjing Rd; 南京西路170号; s ¥850, d ¥1350-1450, ste ¥2700-6500; ❋; Ⓜ People's Sq) The Park Hotel is one of Shànghǎi's most famous art deco heritage spots with a positively supreme location, but it remains stuck in an old-fashioned groove like a scratched record. Staff members are friendly, though, and 10% discounts are common.

PACIFIC HOTEL
HISTORIC HOTEL **$$**

Map p296 (金门大酒店; Jīnmén Dàjiǔdiàn; ☑6327 6226; http://pacific.jinjianghotels.com; 108 West Nanjing Rd; 南京西路108号; d ¥988-1988; ❋; Ⓜ People's Sq) Capped by a distinctive clock tower, this historic hotel built in 1926 is strong on both character and style. The neoclassical entrance leads to a marble lobby with attractive ceiling artwork and wood-trimmed corridors with deep-red carpets. The cheaper rooms at the back of the hotel are distinctly dated, but the ones overlooking People's Park have nicer furniture and more space.

★FAIRMONT PEACE HOTEL
HISTORIC HOTEL **$$$**

Map p296 (费尔蒙和平饭店; Fèi'ěrméng Hépíng Fàndiàn; ☑6321 6888; www.fairmont.com; 20 East Nanjing Rd; 南京东路20号; d ¥2300-3800; ❂❋🛜☎; Ⓜ East Nanjing Rd) If anywhere in town fully conveys swish 1930s Shànghǎi, it's the old Cathay, rising imperiously from the Bund. Renamed the Peace Hotel in the 1950s and reopened in 2010 after a protracted renovation, it's reaffirmed its position as one of the city's most iconic hotels. Rooms are decked out in art deco elegance, from light fixtures down to coffee tables.

The entire hotel is cast in the warm, subdued tints of a bygone era. Expect all the luxuries of a top-class establishment, though note that wi-fi and broadband access cost an extra ¥99 per day for guests. Standard rooms come without a view, deluxe rooms with a street view and suites with the coveted river view. The hotel is also home to a luxury spa, two upscale restaurants and several bars and cafes. Even if you're not staying here, it's worth popping in to admire the magnificent lobby (1929), or taking in an evening show at the jazz bar.

★PENINSULA HOTEL
LUXURY HOTEL **$$$**

Map p296 (半岛酒店; Bàndǎo Jiǔdiàn; ☑2327 2888; www.peninsula.com; 32 East Zhongshan No 1 Rd; 中山东一路32号; d/ste ¥2800/5400; ❋@🛜☎; Ⓜ East Nanjing Rd) This spiffing hotel at the Bund's northern end combines art deco motifs with Shànghǎi modernity. It's a grade above many other market rivals, with TVs in the tub, well-equipped dressing rooms (with fingernail driers), valet boxes for dirty clothes, Nespresso machines and fabulous views across the river or out onto the gardens of the former British consulate. Lacquer fittings in rooms create a sumptuous, yet restrained, elegance. Part of the Rockbund development project, it includes an enormous luxury shopping arcade on the ground floor, and a back entrance that leads to the beautifully renovated Yuanmingyuan Rd.

★WALDORF ASTORIA
LUXURY HOTEL **$$$**

Map p296 (华尔道夫酒店; Huáěr Dàofū Jiǔdiàn; ☑6322 9988; www.waldorfastoriashanghai.com; 2 East Zhongshan No 1 Rd; 中山东一路2号; d/ste ¥3100/4600; ❋@🛜☎; Ⓜ East Nanjing Rd) Grandly marking the southern end of the Bund is the former Shànghǎi Club (1910), once the Bund's most exclusive gentlemen's hang-out. The 20 original rooms here have been reconverted to house the Waldorf Astoria's premium suites, six of which look out onto the Huángpǔ River. Behind this heritage building is a new hotel tower, with 252 state-of-the-art rooms.

Each room features touch digital controls, espresso machine, walk-in closet and even a TV in the mirror. There's a pronounced New York–meets-Shànghǎi theme here, from the Peacock Lounge to the cocktail list at the Long Bar.

LES SUITES ORIENT
LUXURY HOTEL **$$$**

Map p296 (东方商旅酒店; Dōngfāng Shānglǚ Jiǔdiàn; ☑6320 0088; www.lessuitesorient.com; 1 East Jinling Rd; 金陵东路1号; d with/without river view ¥2050/ 1900, ste with/without river view ¥2500/2350; ❋@🛜☎; Ⓜ Yuyuan Garden) Located at the southern edge of the Bund, Les Suites Orient is notable as the only hotel on the strip offering standard rooms (Bund Studio) with fantastic river and Bund vistas – in some rooms even the bathtub gets a view. It's housed in a modern 23-storey tower, with hardwood floors and minimalist design adding to the appealingly chic interior. Excellent service.

JW MARRIOTT
TOMORROW SQUARE
LUXURY HOTEL $$$

Map p296 (明天广场JW万豪酒店; Míngtiān Guǎngchǎng JW Wànháo Jiǔdiàn; ☑5359 4969; www.jwmarriottshanghai.com; 399 West Nanjing Rd; 南京西路399号; d from ¥2180; ✻☞☲; MPeople's Sq) Victor Sassoon probably would have traded in his old digs in a heartbeat if he could have stayed in the chairman's suite here. Housed across the upper 24 floors of one of Shànghǎi's most dramatic towers, the JW Marriott boasts marvellously appointed rooms with spectacular vistas and showers with hydraulic massage functions to soak away the stress.

Service and facilities are top-class, with two pools (indoor and outdoor) and an excellent spa. Internet costs ¥120 (¥600 per week) a day for nonmembers.

YANGTZE BOUTIQUE
SHANGHAI
BOUTIQUE HOTEL $$$

Map p296 (朗廷扬子精品宾馆; Lǎngtíng Yángzǐ Jīngpǐn Bīnguǎn; ☑6080 0800; www.theyangtze hotel.com; 740 Hankou Rd; 汉口路740号; d ¥1300-1800; ✻☞; MPeople's Sq) Originally built in the 1930s, this art deco gem has been splendidly refurbished. In addition to period decor, rooms feature deep baths, glass-walled bathrooms (with Venetian blinds) and even tiny balconies – a rarity in Shànghǎi. Check out the sumptuous stained-glass oblong and recessed skylight in the lobby, above a deco-style curved staircase.

The worn carpet in the foyer and on the stairs points to a high volume of traffic and the hotel is frequently booked out. The hammam and sauna in the fabulous Chuan spa are complimentary for guests; breakfast is served in the Italian restaurant, Ciao. Wi-fi costs extra.

GRAND CENTRAL HOTEL
SHANGHAI
HOTEL $$$

Map p296 (上海大酒店; Shànghǎi Dàjiǔdiàn; www.grandcentralhotelshanghai.com; 505 Jiujiang Rd; 九江路505号; s/d ¥2500/2600, ste ¥3300-43,000; ☞☲; MEast Nanjing Rd) Grand and fresh, this is a superb choice. The effortlessly elegant lobby areas – with acres of softly burnished marble and a small forest of fairy-light flecked palm trees overlooked by verandah-style balconies – is a congenial prelude to ample and traditionally styled deluxe rooms, furnished to a high degree of comfort. Discounts are usually more than 50%.

WESTIN SHANGHAI
HOTEL $$$

Map p296 (威斯汀大饭店; Wēisītīng Dàfàndiàn; ☑6335 1888; www.starwoodhotels.com; 88 Middle Henan Rd; 河南中路88号; d from ¥3150; ✻☞☲; MEast Nanjing Rd) Rooms in the newer tower at the top-notch and ace-placed Westin are sleek and contemporary with capacious bathrooms, some with freestanding tubs; rooms in the older tower are the same price, but are a bit more tired and smaller. The signature Westin 'Heavenly Bed' is displayed prominently in the lobby, a picture of comfort. Service throughout is thoughtful and professional.

There's a gym, a pool, a Thai-style spa and a tempting range of popular restaurants. Expect at least 50% discounts. Wi-fi is free; however, broadband costs ¥100 per night.

🛏 French Concession
法租界

BLUE MOUNTAIN
YOUTH HOSTEL
HOSTEL $

(蓝山国际青年旅舍; Lánshān Guójì Qīngnián Lǚshè; ☑6304 3938; www.bmhostel.com; 2nd fl, Bldg 1, 1072 Quxi Rd, French Concession East; 瞿溪路1072号1号甲2楼; dm ¥50-65, d ¥130-200, tr/q ¥240/280; ✻@☞; MLuban Rd) Although slightly out of the action, this excellent hostel is almost next door to Luban Rd metro station, so transport is sorted. Rooms are clean and simple with pine furniture and flooring, TV and kettle. There are women-only, men-only and mixed four-to-eight bed dorms, and there's a wi-fi-enabled bar-restaurant area with free pool table, free movie screenings and a kitchen with microwave.

There's also washing machines and even hairdryers and irons that you can borrow. Staff members speak English and are very friendly. Rooms are ever so slightly pricier in August.

HÀNTÍNG HOTEL
HOTEL $

Map p302 (汉庭酒店; Hàntíng Jiǔdiàn; ☑5465 6633; www.htinns.com; 233 South Shaanxi Rd, French Concession East; 陕西南路233号; s ¥299, d from ¥339; ✻@☞; MSouth Shaanxi Rd, Jiashan Rd) Rooms are a bit small at this budget chain, but they are well kept. This place is all about its French Concession location, not too far from Yongkang Rd bar street. English is limited.

YUÈYÁNG HOTEL
HOTEL $

Map p306 (悦阳商务酒店; Yuèyáng Shāngwù Jiǔdiàn; ☑6466 6767; 58 Yueyang Rd, French Concession West; 岳阳路58号; s ¥188, d ¥268-368; ❄; ⓂHengshan Rd) One of the best budget options in the French Concession that's within easy walking distance of a metro station, Yuèyáng has well-kept spacious rooms with big double beds and laminated flooring. Shower rooms are clean and modern, although, annoyingly, the hot water isn't always piping hot. Expect only small discounts, if any.

MOTEL 268
HOTEL $

Map p302 (莫泰连锁旅店; Mòtài Liánsuǒ Lǚdiàn; ☑5170 3333; www.motel168.com; 113 Sinan Rd, French Concession East; 思南路113号; d ¥279-329, ste ¥389; ❄@; ⓂDapuqiao) You can find decent enough rooms at this rather chipped and functional branch of Motel 268, which has a lift and friendly staff. The location on leafy Sinan Rd is ideally located for those wanting to explore the maze of charming alleyways known as Tiánzǐfáng. Note some rooms are windowless. English is limited.

★ MAGNOLIA BED & BREAKFAST
B&B $$

Map p306 (☑138 1794 0848; www.magnoliabnb shanghai.com; 36 Yanqing Rd, French Concession West; 延庆路36号; r ¥702-1296; ❄@⊙; ⓂChangshu Rd) Opened by Miranda Yao of the cooking school The Kitchen at... (p40), this cosy little five-room B&B is located in a 1927 French Concession home. It's Shànghǎi all the way, with an art deco starting point followed by comfort and stylish design. While rooms are on the small side, they are high-ceilinged and bright. It's a true labour of love.

There are discounts for stays of seven nights or more. There's no front desk, so phone ahead before visiting.

★ QUINTET
B&B $$

Map p306 (☑6249 9088; www.quintet-shanghai. com; 808 Changle Rd, French Concession West; 长乐路808号; d incl breakfast ¥850-1200; ⊖❄⊙; ⓂChangshu Rd) This chic B&B has six beautiful double rooms in a 1930s townhouse that's not short on character. Some of the rooms are small, but each is decorated with style, incorporating modern luxuries such as large-screen satellite TVs and laptop-sized safes, with more classic touches such as wood-stripped floorboards and deep porcelain bathtubs.

Staff members sometimes get a BBQ going on the roof terrace and there's an excellent restaurant on the ground floor. No sign – just buzz on the gate marked 808 and wait to be let in. Be aware there is no elevator.

★ KEVIN'S OLD HOUSE
B&B $$

Map p306 (老时光酒店; Lǎoshíguāng Jiǔdiàn; ☑6248 6800; www.kevinsoldhouse.com; No 4, Lane 946, Changle Rd, French Concession West; 长乐路946弄4号; ste ¥1180-1280; ❄⊙; ⓂChangshu Rd) Housed in a secluded 1927 four-storey French Concession villa, this lovely boutique hotel is an elegant yet affordable place to stay. Six suites are spread throughout the house, each decorated with care, featuring wooden floorboards, traditional Chinese furniture, stylish artwork and a few antiques. There's an upright piano in the entrance. Suites usually go for around ¥950.

ĀNTÍNG VILLA HOTEL
HISTORIC HOTEL $$

Map p306 (安亭别墅花园酒店; Āntíng Biéshù Huāyuán Jiǔdiàn; ☑6433 1188; 46 Anting Rd, French Concession West; 安亭路46号; r ¥1180-1380, ste ¥1580-5580; ❄⊙; ⓂHengshan Rd) On a quiet tree-lined street, this pleasant hotel shares its grounds with a 1936 colonial Spanish–style villa. It offers bright, comfortable rooms, with wi-fi and quality furniture including a chaise longue by the window. Some rooms have balconies and fine views over the lovely garden. Discounts of up to 40% are available.

HILTON HOTEL
HOTEL $$

Map p306 (静安希尔顿饭店; Jìng'ān Xī'ěrdùn Fàndiàn; ☑6248 0000; www.hilton.com; 250 Huashan Rd, French Concession West; 华山路250号; r from ¥1300; ⓂJing'an Temple) A favourite with airline crews and tour groups, the Hilton's standard rooms are a bit old-fashioned, but the deluxe versions – only ¥100 to ¥200 more – have had a modern refit, meaning more style (slick furniture, rainforest showers), more comfort (thick carpets, big beds) and better views. Access to broadband/wi-fi costs ¥120/160 per day.

HÉNGSHĀN PICARDIE HOTEL
HOTEL $$

Map p306 (衡山宾馆; Héngshān Bīnguǎn; ☑6437 7050; www.hengshanhotel.com; 534 Hengshan Rd, French Concession West; 衡山路534号; d incl breakfast ¥1300; ❄@⊙; ⓂHengshan Rd) These former Picardie Apartments (1934) still boast impressive art deco charm, most noticeably in the fine exterior, the rectangular black-and-white floor pattern of the lobby and the 1930s touches throughout. Superior rooms are attractively styled with European-style decor and have character, but do try to get a corner room. The location is good, between Hengshan Rd and Xújiāhuì.

DŌNGHÚ HOTEL
HISTORIC HOTEL $$

Map p306 (东湖宾馆; Dōnghú Bīnguǎn; ☑6415 8158; www.donghuhotel.com; 70 Donghu Rd, French Concession West; 东湖路70号; d US$150-330; ✳🛜; MSouth Shaanxi Rd) Once the home of feared Shànghǎi gangster Du Yuesheng, the historic Dōnghú is divided into several areas and buildings, although only two of them house ordinary guestrooms. The first, an austere 1934 white concrete building, houses the better rooms, although their colour schemes leave a little to be desired. The second, newer building is an ugly, white-tiled affair across the road and has overpriced rooms with cheap carpets and tatty furnishings. Wi-fi in the lobby only. Discounts of up to 50% make this a reliable midrange option.

★LANGHAM XĪNTIĀNDÌ
LUXURY HOTEL $$$

Map p302 (新天地朗廷酒店; Xīntiāndì Lǎngtíng Jiǔdiàn; ☑2330 2288; xintiandi.langhamhotels.com; 99 Madang Rd, French Concession East; 马当路99号; r/ste ¥1600/1840; ✳🛜🏊; MSouth Huangpi Rd) Xīntiāndì has become a magnet for luxury hotels, and they don't come much nicer than this one. Its 357 rooms all feature huge floor-to-ceiling windows, plenty of space to spread out in, and an attention to the minute details that make all the difference: Japanese-style wooden tubs in suites, heated bathroom floors, internet radio and white orchids.

Amenities include the lauded Cantonese restaurant Ming Court (with a surprisingly affordable business lunch and all-you-can-eat dim sum on the weekends), an indoor pool and the award-winning spa, Chuan.

★ANDAZ
LUXURY HOTEL $$$

Map p302 (安达仕酒店; Āndáshì Jiǔdiàn; ☑2310 1234; http://shanghai.andaz.hyatt.com; 88 Songshan Rd, French Concession East; 嵩山路88号; r ¥1820-2820; ✳🛜🏊; MSouth Huangpi Rd) Housed in a tower with retro '70s style windows, this fab hotel's design-led lobby – a trendy pronouncement of metal latticework – suggests an art space, a sensation that persists when you hunt for the open-plan reception (it's on the right). Along curving corridors, guestrooms are cool and modern,

with sinks and bathtubs that glow in different colours and monumental flat-screen TVs.

With room design courtesy of Japanese interior designer Super Potato, all mod cons are operated by tablet, while views of Pǔxī or Pǔdōng – depending on your choice – range out beyond curved and chunky windows. Discounts of up to 35% online.

★LE SUN CHINE
BOUTIQUE HOTEL $$$

Map p306 (绅公馆; Shēn Gōng Guǎn; ☑5256 9977; www.lesunchine.com; No 6, Lane 1220, Huashan Rd, French Concession West; 华山路 1220弄6号; r ¥1980-4380; ✳🛜🏊; MJiaotong University) Originally the home of the Sun family, this renovated 1932 mansion has become one of Shànghǎi's most exclusive boutique properties. Seventeen personalised suites – decorated in a choice of four different colours on four floors – combine an antique-strewn style with all the modern comforts of home.

Relax in the Roman-style pool or steam bath before enjoying a Shanghainese banquet in the highly lauded restaurant. Service is exquisitely refined. You can usually reserve a room in the region of ¥1300.

★88 XĪNTIĀNDÌ
BOUTIQUE HOTEL $$$

Map p302 (88新天地; ☑5383 8833; www.88xintiandi.com; 380 South Huangpi Rd, French Concession East; 黄陂南路380号; r from ¥1700; ✳🛜; MXintiandi, South Huangpi Rd) This stylish boutique Xīntiāndì residence has 53 spacious studios, each decorated with red lamps and antique Chinese cabinets. The central feature of each room is the raised sleeping area, enclosed with curtains, but also noteworthy are the kitchenettes (including microwave) and the top-notch home entertainment system that boasts surround-sound speakers, DVD player and satellite TV.

A small health club overlooks the park; guests also enjoy complimentary access to the indoor pool at the nearby Langham Xīntiāndì.

HÉNGSHĀN MOLLER VILLA
HISTORIC HOTEL $$$

Map p302 (衡山马勒别墅饭店; Héngshān Mǎlè Biéshù Fàndiàn; ☑6247 8881; www.mollervilla.com; 30 South Shaanxi Rd, French Concession East; 陕西南路30号; r from ¥1500, feature room ¥3800; ✳@🛜; MSouth Shaanxi Rd) With enough wood-panelling to level a substantial forest, this fairy-tale castle lookalike, built by Swedish businessman and horse-racing fanatic Eric Moller, is one of Shànghǎi's unique buildings. There are parquet floors in the lobby and a lush garden in the back, while feature rooms are decorated with old Shànghǎi artwork and are well turned out with sumptuous bedding.

Cheaper rooms in the later No 2 extension block have rather small baths and don't put you in the main villa. A bronze horse stands over the spot where Moller is said to have buried his favourite nag.

INTERCONTINENTAL SHANGHAI RUIJIN HOTEL HISTORIC HOTEL **$$$**

Map p302 (上海瑞金洲际酒店; Shànghǎi Ruìjīn Zhōujì Jiǔdiàn; ☎6472 5222; www.ihg.com; 118 Ruijin No 2 Rd, French Concession East; 瑞金二路118号; standard/executive d ¥1320/2310; ❄@📶; Ⓜ South Shaanxi Rd) The InterContinental group has acquired this historic 238-guestroom garden estate, which includes Building No 1, a 1919 red-brick mansion and former residence of Benjamin Morris, one-time owner of *North China Daily News*. Dark-wood panelled corridors lead to enormous, pleasantly appointed rooms. The architecture and the park-like gardens are lovely. The staff's spoken English is fitful.

Jìng'ān 静安

★LE TOUR TRAVELER'S REST HOSTEL **$**

Map p310 (乐途静安国际青年旅舍; Lètú Jìng'ān Guójì Qīngnián Lǚshè; ☎6267 1912; www.letourshanghai.com; 319 Jiaozhou Rd; 胶州路319号; dm ¥70, d ¥260-280, tr/q ¥360/360; ❄@📶; Ⓜ Changping Rd) Housed in a former towel factory, this fabulous youth hostel leaves most others out to dry. You'll pass a row of splendid *shíkùmén* (stone-gate houses) on your way down the alley to get here. The old-Shànghǎi textures continue once inside, with red-brick walls and reproduced stone gateways above doorways leading to simple but smart rooms and six-person dorms (shared bathrooms).

Double rooms are not very spacious, but they have flatscreen TVs and they're clean. Rooms are between ¥10 and ¥30 pricier on Fridays and Saturdays. The ground floor has a table tennis table, a pool table and wi-fi, all of which are free to use, and there's a fine rooftop bar-restaurant with outdoor seating. Bicycles can also be rented here.

Down an alley off Jiaozhou Rd.

SOHO PEOPLE'S SQUARE YOUTH HOSTEL HOSTEL **$**

(苏州河畔国际青年旅社; Sūzhōu Hépàn Guójì Qīngnián Lǚshè; ☎5888 8817; 1307 South Suzhou Rd; 南苏州路1307号; dm with/without bathroom incl breakfast ¥70/60, d incl breakfast ¥238-298; ❄@📶; Ⓜ Xinzha Rd) Occupying a former warehouse along Sūzhōu Creek, this spacious hostel has high ceilings, painted murals on the walls and oodles of laid-back common space. It's a bit out of the way, but only a five-minute walk from the Xinzha Rd metro station on line 1, which runs direct through People's Sq and the French Concession. Laundry and some kitchen facilities available.

JINJIANG INN HOTEL **$**

Map p310 (锦江之星旅馆; Jǐnjiāng Zhīxīng Lǚguǎn; ☎5213 8811; www.jinjianginns.com; 400 Xikang Rd; 西康路400号; s/d from ¥239/299; ❄📶; Ⓜ Changping Rd) Rooms are in excellent shape at this bright and simple chain. Wi-fi in the lobby only. There are two branches in the Bund.

★URBN BOUTIQUE HOTEL **$$$**

Map p310 (☎5153 4600; www.urbnhotels.com; 183 Jiaozhou Rd; 胶州路183号; r from ¥1500; ❄; Ⓜ Changping Rd) China's first carbon-neutral hotel not only incorporates recyclable materials and low-energy products where possible, it also calculates its complete carbon footprint – including staff commutes and delivery journeys – and offsets it by donating money to environmentally friendly projects. Open-plan rooms are beautifully designed with low furniture and sunken living areas exuding space.

Bathtubs are in the bedroom rather than in the bathroom (and sometimes right next to the bed!), while grey slate tiling and textured surfaces gives this luxury boutique hotel a distinctly urban vibe. Check out the cool wall behind reception arranged with a mosaic of well-travelled suitcases.

PÚLÌ LUXURY HOTEL **$$$**

Map p310 (璞丽酒店; Púlì Jiǔdiàn; ☎3203 9999; www.thepuli.com; 1 Changde Rd; 常德路1号; d from ¥3880; ❄📶🏊; Ⓜ Jing'an Temple) With open-space rooms divided by hanging silk screens and an understated beige-and-mahogany colour scheme accentuated by the beauty of a few well-placed orchids, the Púlì is an exquisite choice. The Zen calm and gorgeous design of this 26-storey hotel make another strong case for stylish skyscrapers. Book ahead for discounts of up to 60%.

PORTMAN RITZ-CARLTON   HOTEL $$$

Map p310 (波特曼丽嘉酒店; Bōtèmàn Lìjiā Jiǔdiàn; 6279 8888; www.ritzcarlton.com; 1376 West Nanjing Rd; 南京西路1376号; r from ¥4000; ❀ @ 🖭 ≋; Ⓜ Jing'an Temple) Impeccable service, excellent facilities and a central location make this one of the best business hotels this side of the Huángpǔ River. While it lacks the gorgeous interior design and architectural pizzazz of Shànghǎi's newest crop of five-star hotels, it's nonetheless a first-rate luxury choice. Selling points include two 7th-floor pools, squash and tennis courts, and a gym.

The real reason for staying here, of course, is the business amenities and the surrounding Shànghǎi Centre, which has a medical clinic, excellent restaurants and consulates. Discounts can drop rates by as much as 60%.

🛏 West Shànghǎi

ROCK & WOOD INTERNATIONAL
YOUTH HOSTEL   HOSTEL $

Map p318 (老木国际青年旅舍; Lǎomù Guójì Qīngnián Lǚshè; 3360 2361; No 278, Lane 615, Zhaohua Rd; 昭化路615弄278号; dm ¥55-60, s ¥110, d ¥160-240; ❀ 🖭; Ⓜ West Yan'an Rd) With a serene bamboo-edged pond in its courtyard, and a bright and inviting lounge and bar area, this is a smart and tranquil choice that sees a steady stream of travellers. Rooms and mixed dorms are clean and quiet; the deluxe double comes with four-poster bed; and the staff is welcoming. The cheapest single has shared shower room.

PENTAHOTEL SHANGHAI   HOTEL $$

Map p318 (上海贝尔特酒店; Shànghǎi Bèiěrtè Jiǔdiàn; 6252 1111; www.pentahotels.com; 1525 Dingxi Rd; 定西路1525号; d from ¥700; ❀ @ 🖭; Ⓜ Zhongshan Park) This young and sprightly hotel is built on a snappy design ethos: the reception doubles as a good-looking, cool cafe and bar; bright rooms are comfortable, boutique-style and modish without being lavish; prices are reasonable; and the emphasis is on practicality and zest. Backing it all up is a helpful staff and efficient management. The hotel is very near Zhongshan Park metro station.

NEW WORLD SHANGHAI HOTEL   HOTEL $$

Map p318 (上海巴黎春天新世界酒店; Shànghǎi Bālíchūntiān Xīnshìjiè Jiǔdiàn; 6240 8888; www. shanghai.newworldhotels.com; 1555 Dingxi Rd; 定西路1555号; d from ¥988; ❀ 🖭 ≋; Ⓜ Zhongshan Park) Stylish and excellent value for money, this neat and tastefully presented hotel zeroes in on business travellers, but also appeals to visitors who want more bang for their buck. It seems far out in the west, but it's right by the Zhongshan Park (lines 2, 3 and 4) metro system for quick zips into the centre of things.

Rooms are spacious and modern, and the breakfast buffet is recommended. There's an outdoor swimming pool on the 15th floor and hotel dining options are sound.

MARRIOTT HOTEL HÓNGQIÁO   HOTEL $$

Map p318 (万豪虹桥大酒店; Wànháo Hóngqiáo Dàjiǔdiàn; 6237 6000; www.marriott.com; 2270 Hongqiao Rd; 虹桥路2270号; r from ¥1024; ❀ @ 🖭 ≋; Ⓜ Longxi Rd) This Marriott is a reasonable choice if you're doing business in the Hóngqiáo area. A grand lobby introduces guests to good all-around facilities that include a bright, semicircular swimming pool, tennis court, bar and a number of decent restaurants. While rooms themselves are basic and a bit dated, the rates are reasonable. Broadband in the standard rooms costs extra (¥120 per day).

XĪJIĀO STATE GUEST HOUSE   HOTEL $$

Map p318 (西郊宾馆; Xījiāo Bīnguǎn; 6219 8800; www.hotelxijiao.com; 1921 Hongqiao Rd; 虹桥路1921号; r from ¥1168; ❀ ≋; Ⓜ Longxi Rd) This quiet spot, which has hosted guests as esteemed as Queen Elizabeth II and Mao Zedong, claims to be the largest garden hotel in Shànghǎi. Its 80 hectares include huge lawns, streams, mature trees and a large lake. Standard rooms are nothing special, but facilities include indoor and outdoor tennis courts, a delightful indoor pool and a gym.

🛏 Old Town 南市

★ WATERHOUSE AT
SOUTH BUND   BOUTIQUE HOTEL $$

Map p300 (水舍时尚设计酒店; Shuǐshè Shíshàng Shèjì Jiǔdiàn; 6080 2988; www.waterhouseshanghai.com; 1-3 Maojiayuan Rd, Lane 479, South Zhongshan Rd; 中山南路479弄毛家园路1-3号; d ¥1100-2800; ❀ 🖭; Ⓜ Xiaonanmen) There are few cooler places to base yourself in Shànghǎi than this awfully trendy 19-room, four-storey, South Bund converted 1930s warehouse right by the Cool Docks.

HOTEL RESTRICTIONS

Astonishingly, the majority of hotels in China still do not accept foreigners. To be able to accept foreigners, hotels need to be registered with, and have approval from, the Public Security Bureau (PSB; 公安局; Gōng'ānjú) – the police. Most hotels in China do not have this authorisation, but select hotels do. This can be highly vexing for travellers, especially those who speak Chinese and who enjoy keeping away from tourist hotels. Hotels that are not allowed to house foreigners are often non-chain and much cheaper than the authorised choices, meaning foreigners are forced to spend more money on a room. To ask in Chinese if a hotel accepts foreigners, simply ask: 你收外国人吗 (*nǐ shōu wàiguórén ma*)? We only recommend hotels that accept foreign guests.

Gazing out onto supreme views of Pǔdōng (or into the crisp courtyard), the Waterhouse's natty rooms (some with terrace) are swishly dressed. Service can be wanting, though, and it's isolated from the action.

Fittingly for this revived part of town, the ethos is industrial chic, so it best suits design-conscious guests. A lovely rooftop bar caps it all and trim ground-floor Table No 1 throws in culinary excellence.

HOTEL INDIGO HOTEL $$$

Map p300 (英迪格酒店; Yīngdígé Jiǔdiàn; www.hotelindigo.com; 585 East Zhongshan No 2 Rd; 中山东二路585号; ❄ 🛜 🌐; MXiaonanmen) With its quirkily designed lobby – chairs like birdcages; tree branches trapped in cascades of glass jars; sheets of metal riveted to the wall; modish, sinuously shaped furniture; and funky ceiling lights – towering Hotel Indigo is a stylish South Bund choice. Chic and playful guestrooms are about colourful cushions and whimsical designs, with lovely rugs and spotless bathrooms.

Note that accommodation either looks out onto the Old Town (so-so) or the river (stellar). Service is very helpful and the infinity pool is a dream. Regular discounts tame prices by up to 60%.

🛏 Pǔdōng 浦东

BEEHOME HOSTEL HOSTEL $

Map p312 (宾家国际青年旅舍; Bīnjiā Guójì Qīngnián Lǚshè; ☎5887 9801; www.beehome-hostel.com; Lane 490, No 210 Dongchang Rd; 东昌路490弄210号; dm ¥65, tw/tr ¥258/298, d ¥290-360; ❄ @ 🛜; MDongchang Rd) If you have to live Pǔdōng-side, this well-tended hostel is a leafy and homely oasis in an otherwise innocuous housing estate. It offers basic but clean rooms, all with private bathrooms (even the dorms), and excellent communal areas – a bar-restaurant, a balcony seating area and a cute, tree-shaded courtyard garden.

There's wi-fi throughout, a laundry room, kitchen and bar. The hostel is tricky to find as there's no English sign on the road – it's through the first gate past the China Post (中国邮政; Zhōngguó Yóuzhèng) office as you walk west, through a wooden gateway marked 东园新村 (Dōngyuán Xīncūn).

★MANDARIN ORIENTAL PUDONG HOTEL $$$

Map p312 (上海浦东文华东方酒店; Shànghǎi Pǔdōng Wénhuá Dōngfāng Jiǔdiàn; ☎2082 9908; www.mandarinoriental.com; 111 South Pudong Rd; 浦东南路111号; d from ¥3800; ❄ @ 🛜 🌐; MLujiazui) Slightly tucked away from the Lùjiāzuǐ five-star hotel melee in a sheltered riverside spot, the 362-room Mandarin Oriental is a visual feast, from the beautiful oval chandeliers in the lobby to the multicoloured glass murals (depicting forests) and gorgeous dining choices. All five-star expectations are naturally met, but it's the meticulous service that ices this cake.

Sumptuous rooms aside, there's a 24-hour pool and gym, spa and delicious views. The address may seem a bit stranded, but it's a short walk to the heart of Lùjiāzuǐ and there's a complimentary shuttle bus within the area.

★RITZ-CARLTON SHANGHAI PUDONG LUXURY HOTEL $$$

Map p312 (上海浦东丽思卡尔顿酒店; Shànghǎi Pǔdōng Lìsī Kǎěrdùn Jiǔdiàn; ☎2020 1888; www.ritzcarlton.com; Shànghǎi IFC, 8 Century Ave; 世纪大道8号; d from ¥2800; ❄ @ 🛜 🌐; MLujiazui) From the stingray-skin-effect wallpaper in the lift to its exquisite accommodation and stunning alfresco bar, the deliciously styled 285-room Ritz-Carlton in the Shànghǎi IFC is a peach. The beautifully designed rooms – a blend of feminine colours, eye-catching art deco motifs, chic elegance and dramatic Bund-side views – are a stylistic triumph.

Divided from the room by a screen, delightful open-plan bathrooms feature deep and inviting free standing bathtubs. Service is, unsurprisingly, top-notch.

★ PARK HYATT
LUXURY HOTEL $$$

Map p312 (柏悦酒店; Bóyuè Jiǔdiàn; ✆6888 1234; www.parkhyattshanghai.com; Shànghǎi World Financial Center, 100 Century Ave; 世纪大道100号世界金融中心; d from ¥2500; ✳@🛜🏊; MLujiazui) Spanning the 79th to 93rd floors of the towering Shànghǎi World Financial Center, this soaring hotel sees Pǔdōng's huge buildings (bar the Shànghǎi Tower) dwarfing into Lego blocks as lobby views graze the tip of the Jinmao Tower. Smaller than the Grand Hyatt, it's a subdued but stylish 174-room affair with a deco slant, high-walled corridors of brown-fabric and grey-stone textures.

Rooms are luxurious, with nifty features (mist-free bathroom mirror containing a small TV screen, automatically opening toilet seats). All come with huge TVs, free wifi, free fresh coffee, deep bathtubs, leather chaise lounges, sumptuous beds and outrageously good views. Accessed from the south side of the tower.

JUMEIRAH HIMALAYAS HOTEL
LUXURY HOTEL $$$

Map p313 (卓美亚喜玛拉雅酒店; Zhuóměiyà Xǐmǎlāyǎ Jiǔdiàn; ✆3858 0888; www.jumeirah. com; 1108 Meihua Rd; 梅花路1108号; d from ¥2188; ✳@🛜🏊; MHuamu Rd) With its huge lobby hung with traditional Chinese paintings and a vast overhead screen swarming with hypnotic, colourful patterns above a Chinese pavilion, this hotel is jaw-dropping. Just perusing the lobby landscape art alone is a diversion in culture-lite Pǔdōng, while feng shui-arranged rooms are both gorgeous and spacious, designed with a strong accent on traditional Chinese aesthetics, given a modern twist.

Rooms come with lovely bathrooms, hardwood floors, beds arranged with traditional Chinese pillows, and coffee machines are to hand. Service is prompt and assuring; the swimming pool has underwater music; and an array of fine restaurants rounds out an already superlative picture. Discounts are good, but book ahead.

PUDONG SHANGRI-LA
LUXURY HOTEL $$$

Map p312 (浦东香格里拉大酒店; Pǔdōng Xiānggélǐlā Dàjiǔdiàn; ✆68828888; www.shangri-la.com; 33 Fucheng Rd; 富城路33号; r from ¥2980; ✳@🛜🏊; MLujiazui) The Shangri-La's two towers – one dated, the other more dramatically modern – house an undisputed elegance. The lobby, corridors, restaurants and rooms are tastefully decorated in natural colours. The beds are sumptuous with pillows galore, and marble bathrooms are exquisite. Rooms in the new tower have floor-to-ceiling windows for full-on views.

Rooms are around ¥300 to ¥400 cheaper in the old tower while accommodation across the board is subject to discounts.

GRAND HYATT
LUXURY HOTEL $$$

Map p312 (金茂君悦大酒店; Jīnmào Jūnyuè Dàjiǔdiàn; ✆50491234; www.shanghai.grand.hyatt. com; Jinmao Tower, 88 Century Ave; 世纪大道88号金茂大厦; d from ¥2000-2450; ✳@🛜🏊; MLujiazu) This classy 555-room hotel, spanning the top 34 floors of the majestic Jinmao Tower, remains one of Shànghǎi's finest. Its once unimpeachable standard for quality high-rise hotel living in Shànghǎi attracted inevitable competition, but an ongoing floor-by-floor refurbishment has pepped up rooms. Tang-dynasty poems are inscribed in gold above lovely beds, while espresso machines, smart tan-leather work desks and inviting bathrooms add to the luxury.

Corner rooms are coveted, and the neck-craning 33-storey atrium is always astonishing. Service remains highly attentive; restaurants (such as On 56) are outstanding; and the views stratospheric.

🛏 Hóngkǒu & North Shànghǎi 虹口区·北上海

NAZA INTERNATIONAL YOUTH HOSTEL
HOSTEL $

Map p314 (那宅青年旅舍; Nàzhái Qīngnián Lǚshè; ✆6541 7062; 318 Baoding Rd; 保定路318号; dm ¥75, s/d/tw/f ¥189/229/249/329; ✳@🛜; MDalian Rd) This Hóngkǒu youth hostel has a pleasant light-filled courtyard, and fine communal spaces including a restful bar area with free pool table and a cute cafe. Rooms are a bit scuffed and have basic furniture, but all (apart from some dorms) have TV and en suite bathroom. More expensive rooms come with reproduction antique furniture, including one with a four-poster bed.

Internet is free and the ground floor has wi-fi. Long-let rooms are also available.

⭐ **ASTOR HOUSE HOTEL** HISTORIC HOTEL **$$$**
Map p314 (浦江饭店; Pǔjiāng Fàndiàn; ☎6324 6388; www.astorhousehotel.com; 15 Huangpu Rd; 黄浦路15号; d/tw ¥1280-1680, 'celebrity' r ¥2080, ste ¥2800-4800; ❋@☎; Ⓜ Tiantong Rd) Stuffed with history (and perhaps a ghost or two), this august old-timer shakes up an impressive cocktail from select ingredients: a location just off the Bund; old-world, Shànghǎi-era charm; great discounts; and colossal rooms. The original polished wooden floorboards, corridors and galleries pitch the mood somewhere between British public school and Victorian asylum.

There's enough wood panelling to build an ark; you could shunt a bed into the capacious bathrooms; and some of the rooms on the higher floors have river views. Pop up the stairs and hang a left to a small museum along the corridor to explore the history of the hotel. Discounts of 40% are common.

CHAI LIVING RESIDENCES APARTMENT **$$$**
Map p314 (☎5608 6051; www.chailiving.com; Embankment Bldg, 400 N Suzhou Rd; 苏州北路400号; 3 days/1 week/1 month apt from ¥3300/6000/13,500; ❋☎; Ⓜ Tiantong Rd) If you need a stylish Shànghǎi address, you can't get much better than one of these 16 luxurious, beautifully appointed and individually styled apartments in the Embankment Building. The block is a living, breathing residential Shànghǎi block, and bumping into tenants merely adds authentic charm (although the grotty lift is a real shocker for some).

There's a minimum three-day stay – just enough time to fully savour the outstanding views (none lower than the 5th floor) and decor of each apartment, each with sound-proof German windows. Apartments range from 40 to 200 sq metres, with daily maid service, underfloor heating, kitchens with Nespresso coffee machines and tantalising river views.

🛏 Xújiāhuì & South Shànghǎi 徐家汇·南上海

ASSET HOTEL HOTEL **$**
Map p316 (雅舍宾馆; Yǎshè Bīnguǎn; ☎6438 9900; www.asset-hotel.com; 590 South Wanping Rd; 宛平南路590号; r from ¥360; ❋@; Ⓜ Shanghai Stadium) Housed in a charming yellow-and-white building hidden from the main road by apartments, this higher-end budget option offers smart, clean rooms with free broadband, complimentary mineral water, a fridge, TV and kettle. Rates include breakfast, and discounts reach 45%.

Understand Shànghǎi

Shànghǎi Today

Rapidly becoming a world metropolis, Shànghǎi typifies modern China while being unlike anywhere else in the nation. Awash with cash, ambition and economic vitality, Shànghǎi is, for the movers and shakers of business (and indeed any job-seeking migrant), the place to be. For all its modernity and cosmopolitanism, however, Shànghǎi is part and parcel of the People's Republic of China, and its challenges are multiplying as fast as cocktails are mixed and served on the Bund.

Best on Film

Shanghai Triad (Zhang Yimou; 1995) Stylish take on Shànghǎi's 1930s gangster scene, starring Gong Li.
Empire of the Sun (Steven Spielberg; 1987) Dramatisation of JG Ballard's account of his internment in WWI Shànghǎi as a child.
Suzhou River (Ye Lou; 2000) A disturbing and obsessive narrative of love in modern Shànghǎi.

Best in Print

Five Star Billionaire (Tash Aw) Compelling tale of four Malaysians trying to make the Shànghǎi big-time.
China Cuckoo: How I Lost a Fortune & Found a Life in China (Mark Kitto) Undone by Shànghǎi, Kitto flees to the mountains in this fascinating and charming read.
Life & Death in Shanghai (Nien Cheng) Classic account of the Cultural Revolution, with a Shànghǎi angle.
Shanghai: The Rise & Fall of a Decadent City 1842–1949 (Stella Dong) Rip-roaring profile of the city's good-old, bad-old days.

Money

The Shanghainese may natter about traffic gridlock and chat about the latest celebrity faux pas or political scandal, but what they really talk about is cash. Labelled *xiǎozī* – 'little capitalists' – by the rest of the land, the Shànghǎi Chinese know how to make *qián* (money) and, equally importantly, how to flaunt it. Ever since Shànghǎi first prospered under foreign control, wealth creation has been indivisible from the Shànghǎi psyche. Whether it's the stock market, apartment price tags or the latest Dior evening bag, money's the talk of the town.

Property

Shànghǎi property prices are talked about at bus stops in the same way British people discuss weather. High prices have ramifications for everyone renting (or owning) floor space, from the lowliest McJobber to the wealthiest property tycoon. Amid dark mutterings of a property bubble, the government has repeatedly tried to tame the runaway market with tax and ownership measures to stifle speculation, with limited success, but property prices in relation to income remain higher than in London, New York or Tokyo.

Air Pollution

Shànghǎi's smog woes have long been eclipsed by Běijīng's more caustic readings. In 2013 and 2014, however, Shànghǎi hit back with some of its own record-breaking levels of atmospheric pollutants. In some areas of town, readings were 28 times World Health Organization safe limits. In response, a 2014 announcement declared that 160,000 cars that did not meet emission standards would be swept off Shànghǎi's roads. The city also pledged to eliminate 2500 polluting coal-fired boilers by 2015 in a further bid to clean the worsening air. Local media reports in 2014 even suggested that authorities would start dispensing free antipollution masks to city residents.

Ageing Shànghǎi

For such a seemingly sprightly city, Shànghǎi is ageing fast. In 2011, 23.4% of the city's population was over 60, but by 2030 this will have leaped to more than 30%, with an additional 200,000 people reaching the age of 60 every year. Implemented in 1979, the one-child policy has created a huge bulge of pensioners, around 80% of whom will be looked after by single children. The bulge is set to continue despite new measures, introduced in 2014, permitting Shànghǎi couples to have a second baby if either parent is an only child.

Growth & Urban Density

Over the past two decades, Shànghǎi has grown faster than any other world city, now housing more than 24 million people, and with four times the number of people per sq km than in New York.

Shànghǎi Versus China

Shànghǎi has a fraught relationship with the rest of China. The city has lured a vast army of labourers who work on the lowest-paid rung of the employment ladder. Although their city has always been a haven for outsiders, the Shànghǎi Chinese tend to look down on other Chinese. A non-Shànghǎi accent automatically flags *wàidìrén* (外地人), who may be considered *tǔ* (literally 'earth', meaning rural). Shànghǎi people conversely see themselves as *yáng* (literally 'sea', but meaning 'Western'). This chauvinism is almost an ideology in itself and, despite the glut of immigrant workers, *wàidì* Chinese have to jump through hoops to become a full 'local'. One such route is to marry a Shànghǎi person, and to stay married for at least 10 years.

Political Uncertainties

The city has been a success story of astonishing proportions, but Shànghǎi is part and parcel of a nation facing considerable challenges. The speed of economic growth has slowed, while relations with the East Asia region remain choppy: friction with Japan, Vietnam and the Philippines over contested islands in the East China Sea and South China Sea has steadily grown. In Shànghǎi, as anywhere else in China, the glowing coals of Chinese nationalism are easily stoked. Never far from the surface, anti-Japanese sentiment in Shànghǎi and across China remains a potent and unpredictable force, occasionally flaring into acrimonious demonstrations such as the 2012 protests in Shànghǎi (and across China) over the Diàoyú (Senkaku) Islands. This uncertainty contributed to a 17% decline in the number of Japanese people living and working in Shànghǎi in 2014.

if Shànghǎi were 100 people

98 would be Han Chinese
1 would be non-Han Chinese
1 would be Foreigners

age of residents
(% of population by age)

81   10   9

15-64   65+   0-14

population per sq km

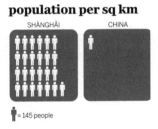

SHÀNGHǍI   CHINA

≈ 145 people

History

In just a few centuries, Shànghǎi went from being an insignificant walled town south of the mouth of the Yangzi River to becoming China's leading and wealthiest metropolis. A dizzying swirl of opium, trade, foreign control, vice, glamour, glitz, rebellion, restoration and money, Shànghǎi's story is a rags-to-riches saga of decadence, exploitation and, ultimately, achievement.

The online resource Virtual Shanghai (www.virtualshanghai.net) is an intriguing treasure trove of old photos, maps, documents, films and specialist information relating to historic Shànghǎi, and includes a blog.

Shànghǎi's Marshy Roots

Up until around the 7th century AD, Shànghǎi was little more than marshland. At that time, the area was known as Shēn (申), after Chunshen Jun, 春申君, a local nobleman from the 3rd century BC; or Hù (沪), after a type of bamboo fishing trap used by fishers. The character *hù* (沪) still identifies the city today – on car number plates, for example – while the city's main football team is known as Shanghai Shenhua (上海申花).

The earliest mention of the name Shànghǎi appears in the 11th century AD and refers to the small settlement that sprang up at the confluence of the Shànghǎi River (long since vanished) and the Huángpǔ River (黄浦江; Huángpǔ Jiāng). Upgraded from village status to market town in 1074, Shànghǎi became a city in 1297 after establishing itself as the major port in the area.

By the late 17th century Shànghǎi supported a population of 50,000, sustained on cotton production, fishing and, thanks to its excellent location at the head of the Yangzi River (长江; Cháng Jiāng), trade in silk and tea.

It All Started with Opium

During the early years of the Qing dynasty (1644–1911), the British East India Company and its later incarnations were trading in the only port open to the West: Canton (now Guǎngzhōu; 广州), south of Shànghǎi. British purchases of tea, silk and porcelain outweighed Chinese purchases of wool and spices, so by the late 18th century the British had decided to balance the books by slipping into India to swap (at a profit)

TIMELINE	453–221 BC	AD 242	960–1126
	Warring States period: the earliest imperial records date from this time, although Neolithic discoveries in Qīngpǔ County suggest human settlement of the region 5900 years ago.	The original Lónghuá Temple is built during the Three Kingdoms Period.	Chinese fleeing the Mongols during the Song dynasty boost the region's population, spurring Shànghǎi on to become the county seat of Jiāngsū in 1291.

silver for opium with which to purchase Chinese goods. The British passion for tea was increasingly matched by China's craving for opium (鸦片; *yāpiàn*), the drug that would virtually single-handedly create latter-day Shànghǎi and earn the city its bipolar reputation as the splendid 'Paris of the East' and the infamous 'Whore of the Orient'.

From a mercantile point of view, the trade in opium – known as 'foreign mud' in China – was an astonishing success, rapidly worming its way into every nook and cranny of Chinese society. Highly addictive and widely available thanks to the prolific efforts of British traders, the drug – smoked via a pipe – quickly became the drug of choice for all sections of the Chinese public, from the lowliest upwards. Jardine & Matheson's highly lucrative trade empire was founded on the opium business.

Opium became the driving force behind Shànghǎi's unstoppable rise and its descent into debauchery; it brought wealth to Shànghǎi's affluent taipans (powerful foreign businesspeople) and lucrative *hongs* (business houses) and fed the city's piercing inequalities. The city became a wanton netherworld of prostitution and vice, violent criminal gangs and corrupt police forces beneath a cartographic constitution of foreign concessions, settlements and Chinese districts.

The Opium War between Great Britain and China was similarly fought in the drug's name and as a pretext to extract the concessions that British opium traders sought from China. The Treaty of Nanking that concluded the First Opium War in 1842 was Shànghǎi's moment of reckoning: its signing spelled the death of old Shànghǎi and the birth of the wild, lawless and spectacularly prosperous endeavour that would rise up over the Huángpǔ River.

The Illegitimate Birth of Shànghǎi

The Treaty of Nanking in 1842 stipulated, among other things: peace between China and Britain; security and protection of British persons and property; the opening of Canton, Fúzhōu, Xiàmén, Níngbō and Shànghǎi, as well as residence for foreigners and consulates in those cities (for the purpose of trade); fair import and export tariffs; the possession of Hong Kong; and an indemnity of US$18 million. Ironically enough, the trade of opium, legal or otherwise, never entered into the treaty.

Following Great Britain's lead, other countries were inspired to join in, including the US and France. In 1843 the first British consul moved into a local house in the Old Town, signalling a foreign presence in the city that would last for the next 100 years.

Of the five port cities in China, Shànghǎi was the most prosperous due to its superb geographical location, capital edge and marginal

By the 1880s, around 10% of the Chinese population smoked opium. No other commodity became so uniquely associated with all of Shànghǎi's spectacular peaks and dismal troughs.

HISTORY THE ILLEGITIMATE BIRTH OF SHÀNGHǍI

1553	1685	1793	1823
The city wall around Shànghǎi's Old Town is constructed to fend off Japanese pirates; 9m high and 5km around, the wall stands until the fall of the Qing dynasty; it's demolished in 1912.	A customs house is opened in Shànghǎi for the first time.	Lord Macartney, George III's envoy to China, is rebuffed by the Qianlong emperor in Chéngdé, sinking British hopes of expanding legitimate trade relations with the 'Middle Kingdom'.	The British import roughly 7000 chests of opium annually, compared with 1000 chests in 1773. With about 63kg of opium per chest, it's enough to keep one million addicts happy.

interference from the Chinese government. Trade and businesses boomed, and by 1850 the foreign settlements housed more than 100 merchants, missionaries and physicians, three-quarters of them British. In 1844, 44 foreign ships made regular trade with China. By 1849, 133 ships lined the shores and by 1855, 437 foreign ships clogged the ports.

Foreigners were divided into three concessions. The original British Concession was north of Bubbling Well Rd (now West Nanjing Rd). The American Concession began life in Hóngkŏu District after Bishop William Boone had set up a mission there. These two concessions later joined to form one large area known as the International Settlement. The French, meanwhile, set up their own settlement south of the British one and to the west of the Old Town, in an area which is still referred to by English speakers as the French Concession.

From regulation to sanitation, everything in Shànghăi was vested in the foreign oligarchies of the Municipal Council and the Conseil d'Administration Municipale, a pattern that was to last as long as the settlements. It was not until the early 1920s that Chinese and Japanese residents (eventually the two largest groups in the settlements) were allowed even limited representation on the council.

From the start, Shànghăi's *raison d'être* was trade. Silks, tea and porcelain were still sailing to the West, and 30,000 chests of opium were being delivered into China annually. Soon great Hong Kong trading houses such as Butterfield & Swire and Jardine & Matheson set up shop, and trade in opium, silk and tea gradually shifted to textiles, real estate, banking, insurance and shipping. Banks in particular boomed; soon all of China's loans, debts and indemnity payments were funnelled through Shànghăi. Buying and selling was handled by Chinese middlemen, known as *compradors* (from the Portuguese), from Canton and Níngbō, who formed a rare link between the Chinese and foreign worlds. The city attracted immigrants and entrepreneurs from across China, and overseas capital and expertise pooled in the burgeoning metropolis.

Foreign ideas were similarly imported. By the 1880s, huge numbers of proselytising American Protestants were saving souls in Shànghăi, while the erudite Jesuits oversaw a flourishing settlement in Xújiāhuì (徐家汇), known locally as Siccawei (or Zikawei).

Gradually sedan chairs and single-wheeled carts gave way to rickshaws and carriages, the former imported from Japan in 1874. Shànghăi lurched into the modern age with gaslights (1865), electricity (1882), motorcars (1895), a cinema and an electric tram (1908), and its first bus (1922).

The Manchu in Běijīng gave only cursory glances to the growth of Shànghăi as all eyes focused on the continued survival of the Qing dynasty, under threat from a barrage of insurgencies that arose from within the rapidly radicalising confines of the Middle Kingdom.

By 1934 Shànghăi was the world's fifth-largest city, home to the tallest buildings in Asia, boasting more cars in one city than the rest of China combined, and providing a haven for more than 70,000 foreigners among a population of three million. Its cosmopolitanism and modernity were encapsulated in the architectural style of art deco.

1839	1842	1843	1846
Tensions between England and China come to a head when British merchants are arrested and forced to watch three million pounds of raw opium being flushed out to sea.	On 29 August Sir Henry Pottinger signs the Treaty of Nanking aboard the *Cornwallis* on the Yangzi River, prising open China's doors and securing Hong Kong.	A supplement to the Treaty of Nanking, the Treaty of the Bogue regulated trade between Britain and China and the terms under which British people could reside in Shànghăi.	Richard's Hotel, the first Western hotel in Shànghăi, opens its doors on the Bund.

Rebellious Youth

Wreathed in opium, sucked dry by local militia, crippled by taxes, bullied by foreign interests and increasingly exposed to Western ideas, Shànghǎi's population was stirring, and anti-Manchu rebellions began to erupt. The first major rebellion to have an impact on Shànghǎi was the Taiping (太平 – literally, 'Supreme Peace'), led by the Hakka visionary Hong Xiuquan. The uprising, which led to 20 million deaths, went down as the bloodiest in human history.

Hong claimed to have ascended to heaven and received a new set of internal organs by a golden-bearded Jehovah, which he used to battle the evil spirits of the world with his elder brother Jesus Christ. Hong's distorted Christian ideology dates from his contact with Christian missionaries in Canton and an identification of his surname (洪; Hóng, meaning 'flood') with the Old Testament deluge. Believing himself chosen, Hong saw the Manchu as devils to be exterminated and set about recruiting converts to establish a Heavenly Kingdom in China. The rebels burst out of Jīntián village in Guǎngxī (广西) in 1851, swept through Guìzhōu (贵州) and succeeded in taking Nánjīng (南京) three years later, where they established their Heavenly Capital (天京; Tiānjīng).

With the Taiping-inspired Small Swords Society entrenched in the Old Town and fearing the seizure of Shànghǎi, the foreign residents organised the Shanghai Volunteer Corps, a force that would repeatedly protect the interests of foreigners in Shànghǎi.

The Taiping threatened again in 1860 but were beaten back by the mercenary armies of Frederick Townsend Ward, an American adventurer hired by the Qing government who was eventually killed in Sōngjiāng in 1862. British and Qing forces joined to defeat the rebels, the Europeans preferring to deal with a corrupt and weak Qing government than with a powerful, united China governed by the Taiping. The

The crossing over Sūzhōu Creek was once undertaken by ferry from three crossing points, until the first proper bridge (Wills' Bridge) was built from wood in 1856, lashing the prosperous British and American settlements together.

HISTORICAL READS

→ *In Search of Old Shanghai* (Pan Ling, 1986)
→ *Shanghai 1937: Stalingrad on the Yangtze* (Peter Harmsen, 2014)
→ *Secret War in Shanghai* (Bernard Wasserstein, 2000)
→ *Old Shanghai: Gangsters in Paradise* (Lynn Pan, 2011)
→ *Shanghai* (Harriet Sergeant, 2002)
→ *Shanghai: The Rise and Fall of a Decadent City 1842–1949* (Stella Dong, 2001)
→ *Through the Looking Glass: China's Foreign Journalists from Opium Wars to Mao* (Paul French, 2009)

1847	1849	1850	1859
Shànghǎi's first library, the Bibliotheca Zi-Ka-Wei in Xújiāhuì, opens.	The French establish their own settlement, known as the French Concession, to the south of the British Concession and beyond the walls of the Chinese Old Town.	The influential English-language weekly newspaper the *North China Herald* is published for the first time (later published in a daily edition as the *North China Daily News*).	By now half of all British troops stationed in Shànghǎi suffer from venereal disease, introduced to Shànghǎi by Westerners and spread by the city's prostitution industry.

Taiping originally banked on the support of the Western powers, but Westerners were ultimately repelled by Hong's heretical concoction.

As rebellions ravaged the countryside, hundreds of thousands of refugees poured into the safety of Shànghǎi's concessions, setting up home alongside the foreigners and sparking a real-estate boom that spurred on Shànghǎi's rapid urbanisation and made the fortunes of many of Shànghǎi's entrepreneurs.

As imperial control loosened, the encroaching Western powers moved in to pick off China's colonial 'possessions' in Indochina and Korea. National humiliation and a growing xenophobia – partly generated by a distrust of Christian missionaries and their activities – spawned the anti-Western Boxer Rebellion, championed in its later stages by the empress dowager, Cixi.

The Boxers were quelled by Western and Japanese troops – who went on to sack Běijīng's Summer Palace – in 1900, but not before the legation quarter in the capital had been devastated. Empress Cixi and her entourage fled to Xī'ān (西安), but returned to Běijīng to face massive indemnities strapped onto the Qing government by the foreign powers.

The weakened state of the country, the death of the empress dowager and the legion of conspiring secret societies marked the end of the tottering Qing dynasty. Shànghǎi renounced the Qing by declaring independence on the wave of public revolt that swept China in 1911, and all men were instructed to shear off their *queues* (long pigtails that symbolised subjection to Manchu authority). But despite the momentous end to China's final dynasty – one that had ruled China for almost 250 years – insular Shànghǎi carried out business as usual, relatively unaffected by the fall of the Qing or the upheavals of WWI. As the rest of China descended into a bedlam of fighting warlords and was plunged into darkness, Shànghǎi emerged as a modern industrial city.

The first railroad in China was the Woosung Railway which opened in 1876, running between Shànghǎi and Wúsōng (吴淞); it operated for less than a year before being dismantled and shipped to Taiwan.

'Paris of the East' Reaches Its Peak

By the first decade of the 20th century, Shànghǎi's population had swelled to one million. As the most elite and cosmopolitan of China's cities, Shànghǎi ensnared capitalists and intellectuals alike, with literature and cinema thriving in the ferment as Chinese intellectuals began to ponder the fate of a modern China.

The foreigners had effectively plucked out prime locations and, using their ever-increasing wealth – the fruits of cheap labour – they established exclusive communities designed after their own countries and dovetailing with their requirements. Vice and crime continued to flourish, assisted by the absence of a paramount police force. The multiple jurisdictions, each representing the laws of the various settlements and

1860s	1863	1882	1882
Cotton emerges as Shànghǎi's chief export.	Shànghǎi's first fire engine arrives and enters service, followed by the launch of the Shànghǎi Volunteer Fire Service three years later.	Shànghǎi's first large beauty pageant for prostitutes is held. The pageant is held every year until 1930.	Shànghǎi (and China) is electrified for the very first time by the British-founded Shànghǎi Electric Company. The Bund is illuminated by electric lights the following year.

SHANGHAIED

If New York was so good they named it twice, then Shànghǎi was so bad they made it an undesirable verb. To shanghai, or 'render insensible by drugs or opium, and ship on a vessel wanting hands', dates from the habit of press-ganging sailors. Men, many of whom were found drunk in 'Blood Alley' (today's Xikou Rd, off modern-day Jinling Rd), were forced onto ships, which then set sail, leaving the comatose sailors no choice but to make up the deficient crew numbers when they sobered up.

the Chinese city, meant that criminals could simply move from one area to another to elude arrest.

Exploited in workhouse conditions, crippled by hunger and poverty, sold into slavery and excluded from the city's high life created by the foreigners, the poor of Shànghǎi developed an appetite for resistance. Intellectuals and students, provoked by the startling inequalities between rich and poor, were perfect receptacles for the many outside influences circulating in the concessions. The *Communist Manifesto* was translated into Chinese and swiftly caught on among secret societies.

In light of the intense dislike that many Chinese felt for foreigners, it may seem ironic that fundamental ideals stemmed from overseas inspirations. Shànghǎi, with its vast proletariat (30,000 textile workers alone) and student population, had become the communists' hope for revolution, and the first meeting of the Chinese Communist Party, where Mao Zedong was present, was held in July 1921 in a French Concession house. Elsewhere, political violence was growing.

In May 1925 resentment spilled over when a Chinese worker was killed in a clash with a Japanese mill manager. In the ensuing demonstrations the British opened fire and 12 Chinese were killed. In protest, 150,000 workers went on strike, which was later seen as a defining moment marking the decline of Western prestige and power.

Strikes and a curfew paralysed the city as the Kuomintang under Chiang Kaishek (with the help of communist supporters under Zhou Enlai) wrested Shànghǎi from the Chinese warlord Sun Chaofang.

Kaishek's aim was not focused on the settlements or even the warlords, but rather his erstwhile allies the communists, whom he then betrayed in an act of breathtaking perfidy. Backed by Shànghǎi bankers and armed by Shànghǎi's top gangster Du Yuesheng, Chiang Kaishek armed gangsters, suited them up in Kuomintang uniforms and launched a surprise attack on the striking workers' militia. Du's machine guns were turned on 100,000 workers taking to the streets, killing as many as 5000. In the ensuing period, known as the White Terror, 12,000 communists were executed in three weeks. Zhou Enlai

1891	1895	1908	1910
The Shànghǎi Sharebrokers Association is established, functioning as Shànghǎi's (and China's) first stock exchange.	The Treaty of Shimonoseki (also called the Treaty of Maguan) concludes the First Sino-Japanese War, forcing China to cede territories (including Taiwan) to Japan.	The Shànghǎi–Nánjīng railway is completed. Covering 193 miles of track, the journey takes around 5½ hours.	Shànghǎi is hit by mob disturbances (called the Plague Riots) in response to anti-plague measures.

and other communists fled to Wŭhàn (武汉), leaving Shànghăi in the hands of the warlords, the wealthy and the Kuomintang.

Nestled away safely in a world of selectively structured law and merciless capitalism, by the 1930s Shànghăi had reached its economic zenith and was soon to begin its fatal downwards slide. Shànghăi had become a modern city replete with art deco cinemas and apartment blocks, the hottest bands and the latest fashions – a place of great energy where two cultures met. Chinese magazines carried ads for Quaker Oats, Colgate and Kodak, while Chinese girls, dressed in traditional *qípáo* (cheongsam; Chinese-style dresses), advertised American cigarettes. Shànghăi's modernity was symbolised by the Bund, Shànghăi's Wall Street, a place of feverish trading and an unabashed playground for Western business sophisticates. To this day the bombastic strip alongside the Huángpŭ River remains the city's most eloquent reminder that modern Shànghăi is a very foreign invention.

The 'Paris of the East' and 'Whore of the Orient' became an increasingly exotic port of call. Flush with foreign cash and requiring neither visa nor passport for entrance, Shànghăi became home to the movers and the shakers, the down-and-out and on-the-run. It offered a place of refuge and a fresh start, and rejected no one. Everyone who came to Shànghăi, it was said, had something to hide. The city had become three times as crowded as London, and the cosmopolitan mix of people was unequalled anywhere in the world.

The Death of Old Shànghăi

Following Japan's invasion of Manchuria in 1931, with anti-Japanese sentiment inflamed and Chinese nationalistic fervour on the rise, the Japanese seized the opportunity to protect their interests. Warships brought in tens of thousands of Japanese troops, who proceeded to take on and defeat the Chinese 19th Route army in Zhábĕi (闸北). The Japanese conducted an aerial bombing campaign against the district, levelling most of its buildings.

After Japan's full-scale invasion of China in 1937, Chiang Kaishek took a rare stand in Shànghăi – and the city bled for it. The Japanese lost 40,000 men, the Chinese anywhere from 100,000 to 250,000.

The International Settlements weren't immune to the fighting, and after Chinese aircraft accidentally bombed the Bund and Nanjing Rd, most foreign residents reacted not by fighting, as they might have done for a colony, but by evacuation. Four million Chinese refugees weren't so lucky.

After intense house-to-house fighting, the Japanese invaders finally subdued Shànghăi in November 1937, allowing their soldiers to proceed to Sūzhōu before advancing on Nánjīng for their infamous occupation of the

In the 1920s and '30s, 25,000 White Russians fled their home country for Shànghăi. By 1935 they formed the city's second-largest foreign community after the Japanese. Ave Joffre (Huaihai Rd) became the heart of the White Russian community, and was lined with Cyrillic signs and cafes serving Shànghăi borscht, blini and black bread. There were Russian cinemas, printing presses and even rival revolutionary and tsarist newspapers.

1912	1920	1921	1927
Republicans pull down Shànghăi's ancient city walls to break links with the ousted Qing dynasty. The Provisional Republican Government of China is established in Nánjīng.	Built to serve the city's first influx of Jewish immigrants, Shànghăi's first synagogue, the Ohel Rachel Synagogue, opens.	The first meeting of the Chinese Communist Party, formed by Marxist groups advised by the Soviet Comintern, takes place in Shànghăi.	Chiang Kaishek takes control of Shànghăi, followed by his 'White Terror', a slaughter of communists, left-wing sympathisers and labour leaders, also known as the 'Shànghăi Massacre'.

SHÀNGHǍI'S GANGSTERS

In Shànghǎi's climate of hedonist freedoms, political ambiguities and capitalist free-for-all, it was perhaps inevitable that the city should spawn China's most powerful mobsters. Ironically, in 1930s Shànghǎi the most binding laws were those of the underworld, with their blood oaths, secret signals and strict code of honour. China's modern-day triads and snakeheads owe much of their form to their Shanghainese predecessors.

One of Shànghǎi's early gangsters was Huang Jinrong, or 'Pockmarked' Huang, who had the enviable position of being the most powerful gangster in Shànghǎi while at the same time holding the highest rank in the French Concession police force. Now sadly closed, Great World (大世界; Dà Shìjiè) opened in 1917 as a place for acrobats and nightclub stars to rival the existing New World building on Nanjing Rd. It soon became a centre for the bizarre and the burlesque under the seedy control of Huang Jinrong in the 1930s before being commandeered as a refugee centre during WWII.

Another famous underworld figure was Cassia Ma, the Night-Soil Queen, who founded a huge empire on the collection of human waste, which was ferried upriver to be sold as fertiliser at a large profit.

The real godfather of the Shànghǎi underworld, however, was Du Yuesheng, or 'Big-Eared' Du as he was known to anyone brave enough to say it to his face. Born in Pǔdōng, Du soon moved across the river and was recruited into the Green Gang (青帮; Qīngbāng), where he worked for Huang. He gained fame by setting up an early opium cartel with the rival Red Gang, and rose through the ranks. By 1927 Du was the head of the Green Gang and in control of the city's prostitution, drug running, protection and labour rackets. Du's special genius was to kidnap the rich and then to negotiate their release, taking half of the ransom money as commission. With an estimated 20,000 men at his beck and call, Du travelled everywhere in a bullet-proof sedan, like a Chinese Al Capone, protected by armed bodyguards crouched on the running boards.

His control of the labour rackets led to contacts with warlords and politicians. In 1927 Du played a major part in Chiang Kaishek's anticommunist massacre and later became adviser to the Kuomintang. A fervent nationalist, his money supplied the anti-Japanese resistance movement.

Yet Du always seemed to crave respectability. In 1931 he was elected to the Municipal Council and was known for years as the unofficial mayor of Shànghǎi. He became a Christian halfway through his life and ended up best known as a philanthropist. When the British poet WH Auden visited Shànghǎi in 1937, Du was head of the Chinese Red Cross.

During the Japanese occupation of Shànghǎi, Du fled to Chóngqìng (Chungking). After the war he settled in Hong Kong, where he died a multimillionaire in 1951. These days you can stay in Du's former Shànghǎi pad, now the Donghu Hotel, or in the building once used as offices by him and Huang, now the exquisite Mansion Hotel. Alternatively, seek out Du's one-time summer retreat in the mountain retreat of Mògānshān in Zhèjiāng province.

HISTORY THE DEATH OF OLD SHÀNGHǍI

1927	1928	1929	1930s
Shànghǎi is designated a municipality for the first time.	Chinese people are finally allowed to visit parks administered by the Shànghǎi Municipal Council.	A masterpiece of art deco design, the iconic Peace Hotel – called Sassoon House when built – is completed on the Bund.	Blood Alley – a sordid domain of whorehouses, seedy bars and all-night vice in the Bund area – is the destination of choice for drunken sailors on shore leave.

Between 1931 and 1941, 20,000 Jews took refuge in Shànghǎi, only to be forced into Japanese war ghettos, and to flee again in 1949. Adding to the mix was a huge influx of Russians seeking sanctuary from the Bolshevik Revolution of 1917. In 1895 the Japanese had gained treaty rights and by 1915 had become Shànghǎi's largest non-Chinese group, turning Hóngkǒu into a de facto Japanese Concession.

city. Under Japanese rule the easy glamour of Shànghǎi's heyday was replaced by a dark cloud of political assassinations, abductions, gunrunning and fear. Espionage by the Japanese, the nationalists, the British and the Americans for wartime information was rife. The rich were abducted and fleeced. Japanese racketeers set up opium halls in the so-called Badlands in the western outskirts of the city, and violent gangs ran rabid.

By December 1941 the hostilities between Japan and the allied powers had intensified abroad, giving the Japanese incentive to take over the foreign settlements in Shànghǎi. Suspect foreigners were taken off for interrogation and torture in notorious prisons such as the Bridgehouse, where JB Powell, editor of the *China Weekly Review,* lost all his toes to gangrene. Prisoners were forced to sit for hours in the cold, with heads lowered, facing Tokyo.

The British and American troops had abandoned Shànghǎi in 1942 to concentrate their energies elsewhere, and the British and American governments, unable to overtake the Japanese, signed over their rights of the foreign settlements to Chiang Kaishek in Chóngqìng in 1943, bringing to a close a century of foreign influence.

After the Japanese surrender in 1945, a few foreigners, released from their internment, tried to sweep out their Tudor-style homes and carry on as before, but priorities and politics had shifted. The gangs, conmen, dignitaries, merchants and anyone else who could had already made their escape to Hong Kong. Those who remained had to cope with biting inflation of 1100%.

By 1948 the Kuomintang was on the edge of defeat in their civil war with the communists, and hundreds of thousands of Kuomintang troops changed sides to join Mao Zedong's forces. In May, Chen Yi led the Red Army troops into Shànghǎi, and by October all the major cities in southern China had fallen to the communists.

In Běijīng on 1 October 1949, Mao Zedong stood atop the Gate of Heavenly Peace, announced that the Chinese people had stood up, and proclaimed the foundation of the People's Republic of China (PRC). Chiang Kaishek then fled to the island of Formosa (Taiwan), taking with him China's gold reserves and the remains of his air force and navy, to set up the Republic of China (ROC), naming his new capital Taipei (台北, Táiběi).

The People's Republic

The birth of the PRC marked the end of 105 years of 'the paradise for adventurers'. The PRC dried up 200,000 opium addicts; shut down Shànghǎi's infamous brothels and 're-educated' 30,000 prostitutes; eradicated the slums; slowed inflation; and eliminated child labour – no easy task. The state took over Shànghǎi's faltering businesses; the

1930s	1931	1932	1935
Cosmopolitan Shànghǎi is the world's fifth-largest city (the largest in Asia), supporting a population of four million. Opium use declines as it goes out of fashion.	In September the Japanese invade Manchuria and by December extend control over the entire area. Shànghǎi's Chinese react with a boycott of Japanese goods.	Japanese naval aircraft bomb Shànghǎi on 28 January.	By now 25,000 White Russians have flocked to Shànghǎi, turning the French Concession into Little Moscow.

racecourse became the obligatory People's Park; and Shànghǎi fell uniformly into step with the rest of China. Under Běijīng's stern hand, the decadence disappeared and the splendour similarly faded.

Yet the communists, essentially a peasant regime, remained suspicious of Shànghǎi. The group lacked the experience necessary to run a big city and resented Shànghǎi's former leadership, which they always regarded as a den of foreign-imperialist-inspired iniquity, a constant reminder of national humiliation, and the former headquarters of the Kuomintang.

SHÀNGHǍI VICE

Underneath the glitz and glamour of 1930s Shànghǎi lay a pool of sweat, blood and crushing poverty. In the words of a British resident, Shànghǎi was 'violent, disreputable, snobbish, mercenary and corrupt'.

The city was often a place of horrific cruelty and brutal violence. After the Small Swords Rebellion, 66 heads, including those of elderly women and children, were stuck up on the city walls. In 1927 striking workers were beheaded and their heads displayed in cages. Up to 80,000 rickshaw pullers worked the littered streets until they dropped, while overcrowded factory workers routinely died of lead and mercury poisoning. In 1934 the life expectancy of the Chinese in Shànghǎi stood at 27 years. In 1937 municipal sanitation workers picked up 20,000 corpses off the streets.

Shànghǎi offered the purely synthetic pleasures of civilisation. Prostitution ran the gamut from the high-class escorts in the clubs of the International Settlement and 'flowers' of the Fuzhou Rd teahouses to the yějī, or 'wild chickens', of Hóngkǒu, who prowled the streets and back alleys. The 'saltwater sisters' from Guǎngdōng specialised in foreigners fresh off the boats. Lowest of the low were the 'nail sheds' of Zhapei, so called because their services were meant to be as fast as driving nails. Lists of the city's 100 top-ranking prostitutes were drawn up annually and listed next to the names of 668 brothels, which went by such names as the 'Alley of Concentrated Happiness'.

Prostitution was not the exclusive domain of the Chinese. The traditional roles were reversed when White Russians turned to prostitution and Chinese men could be seen flaunting Western women. An American madam ran Gracie's, the most famous foreign brothel in town, at 52 Jiangsu Rd, in a strip of brothels called 'The Line'.

Linked to prostitution was opium. At the turn of the century Shànghǎi boasted 1500 opium dens (known locally as 'swallows' nests') and 80 shops openly selling opium. Even some hotels, it is said, supplied heroin on room service. Opium financed the early British trading houses and most of the buildings on the Bund. Later it funded Chinese gangsters, warlord armies and Kuomintang military expeditions. It was true that the police in the French Concession kept a close eye on the drug trade, but only to ensure that they got a reasonable slice of the profits. Not that there was much they could do even if they had wanted to; it was said that a wanted man in 1930s Shànghǎi need only pop into the neighbouring concession to avoid a warrant for his arrest.

1936	1937	1938	1943
Lu Xun, one of China's finest modern novelists and writers, dies of tuberculosis in Shànghǎi.	In an event known as Bloody Saturday, bombs fall onto the foreign concessions for the first time on 14 August, killing more than 2000.	Twenty thousand Jews arrive in Shànghǎi, fleeing persecution in Europe.	The Japanese round up 7600 allied nationals into eight internment camps as the formal foreign presence in Shànghǎi ends.

Perhaps because of this, Shànghǎi, in its determination to prove communist loyalty, became a hotbed of political extremism and played a major role in the Cultural Revolution, the decade of political turmoil that lasted from 1966 to 1976 (although its most ferocious period ended in 1969). Sidelined in Běijīng, it was to Shànghǎi that Mao turned in an attempt to reinvigorate the revolution and claw his way back into power. For most of a decade the city was the power base of the prime movers of the Cultural Revolution, the Gang of Four: Wang Hongwen; Yao Wenyuan (editor of *Shanghai Liberation Army Daily*); Zhang Chunqiao (Shànghǎi's director of propaganda); and Jiang Qing, wife of Mao (and failed Shànghǎi movie actress, formerly known as Lan Ping, who used her position to exact revenge on former colleagues at Shànghǎi Film Studios).

When the clean-up of Sūzhōu Creek was finally completed in 2012, a total of more than a hundred wartime bombs had been dredged from the muck at the river bottom, many dating to the Japanese occupation.

Encouraged by Mao, a rally of one million Red Guards marched through People's Sq, a force of anarchy that resulted in the ousting of the mayor. Competing Red Guards tried to outdo each other in revolutionary fervour – Shanghainese who had any contacts with foreigners were criticised, forced to wear dunce caps, denounced and sometimes killed.

As the Cultural Revolution unfolded, between 1966 and 1970 one million of Shànghǎi's youths were sent to the countryside. Shànghǎi's industries closed; the Bund was renamed Revolution Blvd; and the road opposite the closed Soviet consulate became Anti-Revisionist St. At one point there was even a plan to change the (revolutionary) red of the city's traffic lights to mean 'go'.

In the revolutionary chaos and a bid to destroy the 'four olds' (old customs, old habits, old culture and old thinking), Chinese religion was devastated. Temples were destroyed or converted to factories; priests were conscripted to make umbrellas; monks were sent to labour in the countryside, where they often died; and believers were prohibited from worship. Amid all the chaos, Shànghǎi's concession architecture stood largely preserved, its wealthy occupants merely fading memories of a vanished era.

In 1976, after the death of Mao, the Gang of Four was overthrown and imprisoned. Accused of everything from forging Mao's statements to hindering earthquake relief efforts, the gang's members were arrested on 6 October 1976 and tried in 1980. Jiang Qing remained unrepentant, hurling abuse at her judges and holding famously to the line that she 'was Chairman Mao's dog – whoever he told me to bite, I bit'. Jiang Qing's death sentence was commuted and she lived under house arrest until 1991, when she committed suicide by hanging.

When the Cultural Revolution lost steam, pragmatists such as Zhou Enlai began to look for ways to restore normalcy. In 1972 US president Richard Nixon signed the Shanghai Communiqué at the Jinjiang Hotel. The agreement provided a foundation for increased trade between the US and China, and marked a turning point in China's foreign relations.

1945	1949	1966	1972
After the Japanese surrender, the Kuomintang takes back Shànghǎi, closing treaty ports, and revoking foreign trading and self-governing rights.	Hyperinflation means that one US dollar is worth 23,280,000 yuán. Communist forces take Shànghǎi and the establishment of the People's Republic of China (PRC) is proclaimed.	The Cultural Revolution is launched from Shànghǎi; eventually one million Shanghainese are sent to the countryside. St Ignatius Cathedral finds new employment as a grain store.	US President Nixon visits Shànghǎi as China rejoins the world.

With the doors of China finally reopened to the West in 1979, and with Deng Xiaoping at the helm, China set a course of pragmatic reforms towards economic reconstruction, which would result in consistently strong annual growth rates.

In communist China, however, the rush of economic reform generated very little in the way of political reform. Corruption and inflation led to widespread social unrest, which in 1989 resulted in the demonstrations in Běijīng's Tiān'ānmén Sq.

The demonstrations overtaking the capital spread to Shànghǎi. In the days leading up to 4 June 1989 tens of thousands of students – holding banners demanding, among other things, democracy and freedom – marched from their universities to People's Sq. Hundreds went on hunger strike. Workers joined students to bring chaos to the city by instigating road blocks across more than 100 Shànghǎi streets. But city mayor Zhu Rongji was praised for his handling of events. In contrast to leaders in Běijīng, he didn't take a heavy-handed approach. According to Lynn T White, author of *Unstately Power* (1999), the only serious incident during the unrest was on 6 June when a train outside Shànghǎi Railway Station ran into demonstrators who were trying to block it. Eight people were killed and 30 were injured.

In 1966 a People's Commune, modelled on the Paris Commune of the 19th century, was set up in Shànghǎi. Led by Zhang Chunqiao from headquarters in the Peace Hotel, it lasted just three weeks before Mao, sensing that the anarchy had gone too far, ordered the army to put an end to it.

The Nineties & Noughties

In 1990 the central government began pouring money into Shànghǎi, beginning the city's stunning turnaround. The process was unparalleled in scale and audacity. By the mid-1990s more than a quarter (some sources say half) of the world's high-rise cranes were slowly circling above town. A huge proportion of the world's concrete was funnelled into Shànghǎi as China sucked up a staggering 50% of world production.

Towering over Lùjiāzuǐ, the Oriental Pearl TV Tower was completed in 1994, establishing an architectural template for Pǔdōng that survives today. What followed was a roll-call of skyscraper heavyweights: the Jinmao Tower (1999), Tomorrow Square (2003), Shimao International Plaza (2005) and the Shànghǎi World Financial Center (2008). Shànghǎi's vertical transformation mirrored its growing stature as an international city.

Before the 1990s were spent, the city had already built two metro lines, a light-railway system, a US$2 billion international airport in Pǔdōng, a US$2 billion elevated highway, several convention centres, two giant bridges, several underground tunnels and a whole new city (Pǔdōng).

Always a byword for excess, Shànghǎi had effortlessly outstripped every other city in China by the dawn of the new millennium, bar southern rival Hong Kong. Obsessively comparing itself to Hong Kong, the Huángpǔ River city closed the gap on the ex-British territory with

1976	1989	1990	1995
Mao Zedong dies in September – the same year as the Tángshān earthquake – preparing the way for a rehabilitated Deng Xiaoping to assume leadership of the PRC.	Antigovernment demonstrations in Shànghǎi's People's Sq mirror similar protests in Běijīng's Tiān'ānmén Sq; the demonstrations are broken up.	Pǔdōng discovers it will become a Special Economic Zone (SEZ), converting it, over the next decade, from flat farmland into one of the world's most ultramodern urban landscapes.	Line 1 of the Shànghǎi metro commences operation, with line 2 opening five years later.

breathtaking rapidity during the noughties. The Chinese government deliberately sought to make Shànghǎi the financial centre of Asia, replacing Hong Kong as China's frontier of the future, swinging the spotlight of attention from the ex-colony on to a home-grown success story.

Served by two airports and the world's first Maglev train, Shànghǎi began to command some of the most dizzying salaries in China, with per capita incomes around four times the national average. The metro system was massively expanded, and is, to date, the world's second longest at 538km (running to 14 lines). Pǔdōng was built from the soles up, forging mainland China's most electrifying skyline. Skyscraper residential towers sprouted across the city while car ownership trebled in the five years from 2007. Swelling numbers of residents dwelled in gated villa communities, rewarding themselves with a desirable middle-class standard of living.

Feeding much of this growth was a vast, multimillion-strong army of cheap labour and migrant workers from rural areas. The Bund was redesigned and spruced up while other areas – the Old Town, for example – underwent irreversible overdevelopment.

Despite draconian property taxes designed to hit speculators and purchasers of second flats, Shànghǎi property prices went through the roof in the noughties. The authorities were determined to tame the market to avoid a long-term Japanese-style stagnation, but prices continued to soar, bringing untold wealth to homeowners and speculators alike.

A 2012 survey discovered that fewer than 40% of the city's elementary school children speak the Shànghǎi dialect (Shànghǎihuà) at home, and even then it may be mixed with Mandarin.

TOP SHÀNGHǍI HISTORICAL BIOGRAPHIES

➡ *Captive in Shanghai,* Hugh Collar (1991) – A fascinating personal account of life in the Japanese internment camps in the early 1940s. It's published by Oxford University Press, but is hard to get your hands on.

➡ *Daughter of Shanghai,* Tsai Chin (1989) – Daughter of one of China's most-famous Běijīng opera stars, Chin left Shànghǎi in 1949 and later starred in the film *The World of Suzie Wong* (as the original 'China doll') and in *The Joy Luck Club*. This memoir bridges two worlds during two different times.

➡ *Life and Death in Shanghai,* Nien Cheng (1987) – A classic account of the Cultural Revolution and one of the few biographies with a Shànghǎi angle.

➡ *The Life, Loves and Adventures of Emily Hahn,* Ken Cuthbertson (1998) – A look at the unconventional life of Emily Hahn, who passed through Shànghǎi in 1935 (with her pet gibbon), got hooked on opium and became the concubine of a Chinese poet.

➡ *Red Azalea,* Anchee Min (2006) – A sometimes racy account of growing up in Shànghǎi in the 1950s and 1960s amid the turmoil of the Cultural Revolution.

2004	2007	2009	2011
The world's first commercially operating Maglev train begins scorching across Pǔdōng. Plans for it to connect Běijīng and Shànghǎi are later put to rest.	World markets crash, slowing down – but not halting – Shànghǎi's previously stratospheric rates of economic growth.	Approval is finally given to plans to build a Disneyland in Shànghǎi, scheduled to open in 2015.	The Shànghǎi–Běijīng high-speed rail line enters service, shrinking journey times to 5½ hours.

The Recent Past

After the global financial crisis of 2007 to 2008, the Chinese government's huge fiscal packages, loosening of credit and increased investment in infrastructure protected China and Shànghǎi from economic vicissitudes abroad. The Shànghǎi Tower began construction in November 2008, its concrete form quickly beginning to rise above the sky-high buildings of Pǔdōng.

Some pundits, however, began to see Shànghǎi, and China, at a fork in the road. The formula that served China so well for so long – a cheap workforce, hefty stimulus packages, high investment, endless property price increases and round-the-clock construction – could not go on forever. The Chinese economy continued to grow at a healthy rate, but at a slower clip, growing at 7.8% in 2012, compared to 10.4% in 2010. The breakneck growth patterns of the noughties were clearly unsustainable and a reorientation of the economy became imperative.

The task of the Chinese leadership demanded a more pressing focus on balancing the economy away from its export and high-investment model, rooting out corruption and narrowing the chasm dividing low-wage earners from the wealthy elites. The issue of migrant workers' rights in Shànghǎi and other cities became paramount, as workers sought to bring their rights (education for their children and access to healthcare) closer to native Shanghainese. Meanwhile, atmospheric pollution in Shànghǎi began to occasionally mirror the caustic air of the nation's capital, Běijīng. In December 2013, schoolchildren citywide were ordered indoors and construction was halted as the air quality reached dangerous levels. The burning of coal, car exhaust fumes, factory pollution and weather patterns that confined the smog within the city were all blamed.

Through a bold anti-corruption agenda, the new leadership under Xi Jinping appeared determined to seize the nettle, while recognising that the Chinese Communist Party's legitimacy depended heavily on economic growth. Keeping the economy on track while directing it towards increased domestic consumption (and matching the growing expectations of a Chinese middle class pushing for a fairer society), further rooting out corruption, attempting to tame the rampant property market (as apartment prices put home ownership beyond the reach of most) and cleaning up urban air quality became urgent priorities. This new focus and commitment, however, coincided with a period of increased friction with Japan and Vietnam over competing territorial claims in the South China Sea and the East China Sea, a situation that increasingly threatened to lead to maritime conflict.

Having grown faster than virtually any other Chinese city in the past two decades, Shànghǎi remains the pot of gold at the end of the rainbow for China's swarming migrant workers, who now constitute almost four million of the city's total population of 24 million, and around 40% of the workforce.

HISTORY THE RECENT PAST

2012	2012	2013	2014
Shànghǎi and other cities across China see anti-Japanese demonstrations in response to Japanese claims to the Diàoyú (Senkaku) Islands.	Thaddeus Ma Daqin is detained and stripped of his title as auxiliary bishop of Shànghǎi.	Shànghǎi registers a 6.7% increase in the number of foreign expats coming to the city to live and work.	Shànghǎi issues a health warning and advises children and the elderly to stay indoors as smog engulfs the city.

Arts

You won't be sidestepping spray-can-toting graffiti artists, wayfaring buskers, street-side performers or wild-haired poets handing out flyers but there's enough creativity in Shànghǎi to keep you fired up and traditional Chinese arts are well covered.

Visual Arts

Even if the city's artistic output remains limited, a growing gallery and art-museum scene makes Shànghǎi a vibrant place to join the learning curve for contemporary Chinese art. For political and cultural reasons, Shànghǎi is creatively rather straight-laced and it's rare to see art – such as such as graffiti or street art – that lives beyond the well-defined, clinical gallery environment.

A well-known graffiti wall at Moganshan Rd (M50) – one of the few places in Shànghǎi where you could see graffiti and wall art – was partially demolished in 2013. For info on other graffiti and wall-art sites, see graffitipark.weebly.com.

Contemporary & Modern Art

Notable contemporary Shanghainese artists working across a large spectrum of styles include Pu Jie, with his colourful pop-art depictions of Shànghǎi, video-installation artists Shi Yong and Hu Jieming, and Hángzhōu-born Sun Liang. Wu Yiming creates calmer, more impressionistic works, while Ding Yi is a significant abstract artist whose works employ a repetitive use of crosses. Also look out for works by graphic-design artist Guan Chun, and the diverse works of Chen Hangfeng and Yang Yongliang, which draw inspiration from the techniques and imagery of traditional Chinese painting.

After sizing up contemporary directions in art at the Bund-side Rockbund Art Museum – itself a definitive art deco gem – your next stop should be eclectic M50, Shànghǎi's most cutting-edge and left-field art zone, housed in warehouses near Sūzhōu Creek. It's the city's equivalent of Běijīng's path-breaking 798 Art District. Standout innovative galleries at M50 include island6 and ShanghART. In People's Park, the Shànghǎi Museum of Contemporary Art (MOCA Shànghǎi) is a stimulating venue for art-watching. The collection at the now defunct China Art Museum – formerly housed in the Shanghai Race Club building next to People's Park – has moved to the China Art Palace in the former World Expo Site, in Pǔdōng. Its brazen new home is colossal, but the permanent collection is largely anodyne, although international exhibitions have been a success. The Shànghǎi Gallery of Art, at well-heeled Three on the Bund, is a spacious venue for cerebral and frequently enticing art works.

Link Shanghai (p119) in Tiánzǐfáng is a small but fascinating shop dedicated to selling imaginative work from Chinese artists and local designers.

A stroll around the quaint alleys of Tiánzǐfáng rewards with a smattering of galleries, including the excellent photographic gallery Beaugeste, and a host of small art galleries.

The huge art-centre complex known as Red Town, near Jiāotōng University, focuses on contemporary sculpture, and the thought-provoking displays at the Mínshēng Art Museum are a standout. The Shanghai Chinese Painting Institute at 197 Yueyang Rd also occasionally hosts major exhibitions.

Further afield, check to see what's on at the Shanghai Duolun Museum of Modern Art in Hóngkǒu and earmark a trip to the Gallery Magda Danysz.

In Pǔdōng, the Himalayas Museum, in the organically designed Himalayas Center, is a neat environment for showcasing contemporary art trends.

The hulking yet forward-thinking Power Station of Art (in the 41,000-sq-metre former Nánshì Power Plant) near the Huángpǔ River is the new venue for the Shanghai Biennale, held in November every two years since 1996. Related fringe shows spring up around the same time, and are often of more interest. Outside Biennale years, the China International Arts Festival is an event held in November that brings traditional and modern (Western and Chinese) art, artists and galleries together.

The character 永, which means 'eternal', contains the five fundamental brushstrokes necessary to master calligraphy.

ARTS VISUAL ARTS

Traditional Art

The Shànghǎi Museum puts traditional Chinese art under one roof, with a rare and extensive collection of ancient bronzes, Buddhist sculpture, ceramics, paintings, calligraphy, furniture, ancient jade and ethnic culture. For enthusiasts, an entire day here will only scratch the surface. The Shànghǎi Arts & Crafts Museum is an entertaining and informative choice, with displays of embroidery, paper cutting, lacquer work and jade cutting, with skilled craftsmen and women creating pieces on the spot. For iridescent glassware, the Liúli China Museum has an exquisite collection. Brash propaganda art from the Mao era is the focus of the riveting Propaganda Poster Art Centre, while the foyer of the Jumeirah Himalayas Hotel in Pǔdōng is a virtual art gallery of traditional Chinese paintings.

More traditional art comes from the southern suburb of Jīnshān, which has its own school of untrained 'peasant' painters who have been producing colourful and vibrant paintings for years. Their works have roots in local embroidery designs and contain no perspective; the themes are mostly rural and domestic scenes full of details of everyday life. You can see a selection of paintings from the Jīnshān area in several shops in the Old Town's Old Street, or you can head out to Jīnshān itself. The Sūzhōu Museum in Sūzhōu also has a magnificent collection of traditional Chinese art and is one of the highlights of the town. The new Sūzhōu Art Museum is another impressive space for landscapes, calligraphy and (some modern) Chinese art.

Calligraphy

Although calligraphy (书法; *shūfǎ*) has a place among most languages that employ alphabets, the art of calligraphy in China is taken to unusual heights of intricacy and beauty. Although Chinese calligraphy is beautiful in its own right, the complex infatuation Chinese people have for their written language helps elucidate their great respect for the art.

Chinese calligraphy is the trickiest of China's arts to comprehend for Western visitors, unless they have a sound understanding of written Chinese. The beauty of a Chinese character may be partially appreciated by a Western audience, but for a full understanding it is also essential to understand the meaning of the character in context.

Click on www. chineseposters. net for a fascinating collection of Chinese propaganda posters from 1925 to 2006.

There are five main calligraphic scripts – seal script, clerical script, semicursive script, cursive script and standard script – each of which reflects the style of writing of a specific era. Seal script, the oldest and most complex, was the official writing system during the Qin dynasty and has been employed ever since in the carving of the seals and name chops (stamps carved from stone) that are used to stamp documents.

Expert calligraphers have a preference for using full-form characters (*fántǐzì*) rather than their simplified variants (*jiǎntǐzì*).

Literature

A selection of Lu Xun's books in English, French and German translation can be found in the museum bookshop at the Lu Xun Memorial Hall.

Energised by a vibrant literary scene, Shànghǎi in the 1920s and '30s cast itself as a veritable publishing-industry hub. Sheltered from the censorship of Nationalists and warlords by the foreign settlements, and stimulated by the city's new-fangled modernity and flood of foreign ideas, Shànghǎi hosted a golden era in modern Chinese literature.

Birth of Modern Literature

Although born in Shàoxīng, Lu Xun (1881–1936), China's greatest modern writer, lived in Shànghǎi from 1927 until his death of tuberculosis. One of the first founders of the Shànghǎi-based League of Left-Wing Writers, the highly influential modernist author dragged Chinese literature into the modern era.

Until Lu Xun's radical *Diary of a Madman* in 1918, literary Chinese had been conceived in classical Chinese, a language that represented not Chinese as it was spoken or thought, but as it was communicated by the educated scholarly class. Classical Chinese was a terse, dry and inflexible language that bore little relevance to the real lives of Chinese people. Lu Xun's decision to write his story in vernacular Chinese was a revolutionary act that instantly transformed the literary paradigms of the day, and helped underpin the New Culture Movement (新文化运动; Xīn Wénhuà Yúndòng) which sought to challenge traditional Chinese culture.

Lu Xun's most famous work, the 1921 novella *The True Story of Ah Q* (阿Q正传, *Ā Q Zhèngzhuàn*) – a satirical look at early 20th-century China – is considered a modern masterpiece and was the first piece of literature to entirely utilise vernacular Chinese. Admirers of Lu Xun can visit his Shànghǎi residence.

Writers were not immune to political dangers; Lu Xun's friend Rou Shi was murdered by the Kuomintang in February 1931.

Mao Dun (real name Shen Yanbing; 1896–1981), an active leftist writer in the 1930s, penned *Midnight* (Zǐyè), one of the most famous novels about Shànghǎi. *Rainbow* (1929), by the same author, tells the tale of a young girl from a traditional family background who travels to Shànghǎi on a journey of political awakening.

Ding Ling, whose most famous work is *The Diary of Miss Sophie*, lived in Shànghǎi, as did for a time the writers Yu Dafu and Ba Jin.

For a taste of contemporary Chinese short-story writing in both English and Chinese, buy a copy of *Short Stories in Chinese: New Penguin Parallel Text* (2012).

Eileen Chang (Zhang Ailing; 1920–95) is one of the writers most closely connected to Shànghǎi, certainly among overseas Chinese. Born in Shànghǎi, she lived in the city only from 1942 to 1948 before moving to Hong Kong and then the USA. Seeped in the city's details and moods, her books capture the essence of Shànghǎi. Chang's most famous books include *The Rouge of the North, The Faded Flower, Red Rose and White Rose, The Golden Lock* and *Love in a Fallen City*. Her 1979 novella *Lust, Caution* was made into an award-winning film directed by Ang Lee (director of *Crouching Tiger, Hidden Dragon* and *Brokeback Mountain*) in 2007.

Contemporary Directions

Contemporary voices are more sparse. The most respected Shànghǎi writer today is Wang Anyi (b 1954), whose bestselling novels (in China) include *Love on a Barren Mountain, Baotown* and *Song of Everlasting Sorrow,* the latter following a Shanghainese beauty-pageant winner through four decades from the 1940s. Wang also co-wrote the script for Chen Kaige's film *Temptress Moon*.

More recently, several high school drop-outs gained notoriety, beginning with Mian Mian (b 1970), who vividly described the marginalised underbelly of China in *Candy*. To date this remains her only novel translated into English.

Increasingly known in the West is writer/rally driver/musician/blogger Han Han (b 1982), who skyrocketed to fame before his 18th birthday

SHÀNGHĂI FICTION

→ *Candy,* Mian Mian (2003) – A hip take on modern Shànghăi life, penned by a former heroin addict musing on complicated sexual affairs, suicide and drug addiction in Shēnzhèn and Shànghăi. Applauded for its urban underground tone, but sensational more for its framing of postadolescent themes in contemporary China.

→ *Years of Red Dust: Stories of Shanghai,* Qiu Xiaolong (2010) – Twenty three short stories set against a backdrop of Shànghăi through the decades and in the context of momentous historic events affecting the city and the inhabitants of Red Dust Lane.

→ *Empire of the Sun,* JG Ballard (1984) – An astonishingly well-written and poignant tale based on the author's internment as a child in a Japanese prisoner-of-war camp in Shànghăi, and subsequently made into a film by Steven Spielberg.

→ *Rules for Virgins,* Amy Tan (2013) This 42-page e-novella sensuously explores the life of an apprentice courtesan in 1912 Shànghăi.

→ *Master of Rain,* Tom Bradby (2003) – Atmospheric, noir-ish detective story set in the swinging Shànghăi of the '20s. 'Pockmarked' Huang, a brutally murdered Russian prostitute, and a naive British investigator come together for a real page-turner.

→ *Midnight,* Mao Dun (1933) – In the opening scene of *Midnight,* conservative Confucian Old Man Wu visits his son's home in Shànghăi. The sight of modern women in high-slit skirts and revealing blouses literally shocks him to death. A famed presentation of the social mores of 1920s Shànghăi.

→ *Shanghai: Electric and Lurid City,* Barbara Baker (1998) – An excellent anthology of more than 50 passages of writing about Shànghăi, from its pre-treaty port days to the eve of the 21st century.

→ *Shanghai Girls,* Lisa Lee (2010) – A moving novel about two beautiful sisters whose lives as high-flying models in 1930s Shànghăi are transformed when their father decides to repay his gambling debts by selling the pair to a family in Los Angeles. The book's acclaimed sequel is *Dreams of Joy* (2012).

→ *Five Star Billionaire,* Tash Aw (2013) Longlisted for the Man Booker Prize, Malaysian author Tash Aw's third novel explores the fortunes of four ambitious Malaysian new arrivals to Shànghăi.

→ *The Distant Land of My Father,* Bo Caldwell (2002) – A moving portrayal of the relationship between a daughter and father, and of betrayal and reconciliation, commencing in 1930s Shànghăi.

→ *The Painter from Shanghai,* Jennifer Cody Epstein (2008) – Highly acclaimed debut novel based on the remarkable life of child-prostitute-turned-painter Pan Yuliang.

→ *The Sing-Song Girls of Shanghai,* Han Bangqing (1892) – Delving deeply into the lives of courtesans and prostitutes in fin-de-siècle Shànghăi, this absorbing novel was first published in 1892 but only recently translated into English.

→ *When Red is Black,* Qiu Xiaolong (2004) – A realistic detective story that packs plenty of literary muscle. This is a follow-up Inspector Chen novel (see *Death of a Red Heroine*) and a great snapshot of the changing city seen through Chinese eyes.

→ *When We Were Orphans,* Kazuo Ishiguro (2000) – Subtle and absorbing portrayal of an English detective who sets out to solve the case of his parents' disappearance in Shànghăi, climaxing in war-shattered Hóngkŏu.

with his novel *The Third Gate,* a searing critique of China's educational system. He inspired awe and disgust simultaneously by turning down a scholarship to the prestigious Fùdàn University in order to race cars in Běijīng. Today, Han Han's highly influential blogs are among the most widely read in China.

Sprinkled with snippets from the Shànghǎi dialect (but as yet untranslated), Wang Xiaoying's *Song of a Long Street* (2010) is a vivid portrait of the textures and grain of everyday life in a Shànghǎi backstreet.

Translated into English, *Vicissitudes of Life* (2010) is a collection of stories from contemporary Shànghǎi writers, including Wang Xiaoying, Qiu Maoru and Wang Jiren.

As with Chinese film, fiction dealing with contemporary Shànghǎi is far less successful at filling bookstore shelves than historically set novels. Historical fiction is a safer and far more popular publishing choice, meaning voices on contemporary issues are more marginalised.

Shànghǎi writers today share a common despair about the loss of the Shànghǎi dialect while having to compose in Mandarin (Shanghainese is not written down).

Disappearing Shanghai by Howard W French and Qiu Xiaolong atmospherically captures a vanishing way of life in Shànghǎi's old quarters through thoughtful and tender images and poetry.

Music

Shànghǎi had a buzzing live-music scene in the 1930s, featuring everything from jazz divas to émigré Russian troubadours, but the contemporary scene has been long dominated by Filipino cover bands and saccharine-sweet Canto-pop. Things are changing, though, and while Shànghǎi's live-music scene still lags behind Běijīng's, there are some cracking venues in town where you can catch local bands, the best of which are Yùyīntáng and MAO Livehouse. The sci-fi styled Mercedes Benz Arena in Pǔdōng is the venue for big-name international and Chinese solo artists and bands, including Taylor Swift, The Rolling Stones, Jennifer Lopez, Jessie J, Bruno Mars and Jacky Cheung. Look out for the JUE Festival, a music and art festival held in Běijīng and Shànghǎi in March. Held in Pǔdōng in April, the Shànghǎi Midi Festival is three days of live music and DJs.

Rock

Singing and writing in Shanghainese, Top Floor Circus, who play anything from folk to punk, are legendary on the Shànghǎi music scene. If they're playing while you're in town, do your best to get a ticket. Others worth checking out include Pinkberry (rock), rockers Da Bei, all-girl band Bigger Xifu, blues band Joker, indie band FAF (Forget & Forgive) and rock band Nomad's Land. Torturing Nurse, meanwhile, who make unusual and extremely loud sounds rather than music as such, are China's leading 'noise' band.

Jazz

Shànghǎi's once world-famous jazz scene isn't quite as snappy as it was, but there are still a number of places around town where you can sample the sounds of the 1930s. Cotton Club and JZ Club are the best choices; the latter has a popular branch in Hángzhōu.

The Fairmont Peace Hotel Jazz Bar has been serenading punters for decades; the band has an average age of 80.

Traditional Chinese Music

The *èrhú* is a two-stringed fiddle that is tuned to a low register, providing a soft, melancholy tone. The *húqín* is a higher-pitched two-stringed viola. The *yuèqín,* a sort of moon-shaped four-stringed guitar, has a soft tone and is used to support the *èrhú.* Other instruments you may come across are the *shēng* (reed flute), *pípá* (lute), *gǔzhēng* (zither) and *xiāo* (vertical flute). A good place to hear free traditional music performances is the Shànghǎi Gǔqín Cultural Foundation or at a performance of Chinese opera.

Classical Music

The Shànghǎi Conservatory of Music is a prestigious clearing house of Chinese talent. One of its most famous former students is Liao Changyong, a world-class baritone who has performed with Placido Domingo, among others. Other famous classical-music venues include the Shànghǎi Concert Hall and the Oriental Art Center.

Chinese Opera

Chinese opera, best known for Běijīng opera (京剧; Jīngjù), has a rich and continuous history of some 900 years. Evolving from a convergence of comic and ballad traditions in the Northern Song period, the art brought together a disparate range of forms: acrobatics, martial arts, poetic arias and stylised dance.

Operas were usually performed by travelling troupes, who had a low social status in traditional Chinese society. Chinese law forbade mixed-sex performances, forcing actors to act out roles of the opposite sex. Opera troupes were frequently associated with homosexuality in the public imagination, contributing further to their lowly status.

Formerly, opera was performed mostly on open-air stages in markets, streets, teahouses or temple courtyards.

More than 100 varieties of opera coexist in China today, including Shanghainese opera (沪剧; Hùjù), sometimes called flower-drum opera, which is sung in the local dialect and has its origins in the folk songs

To pick up a traditional Chinese musical instrument such as the *pípá (lute)*, *èrhú* (two-stringed fiddle) or *gǔzhēng* (zither), pop down to Parsons Music on Fenyang Rd near the Shànghǎi Conservatory of Music.

ARTS CHINESE OPERA

AESTHETICS & POLITICS

In reflection of the Chinese character, Chinese aesthetics have traditionally been marked by restraint and understatement, a preference for oblique references over direct explanation, vagueness in place of specificity and an avoidance of the obvious in place of a fondness for the veiled and subtle. Traditional Chinese aesthetics sought to cultivate a reserved artistic impulse, principles that compellingly find their way into virtually every Chinese art form, from painting to sculpture, ceramics, calligraphy, film, poetry, literature and beyond.

As one of the central strands of the world's oldest civilisation, China's aesthetic tradition is tightly embroidered within Chinese cultural identity. For millennia, Chinese aesthetics were highly traditionalist and, despite coming under the influence of occupiers from the Mongols to the Europeans, defiantly conservative. It was not until the fall of the Qing dynasty in 1911 and the genesis of the New Culture Movement that China's great artistic traditions began to rapidly transform. In literature the stranglehold of classical Chinese loosened to allow breathing space for *báihuà* (colloquial Chinese) and a progressive new aesthetic began to flower, ultimately leading to revolutions in all of the arts, from poetry to painting, theatre and music.

It is hard to square China's great aesthetic traditions with the devastation inflicted upon them since 1949. Confucius advocated the edifying role of music and poetry in shaping human lives, but 5th-century philosopher Mozi was less enamoured with them, seeing music and other arts as extravagant and wasteful. The communists took this a stage further, enlisting the arts as props in their propaganda campaigns and permitting the vandalism and destruction of much traditional architecture and heritage. Many of China's traditional skills (such as martial arts lineages) and crafts either died out or went into decline during the Cultural Revolution. Many of these arts have yet to recover fully from this deterioration, even though 'opening up' and reform prompted a vast influx of foreign artistic concepts.

of Pǔdōng. Yueju opera (越剧; Yuèjù) was born in and around Shàoxīng County in neighbouring Zhèjiāng (the ancient state of Yue) province in the early 20th century. Yuèjù roles are normally played by women. Kunju opera (昆剧; Kūnjù) or Kunqu opera (昆曲; Kūnqǔ) originates from Kūnshān, near Sūzhōu in neighbouring Jiāngsū.

Actors portray stylised stock characters who are instantly recognisable to the audience. Most stories are derived from classical literature and Chinese mythology and tell of disasters, natural calamities, intrigues or rebellions. The musicians usually sit on the stage in plain clothes and play without written scores.

China's most legendary 20th-century opera star was Mei Lanfang, who allegedly performed privately for several of Shànghǎi's gangland bosses in the 1930s. The most central venue for appreciating Chinese opera in Shànghǎi is the Yìfū Theatre on Fuzhou Rd.

The lower Yangzi region has a long tradition of storytelling, farce, comic talk and mimicking, all of which were traditionally performed in teahouses. Hángzhōu and Sūzhōu have their own variants. *Píngtán* balladry is a mix of *pínghuà* (Sūzhōu-style storytelling) and *táncí* (ballad singing), accompanied by the *pípá* and *sānxián* (banjo). You can hear samples of various Chinese operas and *píngtán* at the Shànghǎi History Museum in Pǔdōng, or at the Píngtán Museum in Sūzhōu.

The shrill singing and loud percussion of Chinese opera were designed to be heard over the public throng, prompting American writer PJ O'Rourke to compare it to a truck loaded with wind chimes crashing into a set of empty oil drums during a bird-call contest.

Cinema

Early Film

The first screening of any film in China illuminated the garden of a Shànghǎi teahouse in 1896, when Spanish entrepreneur Galen Bocca showed a series of one-reel films to astonished audiences. The city's first cinema opened up in 1908, but before films could reach their glamorous peak in the 1930s, film-makers had to convince the distrustful Shanghainese that it was worth their hard-earned cash. Soon hooked, the city boasted more than 35 cinemas and more than 140 film companies by 1930. Shànghǎi's teahouse culture began to feel the pinch, along with a host of traditional performing arts.

The Golden Age

The 1932 Japanese bombing of the Shànghǎi district of Hóngkǒu had a big effect on the industry, prompting a patriotic fervour epitomised by films coming out of the Lianhua Studio, with its close connections to Chiang Kaishek's Nationalist Party.

Shànghǎi's golden age of film-making reached its peak in 1937 with the release of *Street Angel,* a powerful drama about two sisters who flee the Japanese in northeast China and end up as prostitutes in Shànghǎi, and *Crossroads,* a clever comedy about four unemployed graduates. There was still time, however, after WWII and before the Chinese Communist Party (CCP) took over in 1949, for a final flowering. *A Spring River Flows East,* dubbed the *Gone with the Wind* of Chinese cinema, and *Springtime in a Small Town,* another wartime tear jerker, remain popular films today.

The Shànghǎi International Film Festival (www.siff. com) celebrates international and locally produced films in June every year.

Shànghǎi Cinema Today

China's film industry was stymied after the Communist Revolution, which sent film-makers scurrying to Hong Kong and Taiwan, where they played key roles in building up the local film industries that flourished there. Chinese film-makers need to work against a system of censorship that famous director Feng Xiaogang has termed 'ridiculous'. Today's movie-goers are scarce, as DVD piracy and internet downloads upset the economics of domestic film-making.

More innovative film studios in Xī'ān and Běijīng have captured much of the international acclaim of contemporary Chinese film. Co-productions have been more successful for the Shànghǎi Film Studios, which in 2001 moved from its central location in Xújiāhuì to the far-western city district of Sōngjiāng.

One critical success was *The Red Violin*, a coproduction between Canada and Shànghǎi. Shànghǎi-born Vivian Wu (Wu Junmei; *The Last Emperor, The Pillow Book*) returned to her native city with her husband, director Oscar L Costo, in order to focus on their production company, MARdeORO Films. It produced the well-received *Shanghai Red*, starring Wu and Ge You *(Farewell My Concubine, To Live)*, in 2006. Another actress hailing from Shànghǎi is Joan Chen (Chen Chong), who started her career at the Shànghǎi Film Studios in the late 1970s.

Shànghǎi's independent films are scarce. Look out for Ye Lou's *Suzhou River* (Sūzhōu Hé) and Andrew Chen's *Shanghai Panic* (Wǒmen Hàipà). Both were shot with digital cameras and are notable for showing a decidedly unglamorous and more realistic side of the city.

Chen Yifei's 1920s period drama *The Barber* (aka *The Music Box*) was released posthumously in 2006, while Taiwanese-born Oscar-winning director Ang Lee *(Crouching Tiger, Hidden Dragon* and *Brokeback Mountain)* released *Lust, Caution* in 2007. A controversial tale of sex and espionage set in WWII Shànghǎi, based on the 1979 novella by Eileen Chang, the award-winning film was heavily censored for its mainland China release. Wayne Wang's 2011 release *Snow Flower and the Secret Fan* is partly set in contemporary Shànghǎi, with scenes set in the Peninsula Hotel, among other locations.

The Old Film Café in Hóngkǒu, housed in a beautiful three-storey brick building with charming wooden interior, shows old Shànghǎi films on demand, although few have English subtitles.

ARTS FASHION

Fashion

The Shanghainese have the reputation of being the most fashionable people in China. 'There's nothing the Cantonese won't eat', one version of a popular Chinese saying goes, 'and nothing the Shanghainese won't wear.' The generation gap is perhaps starker here, though, than anywhere else: you're still quite likely to see locals wandering around their neighbourhood dressed in very comfortable (but extremely uncool) pyjamas and slippers, but Shànghǎi has breathtaking, voguish pockets and young Shànghǎi women ooze glamour in even the cheapest skirts and blouses.

On the street, Chinese-language lifestyle magazines such as *Shanghai Tatler, Elle, Vogue, Harper's Bazaar* and *Marie Claire* crowd every corner newsstand. Christian Dior, Gucci and Louis Vuitton shops glut Shànghǎi's top-end malls, while trendy boutiques line French Concession streets such as Changle Rd, Xinle Rd and Nanchang Rd.

Shànghǎi still has a long way to go just to catch up with its own 1930s fashion scene, however, when images of Chinese women clad in figure-hugging *qípáo* (cheongsam) gave rise to its epithet as the 'Paris of the East'.

Shanghai Fashion Week (www.shanghaifashionweek.com) is a biannual event showcasing the work of local, national and international designers. There is also the city-sponsored, month-long International Fashion Culture Festival in March or April.

Martial Arts

China lays claim to a bewildering range of martial-arts styles, from the flamboyant and showy, inspired by the movements of animals or insects (such as Praying Mantis Boxing), to schools empirically built upon the science of human movement (eg Wing Chun). Some pugilists stress a mentalist approach while others put their money on physical power. On the outer fringes are the esoteric arts, abounding with metaphysical feats, arcane practices and closely guarded techniques.

Many fighting styles were once secretively handed down for generations within families and it is only relatively recently that outsiders have been accepted as students. Some schools, especially the more obscure styles, have been driven to extinction partly due to their exclusivity.

Unlike Western fighting arts – such as Savate, kickboxing, boxing, wrestling etc – Chinese martial arts are deeply impregnated with religious and philosophical values. Closely linked to martial arts is the practice of *qìgōng,* a technique for cultivating and circulating *qì* around the body. *Qì* can be developed for use in fighting to protect the body, as a source of power, or for curative and health-giving purposes.

Shànghǎi's parks are good places to go to look for teachers of taichi and *wǔshù* (martial arts), although language may be a barrier. Check the listings of entertainment magazines such as *That's Shanghai, City Weekend* or *Time Out Shanghai* for classes, or check for courses at the Lóngwǔ Kung Fu Center (p125), the Wǔyì Chinese Kungfu Centre (p125) or the Míngwǔ International Kungfu Club (p176).

As well as being an annual gay festival, Shanghai Pride (www.shpride.com) is a week-long celebration of creativity across all media.

Above: Oriental Pearl TV Tower (p147) in Pǔdōng

Architecture in Shànghǎi

Jaw-dropping panoramas of glittering skyscrapers are its trump card, but Shànghǎi is no one-trick pony: the city boasts a diversity of architectural styles that will astound most first-time visitors. Whether you're an art deco hound, a neoclassical buff, a fan of English 1930s suburban style villas, 1920s apartment blocks or Buddhist temple architecture, Shànghǎi has it covered.

Modern Skylines

Charm and panache may ooze from every crevice of its concession-era villas, *shíkùmén* (stone-gate) buildings, *lǐlòng* lanes and art deco marvels, but for sheer wow factor, look to the city's modern skyline. Shànghǎi's tall towers get all the media attention, but many of the city's most iconic and noteworthy contemporary buildings are low-rise.

High-Rise Shànghǎi

Like Hong Kong before it, Shànghǎi has filled its horizons with forests of soaring towers that capture a brash and sophisticated zeitgeist. The grandiose Bund may forever recall the indignity of foreign control, but Pǔdōng – and more specifically Lùjiāzuǐ – concerns itself with the future, and that's a future made in and by China.

Pǔdōng only dates to the early 1990s, so don't expect the sheer variety of New York skyscraper architecture. But some of the world's very tallest buildings erupt from Shànghǎi's notoriously boggy terrain, including the astonishing Shànghǎi Tower in Lùjiāzuǐ, the world's second-tallest building at the time of writing. To carry the load of the glass skin around the tower, an innovative curtain wall was devised, which is suspended from floors above and then stabilised with struts and hoop rings.

The 632m-high Gensler-designed Shànghǎi Tower's spiraling glass-coated form is the dominant structure of a triumvirate of skyscraping towers that also includes the breathtaking Shànghǎi World Financial Center (SWFC), another of the world's tallest buildings since it was completed in 2008. Metallic, glass, uncompromising and audaciously designed, the SWFC tower is a further brash testament to money and ambition. The original design incorporated a circle at its top, where the 'bottle-opener' trapezoid aperture (which reduces the wind pressure) sits, but this design was shouted down by local fears that it would recall the Japanese flag.

The most attractive and elegant of the three towers is the smallest: but it's no lightweight. Replete with Chinese symbolism, the pagoda-like 421m-high Jinmao Tower has 88 floors (eight is a lucky number), while its 13 stepped bands allude to Buddhist imagery. Designed by Adrian Smith of Skidmore, Owings & Merrill, the Jinmao Tower remains one of Shànghǎi's most interesting and notable buildings. On floors 53 to 87, the Grand Hyatt contains the world's highest atrium, a breathtaking architectural feat, while the world's longest laundry chute runs dirty sheets and pillowcases down the length of the tower.

Don't overlook Pǔxī on the far side of the river, where there's a vigorous collection of modern architecture, including claw-like Tomorrow Square, rocketing nefariously over People's Sq. The fifth tallest building in Shànghǎi and completed in 2003, the tower begins as a square before morphing into a diagonal square, topped with a pincer-like formation. On the other side of People's Sq rises the slightly taller, but not as architecturally interesting, Shimao International Plaza.

With such a meteoric construction agenda and an anything-goes attitude, designs can occasionally misfire and disappointments litter the streets. The Oriental Pearl TV Tower, the curious crown atop the Bund Center (88 Middle Henan Rd) and the Radisson Blu Hotel Shanghai New World (88 West Nanjing Rd) are all dubious additions.

> Shànghǎi's notoriously boggy firmament – a clay-based, river-delta type – meant the Shànghǎi Tower had to be built upon 831 reinforced concrete bores buried deep in the ground.

SHÀNGHǍI'S SKYSCRAPERS

Shànghǎi's tallest buildings (in order of height):

➤ Shànghǎi Tower (p146) Brand-new and rising supreme over Lùjiāzuǐ; 121 storeys.

➤ Shànghǎi World Financial Center (p145) A colossal, shimmering bottle-opener at the heart of Lùjiāzuǐ; 101 storeys.

➤ Jinmao Tower (p147) Crystalline, art deco–inspired pagoda and Shànghǎi's most attractive tower; 88 storeys.

➤ Plaza 66 Tower One (p141) One of Pǔxī's tallest buildings, best known for its exclusive mall slung out below; 66 storeys.

➤ Tomorrow Square (p68) Dramatically futuristic aluminium-and-glass tower climbing into the skies above People's Sq; 55 storeys.

Shànghăi World Financial Center (p145; designed by Kohn Pedersen Fox Associates)

Low-Rise Shànghăi

In the Pǔdōng-side former World Expo site, the staggering flying-saucer-shaped Mercedes-Benz Arena looks like it's refuelling after a warp-speed voyage from Alpha Centauri. It's well worth seeing at night, but it looks like it might actually take off in a tornado. The nearby up-turned red-pyramid design of the China Art Palace (the former China Pavilion) is another distinctive architectural icon of the site. In 2012 the pavilion was reinvented as a modern-art museum, guaranteeing it a second wind. Unfortunately, most of the other World Expo pavilions – including the staggeringly inventive UK Pavilion – were dismantled after the event, but a few are still standing. On the other side of the river, the Nánshì Power Plant has found a dramatic new interpretation as the Power Station of Art.

Also in Pǔdōng, the Arata Isozaki–designed Himalayas Center – attached to the Jumeirah Himalayas Hotel – is a highly complicated, organic-looking and challenging form in an otherwise uniform neighbourhood of Shànghăi.

A stroll around People's Sq in Pǔxī introduces you to three of the city's most eye-catching designs. The Shànghăi Urban Planning Exhibition Hall is capped with a distinctive roof with four 'florets'. The nearby Shànghăi Grand Theatre combines Chinese sweeping eaves with a futuristic employment of plastic and glass. Opposite this pair is the uniquely designed Shànghăi Museum, resembling an ancient Chinese cooking vessel known as a *dǐng*.

Other low-rise modern Shànghăi structures with spectacular interiors or exteriors include Pǔdōng International Airport Terminal 1 and Shànghăi Hóngqiáo Railway Station.

China Pavilion (designed by He Jingtang) at the 2010 World Expo site (p151)

Elsewhere, conversions of industrial buildings have breathed new life into disused structures. 1933 in Hóngkǒu is a highly photogenic modern structure, given a new and invigorating lease of life. This former slaughterhouse has been trendily converted to house boutiques, bars, shops and restaurants among its silent, concrete overture of flared columns, sky-bridges and ramps. It's only disadvantage is that it's a bit isolated, but it's one of the top architectural highlights of Shànghǎi.

Don't also overlook hotels, where funky modern architecture and snappy interior design find a creative harmony. While making a ground-breaking push into sustainability among Shànghǎi's hotels, URBN also captures a unique take on Shànghǎi's local aesthetic, with a highly modern and trendy finish. All steel, exposed concrete and brickwork, the Waterhouse at South Bund presents cutting-edge work from Shànghǎi's architectural firm NHDRO, combining industrial and modern aesthetics in this former Japanese army headquarters and warehouse near the river. The 40-floor Bulgari Hotel (due to open in 2015) north of Sūzhōu Creek won't exactly be low-rise, but it won't be in chart-topping high-rise territory either. Set to transform this part of Zháběi, the tower is designed by Foster+Partners, with interior design from architectural firm Antonio Citterio Patricia Viel and Partners. The former Chinese Chamber of Commerce is a notable historic building incorporated into the Bulgari design for the area.

Shànghǎi shopping malls can also be showstoppers in their own right. The interior design of the superduper IAPM Mall on Middle Huaihai Rd is fantastic and worth a look, even if you're not out to buy anything.

Shànghǎi's vast bridges, including the enormous Lúpǔ Bridge, which combine length and height in equal measure, are also sights worth seeing.

Concession Architecture

For many foreign visitors, Shànghǎi's modern architectural vision is a mere side salad to the feast of historic architecture lining the Bund and beyond. Remnants of old Shànghǎi, these buildings are part of the city's genetic code, inseparable from its sense of identity as the former 'Paris of the East'.

Classical & Neoclassical

Although the Bund contains the lion's share of Shànghǎi's neoclassical designs, among the most impressive is the Shànghǎi Race Club Building (till recently the Shànghǎi Art Museum) in People's Sq. It's a beautiful building with a clock tower and once formed part of the main stand at the old racecourse. Another standout building is the British-designed General Post Office, home of the Post Office Museum, completed in 1924. See p58 for details of the most famous neoclassical buildings on the Bund.

In the 1920s the British architectural firm of Palmer & Turner designed many of Shànghǎi's major buildings (13 structures on the Bund alone), including the neoclassical Hongkong and Shanghai Banking Corporation (HSBC) building, the Yokohama Specie Bank, the Custom House and other gems.

The Shànghǎi Exhibition Centre is a triumphant example of Soviet neoclassical architecture.

Villa Architecture

The tree-lined streets of the French Concession house a delightful collection of magnificent residential early-20th-century villa architecture, much of which has been well preserved. Standout examples include the Mansion Hotel, the Moller House, InterContinental Shanghai Ruijin Hotel, Āntíng Villa Hotel and Fu 1039.

Art Deco

The late 1920s saw the arrival of art deco and its sophisticated, modish expressions of the machine age in Shànghǎi. It was one of Shànghǎi's architectural high-water marks, with the city boasting more art deco buildings than any other city in the world. For a comprehensive lowdown on the style, turn to *Shanghai Art Deco* by Deke Erh and Tess Johnston.

Art deco buildings of note include the Fairmont Peace Hotel, the Paramount Ballroom, Broadway Mansions, the Cathay Theatre, the Liza Building at 99 East Nanjing Rd, the Savoy Apartments at 209 Changshu Rd, the Picardie Apartments (now the Hengshan Hotel) on the corner of Hengshan Rd and Wanping Rd, the Embankment Building (housing Chai Living Residences), the Bank of China building on the Bund, and the French Concession building that contains the James Cohan art gallery, among dozens of others.

Shoddy construction quality in China is common-place. In 2009, a newly built 13-storey residential block – its windows fitted and already exterior tiled – simply fell over in Shànghǎi, killing one worker.

ARCHITECTURE IN SHÀNGHǍI CONCESSION ARCHITECTURE

BUILDING THE BUND

The Bund – Shànghǎi's most famous esplanade of concession buildings – was built on unstable foundations due to the leaching mud of the Huángpǔ River. Bund buildings were first built on concrete rafts that were fixed onto wood pilings, which were allowed to sink into the mud. Because of the lack of qualified architects, some of the earliest Western-style buildings in Shànghǎi were partially built in Hong Kong, shipped to Shànghǎi, then assembled on site.

Above: Art deco building on the Bund (p56)
Left: Restored *shíkùmén* (stone-gate houses) in Xīntiāndì (p96)

Strongly associated with art deco (although he also used earlier styles), Ladislaus Hudec (1893–1958) was a Hungarian who came to Shànghǎi in 1918 after escaping while en route to a Russian prisoner-of-war camp in Siberia. The Park Hotel, Grand Theatre, China Baptist Publication Society, the Green House and other art deco buildings all owe their creation to Hudec.

The Rockbund Art Museum is a further magnificent example of art deco architecture, complete with Chinese design motifs such as the eight-trigram windows. The museum is on Yuanmingyuan Rd, itself a long gallery of art deco classics.

Lòngtáng & Shíkùmén

Even though Shànghǎi is typified by its high-rise and uniform residential blocks, near ground level the city comes into its own with its low-rise *lòngtáng* and *shíkùmén* architecture. Here, both Western and Asian architectural motifs were synthesised into harmonious, utilitarian styles that still house a large proportion of Shànghǎi's residents.

Lòngtáng

In the same way that Běijīng's most authentic features survive among its homely (but far older and entirely non-European) *hútòng* alleyways, so Shànghǎi's *lòngtáng* (or *lǐlòng*) lanes are the historic city's representative architectural feature. *Lòngtáng* (弄堂) are the back alleys that form the building blocks of living, breathing communities, supplying a warm and charming counterpoint to the abstract and machine-like skyscrapers rising over the city. Sadly, these alleys and their signature buildings, the *shíkùmén* (stone-gate houses), have offered little more than feeble resistance against developers who have toppled swathes of *shíkùmén* to make way for more glittering projects. But if you want to find Shànghǎi at its most local, community-spirited, neighbourly (and also at its quietest), more than enough *lòngtáng* survive off the main drag for you to savour their slow-moving tempo.

Shíkùmén

Following the devastation of the Taiping Rebellion in 1853, some 20,000 Chinese fled into the International Settlements. Sensing a newly arrived cash cow, the British decided to scrap the law forbidding Chinese from renting property in the concessions, and foreigners from developing real estate. British and French speculators built hundreds of houses in what became Shànghǎi's biggest real-estate bonanza. The result was *shíkùmén* (石库门) – literally 'stone gate' – referring to the stone porticos that fronted these buildings and the alleys that led to them.

Shànghǎi *shíkùmén* architecture is a unique mixture of East and West, a blend of the Chinese courtyard house and English terraced housing. Typical *shíkùmén* houses were two to three storeys tall and fronted by an imposing stone-gate frame topped with a decorated lintel enclosing two stout wooden doors (frequently black), each decorated with a bronze handle. The lintel was sometimes elaborately carved with a dictum in Chinese, usually four characters long. At the entrance to the alley there was often a *yānzhǐdiàn* (烟纸店) – literally a 'tobacco and paper shop' – where residents could pick up provisions round the clock.

Shíkùmén were originally designed to house one family, but Shànghǎi's growth and socialist reorientation led to them being sublet to many families, each of which shared a kitchen and outside bathroom to complement the *mǎtǒng* (chamber pot). For the Shanghainese, a single-family kitchen and separate bedrooms remained a dream until the 1990s.

An art deco classic, the Paramount Ballroom is haunted by the ghost of a young girl who refused to dance with a Japanese soldier (although others say it was gangster Du Yuesheng), who shot her dead.

ARCHITECTURE IN SHÀNGHǍI LÒNGTÁNG & SHÍKÙMÉN

Jade Buddha Temple (p128)

Shànghǎi is not an ancient city like Běijīng. The city's oldest house is a courtyard home called Shū Yǐn Lóu (书隐楼) in the Old Town, dating to the 18th century and named after a library. It's located at 77 Tiandeng Nong.

Shíkùmén made up 60% of Shànghǎi's housing between the 1850s and the 1940s; they can be found across historic Shànghǎi, but are most prevalent in the French Concession, Jìng'ān, Hóngkǒu and parts of the Old Town. One of the most charming *shíkùmén* areas is in the boutique-littered Tiānzǐfáng area in the French Concession. Xīntiāndì is a restored, but more synthetic, *shíkùmén* area housing the absorbing Shíkùmén Open House Museum.

Two other *shíkùmén* areas well worth exploring are Zhang Garden, east of the intersection between West Nanjing Rd and Shimen No 1 Rd, and Cité Bourgogne, on the northeast corner of the crossing between West Jianguo Rd and South Shaanxi Rd. See the Local Knowledge interview with Sue Anne Tay on p99.

Religious Architecture

Following the tumultuous destruction of religious beliefs, practices and architecture that characterised the Mao era, religion has enjoyed a powerful resurgence in Shànghǎi (as it has nationwide) from the 1980s to the present day. The city's most standout buildings may serve Mammon, but many of Shànghǎi's most impressive religious buildings are once again active places of worship.

Temples

The place of prayer for Buddhist, Taoist or Confucian worshippers, Chinese *sìmiào* (寺庙; temples) tend to follow a strict, schematic pattern. Most importantly, all are laid out on a north–south axis in a series of halls, with the main door of each hall facing south.

One striking difference from Christian churches is the open-plan design of temples, with buildings interspersed with breezy open-air

SHÀNGHĂI'S BEST TEMPLES, CHURCHES & SYNAGOGUES

➡ **Jade Buddha Temple** (p128) Shànghăi's best-known shrine, housing a serene effigy of Sakyamuni (Buddha).

➡ **Jìng'ān Temple** (p130) Impressively restored, this Buddhist temple is a major Jìng'ān landmark.

➡ **Chénxiānggé Nunnery** (p82) One of the Old Town's most sacred sites.

➡ **Shĕshān Basilica** (p197) Standing sublimely atop a hill just outside town.

➡ **Ohel Moishe Synagogue** (p159) Jewish Shànghăi's most significant site of religious heritage.

courtyards. This allows the climate to permeate; seasons therefore play an essential role in defining the mood. The open-air layout furthermore allows the *qì* (气; energy) to circulate, dispersing stale air and allowing incense to be burned liberally.

Buddhist temples of architectural note include the Jade Buddha Temple, with its striking yellow-and-red walls; the Jìng'ān Temple, a recent rebuild of one of Shànghăi's first temples (c AD 247); and the Old Town's lovely Chénxiānggé Nunnery.

An important Taoist temple is the Temple of the Town God in the Old Town, a neighbourhood which is also home to the large Confucian Temple, lovingly restored in the 1990s.

Chronicling the changing face of Shànghăi and its impact on the people who live here, *Shanghai Street Stories* (www.shanghai streetstories. com) is a terrific resource for anyone interested in the architectural heritage of the city.

Churches

Churches in Shànghăi reflect the long Christian presence in this historically cosmopolitan city. After St Ignatius Cathedral and Shĕshān Basilica, other churches of note are the beautiful Russian Orthodox Mission Church, with its blue domes; the pretty Dŏngjiādù Cathedral, Shànghăi's oldest church (c 1853); the disused St Nicholas Church (1934); and the delightful St Joseph's Church (c 1862; 36 South Sichuan Rd), with its Gothic spires, now located within the grounds of a school.

Mosques

The main active mosque in Shànghăi is the Peach Garden Mosque, built in the Old Town in 1917. While not particularly impressive architecturally, it is nevertheless an interesting mix of styles with its neoclassical-like facade, Islamic green domes and mixture of Arabic lettering and Chinese characters.

Synagogues

Of the seven synagogues once built in Shànghăi, only two remain. The renovated Ohel Moishe Synagogue is now the absorbing Shànghăi Jewish Refugees Museum. Of more authentic charm is the rather neglected, ivy-cloaked Ohel Rachel Synagogue in Jìng'ān, which was Shànghăi's first synagogue (1920), but it is generally not open to visitors.

Religion & Belief

Religious belief may not dominate contemporary Shànghǎi life, but faith still exercises a powerful hold over the spiritual imagination, and the city is home to a large and disparate brood of temples, churches and mosques.

During the Cultural Revolution, many Christian Churches in Shànghǎi and around China served as warehouses or factories and were gradually rehabilitated in the 1980s. St Ignatius Cathedral was enlisted for the storage of grain.

Buddhism

Although Buddhism (Fójiào) originated in India, so is not an indigenous Chinese faith, it is the religion most deeply associated with China, Tibet and Chinese culture. Its influence today may be a mere shadow of its Tang dynasty apogee, and the religion was heavily bruised by the Cultural Revolution (1966–76), but Buddhism is widely practised in today's Shànghǎi, where several notable Buddhist temples can be visited.

As with many church-goers in the West, many Shànghǎi Buddhists are 'cultural Buddhists' rather than devout believers who live their lives according to strict religious rules.

Shànghǎi temples may lack the history and scale of their counterparts elsewhere in China (take Běijīng, for example), but they can be fascinating places to watch local people light *shāo xiāng* (incense) to worship Buddha, Guanyin (p85) and other deities. For more impressive Buddhist temples, head to Hángzhōu's fabulous Língyǐn Temple or Sūzhōu's huge West Garden Temple.

Taoism

The home-grown philosophy-cum-religion of Taoism (Dào Jiào) is entirely Chinese, but exercises less of an influence over the minds of modern-day people in Shànghǎi and China than Buddhism.

In its simplest, purest and most philosophical form, Taoism draws from *The Classic of the Way and its Power* (Taote Jing; Daode Jing), penned by the sagacious Laotzu (Laozi; c 580–500 BC) who left his writings with the gatekeeper of a pass as he headed west on the back of an ox. Some Chinese believe his wanderings took him to a distant land in the west where he became Buddha.

Taoists seek to live by bringing their lives into harmony with the 'Way' (道; *dào*) and in so doing attain fulfillment. In its more religious manifestations, Taoism is fused with superstitious beliefs in a domain overseen by myriad deities, including the Money God, the Fire God and Guandi.

Taoist temples are similar to Buddhist temples in layout, and although the pantheon of deities differs, the main hall in each type of temple is usually dominated by a trinity of large statues. Taoist monks wear squarish trousers and jacket, with their hair grown long and twisted into a topknot, while Buddhist monks wear robes and shave their heads.

As with Buddhist temples, Shànghǎi has far fewer examples of Taoist temples than elsewhere in China, and none of any great age or heritage, apart from the Temple of the Town God in the Old Town.

Confucianism

A mainstay of Chinese civilisation for the past two thousand years, Confucianism (Rújiā Sīxiǎng) is a humanist philosophy (rather than a religion) based upon the teachings of Confucius (Kǒngzǐ), a 6th-century-BC philosopher who lived during a period of incessant warfare and strife. Confucius' disciples gathered his ideas in the form of short aphorisms and conversations, forming the work known as the *Analects* (Lúnyǔ).

In its quest for social harmony and the common good, Confucianism advocated codes of conduct and systems of obedience with an emphasis on the five basic hierarchical relationships: father-son, ruler-subject, husband-wife, elder-younger, and friend-friend. Confucius believed that if each individual carried out his or her proper role in society (ie, a son served his father respectfully while a father provided for his son, a subject served his ruler respectfully while a ruler provided for his subject, and so on) social order would result.

Confucianism eventually permeated every level of society, and an intimate knowledge of the Confucian classics was a prerequisite to a life in officialdom.

What started off as a fresh and radical philosophy later became conservative, reactionary and an obstacle to change. Confucius' thinking came under vitriolic attack during the Cultural Revolution; the sage has been officially rehabilitated into modern Chinese society, however, and even though his influence and prestige has waned, Confucius' social ethics have resurfaced in government propaganda, where they lend authority to the leadership's emphasis on 'harmony' (*héxié*).

Shànghǎi's historic Confucius Temple is, like many other temples, in the Old Town, a quiet and unruffled corner of the city.

> Confucius Institutes around the world aim to internationally promote Chinese language and culture, while simultaneously developing China's cultural influence abroad.

Christianity

Christianity (Jīdū Jiào) first arrived in China with the Nestorians, a sect from ancient Persia that split with the Byzantine Church in AD 431, who travelled to China via the Silk Road in the 7th century. Much later, in the 16th century, the Jesuits appeared and were popular figures at the imperial court, although they made few converts; they were later very active in Shànghǎi, especially in Xújiāhuì. Large numbers of Catholic and Protestant missionaries established themselves in China in the 19th century, but bore the brunt of much antiforeigner feeling during the Boxer Rebellion and other anti-Western spasms.

In today's Shànghǎi (and China), Christianity is a burgeoning faith, perhaps uniquely placed to expand due to its industrious work ethic, associations with economically developed nations, and its emphasis on human rights and charitable work. Some estimates point to as many as 100 million Christians in China; however, the exact number is hard to calculate as many groups – outside the four official Christian organisations – lead a strict underground existence in what are called 'house churches'.

MONEY, TRADE & REBELLION

Born of money and trade and for so long a byword for exploitation, ill-gotten gains and vice, Shànghǎi is a city whose most prominent buildings – both historically and today – were shrines and temples to Mammon. Conversely, however, the city has also served as a crucible for newfangled – and often potent – ideas, many imported from overseas. For starters, the Chinese Communist Party was conceived here in 1921 and went on to stridently undermine religious belief during the zealous Mao Zedong years.

NATIONALISM

In today's Shànghǎi, '-isms' (主义; zhǔyì or 'doctrines') are often frowned upon. 'Intel-lectualism' is suspect as it may clash with political taboos. 'Idealism' is nonpragmatic and potentially destructive, as Maoism showed.

Some argue that China's one-party state has reduced thinking across the spectrum via propaganda and censorship. This has, however, helped spawn another '-ism': nationalism.

Nationalism is not restricted to Chinese youth but it is this generation – with no experience of the Cultural Revolution's terrifying excesses – which most closely identifies with its message. The fènqīng (angry youth) have been swept along with China's rise; while they are no lovers of the Chinese Communist Party (CCP), they yearn for a stronger China that can stand up to 'foreign interference'.

The CCP actively encourages strong patriotism, but is nervous about its sublimation into nationalism and its potential for disturbance. With China's tendency to get quickly swept along by passions, nationalism has become an often unseen but quite potent force, with anti-Japanese disturbances occurring in Shànghǎi and other cities.

Islam

David Aikman's *Jesus in Beijing: How Christianity is Transforming China and Changing the Global Balance of Power* (2003) predicts almost one-third of Chinese turning to Christianity within the next few decades.

Islam (Yīsiīlán Jiào) in China dates to the 7th century, when it was first brought to China by Arab and Persian traders along the Silk Road. Later, during the Mongol Yuan dynasty, maritime trade increased, bringing new waves of merchants to China's coastal regions. It is estimated that 1.5% to 3% of Chinese today are Muslim. Shànghǎi's most famous mosque is the Peach Garden Mosque in the Old Town.

Judaism

Although Shànghǎi was never a base for Chinese Judaism (Yóutài Jiào) – like Kāifēng in north China's Hénán province – the city has a long and splendid history of Jewish immigration from overseas. Hóngkǒu contains several reminders of the Jewish Quarter there, especially around Zhoushan Rd, including the Ohel Moishe Synagogue.

See p163 for more on Shànghǎi's Jewish history.

Survival Guide

Transport

ARRIVING IN SHÀNGHĂI

Most international passengers reach Shànghăi by air. The city has two airports: Pǔdōng International Airport to the east and Hóngqiáo International Airport on the other side of the city to the west, with most international passengers arriving at the former. Shànghăi is China's second-largest international air hub (third-largest including Hong Kong) and if you can't fly direct, you can go via Běijīng, Hong Kong or Guǎngzhōu (and a host of lesser international airports in China).

➡ From the US west coast figure on a 13- to 14-hour flight to Shànghăi or Běijīng, and an additional hour or more to Hong Kong.

➡ From London Heathrow it's about an 11-hour flight to Běijīng and 12 to 13 hours to Shànghăi and Hong Kong.

➡ Daily (usually several times a day) domestic flights connect Shànghăi to every major city in China.

➡ Shànghăi is linked to the rest of China by an efficient rail network (with numerous high-speed lines) and, to a far lesser extent, long-distance buses.

➡ Shànghăi can be reached by ferry from Osaka, Kobe and Nagasaki in Japan.

Flights, cars and tours can be booked online at lonelyplanet.com.

Pǔdōng International Airport

Pǔdōng International Airport (PVG; 浦东国际机场; Pǔdōng Guójì Jīchǎng; ☑6834 1000, flight information 96990; www.shairport.com) is located 30km southeast of Shànghăi, near the East China Sea. All international flights (and some domestic flights) operate from here. If you're making an onward domestic connection from Pǔdōng International Airport, it's crucial that you find out whether the domestic flight leaves from Pǔdōng or Hóngqiáo, as it will take at least an hour to cross the city.

There are two main passenger terminals, which are easy to navigate. A satellite terminal is due to start operating in 2015. Departures are on the upper level and arrivals on the lower level, where there is a tourist information counter.

Banks and ATMs Located throughout the airport, on both sides of customs.

China Post (中国邮政; Zhōngguó Yóuzhèng) Offices are located in the arrivals and departures halls.

Left luggage Located in the arrivals and departures halls

CLIMATE CHANGE & TRAVEL

Every form of transport that relies on carbon-based fuel generates CO_2, the main cause of human-induced climate change. Modern travel is dependent on aeroplanes, which might use less fuel per kilometre per person than most cars but travel much greater distances. The altitude at which aircraft emit gases (including CO_2) and particles also contributes to their climate change impact. Many websites offer 'carbon calculators' that allow people to estimate the carbon emissions generated by their journey and, for those who wish to do so, to offset the impact of the greenhouse gases emitted with contributions to portfolios of climate-friendly initiatives throughout the world. Lonely Planet offsets the carbon footprint of all staff and author travel.

TAKING THE SHÀNGHǍI MAGLEV TRAIN

If you need to reach or depart Pǔdōng International Airport chop-chop, Shànghǎi's futuristic **Maglev** (磁浮列车; Cífú Lièchē; www.smtdc.com; economy one-way/return ¥50/80, with same-day air ticket ¥40, children under/over 1.2m free/half-price) train comes with a top speed of 430km/h. Launched in 2003, it's the world's sole Maglev (magnetic levitation) train in commercial operation. In place of conventional wheels, the Sino-German train's carriages are supported above the tracks by a magnetic field. Carriages have simple interiors with ample legroom and, perhaps tellingly, no seatbelts. LED meters notch up the rapidly escalating velocity, although the train starts to decelerate around five minutes into its eight-minute cruise, in preparation for arrival. When it hits peak velocity, taxis heading in the same direction in the adjacent freeway fast lane appear to be driving backwards.

The Maglev train only takes you as far as the terminus at Longyang Rd station in Pǔdōng, from where you'll have to disembark and lug your bags onto the metro system to continue your journey. Nonetheless, a trip on the train is thrilling and a return trip to the airport is a fun outing for kids and the family. From a transportation point of view, the Maglev has competition from metro line 2, which travels all the way into town from Pǔdōng International Airport and on to Hóngqiáo Airport Terminal 2, via the city centre.

and open from 6am to 9.30pm. Charges are from ¥10 to ¥30 (up to four hours), or ¥50 per day.

Hotel The **Merry Lin Air Terminal Hotel** (大众美林阁空港宾馆; Dàzhòng Měilín Gékōng Gǎng Bīnguǎn; ☑3879 9999; 6hr from ¥198, 24hr from ¥298) is located between terminals 1 and 2, in front of the Maglev ticket office.

Shuttle buses Connect the terminals, stopping at doors 1 and 8 (terminal 1) and doors 23 and 27 (terminal 2).

Wi-fi Available, but you have to purchase time.

Maglev

The warp-speed **Maglev** (磁浮列车; Cífú Lièchē; www.smtdc.com; economy one-way/return ¥50/80, with same-day air ticket ¥40, children under/over 1.2m free/half-price) runs from Pǔdōng International Airport to Longyang Rd metro stop (just south of Century Park) on metro line 2 in eight minutes, running every 20 minutes in both directions roughly between 6.45am and 9.40pm.

Metro

Metro line 2 zips from Pǔdōng International Airport to Hóngqiáo International Airport, passing through central Shànghǎi. You will, however, need to disembark at Guanglan Rd station and transfer to another train on the same platform to continue your journey. Pǔdōng International Airport is a long way out: it takes about 45 minutes to People's Sq (¥7) and 1¾ hours to Hóngqiáo International Airport (¥8).

Airport Buses

Airport buses take between 60 and 90 minutes to reach destinations in Pǔxī, west of the Huángpǔ River. Buses drop off at all departure halls and pick up outside arrivals, at both terminals 1 and 2, leaving the airport roughly every 15 to 30 minutes from 7am to 11pm and heading to the airport from roughly 5.30am to 9.30pm (bus 1 runs till 11pm). The most useful buses:

Airport bus 1 (¥30) Links Pǔdōng International Airport with Hóngqiáo International Airport (terminals 1 and 2)

Airport bus 2 (¥22) Links Pǔdōng International Airport with the (largely disused) **Airport City Terminal** (机场城市航站楼; Jīchǎng Chéngshì Hángzhànlóu; Map p310; West Nanjing Rd), east of Jìng'ān

Temple; useful for reading Jìng'ān district.

Airport bus 5 (¥16 to ¥22) Links Pǔdōng Airport with Shànghǎi Railway Station via People's Sq.

Airport bus 7 (¥20) runs to Shànghǎi South Railway Station.

Midnight line (¥16 to ¥30) Operates from 11pm to the last arrival, running to Hóngqiáo Airport terminal 1 via Longyang Rd metro station to Shimen No 1 Rd and Huashan Rd.

Taxi

Rides into central Shànghǎi cost around ¥160 and take about an hour; to Hóngqiáo airport it costs around ¥200. Most Shànghǎi taxi drivers are honest, but ensure they use the meter. Avoid monstrous overcharging by using the regular taxi rank outside the arrivals hall.

Hotel Shuttle Buses

Most top-end and some mid-range hotels operate shuttle buses to and from their hotels at fixed times (roughly ¥40 to Pǔdōng International Airport). Enquire at the rows of hotel desks in the arrivals hall or contact your hotel beforehand.

Long-Distance Buses

Regular buses run to Sūzhōu (苏州; ¥84, three hours, 17 per day) and Hángzhōu (杭州; ¥100, three hours, six per day) from the long-distance bus stop at the airport.

Hóngqiáo International Airport

Eighteen kilometres west of the Bund, **Hóngqiáo International Airport** (SHA; 虹桥国际机场; Hóngqiáo Guójì Jīchǎng; ☑5260 4620, flight information 6268 8899; www.shairport.com; Ⓜ Hongqiao Airport Terminal 1, Hongqiao Airport Terminal 2) has two terminals: the older and less-used terminal 1 (east terminal; halls A and B) and the new and sophisticated terminal 2 (west terminal; attached to Shànghǎi Hóngqiáo Railway Station), where most flights arrive. If flying domestically within China from Shànghǎi, consider flying from here; it is closer to central Shànghǎi than Pǔdōng International Airport. If transferring between Hóngqiáo and Pǔdōng International Airports, note they are a long way (1¾ hours) apart.

ATMs Located at most exits and accept international cards.

China Post (中国邮政; Zhōngguó Yóuzhèng) An office is located in the departures hall.

Information counters (虹桥国际机场咨询服务处; Hóngqiáo Guójì Jīchǎng Zīxún Fúwùchù; ⏱5.30am-11pm) Staff can assist by booking discounted accommodation, providing free maps, offering advice on transportation into town and writing the Chinese script for a taxi.

Luggage storage Available in the departure halls and arrivals hall of both terminals, operating between 7am and 8.30pm. Bags must be locked and a passport or ID is required.

Shuttle buses Run frequently (from 6am to 11pm) between terminals 1 and 2, taking 13 minutes.

Wi-fi Accessible by using the password provided at an information counter.

Terminal 2
METRO
Terminal 2 is connected to downtown Shànghǎi by lines 2 and 10 (30 minutes to People's Sq) from Hóngqiáo International Airport terminal 2 metro station; both lines run through East Nanjing Rd station (for the Bund). Line 2 runs to Pǔdōng and connects with Pǔdōng International Airport (¥8; 1¾ hours) and Longyang Rd metro station, south of Century Park, from where you can hop aboard the Maglev. The next stop west from Hóngqiáo Airport terminal 2 is Hóngqiáo Railway Station (connected to the airport and accessible on foot).

TAXI
A taxi to the Bund will cost around ¥70; to Pǔdōng International Airport, around ¥200. Avoid taxi sharks.

BUS
Airport bus 1 (¥30, from 6am to 9.30pm) Runs to Pǔdōng International Airport.

Bus 941 (¥6, from 5.30am to 11pm) Runs to the main Shànghǎi Railway Station.

Night buses 316 (from 11am to 5pm) and **320** (from 11am to 5pm) Run to East Yan'an Rd near the Bund.

LONG-DISTANCE BUS
The long-distance bus station at terminal 2 runs to myriad destinations, including Sūzhōu, Nánjīng, Qīngdǎo, Túnxī (for Huángshān), Hángzhōu and Dēngfēng (for the Shaolin Temple).

TRAIN
Attached to terminal 2, Shànghǎi Hóngqiáo Railway Station has high-speed G-class trains to Hángzhōu, Sūzhōu, Nánjīng and Běijīng.

Terminal 1
METRO
Hóngqiáo Airport terminal 1 is the next stop east on line 10 from Hóngqiáo Airport terminal 2 metro station. Change to line 2 for the metro to Pǔdōng International Airport (¥8).

BUS
Airport shuttle bus (¥4, from 7.50am to 11pm) Runs from Hóngqiáo Airport terminal 1 to the largely defunct **Airport City Terminal** (机场城市航站楼; Jīchǎng Chéngshì Hángzhànlóu; Map p310; West Nanjing Rd) in Jìngān; it's useful for accessing the Jìngān area.

Airport bus 1 (¥30, 6am to 9.30pm) Runs to Pǔdōng International Airport.

Bus 925 (¥4, 5.30am to 10.30pm) Runs to People's Sq via Hongmei Rd and Shimen No 1 Rd.

Bus 941 (¥6, 5.30am to 11pm) Links Hóngqiáo International Airport with the main Shànghǎi Railway Station.

Bus 938 (¥7, 6am to midnight) Runs to Yángjiādù in Pǔdōng via Hongxu Rd, North Caoxi Rd and South Xizang Rd.

Bus 806 (¥5, 6am to 11pm) Runs to Lùpǔ Bridge in the south of Pǔxī.

TAXI
Taxi queues can be long from terminal 1; it can be quicker to take the metro or the bus. Avoid taxi sharks.

Train

China's rail service is gargantuan, excellent and more than a little mind-boggling. Colossal investment over recent years has pumped up the high-speed network. The rail network today totals more than 100,000km in length, including 11,000km of high-speed rail. The only 'international' train to arrive in Shànghǎi is the T99 from Kowloon in Hong Kong. Train is, however, an excellent way to arrive in Shànghǎi from other parts of China. You can also take a train from Shànghǎi to Lhasa, Tibet (when Tibet is accessible).

➠ Trains are generally highly punctual and are usually a safe way to travel.

➠ Train stations are often conveniently close to the centre of town.

➠ Travelling in sleeper berths at night often means you can arrive at your destination first thing in the morning, saving a night's hotel accommodation.

Railway Stations

The new and sophisticated **Shànghǎi Hóngqiáo Railway Station** (上海虹桥站; Shànghǎi Hóngqiáo Zhàn) is Asia's largest train station. It is located at the western end of metro line 10 and on line 2, near Hóngqiáo International Airport. It's the terminus for the high-speed G-class trains and other trains and includes services to Běijīng (¥555, very regular), Hángzhōu (¥78, very regular), Nánjīng South (¥140, frequent) and Sūzhōu (¥40, regular).

The vast, hectic and sprawling **Shànghǎi Railway Station** (上海火车站; Shànghǎi Huǒchē Zhàn; Map p309; ☑6317 9090; 385 Meiyuan Rd), located in the north of town, is easily reached by metro lines 1, 4 and 3 and has G-class, D-class and express trains to Běijīng (¥311, three daily), Hángzhōu (¥93, four daily), Hong Kong (¥226, 6.20pm), Huángshān (¥94, two daily), Nánjīng (¥140, frequent), Sūzhōu (¥40, frequent) and Xī'ān (¥182, 10 daily).

Modern **Shànghǎi South Railway Station** (上海南站; Shànghǎi Nánzhàn; ☑9510 5123; 200 Zhaofeng Rd) is easily accessed on metro lines

1 and 3. It has trains largely to southern and southwestern destinations including Guìlín (¥351, four daily) and Hángzhōu (¥29, frequent).

A few trains also leave from the renovated West Station (上海西站; Shànghǎi Xīzhàn), including trains to Nánjīng; however, it's less convenient.

Train Tickets

Although procuring tickets for nearby destinations (such as Sūzhōu and Hángzhōu) and high-speed train tickets is often straightforward, buying rail tickets in Shànghǎi and China can be very troublesome.

➠ Foreigners need their passports when buying a ticket (the number gets printed on your ticket) at all train ticket offices.

➠ Never aim to get a hard-sleeper (or increasingly, soft-sleeper) ticket on the day of travel – plan a few days ahead.

➠ Most tickets can be booked in advance between two and 18 days (and sometimes longer) prior to your intended date of departure.

➠ Automated ticket machines at Shànghǎi Railway Station and other train stations require Chinese ID and your passport will not work; you will need to queue at the ticket window.

➠ You can use C**Trip** (☑400 619 9999; http://english.ctrip. com), **China Highlights** (www. chinahighlights.com) and **China DIY Travel** (www.china-diy-travel.com) to buy tickets online.

➠ Prepare to queue for a long time at the train station.

➠ Ticket purchases at stations and ticket offices can only be made in cash.

➠ Tickets for travel around Chinese New Year and during the 1 May and 1 October holiday periods can be very hard to find, and prices increase on some routes.

➠ Tickets on many routes (such as to Lhasa, Tibet) can be very

hard to find in July and August so prepare to fly instead.

➠ Try to use the small train ticket offices dotted around town or get your hotel to book you a ticket.

➠ Avoid black-market tickets – your passport number must be on the ticket.

➠ There are no refunds for lost train tickets, so hold on to them tightly.

➠ You can get refunds on tickets before your train departs, but will be charged between 5% and 20% depending on how late you leave it till you return your ticket. There is a ticket returns window at most train stations.

Classes

The most comfortable way to get to destinations around Shànghǎi (such as Sūzhōu and Hángzhōu) is by high-speed train, which assures you a comfortable seat and regular and punctual departures.

On swish high-speed G-class, D-class and C-class trains seating classes are straightforward:

➠ 1st class (一等; yīděng)
➠ 2nd class (二等; è rděng)
➠ Business class (商务座; shāngwù zuò)
➠ VIP class (特等座; tèděng zuò)

For most other slower (T-class, K-class, some Z-class and other) Chinese trains, you have the following choice of ticket types:

➠ Hard seat (硬座; yìngzuò)
➠ Hard sleeper (硬卧; yìngwò)
➠ Soft seat (软座; ruǎnzuò)
➠ Soft sleeper (软卧; ruǎnwò)

On non-high-speed trains, numbered soft seats are more comfortable than hard seats. Hard-seat class is not available on the high-speed C-, D- and G-class trains, and is only found on T- and

K-class trains, and trains without a number prefix; a handful of Z-class trains have hard seats. Hard-seat class generally has padded seats, but it's often unclean and noisy, and painful on the long haul. Since hard seat is the only class most locals can afford, it's packed to the gills.

For overnight trips to further destinations, hard sleepers are easily comfortable enough, with only a fixed number of people allowed in the sleeper carriage. They serve very well as an overnight hotel.

The hard-sleeper carriage consists of doorless compartments with half-a-dozen bunks in three tiers and foldaway seats by the windows. Sheets, pillows and blankets are provided. Carriages are nonsmoking, although smokers congregate between carriages. Competition for hard sleepers is keen, so reserve early. Prices vary according to which berth you get: upper (cheapest), middle or lower berth.

Soft sleepers cost twice the price of hard sleepers, and come with four comfortable bunks in a closed, carpeted compartment.

Buying Tickets

There are several options for getting hold of train tickets in Shànghǎi. You can queue at the ticket offices (售票厅; *shòupiàotīng*) at train stations, but brace for a long wait. There are two ticket halls at the Shànghǎi Railway Station, one in the main building (same-day tickets) and another on the east side of the square (advance tickets). One counter should have English-speaking staff.

Your hotel will be able to obtain a ticket for you; however, a surcharge may be levied.

Tickets can be purchased for a small surcharge from travel agencies. You can also book tickets online using **CTrip** (☑400 619 9999; http://english.ctrip.com), which will then be delivered to your address in China, but your cannot buy e-tickets, print them out or collect them. **China Highlights** (www.chinahighlights.com) offers a similar service, but can also deliver e-tickets by email.

Hard-seat and hardsleeper train tickets can be purchased for a small ¥5 commission from train ticket offices (火车票预售处; *huǒchēpiào yùshòuchù*), which are normally open between around 8am and 5pm or 6pm, sometimes with a break for lunch.

Train information is available over the phone in Chinese only (☑800 820 7890).

Bund Train Ticket Office (Map p296; 384 Middle Jiangxi Rd; 江西中路384号; ☺8am-8pm) Central train ticket office, not far from the Bund.

French Concession West Train Ticket Office (Map p306; 12 Dongping Rd; ☺8am-noon & 1-6pm Mon-Fri, 9am-noon & 1-5.30pm Sat & Sun) Handy ticket office located in the west of the French Concession.

Hengfeng Rd Train Ticket Office (Map p309; 822 Hengfeng Rd; 恒丰路; ☺8am-7pm) If you can't handle the queues at Shànghǎi Railway Station, this small office under the bridge a short walk west is very useful.

Jìng'ān Train Ticket Office (Map p310; 77 Wanhangdu Rd; 万航渡路77号; ☺8am-5pm) Useful train ticket office, located to the west of Jing'ān Temple.

Lùjiāzuǐ Train Ticket Office (1396 Lujiazui Ring Rd; 陆家嘴环路1396号; ☺8am-7pm) Handy train ticket office, situated at the heart of Lùjiāzuǐ, not far from the Oriental Pearl TV Tower.

Online Timetables & Useful Websites

China DIY Travel (www.china-diy-travel.com)

China Highlights (www.china-highlights.com)

CTrip (☑400 619 9999; http://english.ctrip.com)

Seat 61 (www.seat61.com/china.htm)

Travel China Guide (www.travelchinaguide.com)

Bus

As trains are fast, regular and efficient, and traffic on roads unpredictable, travelling by bus is not a very useful way to leave or enter Shànghǎi, unless you are visiting local water towns. Buses to Běijīng take between 14 and 16 hours: it is far faster and more comfortable (but more expensive) to take the 5½-hour high-speed G-class trains to the capital, or even the eight-hour D-class trains.

The huge **Shànghǎi South Long-Distance Bus Station** (上海长途客运南站; Shànghǎi Chángtú Kèyùn Nánzhàn; ☑5436 2835; www.ctnz.net; 666 Shilong Rd; Ⓜ Shanghai South Railway Station) serves cities in south China, including Hángzhōu (¥68, regular), Nánjīng (¥105, five daily), Nánxún (¥47, 11 daily, take the bus for Húzhōu – 湖州), Sūzhōu (¥38, regular), Wūzhèn (¥49, 11 daily), Xītáng (¥32, 12 daily) and Zhōuzhuāng (¥25, two daily).

Although it appears close to Shànghǎi Railway Station, the vast **Shànghǎi Long-Distance Bus Station** (上海长途汽车客运总站; Shànghǎi Chángtú Qìchē Kèyùn Zǒngzhàn; Map p309; ☑6605 0000; www.kyzz.com.cn; 1666 Zhongxing Rd; 中兴路1666号; Ⓜ Shanghai Railway Station) is a pain to get to, but has buses to every-where, including very regular buses to Sūzhōu (¥38) and Hángzhōu (¥68), as well as Nánjīng (¥97, 12

SHÀNGHĂI BY BOAT

Shànghăi Port International Cruise Terminal (上海港国际客运中心; Shànghăi Găng Guójì Kèyùn Zhōngxīn; Gaoyang Rd; 高阳路) Located north of the Bund and mostly serves cruise ships. A few international passenger routes serve Shànghăi, with reservations recommended in July and August. Passengers must be at the harbour three hours before departure to get through immigration.

China-Japan International Ferry Company (中日国际轮渡有限公司; Zhōngguó Guójì Lúndù Yǒuxiàn Gōngsī; Map p314; ☑6595 6888, 6325 7642; www.chinajapanferry.com; 18th fl, Jin'an Bldg, 908 Dongdaming Rd, 东大明路908号金岸大厦; tickets from ¥1300, plus ¥150 fuel surcharge) Has staggered departures every week to either Osaka or Kobe (44 hours) in Japan on Saturdays at 12.30pm. Fares range from ¥1300 in an eight-bed dorm to ¥6500 in a deluxe twin cabin.

Shànghăi International Ferry Company (上海国际轮渡; Shànghăi Guójì Lúndù; Map p314; ☑6595 8666; www.shanghai-ferry.co.jp/english/; 15th fl, Jin'an Bldg, 908 Dongdaming Rd; 东大明路908号金岸大厦; tickets from ¥1300, plus ¥150 fuel surcharge) Has departures to Osaka (44 hours) on Tuesdays at 11am. Fares range from ¥1300 in an eight-bed dorm to ¥6500 in a deluxe twin cabin.

daily), Zhōuzhuāng (¥25, six daily) and Běijīng (¥354, 4pm). It's easiest to catch a cab here.

Regular buses also depart for Hángzhōu (¥100, two hours) and Sūzhōu (¥84, two hours) from Pǔdōng International Airport. Buses for Hángzhōu, Sūzhōu and a host of destinations also leave from the **Hóngqiáo Long-Distance Bus Station** (长途客运虹桥站; Chángtú Kèyùn Hóngqiáozhàn) at Hóngqiáo Airport Terminal 2.

From the **Shànghăi Sightseeing Bus Centre** (上海旅游集散中心; Shànghăi Lǚyóu Jísàn Zhōngxīn; Map p316) at Shànghăi Stadium, you can join tours to Sūzhōu, Hángzhōu, Tónglǐ, Zhōuzhuāng, Zhūjiājiǎo and other destinations around Shànghăi.

GETTING AROUND SHÀNGHĂI

The best way to get around town is by taxi or metro. The rapidly expanding metro and light railway system works like a dream; it's fast, efficient and inexpensive. Rush hour on the metro operates at overcapacity, however, and you get to savour the full meaning of the big squeeze. Taxis are ubiquitous and cheap, but flagging one down during rush hour or during a rainstorm requires staying power of a high order.

With a wide-ranging web of routes, buses may sound tempting, but that's before you try to decipher routes and stops or attempt to squeeze aboard during the crush hour. Buses also have to contend with the increasing solidity of Shànghăi's traffic, which can slow movement to an agonising crawl.

Bicycles are good for small neighbourhoods but distances are too colossal for effective transport about town. Walking around Shànghăi is only really possible within neighbourhoods, and even then the distances can be epic and tiring.

Bicycle

If you can handle the fumes and menace of Shànghăi's intimidating traffic, cycling is a good way to get around town, but you will need to link it in with public transport.

➡ Bikes are banned from some major roads, so cyclists often surge down the pavements (sidewalks) of busy streets.

➡ Cars will give you little room; if you're new to Shànghăi, allow a few days to adjust.

➡ Make sure that you have your own bicycle cable lock and try to leave your bike at bike parks (available at most shopping areas and subway stations for ¥0.50): an attendant will keep an eye on your wheels.

➡ Cyclists never use lights at night and Chinese pedestrians favour dark clothing, so ride carefully.

Several hostels around town, including **Le Tour Traveler's Rest** (乐途静安国际青年旅舍; Lètú Jìng'ān Guójì Qīngnián Lǚshè; Map p310; ☑6267 1912; www.letourshanghai.com; 319 Jiaozhou Rd; 胶州路319号; dm ¥70, d ¥260-280, tr/q ¥360/360; ❋ @ ☏; ⓂChangping Rd), can rent you a bike. You can buy a trashy mountain bike for as little as ¥250 to ¥300 at supermarkets and hypermarkets such as Carrefour.

Purchased bikes need to be taxed, with a disc (available at bike shops) displayed. **Factory Five** (Map p306; http://wearefactoryfive.com; 876 Jiangsu Rd; 江苏路876号; ⏱ 10.30am-9pm Tue-Fri, 1-7pm Sat-Sun; ⓂJiangsu Rd) sells beautiful custom bikes and **Giant** (捷安特; Jiéāntè; Map p316; ☑6426 5119; 666 Tianyaoqiao Rd; ◷9am-8pm) is one of China's largest chains for most of your biking needs. **BOHDI** (☑5266 9013; www. bohdi.com.cn; tours ¥220) and **SISU** (☑5059 6071; www.sisucycling.com; tours ¥150) also sell and rent quality bikes.

The city has a public bike-hire scheme called Forever Public Bike Hire Scheme (bikes per hour ¥4), launched for the World Expo in 2010. It's far more limited than the fantastic system in Hángzhōu (the world's largest) and has not proved a success, especially for visitors due to registration difficulties, a lack of docking stations in tourist areas and a Chinese-language-only website.

To register for a card (¥300 deposit and ¥100 credit), you will need to take your passport to the **Xújiāhuì Tourist Information Center** (徐家汇旅游咨询中心; Xújiāhuì Lǚyóu Zīxún Zhōngxīn; Map p316; 1068 Zhaojiabang Rd; 肇嘉浜路1068号; ◷9.30am-4.30pm) or the **Wukang Road Tourist Information Center** (武康路旅游咨询中心; Wǔkāng Lù Lǚyóu Zīxún Zhōngxīn; Map p306; 393 Wukang Rd; 武康路393号; ◷9am-5pm; Ⓜ Shanghai Library).

Boat

Ferries cross the Huángpǔ River between Pǔxī on the west bank and Pǔdōng on the east. Most useful is the **Jinling Rd Ferry** (☑6326 2135; 127 East Zhongshan No 2 Rd; 中山东二路127号; one way ¥2), which operates between the southern end of the Bund and Dongchang Rd in Pǔdōng, running every 15 minutes from 7am to 10pm. Tickets are sold at the kiosks out front. The **Fuxing Road Ferry** (复兴路轮渡站; Fùxīng Lù Lúndùzhàn; Map p300; one way ¥2)runs from Fuxing Rd north of the Cool Docks in the South Bund to Dongchang Rd. Ferries run every 10 to 20 minutes from 5am to 11pm.

Bus

Although sightseeing buses can be extremely handy, the huge Shànghǎi public bus system is unfortunately very hard for non-Chinese-speaking or -reading foreigners to use. Bus-stop signs and routes are in Chinese only. Drivers and conductors speak little, if any, English, although onboard announcements in English will alert you to when to get off. The conductor will tell you when your stop is arriving, if you ask. Bus stops are widely spaced and your bus can race past your destination and on to the next stop up to a kilometre away. Suburban and long-distance buses don't carry numbers – the destination is in characters.

➡ Air-con buses (with a snowflake motif and the characters 空调 alongside the bus number) cost ¥2 to ¥3. The far rarer buses without air-con cost ¥1.5.

➡ For buses without conductors, drop your cash into the slot by the driver. Always carry exact money; no change given.

➡ The swipe-able Transport Card works on many but not all bus routes.

➡ Try to get on at the terminus (thus guaranteeing yourself a seat), avoid rush hours, and stick to a few tried-and-tested routes.

➡ If you can't speak Chinese, have your destination written down in Chinese to show the driver, conductor or even a fellow passenger.

➡ Be alert to pickpockets, especially during the rush-hour squeeze.

➡ Buses generally operate from 5am to 11pm, except for 300-series buses, which operate all night.

➡ For English-language bus routes in town, go to http://msittig.wubi.org/bus.

SIGHTSEEING BUSES

City Sightseeing Buses (都市观光; Dūshì Guānguāng; ☑40082 06222; www.springtour.com; tickets ¥30; ◷9am-8.30pm summer, to 6pm winter) Tickets for the hop-on, hop-off, open-top buses last 24 hours. Besides enabling you to tour Shànghǎi's highlights, they're a great way to get around the centre of town and Pǔdōng. A recorded commentary runs in eight languages; just plug in your earphones (supplied). Buses have stops across central Shànghǎi, including the Bund, the Old Town and People's Sq.

Big Bus Tours (上海观光车; Shànghǎi Guānguāngchē; ☑6351 5988; www.bigbustours.com; adult/child US$48/32) Operates hop-on, hop-off services, lassoing the sights along 22 stops across two routes. Tickets are valid for 48 hours and include a 90-minute boat tour of the Huángpǔ River, entry to the Jade Buddha Temple and admission to the 88th-floor observation tower of Jinmao Tower.

Car

It is possible to hire a car in Shànghǎi, but the bureaucratic hurdles are designed to deter would-be foreign drivers – you can't simply pick up a car at Pǔdōng International Airport and hit the road. You will need a temporary or long-term Chinese driving licence.

If your visa is for less than 90 days, **Hertz** (☑6085 1900; www.hertzchina.com) or **Avis** (☑6229 1118; www.avischina.com) can help you apply for a temporary Chinese driving licence, but this takes up to a week to arrange and includes a physical exam.

If your visa exceeds 90 days, you can apply for a long-term Chinese driving licence, but this takes up to a month to arrange and includes a theory text plus medical exam.

Residents can apply for a Chinese licence at their local Public Security Bureau (PSB; 公安局; Gōng'ānjú) or the Shànghǎi Transport Bureau (www.jt.sh.cn).

For most visitors, it is more advisable to hire a car and a driver. A Volkswagen Santana with driver and petrol starts at around ¥600 per day; it is likely to be cheaper to hire a taxi for the day. Ask for more information at your hotel.

Metro

The **Shànghǎi metro** (上海地铁; Shànghǎi Dìtiě; www.shmetro.com) is fast, cheap, clean and easy, though hard to get a seat at the best of times (unless you get on at the terminus). The rush hour sees carriages filled to overcapacity, but trains are frequent and the system has been rapidly expanded to envelop more and more of the city.

➡ There are 14 lines serving more than 300 stations with an extra 175km planned to be added to the network by 2015.

➡ Metro maps are available at most stations. The free tourist maps also have a small metro map printed on them, and there's an English section on the metro website.

➡ Metro station exits can be confusing, so look for a street map (usually easy to find) in the ticket hall before exiting to get your bearings.

➡ To find a metro station look for the red M.

➡ The *Explore Shanghai* app helps you calculate how long your journey will take, how much it will cost and where the nearest metro station is.

Key Metro Lines

The most useful lines for travellers are 1, 2 and 10. Lines 1 and 2 connect at People's Sq interchange, the city's busiest station. TV screens at stations count down the wait to the next train.

Line 1 (一号线; yīhào xiàn) Runs from Fujin Rd in the north, through Shànghǎi Railway Station and People's Sq, along Middle Huaihai Rd, through Xújiāhuì and Shànghǎi South Railway Station to Xīnzhuāng in the southern suburbs.

Line 2 (二号线; èrhào xiàn) Runs from East Xujing in the west via Hóngqiáo Railway Station and Hóngqiáo International Airport terminal 2 to Pǔdōng International Airport in the east, passing through Jìng'ān, People's Sq, East Nanjing Rd (and the Bund district) in the centre of town, going under the Huángpǔ River and on to Longyang Rd, the site of the Maglev terminus, before terminating at Pǔdōng International Airport.

Line 10 (十号线; shíhào xiàn) Runs from Hóngqiáo Railway Station in the west through Hóngqiáo International Airport terminal 2 and terminal 1 before zipping through the French Concession, the Old Town, the Bund area and Hóngkǒu before terminating at Xinjiangwancheng.

Fares & Tickets

➡ Tickets range from ¥3 to ¥15, depending on the distance.

➡ Tickets are generally only sold from coin- and note-operated machines.

➡ Service counters will provide you with change if your bills are not accepted.

➡ Keep your ticket until you exit.

➡ When entering the metro, swipe your card across the turnstile sensor for access; when exiting, enter it into the slot, where it will be retained.

➡ The rechargeable Transport Card can be used on the metro, some buses, ferries and all taxis.

➡ One-day (¥18) and three-day travel passes (¥45) for use on the metro are available from service counters in stations.

➡ There can be huge distances between different lines at interchange stations, such as between line 9 and 1 at Xújiāhuì station, so factor this into you journey time.

➡ A growing number of stations have coin-operated toilets.

Operating Hours

There's one main shortcoming to the metro system: it stops running relatively early in the night. Most lines begin their final run between 10pm and 10.30pm (some earlier), so anyone out later than 11pm will need to catch a cab home.

Taxi

Shànghǎi has around 45,000 taxis. Most are Volkswagen Santanas, some are Volkswagen Passats; there's a fleet of Mercedes-Benz taxis and a 4000-strong fleet of spacious and comfortable white Volkswagen Touran taxis. Shànghǎi's taxis are reasonably cheap, hassle-free and generally easy to flag down except during rush hour and in summer storms.

TRANSPORT CARDS & TOURIST PASSES

If you are making more than a fleeting trip to Shànghǎi, it's worth getting a Transport Card (交通卡; Jiāotōng Kǎ) . Available at metro stations and some convenience stores, cards can be topped up with credit and used on the metro, some buses and ferries, and also in taxis. Credit is electronically deducted from the card as you swipe it over the sensor, equipped at metro turnstiles and near the door on buses; when paying your taxi fare, hand it to the taxi driver, who will swipe it. Cards don't save you money, but will save you from queuing for tickets or hunting for change. A refundable deposit of ¥20 is required. Other handy cards include a one-day tourist pass (¥18), which offers unlimited travel on the metro for one day, and the three-day travel pass (¥45), also for use on the metro system. Both passes are available at metro stations.

➡ Drivers can be inept at navigating, even to obvious places. Some stick to main roads and have little grasp of shortcuts. Avoid total novices by examining the number of stars below the driver's photo on the dashboard; stars range from one to five in order of expertise (and English-language skills).

➡ Taxi drivers (mostly male) are mostly honest, but you should always go by the meter. The driver should push the meter down to start it when you get in the cab.

➡ Taxis may not have rear seatbelts, in which case sit up front.

➡ Taxis can't take the tunnel to Lùjiāzuǐ in Pǔdōng from 8am to 9.30am and 5pm to 6.30pm.

➡ Fares are metered. Flag fall is ¥14 for the first 3km, and ¥2.4 per kilometre thereafter; there is no need to tip. A ¥1 fuel surcharge is included in the price.

➡ A night rate operates from 11pm to 5am, when the flag fall is ¥18, then ¥3.10 per kilometre.

➡ Pay by cash (xiànjīn) or use a Transport Card.

➡ At night you can tell if a taxi is empty by the red 'for hire' sign on the dashboard of the passenger side.

➡ Ask for a printed receipt, which gives the fare and the driver and car number, the distance travelled, waiting time and the number to call if there are any problems or if you left something in the taxi.

➡ If you don't speak Chinese, take a Chinese-character map, have your destination written down in characters or pack your destination's business card. Alternatively, download the handy Shanghai Taxi Guide and Offline Maps app to show your driver your destination.

➡ Use your mobile to phone your local contact (or the 24-hour tourist hotline – ☑962 288) in Shànghǎi and ask him or her to give instructions to the driver.

➡ It also helps if you have your own directions and sit in the front with a map, looking knowledgeable (to deter circuitous, looping detours).

➡ Shànghǎi's main taxi companies include turquoise-coloured Dàzhòng (大众; ☑96822), gold Qiángshēng (强生; ☑6258 0000) and green Bāshì (巴士; ☑96840).

➡ For taxi complaints, phone ☑962 000.

➡ Motorcycle taxis wait at some intersections and metro stations to whisk travellers off to nearby destinations. Most trips cost less than ¥10.

TOURS

Fun and handy bus tours of Shànghǎi that cover the top sights of Pǔxī and Pǔdōng include **City Sightseeing Buses** (都市观光; Dūshì Guānguāng; ☑40082 06222; www.springtour.com; tickets ¥30; ⊙9am-8.30pm summer, to 6pm winter) and **Big Bus Tours** (上海观光车; Shànghǎi Guānguāngchē; ☑6351 5988; www.bigbustours.com; adult/child US$48/32). Other intriguing tours include:

BOHDI (☑5266 9013; www.bohdi.com.cn; tours ¥220) Night-time cycling tours on Tuesdays from March to November and trips around the region.

China Cycle Tours (☑1376 111 5050; www.chinacycletours.com; half-day tours from ¥400) City and rural tours in Shànghǎi and Sūzhōu.

Insiders Experience (☑138 1761 6975; www.insidersexperience.com; from ¥800) Fun motorcycle-sidecar tours of the city for up to two passengers, setting off from the Andaz in Xīntiāndì (but can pick up from anywhere, at extra cost).

Newman Tours (新漫; Xīnmàn; ☑138 1777 0229; www.newmantours.com; from ¥190) Bund tour, gangster tour, ancient Shànghǎi tour, ghost tour and a host of other informative and fun walking jaunts around the city. Also covers Hángzhōu and Sūzhōu.

SISU (☑5059 6071; www.sisucycling.com; tours ¥150) Night-time cycling tours on Wednesdays and trips out of town.

Directory A–Z

Business Travellers

Business Cards

Business name cards are absolutely crucial, even if you're not on business. Don't be left high and dry when name cards are being dealt around. Try to get your name translated into (simplified) Chinese and printed on the reverse of the card. Chinese pay particular attention to the quality of business cards, so aim for a good finish. When proffering and receiving business cards, emulate the Chinese method of respectfully using the thumb and forefinger of both hands. Buying a name-card wallet is also recommended.

Useful Organisations

If you're in town on business or looking for commercial opportunities, Shànghǎi has commercial offices that should be able to assist.

American Chamber of Commerce (AmCham; 上海美国商会; Shànghǎi Měiguó Shānghuì; Map p310;☑6279 7119; www.amcham-shanghai. org; Room 568, Shànghǎi Centre, 1376 West Nanjing Rd; 南京西路1376号568室) This office only helps members.

Australian Chamber of Commerce (AustCham Shanghai; 澳大利亚商会; Àodàliyǎ Shànghuì; Map p300;

☑6248 8301; www.austcham-shanghai.com; Suite 1101b, Silver Court, 85 Taoyuan Rd; 桃源路85号永银大厦1101B室)

British Chamber of Commerce (BritCham; 上海英国商会; Shànghǎi Yīngguó Shānghuì; Map p310;☑6218 5022; www.britishchamber-shanghai.org; 5th fl, 863 West Nanjing Rd; 南京西路863号5楼) Inside the Marks & Spencer building.

China Britain Business Council (英中贸易协会; Yīngzhōng Màoyì Xiéhuì; Map p310;☑6218 5183; www.cbbc. org; Room 1701-1702, Westgate Tower, 1038 West Nanjing Rd; 南京西路1038号1701-1702室)

European Union Chamber of Commerce in China (中国欧盟商会; Zhōngguó Ōuméng Shānghuì; Map p302;☑6385 2023; www. euccc.com.cn; Room 2204, Shui On Plaza, 333 Middle Huaihai Rd; 淮海中路333号2204室)

US Commercial Center (Map p310;☑6279 7640; Room 631, Shànghǎi Centre, 1376 West Nanjing Rd; 南京西路1376号631室) The overseas office of the US Department of Commerce; can assist US businesses with finding Chinese business partners.

US-China Business Council (美国贸易全国委员会; Měiguó Màoyì Quánguó

Wěiyuánhuì; Map p310;☑6288 3840; www.uschina.org; Room 1301, 1701 West Beijing Rd; 北京西路1701号1301室)

Business Hours

Businesses in China close for the week-long Chinese New Year (usually in February) and National Day (beginning 1 October). Our reviews don't list business hours unless they differ significantly from standard hours.

Bank of China (中国银行; Zhōngguó Yínháng) Branches usually open weekdays from 9.30am to 11.30am and 1.30pm to 4.30pm. Some branches also open Saturdays and Sundays. Most Bank of China branches have 24-hour ATMs.

Bars Some open in the morning; otherwise, hours are from around 5pm to 2am.

China Post (中国邮政; Zhōngguó Yóuzhèng) Most major China Post offices open daily from 8.30am to 6pm, and sometimes until 10pm. Local branches of China Post close at weekends.

Museums Most open on weekends; a few close on Mondays. Ticket sales usually stop 30 minutes before closing.

Offices and government departments Generally open

Monday to Friday from 9am to noon and 2pm to 4.30pm.

Restaurants Most open from 11am to 10pm or later; some open from 10am to 2.30pm, with an afternoon break before opening again from 5pm to 11pm or later.

Shops Malls and department stores generally open from 10am to 10pm.

Cultural Centres

The following are useful places to keep you culturally connected to your home country and to fellow expats. They are also a good place to meet internationally minded Shanghainese.

Alliance Française (上海法语培训中心; Shànghǎi Fǎyú Péixùn Zhōngxīn; ✓6357 5388; www.afshanghai.org; 5th & 6th fl, 297 Wusong Rd; 吴淞路297号5; ☺8.30am-8.30pm Mon-Thu, to 7pm Fri, to 6.30pm Sat, to 5pm Sun) On hand is a large French library with magazines, newspapers, DVDs and music CDs; exhibitions, music concerts and literary events are also held here. The centre offers French- and Chinese-language courses. There is a branch (✓6226 4005; 2nd fl, 155 Wuyi Rd; ☺8.30am-8.30pm Mon-Thu, to 5pm Fri, to 6pm Sat, to 4pm Sun) in the west of town and another branch (✓6782 7961; 20-22, Lane 58, Longteng Rd; ☺11am-6.30pm Mon-Fri, 9am-6.30pm Sat & Sun) in Sōngjiāng.

British Council (英国文化教育处; Yīngguó Wénhuà Jiàoyù Chù; Map p306; ✓6192 2626; Cultural & Education Section of the British Consulate-General, Unit 18-19, 20th fl The Center, 989 Changle Rd; 长乐路989号; Ⓜ Changshu Rd) Of interest mainly to Chinese wishing to study in the UK, but also supports

arts and cultural programs in China. Phone ahead as the office does not offer drop-in access.

Goethe Institute (歌德学院; Gēdé Xuéyuàn; Map p296; ✓6391 2068; www.goethe.de/china; Room 102a, Cross Tower, 318 Fuzhou Rd; 福州路318号102A室) Has a useful library, film screenings, internet access and German courses.

US Consulate Bureau of Public Affairs (Map p310; ✓6279 7662; Room 532, Shànghǎi Centre, 1376 West Nanjing Rd; 南京西路1376号532室) Has a reading room with American newspapers and periodicals.

Customs Regulations

Chinese customs generally pay tourists little attention. There are clearly marked green channels and red channels. Importation of fresh fruit or cold cuts is prohibited. Pirated DVDs and CDs are illegal exports from China as well as illegal imports into most other countries. If they are found they will be confiscated.

Objects considered to be antiques require a certificate and a red seal to clear customs when leaving China. Anything made before 1949 is considered an antique, and if it was made before 1795 it cannot legally be taken out of the country.

Duty-free allowances:

➡ 400 cigarettes (or 100 cigars or 500g of tobacco)

➡ 1.5L of alcoholic beverages

➡ 50g of gold or silver

➡ ¥20,000 in Chinese currency; there are no restrictions on foreign currency but declare any cash that exceeds US$5,000 or its equivalent in another currency.

Electricity

220V/50Hz

220V/50Hz

Embassies & Consulates

Most consulates defer to their embassies in Běijīng. Most consulates have efficient websites with useful information, such as doing business in Shànghǎi, cultural relations, events and downloadable maps of town.

If you are planning a trip to Southeast Asia, you'll have to go to Běijīng or Hong Kong for a visa for Vietnam, Laos or Myanmar (Burma). There is a Vietnamese consulate in Kūnmíng (in Yúnnán province), as well as Thai, Lao and Myanmar (Burmese) consulates in Kūnmíng.

Australian Consulate
(澳大利亚领事馆; Àodàliyà Lǐngshìguǎn; Map p310; ☑021-2215 5200; www.shanghai.china.embassy.gov.au; 22nd fl, CITIC Sq, 1168 West Nanjing Rd; 南京西路1168号22楼; ⊙8.30am-5pm Mon-Fri)

Canadian Consulate
(加拿大领事馆; Jiānádà Lǐngshìguǎn; Map p310; ☑021-3279 2800; www.shanghai.gc.ca; 8th fl, 1788 West Nanjing Rd; 南京西路1788号8楼; ⊙8.30am-noon & 1-5pm)

French Consulate (法国领事馆; Fǎguó Lǐngshìguǎn; Map p318; ☑021-6010 6300; www.consulfrance-shanghai.org; 8th fl, Bldg A, Soho Zhongshan Plaza, 1055 West Zhongshan Rd; 中山西路1055号中山广场A座18楼; ⊙8.15am-12.15pm Mon, 8.45am-12.15pm Tue-Fri)

German Consulate
(德国领事馆; Déguó Lǐngshìguǎn; Map p306; ☑021-3401 0106; www.shanghai.diplo.de; 181 Yongfu Rd; 永福路181号)

Irish Consulate (爱尔兰领事馆; Ài'ěrlán Lǐngshìguǎn; Map p310; ☑021-6010 1360; www.embassyofireland.cn; 700a Shànghǎi Centre, 1376 West Nanjing Rd; 南京西路1376号700a室; ⊙9.30am-12.30pm & 2-5.30pm)

Japanese Consulate
(日本领事馆; Rìběn

PRACTICALITIES

Magazines

Stacked up in bars, restaurants and cafes, free expat entertainment and listings magazines cover all bases:

➡ **City Weekend** (www.cityweekend.com.cn/shanghai) Glossy bimonthly.

➡ **That's Shanghai** (http://online.thatsmags.com/city/shanghai) Info-packed monthly.

➡ **Time Out Shanghai** (www.timeoutshanghai.com) Well-written and authoritative monthly.

Newspapers

Imported English-language newspapers can be bought from five-star-hotel bookshops or read online. The Shànghǎi-published English-language newspaper the *Shanghai Daily* (www.shanghaidaily.com) is a better read than the insipid national *China Daily* (www.chinadaily.com.cn), but is nevertheless censored.

Radio

Websites can be jammed but it's possible to listen to the following:

➡ **BBC World Service** (www.bbc.co.uk/worldserviceradio/on-air)

➡ **Voice of America** (www.voa.gov)

Smoking

From 2010, antismoking legislation in Shànghǎi demanded that a number of public venues (including hospitals, schools, bars and restaurants) are required to have designated nonsmoking areas and install signs prohibiting smoking.

TV

Your hotel may have ESPN, Star Sports, CNN or BBC News 24. You can also tune into the (censored) English-language channel CCTV9 (Chinese Central TV).

Weights & Measures

China officially subscribes to the international metric system, but you will encounter the ancient Chinese weights and measures system in markets. The system features the *liǎng* (tael, 50g) and the *jīn* (catty, 0.5kg). There are 10 *liǎng* to the *jīn*.

Língshǐguǎn; Map p318;☏021-5257 4766; www.shanghai.cn.emb-japan.go.jp; 8 Wanshan Rd; 万山路8号; ⊙9am-12.30pm & 1.30-5.30pm Mon-Fri)

Netherlands Consulate
(荷兰领事馆; Hélán Língshǐguǎn; Map p318;☏021-2208 7288; www.holland-inchina.org; 10th fl, Tower B, Dawning Center, 500 Hongbaoshi Rd; 红宝石路500号东银中心东塔10楼; ⊙9am-noon & 1-5.30pm Mon-Fri)

New Zealand Consulate
(新西兰领事馆; Xīnxīlán Língshǐguǎn; Map p306;☏021-5407 5858; www.nzembassy.com; Room 1605-1607A, 16th fl, The Centre, 989 Changle Rd; 长乐路989号1605-1607A室; ⊙8.30am-5pm Mon-Fri)

Russian Consulate (俄罗斯领事馆; Èluósī Língshǐguǎn; Map p314;☏021-6324 2682; www.rusconshanghai.org.cn; 20 Huangpu Rd; 黄浦路20号; ⊙9.30am-noon Mon, Wed & Fri)

Singapore Consulate
(新加坡领事馆; Xīnjiāpō Língshǐguǎn; Map p318;☏021-6278 5566; www.mfa.gov.sg/shanghai; 89 Wanshan Rd; 万山路89号; ⊙8.30am-noon & 1-5pm)

Thai Consulate (泰王国领事馆; Tàiwángguó Língshǐguǎn; Map p310;☏021-6288 3010; www.thaishanghai.com; 15th fl, 567 Weihai Rd; 威海路567号15楼; ⊙visa office 9.30-11.30am Mon-Fri)

UK Consulate (英国领事馆; Yīngguó Língshǐguǎn; Map p310;☏021-3279 2000; http://ukinchina.fco.gov.uk; Room 319, 3rd fl, Shànghǎi Centre, 1376 West Nanjing Rd; 南京西路1376号301室; ⊙8.30am-5.30pm Mon-Fri)

US Consulate (美国领事馆; Měiguó Língshǐguǎn; Map p306;☏021-6279 7662; http://shanghai.usembassy-china.org.

cn; 1469 Middle Huaihai Rd; 淮海中路1469号乌鲁木齐路) Consulate-general.

US Consulate (美国领事馆; Měiguó Língshǐguǎn; Map p310; ☏after-hour emergency for US citizens 021-3217 4650; http://shanghai.usembassy-china.org.cn; 8th fl, Westgate Tower, 1038 West Nanjing Rd; 南京西路1038号8楼; ⊙8.15-11.30am & 1.30-3.30pm Mon-Fri) US citizen services and visas.

Emergency
Ambulance (☏120)
Fire (☏119)
Police (☏110)

Gay & Lesbian Travellers

Local law is ambiguous on this issue; generally the authorities take a dim view of gays and lesbians but there's an increasingly confident scene, as evinced by gay bars and the annual event-stuffed Shanghai Pride (www.shpride.com), now five years old. Shànghǎi heterosexuals are not, by and large, particularly homophobic, especially among the under-40s.Young Chinese men sometimes hold hands; this carries no sexual overtones.

For up-to-date information on the latest gay and lesbian hot spots in Shànghǎi and elsewhere throughout China, try Utopia (www.utopia-asia.com/chinshan.htm). For further tips, check out Travel Gay Asia (www.travelgayasia.com).

Health

Health concerns for travellers to Shànghǎi include worsening atmospheric pollution (the city's pollution index has ranged up to 31 times the levels recommended by international

health officials), traveller's diarrhoea and winter influenza. You can find a more than adequate standard of medical care in town, providing you have good travel insurance.

If you have arrived from South America or Central Africa you are required to show proof of a yellow-fever vaccination within the last 10 years.

It's a good idea to consult your own government's official travel-health website before departure.

Australia (www.dfat.gov.au/travel)

Canada (www.travelhealth.gc.ca)

New Zealand (www.mfat.govt.nz/travel)

UK (www.gov.uk/foreign-travel-advice/china) Search for travel in the site index.

USA (www.cdc.gov/travel)

Recommended Vaccinations

You should see your doctor at least three months before your trip in order to get your vaccinations in time. The following immunisations are recommended for Shànghǎi.

Diphtheria and tetanus (DT) Booster of 0.5ml every 10 years. It will cause a sore arm and redness at the injection site.

Hepatitis A & B (combined in Twinrix) The dose is 1ml at day one, day 30 and six months. Minimal soreness at injection site. You are not immune until after the final shot. If you don't have time for the six-month booster you will be fully immune for one year for hepatitis A after the second shot and have some immunity for hepatitis B. You may be able to get the third shot at an international medical clinic while travelling.

Influenza Dose of 0.5ml is recommended if you are trav-

SMARTPHONE & TABLET APPS

Handy Android and iPhone Apps for Shànghǎi for your smartphone or tablet include the following:

Air Quality China Check the China Air Quality Index for major cities in China, including Shànghǎi. Free.

City Weekend The app with an ever-updated database of Shànghǎi restaurant, bar and club listings. Free.

Pleco (www.pleco.com) Fantastic and resourceful app for making sense of Chinese with OCR (Optical Character Recogniser) function: point your smartphone camera at a Chinese character and it will translate it for you. Also has flashcards, handwriting recogniser and audio pronunciation. Free.

Shanghai Toilet Guide When you need one, pronto. Free.

WeChat Chinese people largely use this app to send voice messages, texts and pictures at no cost. Free.

---

elling in the winter months, and especially if you are over 60 years of age or have a chronic illness. It should not be given if you are allergic to eggs. Immunity lasts for one year.

Japanese encephalitis A series of three shots over one month; only advised if you plan on being in rural areas for longer than a month. Immunity will last for three years. As there is a risk of an allergic reaction to the second and third shots, you must remain close to medical care after you receive these.

Polio Dose of 0.5ml syrup orally every 10 years. There are no side effects.

Typhoid Booster of 0.5ml every three years. Minimal soreness at the injection site. At the time of writing there was a worldwide shortage, so plan ahead.

Do not have any of these immunisations if you are pregnant or breastfeeding. It is possible to have a shot of gamma globulin in pregnancy, which gives short-term (four to five months) protection against hepatitis and other viral infections. It is not a common thing to do because it is derived from blood products.

Common Diseases
HEPATITIS A
This virus is common in Shànghǎi and is transmitted through contaminated water and shellfish. It is most commonly caught at local seafood restaurants. Immunisation is important and will prevent it. If you do get hepatitis A, it means six to eight weeks of illness and future intolerance to alcohol.

HEPATITIS B
While this is common in the Shànghǎi area, it is transmitted only by unprotected sex, sharing needles, treading on a discarded needle or receiving contaminated blood. Always use a condom, never share needles and always protect your feet on commonly visited beaches. Vaccination against hepatitis B before you travel is a wise option as it can be a chronic, debilitating illness.

JAPANESE ENCEPHALITIS
Mosquitoes that feed on birds carry this potentially fatal virus, hence it is limited to rural areas of China, particularly near rice fields. It is most common in summer and autumn. Vaccination is recommended if you are travelling in rural areas for longer than one month.

TRAVELLER'S DIARRHOEA
This is the most common disease that a traveller will encounter throughout Asia. Many different types of organisms, usually bacteria (eg *E. coli*, salmonella), are responsible and the result is sudden diarrhoea and vomiting, or both, with or without fever. It is caught from contaminated food or water.

TYPHOID FEVER
Caused by salmonella bacteria, typhoid fever is common throughout China and is caught from faecally contaminated food, milk and water. It manifests as fever, headache, cough, malaise and constipation or diarrhoea. Treatment is with quinolone antibiotics, and a vaccine is recommended before you travel.

Environmental Hazards
POLLUTION
The air quality in Shànghǎi can be appalling, and can ruin your holiday, especially if you are sensitive to impurities in the air. If you suffer from asthma or other allergies you may anticipate a worsening of your symptoms in Shànghǎi and you may need to increase your medication. Eye drops may be a useful addition to your travel

kit, and contact-lens wearers may have more discomfort here. Check levels before you fly; click on http://aqicn.org/city/shanghai/ for the latest reading

WATER
Don't drink tap water or eat ice. Bottled water is readily available. Boiled water is OK.

Online Resources
There is a wealth of travel-health advice on the internet. Lonelyplanet.com is a good place to start. The WHO publishes a book called *International Travel and Health*, which is revised annually and is available online at www.who.int/publications/en.

Internet Access
The Chinese authorities remain mistrustful of the internet, and censorship is heavy-handed. Around 10% of websites are blocked; sites such as Google may be slow, while social-networking sites such as Facebook and Twitter are blocked (as is YouTube). Newspapers such as the *Guardian* and the *New York Times* are also blocked, as is *Bloomberg*. Users can get around blocked websites by using a VPN (Virtual Private Network) service such as Astrill (www.astrill.com).

Occasionally email providers can go down, so having a back-up email address is advised.

The majority of hostels and hotels have broadband internet access, and many hotels, cafes, restaurants and bars are wi-fi enabled. The wi-fi icon is used in Lonely Planet reviews where it is available. Remember that wi-fi is generally unsecured, so take care what kind of information you enter if you're using a wireless connection.

Internet Cafes
Internet cafe charges start at around ¥3 per hour; the cafes are typically either open 24 hours or from 8am to midnight.

You will need some form of ID to register so take your passport. Some internet cafes in Shànghǎi and surrounding provinces may require Chinese ID to get online, thus barring foreign users (which can leave you stuck if you need to respond to emails), so be prepared for this possibility.

Internet cafes are scarce in touristy areas – it's more convenient to get online at your hotel or at a wi-fi hot spot. If stuck, you can find several internet cafes near Shànghǎi train station; look for the characters *wǎngbā* (网吧).

Legal Matters
China does not officially recognise dual nationality or the foreign citizenship of children born in China if one of the parents is a PRC (People's Republic of China) national. If you have Chinese and another nationality you may, in theory, not be allowed to visit China on your foreign passport. In practice, Chinese authorities are not switched on enough to know if you own two passports, and should accept you on a foreign passport. Dual-nationality citizens who enter China on a Chinese passport are subject to Chinese laws and are legally not allowed consular help. If over 16 years of age, carry your passport with you at all times as a form of ID.

China takes a particularly dim view of opium and all its derivatives; trafficking in more than 50g of heroin can lead to the death penalty. Foreign-passport holders have been executed in China for drug offences.

The Chinese criminal justice system does not ensure a fair trial and defendants are not presumed innocent until proven guilty. China conducts more judicial executions than the rest of the world combined, up to 10,000 per year according to some reports. If arrested, most foreign citizens have the right to contact their embassy.

TCM
Traditional Chinese Medicine (TCM) views the human body as an energy system in which the basic substances of *qì* (气; vital energy), *jīng* (精; essence), *xuè* (血; blood) and *tǐyè* (体液; body fluids, blood and other organic fluids) function. The concept of *yīn* (阴; yin) and *yáng* (阳; yang) is fundamental to the system. Disharmony between yin and yang or within the basic substances may be a result of internal causes (emotions), external causes (climatic conditions) or miscellaneous causes (work, exercise, stress etc). Treatment includes acupuncture, massage, herbs, diet and *qìgōng* (气功), which seeks to bring these elements back into balance. Treatments can be particularly useful for treating chronic diseases and ailments such as fatigue, arthritis, irritable bowel syndrome and some chronic skin conditions.

Be aware that 'natural' does not always mean 'safe'; there can be drug interactions between herbal medicines and Western medicines. If using both systems, ensure you inform both practitioners what the other has prescribed.

Gambling is officially illegal in mainland China.

Distributing religious material is illegal in mainland China.

Medical Services

Medical & Dental Clinics

Shànghǎi is credited with the best medical facilities and most advanced medical knowledge in mainland China. The main foreign embassies keep lists of the English-speaking doctors, dentists and hospitals that accept foreigners.

Arrail Dental (瑞尔齿科; Ruì'ěr Chǐkē; Map p302; 5396 6539; www.arrail-dental.com; 2nd fl, 2 Corporate Ave, 202 Hubin Rd; 湖滨路202号企业天地商业中心2号楼2楼) For all dental work, cosmetic dentistry, dental implants, orthodontics and children's dental care.

Huádōng Hospital (华东医院外宾门诊; Huádōng Yīyuàn Wàibīn Ménzhěn; Map p306; 6248 3180 ext 63208; Foreigners Clinic, 2nd fl, Bldg 3, 221 West Yan'an Rd; 延安西路221号3号楼2层; 24hr emergency) Foreigners' clinic on the 2nd floor of building 3.

Huàshān Hospital (华山医院国际医疗中心; Huàshān Yīyuàn Guójì Yīliáo Zhōngxīn; Map p306; 5288 9998; www.sh-hwmc.com.cn; 12 Middle Wulumuqi Rd; 乌鲁木齐中路12号) Hospital treatment and outpatient consultations are available at the 8th-floor foreigners' clinic, the Huashan Worldwide Medical Center (华山医院国际医疗中心; Huàshān Yīyuàn Guójì Yīliáo Zhōngxīn; 6248 3986; www.sh-hwmc.com.cn; 8am-10pm), and there's 24-hour emergency treatment on the 15th floor in building 6.

International Peace Maternity Hospital (国际妇幼保健院; Guójì Fùyòu Bǎojiànyuàn; Map p316; 6407 0434; 910 Hengshan Rd; 衡山路910号) Specialist hospital providing maternal care and child health care.

Parkway Health (以极佳医疗保健服务; Yǐjíjiā Yīliáo Bǎojiàn Fúwù; 24hr hotline 6445 5999; www.parkwayhealth.cn) Seven locations around town including Hóngqiáo (以极佳医疗保健服务; Yǐjíjiā Yīliáo Bǎojiàn Fúwù; Map p318; Unit 30, Mandarine City, 788 Hongxu Rd; 虹许路788号30室) and Jing'an (以极佳医疗保健服务; Yǐjíjiā Yīliáo Bǎojiàn Fúwù; Map p310; Suite 203, Shànghǎi Centre, 1376 W Nanjing Rd; 南京西路1376号203室). Offers comprehensive private medical care from internationally trained physicians and dentists. Members can access after-hours services and an emergency hotline.

Ruìjīn Hospital (瑞金医院; Ruìjīn Yīyuàn; Map p302; 6437 0045; www.rjh.com.cn/chpage/c1352/; 197 Ruijin No 2 Rd; 瑞金二路197号) Teaching hospital under the Shànghǎi Jiāotōng University School of Medicine.

Shànghǎi United Family Hospital (上海和睦家医院; Shànghǎi Hémùjiā Yīyuàn; 2216 3900, 24hr emergency 2216 3999; http://shanghai.ufh.com.cn; 1139 Xianxia Rd; 仙霞路1139号) This Western-owned and -managed hospital is a complete private hospital, staffed by doctors trained in the West. Medical facilities run to inpatient rooms, operating rooms, an intensive-care unit, birthing suites and a dental clinic.

Pharmacies

The handy Hong Kong store **Watson's** (屈臣氏; Qūchénshì; Map p306; 6474 4775; 787 Middle Huaihai Rd;

淮海中路787号) can be found in the basements of malls all over town (there's a branch in Westgate Mall). It sells imported toiletries and a limited range of simple, over-the-counter pharmaceuticals.

For harder-to-find foreign medicines, try any pharmacy (药房; yàofáng), easily identified by a green cross outside; some have service through the night (via a small window). Nearly all pharmacies stock both Chinese and Western medicines. You may not need a doctor's prescription for some medicines you need a prescription for at home (eg antiobiotics), especially outside Shànghǎi, but check at the pharmacy.

Traditional Chinese Medicine (TCM)

Traditional Chinese medicine (TCM) is extremely popular in Shànghǎi, both for prevention and cure. There are many Chinese medicine shops, but English is not widely spoken. Chiropractic care, reflexology and acupuncture are popular, but check that disposable needles are used.

Body and Soul TCM Clinic (Map p300; 5101 9262; www.tcm-shanghai.com; ste 5, 14th fl, Anji Plaza, 760 S Xizang Rd; 西藏南路760号安基大厦14层5室; 9am-6pm Mon, Wed & Fri, to 8pm Tue & Thu, 10am-3pm Sat) International staff integrating TCM and Western medical practices. There are three clinics in town. Acupuncture and tuīná (traditional) massage available.

Lónghuá Hospital Shanghai University of Traditional Chinese Medicine (龙华中医院; Lónghuá Zhōngyīyuàn; Map p316; 6438 5700; 725 S Wanping Rd; 零陵路725号) A kilometre northeast of Shànghǎi Stadium. A full range of TCM therapies and treatments.

Shànghǎi Qìgōng Institute (上海气功研究所;

Shànghǎi Qìgōng Yánjiùsuǒ; Map p302;☑6387 5180, ext 220; top fl, 218-220 Nanchang Rd; 南昌路218-220号; ⊗8am-4.30pm) Part of Shànghǎi's TCM school, the Qìgōng Institute offers *qìgōng* (*qì*-energy development) treatments and massage (¥280), as well as acupuncture sessions (¥280). No English is spoken; call for an appointment.

Shǔguāng Hospital (曙光医院; Shǔguāng Yīyuàn; Map p302;☑6385 5617; 185 Pu'an Rd; 普安路185号) Situated next to Huaihai Park, this hospital has a full range of TCM healthcare. The hospital is affiliated with the Shanghai University of Traditional Chinese Medicine.

Money

The Chinese currency is known as rénmínbì (RMB), or 'people's money'. Officially, the basic unit of RMB is the yuán (¥), which is divided into 10 jiǎo, which again is divided into 10 fēn. In spoken Chinese the yuán is referred to as *kuài* and jiǎo as *máo*. The fēn has so little value that it is rarely used these days. It's generally a good idea to keep ¥1 coins on you for the metro (some ticket machines frequently take only coins) and buses.

The Bank of China (中国银行; Zhōngguó Yínháng) issues RMB bills in denominations of one, two, five, 10, 20, 50 and 100 yuán. Coins come in denominations of one yuán; five and one jiǎo; and one, two and five fēn (the last are rare). Paper versions of the coins circulate, but are disappearing.

ATMs

ATMs that take foreign cards are plentiful, but it's generally safest to use Bank of China (中国银行; Zhōngguó Yínháng), the Industrial and Commercial Bank of China

(工商银行; ICBC) and HSBC (汇丰银行) ATMs, many of which are 24-hour. Many top-end hotels also have ATMs, as do malls, department stores and some metro stations. All ATMs accepting international cards have dual language ability.

Changing Money

You can change foreign currency at money-changing counters at almost every hotel and many shops, department stores and large banks such as the Bank of China and HSBC, as long as you have your passport; you can also change money at both Pǔdōng International Airport and Hóngqiáo International Airports. Some top-end hotels will change money only for their guests. Exchange rates in China are uniform wherever you change money, so there's little need to shop around. The Bank of China charges a 0.75% commission to change cash and travellers cheques. Some Bank of China ATMs are also Forex-equipped.

Whenever you change foreign currency into Chinese currency you will be given a money-exchange voucher recording the transaction. You need to show this to change your yuán back into any foreign currency. Changing Chinese currency outside China is a problem, though it's quite easily done in Hong Kong.

There's a branch of **American Express** (Map p310; ☑6279 8082; ⊗9am-noon & 1-5.30pm) in Jìng'ān, and Amex cardholders can also cash personal cheques with their card at branches of the Bank of China, China International Trust & Investment Corporation (Citic), the Bank of Communications or ICBC.

Counterfeit Bills

Very few Chinese will accept a ¥50 or ¥100 note without first checking to see if it's a fake. Many shopkeepers will run notes under an ultra-violet light, looking for signs of counterfeiting. Visually

checking for forged notes is hard unless you are very familiar with bills, but be aware that street vendors may try to dump forged notes on you in large-denomination change.

Credit Cards

Credit cards are more readily accepted in Shànghǎi than in other parts of China. Most tourist hotels will accept major credit cards (with a 4% processing charge) such as Visa, Amex, MasterCard, Diners and JCB, as will banks, upper-end restaurants and tourist-related shops. Credit hasn't caught on among most Chinese, and most local credit cards are in fact debit cards. Always carry enough cash for buying train tickets and emergencies.

Check to see if your credit-card company charges a foreign transaction fee (usually between 1% and 3%) for purchases in China.

Call your card's emergency contact number in case of loss or theft.

American Express (Map p310;☑6279 8082; ⊗9am-noon & 1-5.30pm) Out of business hours, call the 24-hour refund line (☑852-2811 6122) in Hong Kong.

MasterCard (☑108-00-110 7309)

Visa (☑108-00-110 2911)

Tipping

Tipping is generally not expected, although staff are becoming used to it in upscale restaurants, where most people round up the bill. In general there is no need to tip if a service charge has already been added. Hotel porters may expect a tip; taxi drivers do not.

Travellers Cheques

As ATMs are so plentiful and easy to use in Shànghǎi, travellers cheques are far less popular than they once were. Stick to the major companies such as Thomas Cook, American Express and Citibank.

Post

The larger tourist hotels and business towers have convenient post offices from where you can mail letters and small packages. China Post (中国邮政; Zhōngguó Yóuzhèng) offices and post boxes are green.

Useful branches of China Post:

Main China Post office (中国邮政; Zhōngguó Yóuzhèng; Map p314; ☑6393 6666; 276 North Suzhou Rd; 苏州北路276号; ☺7am-10pm)

China Post Xīntiāndì (中国邮政; Zhōngguó Yóuzhèng; Map p302; Xingye Lu) Opposite the Site of the 1st National Congress of the CCP.

Shànghǎi Centre (中国邮政; Zhōngguó Yóuzhèng; Map p310; 1376 West Nanjing Rd)

Letters and parcels take about a week to reach most overseas destinations; Express Mail Service (EMS) cuts this down to three or four days. Courier companies can take as little as two days. Ubiquitous same-day courier companies (快递; kuàidì) can express items within Shànghǎi from around ¥6 within the same district.

Public Holidays

Many of the following are nominal holidays and do not qualify for a day off work.

New Year's Day (Yuándàn) 1 January.

Spring Festival (Chūn Jié) 19 February 2015, 8 February 2016, 28 January 2017. Also known as Chinese New Year. Officially three days, but generally a week-long break.

Tomb Sweeping Day (Qīngmíng Jié) First weekend in April. A three-day weekend.

International Labour Day (Láodòng Jié) 1 May. Three-day holiday.

Dragon Boat Festival (Duānwǔ Jié) 20 June 2015, 9 June 2016, 30 May 2017.

Mid-Autumn Festival (Zhōngqiū Jié) 27 September 2015, 15 September 2016, 4 October 2017.

National Day (Guóqìng Jié) 1 October. Officially three days, but often morphs into a week-long vacation.

Safe Travel

Shànghǎi feels very safe, and crimes against foreigners are rare. Don't, however, end up in an ambulance: Chinese drivers never give way.

If you do have something stolen, you need to report the crime at the district Public Security Bureau (PSB; 公安局; Gōng'ānjú) office and obtain a police report.

Crossing the road is probably the greatest danger: develop avian vision and a sixth sense to combat the shocking traffic. The green man at traffic lights does not mean it is safe to cross. Instead, it means it is *slightly safer* to cross, but you can still be run down by traffic allowed to turn on red lights. Bicycles and scooters regularly flout all traffic rules, as do many cars. Bicycles, scooters, mopeds and motorbikes freely take to the pavements (sidewalks), as occasionally do cars. Older taxis only have seatbelts in the front passenger seat. Watch out for scooters whizzing down Shànghǎi roads – especially on streets without lighting – without lights at night.

Be careful when taking a taxi alone late at night, as foreigners have been sexually assaulted and robbed. Stick to the larger taxi firms such as the light turquoise **Dàzhòng** (大众; ☑96822), gold **Qiángshēng** (强生; ☑6258 0000), white Jǐnjiāng or green **Bāshì** (巴士; ☑96840) taxis and avoid black-market cabs. A registered taxi should always run on a meter and have a licence displayed on the dashboard.

Other street hazards include spent neon-light tubes poking from litter bins, open manholes with plunging drops, and welders showering pavements with burning sparks. Side streets off the main drag are sometimes devoid of street lights at night, and pavements can be crumbling and uneven.

Scams

Preying on visitors to the Bund, East Nanjing Rd, People's Sq and elsewhere, Shànghǎi's number one scam ruins the holidays of hundreds of foreigners. A couple (or an individual) of English-speaking girls approach single men and ask to be photographed using their mobile phone, then insist on taking the victim to a traditional Chinese teahouse, where they are left to pay eye-watering and heart-stopping bills (hundreds of dollars, usually payable by credit card). Some of the massage services offered to visitors on East Nanjing Road will similarly scam you out of large chunks of your holiday budget in the presentation of a huge bill. Just say no.

Watch out for taxi scams, especially at Pǔdōng International Airport and outside the Maglev terminal at Longyang Rd metro station. Aim for larger taxi firms and insist on using the meter to avoid taxi sharks.

Taxes

All four- and five-star hotels and some top-end restaurants add a service charge of 10% or 15%, which extends to the room and food; all other consumer taxes are included in the price tag.

Telephone

Using a mobile phone is naturally most convenient. If you have the right phone (eg BlackBerry, iPhone, Android) and are in a wi-fi zone, **Skype** (www.skype.com) and **Viber** (www.viber.com) can make calls either very cheap or free.

Long-distance phone calls can be placed from hotel-room phones, though this is expensive without an internet phonecard (IP card; IP卡). You may need a dial-out number for a direct line. Local calls should be free.

Phones are also sometimes attached to magazine kiosks or small shops. Just pick up the phone, make your call, and then pay the attendant (usually five *máo* for a local call). If dialling long-distance within China from Shànghǎi, prefix the number with 17909 for cheaper rates.

Most international calls cost ¥8.20 per minute or ¥2.20 to Hong Kong. You are generally required to leave a ¥200 deposit for international calls.

Note the following country and city codes:

Běijīng (☑010)

People's Republic of China (☑00 86)

Shànghǎi (☑021)

If calling Shànghǎi or Běijīng from abroad, drop the first zero.

The following numbers are useful:

Enquiry about international calls (☑106)

Local directory enquiries (☑114)

Weather (☑12121)

Mobile Phones

You can certainly take your mobile phone to China, but ensure it is unlocked, which means you can use another network's SIM card in your phone. Purchasing a SIM card in Shànghǎi is straightforward: pick one up from a branch of China Mobile (中国移动; Zhōngguó Yídòng); branches are widespread.

Mobile-phone shops (手机店; *shǒujīdiàn*) can sell you a SIM card, which will cost from ¥60 to ¥100 and will include ¥50 of credit. SIM cards are also available from newspaper kiosks (报刊亭; *bàokāntíng*). When this runs out, you can top up the number by buying a credit-charging card (充值卡; *chōngzhí kǎ*) for ¥50 or ¥100 worth of credits.

The Chinese avoid the number four (*sì;* which sounds like but has a different tone from the word for death – *sǐ*) and love the number eight (*bā*). Consequently, the cheapest numbers tend to contain numerous fours and the priciest have strings of eights.

Buying a mobile phone in Shànghǎi is also an option as they are generally inexpensive. Cafes, restaurants and bars in larger towns and cities are frequently wi-fi enabled.

Phonecards

The internet phonecard (IP card; IP卡) connects via the internet and is much cheaper than dialling direct. You can use any home phone, some hotel and some public phones (but not card phones), or a mobile phone to dial a special telephone number and follow the instructions (there is usually an English option).

Cards can be bought at newspaper kiosks, but are far less available than they used to be. Cards come in denominations of ¥50, ¥100, ¥200 and ¥500 – but they are always discounted, with a ¥100 card costing in the region of ¥35 to ¥40. Check that you are buying the right card. Some are for use in Shànghǎi only, while others can be used around the country. Check that the country you wish to call can be called on the card.

Generally, a safe bet is the CNC 10-country card (国际十国卡; *guójì shíguókǎ*), which can be used for calls to the USA, Canada, Australia, New Zealand, Hong Kong and Macau, Taiwan, England, France, Germany and some East Asian countries. Check the expiry date. If you're travelling around China, check it can be used outside the city or province you buy it in.

Time

Time throughout China is set to Běijīng local time, which is eight hours ahead of GMT/UTC. There is no daylight-saving time.

When it's noon in Shànghǎi, it's 8pm (the day before) in Los Angeles, 11pm (the day before) in Montreal and New York, 4am (the same day) in London, 5am in Frankfurt, Paris and Rome, noon in Hong Kong, 2pm in Melbourne and 4pm in Wellington. Add one hour to these times during the summer.

Toilets

Shànghǎi has plenty of public toilets. Often charging a small fee, they run from the sordid to coin-operated portaloos and modern conveniences. The best bet is to head for a top-end hotel, where someone will hand you a towel, pour you some aftershave or exotic hand lotion and wish you a nice day.

➡ Fast-food restaurants can be lifesavers.

➡ Always carry an emergency stash of toilet paper, as many toilets are devoid of it.

➡ Growing numbers of metro stations have coin-operated toilets.

➡ Toilets in hotels are generally sitters, but expect to find squatters in many public toilets.

➡ Remember the Chinese characters for men (男) and women (女).

Tourist Information

The best resource for tourist information or possibly a map of town should be your hotel concierge. For competent English-language help, call the **Shànghǎi Call Centre** (☏962 288), a free 24-hour English-language hotline that can respond to cultural, entertainment or transport enquiries (and even provide directions for your cab driver).

Shànghǎi has about a dozen or so rather useless **Tourist Information & Service Centres** (旅游咨询服务中心; Lǚyóu Zīxún Fúwù Zhōngxīn) where you can at least get free maps and (sometimes) information. Branches:

The Bund (Map p296; ☏6357 3718; 518 Jiujiang Rd; 九江路518号; ◷9.30am-8pm; Ⓜ East Nanjing Rd) Beneath the Bund promenade, opposite the intersection with East Nanjing Rd.

French Concession (Map p302; ☏5386 1882; 138 S Chengdu Rd; 成都南路138号; ◷9am-8.30pm)

Huángpǔ (☏6357 3718; 518 Jiujiang Rd; 九江路518号; ◷9.30am-8pm)

Jìng'ān (Map p310; ☏6248 3259; Lane 1678, 18 West Nanjing Rd; 南京西路1678弄18号; ◷9am-5pm)

Old Town (Map p300; ☏6355 5032; 149 Jiujiaochang Rd; 旧校场路149号; ◷9am-7pm) Southwest of Yùyuán Gardens.

Pǔdōng (Map p312; ☏3878 0202; Base of Oriental Pearl TV Tower; 东方明珠广播电视塔1楼; ◷9am-5pm)

There is also the useful **Shanghai Information Centre for International Visitors** (Map p302; ☏6384 9366; Xīntiāndì South Block, Bldg 2, Xingye Rd; ◷10am-10pm).

The **tourist hotline** (☏962 020) offers a limited English-language service.

Travel Agencies

The following agencies can help with travel bookings.

CTrip (☏400 619 9999; http://english.ctrip.com) An excellent online agency, good for hotel and flight bookings.

eLong (☏400 617 1717; www.elong.net) Hotel and flight bookings.

Travellers with Disabilities

Shànghǎi's traffic and the city's overpasses and underpasses are the greatest challenges to disabled travellers. Many metro stations have lifts to platforms but escalators may only go up from the ticket hall to the exit, and not down. Pavements on lesser roads may be cluttered with obstacles.

That said, an increasing number of modern buildings, museums, stadiums and most new hotels are wheelchair accessible. Try to take a lightweight chair for navigating around obstacles and for collapsing into the back of taxis. Top-end hotels have wheelchair-accessible rooms but budget hotels are less well prepared. Disabled travellers are advised to travel with at least one able-bodied companion.

China's sign language has regional variations, as well as some elements of American Sign Language (ASL), so foreign signers may have some problems communicating in sign language.

Visas

For everyone apart from citizens of Japan, Singapore, Brunei, San Marino, Mauritius, the Seychelles and the Bahamas, a visa is required for visits to the People's Republic of China, although 72-hour visa-free transit in Shànghǎi (and Běijīng plus five other cities with international airports) is available.

Visas are easily obtainable from Chinese embassies, consulates or Chinese Visa Application Service Centres abroad. Getting a visa in Hong Kong is also an option. Most tourists are issued with a single-entry visa for a 30-day stay, valid for three months from the date of issue. Your passport must be valid for at least six months after the expiry date of your visa (nine months for a double-entry visa) and you'll need at least two entire blank pages in your passport for the visa. For children under the age of 18, a parent must sign the application form on their behalf.

The visa application process has become more rigorous and applicants are required to provide the following:

➡ A copy of your flight confirmation showing onward/return travel.

➡ For double-entry visas, you need to provide flight confirmation showing all dates of entry and exit.

➡ If staying at a hotel in China, you must provide confirmation from the hotel (this can be cancelled later if you stay elsewhere).

➡ If staying with friends or relatives, you must provide a copy of the information page of their passport, a copy of their China visa and a letter of invitation from them.

Prices for a standard single-entry 30-day visa (not including Chinese Visa Application Service Centre administration fees):

➡ £30 for UK citizens

➡ US$140 for US citizens

➡ US$30 for all other nationals

COMMON VISA CATEGORIES

The most common categories of ordinary visas are as follows:

TYPE	DESCRIPTION	CHINESE NAME
C	flight attendant	chéngwù
D	resident	dìngjū
F	business or student (less than 6 months)	fǎngwèn
G	transit	guòjìng
J1	journalist (more than 6 months)	jìzhě1
J2	journalist (less than 6 months)	jìzhě2
L	travel	lǚxíng
M	commercial & trade	màoyì
Q1	family visit (more than 6 months)	qīnshǔ1
Q2	family visit (less than 6 months)	qīnshǔ2
R	needed skills/talents	réncái
S1	visit to foreign relatives/private (more than 6 months)	sīrén1
S2	visit to foreign relatives/private (less than 6 months)	sīrén2
X1	student (more than 6 months)	xuéxí1
X2	student (less than 6 months)	xuéxí2
Z	working	rènzhí

Double-entry visas:
➡ £45 for UK citizens
➡ US$140 for US citizens
➡ US$45 for all other nationals
Six-month multiple-entry visas:
➡ £90 for UK citizens
➡ US$140 for US citizens
➡ US$60 for all other nationals
A standard 30-day single-entry visa can be issued within three to five working days. With China becoming increasingly popular as a travel and business destination, queues at Chinese embassies and consulates are getting longer. In many countries, the visa service has been outsourced from the Chinese embassy to a **Chinese Visa Application Service Centre** (www.visaforchina.org), which levies an extra administration fee. In the case of the UK, a single-entry visa costs £30, but the standard administration charge levied by the centre is an additional £36 (three-day express £48, postal service £54). In some countries, such as the UK, France, the US and Canada, there is

more than one service centre nationwide, so check the website for your nearest centre. Visa Application Service Centres are open Monday to Friday. You generally pay for your visa in cash (or debit card) when you collect it.

At least one passport-sized photo of the applicant is required. When asked about your itinerary on the application form, if you are planning on travelling from Shànghǎi, list standard tourist destinations. Many travellers planning trips to Tibet or western Xīnjiāng leave them off the form as the list is non-binding, but their inclusion may raise eyebrows; those working in media or journalism often profess a different occupation to avoid having their visa refused or being given a shorter length of stay than requested.

A growing number of visa-arranging agents can do the legwork and deliver your visa-complete passport to you. In the US, many people use the **China Visa Service Center** (☑ in the US 800 799 6560; www.mychinavisa.com), which offers prompt service.

The procedure takes around 10 to 14 days. **CIBT** (www.uk.cibt.com) offers a global network and a fast and efficient turnaround.

A 30-day visa is activated on the date you enter China, and must be used within three months of the date of issue. Longer-stay visas are also activated upon entry into China. Officials in China are sometimes confused over the validity of the visa and look at the 'valid until' date. On most 30-day visas, however, this is actually the date by which you must have *entered* the country, not left.

Although a 30-day length of stay is standard for tourist visas, 60-day, 90-day, six-month and 12-month multiple-entry visas are also available. If you have trouble getting more than 30 days or a multiple-entry visa, try a local visa-arranging service or a travel agency in Hong Kong.

A business visa is multiple-entry and valid for three to six months from the date of issue, depending on how much you paid for it.

Note that if you go to China, on to Hong Kong or

Macau and then to Shànghǎi, you will need a double-entry visa to get 'back' into China from Hong Kong or Macau, or you will need to reapply for a fresh visa in Hong Kong.

When you check into a hotel, there is usually a question on the registration form asking what type of visa you have. The letter specifying your visa category is usually stamped on the visa itself.

Residence Permit

The 'green card' is a residence permit issued to English teachers, businesspeople, students and other foreigners who are authorised to live in the PRC. Green cards are issued for a period of one year.

To get a residence permit you first need to arrange a work permit (normally obtained by your employer), health certificate and temporary 'Z' visa. If your employer is organised, you can arrange all of this before you arrive in Shànghǎi.

You then go to the Public Security Bureau (PSB; 公安局; Gōng'ānjú) with your passport, health certificate, work permit, your employer's business registration licence or representative office permit, your employment certificate (from the Shanghai Labour Bureau), the temporary residence permit of the hotel or local PSB where you are registered, passport photos, a letter of application from your employer and around ¥400 in RMB. In all, the process usually takes from two to four weeks. Expect to make several visits and always carry multiple copies of every document. Each member of your family needs a residence permit and visa. In most cases, your employer will take care of much of the

process for you. If not, check expat websites for the latest updates to the process.

Shànghǎi Visa-Free Transit

Citizens from a number of countries including the USA, Australia, Canada, New Zealand, Germany, Sweden and France can transit through Shànghǎi through Pǔdōng International Airport and Hóngqiáo International Airport for up to 72 hours without a visa as long as they have visas for their onward countries and proof of seats booked on flights out of China. Your departure point and destination should not be in the same country. Note also that you are not allowed to visit other cities in China during your transit.

Travel in China

Most of China is accessible on a standard Chinese visa. A small number of restricted areas in China require an additional permit from the PSB. In particular, permits are required for travel to Tibet, a region that the authorities can suddenly bar foreigners from entering.

Visa Extensions

Extensions of 30 days are given for any tourist visa. You may be able to wrangle more with reasons such as illness or transport delays, but second extensions are usually only granted for a week, on the understanding that you are leaving. Visa extensions take three days and cost ¥160 for most nationalities and ¥940 for Americans (reciprocity for increased US visa fees). The fine for overstaying your visa is up to ¥300 per day.

To extend a business visa, you need a letter from a

Chinese work unit willing to sponsor you. If you're studying in China, your school can sponsor you for a visa extension.

Visa extensions in Shànghǎi are available from the **Public Security Bureau** (PSB; 公安局; Gōng'ānjú; Map p313; ☑2895 1900; 1500 Minsheng Rd; 民生路1500号; ☉9am-5pm Mon-Sat) and can be completed online.

Women Travellers

Chinese men are neither macho nor generally disrespectful of women, but women still need to keep their wits about them in Shànghǎi, especially after dark. They city is very cosmopolitan, so women can largely wear what they like.

Tampons can be bought everywhere, although it is advisable for you to bring your own contraceptive pills.

Work

It's not too difficult to find work in Shànghǎi, though technically you will need a work visa. You should arrive in Shànghǎi with enough funds to keep you going for at least a few weeks until a job opens up. Being able to speak Chinese is increasingly an important string to your bow. Examine the classified pages of the expat magazines and websites for job opportunities. Modelling and acting can be quite lucrative – especially if you find a decent agent – and teaching English is perennially popular. Bear in mind that most big companies tend to recruit from home, offering comfortable expat packages.

Language

Discounting its many ethnic minority languages, China has eight major dialect groups: Pǔtōnghuà (Mandarin), Yue (Cantonese), Wu (Shanghainese), Minbei (Fuzhou), Minnan (Hokkien-Taiwanese), Xiang, Gan and Hakka. Each of them also divides into subdialects.

Mandarin, which the Chinese themselves call Pǔtōnghuà (meaning 'common speech') is considered the official language of China. Most of the population speaks Mandarin, so you'll find that knowing a few basics in Mandarin will come in handy in Shànghǎi (as well as in many other parts of the country) which is why we've included it in this chapter.

For some more information about Shanghainese, see the boxed text, p277.

Writing

Chinese is often referred to as a language of pictographs. Many of the basic Chinese characters are highly stylised pictures of what they represent, but around 90% are compounds of a 'meaning' element and a 'sound' element.

A well-educated, contemporary Chinese speaker might use between 6000 and 8000 characters. To read a Chinese newspaper you need to know 2000 to 3000 characters, but 1200 to 1500 would be enough to get the gist.

Theoretically, all Chinese dialects share the same written system. In practice, Cantonese adds about 3000 specialised characters and many dialects don't have a written form at all.

WANT MORE?

For in-depth language information and handy phrases, check out Lonely Planet's *China Phrasebook* and *Mandarin Phrasebook*. You'll find them at **shop.lonelyplanet. com**.

Pinyin & Pronunciation

In 1958 the Chinese adopted Pinyin, a system of writing Mandarin using the Roman alphabet. The original idea was to eventually do away with Chinese characters, but over time this idea was abandoned.

Pinyin is often used on shop fronts, street signs and advertising billboards. However, in the countryside and the smaller towns you may not see a single Pinyin sign anywhere, so unless you speak Chinese you'll need a phrasebook with Chinese characters.

In this chapter we've provided Pinyin alongside the Mandarin script. Below is a brief guide to the pronunciation of Pinyin letters.

Vowels

a	as in 'father'
ai	as in 'aisle'
ao	as the 'ow' in 'cow'
e	as in 'her' (without 'r' sound)
ei	as in 'weigh'
i	as the 'ee' in 'meet' (or like a light 'r' as in 'Grrr!' after c, ch, r, s, sh, z or zh)
ian	as the word 'yen'
ie	as the English word 'yeah'
o	as in 'or' (without 'r' sound)
ou	as the 'oa' in 'boat'
u	as in 'flute'
ui	as the word 'way'
uo	like a 'w' followed by 'o'
yu/ü	like 'ee' with lips pursed

Consonants

c	as the 'ts' in 'bits'
ch	as in 'chop', with the tongue curled up and back
h	as in 'hay', articulated from further back in the throat
q	as the 'ch' in 'cheese'
sh	as in 'ship', with the tongue curled up and back
x	as the 'sh'in 'ship'
z	as the 'ds' in 'suds'
zh	as the 'j' in 'judge', with the tongue curled up and back

The only consonants that occur at the end of a syllable are n, ng and r. In Pinyin, apostrophes are occasionally used to separate syllables in order to prevent ambiguity, eg the word píng'ān can be written with an apostrophe after the 'g' to prevent it being pronounced as pín'gān.

Tones

Mandarin is a language with a large number of words with the same pronunciation but a different meaning. What distinguishes these homophones (as these words are called) is their 'tonal' quality – the raising and the lowering of pitch on certain syllables. Mandarin has four tones – high, rising, falling-rising and falling, plus a fifth 'neutral' tone that you can all but ignore. Tones are important for distinguishing meaning of words – eg the word ma has four different meanings according to tone: mā (mother), má (hemp, numb), mǎ (horse), mà (scold, swear). Tones are indicated in Pinyin by the following accent marks on vowels: ā (high), á (rising), ǎ (falling-rising) and à (falling).

Basics

When asking a question it is polite to start with qǐng wèn – literally, 'May I ask?'.

Hello.	你好。	Nǐhǎo.
Goodbye.	再见。	Zàijiàn.
How are you?	你好吗?	Nǐhǎo ma?
Fine. And you?	好。你呢?	Hǎo. Nǐ ne?
Excuse me.	劳驾。	Láojià.
Sorry.	对不起。	Duìbùqǐ.
Yes./No.	是。/不是。	Shì./Bùshì.
Please ...	请……	Qǐng ...
Thank you.	谢谢你。	Xièxie nǐ.
You're welcome.	不客气。	Bù kèqi.

What's your name?
你叫什么名字? Nǐ jiào shénme míngzi?

My name is ...
我叫…… Wǒ jiào ...

Do you speak English?
你会说英文吗? Nǐ huìshuō Yīngwén ma?

I don't understand.
我不明白。 Wǒ bù míngbái.

Accommodation

Do you have a single/double room?
有没有（单人/套）房? Yǒuméiyǒu (dānrén/tào) fáng?

How much is it per night/person?
每天/人多少钱? Měi tiān/rén duōshǎo qián?

KEY PATTERNS

To get by in Mandarin, mix and match these simple patterns with words of your choice:

How much is (the deposit)?
(押金)多少? (Yājīn) duōshǎo?

Do you have (a room)?
有没有(房)? Yǒuméiyǒu (fáng)?

Is there (heating)?
有(暖气)吗? Yóu (nuǎnqi) ma?

I'd like (that one).
我要(那个)。 Wǒ yào (nàge).

Please give me (the menu).
请给我(菜单)。 Qǐng gěiwǒ (càidān).

Can I (sit here)?
我能(坐这儿)吗? Wǒ néng (zuòzhèr) ma?

I need (a can opener).
我想要(一个开罐器)。 Wǒ xiǎngyào (yīge kāiguàn qì).

Do we need (a guide)?
需要(向导)吗? Xūyào (xiàngdǎo) ma?

I have (a reservation).
我有(预订)。 Wǒ yǒu (yùdìng).

I'm (a doctor).
我(是医生)。 Wǒ (shì yīshēng).

air-con	空调	kōngtiáo
bathroom	浴室	yùshì
bed	床	chuáng
campsite	露营地	lùyíngdì
guesthouse	宾馆	bīnguǎn
hostel	招待所	zhāodàisuǒ
hotel	酒店	jiǔdiàn
window	窗	chuāng

Directions

Where's a (bank)?
(银行)在哪儿? (Yínháng) zài nǎr?

What's the address?
地址在哪儿? Dìzhǐ zài nǎr?

Could you write the address, please?
能不能请你把地址写下来? Néngbuneng qǐng nǐ bǎ dìzhǐ xiě xiàlái?

Can you show me where it is on the map?
请帮我找它在地图上的位置。 Qǐng bāngwǒ zhǎo tā zài dìtú shàng de wèizhi.

Go straight ahead.
一直走。 Yìzhí zǒu.

Turn left/right.
左/右转。 Zuǒ/Yòu zhuǎn.

Question Words

What?	什么?	Shénme?
When?	什么时候	Shénme shíhòu?
Where?	哪儿?	Nǎr?
Which?	哪个?	Nǎge?
Who?	谁?	Shuí?
Why?	为什么?	Wèishénme?

at the traffic lights	在红绿灯	zài hónglùdēng
behind	背面	bèimiàn
far	远	yuǎn
in front of ...	……的前面	... de qiánmian
near	近	jìn
next to	旁边	pángbiān
on the corner	拐角	guǎijiǎo
opposite	对面	duìmiàn

Eating & Drinking

What would you recommend?
有什么菜可以推荐的? — Yǒu shénme cài kěyǐ tuījiàn de?

What's in that dish?
这道菜用什么东西做的? — Zhèdào cài yòng shénme dōngxi zuòde?

That was delicious.
真好吃。 — Zhēn hǎochī.

The bill, please!
买单! — Mǎidān!

Cheers!
干杯! — Gānbēi!

I'd like to reserve a table for ...	我想预订一张……的桌子。	Wǒ xiǎng yùdìng yīzhāng ... de zhuōzi.
(eight) o'clock	(八)点钟	(bā) diǎn zhōng
(two) people	(两个)人	(liǎngge) rén

I don't eat ...	我不吃……	Wǒ bùchī ...
nuts	果仁	guǒrén
poultry	家禽	jiāqín
red meat	牛羊肉	niúyángròu

Key Words

bar	酒吧	jiǔbā
bottle	瓶子	píngzi
bowl	碗	wǎn
breakfast	早饭	zǎofàn
cafe	咖啡屋	kāfēiwū
(too) cold	(太)凉	(tài) liáng
dinner	晚饭	wǎnfàn
food	食品	shípǐn
fork	叉子	chāzi
glass	杯子	bēizi
hot (warm)	热	rè
knife	刀	dāo
local specialties	地方小吃	dìfāng xiǎochī
lunch	午饭	wǔfàn
market	菜市	càishì
menu (in English)	(英文)菜单	(Yīngwén) càidān
plate	碟子	diézi
restaurant	餐馆	cānguǎn
(too) spicy	(太)辣	(tài) là
spoon	勺	sháo
vegetarian food	素食食品	sùshí shípǐn

Meat & Fish

beef	牛肉	niúròu
chicken	鸡肉	jīròu
duck	鸭	yā
fish	鱼	yú
lamb	羊肉	yángròu
pork	猪肉	zhūròu
seafood	海鲜	hǎixiān

Fruit & Vegetables

apple	苹果	píngguǒ
banana	香蕉	xiāngjiāo
carrot	胡萝卜	húluóbo
celery	芹菜	qíncài
cucumber	黄瓜	huángguā
fruit	水果	shuǐguǒ
grape	葡萄	pútáo
green beans	扁豆	biǎndòu
mango	芒果	mángguǒ
mushroom	蘑菇	mógū
onion	洋葱	yáng cōng
orange	橙子	chéngzi

Signs

入口	Rùkǒu	**Entrance**
出口	Chūkǒu	**Exit**
问讯处	Wènxùnchù	**Information**
开	Kāi	**Open**
关	Guān	**Closed**
禁止	Jìnzhǐ	**Prohibited**
厕所	Cèsuǒ	**Toilets**
男	Nán	**Men**
女	Nǚ	**Women**

pear	梨	lí
pineapple	凤梨	fènglí
plum	梅子	méizi
potato	土豆	tǔdòu
radish	萝卜	luóbo
spring onion	小葱	xiǎo cōng
sweet potato	地瓜	dìguā
vegetable	蔬菜	shūcài
watermelon	西瓜	xīguā

Other

bread	面包	miànbāo
butter	黄油	huángyóu
egg	蛋	dàn
herbs/spices	香料	xiāngliào
pepper	胡椒粉	hújiāo fěn
salt	盐	yán
soy sauce	酱油	jiàngyóu
sugar	砂糖	shātáng
tofu	豆腐	dòufu
vinegar	醋	cù
vegetable oil	菜油	càiyóu

Drinks

beer	啤酒	píjiǔ
coffee	咖啡	kāfēi
(orange) juice	(橙)汁	(chéng) zhī
milk	牛奶	niúnǎi
mineral water	矿泉水	kuàngquán shuǐ
red wine	红葡萄酒	hóng pútáo jiǔ
rice wine	米酒	mǐjiǔ
soft drink	汽水	qìshuǐ
tea	茶	chá
(boiled) water	(开)水	(kāi) shuǐ

SHANGHAINESE

Shanghainese has around 14 million speakers. As one of the dialects of Wu Chinese, it is similar to the dialects of Níngbō, Sūzhōu and Kūnshān. It is not mutually intelligible with other Wu dialects nor with Standard Mandarin. Nonetheless, it is infused with elements of Mandarin. The younger generation of Shànghǎi residents uses Mandarin expressions and, with government campaigns to encourage the use of Mandarin only, some fear for the future of the dialect. However, while it is rarely heard in schools or in the media, it remains a source of pride and identity for many Shànghǎi natives. Travellers will be perfectly fine using Mandarin in Shànghǎi.

white wine	白葡萄酒	bái pútáo jiǔ
yoghurt	酸奶	suānnǎi

Emergencies

Help!	救命！	Jiùmìng!
I'm lost.	我迷路了。	Wǒ mílù le.
Go away!	走开！	Zǒukāi!

There's been an accident.
出事了。　　　　　Chūshì le.

Call a doctor!
请叫医生来！　　　Qǐng jiào yīshēng lái!

Call the police!
请叫警察！　　　　Qǐng jiào jǐngchá!

I'm ill.
我生病了。　　　　Wǒ shēngbìng le.

Where are the toilets?
厕所在哪儿？　　　Cèsuǒ zài nǎr?

Shopping & Services

I'd like to buy ...
我想买……　　　　Wǒ xiǎng mǎi ...

I'm just looking.
我先看看。　　　　Wǒ xiān kànkan.

Can I look at it?
我能看看吗？　　　Wǒ néng kànkan ma?

I don't like it.
我不喜欢。　　　　Wǒ bù xǐhuan.

How much is it?
多少钱？　　　　　Duōshǎo qián?

That's too expensive.
太贵了。　　　　　Tàiguì le.

Can you lower the price?
能便宜一点吗？　　Néng piányi yīdiǎn ma?

There's a mistake in the bill.
帐单上有问题。　　Zhàngdān shàng yǒu wèntí.

ATM	自动取款机	zìdòng qǔkuǎn jī
internet cafe	网吧	wǎngbā
post office	邮局	yóujú
tourist office	旅行店	lǚxíng diàn

Time & Dates

What time is it?
现在几点钟？　　　Xiànzài jǐdiǎn zhōng?

It's (10) o'clock.
(十)点钟。　　　　(Shí) diǎn zhōng.

Half past (10).
(十)点三十分。　　(Shí) diǎn sānshífēn.

Numbers

1	一	yī
2	二/两	èr/liǎng
3	三	sān
4	四	sì
5	五	wǔ
6	六	liù
7	七	qī
8	八	bā
9	九	jiǔ
10	十	shí
20	二十	èrshí
30	三十	sānshí
40	四十	sìshí
50	五十	wǔshí
60	六十	liùshí
70	七十	qīshí
80	八十	bāshí
90	九十	jiǔshí
100	一百	yībǎi
1000	一千	yīqiān

morning	早上	zǎoshang
afternoon	下午	xiàwǔ
evening	晚上	wǎnshàng
yesterday	昨天	zuótiān
today	今天	jīntiān
tomorrow	明天	míngtiān
Monday	星期一	xīngqī yī
Tuesday	星期二	xīngqī èr
Wednesday	星期三	xīngqī sān
Thursday	星期四	xīngqī sì
Friday	星期五	xīngqī wǔ
Saturday	星期六	xīngqī liù
Sunday	星期天	xīngqī tiān

Transport

boat	船	chuán
bus (city)	大巴	dàbā
bus (intercity)	长途车	chángtú chē
plane	飞机	fēijī
taxi	出租车	chūzū chē
train	火车	huǒchē
tram	电车	diànchē

I want to go to ...
我要去……　　Wǒ yào qù ...

Does it stop at ...?
在……能下车吗？　　Zài ... néng xià chē ma?

At what time does it leave?
几点钟出发？　　Jǐdiǎnzhōng chūfā?

At what time does it get to ...?
几点钟到……？　　Jǐdiǎnzhōng dào ...?

I want to get off here.
我想这儿下车。　　Wǒ xiǎng zhèr xiàchē.

When's the first/last (bus)?
首趟/末趟 (车)　　Shǒutàng/Mòtàng (chē)
几点走？　　jǐdiǎn zǒu?

A ... ticket to (Dàlián).	一张到 (大连) 的 ……票。	Yīzhāng dào (Dàlián) de ... piào.
1st-class	头等	tóuděng
2nd-class	二等	èrděng
one-way	单程	dānchéng
return	双程	shuāngchéng
aisle seat	走廊的座位	zǒuláng de zuòwèi
ticket office	售票处	shòupiàochù
timetable	时刻表	shíkè biǎo
window seat	窗户的座位	chuānghu de zuòwèi
bicycle pump	打气筒	dǎqìtóng
child seat	婴儿座	yīng'érzuò
helmet	头盔	tóukuī
mechanic	机修工	jīxiūgōng
petrol	汽油	qìyóu
service station	加油站	jiāyóu zhàn
I'd like to hire a ...	我要租一辆……	Wǒ yào zū yīliàng ...
4WD	四轮驱动	sìlún qūdòng
bicycle	自行车	zìxíngchē
car	汽车	qìchē
motorcycle	摩托车	mótuochē

Does this road lead to ...?
这条路到……吗？　　Zhè tiáo lù dào ... ma?

How long can I park here?
这儿可以停多久？　　Zhèr kěyǐ tíng duōjiǔ?

The car has broken down.
汽车是坏的。　　Qìchē shì huài de.

I have a flat tyre.
轮胎瘪了。　　Lúntāi biě le.

I've run out of petrol.
没有汽油了。　　Méiyou qìyóu le.

GLOSSARY

arhat – Buddhist, especially a monk who has achieved enlightenment

běi – north

biéshù – villa

bīnguǎn – tourist hotel

bówùguǎn – museum

cāntīng – restaurant

CCP – Chinese Communist Party; founded in Shànghǎi in 1921

cheongsam – see *qípáo*

Chiang Kaishek – (1887–1975) leader of the Kuomintang, anticommunist and head of the nationalist government from 1928 to 1949

chop – carved name seal that acts as a signature

Confucius – (551–479 BC) legendary scholar who developed the philosophy of Confucianism, which defines codes of conduct and patterns of obedience in society

Cultural Revolution – a brutal and devastating purge of the arts, religion and the intelligentsia by Mao's *Red Guards* and later the *PLA* from 1966 to 1970, it officially ended in 1976.

dàdào – boulevard, avenue

dàfàndiàn – large hotel

dàjiē – avenue

dàjiǔdiàn – large hotel

dàshà – hotel, building

Deng Xiaoping – (1904–97) considered to be the most powerful political figure in China from the late 1970s until his death; Deng's reforms resulted in economic growth, but he also instituted harsh social policies and authorised the military force that resulted in the Tiān'ānmén Square incident in Běijīng in 1989

dōng – east

fàndiàn – hotel, restaurant

fēn – one-tenth of a *jiǎo*

fēng – peak

fēng shuǐ – geomancy, literally 'wind and water'; the art of using ancient principles to maximise the flow of *qì* (universal energy)

Gang of Four – members of a clique, headed by Mao's wife, Jiang Qing, who were blamed for the *Cultural Revolution*

gé – pavilion, temple

gōngyuán – park

gùjū – house, home, residence

gǔzhèn – ancient town

hé – river

hú – lake

huā – flower tea

jiāng – river

jiǎo – unit of currency, one-tenth of a *yuán*

jiē – street

jié – festival

jīn – unit of measurement (500g)

jìniànguǎn – memorial hall

jiǔdiàn – hotel

jū – residence, home

kuài – in spoken Chinese, colloquial term for the currency, *yuán*

Kuomintang – *Chiang Kaishek's* Nationalist Party; the dominant political force after the fall of the Qing dynasty

liǎng – unit of measurement (50g)

lǐlòng – alleyway

lòngtáng – narrow alleyway, or *lǐlòng*; lòngtáng is the preferred term used in Shànghǎi

lóu – tower

lǜchá – green tea

lù – road

luóhàn – see *arhat*

máo – in spoken Chinese, colloquial term for the *jiǎo*

Mao Zedong – (1893–1976) leader of the early communist forces, he founded the *PRC* and was party chairman until his death

mǎtou – dock

mén – gate

miào – temple

nán – south

PLA – People's Liberation Army

pǔ'ěr – post-fermented, dark tea from Yúnnán (pu-erh)

PRC – People's Republic of China

PSB – Public Security Bureau; the arm of the police force set up to deal with foreigners

qiáo – bridge

qípáo – the figure-hugging dress worn by Chinese women (also called a cheongsam)

Red Guards – a pro-Mao faction that persecuted rightists during the *Cultural Revolution*

renminbi – literally 'people's money', the formal name for the currency; shortened to RMB

RMB – see *Renminbi*

shān – mountain

shì – city

shìchǎng – market

shíkùmén – stone-gate house; a blend of Chinese courtyard housing and English terraced housing

sì – temple, monastery

Sun Yatsen – (1866–1925) first president of the Republic of China; loved by republicans and communists alike

tǎ – pagoda

taichi – slow-motion shadow-boxing

Taiping Rebellion – rebellion (1850–64) that attempted to overthrow the Qing dynasty

tíng – pavilion

wūlóng – oolong tea

xī – west

yuán – Chinese unit of currency, the basic unit of RMB; garden

zhōng – middle

Zhou Enlai – an early comrade of Mao's, Zhou exercised the most influence in the day-to-day governing of China following the *Cultural Revolution*

MENU DECODER

bīng 冰 ice
bīngqílín 冰淇淋 ice cream
cù 醋 vinegar
dòufu 豆腐 tofu
hànbǎobāo 汉堡包 hamburger
huángguā 黄瓜 cucumber
huángyóu 黄油 butter
hújiāofěn 胡椒粉 pepper
jiàngyóu 酱油 soy sauce
jīdàn 鸡蛋 egg
jīròu 鸡肉 chicken
làjiāo 辣椒 chilli
lāmiàn 拉面 pulled noodles
miànbāo 面包 bread
niúròu 牛肉 beef
pángxiè 螃蟹 crab
qiézi 茄子 aubergine
qíncài 芹菜 celery
qīngcài 青菜 green vegetables
sèlā 色拉 salad
shāokǎo 烧烤 barbecue
shǔtiáo 薯条 chips
sùcài 素菜 vegetables
tāng 汤 soup
táng 糖 sugar
tǔdòu 土豆 potato
wèijīng 味精 MSG
xīhóngshì 西红柿 tomato
yán 盐 salt
yángròu 羊肉 lamb
yángròuchuàn 羊肉串 lamb kebab
yāzi 鸭子 duck
yóuyú 鱿鱼 squid
zhōu 粥 rice porridge (congee)
zhūròu 猪肉 pork

Rice Dishes 米饭

báifàn 白饭 steamed white rice
chǎofàn 炒饭 fried rice
jīdàn chǎofàn 鸡蛋炒饭 fried rice with egg

Soup 汤

húntun tāng 馄饨汤 won ton (dumpling) soup
jīdàn tāng 鸡蛋汤 egg drop soup
sānxiān tāng 三鲜汤 three kinds of seafood soup
suānlà tāng 酸辣汤 hot and sour soup
xīhóngshì jīdàntāng 西红柿鸡蛋汤 tomato and egg soup

Vegetable Dishes 素菜

báicài xiān shuānggū 白菜鲜双菇 bok choy and mushrooms
cuìpí dòufu 脆皮豆腐 crispy skin bean curd
dìsānxiān 地三鲜 cooked potato, aubergine and green pepper
háoyóu xiāngū 蚝油鲜菇 mushrooms in oyster sauce
hēimù'ěr mèn dòufu 黑木耳焖豆腐 bean curd with mushrooms
jiǔcài jiǎozi 韭菜饺子 chive dumplings
shāo qiézi 烧茄子 cooked aubergine (eggplant)
tángcù ǒubǐng 糖醋藕饼 lotus root cakes in sweet-and-sour sauce

Seafood 海鲜

chāngyú 鲳鱼 pomfret
chǎo huángshàn 炒黄鳝 fried eel
cōngsū jìyú 葱酥鲫鱼 braised carp with onion
dàzhá xiè 大闸蟹 hairy crabs
fúróng yúpiàn 芙蓉鱼片 fish slices in egg white

gānjiān xiǎo huángyú 干煎小黄鱼 dry-fried yellow croaker
guōbā xiārén 锅巴虾仁 shrimp in sizzling rice crust
héxiāng báilián 荷香白鲢 lotus-flavoured silver carp
hóngshāo shànyú 红烧鳝鱼 eel soaked in soy sauce
huángyú 黄鱼 yellow croaker
jiāng cōng chǎo xiè 姜葱炒蟹 stir-fried crab with ginger and scallions
jiǔxiāng yúpiàn 酒香鱼片 fish slices in wine
mìzhī xūnyú 蜜汁熏鱼 honey-smoked carp
níngshì shànyú 宁式鳝鱼 stir-fried eel with onion
qiézhī yúkuài 茄汁鱼块 fish fillet in tomato sauce
qīngzhēng guìyú 清蒸鳜鱼 steamed Mandarin fish
sōngjiānglúyú 松江鲈鱼 Songjiang perch
sōngshǔ guìyú 松鼠鳜鱼 squirrel-shaped Mandarin fish
sōngzǐ guìyú 松子鳜鱼 Mandarin fish with pine nuts
suānlà yóuyú 酸辣鱿鱼 hot-and-sour squid
yóubào xiārén 油爆虾仁 fried shrimp
zhá hēi lǐyú 炸黑鲤鱼 fried black carp
zhá yúwán 炸鱼丸 fish balls

Home-Style Dishes 家常菜

biǎndòu ròusī 扁豆肉丝 shredded pork and green beans
fānqié chǎodàn 番茄炒蛋 egg and tomato
hóngshāo qiézi 红烧茄子 red-cooked aubergine

huíguō ròu 回锅肉
double-cooked fatty pork

jiācháng dòufu 家常豆腐
'home-style' tofu

jīngjiàng ròusī 精酱肉丝
pork cooked with soy sauce

níngméng jī 柠檬鸡
lemon chicken

niúròu miàn 牛肉面
beef noodles in soup

páigǔ 排骨 ribs

sùchǎo biǎndòu 素炒扁豆
garlic beans

sùchǎo sùcài 素炒素菜
fried vegetables

tiěbǎn niúròu 铁板牛肉
sizzling beef platter

yángcōng chǎo ròupiàn 洋葱炒肉片
pork and fried onions

yúxiāng qiézi 鱼香茄子
fish-flavoured aubergine

Shanghainese Dishes 上海菜

hǔpíjiānjiāo 虎皮尖椒
tiger skin chillies

jīngcōng ròusī jiá bǐng 京葱肉丝夹饼
soy pork with scallions in pancakes

jīngdū guō páigǔ 京都锅排骨
Mandarin-style pork ribs

sōngrén yùmǐ 松仁玉米
sweet corn and pine nuts

sōngzǐ yā 松子鸭
duck with pine nuts

xiāngsū jī 香酥鸡
crispy chicken

xiánjī 咸鸡
cold salty chicken

xiǎolóngbāo 小笼包
little steamer buns

xièfěn shīzitóu 蟹粉狮子头
lion's head meatballs with crab

yóutiáo niú ròu 油条牛肉
fried dough sticks with beef

zuìjī 醉鸡 drunken chicken

Hángzhōu Dishes 杭州菜

dōngpō bèiròu 东坡焙肉
Dongpo pork

héyè fěnzhēng ròu 荷叶粉蒸肉
steamed pork wrapped in lotus leaf

jiào huā jī 叫化鸡
beggar's chicken

lóngjǐng xiārén 龙井虾仁
Longjing stir-fried shrimp

shāguō yútóu dòufu 沙锅鱼头豆腐
earthenware-pot fish-head tofu

xīhú chúncài tāng 西湖莼菜汤
West Lake water shield soup

xīhú cùyú 西湖醋鱼
West Lake fish

Cantonese Dishes 粤菜

chǎomiàn 炒面 chow mein

chāshāo 叉烧 cha siu

diǎnxīn 点心 dim sum

guōtiē 锅贴 fried dumplings

háoyóu niúròu 蚝油牛肉
beef with oyster sauce

kǎo rǔzhū 烤乳猪
crispy suckling pig

mìzhī chāshāo 蜜汁叉烧
roast pork with sweet syrup

tángcù lǐjī/gǔlǎo ròu 糖醋里脊/古老肉
sweet-and-sour pork fillets

xiāngsū jī 香酥鸡
crispy chicken

Sichuanese Dishes 川菜

dàndànmiàn 担担面
Dandan noodles

gōngbào jīdīng 宫爆鸡丁
spicy chicken with peanuts

málà dòufu 麻辣豆腐
spicy tofu

mápó dòufu 麻婆豆腐
tofu and pork crumbs in a spicy sauce

shuǐ zhǔ niúròu 水煮牛肉
fried and boiled beef, garlic sprouts and celery

suāncàiyú 酸菜鱼
boiled fish with pickled vegetables

yuānyāng huǒguō 鸳鸯火锅
Yuanyang hotpot

yúxiāng ròusī 鱼香肉丝
fish-flavoured meat

Běijīng & Northern Dishes 京菜和北方菜

běijīng kǎoyā 北京烤鸭
Peking duck

jiǎozi 饺子 dumplings

mántou 馒头 steamed buns

ròu bāozi 肉包子
steamed meat buns

shuàn yángròu huǒguō 涮羊肉火锅 lamb hotpot

sùcài bāozi 素菜包子
steamed vegetable buns

Drinks 饮料

báijiǔ 白酒 white spirits

dòunǎi 豆奶 soya milk

hóngchá 红茶
Western (black) tea

júhuā chá 菊花茶
chrysanthemum tea

lǜ chá 绿茶 green tea

mǐjiǔ 米酒 rice wine

nǎijīng 奶精 coffee creamer

yēzi zhī 椰子汁 coconut juice

zhēnzhū nǎichá 珍珠奶茶
bubble tea

Behind the Scenes

SEND US YOUR FEEDBACK

We love to hear from travellers – your comments keep us on our toes and help make our books better. Our well-travelled team reads every word on what you loved or loathed about this book. Although we cannot reply individually to your submissions, we always guarantee that your feedback goes straight to the appropriate authors, in time for the next edition. Each person who sends us information is thanked in the next edition – the most useful submissions are rewarded with a selection of digital PDF chapters.

Visit **lonelyplanet.com/contact** to submit your updates and suggestions or to ask for help. Our award-winning website also features inspirational travel stories, news and discussions.

Note: We may edit, reproduce and incorporate your comments in Lonely Planet products such as guidebooks, websites and digital products, so let us know if you don't want your comments reproduced or your name acknowledged. For a copy of our privacy policy visit lonelyplanet.com/privacy.

OUR READERS

Many thanks to the travellers who used the last edition and wrote to us with helpful hints, useful advice and interesting anecdotes: Thomas Chabrieres, Diana Cioffi, Matti Laitinen, Stine Schou Lassen, Cristina Marsico, Rachel Roth, Tom Wagener

AUTHOR THANKS
Damian Harper

Thanks to Dai Min, Margaux, Alvin and Edward, Chris Pitts, Daniel McCrohan, David Eimer, Edward Li, John Zhang, Jimmy Gu and Liu Meina. Much gratitude also to Jiale and Jiafu for everything, as always. Last but not least, a big thanks, of course, to the people of Shanghai for making their city so fascinating.

Dai Min

Massive thanks to Dai Lu, Li Jianjun and Cheng Yuan for all their help and support while in Shanghai, your assistance was invaluable. Gratitude also to Wang Ying and Ju Weihong for helping out big time and a huge thank you to my husband for everything.

ACKNOWLEDGEMENTS

Cover photograph: Oriental Pearl TV Tower and Shànghǎi Ocean Aquarium, Luigi Vaccarella/4Corners
Illustration pp58-9 by Michael Weldon.

THIS BOOK

This 7th edition of Lonely Planet's *Shanghai* guidebook was researched and written by Damian Harper and Dai Min. The 6th edition was written by Damian Harper and Christopher Pitts, and the 5th edition was written by Christopher Pitts and Daniel McCrohan. This guidebook was produced by the following:

Destination Editor Megan Eaves
Commissioning Editor Joe Bindloss
Coordinating Editor Susan Paterson
Product Editor Kate Kiely
Senior Cartographer Julie Sheridan
Book Designer Virginia Moreno
Assisting Editors Melanie Dankel, Jodie Martire
Cartographer Rachel Imeson

Assisting Book Designer Jennifer Mullins
Cover Researcher Naomi Parker
Thanks to Anita Banh, Kate Chapman, Ryan Evans, Justin Flynn, Larissa Frost, Jouve India, Andi Jones, Lucie Monie, Wayne Murphy, Claire Naylor, Martine Power, Averil Robertson, Dianne Schallmeiner, Samantha Tyson, Diana Von Holdt, Juan Winata, Lauren Wellicome

See also separate subindexes for:

✘ **EATING P287**

🍷 **DRINKING & NIGHTLIFE P288**

☆ **ENTERTAINMENT P289**

📖 **SHOPPING P289**

🛏 **SLEEPING P290**

Index

✕ EATING

🛏 SLEEPING

Sights 000
Map Pages **000**
Photo Pages **000**

 SPORTS & ACTIVITIES

Shànghǎi Maps

Sights
- ⦿ Beach
- ⦿ Bird Sanctuary
- ⦿ Buddhist
- ⦿ Castle/Palace
- ⦿ Christian
- ⦿ Confucian
- ⦿ Hindu
- ⦿ Islamic
- ⦿ Jain
- ⦿ Jewish
- ⦿ Monument
- ⦿ Museum/Gallery/Historic Building
- ⦿ Ruin
- ⦿ Shinto
- ⦿ Sikh
- ⦿ Taoist
- ⦿ Winery/Vineyard
- ⦿ Zoo/Wildlife Sanctuary
- ⦿ Other Sight

Activities, Courses & Tours
- ⦿ Bodysurfing
- ⦿ Diving
- ⦿ Canoeing/Kayaking
- ⦿ Course/Tour
- ⦿ Sento Hot Baths/Onsen
- ⦿ Skiing
- ⦿ Snorkelling
- ⦿ Surfing
- ⦿ Swimming/Pool
- ⦿ Walking
- ⦿ Windsurfing
- ⦿ Other Activity

Sleeping
- ⦿ Sleeping
- ⦿ Camping

Eating
- ⦿ Eating

Drinking & Nightlife
- ⦿ Drinking & Nightlife
- ⦿ Cafe

Entertainment
- ⦿ Entertainment

Shopping
- ⦿ Shopping

Information
- ⦿ Bank
- ⦿ Embassy/Consulate
- ⦿ Hospital/Medical
- @ Internet
- ⦿ Police
- ⦿ Post Office
- ⦿ Telephone
- ⦿ Toilet
- ⦿ Tourist Information
- ● Other Information

Geographic
- ⦿ Beach
- ⦿ Hut/Shelter
- ⦿ Lighthouse
- ⦿ Lookout
- ▲ Mountain/Volcano
- ⦿ Oasis
- ⦿ Park
-)(Pass
- ⦿ Picnic Area
- ⦿ Waterfall

Population
- ⦿ Capital (National)
- ⦿ Capital (State/Province)
- ⦿ City/Large Town
- ⦿ Town/Village

Transport
- ⦿ Airport
- ⦿ Border crossing
- ⦿ Bus
- ⦿ Cable car/Funicular
- ⦿ Cycling
- ⦿ Ferry
- Ⓜ Metro/MTR/MRT station
- ⦿ Monorail
- Ⓟ Parking
- ⦿ Petrol station
- ⓢ Skytrain/Subway station
- ⦿ Taxi
- ⦿ Train station/Railway
- ⦿ Tram
- Ⓤ Underground station
- ● Other Transport

Note: Not all symbols displayed above appear on the maps in this book

Routes
- Tollway
- Freeway
- Primary
- Secondary
- Tertiary
- Lane
- Unsealed road
- Road under construction
- Plaza/Mall
- Steps
-)═══(Tunnel
- Pedestrian overpass
- Walking Tour
- Walking Tour detour
- Path/Walking Trail

Boundaries
- International
- State/Province
- Disputed
- Regional/Suburb
- Marine Park
- Cliff
- Wall

Hydrography
- River, Creek
- Intermittent River
- Canal
- Water
- Dry/Salt/Intermittent Lake
- Reef

Areas
- Airport/Runway
- Beach/Desert
- Cemetery (Christian)
- Cemetery (Other)
- Glacier
- Mudflat
- Park/Forest
- Sight (Building)
- Sportsground
- Swamp/Mangrove

MAP INDEX

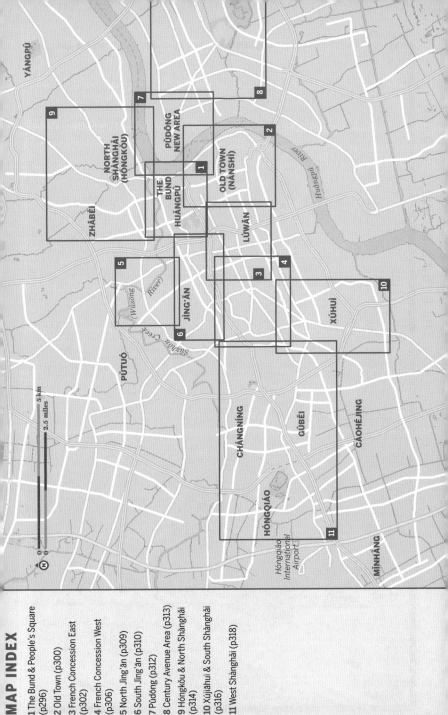

YÁNGPǓ

NORTH SHÀNGHǍI (HÓNGKǑU)

ZHÁBĚI

PǓDŌNG NEW AREA

THE BUND

HUÁNGPǓ

OLD TOWN (NÁNSHÌ)

LŪWĀN

Huángpǔ River

PǓTUÓ

Wúsōng River

Sūzhōu Creek

JÌNG'ĀN

XÚHUÌ

CHÁNGNÍNG

GǓBĚI

CÁOHÉJĪNG

HÓNGQIÁO

Hóngqiáo International Airport

MǏNHÁNG

5 km

2.5 miles

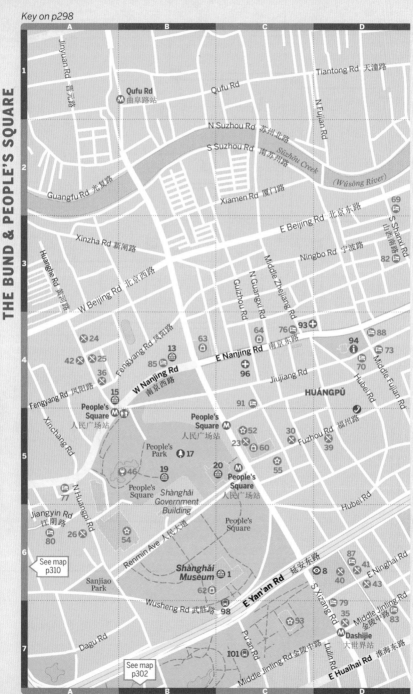

A   B   C   D

1

Jinyuan Rd 晋元路

Tiantong Rd 天潼路

Qufu Rd
曲阜路站

Qufu Rd

N Fujian Rd

N Suzhou Rd 苏州北路

2

S Suzhou Rd 南苏州路

Sūzhōu Creek

Guangfu Rd 光复路

Xiamen Rd 厦门路

(Wúsōng River)

69
S Shanxi Rd 山西南路

E Beijing Rd 北京东路

Xinzha Rd 新闸路

Ningbo Rd 宁波路

82

3

Huanghe Rd 黄河路

W Beijing Rd 北京西路

Guizhou Rd

N Guangxi Rd

Middle Zhejiang Rd

24

63

64   76   93

88

Fengyang Rd 凤阳路

13

E Nanjing Rd 南京东路

94

73

42   25

85

70

Middle Fujian Rd

36

W Nanjing Rd
南京西路

96

Jiujiang Rd

HUÁNGPǓ

Hubei Rd

4

Fengyang Rd 凤阳路

15

91

Xinchang Rd

People's
Square
人民广场站

People's
Square
人民广场站

52

30

Fuzhou Rd 福州路

23   60

39

5

People's
Park

17

20

55

46

19

People's
Square

Shànghǎi
Government
Building

People's
Square
人民广场站

77

N Huangpi Rd

People's
Square

Hubei Rd

Jiangyin Rd
江阴路

26

54

80

Renmin Ave 人民大道

6

See map
p310

Shànghǎi
Museum

1

87   41   E Ninghai Rd

8

40   43

Sanjiao
Park

62

E Yan'an Rd 延安东路

S Xizang Rd

79

Dagu Rd

Wusheng Rd 武胜路

98

35
Middle Jinling Rd
金陵中路   83

53

Dashijie
大世界站

7

See map
p302

101

Pu'an Rd

Middle Jinling Rd 金陵中路

Liulin Rd

E Huaihai Rd 淮海东路

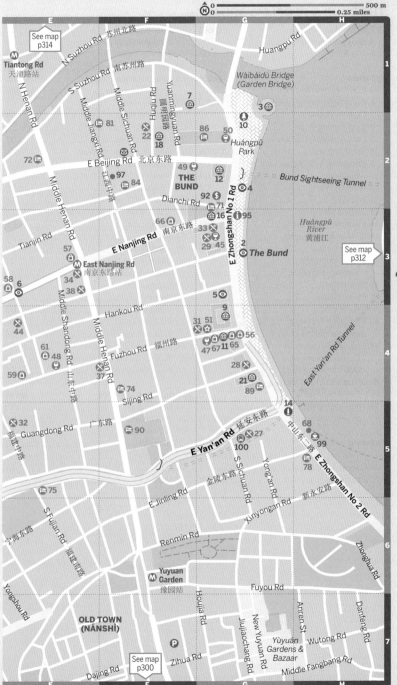

THE BUND & PEOPLE'S SQUARE *Map on p296*

THE BUND & PEOPLE'S SQUARE

OLD TOWN

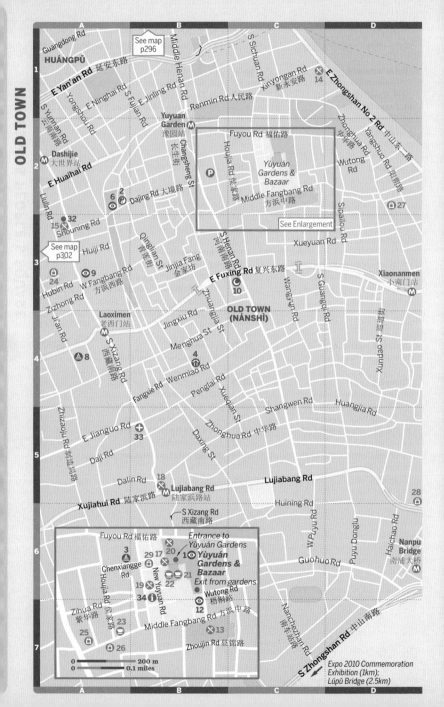

See map p296

HUÁNGPÚ

Guangdong Rd

E Yan'an Rd 延安东路

Yongshou Rd

S Yunnan Rd 云南南路

E Ninghai Rd

E Jinling Rd

E Fujian Rd

Middle Henan Rd

Renmin Rd 人民路

S Sichuan Rd

Xinyongan Rd 新永安路

✈ 14

E Zhongshan No 2 Rd 中山东二路

1

Dashijie 大世界站 Ⓜ

2

E Huaihai Rd

Liulin Rd

Yuyuan Garden 豫园站 Ⓜ

Changsheng St 长生街

Fuyou Rd 福佑路

Ⓟ

Houjia Rd 侯家路

Yùyuán Gardens & Bazaar

Zhonghua Rd 华路

Middle Fangbang Rd 方浜中路

Wutong Rd

27 🔒

2 ◉

6 ◉

Dajing Rd 大境路

15

32

Shouning Rd

Qingtian St 青莲街

Jinjia Fang 金家坊

S Henan Rd 河南南路

E Fuxing Rd 复兴东路

Xueyuan Rd

Sipailou Rd

Xiaonanmen 小南门站 Ⓜ

3

See map p302

24 🔒

Hubin Rd

9 🚻

W Fangbang Rd 方浜西路

Zizhong Rd

Ji'an Rd

Huiji Rd

10 ◉

OLD TOWN (NÁNSHÌ)

Wangyun Rd

S Guangqi Rd

Xundao St 蟹道街

4

Laoximen 老西门站 Ⓜ

S Xizang Rd 西藏南路

Jingxiu Rd

Menghua St

Zhuangjia St

Wenmiao Rd

4 ◉ 🅣

8 ♨

Fangxie Rd

Penglai Rd

Xueqian St

Shangwen Rd

Huangjia Rd

5

Zhizaoju Rd 制造局路

E Jianguo Rd

Daji Rd

Daxing St

Zhonghua Rd 中华路

33 ➕

Dalin Rd

18

Lujiabang Rd

Ⓜ 陆家浜路站

6

Xujiahui Rd 陆家浜路

S Xizang Rd 西藏南路

Lujiabang Rd

Huining Rd

W Puyu Rd

Guohuo Rd

Puyu Donglu

Haichao Rd

28 🔒

Nanpu Bridge 南浦大桥 Ⓜ

Enlargement:

Fuyou Rd 福佑路

Entrance to Yùyuán Gardens

3

Chenxiangge Rd

Houjia Rd 侯家路

New Yuyuan Rd

29 **17** **20**

1 ◉ **Yùyuán Gardens & Bazaar**

19 🍴

22

21

Exit from gardens

Wutong Rd 梧桐路

34 ℹ

12 ◉

25 🔒

Zihua Rd 紫华路

23

Middle Fangbang Rd 方浜中路

13 🍴

26 🔒

Zhoujin Rd 昼锦路

0 _____ 200 m
0 _____ 0.1 miles

S Zhongshan Rd 中山南路

Nanchezhan Rd 南车站路

Expo 2010 Commemoration Exhibition (1km); Lúpǔ Bridge (2.5km)

Key on p304

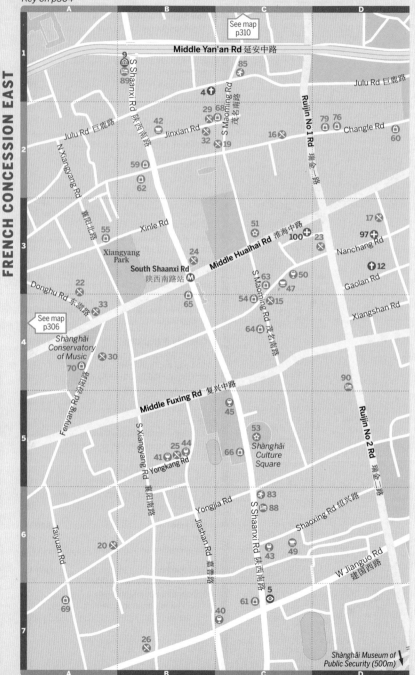

FRENCH CONCESSION EAST

See map
p310

Middle Yan'an Rd 延安中路

1

9

S Shaanxi Rd 陕西南路

89

85

Julu Rd 巨鹿路

4

29 68

S Maoming Rd 茂名南路

Ruijin No 1 Rd 瑞金一路

79 76

Changle Rd

60

Julu Rd 巨鹿路

42

Jinxian Rd

N Xiangyang Rd

2

32

19

16

59

62

55

Xinle Rd

51

17

100

23

97

3

Xiangyang
Park

24

Middle Huaihai Rd 淮海中路

S Maoming Rd 茂名南路

Nanchang Rd

12

South Shaanxi Rd
陕西南路站

63

50

Gaolan Rd

22

54

15

47

Donghu Rd 东湖路

33

65

64

Xiangshan Rd

See map
p306

Fenyang Rd 汾阳路

4

Shànghǎi
Conservatory
of Music

30

70

90

Middle Fuxing Rd 复兴中路

Ruijin No 2 Rd 瑞金二路

45

5

S Xiangyang Rd 襄阳南路

25 44

53

41

Yongkang Rd

66

Shànghǎi
Culture
Square

Taiyuan Rd

20

Yongjia Rd

Jiashan Rd 嘉善路

S Shaanxi Rd 陕西南路

83

88

6

49

43

Shaoxing Rd 绍兴路

W Jianguo Rd
建国西路

5

61

69

40

7

26

Shànghǎi Museum of
Public Security (500m)

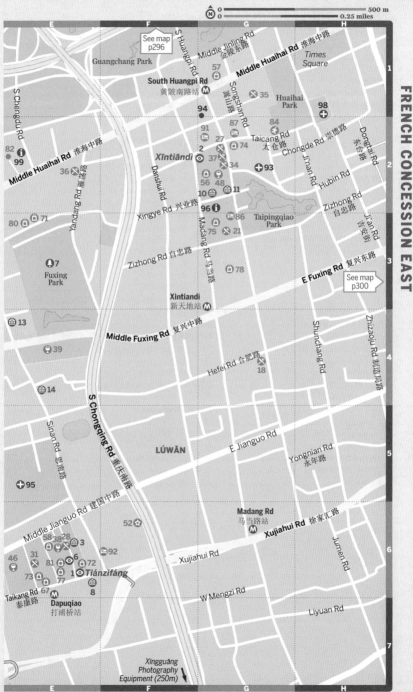

0
500 m
0
0.25 miles

See map
p296

Guangchang Park

S Huangpi Rd

Middle Jinling Rd
金陵东路

Middle Huaihai Rd 淮海中路

Times
Square

1

S Chengdu Rd

South Huangpi Rd
黄陂南路站

57

Songshan Rd 嵩山路

35

Huaihai
Park

98

Middle Huaihai Rd 淮海中路

94

91
2

87
27

84
Taicang Rd
太仓路

Chongde Rd 崇德路

Ji'nan Rd

Dongtai Rd
东台路

36

Xīntiāndì

37
34

74

93

Hubin Rd

Danshui Rd

56 48
10 11

Zizhong Rd
自忠路

80
71

Xingye Rd 兴业路

96

86

Taipingqiao
Park

Ji'an Rd
吉安路

Yandang Rd 雁荡路

Madang Rd 马当路

75
21

7

Fuxing
Park

Zizhong Rd 自忠路

78

E Fuxing Rd 复兴东路

3

See map
p300

13

Xintiandi
新天地站

Zhizaoju Rd 制造局路

39

Middle Fuxing Rd 复兴中路

Hefei Rd 合肥路

18

Shunchang Rd

4

14

S Chongqing Rd 重庆南路

Sinan Rd 思南路

LÚWĀN

E Jianguo Rd

Yongnian Rd
永年路

5

95

Middle Jianguo Rd 建国中路

52

Madang Rd
马当路站

Xujiahui Rd 徐家汇路

58 38 28
3
46
31
81
6
72
92

Tiánzǐfáng

Xujiahui Rd

Jumen Rd

6

73
1
77
8

67
Tiánzǐfáng

Taikang Rd
泰康路

Dapuqiao
打浦桥站

W Mengzi Rd

Liyuan Rd

7

*Xīngguāng
Photography
Equipment (250m)*

E
F
G
H

FRENCH CONCESSION EAST *Map on p302*

Sports & Activities   (p125)

Sleeping   (p205)

Information   (p261)

Key on p308

FRENCH CONCESSION WEST

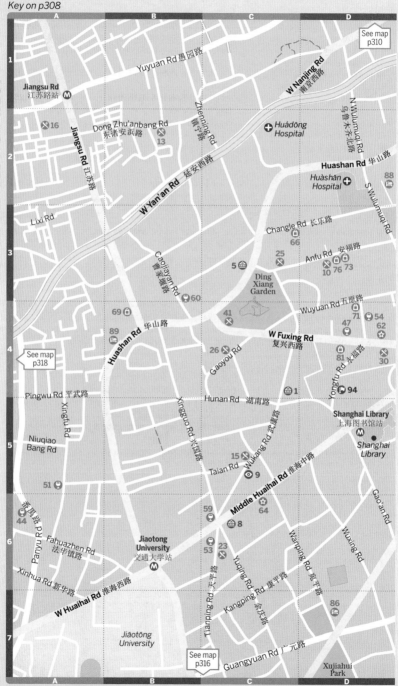

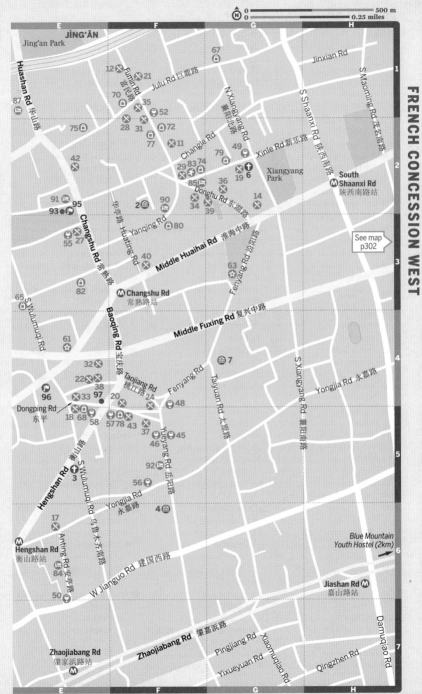

JÌNG'ĀN
Jing'an Park

Huashan Rd 华山路

Jing'an Park

Furin Rd 富民路
Julu Rd 巨鹿路

Jinxian Rd

S Maoming Rd 茂名南路

N Xiangyang Rd 襄阳北路

Changle Rd

Xinle Rd 新乐路

S Shaanxi Rd 陕西南路

S Shaanxi Rd 陕西南路

Xiangyang Park

South Shaanxi Rd
陕西南路站

Donghu Rd 东湖路

Changshu Rd 常熟路

Yanqing Rd

Huating Rd 华亭路

Middle Huaihai Rd 淮海中路

Fenyang Rd 汾阳路

See map p302

Changshu Rd
常熟路站

Baoqing Rd 宝庆路

Middle Fuxing Rd 复兴中路

S Wulumuqi Rd

S Wulumuqi Rd 乌鲁木齐南路

Taojiang Rd
桃江路

Fenyang Rd

Taiyuan Rd 太原路

S Xiangyang Rd 襄阳南路

Yongjia Rd 永嘉路

Dongping Rd
东平

Hengshan Rd 衡山路

Yueyang Rd 岳阳路

Yongjia Rd
永嘉路

Hengshan Rd
衡山路站

Anting Rd 安亭路

Blue Mountain
Youth Hostel (2km)

Jiashan Rd
嘉山路站

W Jianguo Rd 建国西路

Zhaojiabang Rd
肇家浜路站

Zhaojiabang Rd 肇嘉浜路

Pingjiang Rd

Xiaomuqiao Rd 小木桥路

Yixueyuan Rd

Qingzhen Rd

Damuqiao Rd

FRENCH CONCESSION WEST *Map on p306*

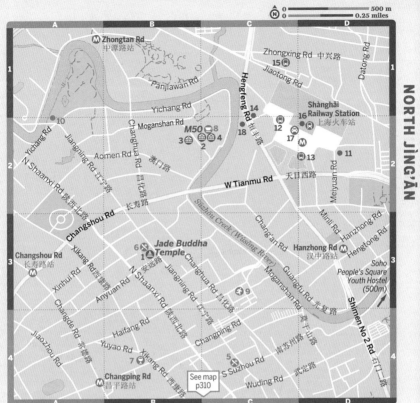

SOUTH JÌNG'ĀN

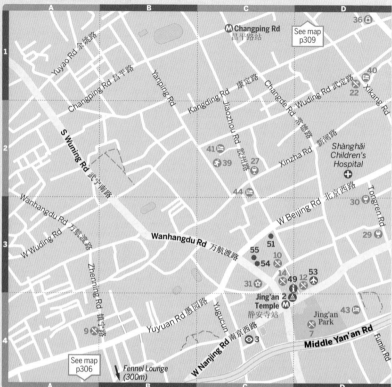

M Changping Rd
昌平路站

See map
p309

Shànghǎi
Children's
Hospital

Wanhangdu Rd 万航渡路

Jìng'an
Temple
静安寺站

Jìng'an
Park

Fennel Lounge
(300m)

See map
p306

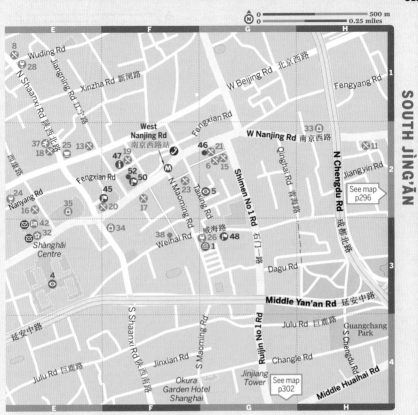

PŬDŌNG

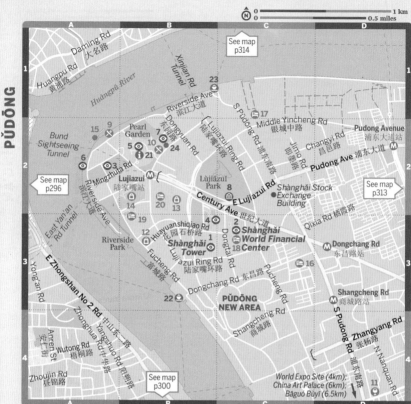

HÓNGKŎU & NORTH SHÀNGHǍI

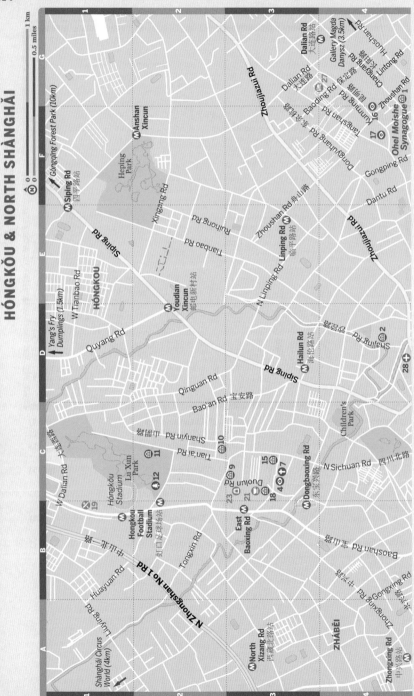

Shànghǎi Circus World (4km)

N Zhongshan No 1 Rd

Luyang Rd
Huayuan Rd

W Dalian Rd
大连西路

Yang's Fry Dumplings (1.5km)

Göngqing Forest Park (10km)

Quyang Rd

W Tianbao Rd

HÓNGKŎU

Siping Rd
四平路站

Heping Park

Anshan Xincun

Xingang Rd

Tianbao Rd

Ruihong Rd

Siping Rd

Youdian Xincun
邮电新村站

Qinguan Rd

Bao'an Rd 宝安路

Tian'ai Rd
Shanyin Rd 山阴路

Lu Xun Park

Hóngkŏu Stadium

Hongkou Football Stadium
虹口足球场站

Tongxin Rd

Duolun Rd

East Baoxing Rd

Qingyang Rd 舟山路

Zhoushan Rd

N Linping Rd Linping Rd
临平路站

Hailun Rd
海伦路站

N Sichuan Rd 四川北路

Dongbaoxing Rd
东宝兴路

Baoshan Rd 宝山路

Zhongxing Rd
中兴路站

Zhongxing Rd

ZHÁBĚI

N Xizang Rd
西藏北路站

Zhoujiazui Rd

Dalian Rd
大连路

Dalian Rd
大连路

Baoding Rd 保定路

Changyang Rd 长阳路

Kunming Rd
昆明路

Tangshan Rd 唐山路

Dongjuhang Rd

Gongping Rd

Dantu Rd

Zhoujiazui Rd

Gallery Magda Danysz (3.5km)

Lintong Rd

Huoshan Rd

Zhoushan Rd站

Ohel Moishe Synagogue

Shajing Rd

Children's Park

2

28

27

17

19

11
12
9
10
15
7
23
21
18
4

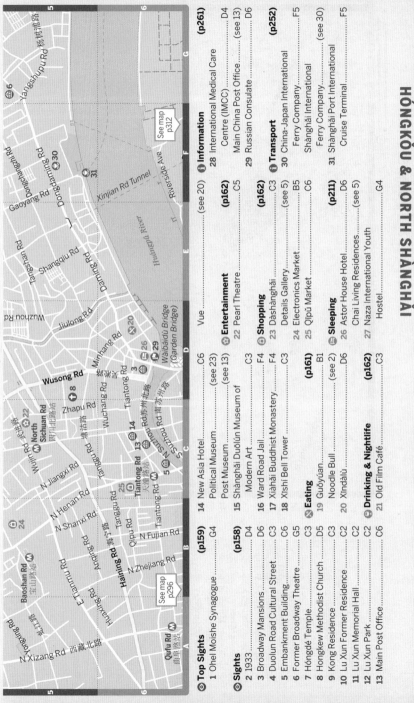

◎ Top Sights (p159)

1 Ohel Moishe Synagogue G4

◎ Sights (p158)

2 1933 .... D4
3 Broadway Mansions D6
4 Duolun Road Cultural Street C3
5 Embankment Building F4
6 Former Broadway Theatre G5
7 Hóngdé Temple C3
8 Hongkew Methodist Church D5
9 Kong Residence C3
10 Lu Xun Former Residence C2
11 Lu Xun Memorial Hall C2
12 Lu Xun Park C2
13 Main Post Office C6
14 New Asia Hotel C6
15 Shànghăi Duōlún Museum of
  Modern Art C3
16 Ward Road Jail D6
17 Xiàhăi Buddhist Monastery C6
18 Xīshí Bell Tower G5

✕ Eating (p161)

19 Guōyuán B1
20 Noodle Bull .... (see 2)
20 Xīndàlù D6

◎ Drinking & Nightlife (p162)

21 Old Film Café C6

Post Museum .... (see 23)
Political Museum .... (see 13)
Vue .... (see 20)

✪ Entertainment (p162)

22 Pearl Theatre C5

⊙ Shopping (p162)

23 Dàshànghăi C3
 Details Gallery .... (see 5)
24 Electronics Market B5
25 Qīpǔ Market C6

⊙ Sleeping (p211)

26 Astor House Hotel D6
 Chai Living Residences .... (see 5)
27 Naza International Youth
  Hostel G4

❶ Information (p261)

28 International Medical Care
  Centre (IMCC) D4
 Main China Post Office .... (see 13)
29 Russian Consulate D6

❶ Transport (p252)

30 China-Japan International
  Ferry Company F5
 Shànghăi International
  Ferry Company .... (see 30)
31 Shànghăi Port International
  Cruise Terminal F5

See map p312

See map p296

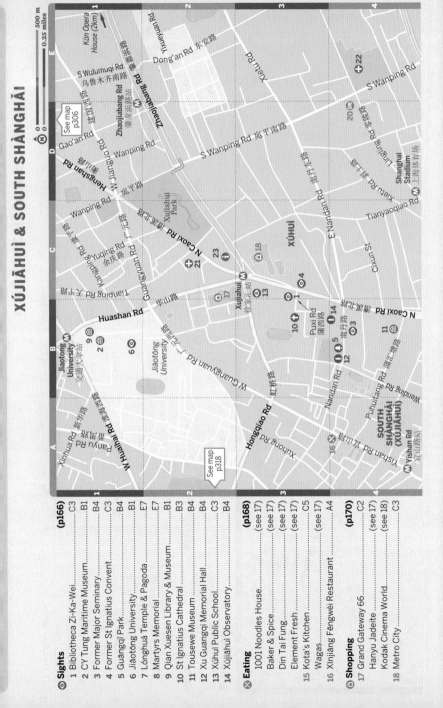

XŪJIĀHUÌ & SOUTH SHÀNGHǍI

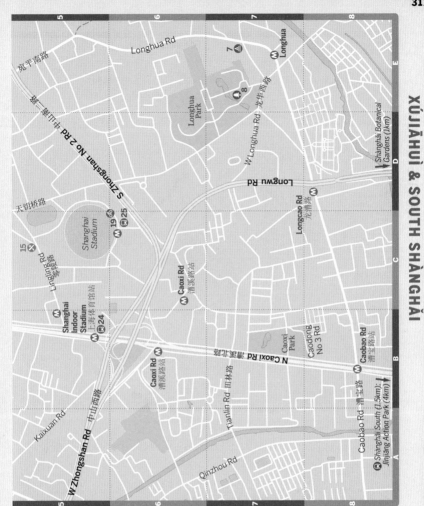

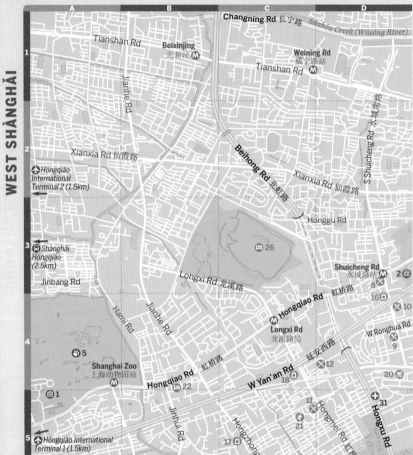

WEST SHÀNGHǍI

Our Story

A beat-up old car, a few dollars in the pocket and a sense of adventure. In 1972 that's all Tony and Maureen Wheeler needed for the trip of a lifetime – across Europe and Asia overland to Australia. It took several months, and at the end – broke but inspired – they sat at their kitchen table writing and stapling together their first travel guide, *Across Asia on the Cheap*. Within a week they'd sold 1500 copies. Lonely Planet was born.

Today, Lonely Planet has offices in Franklin, London, Melbourne, Oakland, Beijing and Delhi, with more than 600 staff and writers. We share Tony's belief that 'a great guidebook should do three things: inform, educate and amuse'.

Our Writers

Damian Harper

Coordinating author, The Bund & People's Square, French Concession, Jìng'ān, West Shànghǎi, Day Trips from Shànghǎi After graduating with a degree in modern and classical Chinese from London's School of Oriental and African Studies, guidebook writer Damian has lived and worked in Shànghǎi, Běijīng and Hong Kong, travelling the highways and byroads of China. Fascinated by China's coming of age, relishing Shànghǎi's finest xiǎolóngbāo dumplings and shíkùmén buildings, and while hounded by deadlines, Damian has worked on multiple editions of Shanghai.

Read more about Damian at:
lonelyplanet.com/members/damianharper

Dai Min

Old Town, Pǔdōng, Hóngkǒu & North Shànghǎi, Xújiāhuì & South Shànghǎi Dai Min grew up in beer-making Qīngdǎo (Tsingtao) on the Shāndōng coast before hopping on the train north to university in Běijīng to read English. She moved to the UK in the 1990s, then to Shànghǎi for two years in the midnoughties, living on the gritty cusp of the French Concession and, for a while, in West Shànghǎi. Regularly returning to visit her sister in Pudong, Dai Min has contributed to several editions of the Lonely Planet *China* guide and also works as a freelance English–Chinese translator (and multitasking mum). Dai Min also wrote the Eating, Drinking & Nightlife, Entertainment, Shopping, Sleeping, Transport and Directory chapters.

Published by Lonely Planet Publications Pty Ltd
ABN 36 005 607 983
7th edition – Apr 2015
ISBN 978 1 74321 571 5
© Lonely Planet 2015   Photographs © as indicated 2015
10 9 8 7 6 5 4 3 2 1
Printed in China

Although the authors and Lonely Planet have taken all reasonable care in preparing this book, we make no warranty about the accuracy or completeness of its content and, to the maximum extent permitted, disclaim all liability arising from its use.

32953012584027